Saint-Porchaire Ewer
White paste earthenware, lead-glazed
H. 35.6 cm., W. 13.6 cm.
France, Saint-Porchaire, ca. 1540–1567
The Cleveland Museum of Art, Purchase
from the J.H. Wade Fund 53.363.

EUROPEAN DECORATIVE ARTS
1400-1600

an annotated bibliography

Reference Publications in
ART HISTORY
Marilyn Aronberg Lavin, Editor
Italian Renaissance

EUROPEAN DECORATIVE ARTS
1400-1600

---

an annotated bibliography

PATRICK M. DE WINTER

REFERENCE PUBLICATIONS
IN
ART HISTORY

G. K. Hall & Co, 70 Lincoln Street, Boston, Massachusetts

Library of Congress Cataloging-in-Publication Data

de Winter, Patrick M., 1939-
European decorative arts, 1400-1600.

(Reference publications in art history)
Includes indexes.
1. Decorative arts, Gothic—Bibliography.
2. Decorative arts, Renaissance—Bibliography.
I. Title. II. Series.
Z5956.D3D38 1988 [NK1840] 016.745′094 87-31071
ISBN 0-8161-8612-X

Contents

Contents

Contents

Contents

Contents

Contents

Contents

Contents

Contents

Contents

Contents

Contents

Contents

Contents

Contents

Contents

Contents

The Author

Patrick M. de Winter earned a Ph.D. degree in Art History from the Institute of Fine Arts, New York University, and at present is curator of the medieval and Renaissance collections at The Cleveland Museum of Art. He is the author of three books and over two dozen articles dealing with a variety of art historical topics. A fellow of the Society of Antiquaries of London, he divides his time between the United States, Paris, and Florence.

Introduction

In this volume have been gathered over twenty-two hundred annotated references to selected published material dealing with the various types of furnishings made for the church, the palace, and the home, as well as with objects used for personal adornment, produced in Europe during the time that spans the late Gothic and Renaissance periods.

The intention in compiling this work has been twofold. The first is identical to that of other volumes in the series, namely to select and call attention to a specialized body of literature to persons conducting academic research in art history. The second, no less significant, is to present this material in such a manner that is will also be a useful tool for collectors whose needs are generally more pragmatic and whose interests are more focused in scope.

Decorative Arts, essential component in the title of this book, is a broad term that encompasses a wide array of different man-made creations. Evolved as recently as the late nineteenth century, it designates a body of objects that are aesthetically wedged, but with overlaps, between what the eighteenth century academicians have dubbed the "noble" or "fine" arts — painting, scultpure, architecture — and the pure crafts generally associated solely with utilitarian purposes. Most often found in current literature, the adjective *decorative* has been nearly interchangeably used with the somewhat belittling qualifiers *useful, minor,* or *applied,* or has been substituted by the manifestly more positive term *objets d'art* used by the French and its less successful translation *works of art* favored in the parlance of British and American auction houses. Most of these composites, however, are very similar in that each to some degree implies a value judgment.

While the adjective *decorative* in current usage implies little but ornamentation, the term *decorative art* as a whole more broadly suggests a preoccupation with criteria of shape, material, and color. With clear emphasis on fine design; harmony of form, pattern, and technique; and excellence of execution, the decorative arts are often masterpieces of aesthetic creation. The relative scarcity of extant objects from the fifteenth and sixteenth centuries, however, combined with a perennial fascination for this historically rich and tumultuous period of European history, has led many collectors and art museums, as well as some art historians, to include in their collections or studies a fair number of objects that can more readily be classified as artifacts than as aesthetic milestones. A fair sampling of the literature dealing with this aspect of the history of objects is also included in the bibliography. In incorporating this material we follow the tradition of such well-established bibliographical guides as RAA (see entry 38) and RILA (see entry 39). Intrinsically meshed with the civilization that created them, both the zenith and the nadir of the decorative arts certainly provide insight into the political, social, and economic climate, as well as the aesthetic standards, of the time and place in which they were produced.

The creation of decorative arts in any given period is clearly bound to some degree to life-style and the practice of collecting. Until 1400 interiors had been Spartan with rudimentary furnishings limited to beds, tables, benches, and coffers, the fireplace generally constituting a fixed point of reference. Plate was reserved for the table and sideboard of the prince, and its purpose was primarily ostentatious in nature rather than utilitarian or for personal satisfaction. From 1400 onward, a dramatic concentration of personal wealth resulting from a series of catastrophic epidemics, combined with a sharp growth of mercantilism as well as a rising urban population, created a ready patronage, which, in seeking the balm of increased comfort, fostered the development of specialized workshops that catered to embellishing the home.

Fifteenth- and sixteenth-century collectors offer an enduring topic for study. Among medieval and Renaissance pioneers in the field are Jean de Berry in Bourges; the Valois dukes of Burgundy in Dijon, Brussels, and Bruges; many of the pontiffs in Rome; the Medicis in Florence; Margaret of Austria in Malines; Francis I in Paris; Isabella d'Este in Mantua; Archduke Ferdinand of Tyrol in Innsbruck; Elector Augustus of Saxony in Dresden; the Fugger family in Augsburg; William IV, duke of Bavaria in Munich; and Emperor Rudolph II in Prague. Collecting for these grandees served a threefold purpose: intellectual and aesthetic satisfaction; prestige and political advancement; and utility. Soon following in their wake was a host of other avid collectors—to be sure less wealthy—owners of houses with crowded interiors similar to those depicted by the Flemish masters, filled with angular Gothic furniture on which rest bottles, boxes, dinanderie, and sundry objects, or others whose houses were more sparsely furnished, as in the views of Italian artists such as Carpaccio, and in which the prized collector's items such as small bronzes were isolated and thus focused against the more neutral interior. A relationship between the home and its occupants became a reality of daily life as well as an explicit statement of taste. Inventories, records of correspondence, and historical accounts afford countless glimpses of the passions and rapacity of these collectors for the unsurpassed maiolica ware of Italian and Spanish centers, the sumptuous tapestries woven in Brussels and Flanders, and the distinctive plate of English silversmiths. In addition to these decorative arts, the Renaissance collector had an encyclopedic interest in curiosities and rarities, which included antiquities, automatons, scientific instruments, as well as such naturalia as stuffed crocodiles and exotic birds, fossils, and uncommon stones. Sabba da Castiglione, a Milanese gentleman who died in 1554 and a kinsman of the famed Baldassare, devotes part of his memoirs to a description of what the interior of the house of a man of good breeding should be—filled with tapestries, cabinets, goldsmith works, small sculptures, and precious or unusual objects. In 1565 with his *Inscriptiones vel tituli teatri amplissimi,* Samuel van Quiccheberg of Antwerp completed the first manual dealing with the proper arrangement of a collection. By the end of the century La Croix du Maine prepared a guide of celebrated collections, the title of which reads in translation, "The Most Renowned Library and Cabinets (Which Some Call Chambers of Marvels) of France."

To a large extent, Gothic and Renaissance decorative arts lost their appeal during the seventeenth and eighteenth centuries during which time as much seems to have been senselessly destroyed as during the major moments of religious and social upheaval. It was in the nineteenth century that members of the upper middle class, looking for psychological roots and confronted with the new age of the machine, developed a near passion for Gothic and Renaissance objects. This took place from the 1830s onward, fueled by the romantic movement. It was at this time that were formed prominent collections of fifteenth and sixteenth century decorative arts, such as those of Carrand, Sellière, and Spitzer in France, and those of Hamilton, Fountaine, and the Rothschilds in England. These collectors—enlightened and indefatigable *curieux* rather than mere *amateurs*—soon hired the services of encyclopedic historians such as Müntz, Labarte, and Molinier to catalog their collections. To a large degree the publications that ensued laid the groundwork for modern scientific studies of the decorative arts. The next step in the evolution of decorative arts collecting was in the form of judicious purchases by public institutions and generous bequests that brought about the foundation of museums such as the South Kensington Museum (later renamed the Victoria and Albert Museum) in London in 1850, the Kunstgewerbemuseum in Berlin in 1867, and the Société du Musée des Arts Décoratifs in Paris in 1880. At the same time, already existing large holdings of decorative arts such as the imperial collection in Vienna—which segregated holdings into two distinct institutions—art museums and science museums—began to be reassessed according to scientific criteria. The next major development occurred in the early twentieth century with larger groups of collectors, whose names will be found in the pages that follow, and with the emergence of methodical and rigorous scholarship.

By and large though, until the 1950s, the research necessary for fundamental studies of decorative arts remained more approximate than in the so-called fine arts; objects need to be handled rather than simply contemplated, and their material and manufacturing process thoroughly examined. Recent years have witnessed favorable advances. As a result, not only Renaissance goldsmiths but contemporary makers of intarsia furniture and maiolica, for example, have increasingly been given artistic personalities; they are artist-craftsmen whose style and evolution are studied and partially reconstructable.

This bibliography presents the significant literature produced well over a century with emphasis on works written between 1960 and 1986. Major learned periodicals have been carefully combed; regional publications, on the other hand, have oftentimes been difficult to locate. What has been available to me has varied from country to country; I have, for example, had little access to literature from Eastern European countries.

Nearly all works included in this bibliography are in Western languages; for Russian works, transliterated forms are given from the Cyrillic into the Roman alphabet. Since this volume is addressed to the English-speaking reader, whenever possible it is English versions or translations that are listed.

The general plan of the volume is pragmatic, adopted from the natural flow of subject entries from the general to the specific. Because of space limitations, theoretical writings of the fifteenth-sixteenth century that deal with the decorative arts, such as the famed treatise of Cellini on goldsmith works, Cipriano Piccolpasso's *Tre libri dell'arte del vasajo,* Bernard Palissy's memoirs, or Pomponius Gauricus's *De sculptura* dealing primarily with small-scale bronze sculpture, have not been included. The same is true for inventories of fifteenth-sixteenth-century collections noted for their objets d'art (they are listed in Fernand de Mély and Edmund Bishop, *Bibliographie générale des inventaires imprimés,* 3 vols., Paris, 1892-95, with additions in subsequent compilations). Purposefully excluded are certain classes of objects such as palmesels, which are akin to large-scale sculpture; mosaics, and marble floors, which are an intrinsic part of architecture; stained glass covered in another volume of the G.K. Hall series; and coins, since numismatics is a specialized field largely involved with questions not pertinent to our concerns.

For the sake of clarity, it was decided to use adjectives of modern nationalities as means of classifications (e.g. Italian, French) rather than the geography of often parceled states prevalent during the fifteenth and sixteenth centuries. In the case of modern Belgium, comprised of what was formerly Flanders, Brabant, the Meuse Valley, the Bishopric of Liège, the Free city of Tournai, etc., the noun Belgium has been given (with adjectives Flemish, Brabantine, etc. in parenthesis) to indicate the diversity of its past, while English, Scottish, Welsh, and Irish appear under the heading British Isles. The same criterion has been used for the U.S.S.R. (comprised of fifteen states, eight of which are part of Europe). The former Kingdom of Bohemia appears under Czechoslovakia. Objects of Danish, Finnish, Norwegian, and Swedish origin are classified under the geographical heading Scandinavia.

Research for this project was primarily carried out at the libraries of the Kunsthistorisches Institute in Florence, the Hertziana in Rome, the Bibliothèque nationale in Paris, the New York Public Library and The Cleveland Museum of Art. Appreciative words go to the librarians of these and other institutions.

This volume has vastly benefited from the organizational skills of my wife, from the unflinching assistance of Stephen Fliegel, and, at an early stage, from the contributions of Joseph R. Bliss. May the indulgent reader profit from the toil of the author, who at the completion of this work shared the feelings of the Parisian medieval scribe Henri de Trévou, who exclaimed with relief in the closing paragraph of one of the manuscripts he painfully transcribed: "Or est ci fini nostre livre, Benoît soit Dieu, je en suis délivré" (Thus our book comes to an end; blessed be the Lord that I am delivered of it).

Notes on Organization of the Bibliography

The works listed are divided into the following categories:

1. Dictionaries and Encyclopedias

2. Biographical Dictionaries

3. Surveys and Histories

4. Bibliographical Guides

5. General References to Auction Catalogs

6. Permanent Collections

7. Exhibition Catalogs

8. Private Collection, Auction, and Dealer Catalogs

Classification headings are given in the plural (e.g., [3] Surveys and Histories) – even when there is only one entry, in order to maintain uniformity.

Entries within each subdivision are listed alphabetically. When there are two or more entries for one location under (6) Permanent Collections or (8) Private Collection, Auction, and Dealer Catalogs, they are listed chronologically.
Example:
Paris

MUSÉE DU LOUVRE

52   *Donation du Baron Charles Davillier: Catalogue des objets Éxposés au Musée du Louvre.* Catalog by Louis Courajod and Émile Molinier. Paris: Imprimeries Réunies, 1885.

53   *Collection Paul Garnier: Horloges et montres, ivoires et plaquettes.* Catalog by Gaston Migeon. Paris: Hachette, 1917.

PETIT PALAIS

55   MIGEON, GASTON. "Les Objets d'art de la Collection Dutuit." *Les Arts* 11 (1902):22-32.

Permanent collection and exhibition catalogs—listed chronologically—have been entered first by title of the work followed by the name of the author. Works dealing with a particular collection that are not catalogs have been listed first by the name of the author.
Example:
London

BRITISH MUSEUM

49   *The Waddesdon Bequest: Catalogue of the Works of Art Bequeathed to the British Museum by Baron Ferdinand Rothschild, M.P., 1898,* by Charles Hercules Read. London: Trustees of the British Museum, 1902.

49a   *TAIT, HUGH. The Waddesdon Bequest: The Legacy of Baron Ferdinand Rothschild to the British Museum.* London: British Museum Publications, 1981.

An exhibition catalog entirely devoted to a specific permanent or private collection is listed under that collection regardless of where the exhibition was held.
Example:
New York

METROPOLITAN MUSEUM OF ART

1521   *The Art of Chivalry: European Arms and Armor from the Metropolitan Museum of Art.* Exhibition held in Seattle at the Seattle Art Center, [the Denver Art Museum, Witte Museum in San Antonio, Minneapolis Institute of Arts, and Detroit Institute of Arts].

When a private collection name is not specified, the work is listed in (3) Surveys and Histories, rather then in (8) Private Collection, Auction, and Dealer Catalogs.
So as not to overburden the text, cross-references have been selective. The index, in terms of specific artists, is not exhaustive; only those who are mentioned in the text receive an entry. Chapters 1-5 include works that deal with two or more media. The reader who wishes to make a thorough survey of any one medium should therefore consult, in addition to the specific relevant chapter, Chapters 1-5 as well as those dealing with closely related media.

Note:
Although great care was taken by the author and the publisher to reproduce all accents, for mechanical reasons some used in Scandinavian and Slavic languages could not be typeset.

I. General References to More Than One Country and More Than One Medium

1. DICTIONARIES AND ENCYCLOPEDIAS OF DECORATIVE ARTS

1   BOGER, LOUISE ADE, and BOGER, H. BATTERSON. *The Dictionary of Antiques and the Decorative Arts: A Book of Reference for Glass, Furniture, Ceramics, Silver, Periods, Styles, Technical Terms, Etc.* New York: Charles Scribner's Sons, 1957. 560 pp., 32 b&w pls., with several illus. on each, numerous line drawings.
       Alphabetically arranged concise entries for terms, forms, styles, shapes, techniques, main centers of production, artists, makers. Twenty-page repertory of main subjects (e.g., arms and armor, carpets and rugs, ceramics, etc.) with listing of relevant terminology. Bibliography.

2   BOSC, ERNEST. *Dictionnaire de l'art, de la curiosité et du bibelot.* Paris: Librairie de Firmin-Didot et Cie, 1883. 695 pp., 709 line drawings. Reprint. New York and London: Garland Publishing, 1979.
       Discursive and somewhat dated dictionary of the applied arts that is nonetheless useful for the clarity of its illustrations, for its citations of inventories, and particularly for the list of 19th-century collections found in the appendix.

3   BURTY, PHILIPPE. *Chefs-d'oeuvre of the Industrial Arts.* Edited and with translation revised by W. Chaffers. London: Chapman & Hall, 1869. 391 pp., 56 full-page engravings, numerous others in text. (Originally published as *Chefs-d'oeuvre des arts industriels.* Paris: Paul Ducrocq, 1866. 599 pp., 200 engravings.)
       Pioneering work dedicated to the decorative arts. In discursive and chatty manner, the author covers ceramic art (terra cotta, enameled faience, porcelain), glass (table glass, window glass), enamel, metals (bronze and iron, jewelry, and plate), tapestry, and carpets. Line drawings illustrate objects, generally in private collections, of the mid-19th century.

4   *The Connoisseur Complete Encyclopedia of Antiques.* 2d rev. ed. London: Connoisseur, 1975. 704 pp., numerous color and b&w figs. (1st ed. 1952.)

Alphabetically arranged by type of object, each with brief historic essay(s) tracing origin, development, styles, etc., often within specific countries or periods, and followed by glossary of terms, types, forms, and styles, as well as entries for major makers, designers, centers of production.

5   *The Dictionary of Art*. Edited by Hugh Brigstocke, with contributions by about 2,000 authors. London: Macmillan; New York: Grove's Dictionaries. To be published in 1991 with 28 vols. projected, each consisting of 992 pp., and a total of 25 million words and 20,000 b&w figs.
        Comprehensive dictionary of about fifteen thousand individual articles planned to serve as a fundamental work of reference to the visual arts.   According to the 1985 prospectus, 3 million words will be devoted to "design, garden history, interior decoration and major decorative art forms."

6   DIRSZTAY, PATRICIA. *Church Furnishings: A NADFAS Guide.* London: Routledge & K. Paul, 1978, 246 pp., 500 figs.
        Dictionary of terms, types, styles, periods. Of interest for the period 1400-1600, are, for example, the entries dealing with ceramics, costumes, crosses and crucifixes, decorative motifs, frames, metalwork, textiles, vestments and alter cloths, and woodwork.

7   *Encyclopedia of World Art*. Edited by Massimo Pallottino. Many contributors. 15 vols. New York, Toronto, London: McGraw-Hill, 1959-83. Each volume approximately 450 pp., over 500 pls., many in color.
        Series of articles on leading artists, schools, concepts, principal artistic media, etc. Specifically pertinent to 15th- 16th-century decorative arts are the following entries: in vol. 1, arms and armor, cols. 730-55, pls. 436-55; 3, ceramics, cols. 186-326, pls. 120-73, coins and medals, cols. 699-748, pls. 393-416; 4, costumes, cols. 14-54, pls. 8-33, emblems and insignia, cols. 710-34, pls. 393-404, enamels cols. 734-48, pls. 405-19; 5, furniture, cols. 687-747, pls. 425-64; 6, games and toys, cols. 1-18, pls. 1-12, gems and glyptics, cols. 44-80, pls. 33-52, glass, cols. 367-98, pls. 218-40, gold- and silverwork, cols. 399-459, pls. 241-88, graphic arts (includes bookbindings), cols. 666-717, pls. 403-24; 7, household objects, cols. 610-50, pls. 311-46; 8, inlay, cols. 126-35, pls. 77-90, interior decoration and design, cols. 183-211, pls. 91-118, ivory and bone carving, cols. 757-86, pls. 235-50; 9, liturgical and ritual objects, cols. 270-315, pls. 156-78, metalwork, cols. 790-827, pls., 497-521; 12, scientific and mechanical works, cols. 797-816, pls. 455-80, seals, cols. 840-58, pls. 532-34; 13, table and food, cols. 884-93, pls. 367-74, tapestry and carpets, cols. 909-65, pls. 391-434; 14, textiles, embroidery, and lace, cols. 1-37, pls. 1-34, utensils and tools, cols. 682-92., pls. 269-85; 15, index.

8   FLEMING, JOHN, and HONOUR, HUGH. *The Penguin Dictionary of Decorative Arts.* London: Penguin Books, 1977. 896 pp., over 1,000 b&w figs.
        Furniture and furnishings in Europe from the Middle Ages to the present and in North America from Colonial period onward (excluded are musical and scientific instruments and articles of personal adornment). Numerous entries define stylistic and technical terms, describe materials and techniques, and provide biographies of main designers and makers and brief histories of leading factories. Short bibliographical references within entries. Appendixes of marks.

9   HAVARD, HENRY. *Dictionnaire de l'ameublement et de la décoration depuis le XIIIe*
     siècle jusqu'à nos jours. 4 vols. 2d enl. and rev. ed. Vol. 1, *A-C,* 1086 cols., 803 b&w figs.,
     64 pls.; vol. 2, *D-H,* 1050 cols., 64 pls., 956 b&w figs.; vol. 3, *I-O,* 1222 cols., 64 pls., 888
     b&w figs.; vol. 4, *P-Z,* 1638 cols., 65 pls., 971 b&w figs. Paris: Maison Quantain, [1894]
     (1st ed. 1887-90.)
         Important if somewhat verbose encyclopedic dictionary of mostly French furniture
     and furnishings with numerous entries dealing with utensils, tools, materials, architectural and
     decorative elements, terms, etc., but not artists or individual craftsmen. Gothic and Renais-
     sance subjects. Topics are clearly illustrated with line drawings and plates, many hand-
     colored, of major examples.

10   *McGraw-Hill Dictionary of Art*. Edited by Bernard S. Myers, assisted by Shirley D. Myers.
     Signed entries by many contributors. 5 vols. Vol. 1, *AA-CEY,* 535 pp.; vol. 2, *CEZ-GRE,*
     565 pp.; vol. 3, *GRE-MAS,* 567 pp.; vol. 4, *MAS-ROT,* 565 pp.; vol. 5, *ROU-ZYL,* 574 pp.;
     numerous pls. and figs., many in color. New York, Toronto, London, Sydney, Johannes-
     burg: McGraw Hill Book Co., 1969.
         Useful introductory reference to all the visual arts covering broad aspects of the
     decorative arts. Entries tend to be short overviews providing some general bibliographical
     reference. Well illustrated.

11   *The Oxford Companion to the Decorative Arts*. Edited by Harold Osborne. Oxford:
     Clarendon, 1975. 879 pp., 60 line drawings, 400 b&w figs.
         Decorative arts dictionary with numerous entries on particular crafts (e.g., arms and
     armor, ceramics, clocks, costume, embroidery, enamels, glass, jewelry, lace, leather, metal,
     woodcarving, etc.), periods or cultures, schools, styles; description of materials, tools, techni-
     ques; biographies of leading craftsmen. Fifteen-page bibliography.

12   RIS-PAQUOT, [OSCAR E.]. *Dictionnaire encyclopédique des marques et monogrammes,*
     chiffres, lettres initiales, signes figuratifs, etc. contenant 12,156 marques.... 2 vols. Vol. 1, *A-*
     I, 272 pp.; vol. 2, *J-Z,* 414 pp., 3 pls. of engravings. Paris: Laurens, [1928]. Reprint. New
     York: Burt Franklin, [1964].
         12,156 makers' marks found on a variety of works of art produced in all European
     countries from the 15th through the 19th century and including armor, ceramics, goldsmith
     work, enamels, nielli, pewter and other metalwork, clocks, furniture, waxes, bindings, ivory,
     mother-of-pearl, tapestries and other textiles.

13   ROUAIX, PAUL. *Dictionnaire des arts décoratifs à l'usage des artisans, des artistes, des*
     amateurs et des écoles. Paris: À la Librairie Illustrée, (1885). 1,049 pp., 541 engravings.
         Informative if somewhat dated general dictionary of the decorative arts. Includes
     entries on furniture, arms and armor, jewelry, embroidery and lace, garments, enamels, earth-
     enware, goldsmith work, porcelain, ironwork, tapestries, and glass from all Western countries
     with emphasis on French material.

2. BIOGRAPHICAL DICTIONARIES

14   THIEME, ULRICH, and BECKER, FELIX, eds. *Allgemeines Lexikon der bildenden*
     Künstler von der Antike bis zur Gegenwart. Contributions by 300 authors. 37 vols. Leip-
     zig: VEB E.A. Seeman, 1907-50. Each volume approximately 600 pp., no illus.
         The most exhaustive dictionary of artists (from antiquity to modern times) to date.
     The fact that most entries are by the leading specialist in the field at the time of publication
     means well-conceived, informative, and thought-provoking texts even if the material may now

be partially outdated. An updated edition is under preparation in Leipzig. Bibliographical references. Vols. 1-36, A-Z; vol. 37, anonymous artists known by their major work, trademark, monograms, etc.

3. SURVEYS AND HISTORIES

Books

15   ALEXANDRE, ARSÈNE. *Histoire de l'art décoratif du XVIe siècle à nos jours.* Paris: Laurens, [1892]. 336 pp., 60 chromolithographs, 528 line drawings.
    Pioneering and well-illustrated history of most aspects of the decorative arts from the 16th through the 19th century: furniture making, metalsmithing, ceramic- and glass-making, textiles.

15a   ALLEMAGNE, HENRY RENÉ D'. *Les Accessoires du costume et du mobilier depuis le treizième jusqu'au milieu du dixneuvième siècle.* 3 vols. Paris: Schemit, 1928. 567 pp., 393 b&w pls. including 3,000 figs. (continuous pagination). Reprint. New York: Hacker, 1970.
    Encyclopedic publication surveying accessories for costume and furniture as well as tools, from the 13th to the mid-19th century. Most objects discussed and illustrated are in the author's (see entry no. 126) and other private collections (Figdor [see entry 102], Gélis, Richebé, etc.) supplemented with objects from the Musée des Arts Décoratifs. Vol. 1 includes, of the 15th-16th century, jewelry—rings, bracelets, earrings—buttons, seals, mirrors, purses, boxes and caskets, luminaries; vol. 2, tools, scientific instruments, eyeglasses, clocks and watches, kitchen and other household utensils including mortars. Vol. 3 is mainly composed of lengthy captions for the plates.

16   *Antiques: Traditional Techniques of the Master Craftsmen, Furniture, Glass, Ceramics, Gold, Silver, and Much More.* Edited by Elizabeth Drury. Introduction by Philippa Glanville. Contributions by fifteen authors. London: Roxby Art Publishing, 1986. 224 pp., numerous color and b&w figs.
    Useful introduction to the subject. Many of the techniques—which are discussed in brief paragraphs—were developed or used in 15th-16th-century Europe.

17   APPUHN, HORST. *Schatzkammern in Deutschland, Österreich und Schweiz: Führer zu kirchlichen und weltlichen Kostbarkeiten.* Düsseldorf: ECON Taschenbuch, 1984. 288 pp., numerous figs., some in color.
    Useful concise guide listing the contents (generally goldsmith work) of church treasures in Germany, Austria, and Switzerland. Although many of the essential works antedate the year 1400, the volume clearly suggests the wealth of late Gothic objects in ecclesiastical foundations of these regions. Includes bibliography and glossary.

18   DEUCHLER, FLORENS. *Die Burgunderbeute: Inventar der Beutestüke aus den Schlachten von Grandson, Murten und Nancy 1476/1477.* Bern: Stämpfli, 1963. 440 pp., 10 color figs., 378 b&w figs.
    The Burgundian spoils that fell into the hands of the Swiss after their victories at Grandson, Murten, and Nancy in 1476-77. Historical essay, transcription of inventories, catalog of 340 items including the seals, jewels, and plate of Charles the Bold, ecclesiastical

goldsmith work, tapestries, liveries and vestments, flags and pennants, cannons, shields, armor, and swords. Addenda on heraldry, flags, and the household of Charles the Bold. (See also entry 94.)

19   EVANS, JOAN. *Pattern: A Study of Ornament in Western Europe from 1180 to 1900.* 2 vols. Oxford: Clarendon, 1931. 1: 215 pp., 252 b&w figs.; 2: 264 pp., 183 b&w figs.
      Study of the conditions of artistic creation in the decorative arts. Progress and change in the applied arts emanating from centers of intellectual thought. The influence and spread of "patterns" as proportion, form, and color. Vol. 1 deals with the Gothic period and examines, among other topics, the relationship of architectural elements to metalwork. Vol. 2, pp. 1-22, deals with the Renaissance in France and Italy: motifs on armors and maiolica in relation to capitals, friezes, etc.

20   FALKE, JACOB VON. *Art in the House. Historical, Critical, and Aesthetical Studies on the Decoration and Furnishing of the Dwelling.* Translated, edited, and annotated by Charles C. Perkins. Boston: L. Prang, 1879. 374 pp., 5 chromolithographs, 55 b&w pls., 166 engravings.
      Older and somewhat trudging history of the decoration and furnishings of the patrician household from antiquity through the 18th century. Still valuable for its discussion of the varied perceptions and use of interior spaces and the decor of ceilings and walls in addition to actual furnishings, tableware, etc.

21   *Geschichte des Kunstgewerbes aller Zeiten und Völker.* Edited by H. Th. Bossert. 6 vols. Vol. 5 (1932), 480 pp., numerous b&w figs.; vol. 6 (1935), 422 pp., 1 color pl., 27 b&w pls., numerous b&w figs. Berlin-Charlottenburg: Ernst Wasmuth, 1928-35.
      Authoritative history of applied arts from early times through the 1920s. Vol. 5, pp. 367-480, by Heinrich Kohlhausen, deals with 14th-15th-century northern goldsmith works, bronze, lead, pewter, iron, leather, flags, furniture, silks, embroideries, ceramics, glass, and ivory. Vol. 6, pp. 1-75, by Edmund Wilhelm Braun-Troppau, deals with the Rennaissance period in Italy, Spain, France, and Germany—furniture, metalwork, maiolica, and textiles.

22   GRÖBER, KARL. *Kinderspielzeug aus alter Zeit: Eine Geschichte des Spielzeugs.* Berlin: Deutscher Kunstverlag, 1928. 68 pp., 12 color pls., 306 b&w figs.
      A history of toys from ancient times through the 19th century. Pp. 10-21 deal with the medieval and Rennaissance periods. Most useful are figs. 27-41 and color pls. III-IV illustrating one ca. 1450 clay figurine, several 16th-century wood and metal knights on horseback, female dolls in lavish costumes, and several doll houses dating to ca. 1600.

23   HAMLIN, A.D.F. *A History of Ornament.* 2 vols. Vol. 1, *Ancient and Medieval* (1916), 406 pp., 401 b&w figs., 23 pls., some in color; vol. 2, *Renaissance and Modern* (1923), 521 pp., 464 b&w figs., 24 pls., some in color. New York: Century Co.
      Standard, authoritative study of the origins and progressive developments of decorative design in the West from ancient times to the 20th century. Vol. 1, pp. 282-392, pls. XVII-XXII, deals with the Gothic period; vol. 2, pp. 1-252, pls. I-XIV, deals with the Renaissance.

24   HEINTSCHEL, HELLA, and DAWID, MARIA. *Lampen, Leuchter, Laternen seit der Antike.* Innsbruck: Pinguin; Frankfurt: Umschau, 1975. 31 pp. with 35 line drawings, 30 color pls., 107 b&w figs.

Survey of lamps, candlesticks, and chandeliers from antiquity to the 20th century; includes 15th- and 16th-century German, Italian, and French ecclesiastical and domestic fixtures (pp. 16-21); ten of the text figures and twenty-one of the plates illustrate 15th- and 16th-century pieces.

25 *Illustrierte Geschichte des Kunstgewerbes.* Edited by Georg Hermann Lehnert. 2 vols. Vol. 1, [Gothic and Renaissance], 666 pp., 28 color pls., several b&w pls., 531 b&w figs. Berlin: Martin Oldenbourg, [1907-9].

Scholarly history of the applied arts covering all civilizations and periods through the 19th century written by a team of well-known authorities. Vol. 1, pp. 361-422, by Otto von Falke, deals with late Gothic 15th century; pp. 423-542, by Georg Swarzenski, covers the Renaissance in Italy; pp. 543-656, by Wilhelm Behnecke, deals with the Renaissance north of the Alps.

26 JACQUEMART, ALBERT. *A History of Furniture.* Translated and edited by Mrs. Bury Palliser. London: Chapman & Hall; New York: Scribner, Welford, & Armstrong, 1878. 487 pp., 170 line drawings.

An early study not only of furniture (different types, of carved wood, of intarsia, incorporating bronze panels, etc.) but of other interior furnishings as well: tapestries, embroideries, textiles, stamped and painted leather, bronze, ivory, terra cotta, enamels, glass, jewelry, and other goldsmith works; several lists of recorded craftsmen in each field. Of value for illustrations of those objects said to be in private collections.

27 LABARTE, JULES. *Histoire des arts industriels au moyen âge et à l'époque de la Renaissance.* 4 vols., plus 2-vol. album of pls. Vol. 1 (1864), 548 pp.; vol. 2 (1864), 613 pp.; vol. 3 (1865), 718 pp.; vol. 4 (1866), 825 pp.; some line drawings in each volume. Plate albums (1864), 148 chromolithographs of major examples of type of objects, each accompanied by a descriptive entry. Paris: A. Morel.

Early standard and broad history of the decorative arts from the 4th century through the Renaissance. Vol. 1: sculpture (including ivory and wood, metalwork, glyptic arts, goldsmith work); vol. 2: goldsmith work continued, locks; vol. 3: manuscripts, painting on glass, enamel; vol. 4: enamel continued, mosaics, embroideries, tapestries, damascening, ceramics, glass, arms and armor, clocks and watches, secular and ecclesiastical furnishings and furniture; concludes with a 114- page index.

28 MOLINIER, ÉMILE. *Histoire générale des arts appliqués à l'industrie.* Vol. 2, *Les Meubles du Moyen Age & de la Renaissance, les sculptures microscopiques, les cires.* Paris: E. Lévy et Cie, [1897]. 244 pp., 22 b&w pls., 144 b&w figs.

Pioneering work on 15th-century furniture in France (pp. 20-31), Germany (35-43), and Flanders, Spain, and England (44-58), and on Renaissance furniture in Italy (59-84, includes choir stalls), and France (85-187). Also, small carved objects (caskets, combs, rosary beads, mirror frames, medals) of wood (188-218), and waxes (219-35). No index.

29 MORANT, HENRY DE. *Histoire des arts décoratifs des origines à nos jours.* Includes supplemental chapter by Gérald Gassoit-Talabot. Paris: Hachette, 1970. 574 pp., 768 illus., some in color.

Synoptic overview of decorative arts through the ages in most parts of the world. The Gothic period is discussed pp. 278-307; the Renaissance, 308-31. Includes a repertory of museums (listed by country) that have a collection of decorative arts.

30   SCHEICHER, ELISABETH. *Die Kunst- und Wunderkammern der Habsburger.* Vienna, Munich, Zurich: Molden, 1979. 207 pp., 106 color figs., 99 b&w figs.
      Precious and often major objects primarily in the Kunsthistorisches Museum, Vienna, and in the Castle of Ambras at Innsbruck, owned by or connected to the Hapsburg imperial family. Particularly important mannerist goldsmith work, jewels, ivories, ceramics, clocks, wax portraits, small bronzes, and curios. Excellent photographs of many objects never before reproduced in color.

31   SCHLOSSER, JULIUS VON. *Die Kunst- und Wunderkammern der Spätrenaissance.* Leipzig: Klinkhardt & Biermann, 1908. 146 pp., 102 b&w figs.
      Basic work dealing with the Renaissance "Kunst- und Wunderkammer" collecting phenomena involving aesthetics, rarity, and magical quality of art works and artifacts based on examples in the Hapsburg collections and on others elsewhere that are related.

32   SINGLETON, ESTHER. *Dutch and Flemish Furniture.* London: Hodder & Stoughton, 1907. 338 pp., 105 b&w illus.
      Overview, somewhat dated, of Dutch and Flemish furniture of the 13th-19th century including textiles, ornaments, goldsmith work, and musical instruments; reference to contemporary literary descriptions and inventories; chap. 2, pp. 31-62, deals with pieces from the Burgundian courts; chap. 3, 63-96, discusses the household of Margaret of Austria, Dutch and Flemish furniture (domestic and ecclesiastical) and Flemish tapestries, and Italian furniture, chap. 4, 97-129, discusses furnishings at the court of Mary of Hungary, Flemish furniture, glass, and musical instruments.

Articles

33   HACKENBROCH, YVONNE. "Some Portraits of Charles V." *Metropolitan Museum of Art Bulletin* 27 (1969): 323-32, 20 b&w figs.
      Hat jewels, pendants, cameos, medals, and coins of the 16th century in public and private U.S. and European collections, by Gian Maria Pomedello, Hans Reinhart the Elder, Giovanni Bernardi, etc., many after portraits by Titian, Leone Leoni, and van Orley.

34   KRIS, ERNEST. "Der Still 'rustique': Die Verwendung des Naturabgusses bei Wenzel Jamnitzer und Bernard Palissy." *Jahrbuch der kunsthistorischen Sammlungen in Wien* 1 (1926): 137-208, 68 b&w figs.
      Direct quotations from the animal (mostly reptiles and insects) and vegetable world in the works of Renaissance artists beginning with the Paduan bronzes of Riccio and his school to the goldsmith productions of Wenzel Jamnitzer in Nuremberg, the ceramics of Bernard Palissy in Paris, the bronzes of Giambologna in Florence, and their followers.

4. BIBLIOGRAPHICAL GUIDES

35   ARNTZEN, ETTA, and RAINWATER, ROBERT. *Guide to the Literature of Art History.* Chicago: American Library Association; London: Art Book Company, 1980. 634 pp.
      Most recent (material up to 1977), well-organized general bibliography on the visual arts superseding Mary W. Chamberlain's *Guide to Art Reference Books* (Chicago: American Library Association, 1959). Section P, pp. 384-477, comprises 721 entries dealing with the decorative and applied arts of all periods and countries. Good cross-referencing and copious index.

36   EHRESMANN, DONALD L. *Applied and Decorative Arts: A Bibliographic Guide to Basic Reference Works, Histories, and Handbooks.* Littleton, Colo.: Libraries Unlimited, 1977. 232 pp.

    Useful, if rather broad, bibliography comprising 1,240 references with short annotations to books published between 1875 and 1975, covering all countries and periods, excluding all periodical articles, permanent collection and exhibition catalogs. Author and subject indexes.

37   FRANKLIN, LINDA CAMPBELL. *Antiques and Collectibles: A Bibliography of Works in English, 16th Century to 1976.* Metuchen, N.J., and London: Scarecrow, 1978. 1,091 pp.

    Bibliographical listing of English language books, pamphlets, and exhibition catalogs dealing with collectibles; entries are arranged by subject matter and alphabetically by author within each area; includes listings for major decorative arts of the period 1400-1600 (furniture, ceramics, glass, silver and gold, woodwork, metalwork, ivory, gems, jewelry, costumes, textiles, arms and armor, etc.); location guide for many books published before 1925.

38   *RAA (Répertoire d'art et d'archéologie).* Paris: Éditions du Centre National de la Recherche Scientifique. 1st ser., vols. 1-68 (1910-64); n.s., vols. 1-22 (1965-86).

    The most comprehensive international bibliography of the visual arts from Early Christian times to 1939. Published quarterly, it comprises entries [in French] produced by the staff. Classified listing of the material (see section E, *Arts décoratifs,* of chapters 02, "Histoire générale de l'Art"; 03, "Moyen Age"; and 04, "Renaissance"). Concludes with subject and author indexes. *RAA* is expected to merge forces with *RILA* in 1988 to form a new publication.

39   *RILA (Répertoire international de la littérature de l'art. International Repertory of the Literature of Art).* Williamstown, Mass.: [A Getty Art History Information Program]. Published by-yearly; 1st vol. 1975.

    Abstracts of current books, Festschriften, catalogs, and articles from many periodicals. Entries are by staff or solicited from individual authors. Each issue includes complete subject and author indexes. For general works on decorative arts, see sec. 18, for those of medieval times, sec. 58, those of the Renaissance, sec. 68. *RILA* is expected to merge with RAA by 1988 to form a single publication with entries either in English or French.

40   *The Worldwide Art Catalogue Bulletin.* Boston: Worldwide Books. Quarterly periodical; 1st vol. 1964; present editor Anne Weisman.

    Analyzes, in a long paragraph, the content of exhibition catalogs dealing with the fine arts, architecture, archaeology, decorative arts, applied arts, graphics, and art education. A very useful tool, although the thoroughness of entries varies. Well indexed. Most catalogs are available and marketed by the publisher, Worldwide Books.

5. GENERAL REFERENCES TO AUCTION CATALOGS

41   BLANC, CHARLES. *Le Trésor de la curiosité tiré des catalogues de vente de tableaux, dessins, estampes, livres, marbres, bronzes, ivoires, terres cuites, vitraux, médailles, armes, porcelaines, meubles, émaux, laques et autres objets d'art.* 2 vols. Paris: Ve Jules Renouard, 1857-58. 1: 480 pp., 2: 636 pp. Some engravings in each volume.

    Valuable synoptic repertory of art auctions held in France from 1737 until 1855 gathered from catalogs, many of which are virtually impossible to locate today. Each entry is headed by the name of the consignor about whom some biographical information is often furnished. Although the compiler's primary concern is to record the sale of paintings and drawings, he also mentions, if more cursorily, the presence in most sales of some decorative arts objects — furniture, ceramics, goldsmith work, etc. — and is most informative in terms of bronze statuettes and medals.

42 LUGT, FRITZ. *Répertoire des catalogues de ventes publiques intéressant l'art ou la curiosité.* 3 vols.. Vol. 1, *Vers 1600-1825* (1938), 496 pp.; vol. 2, *1826-1860* (1953), 749 pp.; vol. 3, *1861-1900* (1964), 789 pp. The Hague: Martinus Nijhoff.

Standard compendium and a major tool for the study of collecting, listing a total of 58,704 art auctions held in Europe and the U.S. These are arranged chronologically with a brief mention of general content of the sale, each volume concluding with an index of collections.

43 PARIS, BIBLIOTHÈQUE FORNEY. *Catalogue des catalogues de ventes d'art.* 2 vols. Boston: G.K. Hall, 1972. 1: 820 pp.; 2: 824 pp.

Photomechanical reproduction of some fifty thousand catalog cards of public auctions in this Paris library. This publication completes and expands Lugt's *Répertoire* (see previous entry). The classification is as follows: Part 1: collectors, alphabetically listed; part 2: places of auctions, alphabetically listed; part 3: dates of auctions (1778-1971), chronologically listed; part 3: dates of auctions (1778-1971), chronologically presented.

44 REDFORD, GEORGE. *Art Sales: A History of Sales of Pictures and Other Works of Art with Notices of the Collections Sold, Names of Owners, Title of Pictures, Prices and Purchases, Arranged under the Artists of the Different Schools in Order of Date....* 2 vols. London: [Bradbury, Agnew & Co.], 1888. 1:497 pp., 19 b&w illus.; 2:357 pp., 2 b&w illus.

Classic reference to important fine arts auctions held in England from the 16th century until 1888 with emphasis on the 19th century. Vol. 1 provides digests of sales catalogs or reprints of reviews from newspapers — especially from the London *Times* — in the 1870s-80s. Described therein are many collections of decorative arts objects as well as specific items. Vol. 2 comprises lists of drawings and oil and watercolor paintings only.

45 ROBERTS, W. *Memorials of Christie's: A Record of Art Sales from 1766 to 1896.* 2 vols. London: George Bell & Sons, 1897. 1:340 pp., 1 chromolithograph, 10 engravings, 13 line drawings; 2:375 pp., 53 b&w pls., 1 line drawing.

Synoptic description of the collections that were auctioned off at Christie's in London, listing all major items and prices fetched. Important overview of collecting in England. Though the major emphasis is on painting, the volumes are to some extent useful for tracing types of decorative arts objects (see index), if not specific ones, since descriptions are generally cursory.

II. Multi Country, Multimedia: Permanent Collections

In addition to the literature listed below, the reader is advised to consult more general museum publications as well as year-end reports, which usually list the institution's new acquisitions

AUSTRALIA

Melbourne

NATIONAL GALLERY OF VICTORIA

46   *Decorative Arts from the Collections of the National Gallery of Victoria.* Catalog by Terence Lane and four other contributors.   Melbourne: National Gallery of Victoria, 1980.   123 pp., 37 color figs., 66 b&w figs.

Includes Italian verre églomisé diptych of ca. 1400, a maiolica piece from each: Orvieto, Florence, Urbino (by Francesco Xanto da Rovigo), a Paduan bronze statuette of David, a London-made chalice and paten of 1535, lace from Venice of the 16th century, a Limoges plaque of the mid-16th century, and a German glass beaker of 1593.

AUSTRIA

Vienna

KUNSTHISTORISCHES MUSEUM

47   *The Kunsthistorische Museum Vienna: The Treasury and the Collection of Sculpture and Decorative Arts.* Catalog by Manfred Leithe-Jasper and Rudolf Distelberger.   London: Philip Wilson, 1982.   128 pp., 284 color illus.

Illustrated handbook of the most important objects in this well-known collection with brief introduction.   301 short entries with color reproductions describe metalwork, ivory, jewels, arms and armor, textiles, enamel, rock-crystal objects dating from the early Middle Ages to the 19th century.   Many examples date from the period 1400-1600.   Supplemented by the newly published and more detailed *Weltliche und Geistliche Schatzkammer, Bildführer* by

Rotraud Bauer, Rudolf Distelberger, Stefan Krenn, Manfred Leithe-Jasper, Karl Schütz, and Helmut Trnek (Vienna: Residenz Verlag, 1987), 352 pp., many color and b&w illus., that provides extensive entries and bibliographical references.

BELGIUM

Brussels

MUSÉES ROYAUX D'ART ET D'HISTOIRE

48   *Les Musées Royaux du Parc de Cinquantenaire et de la Porte de Hal à Bruxelles: Armes et armures, industries d'art.* 28 unbound fascicles. Catalog by J. Destrée, A.J. Kymeulen, and Alex Honnotiau. Brussels: A.J. Kymeulen, n.d. Unpaginated, 128 b&w pls.

Each fascicle presents four/five pieces from the major decorative arts and arms and armor collections in Brussels, each one illustrated. Includes prime examples of 15th- and 16th-century European arms and armor, enamels, maiolica, furniture, glass (Venetian), leatherwork, metalwork, small-scale sculpture, stoneware, and textiles; brief essays complement the large black and white plates.

BRITISH ISLES (ENGLAND)

London

BRITISH MUSEUM

49   *The Waddesdon Bequest: Catalogue of the Works of Art Bequeathed to the British Museum by Baron Ferdinand Rothschild, M.P., 1898,* by Charles Hercules Read. London: Trustees of the British Museum, 1902. 145 pp., 55 b&w pls., 42 b&w figs.

Among the 265 entries are a few highly important late Gothic pieces and many exceptional Renaissance objects including a large collection of Limoges enamels, German jewels of Italian inspiration, and a series of German secular plate, boxwood carving and portrait medallions; also some arms and armor including the Demidoff Shield by Giorgio Ghisi and some Venetian glass as well as Italian maiolica.

49a   TAIT, HUGH. *The Waddesdon Bequest: The Legacy of Baron Ferdinand Rothschild to the British Museum.* London: British Museum Publications, 1981. 96 pp., 16 color pls., 72 b&w figs.

Selection of outstanding late Gothic-Renaissance objects from the Waddesdon bequest. Comprising about three hundred works of mostly secular court art, the collection includes: miniature boxwood carvings; an enameled and gilt reliquary commissioned by Jean de Berry; a silver and gilt bookcover; a chalcedony cup; Venetian glass; maiolica from Urbino; Limoges painted enamels by Jean de Court, the Aeneid Master, Léonard Limosin, etc.; enameled jewelry and pocket miniatures; Italian and German gilt-silver vessels (plates, tankards, horns, and ewers).

VICTORIA AND ALBERT MUSEUM

50   *Catalogue of the Soulages Collection; Being a Descriptive Inventory of a Collection of Works of Decorative Art, Formerly in the Possession of M. Jules Soulages of Toulouse,* by J.C. Robinson. London: Chapman & Hall, 1856. 213 pp., 9 b&w pls.

Early and famed collection subsequently acquired for the museum of mostly Italian decorative arts dating from the 15th through 17th century formed between 1830 and 1840. Catalog includes 749 entries among which are 167 Italian maiolica pieces from all centers; 23 Palissy wares; 10 Swiss, Italian, and Flemish stonewares; 91 Venetian glass ewer, tazze, dishes, etc.; 48 knives, forks, spoons, coffers, ivories, utensils; 25 painted Limoges enamels; 86 salvers, fire-dogs, candlesticks, doorknockers, lamps, bells, statuettes, and various utensils such as scissors, corkscrews, clocks, and sundials, stone and marble sculpture, silver stained glass; 106 medals of the Quattro- and Cinquecento, paintings; 20 items of textiles and tapestries; 80 pieces of Venetian, Tuscan, French, furniture of the Renaissance; 60 frames and other items of interior furnishings. Appendix A: facsimiles of signatures of Master Giorgio, traced from pieces in the Soulages collection; appendix B: maiolica by the Fontana family.

WALLACE COLLECTION

51   *Sculpture, Marbles, Terra-Cottas and Bronzes, Carvings in Ivory and Wood, Plaquettes, Medals, Coins, and Wax-Reliefs.* Catalog by J.G. Mann. London: His Majesty's Stationery Office, 1931. 262 pp., 100 b&w pls.

      Eight-page introduction examining the formation and composition of the collection and surveying techniques of metal casting, is followed by 466 comprehensive but concise catalog entries of works dating from ancient Greece to the 19th century. Of the period 1400-1600 are Italian and French terra cottas (cat. nos. 52-59); Italian (62-131), German (238, 242), and Spanish (239-41) bronze objects and statuettes; German ivories (256-57, 259), wood carvings (273-75, 277-82, 284-93); Italian (298-317) and German (318-20) bronze plaquettes; Italian (328-60), French (361-75), and German, Flemish, and Dutch medals (399-410, 412-13).

FRANCE

Paris

MUSÉE DU LOUVRE

52   *Donation du Baron Charles Davillier: Catalogue des objets exposés au Musée du Louvre.* Catalog by Louis Courajod and Émile Molinier. Paris: Imprimeries réunies, 1885. 310 pp., 31 line drawings.

      Collection of 582 works bequeathed to the Louvre by the collector Charles Davillier, many of which are today among the most treasured of the "Département des objets d'art." Includes ivories and bone carvings, bronze plaquettes and statuettes, many Italian medals, rings, paxes, reliquaries, monstrances, Limoges enamels, Hispano-Moresque and Italian maiolica, St.-Porchaire ware, verre églomisé, glass, furniture, leather, and textiles. Catalog with descriptive entries with minimal scholarly apparatus.

53   *Collection Paul Garnier: Horloges et montres, ivoires et plaquettes.* Catalog by Gaston Migeon. Paris: Hachette, 1917. 112 pp., 48 b&w pls.

      Clocks and watches and plaquettes in the Garnier Collection of the Louvre. Catalog entries 1-4, 9-11, 25, 29, 39 are of fine French 16th-century watches made in the workshops of Blois, Loches, Paris, Rouen, and Nérac; 65 is of an engraved silver 15th-century plaque; 66-71 are 15th-16th-century Italian bronze plaquettes attributed to Riccio, Ulocrino, etc.

54   *Nouvelles acquisitions de Département des Objets d'art 1980-1984.* Catalog by Daniel Alcouffe et al. Paris: Réunion des Musées Nationaux, 1985. 195 pp., 12 color pls., numerous b&w figs.

Catalog of 105 additions, all illustrated, often with details, made to the collection of decorative arts in the years 1980-84. Catalog nos. 14-15 are large Brussels tapestries of ca. 1500; 16, an Oudenaarde tapestry of a boar hunt of ca. 1600; 17A-D, 16th-century Italian nielloed cutlery bearing the arms of Cosimo I de' Medici; 18, a 16th-century South German metal casket; 19, a bronze statuette of a monkey (ca. 1570) by Giambologna.

PETIT PALAIS

55 MIGEON GASTON. "Les Objets d'art de la Collection Dutuit." *Les Arts* 11 (1902):22-32, 19 b&w figs. (9 additional figs. of decorative art objects in preceding articles about other media in the Dutuit Collection).
Brief overview of some of the highlights of the Dutuit Collection, which became part of the permanent holdings of the Petit Palais. Dating of the 15th-16th century are some bronzes, enamels by Nardon Pénicaud, Italian maiolica, Palissy and St.-Porchaire ware, etc.

55a *La Collection Dutuit au Petit Palais des Champs-Élysées: Histoire de la collection.* Edited and with introduction by Georges Cain. 2 vols. in 10 parts. Paris: Goupil & Cie, 1903. Vols. 1 & 2: 37 pp., 10 photo-engraved color pls., 23 hand-painted pls., 67 b&w pls.
Part 1: brief history and survey of the collection. Part 5: eleven plates, with accompanying entries by Édouard Rahir, of mostly 16th-century French bookbindings; part 6: twelve plates, with entries by Gaston Migeon and Jean Robiquet, of French, primarily 16th-century, enamels; parts 8 and 9: eighteen plates with entries by Migeon and Robiquet of Italian maiolica and St.-Porchaire ware; part 10: ten plates with entries by Migeon and Robiquet, of various objects including several 16th-century bronzes and other metalwork and jewelry.

Reims

CATHÉDRALE NOTRE-DAME

56 CERF, [ABBÉ]. *Trésor de la Cathédrale de Reims.* Paris: Veuve-Levrault & Fils, 1867. Unpaginated, 88 b&w pls.
Once the wealthiest church treasury of France, it still includes, despite the many losses sustained in 1793, important examples of goldsmith works from the 11th to the 18th century. Volume includes many 15th-16th-century reliquaries, ostensories, nefs, chalices, crosses, and embroidered vestments.

GERMANY

Berlin

STAATLICHE MUSEEN

57 *Die Bildwerke in Bronze und in anderen Metallen, Arbeiten in Perlmutter und Wachs, geschnittene Steine.* Catalog by E.F. Bange. Vol. 2 of *Die Bildwerke des deutschen Museums,* edited by Theodore Demmler. Berlin and Leipzig: Walter De Gruyter & Co., 1923. 177 pp., 49 b&w pls., 156 b&w figs.
Catalog of over eight thousand three-dimensional objects in bronze and other metals as well as carved mother-of-pearl, wax, and engraved stone from Germany, the Netherlands, and France dating from the 12th to the 18th century and arranged chronologically and by country. Includes numerous and often major 15th-16th-century statuettes and busts, plaques

and plaquettes, wax portrait reliefs, mother-of-pearl roundels (devotional subjects and portraits). Works described therein are now either in the Kunstgewerbemuseum of West or East Berlin or else were lost or destroyed in 1945.

STAATLICHE MUSEEN PREUSSISCHER KULTURBESITZ, KUNSTGEWERBEMUSEUM.

58   *Europäisches Kunsthandwerk vom Mittelalter bis zur Gegenwart: Neuerwerbungen 1959-1969.* Exhibition catalog by Franz-Adrian Dreier et al. Berlin: Kunstgewerbemuseum, 1970. 179 pp., 16 color pls., 153 b&w figs.

144 additions of decorative art objects from the Middle Ages to modern times made to the collections during the decade 1959-69. Numbers 6-54 are mostly of the 15th-16th century and include candlesticks, an amethyst double cup in a goldsmith mount, leather objects, Venetian enamel, ecclesiastical vestments, tapestries, Spanish lustreware, Italian maiolica, standing cups, plaquettes, etc.

59   *Kunstgewerbemuseum Berlin.* Catalog edited by Monika Bierschenk, with entries by seven contributors. Berlin: Staatliche Museum Preussischer Kulturbesitz, 1985. 260 pp., 50 color pls., numerous b&w figs.

Permanent collection catalog of the Berlin museum of decorative arts in its new and recently inaugurated location. Description of 349 objects in ten galleries; catalog nos. 30-104, 107-17, 120-21, 125-26, 133-35, 141, 143-44, 146, 148-52, 158-61, and 163 are 15th-16th-century French, Italian, German, Spanish, and Swiss objects, including Limoges enamels, Italian maiolica, Venetian glass, bronzes, furniture, and religious and secular goldsmith works.

Cologne

KUNSTGEWERBEMUSEUM

60   *Die Sammlung Clemens.* Catalog of the exhibition held at the Overstolzenhaus, Rheingasse, by Brigitte Klesse, Hanns-Ulrich Haedeke, and Heinke Griese. Cologne: Kunstgewerbemuseum, 1963. 166 pp., 65 b&w pls.

Retrospective exhibition of the collection of Wilhelm Clemens which, after his death in 1934, was bequeathed to the museum of decorative arts of Cologne. The majority of the 924 items cataloged date of the 15th-16th century and include painting, sculpture, Spanish and Italian ivories, German and Italian bronze statuettes (Meit, Giambologna workshop, etc.) and many plaquettes (Moderno, Leoni, Belli, Flötner, etc.), medals (de' Pasti, Candida, Sperandio, Bellano, Leoni, Gebel, etc.), 15th-century seals and pilgrim badges, clasps, brooches of mother-of-pearl, etc., rings, jewels and amulets, cups, dishes, and flagons of tin, bronze, copper, and iron, shields, arms and armor, hunting gear, German ceramics and glass, furniture, tapestries (mostly Swiss) and other textiles.

Dresden

MUSEUM FÜR KUNSTHANDWERK

61   *Kunsthandwerk der Gotik und Renaissance 13. bis. 17. Jahrhundert.* Catalog forward and metalwork entries by Günter Reinheckel, other contributions by Gisela Haase, Klause-Peter Arnold, and Ursula Hennig. Dresden: Staatliche Kunstsammlungen Dresden, 1981. 191 pp., 234 b&w figs. with many details.

Entries for 234 selected objects from the collection including 15th-16th-century German furniture and woodcarving (figurines, portable altars, paneling, chairs, cabinets, caskets, etc.); Venetian and Bohemian glass (flasks, pokals, tankards, etc.); German ceramics (tiles, pitchers, tankards) and Italian maiolica; German metalwork (liturgical objects, candlesticks, bells, tankards, small bronzes [some Italian], bowls, etc.); also a few Italian and German textile fragments, a bookcover, and a leather casket.

STAATLICHE KUNSTSAMMLUNGEN DRESDEN

62   *The Splendor of Dresden: Five Centuries of Art Collecting.* Exhibition held at the National Gallery of Art, Washington; The Metropolitan Museum of Art, New York; The Fine Arts Museum of San Francisco. Catalog edited by J. Carter Brown, Philippe de Montebello, and Ian McKibbin White; essays and catalog entries by Joachim Menzhausen, et al. New York: Metropolitan Museum of Art, 1978; Dresden: State Art Collections, 1978. 278 pp., 29 color figs., 248 b&w figs.

628 outstanding works from eight museums of the State Art Collections of Dresden ranging from the 14th to the 20th century and selected to explore the history of art collecting from the 16th-century Kunstkammer and armory to the specialized royal art galleries of the 18th century and finally to the reorganization of the collections into public museums in the 19th-20th centuries. Of the 15th-16th century are goldsmith works (drinking horn, nautilus cups, writing caskets, etc., catalog nos. 22-27, 39-42, 241-54, 256-60), jewels (German, 294-99), bronzes (Filarete, Adriaen de Vries, Giovanni Francesco Susini, etc., 47-52, 506-7), ivories (53-60, 66), amber (70), tools (saws, planes, etc., 73-91), furniture (94-96), and arms and armor (German, French, Spanish, Italian, 138-48, 150-52, 158-62, 166-74, 177-78, 183-84, 191-93).

Munich

BAYERISCHES NATIONALMUSEUM

63   *Kunst und Kunsthandwerk: Meisterwerk im Bayerischen Nationalmuseum München. Festschrift zum hundertjährigen Bestehen des Museums 1855-1955.* Essay by Oskar Lenz. Munich: F. Bruckmann KG, 1955. 82 pp., 8 color pls., 188 b&w figs.

Highlights of the collection for the centennial of the Bayerischen Nationalmuseum. 179 catalog entries, many of objects of the 15th-16th century: goldsmith works, armor, tapestries, furniture, bronze and other metalwork, rock crystal, jewelry, textiles (costume), scientific instruments; thirty-page essay outlining the history of the institution.

RESIDENZ

64   BRUNNER, HERBERT. *Die Kunstschätze der Münchner Residenz.* Munich: Süddeutscher Verlag, 1977. 360 pp., 52 color figs., 334 b&w figs.

Detailed, well-illustrated publication on the collection and history of the palace where the Bavarian rulers resided. The famous Treasury, which houses major late Gothic and Renaissance goldsmith works as well as ecclesiastical vestments, is described pp. 127-94. The Silver Room, which includes a few Renaissance pieces of Nuremberg plate, is discussed pp. 195-210. Also of the 16th century in the Residenz are examples of Faenza and Urbino maiolica and a few 16th-century Brussels tapestries.

64a   *Schatzkammer der Residenz München.* Edited by G. Hojer and H. Stierhof, Munich: Bayerische Verwaltung der Staatlichen Schlösser, Gärten und Seen, 1981. 64 pp., 15 color figs., 51 b&w figs. (An abridged, earlier English version, compiled by H. Brunner, translated by M.D. Senft-Howie, exists as: *The Treasury in the Residenz Munich*. Munich: Bayerische Verwaltung der Staatlichen Schlösser, Gärten und Seen, 1977. 62 pp., 24 b&w pls.)

Checklist of 1,258 objects in the Residenz treasury. Numbers 17-106, 174-80, 204-7, 232-33, 235, 321-52, 377-78, 390-412, 414-19, 455, 459-66, 469-70, 478-87, 493-94, 504-10, 517-23, 551, 554, 559-97, 600, 608-30, 635-44, 647-50, 652 are of French, Flemish, Italian, and mostly German precious objects including jewelry, ecclesiastical implements, vessels of rock crystal and of precious stones, and insignia.

Nuremberg

GERMANISCHES NATIONALMUSEUM

65 *Die Werke plasticher Kunst*. Catalog by Walter Josephi. Nuremberg: Germanischen Nationalmuseums, 1910. 499 pp., 64 b&w pls., 160 b&w text figs.

Three-dimensional objects in the permanent collection — among which are 15th-16th-century clay, gesso, and papier-maché statuettes produced in Germany (mostly Nuremberg) and Westphalia (cat. nos. 87-115); 15th-16th-century German bronzes, made particularly in Nuremberg, many given to the workshop of Peter Vischer (150-67); 15th-16th-century gilt-silver German corpuses and a Romulus and Remus group (185-87); 15th- 16th-century Italian, German, and French ivories (641-53); 15th-century mother-of-pearl reliefs (667-82); and 16th-century waxes made in Nuremberg (688-95), all described in detailed entries.

Regensburg

DOMSCHATZ

66 *Der Regensburger Domschatz*. Catalog by Achim Hubel. Munich and Zurich: Schnell und Steiner, 1976. 326 pp., 20 color pls., 22 b&w pls.

Comprehensive catalog of the cathedral treasury of Regensburg. Of the 179 entries for chalices and ciboriums, monstrances, altar implements, reliquaries, textiles (vestments and altar cloths), paintings, several date of the period 1400-1600. Preceded by a seventy-eight-page essay on the history of the collection.

HUNGARY

Esztergom

FÖSZÉKESEGYHÁZI KINCSTÁR

67 *Der Domschatz von Esztergom*. Catalog by Pál Cséfalvay. Budapest: Corvina Kiadó, 1984. 32 pp., 70 b&w pls.

Catalog of seventy objects in the cathedral treasury of Esztergom, of which nos. 11-31, 51-66 are of the period 1400-1600. Includes the Calvary Reliquary (Paris, 1402) of Matthias Corvinus, a Rhenish drinking horn of 1408, and Hungarian chalices, monstrances, morses, as well as embroidered liturgical vestments.

ITALY

Florence

MUSEO DEGLI ARGENTI

68   *Il Museo degli Argenti a Firenze.* Catalog by Cristina Piacenti Aschengreen. Milan: Electa, 1968. 241 pp., 41 color illus., 64 b&w illus.

Catalog with entries for all 2,049 ivories, cameos, gems, rock crystal, and goldsmith works ranging from the Byzantine period to the 19th century with many of the outstanding examples dating of the 1500s. Forty-one-page introduction traces history of the collection founded by Piero de' Medici.

MUSEO STIBBERT

69   *Il Museo Stibbert a Firenze.* 4 vols. in 7 parts. Catalog by Henry Russell Robinson, Giuseppe Cantelli, Lionello Giorgio Boccia, Fosco Maraini; edited by Ugo Procacci. Vol. 1, *Armi e armature orientali* (1974); Vol. 2, *Catalogo* (1974), part 1, 285 pp.; part 2, 57 color figs., 366 b&w figs.; vol. 3, *L'armeria europa* (1975), part 1, 259 pp., 17 b&w figs., 13 pp. of armorers' marks; part 2, 621 figs., some color; Vol. 4, *I depositi e l'archivio* (1976), part 1, 275 pp., 75 b&w figs.; part 2, 133 color figs., 387 b&w figs. Milan: Electa.

Description of the important holdings of the eclectic collection formed by Federico Stibbert (1838-1906) converted into a public museum in its original setting. Vol. 1 deals with Oriental armor. Vol. 2 describes the furnishings of the Palazzo Stibbert including 15th-16th-century cassoni, chairs, clocks, small-scale bronzes, paxes, and plaquettes (Moderno, IO.F.F, Flötner, Michelet Saulmon, etc.), Italian chalices and reliquaries, Florentine and other Italian textiles, pastiglia boxes, a Venetian leather box, German metal boxes, knives, and forks. Vol. 3 covers major collection of arms and armor featuring outstanding Italian and German full and half suits and maces, as well as Spanish, Italian, and German swords, lances, halberds, morions, and firearms. Vol. 4 deals with paintings, drawings, and prints as well as 16th-century frames, pastiglia boxes, Ferrarese metal ornaments, maiolica from Deruta, fragments of carved bone decoration by the Embriachi, floral tapestries, damasks, and embroideries.

Milan

MUSEO DEL DUOMO

70   *Tesoro e Museo del Duomo.* Catalog by Rossana Brivio and Mia Mirabella Roberti. 2 vols. Milan: Electa, 1978. 1: 373 pp., 43 color illus., 640 b&w illus.; 2: 471 pp., 38 color illus., 1,151 b&w illus.

Among the rich holdings of the Milan cathedral museum are reliquaries, chalices, crosses, monstrances, and other liturgical precious objects as well as bronze candelabra, stalls, tapestries (Flemish), and vestments of the Renaissance. See vol. 1 passim.

70a   *Il Duomo di Milano, museo d'arte sacra.* Edited by Ernesto Brivio, with contributions by Chiara Buss, Enrico Cattaneo, and Gian Guido Sambonet. Milan: Banca Popolare di Milano, 1981. 222 pp., 64 color figs., 170 b&w figs.

Precious metalwork, vestments, hangings, and sculpture in the Milan cathedral treasury and museum; choir and altar stalls of the cathedral, tabernacles, pulpit, and stained glass. Useful for illustration and when used in conjunction with the preceding entry.

MUSEO POLDI PEZZOLI

71   *Il Museo Poldi Pezzoli.* Catalog by Guido Gregorietti, Lionello Giorgio Boccia, Antonio Frova, Alessandra Mottola Molfino, and Franco Russoli. Milan: Cassa di Risparmio delle Provincie Lombarde, 1972. 309 pp., 240 color figs., 281 b&w figs.

Twenty-three-page historical introduction on this family of major Italian collectors, the Pezzoli and Poldi Pezzoli, followed by five chapters on the varied areas of this highly important collection. Decorative art objects of the period 1400-1600 include Italian, German, and French arms and armor (pp. 34-55, 62-67), Limoges (120-22), and Italian (125-29) enamels, mounted cups, pax, jewelry caskets (130-34), knives and forks (136-38), watches (138-40), jewelry (147-53), Italian furniture (162-66) and textiles (172-79), Brussels tapestries (180-81), and Venetian glass (190-94).

72   *Orologi, oreficerie.* Edited by Carlo Pirovano with entries by Giuseppe Brusa, Guido Gregorietti, Giuliana Cavalieri Manasse, Elisabetta Roffia, and Tullio Tomba. Vol. 2 of museum catalogs. Milan: Electa, 1981. 451 pp., 59 color figs., 300 b&w figs.

Within the museum's permanent collection of clocks and jewelry are some 16th-century solar clocks (cat. nos. 1, 3-4, pp. 15-18; figs. 1-2, 4-6, pp. 29-31), 16th-century mechanical clocks (nos. 1-14, pp. 131-37; figs. 1-24, pp. 157-68), and 15th-16th-century jewelry (mostly Italian, several French, and a few German, Spanish, and English, pendants, necklaces, rings, belts, altar crosses, pax, paten, enamels [including several Limoges]), reliquaries, mounted rock-crystal covered cups, candlesticks, bucket, small caskets (leather, wood, ivory, enamel), knives and forks, nos. 82-94, 100-101, 150-73, 196-200, 211-25, 232-33, 250-62, 290-93, 301-17, pp. 276-79, 284-87, 289-91, 293-99, 301-3, 306, 433-34; figs. 92-103, 105, 111-12, 115, 161-86, 211-13, 215-18, 234-53, 264-65, 279-91, 317-20, 336-47, 354-56, pp. 338-44, 346-48, 362-67, 376-80, 388-98, 404, 410-13, 421-23, 427-29, 431-32.

73   *Ceramiche, vetri, mobile e arredi.* Edited by Carlo Pirovano, with entries by Laura Brambilla, Lucia Caterina, Carla Di Benedetto, Giuliana Cavalieri Manasse, Giovanni Mariacher, Elisabetta Roffia, Giovanna Ventrone Vassallo, and Annalisa Zanni. Vol. 3 of museum catalogs. Milan: Electa, 1983. 473 pp., 55 color figs., 652 b&w figs.

Within the museum's permanent collection of ceramics, glass, furniture, and furnishings, are several 16th-century Venetian glass bowls, beaker, lamps, bottles, etc. (cat. nos. 37-80, pp., 172-77; figs. 37-80, pp., 212-32) and Italian 16th-century furniture—cassoni, tables, chests, chairs, caskets, etc.—nos. 1-19, pp. 311-15; figs. 1-24, pp. 341-57).

Rome (Vatican)

MUSEI E GALLERIE PONTIFICIE

74   *The Vatican Collections: The Papacy and Art.* Exhibition held in New York at The Metropolitan Museum of Art, at The Art Institute of Chicago, and at The Fine Arts Museums of San Francisco. Catalog with numerous contributors. New York: Metropolitan Museum of Art and Harry N. Abrams, 1982. 255 pp., 165 color figs., 111 b&w figs.

Catalog of 168 works, often major and from various origins, owned by the Vatican. Relevant to the 15th-16th century are catalog nos. 14-19 (tapestries), 22-24 (famed candlestick and cross by Gentili), 25 (altar frontal and vestments), 47-53 (niello, goldsmith works, rock crystal by Belli, and an ivory descent from the cross by Nicolas Mostaert).

Turin

MUSEO CIVICO D'ARTE ANTICA, PALAZZO MADAMA

75   MALLÉ, LUIGI. *Palazzo Madama in Torino.* Vol. 2, *Le collezioni d'arte.* Turin: Tipografia Torinese, 1970. 502 pp., 59 color pls., 562 b&w figs.
   The rich holdings of this museum include some 16th-century Limoges and Italian enamels, some important Spanish lustreware, Faenza, Gubbio, Deruta, Castel Durante maiolica, furniture (especially Venetian intarsia chest), 15th-16th-century verres églomisés, reliquaries, monstrances, goldsmith ornaments, small Paduan, Venetian bronzes, leather boxes and bindings.

76   *Smalti-avori del Museo d'Arte Antica.* Catalog by Luigi Mallé. Turin: Museo d'Arte Antica, 1969. 354 pp., 6 color figs., 235 b&w figs.
   Catalog of permanent collection of enamels and ivories. Forty-three-page essay deals with enamelwork from origins to 20th century (see pp. 33-47 for European works of 1400-1600); catalog includes 15th- and 16th-century Italian and French translucent and painted enamels (monstrances, cups, goblets, plates, reliquaries, caskets, pendants, etc., pp. 99-111, pls. 41-70). Seventy-page essay deals with ivories (see pp. 237-48, 251-52, 266-67 for French, Italian, German, Spanish, and Portugese works of 1400-1600); catalog includes 15th and 16th-century Italian (mostly), French, German, Flemish, and Spanish works (statuettes, altars, caskets, combs, etc., pp. 301-26, pls. 141-83).

76a   *Vetri—vetrate—cristalli di rocca e pietre dure.* Catalog by Luigi Mallé. Turin: Museo Civico di Torino, 1971. 406 pp., 20 color figs., 198 b&w figs.
   Catalog of glass, stained glass, jade, rock crystal and semiprecious stones in the museum. Particularly important are Venetian glass objects and a few carved rock crystals. Each section is preceded by an essay.

MALTA

Valetta

CHURCH OF ST. JOHN

77   OMAN, CHARLES. "The Treasure of the Conventional Church of St. John at Malta." *Connoisseur* 173 (1970), part 1, 101-7, 14 b&w figs.; part 2, "Plate Used at Services," 177-85, 19 b&w figs.; part 3, "The Plate about the Church and the Robbery of the Treasure," 244-49, 8 b&w figs.
   History of the order's collection of goldsmith works (formerly owned by the Church of St. Anthony Abbot in Vittoriosa and various chapels in Malta and Gozo). Most pieces, which are now lost, are described in the 574-page inventory dated 1756 with twenty-one water-color drawings, listing several 15th-16th-century objects, mostly from Italy but also of Russian, German, French, and Spanish origin: reliquaries, processional and altar crosses, chalice, bishop's mitre, jewelry for the icon of Our Lady of Filermo.

SPAIN

Escorial

MONASTERIO SAN LORENZO

78   JUNQUERA, PAULINA. "Ornamentos sagrados y relicarios del Real Monasterio de San Lorenzo." *Goya* 56/57 (1963):180-90, 1 color fig., 15 b&w figs.
         10th- to 16th-century religious objects in the Monastery of San Lorenzo of El Escorial. Among those of the 15th-16th century are embroidered copes, dalmatics, and altar frontals of the Escorial workshops, a German 15th-century arm reliquary, a Spanish 16th-century head reliquary, and a few Portuguese and Italian 16th-century shrines.

Madrid

MUSEO LÁZARO GALDIANO

79   *La Colleccion Lázaro de Madrid.* Introduction by William Ruck. 2 vols. Madrid: España Moderna, 1926-27. 1:495 pp., 458 b&w figs.; 2:547 pp., 598 b&w figs.
         Photographic presentation interspersed with laudatory commentaries on Spain's most famous 19th-century private collection, subsequently turned into a museum. Holdings by and large of high quality, are primarily Spanish, followed by French, Italian, and German. Includes 15th-16th-century ecclesiastical and secular goldsmith works (mostly mudejar in style), jewels, Spanish furniture, stalls, and other woodcarvings, Italian medals and plaquettes, Spanish keys, a 16th-century clock, amulets from Santiago, a Flemish reliquary, lustreware and azuelos, Italian maiolica (plate by Master Giorgio), Spanish bookbindings, altar frontals, silk, lace, and other textiles including vestments. Concludes with general index by medium only.

79a   *Coleccão Lázaro de Nova Iorque.* Exhibition held in Lisbon, Museu Nacional de Arte Antiga. 2d ed. Lisbon: Museu Nacional de Arte Antiga, 1945. 57 pp., 41 b&w pls.
         Showing of a selection (332 items) from the collection of José Lazaro (Galdiano) that had been brought to New York subsequent to the 1926-27 Madrid catalog.

79b   *Guia abreviada del Museo Lázaro Galdiano* by José Camón Aznar. Madrid: Fundacion Lázaro Galdiano, 1951. 163 pp., 40 b&w pls.
         Brief guide to this museum in which are emphasized several important pieces of 15th-16th-century goldsmith work: the pokal of Matthias Corvinus, a French reliquary, one of the Aldobrandini cups, rock-crystal vessels, etc.

U.S.A.

Cincinnati

TAFT MUSEUM

80   *Taft Museum Catalogue.* Cincinnati: Cincinnati Institute of Fine Arts, n.d. 205 pp., 41 b&w figs.
         572 entries, among which an important collection of Limoges Renaissance enamels (nos. 21-32, 89-100, 108, 110, 112, 115, 119-126, 134-57, 167-68, 171-80, 550, 555) including the "Monvaerni" Crucifixion triptych, Italian 16th-century carved rock crystal (246-51, 260-61, 263, 265-66, 276), and Italian and German 16th-century pendants (253-55, 257-59), German hone-

stones (43-44, 504), and a gold cup (270). Also, Italian maiolica (107, 109, 111, 113, 117, 187-95), a St.-Porchaire salt (256), French Renaissance chairs (493-94), and a 16th-century Flemish tapestry.

Los Angeles

LOS ANGELES COUNTY MUSEUM OF ART

81   SCHRODER, TIMOTHY. "Decorative Arts of the Renaissance." *Apollo* 124 (1986):404-9, 3 color figs., 5 b&w figs.
      Overview of holdings consisting of Italian and Hispano-Moresque maiolica, Palissy ware, Limoges enamels, "the Methuen Cup" (a 16th-century gilt-silver Scottish vessel). Most of these items were once in the William Randolph Hearst Collection.

Louisville

J.B. SPEED MUSEUM

82   COMSTOCK, HELEN. "The Satterwhite Collection of Gothic and Renaissance Art." *Connoisseur* 128 (1951):132-36, 8 b&w figs.
      Describes some of the outstanding pieces from the collection of Preston Pope Satterwhite, since bequeathed to this museum, comprised of decorative arts objects of the Middle Ages and Renaissance: a 15th-century Sienese enameled chalice; a French architectural reliquary of the 15th century; a Flemish tapestry of ca. 1500 (Brussels); a cassone (Rome, ca. 1550); bronze statuettes attributed to Cellini and Giambologna, etc.

New York

METROPOLITAN MUSEUM OF ART

83   *The Jack and Belle Linsky Collection in The Metropolitan Museum of Art.* Contributions by Olga Raggio, James D. Draper, Carmen Gómez-Moreno, Clare Vincent, Jessie McNab, et al. New York: Metropolitan Museum of Art, 1984. 361 pp., 74 color figs., numerous b&w figs.
      The essential part of a former major New York collection. Among the 336 items bequeathed, nos. 48-100 are mostly medieval and Renaissance French enamels, Venetian glass, Italian and German small-scale sculpture (by Antico, Riccio, Severo da Ravenna, Giambologna, Gerhard, Kern, etc.), mortars by the Grandis, carnelian and rock-crystal cups, German and Spanish jewels. For the portion of the collection that was auctioned, see entry 170.

84   *The Middle Ages: Treasures from The Cloisters and The Metropolitan Museum of Art.* Exhibition catalog by Vera K. Ostoia. Los Angeles: Los Angeles County Museum of Art, 1969. 265 pp., 15 color pls., 117 b&w figs.
      Highlights of the medieval collection ranging from the 3d to the 16th centuries. For 15th-16th centuries, see cat. nos. 84 to 118, including a monstrance, maiolica, Hispano-Moresque lustreware, tapestries, a gilt-silver crozier head, carved boxwood base, glassware, a brass lectern, ewers, chalice, mazer, boxwood triptych, pendant, etc. This exhibition also traveled to The Art Institute of Chicago.

85 *Highlights of the Untermyer Collection of English and Continental Decorative Arts.* Contributions by Yvonne Hackenbroch, William D. Rieder, Carmen Gómez-Moreno, James D. Draper, et al. New York: Metropolitan Museum of Art, 1977. 216 pp., 244 b&w figs.

388 entries include: 16th-century English silver (pp. 11-17, cat. nos. 1-11) and furniture (pp. 67-68, nos. 109-11); 15th- and 16th-century Austrian, Burgundian, English, German, Italian, and Netherlandish metalwork (tableware, water vessels, candleholders, mortars, small bronzes, andirons, a total of thirty-four pieces, pp. 149-74); Italian mandora (p. 150, no. 286); English, French, Flemish, and Italian textiles (panels, tapestries, table carpets, cushion covers, coifs, pp. 188-95, nos. 343-56).

Sarasota

JOHN AND MABLE RINGLING MUSEUM OF ART

86 *500 Years of Decorative Arts from the Ringling Collections, 1350-1850.* Exhibition catalog by Cynthia Duval. Sarasota: John and Mable Ringling Museum of Art Foundation, 1981. 175 pp., 133 b&w figs.

Presentation of 157 objects from the museum's permanent collections, including 16th-century French clocks, Italian and French wax portraits in metal mounts, Italian and Spanish maiolica, 15th-century German monstrances, ewers, and coconut cup, pax incorporating Moderno plaquette, 16th-century Florentine and Flemish furniture.

U.S.S.R.

Moscow

ORUZHÉINAYA PALÁTA

87 *The Armoury Chamber,* by V. Goncharenko and V. Narozhnaya. Translated by Natalie Ward. Moscow: Progress, 1976. 181 pp., 16 color pls., 122 b&w figs.

Pocket guide incorporating the former treasury of the tsars, as well as Russian and Western art objects ranging from the 12th century to modern times; 15th- and 16th-century Western works include arms and armor, textiles, goldsmith works (mostly Nuremberg and Augsburg pokals, ewers, nautilus cups, etc.), the 16th-century ivory throne of Ivan the Terrible.

III. Multi Country, Multimedia: Exhibition Catalogs

Dealers' catalogs are in Chapter IV

AUSTRIA

Vienna

KUNSTHISTORISCHES MUSEUM

88 *Europäische Kunst um 1400.* Vienna: Kunsthistorisches Museum, 1962. 536 pp., 160 b&w pls. (A French version of this exhibition catalog was published as: *L'Art européen vers 1400,* 470 pp., 160 b&w pls.; it does not include, however, bibliographical references for catalog entries.)

International European Gothic style art of around 1400. Preceded by a sixty-five-page socioeconomic introduction, the catalog includes 601 objects often of major importance and borrowed from European and North American museums. The material is organized by medium and subdivided by country of origin, each classification preceded by an introduction. Represented are goldsmith works and related objects such as caskets, candelabra (entries 437-513, 600-601); textiles (514-42); arms and armor (543-62); medals, coins, and seals (563-93).

BELGIUM

Brussels

PALAIS DES BEAUX-ARTS

89 *Le Siècle de Bourgogne.* Exhibition catalog by Pierre Quarré, R. van Luttervelt, et al. Brussels: Ministère de l'Instruction Publique, 1951. 109 pp., 72 b&w pls.

274 art works of the late 14th-early 16th century produced for or around the court of Burgundy. A variant of the Amsterdam exhibit *Bourgondische Pracht* (see entry 92).

Ghent

MUSÉE DES BEAUX-ARTS

90   *Charles-Quint et son temps.* 2d ed. Essays by H. Nowé and Georges Chabot, biographies
and exhibition catalog entries by E. Bille-de Met. Ghent: Éditions de la Connaissance,
1955. 188 pp., 137 b&w figs.
    Dedicated to Emperor Charles V of Spain, born in Ghent: brief biography on the
monarch and contemporaries; essays on the arts during his reign; catalog of 547 objects, including medals and seals by Dürer, Leone Leoni, and others (nos. 392-412b), arms and armor
(430-38), faience (482-89), and furniture (490-513).

BRITISH ISLES (ENGLAND)

Manchester

91   *Art Treasures of the United Kingdom from the Art Treasures Exhibition, Manchester.* Exhibition catalog edited by J.B. Waring, with essays by Owen Jones, Digby Wyatt, A.W.
Franks, J.B. Waring, J.C. Robinson, and G. Scharf. London: Day & Son, 1858. 233 pp.,
100 chromolithographs and woodcuts.
    Commemorative publication of the 1857 exhibition. Extremely valuable for the his-
tory of taste and record of ownership of important objects. Includes tables, essays followed
by colored line engravings, lithographic plates on: sculpture (actually ivory statuettes and
panels, small bronzes, terra cottas), ceramic art (including Hispano-Moresque ware, Flemish
stoneware), vitreous art (including Venetian and German glass, Limoges enamels), metallic
art (goldsmith work, keys, lock, watches, jewels, liturgical bronze implements, arms and
armor, etc.), textiles (silks, embroideries, vestments, tapestries), and secular Renaissance furniture.

NETHERLANDS

Amsterdam

RIJKSMUSEUM

92   *Bourgondische Pracht van Philips de Stoute tot Philips de Schone.* Exhibition catalog by R.
van Luttervelt, J.H.M. Terwindt, and A.M.L.E. Erkelens. Amsterdam: Rijksmuseum,
1951. 119 pp., 64 b&w figs.
    309 art works of the late 14th-early 16th century connected with the patronage of the
court of Burgundy and of Maximilian I, produced in Flanders, France, Germany, and Italy. In
addition to paintings, sculptures, and manuscripts, includes ivories, important goldsmith
works, the clock of Philip the Good, furniture, tapestries, and vestments from public and
private collections. Cursory catalog entries.

's Hertogenbosch

93   *De oude kerkelijke kunst in nederland gedenkboek van de nationale tentoonstelling te
      's Hertogenbosch in 1913. Afbeeldingen der belangrijkste voorwerpen / L'Art religieux ancien
      aux Pays-Bas. Mémorial de l'exposition nationale de Bois-le-Duc 1913.* Catalog by J.S.
      Frederiks, Jan Kalf, and six other contributors. 's Hertogenbosch: C.N. Teulings, 1914.
      213 pp., 72 b&w pls. Text in Dutch and French.
         Useful retrospective publication of an exhibition of 163 Dutch medieval and Renais-
      sance art works of religious (mostly ecclesiastical) nature in treasuries of synagogues and chur-
      ches, as well as private collections, of the Netherlands. Includes paintings, textiles, goldsmith
      works, dinanderie, and sculpture.

SWITZERLAND

Bern

BERNISCHES HISTORISCHES MUSEUM

94   *Die Burgunderbeute und Werke burgundischer Hofkunst.* Exhibition catalog by Florens
      Deuchler and several other contributors. Bern: Bernisches Historisches Museum, 1969.
      339 pp., 1 color pl., 359 b&w figs. (A bilingual French/English summary of this catalog
      was edited by H. Matile, and translated by P.E. Schazmann, and by B.M. Charleston and
      Ruth Cecil, respectively: *Le Butin des guerres de Bourgogne et oeuvres d'art de le cour de
      Bourgogne/The Burgundian Booty and Works of Burgundan Court Art,* 184 pp., 34 b&w pls.)
         Many of the 255 items cataloged represent the Burgundian spoils gathered by the
      Swiss after their victories over Duke Charles the Bold in 1476-77. (See Deuchler, *Burgunder-
      beute,* entry 18.) Complemented with contemporary paintings, coins, stained glass, tapestries,
      and sculpture in Swiss collections.

U.S.A.

Ann Arbor

UNIVERSITY OF MICHIGAN MUSEUM OF ART

95   *Images of Love and Death in Late Medieval and Renaissance Art.* Exhibition catalog by
      William R. Levin, with essays by Clifton C. Olds and Ralph G. Williams. Ann Arbor:
      University Publications/University of Michigan, 1976. 139 pp., 68 b&w pls.
         Two essays examining the themes in art (pp. 3-6) and literature (pp. 7-39) followed
      by entries for ninety-four objects of varied media from public and private U.S. collections. Of
      decorative arts of the period 1400-1600 are French and Franco-Flemish textiles and tapestries
      (nos. 61-63, pp. 101-4), French and Flemish ivories (nos. 65, 72-73, 76, 78, pp. 105, 111, 113-
      115), English, Flemish, and German chaplets and rosaries (nos. 84-85, 87-91, pp. 118-24), an
      English bridal casket (no. 92, p. 124), a Castel Durante roundel (no. 93, pp. 124-125), and a
      15th-century wood comb (no. 94, pp. 125-26).

Lawrence

UNIVERSITY OF KANSAS MUSEUM OF ART [SPENCER MUSEUM OF ART]

96 *The Waning of the Middle Ages: An Exhibition of French and Netherlandish Art from 1350 to 1500 Commemorating the Fiftieth Anniversary of the Publication of "The Waning of the Middle Ages" by Johan Huizinga.* Exhibition catalog by J.L. Schrader. Lawrence: University of Kansas Museum of Art, 1969. 102 pp., 1 color pl., 76 b&w pls.

    Includes 138 concisely written entries dealing with French or Flemish works lent by American institutions, collectors, and dealers: ivories (boxes, panels, comb), miniatures, a-quamanile, metal caskets, ecclesiastical embroideries, paintings, drawings, sculpture, tapestries, paneling, a purse handle, a falcon hood stand.

New York

METROPOLITAN MUSEUM OF ART – CLOISTERS

97 *The Secular Spirit: Life and Art at the End of the Middle Ages.* Exhibition catalog introduction by Timothy B. Husband and Jane Hayward, with essays and entries by many authors. New York: E.P. Dutton & Co., 1975. 287 pp., 15 color pls., 344 b&w figs.

    320 objects of secular character from the later Middle Ages (1300-1550) from North American museums and private lenders; arranged in eight sections, each presenting a different socioeconomic, scientific, or cultural theme; catalog includes a wide assortment of objects: candlesticks, small caskets, utensils, cutlery, dishes, vessels, costumes, jewelry, arms, musical and scientific instruments, coins, tapestries, clocks, etc., with essays and selected bibliography.

San Francisco

CALIFORNIA PALACE OF THE LEGION OF HONOR

98 *The Triumph of Humanism: A Visual Survey of the Decorative Arts of the Renaissance.* Exhibition catalog introduction by D. Graeme Keith, with contributions by Charles Avery, Jessie McNab Dennis, David DuBon, Stephen V. Grancsay, Yvonne Hackenbroch, Paul Needham, Clare Vincent, and William D. Wixom. San Francisco: Fine Arts Museums of San Francisco, 1977. 96 pp., 8 color pls., 111 b&w figs.

    Checklist of 286 objects in the exhibition from U.S. museums and collections and from the Victoria and Albert; short essays on the patronage of the Medicis (pp. 17-25), Italian small bronzes (26-34), European goldsmith work and jewelry (35-42), arms and armor (43-51), timepieces and scientific instruments (52-58), ceramics, glass and enamels (59-67), furniture and woodcarvings (68-73), and tooled bookbindings (74-80).

Worcester, Mass.

WORCESTER ART MUSEUM

99 *The Virtuoso Craftsman: Northern and European Design in the Sixteenth Century.* Exhibition catalog by John David Farmer. Worcester: Worcester Art Museum, 1969. 210 pp., 108 b&w illus.

108 examples of the decorative arts in France, England, the Netherlands, and Germany epitomizing Renaissance and mannerist taste and drawn from U.S. museums and private collections: gold- and silversmiths' works, enamels, jewelry, astronomical instruments, boxwood medallion, tapestry, carved gemstone vessels, ceramics, glassware, armor, ivory, engravings, etc. Detailed entries placing objects in context of contemporary art and society, mentioning comparative material, and providing biographical sketches of identified artists.

U.S.S.R.

Leningrad

100   PRACHOFF, ADRIEN. *Album de l'exposition rétrospective d'objets d'art, de 1904, à St.-Pétersbourg.* . . . St. Petersburg: S-té Golicke & A. Willborg, 1907. 308 pp., 138 b&w text figs., 19 pls, some in color.

Commemorative publication of the 1904 exhibition of decorative arts held in the private museum of Baron Stiegler in St. Petersburg. Important since most of the objects discussed were then in Russian or Austrian private collections. Deals mostly with the 18th century but includes a St.-Porchaire salt, a Spanish silver cross of the 15th century, Nuremberg goldsmith work, a Lübeck silver statuette of St.-George by Berndt Heynemann dated 1507, a 16th-century Russian cross, icons, jewels, Limoges painted enamels, a 15th-century Italian round box, a 16th-century tapestry with the genealogy of the counts of Sternberg.

IV. Multi Country, Multimedia: Private Collection, Auction, and Dealer Catalogs

Arranged alphabetically first by country of location, then by collection name. Collection catalogs have been listed alphabetically by author; sales catalogs, by title.

AUSTRIA

CASTIGLIONI COLLECTION

101 *Collections Camillo Castiglioni de Vienne.* 2 vols. Sale held in Amsterdam by Frederick Muller & Cie, 17-20 November 1925. Vienna: Frederick Muller & Cie; Ant. W.M. Mensing, 1925. 1:65 pp., 76 b&w pls.; 2:71 pp., 75 b&w pls.

Important collection best known for its Italian and Flemish painting, but which also included Italian Renaissance furniture: cabinets, chests, chairs (vol. 1, nos. 132-215; vol. 2, nos. 180-234); a 15th-century reliquary chalice from Siena (1, nos. 232-33); various German and Venetian goldsmith works (1, nos. 234-47, 259-64); Flemish tapestries (1, nos. 266-70); the collection of small Renaissance bronzes cataloged in 1923 by Planiscig (see entry 1184); leather objects (1, nos. 396-407); Italian and German arms of the 16th century (2, nos. 409-60); German and Italian andirons, pewter plate and bottle (2, nos. 461-88); Hispano-Moresque, German, and Italian ceramics (2, nos. 499-505).

FIGDOR COLLECTION

102 *Die Sammlung Dr. Albert Figdor,* edited by Otto von Falke. 5 vols. Sale held in Vienna by Artaria & Co./Glückselig G.M.B.H. and Paul Cassirer 11-13 June (vols. 1-2), 29-30 September (vols. 3-5), 1930. Vol. 1, by von Falke, 507 lots, 76 b&w pls.; vol. 2, by August Schestag, 303 lots, 80 b&w pls.; vol. 3, by Max J. Friedländer, 118 lots, 64 b&w pls.; vol. 4, by Leo Planiscig and Theodor Demmler, 179 lots, 52 b&w pls.; vol. 5, by von Falke and Planiscig, 273 lots, 84 b&w pls.

Dispersal of major collection mainly comprised of medieval and Renaissance art. Vol. 1: Netherlandish, Swiss, French, Flemish, and German tapestries, ecclesiastical vestments (mostly Italian), embroideries; pewter plates, flasks, and other vessels; gold- and silversmith works (mazers, coconut cups, nautilus cup, drinking horn, gilt-bronze statuettes); liturgical objects (chalices, ciboria, monstrances), crucifixes. Vol. 2: furniture (assortment of European chairs, table, chests, cassoni—some richly decorated with carving, intarsia, etc.). Vol. 3: paintings. Vol. 4: sculpture, including round mirror frame by Lucca della Robia and several 16th-century German wood medallions. Vol. 5: small carved wooden caskets; bronze caskets, bells, mortars, brass ewers, tankard, plates; bronze armorial plates.

RUHMANN COLLECTION

103   BORN, WOLFGANG. "Five Centuries of Glass—I. The Franz Ruhmann Collection at Vienna." *Connoisseur* 101 (1938):10-14, 10 b&w figs.
    Selection of 15th-16th-century examples from this extensive private collection of about five hundred glass objects: a Venetian enameled-glass goblet of ca. 1490; two German "cabbage-stalk" glass reliquaries, ca. 1500 and 1520; a German barrel-shaped glass (16th century), and a German humpen dated 1541. (Part 2 deals with 18th-19th-century pieces.)

SCHWARZ COLLECTION

104   *Sammlung Hans Schwarz, Wien: Werke der bildenden Kunst und des Kunstgewerbes des XIII. bis XVIII. Jahrhunderts.* Sale held in Berlin at Rudolph Lepke's Kunst-Auctions-Haus 8-9 November 1910. 51 pp., 44 b&w pls.
    Viennese collection comprised of 313 lots including important paintings, major German sculptures, wood reliefs, and statuettes dating mostly of late Gothic times. Of the same period are also bronze mortars and plaques, metal engraved caskets, locks, elements of armor, arms, furniture, lighting fixtures, Italian maiolica, Austrian tiles, and Rhenish salt-glazed ware.

STRAUSS (MAX) COLLECTION

105   *Nachlass Dr. Max Strauss Wien. Venezianisches Glas, Keramic, Bronzen, Silber, Etc.* Sale held in Vienna by Gluckselig G.M.B.H. at the Auktionhaus für Altertümer 2-4 November 1925. Introduction by Robert Schmidt. 91 pp., 26 b&w pls., 462 b&w figs.
    Dispersal of major collection of Kleinkunst (444 lots, many dating of the 16th century): ceramics (Rhenish stoneware, Raeren and Siegburg vessels, Italian maiolica, Palissy ware); Venetian glass (bowls, tazze, goblets, pokals, etc.); early clocks (lots 417-19); Italian bronze statuettes (423-30); some German pewter and goldsmith works. All illustrated.

WEINBERGER COLLECTION

106   *Versteigerung der hinterlassenen Sammlung des Herrn Emil Weinberger, Wien.* Catalog by Richard Ernst, Ludwig Baldass, Ernst Kris. Sale held in Vienna by Auktionhaus C.J. Wawra, Auktionhaus Glückselig G.M.B.H., and Kunsthändler Richard Leitner 22-24 October 1929. 116 pp., 525 b&w figs.
    Selection of 471 lots from the estate of Emil Weinberger of Vienna. Includes 15th-16th-century Rhenish and other German and Austrian ceramics (lots 1-24), Italian maiolica (30-52), Spanish lustreware plate (53), German glass (59-61), mostly German plate, caskets, ecclesiastical and devotional goldsmith works (82, 90, 96-100, 123, 129-30, 137), bronze medals (by Hans Reinhardt) and statuettes (by Riccio, Giambologna, etc.) (139-46, 151-55, 157-76, 178-85, 187, 190-97), clocks and astronomical instruments (198-208, 247-48), Embriachi bone,

ivory, and boxwood carvings (249-61), Limoges enamels (262-68), leatherworks (271-72), iron caskets (282-84), Arras tapestry dated of ca. 1430 (293) and several other textiles, Italian, French, German, and Spanish furniture (380-86, 388-90, 394-412, 415, 417, 424-25).

BRITISH ISLES (ENGLAND)

BERNAL COLLECTION

107   *Catalogue of the Celebrated Collection of Works of Art from the Byzantine Period to that of Louis Seize, of That Distinguished Collector, Ralph Bernal, Esq., Deceased; Also, of the Beautiful Decorative Furniture and Service of Plate.* Sale held in London at Christie's 5 March 1855. 357 pp., numerous photogravure illus.

Sale of a famous collection comprising 4,294 lots which in addition to paintings and porcelain included over 300 pieces of late medieval and Renaissance goldsmith works, enamels, 350 Italian maiolica items, some 50 Palissy wares, other ceramics, over 500 items of glass (especially Venetian, German, and Flemish), over 150 lots of arms and armor. Also jewels, ancient keys, clocks, ivories. Each lot is cursorily described; some of the most important items are illustrated with a line drawing.

CLARK COLLECTION

108   *Paintings and Works of Art from the Collections of the Late Lord [Kenneth] Clark of Saltwood, O.M., C.H., K.C.B.* Sale held in London at Sotheby's 27 June, 3 and 5 July 1984. 234 pp. (unpaginated), 51 color figs., 137 b&w figs.

Among the 200 lots are some Italian medals (lots 133, 135-37, 139), a bronze roundel (138), and plaquettes (140-42), a small casket inset with Italian Renaissance cameos and intaglios (131), a 16th-century German bronze dragon (132), and Italian maiolica (144-57).

COLWORTH COLLECTION

109   *Catalogue of the Renowned Collection of Works of Art Chiefly Formed by the Late Hollingworth Magniac, Esq. (Known as the Colworth Collection). . . .* Sale held in London at Christie's 2, 4 July 1892. 250 pp., 52 b&w figs.

Sale of a major English collection, which includes 1,554 lot numbers (often subdivided) that are unevenly described, often without a date provided. The following lots appear largely pertinent to 15th-16th-century decorative arts: 195-215, 335-66, 640-716, 786-803, ecclesiastical and secular goldsmith work; 215A-28, Italian bronze medals, statuettes, doorknocker, etc.; 229-50, 384-403, 509-28, important Limoges and other painted enamels; 260-61, ivories; 261B-83, 771-85, honestone, boxwood carvings, etc.; 284-300, 427-39, 572-86, important Italian, Flemish, and German furniture (cabinets, cassoni, Venetian mirrors, etc.); 367-79, 469-92, 633-38, Italian maiolica; 404-26, German glass; 440-68, 599-632, German and Flemish ceramics; 493, a St.-Porchaire ewer; 529-71, 831-69, Venetian glass; 717-48, 871-922, 944-1046, arms and armor; 804-30, Palissy ware; 948-69, Hispano-Moresque ware.

FITZHENRY COLLECTION

110   *Catalogue of the Collection of Works of Art Chiefly of the Medieval and Renaissance Periods Formed by J.H. Fitzhenry, Esq.* Sale held in London at Christie's 18-19, 24-26 November 1913. 97 pp., 8 b&w pls.

Dispersal of this London collection (792 lots), the greater part of which had previously been on loan to the Victoria and Albert Museum. Of the period 1400-1600 are: examples of Italian maiolica (lots 1-21); Limoges painted enamels (42-52) by Pierre Courteys, Pénicaud, Jean Laudin; brass candelabra, aquamanile; Florentine, Paduan, and Venetian Renaissance bronze statuettes, knockers, mortars, etc.; small woodcarvings from Flanders, France, and England; Palissy, Nevers, Rouen, and Nîmes ceramics (159-61); molded and stamped leather cases (167-79); French wax portraits (206-7); ecclesiastical goldsmith work from Italy and Germany; various woodworks including carvings and small 15th-century furniture; enameled Venetian goblet and plaque (503, 507); some French, Italian, and German medals and plaquettes.

FOUNTAINE COLLECTION

111   *Catalogue of the Celebrated Fountaine Collection of Majolica, Henry II Ware, Palissy Ware, Nevers Ware, Limoges Enamel. . . .* Sale held in London at Christie's 16-19 June 1884. 66pp., 22 pls. with line drawings.
        Property of the late Andrew Fountaine of Narford Hall (Norfolk) comprised of 574 lots forming, by their individual quality, one of the most famous collections of decorative arts in 19th-century England. Includes 131 Limoges enamels, 321 ceramics (Italian maiolica, Nevers, St.-Porchaire and Palissy ware), 22 ivories, 25 arms, etc.

GWYNN COLLECTION

112   HAYWARD, J.F., and BLAIR, CLAUDE. "The R.T. Gwynn Collections: Medieval Furniture, Armour and Early Clocks." *Connoisseur* 150 (1962):78-91, 1 color fig., 16 b&w figs.
        Includes some 15th-16th-century English chests, a stool, cupboard, chair, and a rare countertable; an important array of 15th-century German helmets, other elements of armor, arms, and a Touraine tapestry of ca. 1510 woven for Le Mans Cathedral.

HAMILTON COLLECTION

113   *The Hamilton Palace Collection.* Sale held in London at Christie's 17, 19-20, 24, 26-27 June, 1, 3-4, 8, 10-11, 15, 17-20 July 1892. Paris: Librairie d'Art; London: Remington & Co., 1882. 240 pp., several b&w pls.
        The noted English collection of 2,116 art works founded by Alexander, tenth duke of Hamilton (1796-1852) and dispersed on the orders of his grandson. The catalog provides only cursory information and practically no dating. Decorative art objects of the period 1400-1600 are: an oval-shaped tazza of hematite in gold enameled mounts; a Flemish cabinet; a Florentine pietre dure mosaic table; silver and gilt-silver plate; Limoges enamels; Italian maiolica; St.-Porchaire ware; Venetian glass.

HEVER COLLECTION

114   *The Hever Castle and the Property of the Lord Astor of Hever.* 2 vols. Sale held in London at Sotheby's 5-6 May 1983. Vol. 1. *Arms and Armour,* 141 pp., 26 color figs., 90 b&w figs.; vol. 2., *Works of Art* 55 color figs., 101 b&w figs.
        Dispersal of a highly important collection. Vol. 1: 194 lots of arms and armor dating from the 15th to the 18th century and including fourteen full suits among which the three-quarter armor made ca. 1540-45 by Giovanni Paola Negroli for Henri II of France (lot 44), and many rare pieces such as the 16th-century openwork jester's helmet (32) and the 16th-century combination daggar and wheel-lock pistol (60). Vol. 2: 179 lots including several dating

of the 15th-16th century such as textiles and tapestries, locks and keys, important Italian and Spanish religious goldsmith works and jewels, a carved sapphire of Elizabeth I attributed to Julien de Fontenary (290).

LAKING COLLECTION

115   *Catalogue of the Collection of Arms and Armor and Objects of Art Formed by Sir Guy Francis Laking, Bart. . . .* Sale held in London at Christie's 19 April 1920. 70 pp., 13 b&w pls.

Dispersal of collection (670 lots) of a former keeper of the King's Armory, of the Wallace Collection, and of the London Museum. Lots 15-143, 205-99 are mostly 15th-16th-century arms and elements of armor; 144-66 are sword pommels; 367-445 bearing the heading "Objects of Art" include some 15th-16th-century plate, ironwork, bronze statuettes, carved panels, a Flemish cabinet, etc.

SHANDON (NAPIER) COLLECTION

116   ROBINSON, J.C.   *Catalogue of the Works of Art Forming the Collection of Robert Napier of West Shandon, Dumbartonshire.* London: Privately Printed at the Chiswick Press, 1865. 326 pp.

Brief citations for 4,937 objects, many of the 15th-16th century, including Italian, French, and German bronzes, carved wood (comb, bellows, frieze), ivory plaques and figurines, rock crystal, coconuts, etc. in gold mounts, Italian rock-crystal medallion intaglio, Limoges enamels, a few Italian and German arms, French and Italian keys, German, Dutch, Italian knives, forks, spoons, works in metal, Venetian glass, Italian maiolica and Hispano-Moresque wares, and earthenware.

117   *Catalogue of the Celebrated Assemblage of Works of Art and Vertu, Known as the Shandon Collection, Formed during the Last Half-Century by That Well-Known Amateur Robert Napier, Esq.* Sale held in London at Christie's 11-14, 16-20 April, 14-18 May, 4-7, 11-12 June 1877. 222 pp.

Dispersal of 3,432 lots, which include silver plate, Italian and other bronze statuettes, etc., furniture, Nevers faience, German stoneware, ivories, Venetian and German glass, Limoges enamels, Hispano-Moresque lustreware, an important series of Italian maiolica, also sgraffito ware, arms, goldsmith and other metalworks. Cursory description of the lots is usually limited to one line.

STOWE MANOR COLLECTION

118   FORSTER, HENRY RUMSEY.   *The Stowe Catalogue.* London: Donald Bogue, 1848. 353 pp., 15 b&w pls.

Commemorative catalog of the sale (3,460 lots) held at the Manor of Stowe (property of the late Richard Grenville, second duke of Buckingham and Chandos) by Christie's of London 15 August-7 October 1848. Includes the best and at that time the largest single collection (109 pieces) of Italian maiolica (lots 50-89, 197-213, 301-40, 476-83, 641-49); also many examples of goldsmith works (rock crystal and other stones in mounts), a good number of which appear to be of the late 16th century (items are not dated and most are only cursorily described), of tapestries, small bronzes (by Giambologna, etc.), arms and armor (233-75). Catalog provides prices and names of purchasers. Index of purchasers.

WHAWELL COLLECTION

119   *Catalogue of the Magnificent Collection of Armour, Weapons and Works of Art, the Property of the late S.J. Whawell, Esq.* Sale held in London at Sotheby's 3 May 1927. 87 pp., 32 b&w pls.

526 lots among which are three-quarter suits including a Greenwich suit (lot 263), composite suits, helmets, shields, firearms including an important harquebus of 1583 made for Francis II, swords, etc. Sale also included pottery (stoneware), medals and plaquetes, ivories, silversmiths' work and metalwork (chalices, standing cups, tankards, a rare Spanish monstrance [459]), woodcarving and furniture.

RECENT MULTI OWNER AUCTIONS

120   *Catalogue of Medieval, Renaissance, and Baroque Works of Art.* Sale held in London at Sotheby's 13 December 1979. 159 pp., 18 color figs., 165 b&w figs.

Embriachi carved bone casket (lot 38); Limoges tazza and plaques (94-96); 16th-century French and German locks and keys (98-102, 112-115); 15th-16th-century leather, iron, wood caskets (135-41, 143, 146-50); Italian, Flemish, and French carved wood reliefs (158-60); bronzes (mostly Italian plaquettes and statuettes) (esp. 162-87, 207-12, 218-21), Roccatagliata, Susini, Riccio school, Da Volterra, etc.

121   *European Medieval, Renaissance, and Baroque Works of Art.* Sale held in London at Sotheby's 3 April 1984. 82 pp., 11 color figs., 100 b&w figs.

279 lots including several 15th-16th-century Netherlandish, German, Italian metalwork objects (lots 73-75, 82, 84-85, 87-88, 92-96, 98-99), a 15th-century Tournai Crucifixion tapestry (100), 15th-16th-century Italian, Spanish, German ecclesiastical objects (127-30, 132, 135-36, 138), German steel casket (147), and 15th-16th-century German, Spanish, French, Italian, and Flemish jewelry (149-52, 154-55, 161, 164-66, 179, 183-87, 192, 207, 228-29, 260, 267, 271, 279).

122   *Important Medieval Works of Art, Renaissance and Baroque Bronzes and Other European Sculpture.* Sale held in London at Sotheby's 11 December 1986. 146 pp., 30 color pls., numerous b&w figs.

Sale includes several small bronzes: a 1400 Flemish Virgin and Child, Italian figures by the circle of Riccio, Severo, etc.; also Renaissance mortars; a 16th-century French Neptune; important late Gothic and Renaissance jewels including the Middleham Pendant; small wood reliefs; four Limoges enamels; German and Spanish metal caskets.

London

P. & D. COLNAGHI & CO., LTD.

123   *Objects for a "Wunderkammer."* Catalog edited by Alvar González-Palacios assisted by Luigi d'Urso, with entries by same and seven other contributors. London: P. & D. Colnaghi & Co., 1981. 371 pp., 40 color pls., 136 b&w figs.

Important dealer's exhibition of 165 decorative arts objects dating mostly of Renaissance times and including metalwork, scientific instruments, watches and clocks, glass beaker, rock crystal, waxes, small-scale sculpture, wood carving, furniture, textiles, draughtsmen, from Italy, France, and Germany.

CZECHOSLOVAKIA

LANNA COLLECTION

124 LEISCHING, JULIUS. *Sammlung Lanna, Prag.* Leipzig: Karl W. Hiersemann, 1909. 201 pp., 50 pls, some in color.

Famed encyclopedic collection including 15th-16th-century French, German, Italian goldsmith works, Limoges enamels, leather boxes, Italian and German bronzes, including many important plaquettes, pewter plate, box and other small wood carvings, a pastiglia box, important Italian maiolica including a Faenza relief, other 16th-century ceramics from Austria, Nuremberg, Silesian and Rhenish earthenware, German mother-of-pearl carvings, French Renaissance tapestries and furniture, some arms.

124a *Sammlung des Freiherrn Adalbert von Lanna, Prag.* 2 vols. Sale held in Berlin at Rudolph Lepke's Kunst-Auctions-Haus 9-16 November 1909; 21-28 March 1911. 1:194 pp., 110 b&w figs.; 2:110 pp., 111 b&w pls.

Sales catalog comprising 3,763 lots. More valuable than the collection catalog as it contains a larger number of illustrations.

FRANCE

ADDA COLLECTION

125 *Collection d'un grand amateur.* Sale held in Paris at Palais Galliera 29-30 November, 1-3 December 1965.   Paris: Maurice Rheims & Philippe Rheims, 1965.   441 pp. (unpaginated), 7 color figs., 401 b&w figs.

Dispersal of a major collection comprised of paintings as well as objects of decorative arts from the late medieval period until the eighteenth century. Of the period 1400-1600, lots 153, 157-59 are German enameled glass; 166-82, Limoges enamels; 183-90, 194-95, English-German silver mounts; 206, 209-12, 222, 224, 229-31, Nuremberg cups; 237, 239, tankards; 252-54, metal chests by Michael Mann; 255-56, 260, 264, 267, 270, clocks; 272-76, Spanish, French, Italian mortars; 278-88, plaquettes of Moderno and others; 289-325, statuettes of Bellano, Severo da Ravenna and other Riccio pupils, Leone Leoni, Roman School, after the antique; 353-60, Italian bells; 361-69, medals; 376-85, 387-412, statuettes after Giambologna, Campagna, Venetian, etc.; lots 456-647 comprise a remarkable collection of Italian maiolica from Caffaggiolo (456-65), Castel Durante (466-78), Castelli (479), Deruta (480-530), Faenza (531-79), Florence (580-84), Forli (585), Gubbio (586-97), Montelupo, Padua, Palermo (598-600), Perugia (601-6), Urbino (607-47); Hispano-Moresque lustreware (648-61).

ALLEMAGNE COLLECTION

126 JANNEAU, GUILLAUME. *La Maison d'un vieux collectionneur.* 2 vols. Paris: Libraire Gründ, 1948. 1:300 pp., 10 b&w pls., numerous line drawings; 2:248 unbound b&w pls.

Presentation of heteroclitic collection amassed by Henry-René d'Allemagne in his Paris house from the 1880s until the 1940s. The text is conceived as a lengthy room-by-room guided tour. First storey includes rooms with several pieces of French furniture, carvings, and iron works of the Renaissance (see pls. XXXII-XXXVI, XLI-XLII, XLVII, XLIX, LII-LVIII and passim); also late Gothic bronze candlesticks, dishes, bronze figures, and ceramics.

BARDAC COLLECTION

127   LEMAN, HENRI. *Collection Sigismond Bardac: Faïences italiennes du XVe siècle; objets de haute curiosité, Moyen Age et Renaissance.* Paris: Librairie Centrale des Beaux-Arts, 1913. 50 pp., 50 hand-colored pls.

Catalog of a private collection comprised of thirty pieces of 15th-16th-century Italian maiolica (from Montelupo, Faenza, Siena, Caffaggiolo, and by the Della Robbias), and twenty varied medieval and Renaissance objects (nine of the 15th-16th century including Venetian glass, Limoges enamel, candlesticks by François Briot, and Venetian helmet attributed to Paolo Rizzo); short descriptive entries.

BASILEWSKY COLLECTION

128   DARCEL, A. and BASILEWSKY, A. *Collection Basilewsky: Catalogue raisonné.* 2 vols. Paris: Vve A. Morel et Cie, 1874. 1:206 pp.; 2:33 color pls., 17 b&w pls.

122-page introduction on the "industrial arts" from the 1st to the 16th century centering on this then major Paris collector; for the 15th century see the section dealing with the Middle Ages, passim (ivory, woodwork, furniture, bronze, goldsmith works, enamels, metalwork, armor—pp. 47-81); for the 16th, see pp. 83-122 (woodwork, furniture, ceramics, bronze, metalwork, enamel, glass, Palissy ware, embroideries and tapestries). 558 catalog entries among which nos. 120-23, 136-37, 157, 159-89, 239, 243-44, 249-50, 253 are of French, Flemish, German, and Italian furniture, liturgical goldsmith works, enamel, metalwork, and armor, and practically all entries from no. 258 to 550 are of German, Italian, and French ivory, carved woodwork, furniture, earthenware, bronze, metalwork, knives, arms, Limoges enamels (nos. 305-49), Spanish and Italian maiolica (nos. 350-442), Palissy ware, glass, tapestry, and embroidery.

COTTREAU COLLECTION

129   HAMEL, MAURICE. "La Collection Cottreau." *Les Arts* 100 (1910):2-31, 52 b&w figs.

Highlights of this important collection of medieval and Renaissance objects, especially of Limoges enamels by Pierre Reymond, Nardon and Jean II Pénicaud, Jean de Court, etc., of Italian maiolica, Palissy ware, cups carved out of semiprecious stone, bronze statuettes, and plaquettes.

129a   *Collection Cottreau: Catalogue des objets d'art et de haute curiosité de l'Antiquité, du Moyen-Age, de la Renaissance, des XVIIe et XVIIIe siècles, faïences italiennes, émaux champlevés et peints de Limoges, ivoires, bronzes, objets de vitrines.* Sale held in Paris at the Galerie George Petit 28-29 April 1910. Paris: Henri Baudoin, 1910. 40 pp.

103 lots among which some Palissy ware (lots 4-7), Italian maiolica (8-29), French 16th-century ivories (36-37), 15th-century Limoges enamels (47-79), small Italian bronzes of the 15th-16th century (86-96), 16th-century gold figurine (103), vessels of semiprecious stone (104-5), silver 16th-century Italian pax (123), small 16th-century Italian caskets in metal or leather (124-26), and 16th-century German tin drinking vessel (127).

DAVILLIER COLLECTION

See entry 52

DUTUIT COLLECTION

See entry 55a

ENGEL-GROS COLLECTION

130   GANZ, PAUL. *L'Oeuvre d'un amateur d'art: La Collection de Monsieur F. Engel-Gros;*
Catalogue raisonné, with the collaboration of Raymond Koechlin, Gaston Migeon, Joseph
Destrée, et al. 2 vols. Geneva: Éditions d'art Boisonnas; Paris: Éditions Jean Budry &
Co., [1925]. 1:476 pp., some text figs.; 2:12 color pls., 141 b&w pls.
       Commemorative catalog of the F. Engel-Gros Collection, which until sold at auction
(Paris: Galerie Georges Petit, 30-31 May, 2 June, 15 December 1921, 19-20 December 1922)
was housed at Château Gundeldingen, Basel, and Château Ripaille on the Lake of Geneva.
       Eclectic collection of a wealthy Alsacian textile manufacturer that includes 15th-16th
century: boots, clothing, and purses; German honestone models for medals; Italian plaquettes
(Moderno, Riccio, etc.); cassoni; German and Swiss stove tiles; Italian and Spanish frames;
French cabinets. The textile holdings are particularly important with Brussels, Arras, Loire
Valley, Upper Rhine and Swedish tapestries; a large collection of 16th-century embroideries
(ecclesiastical and secular) on silk and linen; lace, mostly from Flanders, Italy, and France;
leather bindings of Naples, Venice, made for Jean Grolier, and French and German bindings;
elements of armor, arms including crossbows and firearms; French, Italian, and German silver, bronze and lead medals; coins and seals; some goldsmith works (pyx, cups); Limoges plaques; a musical instrument bearing the monogram of the French king Henri II; a watch; many
rings, dinanderie and pewter; iron keys, etc.; a St.-Porchaire cup; Italian maiolica; Siegburg
jugs; two Hispano-Moresque plates, glass from Venice and Germany, leather containers. Vol.
2 concludes with a list of prices the collection fetched.

FOULC COLLECTION

131   LEMAN, HENRI. *La Collection Foulc: Objets d'art du Moyen Age et de la Renaissance.*
2 vols. Paris: Les Beaux-Arts, 1927. 1:119 pp.; 2:86 b&w pls.
       Catalog of 207 items forming the collection of Edmond Foulc, Paris. Included are:
twenty-five Renaissance bronzes by Bertoldo, Riccio, Bellano, Pollaiuolo, Adriano Fiorentino,
Sansovino, etc., many of which are now in public collections; a seal box made for Duke Charles the Bold of Burgundy; Agnus Dei and other 15th-16th-century boxes, basins; a French
16th-century clock; two wax portraits; a painted Limoges triptych by Pénicaud (now in the
Frick Collection, New York); the alabaster choir screen of the chapel at the Château of Pagny
(now in the Philadelphia Museum of Art); French Gothic and Renaissance sculpture, leather
boxes and bindings, keys, tools, and knives; 16th-century firearms; French carved panels and
furniture (cupboards, chests, chairs, tables, doors) of the 15th-16th century; an outstanding
15th-century French carved alcove; two French and three Florentine tapestries.

KANN (ALPHONSE) COLLECTION

132   *The Alphonse Kann Collection.* 2 parts. Sale held in New York at the American Art Galleries 6-8 January 1927. Unpaginated, numerous b&w pls.
       Pertinent to the 15th-16th century are lots 336-430, which include: Italian bronze pla-
quettes and medals among which are the Heraclius medal; bronze statuettes attributed to Bellano (St. Christopher, etc.), Bertoldo, Riccio, Sansovino, Giambologna, and others; Italian
and Spanish maiolica; some goldsmith work (lots 465-66, 468-74, 477, 490-91); a French
tapestry and German embroidery (492-494); French and Italian furniture (508-18).

KANN (RODOLPHE) COLLECTION

133   MANNHEIM, JULES, and RAHIR, ÉDOUARD. *Catalogue of the Rodolphe Kann Collection.* 2 vols. Vol. 1, *Objets d'art, Middle Ages and Renaissance,* Paris: Privately Printed, 1907. 69 pp., 86 b&w pls.

This large volume of plates and captions includes: fifteen maiolica pieces from Deruta, Urbino, Castel Durante, Gubbio; two 16th-century ivory statuettes; 16th-century carved panels from the Netherlands and Lombardy, a bronze plaque by Vecchietta; bronze mortars and several statuettes (David by Severo); two German table clocks; a large iron frame of the 16th century.

LE ROY COLLECTION

134   MIGEON, GASTON. "La Collection de M. Martin Le Roy." *Les Arts* 10 (1902):2-34, 42 b&w figs.

Overview of this outstanding Paris collection of medieval and Renaissance art including Flemish and French tapestries, an embroidery, small bronzes, furniture, etc.

134a   MARQUET DE VASSELOT, J.-J. et al. *Catalogue raisonné de la Collection Martin Le Roy.* 5 vols. Vol. 1 (1906), *Orfèvrerie et émaillerie,* by Marquet de Vasselot, 94 pp., 1 hand-painted pl., 33 monochrome pls.; vol. 2 (1906), *Ivoires et sculptures,* by Raymond Koechlin; vol. 3 (1907), *Bronzes et objets divers,* by Gaston Migeon, and *Mobilier,* by Louis Metman, 130 pp., 33 monochrome prints; vol. 4 (1908), *Tapisseries et broderies,* by Marquet de Vasselot, 93 pp., 18 monochrome prints; vol. 5 (1909), *Peintures,* by Paul Leprieur and André Pératé, and *Miniatures et dessins,* by André Lemoisne, Paris: [Privately Printed].

Major French collection of 11th-18th-century objects of the turn of the century. Detailed entries for all items in collection. Vol 1: goldsmith works and enamels among which are a Flemish 15th-century gilt-copper tower-shaped box (no. 46) and two Italian 15th-century enameled paxes; vol. 2: ivories and sculpture, none of the former of the 1400-1600 period; vol. 3: bronzes and other objects with nos. 4-27 being Italian, French, Flemish, and Spanish 15th-16th-century bronzes (mortars, statuettes, caskets) and nos. 28-29 being French and Italian 15th-century leather box and sheath; furniture, among which nos. 1-21 are French, Italian, Spanish, and Flemish choir stalls, caskets, dressers, cupboards, door lintel, and chairs; vol. 4: tapestries and embroideries including French, English, and Flemish 15th-16th-century examples (nos. 1-9); vol. 5: paintings, miniatures, drawings.

MANNHEIM COLLECTION

135   *The Collection of the Late Mr. Charles Mannheim. Art Objects: Pottery, Ivories, Enamels, Orfèvrerie, Rock Crystals, Jewellery, Bronzes, Sculpture, Glass.* Paris: Georges Petit, 1910. 55 pp., 38 b&w pls.

Catalog of 164 decorative art objects most of which date of the 15th-16th century. Included are Italian maiolica (nos. 1-41), Spanish lustreware, etc. (42-48), Palissy ware (49-53), ivory statuettes (63-67), Limoges enamels (75-85), reliquary (88), carved rock crystals (97-99), jewelry (104-13), glass from Venice and elsewhere (142-64).

SAMBON COLLECTION

136   *Catalogue des objets d'art et de haute curiosité de l'Antiquité, du Moyen Age, de la Renais-
       sance . . . formant la collection de M. Arthur Sambon.* Sale held in Paris at the Galerie
       Georges Petit 25-28 May 1914. 100 pp., several b&w pls.
              Dispersal of 470 lots including ceramics (nos. 222-73), mostly Italian maiolica, Italian
       ivory beads and crucifix said to be of the 16th century (306-8), reliquaries, enamel plaques,
       paxes, Venetians glass, and miscellaneous objects (336-88), some dating of the period 1400-
       1600. Some Renaissance bronze statuettes (416-58 passim).

SOLTYKOFF COLLECTION

137   *Catalogue des objets d'art et de haute curiosité composant la célèbre collection de Prince Sol-
       tykoff.* Sale held in Paris at the Hôtel Drouot 8-10, 15-17, 22-24, 29-30 April, 1 May 1861.
       Paris: Charles Pillet, 1861. 260 pp., 1 b&w pl.
              Sale of a major collection comprised of 1,109 lots, which include important series of
       late medieval and Renaissance liturgical and devotional goldsmith work, Limoges enamels
       (plaques and plate), French, Flemish, Italian, German furniture (wardrobes, cabinets, chairs,
       mirror frames), clocks, 130 lots of Palissy ware, 2 of St.-Porchaire, a Beauvais platter dated
       1511, German and Flemish earthenware, 115 Italian maiolica pieces, 85 lots of Venetian and
       11 of German glass, German silver plates, cups, ewers, bronze candlesticks, andirons, seals,
       medals by de' Pasti, Pisanello, and French artists. Entries tend to be cursory with little or no
       scholarly apparatus.

SOULAGES COLLECTION

       See entry 50

SPITZER COLLECTION

138   BONNAFFÉ, EDMOND. *Le Musée Spitzer.* Paris: E. Ménard & Cie, 1890. 35 pp., 4
       b&w pls.
              Private collection of the famed colorful art dealer-collector Frédéric Spitzer (1815-
       90) in late-19th-century Paris. Spitzer is held to have selected the best representative
       medieval and Renaissance enamels, furniture, goldsmith works, arms and armor, bronzes,
       tapestries, sculpture, etc., with the apparent intent of forming a museum (for detail of content,
       see following entry; the collection was auctioned off in 1893, see entry 138c).

138a   *La Collection Spitzer: Antiquité, Moyen-Age, Renaissance.* 6 vols. Vol. 1 (1890), 227 pp.,
       52 color pls., 2 b&w pls.; vol. 2 (1891), 223 pp., 49 color pls., 6 b&w pls.; vol. 3 (1891),
       295 pp., 46 color pls., 13 b&w pls.; vol. 4 (1892), 202 pp., 30 color pls., 29 b&w pls.; vol. 5
       (1892), 260 pp., 22 color pls., 30 b&w pls.; vol. 6 (1892), 240 pp., 57 b&w pls.; numerous
       line drawings in all volumes, which are folio-size. Paris: Maison Quantin.
              Catalog of more than four thousand objects constituting the major private collection
       of decorative arts of the 19th century. Vol. 1: fifty-one-page introduction by Eugène Müntz
       provides an overview of the collection established as a private museum; antiquities (pp. 1-17)
       by M. Froehner; ivories (pp. 19-73) by Alfred Darcel (cat. nos. 107-19 are 15th-century and
       nos. 120-42 are 16th-century ivories of French, Italian, German, Spanish, and Flemish origin):
       ecclesiastical bronzes, enamels, and goldsmith works (pp. 75-151) by Léon Palustre (nos. 96-
       146) are 15th-century and nos. 147-85 are 16th-century German, Spanish, Italian, Flemish, and
       French statuettes, crosses, monstrances, morse, paxes, candlesticks, and Limoges enamels);

tapestries (pp. 153-69) by Müntz (nos. 1-6 are 15th-century and nos. 7-23 are 16th-century Italian, Flemish, and Parisian hangings). Vol. 2: Limoges enamels of the 16th century by or attributed to the Pénicauds, Limosin, Poncet, Nouailher, Reymond, Didier, Courteys, and de Court (pp. 1-72, nos. 1-171) by Claudius Popelin; furniture and woodworks (pp. 73-116) by Edmond Bonnaffé (nos. 1-4 are 15th-century and nos. 5-75, 120-32 are 16th-century French, Italian, Spanish, German, Flemish credenze, sideboards, chairs, tables, doors, cabinets, panels, bellows; St.-Porchaire ware (pp. 117-33), nos. 1-7) by Bonnaffé; Palissy ware (pp. 135-58, nos. 1-69) by Émile Molinier; locks and keys (pp. 159-90) by Henry d'Allemagne (nos. 1-11 are French 15th-century locks; nos. 12-17 are French and German 16th-century locks; nos. 1-36 are French and Spanish 16th-century keys); leather (pp. 191-218) by Alfred Darcel (nos. 8-26 are 15th-century and nos. 27-67 are 16th-century French, Italian, Flemish, German, and English caskets, cases, bookslips, sheaths, desk sets). Vol. 3: secular goldsmith works (pp. 1-31) by Darcel (nos. 1-4 are 15th-century and nos. 5-70 are 16th-century German, Spanish, French, and Italian cups, ewers, pokals, tankards, nautilus cups, coconut cups, salts); engraved and embossed metalwork (pp. 33-52) by Molinier (nos. 1-42, 44-48 are 16th-century Italian cabinets, frames, purse handles, and plaques; Italian verres églomisés of the 16th century (pp. 53-73, nos. 1-38) by Molinier; glass (pp. 75-111) by Édouard Garnier (nos. 9-17, 26-27, 40-41, 43-45, 48, 50, 55, 73 are 15th century and nos. 18-25, 28-34, 36-38, 46-47, 49, 51-54, 56-72, 74-85 are 16th-century Venetian goblets, bottles, ewers; nos. 86-94, 101-2, 104-6, 111 are 16th-century Spanish, French, German, and Flemish glass; stained glass (pp. 113-26) by Molinier; jewels and rings (pp. 127-71) by Bonnaffé (no. 1 is a French 16th-century enamel diptych; nos. 2-77 are 15th-century Flemish, Italian, German brooches, morses, crosses, and pendants; nos. 7-13, 49 are 15th-century and nos. 14-47, 50-62, 64, 76-77 are 16th-century rings); earthenware (pp. 173-97) by Arthur Pabst (nos. 1-59 are 16th-century German stoneware); knives, forks, and spoons (pp. 199-248) by d'Allemagne (nos. 2-21, 23, 68-69, 117 are of the 15th century and nos. 22, 24, 27-34, 37-43, 46-51, 56-57, 61, 63-67, 81-83, 85, 87-88, 90-92, 94-98, 101-12, 118-22, 124-25, 127-30, 132-37, 141-44, 147-86, 192, 194-97, 199-200, 204, 206-13 are Italian, German, and French pieces of the 16th century); 16th-century German and Flemish boxwood and honestone small-scale decorative sculpture and medallions (pp. 249-88, nos. 2-192) by Pabst. Vol. 4: Italian maiolica, Hispano-Moresque lustreware and Oriental porcelain (pp. 17-88) by Molinier (nos. 1-210 are 15th- and mostly 16th-century dishes, albarelli, and vases from Caffaggiolo, Faenza, Urbino, Gubbio, Castel Durante, Venice, Deruta; nos. 1-18 are 15th-16th century Spanish pieces); sculpture (pp. 89-122) by Wilhelm Bode including terra cottas (nos. 1-14) mostly by the Della Robbias, and small-scale bronzes from Padua, Florence, Venice, and Nuremberg (nos. 2-54); plaquettes and medals (pp. 123-88) by Molinier (nos. 1-67, 70-77, 103-13 are Italian plaquettes by Riccio, Belli, Moderno, Fra Antonio da Brescia, etc.; nos. 68-69 are by Flötner; nos. 78-95 are German, nos. 96-97, 116 are Flemish, and nos. 99-102 are French plaquettes); medals: ninety-seven are Italian, thirty-one German, and four are French of the 15th-16th centuries; dinanderie (pp. 189-98) by Molinier (nos. 13-21 are of the 15th century, 22-23 are of the 16th century). Vol. 5: gems (pp. 1-24) by Bonnaffé (forty-four 16th-century Italian, French, Spanish, German rock crystal, jasper, chalcedony, sardonyx, porphyry cups, ewers, plates, plaques, medallions); clocks and watches (pp. 25-62) by Palustre (nos. 1-23, 25, 27-28, 30-33, 35-36, 40-50, 57, 60-61, 65, 67 are 16th-century German, French, and Italian clocks, mostly astronomical; nos 2, 4-8, 11-14, 18, 21, 24-31, 34-35, 39-40, 42-43 are 16th-century French, German, and English watches); scientific instruments (pp. 63-122) by Alfred Ernst (nos. 21-24, 28-42, 102, 113, 116, 122-29, 140, 142, 147-48, 150-51, 153, 172-73, 175-76, 179-80 are French, German, and Italian 16th-century astrolabes, sundials, celestial globes, and perpetual calendar); miniatures, paintings, and drawings (pp. 123-61) by Molinier and Léopold Delisle; wax (pp. 163-94) by Gaston Le Breton (nos. 1-24, 26 are Italian portrait medallions); embroidery and textiles (pp. 195-239) by Louis de Farcy (nos. 5-208 are 14th-15th century ecclesiastical vestments, antependiums, tapestries from Italy,

Spain, Portugal, and England); 16th-century Italian pastiglia boxes (pp. 241-48) by Molinier; games (pp. 249-55) by Molinier (nos. 1-4 are 16th- century Venetian and German backgammon and checkerboards). Vol. 6: repeat of the introduction in vol. 1 by Müntz; eighty- three-page introduction on arms and armor by J.-B. Giraud, and 543 entries by Molinier, most of which are of objects of the 15th-16th centuries: complete German and Italian combat and parade suits (nos. 1-9, 15-20), also half armor; helmets (nos. 25-46); various elements of armor often lavishly chiseled (nos. 47-84, 92-93); shields (85-91, 94-96); Spanish, Italian, and German swords (nos. 98-173, 175, 177-78, 188, 191-92, 194-207, 211), daggers (nos. 174-76, 179-81, 184-90, 193, 208-10, 212-27), lances, halberds, etc. (nos. 228-68); maces (269-84); crossbows (nos. 285-97); wheel-lock guns (nos. 297-319, 518), pistols (nos. 335-41, 344); powder horns and ammunition storages (nos. 384- 446); stirrups (nos. 449-91), harnesses (492-517); cannons (nos. 533-38); horns and purses (nos. 539-43).

138b   *La Collection Spitzer: Antiquité, Moyen-Age, Renaissance.* 2 vols. Macon: Protat Frères, 1890-1. 1:561 pp.; 2:543 pp.
        Slightly altered edition of catalog entries in the six-volume deluxe edition. The present volumes, reduced to quarto size, also lack introductory essays and all illustrations.

138c   *Catalogue des objets d'art et de haute curiosité antiques, du Moyen-Age et de la Renaissance composant l'importante et précieuse Collection Spitzer.* Essays by Edmond Bonnaffé and Émile Molinier. 2 vols. 1:282 pp.; 2:273 pp. Sale held in Paris by Paul Chevallier and Charles Mannheim 17 April-16 June 1893.
        Sale catalog of 3,369 lots of this spectacular 19th-century Paris collection comprising innumerable 15th- and 16th-century ivories, religious goldsmith works, tapestries, enamels, Palissy ware, furniture, works in leather, locks and keys, brass objects, Spanish and Italian maiolica, earthenware, gems, medals, bronzes (vol. 1); plaquettes, faience, secular goldsmith works, rock crystal, knives, iron wares, clocks, watches and scientific instruments, waxes, caskets, games, and textiles (vol. 2). Introduced by two essays, the first a reprint of Bonnaffé's 1890 publication (see entry 138), the second by Molinier who reminisces about Spitzer and laments the dispersal as he describes the order in which the collection will be auctioned.

STEIN COLLECTION

139   *Catalogue des objets d'art de haute curiosité et d'ameublement composant l'importante collection de M. Ch. Stein.* Sale held in Paris at the Galerie Georges Petit 10-14 May 1886. Paris: Paul Chevallier, 1886. 103 pp., 33 b&w pls., 43 b&w figs.
        Sales catalog of 410 lots from the collection of Charles Stein (also a dealer) of which nos. 2-240 are comprised of many 15th-16th-century European decorative arts including ivories, Limoges enamels, Italian maiolica, Venetian glass, seals, arms and armor, jewelry, carved rock crystal, liturgical goldsmith utensils, clocks, small caskets, bronze inkwells, statuettes, and plaquettes, the most important of which eventually entered public collections.

140   *Catalogue des objets d'art de haute curiosité . . . composant la collection de feu M. Charles Stein.* Sale held in Paris at the Galerie Georges Petit 8-10 June 1899. Paris: Paul Chevallier, 1899. 80 pp., 29 b&w pls., 25 b&w figs.
        Sales catalog of 352 often highly important lots from Stein's estate; nos. 1-244 are mostly 15th-16th-century Italian maiolica (Gubbio, Urbino, Faenza, Castel Durante), St.-Porchaire and Palissy ware, Limoges enamels, Venetian glass, and French, Flemish, German, Italian, and Spanish religious goldsmith works, jewelry and watches, mirrors, medallions and carved rosary beads, ivory, aquamanile, candlesticks, bronze plaquettes and statuettes, arms, small caskets, furniture, and tapestries; entries often include indication of former collection.

GERMANY

BECKERATH COLLECTION

141   BOMBE, WALTER. "Die Sammlung Adolph von Beckerath." *Cicerone* 8 (1916):167-86, 19 b&w figs.

Brief presentation of a major collection of Italian Renaissance paintings, sculpture, and decorative arts slated to be auctioned the same year.

141a   *Nachlass Adolf von Beckerath, Berlin.* Sale held in Berlin at Rudolph Lepke's Kunst-Auctions-Haus 23-26 May 1916. 149 pp., 85 b&w pls.

Sale of the estate of Adolf von Beckerath (1834-1915), one of Germany's important collectors of decorative arts. Of the 1,178 lots, nos. 157-297 are furniture (Italian chair, mirrors, cabinets) and other woodwork, many of which are of the period 1400-1600; 345-428 are rather bland 16th-17th-century Italian bronze statuettes and plaquettes; 429-754 are mostly Italian albarelli and plate while some are Hispano-Moresque.

BERNHEIMER COLLECTION

142   *Privatsammlung aus dem Nachlass des Konsuls Otto Bernheimer, München: Mittelalterliches und barockes Kuntsgewerbe, Textilien und Teppiche, Möbel, Skulpturen, Gemälde und Graphik, aussereuropäische Kunst.* Sale held in Munich at the Weinmüller Kunstversteigerungshaus 9-10 December 1960. 101 pp., 170 b&w pls.

Sale of the collection (1,243 lots) of the late Otto Bernheimer (1877-1960) of Munich. Diversified holdings include, of the period 1400-1600: bronze and pewter ewers, pitchers and plates, candlesticks; ecclesiastical implements; silver plate and chalices; Limoges painted enamel; a pastiglia box; a chalice carved out of horn; a German ivory casket; tapestries woven in Basel, Franconia, the Rhine region, Brussels, Tournai, Enghien, Oudenaarde, and Wismar; French, Flemish, and English panel embroideries as well as some from Nuremberg, Passau, and Thurgau; ecclesiastical vestments and silks; Italian and Spanish furniture, an Augsburg clock.

BODE COLLECTION

143   *Nachlass Wilhelm von Bode.* Sale held in Berlin by Paul Cassirer 5 November 1929. Catalog edited by Robert Schmidt. Berlin: Paul Cassirer and Hugo Helbing, 1929. 61 pp., 34 b&w pls.

Dispersal of the private collection of Wilhelm von Bode, well-known historian and museum personality. The auction included: (lots 1-58) Italian maiolica (albarelli, drug jars, vases, flasks, and bottles) from Faenza, Florence, Siena, Rome, and Venice; and 16th-century bronze candlesticks and vessels (78-83).

BOHNEWAND COLLECTION

144   SCHMIDT, ROBERT; WINKLER, F.; and FALKE, OTTO VON. *Aus der Sammlung Curt Bohnewand.* Munich: F. Bruckmann K.G., n.d. 157 pp., 1 color pl., 88 b&w figs.

Selection from the collection of Curt Bohnewand of Berlin, which in addition to paintings held eighty-eight decorative arts objects including a series of mostly 16th-century bronze mortars and some German ecclesiastical goldsmith work, Italian maiolica (from Faenza, Urbino, Venice, Siena, Florence, Castel Durante).

GUTMANN COLLECTION

145 FALKE, OTTO VON. *Die Kunstsammlung Eugen Gutmann.* Berlin: Meisenbach Riffarth & Co., 1912. 113 pp., with some text figs., 8 color pls., 67 b&w pls.

Collection of 326 decorative art objects that includes important goldsmith works among which are a small Paris enamel tryptich of ca. 1403 (now in the Rijksmuseum), a famed collection of French, German, and Italian Renaissance pendant jewels, important rock-crystal cups, pokals, Nuremberg seals, clocks, Italian maiolica from Deruta, Gubbio (Giorgio Andreoli), Faenza, Castel Durante, Urbino (Nicola Pellipario, Fontana, Francesco Xanto Avelli), a French Palissy plate and a Limoges enamel plate. (For a partial dispersal catalog of this collection, see entry 164.)

HAINAUER COLLECTION

146 BODE, WILHELM. *Die Sammlung Oscar Hainauer.* Berlin: W. Büxenstein, 1897. 157 pp., 34 b&w pls., 43 b&w text figs. Text in German and English: *The Collection of Oscar Hainauer.* London: Chiswick Press, 1906.

Fifty-seven-page introduction, arranged according to category of objects, discusses the formation of this major late 19th-century collection and the pieces in it in relation to the period and similar examples in other collections (section on bronzes, by Bode; ivories, enamels of Léonard Limosin, by Richard Graul; plaques and medals, by Ulrich Thieme; Italian maiolica by Otto von Falke; church utensils and decoration, tapestry and hangings, by Julius Lessing; furniture and woodcarvings, by Richard Borrmann). 579 catalog entries, among which innumerable 15th-16th-century objects: mostly Italian and some German and French bronzes (nos. 83-129); a Netherlandish (134) and French (139) ivory statuette; many (mostly North Italian) plaquettes and medals (144-280), Italian maiolica (281-369), Rhenish stoneware (370-71, 374, 376, 378-81); German, French, Spanish, Italian, Flemish church furniture and ornaments (382-402, 404-12), brass utensils (436-42), ironwork (462-65, 467-68), furniture (484-552), and textiles (553-65, 571-72, 575-76, 578-82); Limoges enamels (410-34); Flemish and German tapestries (444-50, 460-61); German clocks (469-74).

HULDSCHINSKY COLLECTION

147 *Die Sammlung Oscar Huldschinsky.* Sale held in Berlin by Paul Cassirer 10-11 May 1928. Catalog written in 1908 by Ernst Bange, Hans Huth, Jacob Rosenberg, Grete Ring and edited by Wilhelm von Bode. Berlin: Paul Cassirer and Hugo Helbing, 1928. 215 pp., 83 b&w pls.

Includes (nos. 79-98) bronze statuettes by Giambologna and workshop, Vittoria, and 16th-century Venetian masters; jewelry of the Renaissance (145-46), Florentine and Venetian carved chests, credenze, cabinets, chairs, and tables.

KAUFMANN COLLECTION

148 *Die Sammlung Richard von Kaufmann, Berlin.* 3 vols. Sale held in Berlin by Paul Cassirer 4-5 December 1917. Berlin: Paul Cassirer; Munich: Hugo Helbing, 1917. 3:109 pp., 96 b&w pls.

Sales catalog of a major Berlin collection of the turn of the century. Vol. 3, prefaced by Fritz Goldschmidt, includes bronze plaquettes, reliefs, and statuettes (lots 165-254) by Donatello's circle, Riccio, Flötner, Moderno, Vischer, Giambologna, [Severo]; a boxwood frame, plaques, crozier, etc. (262, 335-49), fragments of ca. 1490 Netherlandish choir stalls (383-84), goldsmith work, mostly devotional (statuettes, agnus dei, crosses, monstrances, reliquaries [416-36]); bronze, copper, and iron implements (aquamanile, candlesticks, etc., also paxes fitted with Limoges plaques, niello work (438-94); Italian maiolica and Rhenish stoneware (509-49); modest examples of Italian, French, and German Renaissance furniture and tapestries (550-604).

MÜHSAM COLLECTION

149 *Sammlung Kommerzienrat Jacques Mühsam, Berlin: Holzplastik, Bronzen, Keramik.* Sale held in Berlin at Rudolph Lepke's Kunst-Auctions-Haus 30 November-1 December 1926. 80 pp., 45 b&w pls.

Dispersal of the collection of 507 lots comprising wood sculpture and furniture, small bronzes, German and Italian tapestries and other textiles, property of the dealer Jacques Mühsam. Includes many 16th-century examples.

OPPENHEIM COLLECTION

150 *Collection Baron Albert Oppenheim, Cöln.* Vol. 2, *Kunstgewerbe.* Sale held in Berlin at Rudolph Lepke's Kunst-Auction-Haus 28-29 October 1914. Catalog by Otto von Falke. Berlin: Rudolph Lepke's Kunst-Auctions-Haus; Munich: Hugo Helbing Kunsthandlung, 1914. 85 pp., 92 b&w pls. Introduction in German, English, and French.

276 lots of decorative art objects collected by von Oppenheim (1834-1912) and displayed as part of his private museum in his patrician house in Cologne. Most important is a large 15th-16th-century (German and some French) ceramic collection (Rhenish stoneware: lots 1-66, 68-70, 73-75; others 85-87, 104-6, 109, 111-13); German and Venetian glass (115-16, 118); Netherlandish embroidery of ca. 1600 (194); Flemish, German, French, and Italian 15th-16th-century furniture (195-97, 199-200, 202-3, 208-12); German and Italian bronzes depicting Cleopatra (222-23).

PANNWITZ COLLECTION

151 *Die Sammlung von Pannwitz München-Kunst und Kunstgewerbe des XV.-XVIII. Jahrhunderts.* Sale held in Munich at the Galerie Helbing 24-25 October 1905. 90 pp., 12 b&w pls., 30 b&w figs.

Among the 509 items auctioned from the von Pannwitz Collection, Munich, are important examples of German Renaissance plate (pokals, nautilus cups, lots 1-46), Italian and German jewelry (52-64), a few Italian bronze statuettes (76-84), and Italian maiolica (252-62).

152 FALKE, OTTO VON, ed. *Die Kunstsammlung von Pannwitz.* Vol. 2, *Skulpturen und Kunstgewerbe.* Munich: F. Bruckmann, 1925. 52 pp., 74 b&w pls.

Brief catalog entries for 463 sculptures and decorative arts objects from the important von Pannwitz Collection of Berlin. Dating of the 15th-16th centuries are bronzes (nos. 1-36), silver and goldsmith works (44-47, 50-54, 56-58, 60-66), Limoges enamels (68-75), Italian maiolica (76-96), German, Swiss, and Flemish silver-stained glass (97-100, 112-14), Italian and French furniture (152-68, 172-74, 184-91), French and Flemish tapestries (193-96), and Italian altar frontals (200-202).

PASSAVANT-GONTARD COLLECTION

153 SWARZENSKI, GEORG, ed. *Sammlung R. von Passavant-Gontard.* Frankfurt Staedelschen Kunstinstituts, 1919. 57 pp., 80 b&w pls.

Summary catalog of major pre-World War II Frankfurt collection of 290 items ranging from antiquity to the Renaissance. It included Embriachi bone carvings, 15th-16th-century Italian goldsmith works (chalices, ewers, jewelry), Renaissance German cups, several Limoges enamels, two glazed terra cottas by the della Robbias, maiolica from Faenza, Deruta, Gubbio, and Urbino, German ceramics with rare examples of Cologne pottery, small bronze statuettes, etc.

153a   SCHILLING, R. "Ausstellung der Sammlung R. v. Passavant-Gontard im Städelschen Kunstinstitut." *Pantheon* 3 (1929): 183-89, 11 b&w figs.
    Highlights of the collection of R. von Passavant-Gontard, Frankfurt, exhibited in the Städel Institut.

SILTEN COLLECTION

154   VOLBACH, W.F. *Die Sammlung Silten.* Berlin: Verlag für Kunstwissenschaft, 1923. 80 pp., with 35 b&w text figs., 32 b&w pls.
    Collection of Paul Ludwig Silten in Berlin. Though many of the 225 entries are of later dates, holdings include 15th-16th-century small bronzes (a Neptune attributed to Giambologna), German boxwood carvings, devotional German statuettes carved out of amber and Italian portrait reliefs modeled in wax, Limoges plaques, honestone, Italian maiolica pieces, plate wrought out of silver, and Italian furniture.

SIMON COLLECTION

155   *Die Sammlung Dr. Eduard Simon, Berlin.* 2 vols. Sale held in Berlin by Paul Cassirer 10-11 October 1929. Catalog by M.J. Friedländer, E.F. Bange, F. Schottmüller, E. Kühnel, and C.F. Foerster. Berlin: Paul Cassirer and Hugo Helbing, 1929. 320 pp., 214 figs.
    Important collection including small bronzes and medals, furniture, textiles, and other decorative arts of the Renassance through the 18th century. Well illustrated.

THEWALT COLLECTION

156   *Katalog der reichhaltigen, nachgelassenen Kunst-Sammlung des Herrn Karl Thewalt in Köln.* Sale held in Cologne, Saale der Bürgergesellshaft, 4-14 November 1903. Cologne: Firma Math. Lempertz, 1903. 156 pp., 30 b&w pls., with many objects illustrated on each, 52 b&w text figs.
    Sales catalog of a sizable and noteworthy collection of mostly late medieval and Renaissance decorative arts objects from the estate of the late Karl Thewalt (died 1902), former mayor of Cologne. 2,329 lots include: ceramics (Rhenish stoneware); glassware (German, Bohemian, Venetian); ivory (plaques, statuettes, diptychs); gold- and silversmiths' work (pokals, coconut and nautilus cups, standing cups, mazers, chalices, spoons, etc.); jewelry, niello and enamel works; bronzes (statuettes, plaquettes); pewter objects; arms and armor; early clocks and astronomical instruments, etc.

ITALY

AGOSTI & MENDOZA COLLECTIONS

157   MILAN, GALLERIA PESARO. *Le Collezioni Agosti e Mendoza* by Gustavo Botta. Milan: Tumminelli & C., 1936. 27 pp., 118 pp.

Collections Agosti and Mendoza slated for dispersal. In addition to paintings and some sculpture these included decorative arts objects (many from the former Chiesa Collection), ivory and Limoges plaques, Italian and Spanish maiolica, Brussels tapestries, liturgical vestments, Renaissance furniture (cabinets, cassoni, tables, credenze).

GRASSI COLLECTION

158 *Italian Art, The Collection of Professor Luigi Grassi: Furniture, Textiles, Sculptures and Jewelry.* Catalog by Giacomo de Nicola and Pietro Toesca. Sale held in New York at the American Art Association 20-22 January 1927. 289 pp., 199 b&w figs.

Sale of the holdings of this dealer-collector whose principal residence had been Florence, comprised of 580 lots of mostly Italian furniture of the 16th century, comparable in quality to the Volpi and Bardini Collections (see entries 226-27, 237-37b). Also includes a variety of household objects: frames; candlesticks; inkwells; wine cooler; mortars (lots 1-49, 199-207, 216-22, 384-88, 496-558); 15th-16th-century slippers (208-15), brocades, damasks, velvets (50-120, 275-308, 384-410); furniture (121-97, 309-83); an ivory inlaid chessboard (223); arms and armor (224-42); tableware in steel and silver (243-61); jewelry (rings: 411-28; pendants: 444-47, 450-58); a German clock (448). Informative entries, often fairly detailed and including mention of former collections. Good illustrations.

MURRAY COLLECTION

159 *Sammlung Murray/Florenz.* Sale held in Berlin by Paul Cassirer, 6-7 November 1929. Sale catalog entries by Robert Schmidt and W.R. Deusch. Berlin: Paul Cassirer and Hugo Helbing, 1929. 97 pp., 51 b&w pls.

Dispersal includes 152 lots of Italian maiolica (Orvieto, Faenza, Tuscany) and Hispano-Moresque ware; three of Italian textiles of the 16th century, a Paduan bronze casket (now in the Bayerischnationalmuseum in Munich) and other metal objects (mostly German) of the 16th century, Italian Renaissance cabinets and chairs (lots 181-232).

PISA COLLECTION

160 OJETTI, UGO. *Catalogue de la Collection Pisa.* 2 vols. Milan: Soc. An. Leonardo, 1937. 1:230 pp.; 2:212 b&w pls. Captions in Italian and French.

Collection formed by Luigi Pisa. Vol. 1: preface and brief catalog entries for 1,673 items. Vol. 2: plates. Includes 1400-1600: Italian furniture (nos. 1-186); Hispano-Moresque earthenware (477-592); wrought iron works (883-948); Brussels tapestries (949-63); textiles, silk vestments, etc. (1033-1133); goldsmith, bronze, and pewter works—processional crosses, reliquaries, candlesticks, mortars, plate, caskets, etc. (1277- 1315, 1342-82).

STROGANOFF COLLECTION

161 POLLAK, LUDWIG, and MUÑOZ, ANTONIO. *Pièces de choix de la collection du Comte Grégoire Stroganoff à Rome.* 2 vols. Rome, 1912. 1:101 pp., 57 b&w pls.; 2:233 pp., 1 color pl., 157 b&w pls.

Collection best known for its paintings and antique and Byzantine objects but including a large Brussels tapestry of the Vices and Virtues; Italian Renaissance bronzes: casket, sea-monster inkwell, a Pollaiuolo(?) statuette, Tribolo, River god; fragments of Flemish stalls; money-changer table; Italian maiolica; pewter ewer and dish attributed to François Briot.

TOLENTINO COLLECTION

162 *The Rare and Artistic Properties Collected by the Connoisseur Signor Raoul Tolentino.* Sale held in New York at the American Art Association 21-24, 26-27 April 1920. Unpaginated, numerous b&w figs.

Sale of the properties of dealer-collector Raoul Tolentino (of Rome?) comprised of 927 lots generally of Italian origin (and some of questionable authenticity judging from the illustrations), which include a Venetian crozier, ivory and inlaid chessboards of the 16th century, Italian maiolica and Hispano-Moresque wares (lots 40-100), wrought iron (115-87), arms and armor (188-219), 16th-century Sienese banners (220-25), bronze statuettes, mortars, reliquaries, copper dishes (228-303) dating mostly to the 15th-16th centuries, furniture (321-584), frames, chairs (straight, Dante, and Savonarola), tables, stands, cabinets, cassoni, stalls, a corner of the Medici Library from Marradi near Florence (583), the Henri IV dining room from the Château of Rosny, near Paris (584—architectural elements, furniture, full suits of armor, arms, furnishings), tapestries, velvets, embroideries for ecclesiastical and domestic use (585- 753), which include 16th- century pieces. Sale concludes with sculpture, paintings, and architectural elements.

Bergamo

GALLERIA LORENZELLI

163 *TRA/E: Teche, pissidi, cofani e forzieri dall'alto mediova al barocco.* Exhibition catalog by Pietro Lorenzilli and Alberto Veca. Bergamo: Galleria Lorenzelli, 1984. 392 pp., 685 figs., some in color.

Collection of nearly 200 objects: reliquaries, sheaths, pyxes, caskets, strong and pastiglia boxes, and other containers, from Italy, France, Germany and elsewhere and dating from the early Middle Ages through the 18th century. Objects are presented through a series of didactic essays in which are discussed and illustrated an important body of comparative material both in private and public collections. This exhibit also traveled to Antiquaria L.T.D., London, in 1985.

LIECHTENSTEIN

Vaduz

LIECHTENSTEIN COLLECTION

164 *Liechtenstein: The Princely Collections.* Exhibition held in New York at The Metropolitan Museum of Art. Catalog by thirteen contributors. German and French translations by Joel Agee and Richard Miller, respectively. New York: Metropolitan Museum of Art, 1985. 390 pp., many color and b&w figs.

Though dominated by paintings and objects of later periods, this selection of 218 works from the collection housed at Vaduz includes a 1587-95 perpetual calendar by Erasmus Habermel of Prague, a late 16th-century casket and tabletops of inlaid hardstones by the workshop of Castrucci, Limoges painted enamel plaques by Pierre Courteys. Good color reproductions.

NETHERLANDS

The Hague

BACHSTITZ GALLERY

165   *The Bachstitz Gallery Collection.* 3 vols. [Berlin, 1921]. 1:11 pp. (essay by G. Gronau), 98
       b&w pls.; 2:82 pp., 131 pls. (one hand-colored); 3:7 pp. (essays by Otto von Falke and G.
       Gronau), 103 pls.
            Large, ostentatious dealer's catalog composed of short essays, series of good plates
       with captions. Vol. 1: paintings and three Brussels tapestries (Solomon and Sheba of ca.
       1490, Continence of Scipio, 16th century); vol. 2: antiquity, Byzantine and Islamic works; vol.
       3: small Renaissance bronzes from the Hollitscher Collection (works by or ascribed to Riccio,
       Cellini, [Severo], a Leonardo follower, Vittoria, Giambologna, Adriaen de Vries, della Porta);
       from the Eugen Gutmann Collection (for which see entry 145): maiolica from Faenza, Castel
       Durante, Deruta, Gubbio (by Giorgio Andreoli), Urbino (by Francesco Xanto Avelli); a 15th-
       century silver statuette of the Virgin from Augsburg; Renaissance goldsmith work—cups from
       Lübeck, Augsburg, globes of heaven and earth, tankards, two clocks; from the Fritz von Ganz
       Collection: important Renaissance jewels (including the so-called Marlborough gems); a
       Venetian bottle and cut rock-crystal vases of the 16th-17th century. Volume concludes with
       18th-century miniatures, various paintings, and a Brussels tapestry of ca. 1550 designed by
       Pieter van Aelst and depicting the story of St. Paul.

SCANDINAVIA (DENMARK)

OLSENS COLLECTION

166   SCHMITZ, HERMANN. *Generaldirektør Ole Olsens Kunstsamlinger.* 2 vols. Munich: F.
       Bruckmann A.-G., n.d. 1:111 pp., 140 b&w pls., 2 pp. of facsimile silversmiths' marks; 2:
       80 pp., 94 b&w pls. Text in Danish/English/German.
            Catalog of the vast (2,042 items) and eclectic collection formed by Ole Olsens, a
       Copenhagen businessman. For the period 1400-1600, most important are the seventy-three
       Limoges painted enamels and fifty-seven Italian maiolica pieces (Deruta, Urbino, Castel
       Durante, and Venice). Also includes several 16th-century rock-crystal vessels in mounts, late
       Gothic ecclesiastical and devotional goldsmith and ivory works from Germany and elsewhere,
       a 16th-century Spanish pendant jewel, two Saxon bookcovers of 1584-1600, humpen, two Palis-
       sy wares, and thirty German stonewares.

SPAIN

SCHEVITCH COLLECTION

167   *Catalogue des objets d'art et de haute curiosité de l'Antiquité, du Moyen Age et de la Renais-
       sance... composant la collection de M. D[mitri] Schevitch.* Sale held in Paris at the Galerie
       Georges Petit 4-7 April 1906. 257 pp., 73 b&w pls.
            Sales catalog with thirty-nine-page introduction by Émile Molinier that scans the
       former Madrid collection, which included, of the 15th-16th century, Hispano-Moresque and
       Valencian lustreware (nos. 33-52), Italian maiolica (53-57), Italian and Spanish secular plate
       (59-72—dishes, cups, ewers, salts), Flemish, Portuguese, Spanish, Italian devotional goldsmith

works (78-100, 102—reliquaries, paxes, plaques, incense burners, monstrance, chalices), wrought iron caskets, lecterns, torches, etc. (112-19), Italian wood caskets (121-25), Italian, French, Spanish, and Flemish ivory figurines, plaques, paxes (158-67), Limoges enamels by the Pénicauds, Nouailher, Reymond, Courteys, Limosin (211-41), Spanish, Italian, French, Georgian, German, jewelry (254-80—belt buckles, medallions, pendants, crosses, rings), Flemish and Spanish terra cotta busts (310-11), Neapolitan wax reliefs by Bernardo Azzolino (313), door panels (315, 327), Italian and Spanish copper and bronze chalices, crosses, reliquaries, plaquette attributed to Moderno, incense burner, paxes, etc. (341-51), English, Italian, Spanish ecclesiastical vestments and textiles (360-73), Italian and Flemish tapestries (397-402).

SWITZERLAND

THYSSEN-BORNEMISZA COLLECTION

168   *Sammlung Schloss Rohoncz.* 2 vols. Exhibition held in Munich at the Neue Pinakothek. Catalog edited by Rudolf Heinemann-Fleischmann. Munich: Neue Pinakothek, 1930. 1:150 pp., 153 b&w pls.; 2:33 pp., 36 b&w pls.

    Exhibition catalog of the Thyssen-Bornemisza Collection now exhibited for the most part at the Villa Favorita in Lugano. Vol. 2, dealing with sculpture and decorative arts, includes German Renaissance boxwood statuettes, Limoges enamel plaques (by the Master of the Orléans Triptych, Pierre and Jean Reymond), German pokals, an Arras tapestry of ca. 1400, 15th-century German, Brussels, and French tapestries, and St. Martin embroidery.

U.S.A.

BARNARD COLLECTION

169   WEINBERGER, MARTIN. *The George Grey Barnard Collection.* New York: Robinson Galleries, Inc., [1941]. 77 pp., 63 b&w pls.

    Catalog of the second Barnard Collection, New York, of 264 items dispersed soon after publication date. Though much is sculpture, eleven entries are of 15th-16th-century caskets (Venetian pastiglia boxes, etc.), twenty-seven woodworks and furniture from 15th-century France, Italy, and Flanders, bronze statuettes and metalwork in copper, brass, and iron, Tuscan tiles, a Palissy Neptune figure, fragments of tapestries, embroideries, and various small-scale utensils.

BLUMENTHAL COLLECTION

170   RUBENSTEIN-BLOCH, STELLA. *Catalogue of the Collection of George and Florence Blumenthal, New York.* Vol. 2, *Sculpture and Bronzes Medieval and Renaissance* (1926), unpaginated. 76 b&w pls.; vol. 3, *Works of Art Medieval and Renaissance (Ivories, Enamels, Majolica, Stained Glass, Etc.)* (1926), unpaginated, 58 b&w pls.; vol. 4, *Tapestries and Furniture Medieval and Renaissance* (1927), unpaginated, 47 b&w pls. Paris: Privately printed.

    Vol. 2: in addition to sculpture, includes small French and Italian bronzes of the 16th century, pls. XLV-LXI and accompanying text; vol. 3: for Limoges enamels of the 16th century, see pls. XVIII-XXIII; for Italian and German goldsmith works of the same period, see pls. XXIV-XXX; a 15th-century leather casket, pl. XXXI; for 15th-century Spanish lustreware, pls. XXXII-XXXIV; Italian 16th-century maiolica, pls. XXXV-XLVI. Vol. 4: for 15th-16th century tapestries, see pls. I-XVII; 16th-century Flemish vestments, pl. XVIII; French furniture of the 15th-16th century, pls. XIX-XXXIII; Spanish 16th-century stall, pl. XXXIV; Italian furniture of the 15th-16th century, pls. XXXV- XLII; 15th-16th-century ironworks from France, Italy and Spain, pls. XLIII-XLVII.

LINSKY COLLECTION

171   *Property from the Jack and Belle Linsky Collection.* Sale held in New York at Sotheby's 21 May 1985. 138 pp., 68 color figs., 74 b&w figs.

Among the 170 lots are a Limoges enamel mirror plaque by Jean de Court (lot 80), Italian bronzes (87-93, including one each by Danese Cattaneo, workshop of Severo da Ravenna, and workshop of Desiderio da Firenze), bronzes after 15th-century models (97-98, 100-101, 103-4), gold 16th-century pendants (118, 128-30), and a gold necklace (134). For the portion of this collection bequeathed, see entry 83.

MARQUAND COLLECTION

172   *Illustrated Catalogue of the Art and Literary Property Collected by the Late Henry G. Marquand.* Sale held in New York at Mendelssohn Hall and the American Art Association 23-24 February 1903. Sales catalog edited by Thomas E. Kirby, with lot entries by various contributors. Unpaginated, 72 b&w figs.

Ostentatious catalog with 2,154 entries of little scientific precision describing an eclectic collection that included some Venetian and Spanish 15th-century glass, important Limoges enamels (nos. 1050-61), Hispano-Moresque ware, a few Italian Renaissance textiles, some Brussels tapestries.

PIERPONT MORGAN COLLECTION

173   PÉRATE, ANDRÉ, and BRIÈRE, GASTON. *Collections Georges Hoentschel aquises par M. J. Pierpont Morgan et prêtées au Metropolitan Museum de New-York.* Vol. 1, *Moyen Age & Renaissance.* Paris: Librairie Centrales des Beaux-Arts, 1908. 46 pp., 72 b&w pls.

Medieval and Renaissance objects bought by J.P. Morgan from the Paris collection of G. Hoentschel and on indefinite loan at the time of publication to the Metropolitan Museum. Includes 15th- and 16th-century choir stalls, lectern, panels, caskets, cupboards, and Flemish tapestries.

173a   *Guide to the Loan Exhibition of the J. Pierpont Morgan Collection.* Exhibition held in New York at The Metropolitan Museum of Art. Catalog introduction by Edward Robinson, gallery descriptions by seven contributors. New York: Metropolitan Museum of Art, 1914. 175 pp., several b&w figures.

Summary guide describing the exhibited holdings of this major American collection of medieval and Renaissance decorative arts subsequently partly dispersed. Includes 15th-16th-century ivories, tapestries, maiolica, liturgical and secular goldsmith works, and bronze statuettes.

174   WILLIAMSON, G.C. *Catalogue of the Collection of Jewels and Precious Works of Art— Property of J. Pierpont Morgan.* London: Chiswick Press, 1910. 183 pp., 95 b&w pls., 13 text figs.

116 entries with sometimes lengthy descriptions. Examples, often important, of the 15th-16th-century include chains, badges, gems, pendants, medals, rosaries, necklaces, medallions, rings, hat ornaments, seals, etc., in a wide variety and combination of precious materials; a 16th-century female wax portrait; boxwood carvings (rosary beads, medallions, diptychs, a figurine, casket, shrine, mirror); Renaissance rock-crystal objects (ewer, reliefs, cross, vases, cups, medallion, paxes); gold and gilt-silver ciborium, chalice, pax, shrine, etc.

SALOMON COLLECTION

175   *The Notable Collection of the Art of the Italian Renaissance and French 18th Century Belonging to the Estate of the Late William Salomon of New York City.* Sale held in New York at the American Art Galleries 4-7 April 1923. Unpaginated, numerous b&w pls.

764 lots including, of the 15th-16th centuries, French and Italian furniture, Italian, French, Flemish, and German plate, textiles, embroidery, ecclesiastical vestments, terra cottas, and a large collection of bronzes attributed to Riccio, Alessandro Vittoria, Bellano, Adriaen de Vries, Pietro Tacca, and Giambologna.

RECENT MULTI OWNER AUCTIONS

176   *Important European Works of Art* (Vol. 1); *European Works of Art, Arms, Furniture, and Tapestries* (Vol. 2). Sale held in New York at Sotheby's 27-28 November 1981. Unpaginated, illus., many in color.

Includes small German, Italian Renaissance bronze statuettes and plaquettes, Limoges enamels, Venetian glass, German humpen, alms dishes and chargers, Spanish, French, and German iron caskets, Italian inlaid and bone caskets, Orvieto, Faenza, Castel Durante, Gubbio, Urbino maiolica, Hispano-Moresque lustreware, Rhenish stoneware, various mortars, arms and armor, Italian furniture, and 16th-century Flemish tapestries.

177   *Fine European Works of Art, Arms and Armour, Furniture and Tapestries, The Property of the Brown University of Art, The Estate of Caroline McFadden Ewing, The Metropolitan Museum of Art, The Estate of Raymond Pitcairn, The Philadelphia Museum of Art, The J. Richard Phillips Collection, The Princeton University Art Museum.* Sale held in New York at Sotheby's 23- 24 November 1984. 155 pp. (unpaginated), 24 color figs., 254 b&w figs.

598 lots, many of 15th-16th century objects: jewelry (lots 12-13, 197, 203); bronze objects, plaques, and statuettes (14-15, 81-84, 88-89, 92, 194, 476-79, 488-91); Flemish, Italian, and French ivories (55-56, 64-65); Limoges enamels (71-77); terra cotta (Andrea della Robbia workshop, 123); Hispano-Moresque lustreware (137-41); Italian maiolica (148-52); German stove tile (156); Italian cuir-bouilli case (207); arms (213, 217, 219-23, 289) and armor (367, 370); French and Italian furniture (436-37, 439-41, 503, 508, 518-22); and Italian and Flemish textiles and tapestries (533-38, 549-53, 555, 557-58, 560, 567-69).

178   *European Works of Art, Armour, Furniture and Tapestries.* Sale held in New York at Sotheby's 10-11 May 1985. Unpaginated, 12 color pls., 242 b&w figs.

Among the 537 lots are: 15th-16th-century ecclesiastical goldsmith works (lots 5-7); Italian (176-79, 186-87, 189, 192, 195, 199, 215-28, 220-21, 225) and German (189-90) bronze statuettes, reliefs, medals, and paxes; Italian (233, 268, 271), and German (231, 234, 253) arms and armor as well as several (236-44, 247-48, 254, 259-60, 269, 272) of unspecified origin; Italian, German, Flemish, and Spanish metalwork (312-16, 318, 320-21, 330-32, 337, 339-40, 342); French, Italian, Flemish, and German caskets (343-44) and wood carvings (357-61, 378-

79); French, Italian, Flemish, Spanish, English furniture (381, 385-92, 395-96, 401, 403-5, 409-12, 419-21, 419-21, 424, 434-35, 437-39, 441, 445B-C, 446, 448-49, 457); Italian chasuble (472); Flemish (492, 500-507, 510, 512-14), Italian (521), and French (526) tapestries.

U.S.S.R.

BOTKINE COLLECTION

179 *Collection M.P. Botkine.* St. Petersburg [Leningrad]: n.p., 1911. 41 pp. with 75 b&w text figs.; 54 color pls.; 49 b&w pls.

Wide assortment of objects of a Leningrad Collection primarily of Italian Renaissance maiolica, bronze door-knockers and furniture, Byzantine ivories and enamels, and Tanagra statuettes. Well illustrated.

V. Single Country, Multimedia

BELGIUM (FLEMISH)

7. EXHIBITION CATALOGS

Detroit

DETROIT INSTITUTE OF ARTS

180   *Flanders in the Fifteenth Century: Art and Civilization. Masterpieces of Flemish Art: Van Eyck to Bosch.* Exhibition catalog introductory essays by Edgar P. Richardson and Richard Kay; catalog entries by Lucie Ninane, Jacqueline Folie, Dorothy E. Miner, Francis W. Robinson, and Albert Schouteet. Translated by Richard M. Stein, assisted by Frank Smolar and Mrs. Robert Shepherd. Detroit: Detroit Institute of Arts; Brussels: Centre National de Recherches Primitifs Flamands, 1960. 467 pp., 9 col pls., 233 b&w figs.

     Multimedia exhibition presenting outstanding examples of late Gothic Flemish art at its zenith drawn from Belgian and U.S. museums. Introductory essays on Flemish paintings in U.S. collections (pp. 27-30), on Flanders in the 15th century (pp. 31-55); 213 detailed entries, often preceded by biographical notes on specific artists. For decorative arts: misericords (cat. nos. 81-84); metalwork (nos. 101-26); goldsmith works, including chalices, monstrances, reliquaries, jewelry and personal ornaments (nos. 127-38); arms and armor (nos. 139-47); textiles, mostly tapestries with some ecclesiastical vestments (nos. 148- 60); furniture (nos. 161-64); a drinking glass (no. 169); matrixes and seals (nos. 173-74, 176-84, 194-95).

Washington

SMITHSONIAN INSTITUTION

181   *Antwerp's Golden Age: The Metropolis of the West in the 16th and 17th Centuries.* Exhibition catalog introduction by Paul N. Perrot, essays by Léon Voet, Frans Baudouin, and Jeanine Lambrechts-Douillez. Washington, D.C.: Smithsonian Institution, 1973. 223 pp., 83 b&w pls.

     Highlights from various institutions in Antwerp of works in all media and including medals and bookbinding. Essays trace history of Antwerp and of each art form.

BRITISH
(ENGLISH AND SCOTTISH)

3. SURVEYS AND HISTORIES

Book

182   *The Tudor Period 1500-1603.* Edited by Ralph Edwards and L.G.G. Ramsey. London: Connoisseur, 1956. 192 pp., 96 b&w pls., numerous line drawings.

Fifteen essays by as many contributors, on different aspects of Tudor art including furniture (pp. 31-44), silver (65-75), pottery, porcelain, and glass (79-88), domestic metalwork (91-98), textiles (101-12), costumes (115-23), jewelry (139-46), and leather (149-56).

Article

183   THOMAS, W.G. MACKAY. "Old English Candlesticks and Their Venetian Prototypes." *Burlington Magazine* 80 (1942):145-51, 17 b&w figs.

15th-16th-century earthenware and metal candlesticks with a design—central drip tray and truncated bell base—borrowed from Venice.

7. EXHIBITION CATALOGS

Edinburgh

NATIONAL MUSEUM OF ANTIQUITIES OF SCOTLAND

184   *Angels, Nobles and Unicorns: Art and Patronage in Medieval Scotland.* Exhibition catalog edited by D.H. Caldwell. Entries by Elizabeth Sharratt, with contributions by Andrea Gilbert, Ruth Summers, Kathryn Morrison, and Jennifer Blakebell. Edinburgh: National Museum of Antiquities of Scotland, 1982. 20 pp., 164 b&w figs.

Catalog of 269 works of art produced in Scotland from 1100 to 1500 now mostly in the Edinburgh National Museum and the Edinburgh Library of Scotland but also in the Glasgow University Library, and other Scottish and English collections. Includes some 15th-16th-century jewels, bronze ewers, pawns, coins, university maces, leather, whalebone caskets, earthenware, seals, and carved panels, made for the Church, lay patronage, or the Crown.

London

BURLINGTON HOUSE

185   *Catalogue of a Collection of Objects of British Heraldic Art to the End of the Tudor Period.* Exhibition catalog by E.E. Dorling, with introduction by Oswald Barron. London: Burlington Fine Arts Club, 1916. 147 pp.

Embroidered hangings, tapestries, tiles, shields, bookbindings, ceramic ware, bench ends, medals, seals, pendants, rings, etc., dating of the 13th to the 16th century (mostly 15th-16th) bearing English coats of arms. Most of the nearly five hundred objects from private British collections, are of English production, but some are from the Continent (e.g. a series of floor tiles from the church of St.-Étienne at Caen, Rhenish Bellarmine jug, Seigburg jugs, etc.).

186   *Catalogue of an Exhibition of Late Elizabethan Art in Conjunction with the Tercentenary of Francis Bacon.* Exhibition catalog contributions by George F. Hill, W.W. Watts, et al. London: Burlington Fine Arts Club, 1926. 100 pp., 50 b&w pls.

Five brief introductory essays followed by a catalog of 183 items from British private collections arranged by medium. In addition to paintings and miniatures, included are 113 decorative arts objects (pp. 65-95), pls. XXVII-XLI): silversmith work (ewers, dishes, cups, spoons); ceramics; rock crystal; coins and medals; jewelry; furniture, glass (verre églomisé), an engraved astrolabe, a closed helmet; textiles (tapestries, embroidery, costumes).

Manchester

CORPORATION OF MANCHESTER ART GALLERY

187   *Exhibition of the Royal House of Tudor.* Exhibition catalog by H.A. Greubar, et al. Manchester: Corporation of Manchester Art Gallery, 1897. 153 pp.

Modest catalog resembling a hand-list for an exhibition of over 843 items illustrating English reigns from the ascent of Henry VII (1485) to the death of Elizabeth I (1603). Nos. 198- 207 are embroideries, 208-318 arms and armor (English but also German and Italian), 370-437 small objects such as seals, inkstand, relics and mementos of historical figures, rings, keys, watches, etc., all in private collections; electrotypes (514-85) and actual (587-627) plate, casts, and impressions of Tudor seals (630-61), large number (no numeration) of coins and medals of the period.

Norwich

CASTLE MUSEUM

188   *Medieval Art in East Anglia 1300-1520.* Exhibition catalog edited by P. Lasko and N.J. Morgan, with entries by Lasko, Morgan, F.W. Cheetham, P. Clabburn, D.J. King, A.H.R. Martindale, and R.M.R. Young. 2d ed. London: Thames & Hudson, 1974. 1 color pl., 20 color figs., 29 b&w figs.

While the main emphasis is on manuscript illumination, there are some examples of other media, including eighteen 15th- 16th-century goldsmith works (a chalice, a pax, communion patens, reliquary, coconut cups), bone crucifix, embroideries, a painted burse, bench ends, and a misericord made in East Anglia or else for East Anglian patrons.

FRENCH

1. DICTIONARIES AND ENCYCLOPEDIAS

189   GAY, VICTOR. *Glossaire archéologique du Moyen Age et de la Renaissance.* 2 vols. Vol. 1, *A-GUY,* Paris: Librarie de la Société Bibliographique, 1887, 806 pp.; vol. 2, *H-Z,* edited by Henri Stein, Paris: Éditions Auguste Picard, 1928, 484 pp. Numerous line drawings throughout.

Comprehensive dictionary of French terms for architectural elements, objects, trades, techniques, concepts, etc., relevant to medieval and Renaissance times. Often includes quotations of dated texts to clarify variations of meaning in different periods.

190   VIOLLET-LE-DUC, E. *Dictionnaire raisonné du mobilier français de l'époque carolin-gienne à la Renaissance.* 6 vols. Paris: Ernst Gründ, 1858-75. 1:443 pp., 391 engravings and line drawings; 2:535 pp., 391 engravings and line drawings; 3:479 pp., 419 engravings and line drawings; 4:507 pp., 378 engravings and line drawings; 5:499 pp., 407 engravings and line drawings; 6:489 pp., 309 engravings and line drawings. Some chromolithographs in each volume.
      Encyclopedic dictionary of the decorative arts and of functional objects from Carolingian times through the 15th century. Entries are descriptive and historic in content (some being very lengthy—e.g., the entry "joyaux" is fifty pages long), include quotations from contemporary texts, and are amply illustrated with engravings. Vol. 1: furniture and furnishings, both secular and ecclesiastical; includes essay/entries on ceremonies, customs, craftsmen, and production of furniture, as well as on particular objects. Vol. 2: secular and ecclesiastical utensils and goldsmith works, musical instruments, games, accouterments for jousts, tournaments, hunting, and dancing, tools. Vols. 3 and 4: garments, vestments, jewelry, and horse trappings. Vols. 5 and 6: arms and armor. All volumes have indexes; no bibliography.

2. BIOGRAPHICAL DICTIONARIES

191   AUDIN, MARIUS, and VIAL, EUGÈNE. *Dictionnaire des artistes et ouvriers d'art du Lyonnais.* 2 vols. Vol. 1, *A-L* (1918), 521 pp.; vol. 2, *M-Z* (1919), 371 pp. Paris: Bibliothèque d'Art et d'Archéologie.
      Comprehensive dictionary of artists active in the regions of Lyon from the late 15th through the 19th century. Entries include biographical data, known works, and bibliographical references. Includes Renaissance goldsmiths, medalists, furniture makers, etc. Concludes with a twenty-two page bibliography and a proper name index.

7. EXHIBITION CATALOGS

Cleveland

CLEVELAND MUSEUM OF ART

192   *Treasures from Medieval France.* Exhibition catalog by William D. Wixon. Cleveland: Cleveland Musum of Art, 1967. 394 pp., 28 color pls., 137 b&w figs.
      Catalog of major exhibition with many lenders. Ten-page introduction followed by 165 entries for secular and ecclesiastical objects ranging from the 8th to the 16th century, including ivories, metalwork, jewelry, enamels, tapestry, etc.; chap. 6 and 7 (pp. 254-345, 63 catalog entries) deal with 15th- and 16th-century objects.

Paris

MUSÉE DES ARTS DÉCORATIFS

193   *Les Trésors des églises de France.* 2d ed. Exhibition catalog introduction by Jean Taralon. Paris: Caisse Nationale des Monuments Historiques, 1965. 629 pp., 8 color pls., 254 b&w pls.
      Brings to light objects in French church treasuries, chiefly of the Middle Ages but also of the 15-16th century, arranged by region. Represented are reliquaries, chalices, censers, processional crosses, caskets, enamels, ivories, tapestries, etc. Six pages of makers' and town marks.

Rouen

MUSÉE DÉPARTEMENTAL DES ANTIQUITÉS DE LA SEINE- MARITIME

194   *Trésors des abbayes normandes.* Exhibition catalog edited by Françoise Debaisieux and Elisabeth Chirol, with contributions by many authors. Rouen: Musée Départemental de la Seine-Maritime, 1979. 544 pp., 4 color pls., 198 b&w figs.

   Deals with the history of, and the intellectual and artistic life in the large abbeys of Normandy from the 8th-19th century. 634 catalog entries include some decorative arts of 1400-1600: seals, church furnishing, ivories, goldsmith works (liturgical objects), tiles, and textiles. Exhibition also traveled to the Musée des Beaux-Arts in Caen.

GERMAN

1. DICTIONARIES AND ENCYCLOPEDIAS

195   *Reallexikon zur deutschen Kunstgeschichte.* Edited by Otto Schmitt, Ernst Gall, Ludwig Heinrich Heydenreich, Hans Martin von Erfa, and Karl-August Wirth. Contributions by many authors. 7 vols. to date. Vol. 1, *A-Baubetrieb,* Stuttgart: J.B. Metzlersche Verlagsbuchhandlung, 1937, 1528 cols., numerous b&w figs. Vol. 2, *Bauer-Buchmalerei,* Stuttgart-Waldsee: Alfred Druckenmüller, 1948, 1524 cols., numerous b&w figs. Vol. 3, *Buchpult-Dill,* Stuttgart: Alfred Druckenmüller, 1954, 1496 cols., 16-page French- German, English-German, and Italian-German dictionary, numerous b&w pls. Vol. 4, *Dinanderie-Elle,* Stuttgart: Alfred Druckenmüller, 1958, 1544 cols., 4-page dictionary. Vol. 5, *Email-Eselstritt,* Stuttgart: Alfred Druckenmüller, 1967, 1536 cols., 2-page dictionary, numerous b&w figs. Vol. 6, *Eselsrücken-Farbe, Farbmittel,* Munich: Alfred Druckenmüller, 197, 1512 cols., 2-page dictionary, numerous b&w figs. Vol. 7 *Farbe, Farbmittel-Fensterlanden,* Munich: C.H. Beck'schen Verlagsbuchhandlung, 1981, 1524 cols., 2-page dictionary, numerous b&w figs.

   Encyclopedia dealing, in well-illustrated, often lengthy entries, with concepts, symbols, ideas, material, objects — often very specific such as Apostelglas, Doppeladler, Doppelbecker — architectural elements, etc., in German art, many applying to the 15th-16th centuries. Particulary useful for outline of history and background information. Includes bibliographical references.

3. SURVEYS AND HISTORIES

Books

196   FALKE, JACOB VON. *Geschichte des deutschen Kunstgewerbes.* Berlin: G. Grote'sche Verlagsbuchhandlung, [1888]. 218 pp., 32 pls., some in color, 96 engravings.

   Older history of German decorative arts of value primarily for a historical perspective on late 19th-century taste and scholarly criteria. The Gothic period (1250-1500) is dealt with on pp. 74-118; the 16th century, pp. 119-68.

197   KOHLHAUSSEN, HEINRICH. *Geschichte des deutschen Kunsthandwerks.* Vol. 5 of *Deutsche Kunstgeschichte.* Munich: F. Bruckmann, 1955. 592 pp., 16 color pls., 543 b&w figs.

Thorough, well-illustrated history of German decorative arts from the 6th century to the 1950s. Pp. 154-287 deal with high and late Gothic periods; pp. 288-434 with Renaissance times. Particularly useful for providing a cohesive image of what was produced in each period.

198 MENZHAUSEN, JOACHIM. *The Green Vaults*. Translated by Marianne Herzfeld and revised by D. Talbot Rice. Leipzig: Edition Leipzig, 1968. 114 pp., 47 color pls., 107 b&w illus.

History of the famed Dresden Treasury; 140 entries highlighting key pieces, over half of the 15th-16th century, in gold, silver, enamel, rock crystal, and other semiprecious stones: cups, bowls, flasks, chalices, crucifixes, caskets, of different origins, mostly German; all illustrated.

199 SCHOLZ, RENATE. *Humpen und Krüge- Trinkgefässe 16.-20. Jahrhundert*. Munich: Keysersche Verlagsbuchhandlung, 1978. 164 pp., 4 color pls., 166 b&w figs.

German tankards and mugs from the 16th to 20th century. Includes 16th-century examples in pewter, silver, earthenware, many stoneware, faience, and glass.

Article

200 FALKE, OTTO VON. "Die Neugotik im deutschen Kunstgewerbe der Spätrenaissance." *Jahrbuch der preuszischen Kunstsammlungen* 40 (1919):75-92, 17 b&w figs.

Revival of Gothic forms at the time of the Reformation as exemplified by trauben pokals (generally double) made in Lüneburg and carved casket panels, drawn primarily from the collections of the Kunstgewerbemuseum, Berlin.

6. PERMANENT COLLECTIONS

Aachen

KAISERSAAL DER RATHAUS

201 *Der Aachner Domschatz*. Exhibiton catalog by Ernst Gunther Grimme, with essays by Erich Stephany. Düsseldorf: L. Schwann, 1972. 418 pp., 22 color pls., 321 b&w pls.

Liturgical and devotional statues, reliefs, crosses, chalices, reliquaries, vestments, etc., from the 9th to the 20th century from the Aachen cathedral treasury, each reproduced. Detailed entries preceded by essay tracing the history of the collection.

7. EXHIBITION CATALOGS

Augsburg

RATHAUS; ZEUGHAUS

202 *Welt im Umbruch: Augsburg zwischen Renaissance und Barock*. 3 vols. Exhibition catalog by thirty-three contributors; essays in vol. 3 by nine contributors. Augsburg: Augsburger Druck- und Verlagshaus, 1980. 1:430 pp., 10 color pls., numerous b&w figs.; 2:546 pp., 23 color pls., numerous b&w figs.; 3:175 pp., several b&w figs.

Important international exhibition of art produced in Augsburg or elsewhere for Augsburg patrons in the 16th and 17th centuries. Vol. 1 includes mostly objects dealing with civic history, but catalog nos. 144-46 are 16th-century German and Italian goldsmith works. Vol. 2: fifteen essays, many dealing with various aspects of the decorative arts in Renaissance and Baroque Augsburg; detailed catalog entries for mostly bronze and wood reliefs, medals, statuettes, small objects (nos. 442-586), goldsmith works (670-815), watches, clocks, and scientific instruments (816-55), small wood cabinets (856-60), textiles, and ceramics (866-74), and arms and armor (875-958). Vol. 3 is a compilation of writings; pertinent to 15th-16th century decorative arts are an essay on silver- and goldsmith work in 16th-century Augsburg (by Helmut W. Seling), and one on armor from Augsburg (by Ortwin Gamber).

Austin

ARCHER M. HUNTINGTON ART GALLERY, THE UNIVERSITY OF TEXAS AT AUSTIN

203   *Nuremberg: A Renaissance City, 1500-1618.* Exhibition catalog by Jeffrey Chipps Smith, with contribution by Guy Fitch Lytle. Austin: University of Texas Press, 1983. 336 pp., 305 b&w illus.
    Underlines the significance of Nuremberg as an artistic center of the 16th century; the impact of the Renaissance and Reformation on the city. Catalog includes 213 objects from various museums (mostly engravings and woodcuts) arranged by artist; for decorative arts objects: plaquettes (nos. 115, 125-35, 200-203); medals (137-57); bronze statuettes (118, 158, 209); a bronze mortar (198); a brass candlestick (199); a carved pearwood relief (204); goldsmiths' works (116, 205-7); also pp. 63-65, 79-85); armor (160-62). Examples by Krug, Vischer, Flötner, Gebel, Deschler, Jamnitzer (Hans and Wenzel), etc.; some design engravings by Hornick, Solis, Zan, Flindt, Zündt, etc. Biographical appendix of important Nuremberg artists not included in exhibition.

Berlin

KUNSTGEWERBEMUSEUM, SCHLOSS KÖPENICK

204   *Kunsthandwerk der Dürerzeit und der deutschen Renaissance.* Exhibition catalog by Werner Schulz, with essays by various contributors. Berlin: Staatliche Museen, 1971. 242 pp., 1 color fig., 174 b&w figs.
    Decorative arts in Germany at the time of Dürer presented through a series of ten essays followed by catalog of 174 pieces lent by East German, Czech, Soviet, and Polish institutions: furniture; jewels, gems, goldsmith work; medals; arms and armor; iron work; cutlery; pewter and brass objects; stove tiles; stoneware pottery; glass; and textiles.

London

BURLINGTON HOUSE

205   *Exhibition of Early German Art.* Exhibiton catalog introduction by Campbell Dodgson. London: Burlington Fine Arts Club, 1906. 207 pp., 70 b&w pls.
    Forty-four-page introductory essay on German artists and schools of the 15th and 16th century. Catalog of 166 items, mostly from private British collections, arranged by medium and, generally, chronologically; as well as paintings, includes many objects (cups, bowls, ewers, dishes, statuettes, rock-crystal vessels, plaquettes, medals, a pearwood tazza, a glass beaker and cover, a pendant, and a tapestry hanging—pls. XLI-XLIX, LII- LXIV, LXVIII).

METROPOLITAN MUSEUM OF ART

206 *Gothic and Renaissance Art in Nuremberg 1300-1550.* Exhibition catalog by Rainer Kahsnitz, William D. Wixom, et al. New York: Metropolitan Museum of Art; Munich: Prestel-Verlag, 1986. 499 pp., 142 color illus., 141 b&w figs.

Catalog of multimedia exhibition includes entries for 278 objects and is preceded by introductory essays summarizing the city's history and outlining specific artistic media. Catalog entries are generally arranged by medium. For decorative arts objects: gold- and silversmiths' work (nos. 46-52, 73-82, 208-12, 263); tapestry (nos. 55-58, 67-69); works in brass and bronze — aquamanile, statuettes, plaquettes, medals — (pp. 75-80, 105-7 nos. 9, 16-22, 45, 97, 183-202, 205, 213-38, 248, 250, 254-56, 258, 261); ceramics (nos. 239-43); a carved boxwood sundial (no. 244); a cast brass astrolabe (no. 245); missal cover with box (no. 54); armor (pp. 101-4, nos. 11, 265-78). Examples, often representing works by the city's most prominent artists, are drawn from European and American collections. Biographical appendix. Exhibition also traveled to the Germanisches Nationalmuseum in Nuremberg.

Trier

DOMSCHATZ

207 *Schatzkunst Trier.* Exhibition Catalog by Franz J. Ronig, Norbert Jopek, et al. Essays by Hans-Wolfgang Kuhn, Anne-Marie Zander, and Hans-Berthold Busse. Trier: Spee-Buchverlag, 1984. 303 pp., 16 color pls., 311 b&w figs.

Three introductory essays (pp. 19-58) deal primarily with post-1600 aspects of the cathedral treasure. Catalog of 301 entries: liturgical objects, ivories, illuminated manuscripts, etc., the bulk from Trier cathedral's permanent holdings but many from parish churches of the Moselle region ranging in date from the 3d through 20th centuries. For the period 1400-1600, see catalog nos. 116-17, 119-47, all German objects including a ciborium, monstrances, censer, reliquaries, chalices, statuettes, crown, gospel bookcovers, also a silver medal representing the Trinity by Hans Reinhart, and a coconut cup.

ITALIAN

MULTI REGION

2. BIOGRAPHICAL DICTIONARIES

208 *Dizionario biografico degli Italiani.* Rome: Istituto della Enciclopedia Italiana fondata da Giovanni Treccani, 1960-. In course of publication. Vol. 30, *COSATTINI-CRISPOLTO* (1984) was last volume avalaible to author. 800 pp. (average) per vol.

Most thorough biographical dictionary dealing exclusively with Italians through the ages. Exhaustive, authoritative entries followed by up-to-date bibliography, by numerous contributors. Very useful information on a great many 15th-16th-century artists.

3. SURVEYS AND HISTORIES

209   BURCKHARDT, JACOB. *The Architecture of the Italian Renaissance.* Translated by James Palmes from *Die Geschichte der Renaissance* published in 1878. Revised and edited by Peter Murray. Chicago: University of Chicago Press, 1985. 311 pp., 351 b&w figs.

Book 2 of this classic study of Italian Renaissance history and culture is devoted to decoration; chap. 3 therein briefly deals with bronze doors, screens, altar-rails, candlesticks, and other objects; chap. 4 is on works in wood—intarsia, choir stalls, doors, wall panelings, frames, furniture; chap. 8 deals with goldsmith work, vessels of semiprecious stones and crystal, adornment, weapons, seals, maiolica, and other ceramics.

210   MÜNTZ, EUGÈNE. *Histoire de l'art pendant la Renaissance.* 3 vols. Vol 1, *Italie: Les Primitifs* (1889), 744 pp., 33 color pls., 514 b&w figs. and line drawings; vol. 2, *Italie: L'Age d'or* (1891), 864 pp., 37 color pls., 531 b&w figs. and line drawings; vol. 3, *Italie: La Fin de la Renaissance* (1895), 757 pp., 32 color pls., 476 b&w figs. and line drawings. Paris: Hachette.

Anthological essay on Italian Renaissance art. Sec. 1 and 2 of each volume deal with patrons, regional schools, traditions, influences, stylistic currents, artistic training; sec. 6 (the smallest and last) deals with the decorative arts—small bronzes, medals, and plaquettes, jewelry, ironworks, glyptic arts, textiles and tapestries.

6. PERMANENT COLLECTIONS

Bologna

MUSEO CIVICO MEDIEVALE

211   *Introduzione al Museo Civico Medievale, Palazzo Ghisilardi-Fava.* Edited by Gian Carlo Cavalli, with contributions by Carlo De Angelis, Renzo Grandi, Paolo Nannelli, and Roberto Scannavini. Bologna: Museo Civico Medievale di Bologna, 1985. 92 pp., 118 figs., some color.

Overview of the museum galleries after a recent reinstallation. Includes catalog of sixty-three Italian objects among which are several of the 15th-16th-century: bone carvings by the Embriachi, Venetian enameled glass, a German ivory saddle, arms and armor, musical instruments, and maiolica.

Chicago

ART INSTITUTE OF CHICAGO

212   WARDWELL, ALLEN, and DAVISON, MILDRED. "Three Centuries of the Decorative Arts in Italy." *Apollo* 84 (1966):179-89, 4 color pls., 17 b&w figs.

Presentation of Italian decorative art objects bequeathed to the institute since 1937 (by Martin A. Ryerson and others): maiolica, a terra cotta Virgin and Child attributed to Giovanni Minelli (early 16th century), a bronze relief of the Annuciation by Alessandro Vittoria, ca. 1583; a Venetian enameled covered cup (16th centtury); an Annunciation tapestry of ca. 1510 for Francesco Gonzaga; etc.

Cleveland

CLEVELAND MUSEUM OF ART

213   WINTER, PATRICK M. DE. "Recent Accessions of Italian Renaissance Decorative Arts." *Bulletin of The Cleveland Museum of Art* 73 (1986), Part 1, "Incorporating Notes on the Sculptor Severo da Ravenna," 74-138, 136 b&w figs.; part 2, 142- 83, 66 b&w figs.
      Reassessment of genesis and attributions of plaquettes in the circle of Donatello, medals produced for Pope Paul II, and of the oeuvre of the Paduan artist, Severo da Ravenna, who produced small-scale bronzes mostly as decoration for the home; works by other 16th-century artists working in bronze: Moderno, IO. F.F., Belli, Master of the Birth of Venus; Venetian glass; badge; jewel; pastiglia boxes (additions to census of 1984, see entry 2148); wax models by Rustici and Fontana; bronze Cristo morto from the workshop of Giambologna.

Milan

CIVICHE RACCOLTE DI ARTE APPLICATA, CASTELLO SFORZESCO

214   *The Sforza Castle Civic Museums, Milan,* by Clelia Alberici, et al. Translated by Leitizia Rucellai. Milan: Federico Garolla, 1984. 156 pp., numerous color and b&w figs.
      Short guide that includes overview of collections of arms and armor (pp. 36-39), furniture and tapestries (44-50), wrought iron, sgraffito ware and other maiolica (90-96), goldsmith and enamel works, ivory, bronzes, glass (102-12), tooled leather (113), tapestries (117-18).

Venice

FONDAZIONE GIORGIO CINI

215   *Dipinti toscani e oggetti d'arte dalla Collezione Vittorio Cini.* Catalog by Federico Zeri, Mauro Natale, and Alessandra Mottola Molfino. Vicenza: Neri Pozza, 1984. 86 pp., 8 color pls., 114 b&w figs.
      Collection that in addition to outstanding paintings and manuscripts includes two folding altars and two boxes of carved bone by the Embriachi Workshop, 16th-century Tuscan furniture and candlesticks, as well as 15th-century Venetian enameled plates and candlesticks.

7. EXHIBITION CATALOGS

Allentown

ALLENTOWN ART MUSEUM

216   *Beyond Nobility: Art for the Private Citizen in the Early Renaissance.* Exhibiton catalog by Ellen Callmann. Allentown: Allentown Art Museum, 1980. 148 pp., 4 color pls., 182 b&w figs.
      Useful catalog of 138 mostly Italian objects from private and public U.S. collections, many published here for the first time. Includes bronze statuettes, medals (Bellano, Donatello, Riccio, Alberti, Pisanello, etc.), and mortars; also textiles, furniture, as well as Embriachi, pastiglia, and leather caskets. Several maiolica pieces from various centers, Venetian glass, and also metal work. As a sequel to this publication and also authored by Callmann, see *Family Pride: The Italian Renaissance House and Its Furnishings,* catalog of an exhibition held at the Hyde Collection, Glen Falls, New York, in 1984. .

Bordeaux

MUSÉE DES ARTS DÉCORATIFS

216a   *Objets d'art italiens de la Renaissance.* Exhibition catalog by Arnaud Bréjon de Lavergnée, Jean-Pierre Reverseau, and Pierre Arizzoli-Clémentel. [Bordeaux, 1975.] 55 pp., 78 b&w figs.
      Group of seventy-nine objects from French public collections: maiolica, bronzes, brass plate, iron caskets, arms and armor, enameling, pastiglia casket, cassone, and Florentine tapestry, cataloged in short but critical and stimulating entries.

Detroit

DETROIT INSTITUTE OF ARTS

217   *Decorative Arts of the Italian Renaissance 1400-1600.* Exhibition catalog compiled by Paul L. Grigaut. Detroit: Detroit Institute of Arts, 1959. 180 pp., 4 color figs., 169 b&w figs.
      435 short catalog entries of often important objects including furniture, ceramics, glass, textiles, arms and armor, bronzes, jewelry, and other metalwork, and manuscripts in North American and European museums and held by U.S. private collections and dealers.

London

BURLINGTON HOUSE

218   *Catalogue of a Collection of Italian Sculptures and Other Plastic Art of the Renaissance.* Exhibition catalog introduction by E.R.D. Maclagan. London: Burlington Fine Arts Club, 1913. 163 pp., 69 b&w pls., often comprising several figs.
      Twelve-page introduction deals with method of producing small-scale sculpture in terra cotta, bronze, and wax as well as gem-carving in the Renaissance. 272 brief entries for sculpture, bronze objects (e.g. inkstands, door-knockers) and statuettes (26 pieces), medals (117 pieces), plaquettes (42 pieces), and wax models and gems (21 pieces), lent from private English collections and the Corporation and Museum of Birmingham, and J. Pierpont Morgan, New York. Many of the pieces included have subsequently passed into British and American public collections.

Toronto

ART GALLERY OF ONTARIO

219   *The Arts of Italy in Toronto Collections 1300-1800.* Exhibition catalog by David McTavish, K. Corey Keeble, Katharine Lochnan, and Sybille Pantazzi. Toronto: Art Gallery of Ontario, 1982. 239 pp., 16 color pls., 188 b&w figs.
      Based on the holdings of the Art Gallery of Ontario, the Royal Ontario Museum, and private collections in the Toronto area. Includes some 16th-century Paduan, Florentine, and Roman bronze statuettes; 15th-century armor; maiolica from Faenza, Castel Durante, Deruta, Urbino, Venice; furniture: Savonarola chair, Tuscan table and chairs; Venetian glass; 16th-century chalice and pax; silks and lace from Lucca, Venice, and Florence.

Tulsa

PHILBROOK ART CENTER

220   *Gloria dell'arte: A Renaissance Perspective.* Exhibition catalog edited by Katherine W.
Paris, with essays by Loren Partridge, Helmut Nickel, J.V.G. Mallet, and Ludovico Bor-
gio. Tulsa: Philbrook Art Center, 1979. 88 pp., 4 color figs., 43 b&w figs.
        Gathering of 171 objects, mostly of 15th-16th-century Italy, from American collec-
tions, the Louvre, British Museum, Victoria and Albert Museum, and the Courtauld Institute.
Includes arms and armor, bronzes, furniture, glass, jewelry, maiolica; short entries.

8. PRIVATE COLLECTION, AUCTION, AND DEALER CATALOGS

GUALINO COLLECTION

221   *Dagli ori antichi agli anni venti: Le collezioni di Riccardo Gualino.* Exhibition held in
Turin at Palazzo Madama, Galleria Sabauda. Catalog edited by Gabriella Borsano and
Tilde Vitta Zelman, with contributions by many authors. Milan: Gruppo Editoriale Electa, 1982. 266 p., 18 color figs., numerous b&w figs.
        Commemorative exhibition reconstructing the holdings of the eclectic collection
formed by the industrial magnate Riccardo Gualino in his neo-Gothic castle of Cereseto, in
the Monferrato, and now largely dispersed (mostly among Italian institutions and specifically
in Turin). In addition to paintings, includes a variety of Italian objects some of which are of
the period 1400- 1600: silks and tapestries; Venetian glass; goldsmith work; maiolica; medals
and plaquettes; furniture (cassoni, chairs, carved panels); textiles.

ORSELLI COLLECTION

222   *The Extensive and Very Valuable Antique Property Belonging to the Well-Known Connoisseur Luigi Orselli.* Sale held in New York at the American Art Association 15-19
February 1921. Unpaginated, some b&w figs.
        Sale of this New York dealer-collector whose holdings (915 lots) partially included
the Volpi and Bardini collections (see entries 226-27, 237-37b). Includes maiolica (lots 1-84),
Florentine terra cotta (85-92), Hispano-Moresque lustreware (93-98), Venetian and Hispano-
Moresque glass (119-24), Italian bronze mortars, bells, horses (128-45), brass and copper
bowls, candlesticks, altar cross (128-57), inlaid and ivory caskets, some wood carvings,
wrought iron candlesticks, andirons, gates (276-346), various textiles including Genoese silks,
Florentine and Venetian embroidered velvets, furniture including 15th-16th- century chairs,
tables, cabinets, stalls, large candlesticks, cassoni, door frames (647-897). Concludes with
tapestries dating mostly of the 17th century.

PEPOLI AND RUSCONI COLLECTIONS

223   *Italian Art of the Quattrocento and High Renaissance: Important Early Furniture, Notable
Sculptures, Bronzes, Paintings, Rich Fabrics.* Edited by Luigi Grassi. Sale held in New
York at the American Art Association 18-19 February 1929. Unpaginated, several b&w
figs.
        Sale of 348 lots drawn primarily from the Pepoli family of Bologna and the Rusconi
family and among which are fine examples of Renaissance furniture including a cabinet table
of 1548 (lot 330) identified as that of the Manchasolia family, various silks, the Erizo armet
and sword of the early 16th century (239-40).

SAVOY AND TOLENTINO COLLECTIONS

224   *Furniture and Works of Art from the Castle Formerly Occupied by the Savoy Family in Ver-zuolo (Piedmont), Italy, and Other Valuable Artistic Property Recently Selected Abroad by the Connoisseur Chevalier Raoul Tolentino.* Sale held in New York in the American Art Association 16-18 February 1922. Unpaginated, some b&w figs.

    565 lots among which furniture is most prevalent (chairs, tables, cabinets, cassoni, beds, stalls, paneling) and is primarily Italian, much of it dating of the 15th and especially of the 16th century. Also candlesticks, small bronzes, wrought iron, and textiles including some 15-16th-century French, Florentine, Ferrarese, and Flemish tapestries. Sale also included paintings and sculpture.

SIMONETTI COLLECTION

225   *Collezioni Simonetti, Roma: Quadri, mobili e oggetti d'arte.* Catalog by Ludovico Pollak. Sale held in Rome at the Casa di Vendite G. Tavazzi 26 April-6 May 1932. 112 pp., 86 b&w pls.

    Dispersal of over 870 items from the collection formed by the painter Attilio Simonet-ti (1843-1925), a pupil of Mariano Fortuny. Includes 15th-16th-century maiolica and tiles, Italian furniture including choir stalls, chairs, cassoni, tables, a pastiglia box, wrought iron works, silks and embroideries.

VOLPI COLLECTION

226   *Catalogue de la vente des objets d'art ancien composant les collections Elie Volpi.* Sale held in Florence by Jandolo & Tavazzi of Rome at the Piazza Dora D'Istria Villino Volpi 25 April-3 May 1910. Rome: Jandolo & Tavazzi, 1910. 74 pp., 131 b&w pls.

    Dispersal of 823 lots—paintings, furniture, and furnishings (principally maiolica)—not included by Volpi in the decor of his Palazzo Davanzati and Villa Pia (see following entry).

VOLPI [DAVANZATI] COLLECTION

227   *Illustrated Catalogue of the Exceedingly Rare and Valuable Art Treasures and Antiquities Formerly Contained in the Famous Davanzati Palace, Florence, Italy, which, together with the Contents of His Villa Pia Were Brought to America by Their Owner Professor Commendatore Elia Volpi, the Recognized European Expert and Connoisseur.* Sale held in New York at the American Art Galleries 21-25, 27-28 November 1916. Unpaginated, several b&w figs.

    The major collection of Italian Renaissance furniture and furnishings in private hands amassed by Elia Volpi and formed while still in Florence comprised of 979 lots including ivories, bronze medals and plaquettes, candlesticks, statuettes, door knocker, cross, reliquary, Paduan burners, maiolica from Orvieto and Faenza, various silks. The actual furniture, lots 262-557, includes examples of every known type. Also a great variety of furnishings including embroideries, tapestries, important maiolica from Caffaggiolo, Faenza, Deruta, and Orvieto (610-94), 16th-century arms, armor, and early firearms (716-805), Venetian glass (806-979), wrought iron, copper, bronze, and brass works, and various textiles of the 16th century.

SINGLE OR REGIONAL CENTERS OF PRODUCTION

FLORENCE AND TUSCANY

3. SURVEYS AND HISTORIES

228 SCHIAPARELLI, ATTILIO. *La casa fiorentina e i suoi arredi nei secoli XIV e XV.* Florence G.C. Sansoni, 1908. Reprint with revision and updating of notes and bibliographical references, as well as additional illustrations, by Maria Sframeli and Laura Pagnetta. 2 vols. Florence: Le Lettere, 1983. 1:325 pp., 174 b&w figs.; 2:113 pp., 10 color pls., 165 b&w pls.

Historical description of Florentine well-to-do houses in the 14th and 15th centuries. Beside sections on architecture, there are short chapters on tapestry and furniture (including intarsia). Particularly useful for the illustrations, many of contemporary paintings.

6. PERMANENT COLLECTIONS

Cleveland

CLEVELAND MUSEUM OF ART

229 *Florence and the Arts: Five Centuries of Patronage.* Exhibition catalog by Edmund P. Pillsbury. Cleveland: Cleveland Museum of Art, 1971. 56 pp., 103 b&w illus.

103 Florentine objects from the permanent collection dating of the 13th-18th centuries; includes 15th- and 16th- century small bronzes (cat. nos. 23, 35-37), furniture (81-90), ceramics (92-99), textiles (100-10), bookcover (102), glass (103); two-page list of other Florentine works in the museum not included in the exhibition.

Florence

MUSEO DEGLI ARGENTI

230 MORASSI, ANTONIO. *Art Treasures of the Medici.* Greenwich, N.Y.: New York Graphic Society , 1963. 38 pp., 55 color pls., 8 b&w figs.

Selection of fifty-five notable examples of goldsmith works and objects of rock crystal and other carved semi-precious stones, representing the salient features of the Treasury of the Medicis; over half date of the 15th-16th century or are ancient works with mounts of these periods. Thirty-five-page introduction traces the founding and growth of the collection and examines the taste of the Medicis and their role as patrons.

MUSEO HORNE

231 *Il Museo Horne a Firenze.* Catalog by Filippo Rossi. Milan: Electa, 1966. 199 pp., 39 color figs. and 135 figs.

Presentation of the collection bequeathed by Herbert Horne (1864-1916), which, in addition to Tuscan paintings and sculptures, includes maiolica from Florence, Faenza, Caffaggiolo, Siena, Castel Durante, Urbino, and Pesaro, a 16th-century straw fan, ironworks, carved bone and ivory (including a frame by the Embriachi Workshop), plaquettes of Riccio and Moderno, chalices, utensils and furniture (especially cassoni) of the late 15th-16th century. Summary catalog, tables.

MUSEO DELL'OPERA DEL DUOMO

232 *Il Museo dell'Opera del Duomo a Firenze.* Vol. 2. Catalog by Luisa Becherucci and Guilia Brunetti. Milan: Electa, [1970]. 309 pp. including 42 color and 230 b&w pls.

Catalog of the cathedral museum including the silver altar of the 14th-15th century, candlesticks, reliquaries, the series of silks embroidered on designs of Antonio Pollaiuolo, and vestments of the 15th-16th century. Extensive bibliography.

7. EXHIBITION CATALOGS

Florence

CONVENTO DI S. MARCO

233 *Mostra del Tesoro di Firenze sacra.* Florence: [Tipocalografia Classica], 1933. 161 pp., 32 b&w pls.

Cursory catalog of a major exhibit of over 1,100 art objects drawn from nearly all the churches of Florence and environs, including paintings, sculpture, goldsmith works, manuscripts, tapestries, vestments, many of the period 1400-1600.

PALAZZO MEDICI-RICCARDI

234 *Mostra Medicea.* Exhibition catalog by Ugo Ojetti, et al. Florence: Editrice Marzocco, 1939. 141 pp., 49 b&w pls.

Art commissioned by the Medicis and their circle from the 15th through the 18th century. In addition to paintings, sculptures, architectural models, and manuscripts, this exhibition of some four hundred objects (cursorily described in the entries) included many Renaissance jewels, goldsmith works (ecclesiastical and secular), semiprecious stones, seals, small bronzes, tapestries, and vestments.

PALAZZO VECCHIO

235 *Palazzo Vecchio: Committenza e collezionismo medicei 1537-1610.* Exhibition catalog edited by Claudia Beltramo Ceppi and Nicoletta Confuorto, with entries by thirty-four contributors. Florence: Edizioni Medicee, 1980. 410 pp., 16 color pls., many unnumbered b&w figs.

Catalog of major international exhibition dealing with 16th-century patronage of the Medicis. Among the 736 items are small bronzes, tapestries, arms and armor, carved semiprecious stones, textiles, maiolica and Medici porcelain, medals, furniture, and goldsmithwork, representing the highest aesthetic achievements of Italian decorative arts of the mannerist period.

S. STEFANO AL PONTE

236 *La comunità cristiana fiorentina e toscana nella dialettica religiosa del Cinquecento.* Exhibition catalog by Antonio Paolucci, with essays by Arnaldo d'Addario, Alessandro Parronchi, Marisa Forlani Conti, and Bruno Pacciani. Florence: Saverio Becocci, 1980. 293 pp., 27 color pls., numerous b&w figs.

Painting, sculpture, goldsmith work, lighting fixtures, furniture, altercloths, vestments produced for Florentine churches and convents of the 16th century when the Medici rulers reached their zenith. Historical essays dealing with the clergy and the Counter-Reformation; catalog comprised of 102 entries.

8. PRIVATE COLLECTION, AUCTION, AND DEALER CATALOGS

BARDINI COLLECTION

237 *Catalogue des objets d'art antiques du Moyen Age et de la Renaissance provenant de la Collection Bardini de Florence* by Stafano Bardini. 2 vols. Paris: Privately printed, 1902. 1:137 pp.; vol 2:128 b&w pls.

Official, detailed catalog (730 entries) announcing to an international audience the sale of this famous collection of mostly Florentine decorative arts at Christie's, London (see following entry). Includes Italian Renaissance bronze statuettes, some shaped as utilitarian objects (inkwell, candlesticks, mortars) by major Paduan, Florentine, and Venetian workshops (catalog nos. 3-106), a major collection of plaquettes by Moderno, Ulocrino, Riccio, Belli, Fra Antonio, Melioli, Sansovino, Flötner, and others (107-426), Italian maiolica from all major centers (427-502), a 15th-century candlestick (569), 14th-16th-century furniture, mostly Italian, among which cabinets, tables, stands, chairs, chests, frames (573-641), 16th- century Flemish, German tapestries (642-45), wax figurines (651-53), Italian, German 16th-century goldsmith work including a rock-crystal cross the mounts of which are attributed to Benvenuto Cellini (654-70).

237a *Catalogue of a Choice Collection of Pictures and Other Works of Art Chiefly Italian, of Medieval and Renaissance Times, the Property of Signor Stefano Bardini of Florence.* Sale held in London at Christie's 26-30 May 1902. 106 pp., 26 b&w pls.

Catalog of the actual sale (reduced to 650 lots). Items not in same order as the collection catalog and more cursorily described but each time reference is made to the earlier publication.

237b *Catalogue of the Beautiful Treasures and Antiquities Illustrating the Golden Age of Italian Art Belonging to the Famous Expert and Antiquarian Signor Stefano Bardini of Florence, Italy.* Sale held in New York at the American Art Galleries 23-27 April 1918. 280 pp., numerous b&w figs.

Sale includes 782 lots, some of which are reintroductions of items withdrawn or not sold during the 1902 Christie's sale (see preceding entry), this being obviously true of the plaquette collection (lots 137-237). Present sale also includes 15th-16th century medals, medallions, and plaquettes (1-47), bronze statuettes, utensils, mortars, knockers, ewers, candlesticks (48-108), wrought iron fire screens, etc. and bronze andirons (109-35), some ecclesiastical goldsmith work, Italian maiolica(257-303), Italian Renaissance furniture (within lots 580-781) among which are chairs, tables, cabinets, frames, cassoni, beds, which by and large are not outstanding.

BENGUJAT [DAVANZATI] COLLECTION

238 *Collezione del Museo di Palazzo Davanzati in Firenze di proprietà del Signor Léopold Bengujat.* Sale held in Florence at the Galleria Bellini 25-30 June 1934. Florence: Luigi and Giuseppe Leonardo Bellini, Francesco Ciardiello, 1934. 60 pp., 64 b&w pls.

Six hundred lots, very succinctly described and only a fraction of which are illustrated, of 15th-16th-century Italian furniture and furnishings, many of the 15th-16th century: chairs, tables, cassoni, credenze, beds, maiolica, Venetian glass, bronzes and other metalwork, comb, embroidery, tapestries, the property of this one-time owner of the Davanzati Palace. Notes on the palace and family in Italian, English, and French.

CHIGI-SARACINI COLLECTION

239   SALMI, MARIO. *Il Palazzo e la collezione Chigi- Saracini.* Siena: Monte dei Paschi di Siena, 1967. 315 pp., 36 color pls., 234 b&w figs.

Collection located in Siena and whose principal holdings are paintings. Includes a chalice, Embriachi caskets and chessboard, plaquettes of Donatello's circle and Boldù, a Roccatagliata(?) Putto, Faenza, Deruta, Castel Durante, Urbino maiolica, a Renaissance cabinet from Brescia, and intarsia furniture.

ROME

3. SURVEYS AND HISTORIES

240   MÜNTZ, EUGÈNE. *Les Arts à la cour des papes pendant le XVe et le XVIe siècle: Recueil de documents inédits tiré des archives et des bibliothèques romaines.* 3 vols. Vol. 1, *Martin V-Pie II, 1417-1464,* 364 pp.; vol. 2, *Paul II, 1464-1471,* 333 pp., 2 b&w pls.; vol. 3, *Sixte IV-Léon X, 1471-1521* [in effect only Sixtus IV, 1471-84], 303 pp., 2 pls. Paris: Ernest Thorin, 1878-82. Reprint [3 vols. in 1]. Hildesheim, Zürich, New York: Georg Olms, 1983.

Unsurpassed study on papal patronage during the 15th century. Vol. 1: Martin V (1417-31), commissions and gifts of goldsmith works (pp. 18-25), tapestries and embroideries (25-31); Eugene IV (1431-47), goldsmith works (53-62), tapestries and embroideries (63-66); Nicholas V (1447-55), goldsmith works (166-79), tapestries and embroideries (179-89); Calixtus III (1455-58), goldsmith works (206-10), embroideries (210), inventory (includes various decorative arts objects 213-19); Pius II (1458-64), goldsmith works (309-18), tapestries and embroideries (318-28), furniture (328-29). Vol. 2: Paul II (1464-71), vestments and tapestries amassed by Paul II (109-23, 128-59, 181-287) and those of his contemporaries in Italy (160-80) and his large collection of goldsmith works, carved gems, bronzes, medals, and coins. Vol. 3: Sixtus IV (1471-84), goldsmith works (239-62), tapestries (262-63), and embroideries (263-67).

240a   MÜNTZ, EUGÈNE. *Les Arts à la cour des papes Innocent VIII, Alexandre VI, Pie III (1484-1503): Recueil de documents inédits ou peu connus.* Paris: Ernest LeRoux, 1898. 303 pp., 10 b&w pls., 60 line drawings. Reprint, n.d.

Resumes the history of papal patronage from 1484. Innocent VIII's (1484-92) goldsmith works (pp. 104-20), tapestries and embroideries (121-31), costumes (132), furniture (132-33); Alexander VI's (1492-1503) goldsmith works (231-41), ceremonial swords (241-42), tapestries and embroideries (246-48).

6. PERMANENT COLLECTIONS

Rome

MUSEO DI PALAZZO VENEZIA

241   ZIPPEL, GIUSEPPE. "Paolo II e l'Arte." *L'arte* 13 (1910): 241-58, 6 b&w figs.

The vast collections amassed here by Paul II, particularly the reliquary of Montalto that bears the pontiff's arms.

242   *Palazzo Venezia: Paolo II e le fabbriche di S. Marco.* Exhibition catalog by Maria Letizia Casanova Uccella. Rome: De Luca, 1980. 189 pp., 1 color pl., numerous b&w figs.
       Traces the construction of the famed Palazzo; studies the many foundation medals as well as the collection of Cardinal Barbo, subsequently Pope Paul II, including carved gems, goldsmith works, a carved panel with the pontiff's arms, his leather traveling box.

7. EXHIBITION CATALOGS

Rome

MUSEO DI PALAZZO VENEZIA

243   *Roma 1300-1875: L'Arte degli anni santi.* Exhibition catalog by Marcello Fagiolo and Maria Luisa Madonna. Milan: Arnoldo Mondadori, 1984. 494 pp., 24 color pls., numerous b&w figs.
       Liturgical and devotional art works related to or produced in connection with the Holy Years; includes some cult implements, most from Roman churches, hard to see in situ and rarely reproduced (ceremonial banners, chalices, reliquary ciboria, altar crosses, copes and altar clothes, etc.), as well as commemorative medals, pilgrim badges, jewels, in addition to prints, painting, and sculpture. Includes representative examples of the 15th-16th centuries.

SARDINIA

3. SURVEYS AND HISTORIES

244   MALTESE, CORRADO. *Arte in Sardegna dal V al XVIII.* With several entries by Renata Serva. [Rome]: De Luca, 1962. 262 pp., 12 color pls., 147 b&w pls.
       Pictorial overview, accompanied by long entries and preceded by twenty-seven page introduction, of art on the island of Sardinia, which includes ecclesiastial and secular goldsmith work and a textile in the cathedral treasury of Cagliari (see pls. 57-64, 106-8): altar crosses, chalice, monstrance, ewer, dish, and embroidered chasuble.

TURIN AND PIEDMONT

6. PERMANENT COLLECTIONS

Turin

MUSEO CIVICO DI TORINO

245   *Mobili e arredi lignei; Arazzi e bozzetti per arazzi.* Catalog by Luigi Mallé. Turin; Museo Civico de Torino, 1972. 570 pp., including 10 color pls, and 409 b&w figs.
       Furniture, woodcarvings, tapestries, and cartoons in the permanent collection, each object illustrated and accompanied by comprehensive but concise entry (unnumbered) including state of conservation. Pp. 38-92 and figs. 2-210 are of 15th-16th-century cassoni, chairs, choir stalls, credenze carved woodwork panels produced mostly in the Piedmont but also in Liguria, Tuscany, Lombardy, and the Veneto. In the tapestry section , pp. 519-21 and figs. 1-6 are three 16th-century Brussels-woven tapestries (a Deposition and two hunting scenes).

VENICE AND THE VENETO

6. PERMANENT COLLECTIONS

Padua

DUOMO

246 MOSCHETTI, ANDREA. "Il tesoro della cattedrale di Padova." *Dedalo* 6 (1925). Part 1:79-109, 1 color pl., 25 b&w figs.; part 2:277-310, 28 b&w figs.

Major holdings in the cathedral treasury ranging from the Early Christian period to the 19th century. Of the 15th-16th century are monstrances, reliquaries, a silver statuette, a reliquary cross of 1435-53 by Pietro da Parma and Tommaso da Bologna, a silver frame (1492) by Anton Francesco della Seta, a bronze bell and pax, ecclesiastical vestments, the bindings of the Gospels of Isidorus by the goldsmith Alvise (1525), two silver vases with detailed openwork, two candlesticks and a cross of rock crystal (ca. 1590).

MUSEO CIVICO

247 *Il Museo Civico di Padova,* by Andrea Moschetti. 2d rev. ed. Padua: Società Cooperativa Tipografica, 1938. 525 pp., 100 b&w pls., 370 b&2 figs. (1st ed. 1925).

Discurvsive presentation of the holdings of the city library, archives, and museum. Includes small Renaissance bronzes — among which the votive urn by Desiderio da Firenze — plaquettes, statuettes various artifacts, maiolica, large medals (Bottacin Collection), some goldsmith work, and ecclesiastical vestments.

7. EXHIBITION CATALOGS

London

VICTORIA AND ALBERT MUSEUM

248 *Splendours of the Gonzaga.* Exhibition catalog edited by David Chambers and Jane Martineau, with twenty-six contributors. London: Victoria and Albert Museum, 1981. 272 pp., 113 color illus, 272 b&w illus.

Patronage and art collecting of the Gonzagas in Mantua; essays on ceramics (pp. 39-43), painted tiles (44-45), small bronzes (46-49), musical instruments (87-94); 282 catalog entries including silver and bronze works, tiles, cermics, furniture, woodwork and jewelry.

Mantua

PALAZZO DUCALE

249 *Tesori d'arte nella terra dei Gonzaga.* Exhibition catalog introduction by Ciro Ferrari with essays and entries by Lionello Giorgio Boccia et al. Milan: Electa, 1974. 199 pp., 7 color pls. 345 b&w figs.

307 works of art in and around Mantua from the 14th through the 18th century. Includes goldsmith works, medals, maiolica, vestments, tapestries, armor, furniture. Useful for overview of local holdings.

Vicenza

PALAZZO BARBARAN DA PORTO

250   *Mostra dell'arredamento del Cinquecento veneto.* Exhibition catalog introduction by Carla Bernardi. Vicenza: Palazzo Barbaran da Porto, 1973. 60 pp., 53 b&w figs.

Over two hundred examples, accompanied by brief entries, of 16th-century furniture and furnishings—carpets, vases, sculpture, paintings, etc.—that graced Palladian houses of the Veneto, and which reflect changing aesthetics and function.

NETHERLANDISH

3. SURVEYS AND HISTORIES

251   BERENDSEN, ANNE. *Het Nederlandse interieur: Binnenhuis, meubelen, tapijten, koper, tin, zilver, glas, porselein en aardewerk van 1450-1820.* Utrecht: Uitgeversmaatschappij W. de Haan N.V., 1950. 264 pp., 340 b&w figs.

Good survey of Dutch interiors, their furniture and furnishings from 1450 until 1820. Pp. 34-55 and figs. 1-72 deal with the 15th-16th centuries: chairs, tables, stands, chests, bronze luminaries and mortars, glassware, and ceramic tiles.

7. EXHIBITION CATALOGS

Zwolle

PROVINCIAAL OVERIJSSELS MUSEUM

252   *Thuis in de late middeleeuwen: Het Nederlands burgerinterieur 1400-1535.* Exhibition catalog entries by J.W.M. de Jong, with introduction by W.J. Walters and essays by R. Meischke and B. Dubbe. Zwolle: Uitgeverij Waanders, 1980. 203 pp., 64 color figs., 290 b&w figs.

Entries for 356 items, presented wtih essays, suggestive of several aspects of life in the houses of burghers within the Netherlands of the period 1400-1535. Mostly household furnishings including brass chandeliers, tools, utensils, chests, mortars, cauldrons, lavabos, chamber pots, chairs, various ceramics, glass, badges, keys, etc., often compared to examples in contemporary paintings.

POLISH

7. EXHIBITION CATALOGS

Kraków

MUZEUM NARODOWE

253   *L'Art à Cracovie entre 1350 et 1550.* Exhibition catalog by Maria Kopffowa, Barbara Miodonska, et al. Kraków: Muzeum Narodowe, 1964. 282 pp., 105 b&w pls.

Exhibition of medieval and Renaissance Polish art marking the foundation of the Jagellonian University of Kraków. Fifty-seven page introduction deals with the history and the intellectual and cultural life of the city; 313 catalog entries include some decorative arts of the 15th-16th centuries: goldsmith works (chalices, monstrances, reliquaries, altar crosses, croziers, miner's horn); metalwork (candelstick, bronze medals, etc.); a ceremonial sword; textiles (vestments and tapestries).

Rome

MUSEO DI PALAZZO VENEZIA

254   *Polonia: Arte e cultura dal medioevo all' illuminismo.* Exhibition held in Rome at Palazzo Venezia. Catalog by Filippa Alberti Gaudioso, et al. Florence: Centro Di, 1975. 286 pp., 9 color figs., 279 b&w figs.
       Polish art from the 13th through 18th centuries. Includes some objects of the period 1400-1600: textiles (vestments and tapestries); metalwork (liturgical vessels, crucifix, reliquary, secular goldsmith works); astronomical instruments. See nos. 17-22, 25-26, 36-39, 40-43.

PORTUGUESE

3. SURVEYS AND HISTORIES

255   SMITH, ROBERT C. *The Art of Portugal 1500-1800.* New York: Meredith Press, [1968]. 320 pp., 17 color pls., 10 maps and plans, 264 b&w figs.
       General introduction to architecture, church woodcarving, sculpture, painting, ceramics (tiles, plates and vessels — chap. 5, pp. 229-63), silver (chap. 6, pp. 264-84), furniture (chap. 7, pp. 285-308), and textiles (chap. 8, pp. 309-12), reflecting strong influences from the Moorish occupation, overseas expansion to Africa and the Orient, and the prosperity that attracted foreign artists to Portugal in the 16th-century.

SPANISH

2. BIOGRAPHICAL DICTIONARIES

256   *Diccionario biográfico de artistas de Cataluña desde da época romana hasta nuestros días.* Edited by J.F. Ráfols [Fontanals] and José Gibert Buch, with entries by ten collaborators. 3 vols. Vol. 1, *A-G* (1951), 566 pp., 32 b&w pls.; vol. 2, *H-R* (1953), 530 pp., 34 b&w pls. vol. 3, *S-Z* and *Supplement* (1954), 628 pp., 46 b&w pls. Barcelona: Editorial Millá, 1951-54.
       Biographical dictionary of painters, draftsmen, engravers, sculptors, architects, smiths, potters, goldsmiths, printers, embroiderers, armorers, glassmakers, etc., of Catalonia from Romanesque to modern times. Each volume has a place and name index and a glossary; no bibliography. Vol. 3 also contains a descriptive repertory of all buildings in Barcelona cited in the biography and monographs on the various branches of art (e.g., goldsmith works, ceramics, etc.) with index of artists chronologically arranged.

3. SURVEYS AND HISTORIES

257   AINAUD DE LASCARTE, JUAN. *Cerámica y vidrio.* Vol. 10 of *Ars hispaniae: Historia universal del arte hispánico.* Madrid: Editorial Plus-Ultra, 1952. 421 pp., 974 b&w figs.

Comprehensive study of Spanish ceramics and glass from the 14th to the 19th centuries. Arranged by geographic location (Valencia, Catalonia, Aragon, Castile, etc.) and then chronologically. Copious illustration of objects from public and private European (mostly Spanish) and U.S. collections.

258 WILLIAMS, LEONARD. *The Arts and Crafts of Older Spain.* 3 vols. Chicago: A.C. McClurg & Co., 1908. 1:289 pp., 61 b&w pls.; 2:263 pp., 77 b&w pls.; 3:282 pp., 32 b&w pls.

Broad sociocultural survey whose primary usefulness is the fact that it is in English. Vol. 1 deals with gold- and silversmith works and jewelry, ironwork, bronzes, arms; Vol. 2, furniture, ivories, pottery, glass; Vol. 3, silk, cloths and woolens, embroidery, tapestry, and lace.

6. PERMANENT COLLECTIONS

DIRECTORY

259 *Museos de Barcelona.* Contributions by many authors. Madrid: Patrimonio Nacional, 1972. 358 pp., many illus., some in color.

Overview of the holdings of Barcelona's many museums. Relevant to 15th-16th-century Spanish decorative arts are the sections dealing with the following collections: Museo de Historia de la Ciudad, Instituto Amatller de Arte Hispánico, Museo de Música, Museo Diocesano y Catedralicio, Museo Militar, Museo de Artes Decorativas, Museo de Cerámica, and Museo Textil.

7. EXHIBITION CATALOGS

Valencia

MUSEO DE BELLAS ARTES

260 *El siglo XV valenciano.* Exhibition catalog by Carlos Soler d'Hyver and Ramón Rodríguez Culebras. Valencia: Museo de Bellas Artes, 1973. 68 pp., 3 color figs., 118 b&w figs.

Surveys the art of Valencia in the 15th century. Twenty- two pages of introductory essays by five contributors on historical, social, and artistic background followed by 145 catalog entries (most illustrated) for paintings, sculpture, and decorative arts (nos. 97-141): ceramics (plates, jars, bowls, tiles); metalwork (crucifixes, monstrance, ciborium, bowl, statuette); furniture (stall, chest); textiles (embroidery).

8. PRIVATE COLLECTION, AUCTION, AND DEALER CATALOGS

LAS ALMENAS COLLECTION

261 *Important Medieval and Early Renaissance Works of Art from Spain: Sculptures, Furniture, Textiles, Tapestries and Rugs, Collection of Conde de las Almenas, Madrid, Spain.* Catalog by Mildred Stapley Byne, Arthur Byne, and Ercole Canessa. Sale held in New York at the American Art Association 13-15 January 1927. 324 pp., several b&w figs.

The major public sale of Spanish art from the collection of José Maria de Palacio, Count de las Almenas, allowed to leave Spain prior to the 1926 law restricting exportation. Among the 447 lots are primary examples of 15th- and 16th-century ecclesiastical and domestic furniture (stalls, thrones, sacristy chests, tables, varguenos, treasure chests, steel cabinets,

Gothic chests with paneling, chairs, beds, cupboards), also important textiles (orphreys, dalmatics, chasubles with embroideries, tapestries), Hispano-Moresque ware, wrought iron, and some goldsmith work in addition to sculpture and manuscript pages.

WEISSBERGER COLLECTIONS

262   *Spanish Art Treasures Collected during Many Years and Owned by Herbert P. Weissberger of Madrid, Spain.... Sale held in New York at the American Art Association 26-30 April 1921.* New York: American Art Association, 1921. Unpaginated, several b&w figs.

Dispersal of a collection of 969 lots partially formed from the Valverde and Lunaza Collections (Madrid), Diez Monterio (Burgos), as well as from conventual Spanish churches: various ceramic albarelli, dishes, holy water fonts, and tiles; bronze, brass; leather objects; important series of Spanish and Italian silks (lots 204-434); also paintings and sculpture. Sale concludes with large collection—often fine—of domestic and ecclesiastical furniture, wrought iron, and some Flemish tapestries (618-969).

SWISS

6. PERMANENT COLLECTIONS

Fribourg

CATHÉDRALE SAINT-NICOLAS

263   *Trésor de la Cathédrale Saint-Nicolas de Fribourg. Der Kirchenschatz des St. Niklausenmünsters in Freiburg.* Exhibition catalog essays by Hermann Schöpfer, Hugo Vonlanthen, Gérard Pfulg, et al. Fribourg: Cathédrale Saint Nicolas, 1983. 300 pp., 7 color figs., 233 b&w figs. French/German text.

Over 160 masterpieces from the cathedral treasury dating from the 15th to the 19th century. Presented in eight sections: liturgical vessels; reliquaries; silver statuary; figurative motifs in goldsmiths' works; secular silver; manuscripts and printed liturgical texts; liturgical vestments; portraits and documents. Descriptive entries explain use of object in the service, and provide stylistic comparisons and bibliography. Appendix of goldsmith techniques; glossaries of liturgical, textile, and metalsmith terms; index of metalsmith works.

U.S.S.R. (LATVIAN, ESTONIAN, AND LITHUANIAN)

2. BIOGRAPHICAL DICTIONARIES

264   CAMPE, PAUL. *Lexikon liv-und kurländischer Baumeister: Bauhandwerker und Baugestalter von 1400-1850.* 2 vols. Stockholm, 1951-57.

A dictionary of architects and craftsmen active in Livonia and Lithuania [Courland] from 1400-1850, chronologically arranged. For alphabetical listing see vol. 1, pp. 509-39, and vol. 2, pp. 541-644. Includes some 15th-16th- century entries.

VI. General Works on Small-Scale Carvings and Wax

A. MULTI COUNTRY OF ORIGIN

3. SURVEYS AND HISTORIES

Book

265   WINTER, F[ERDINAND]. *Die Kämme aller Zeiten von der Steinzeit bis zur Gegenwart.* Liepzig: H.A. Ludwig Degener, 1906. 12 pp., 84 b&w pls. comprising 311 figs. Text in German/English/French.
    Combs of all countries from the Stone Age to present days. Series of plates with notes. Pls. 37-45 include Italian, French, English, Spanish, and German ivory and boxwood examples of the period 1400-1600.

See also entry 28.

Articles

266   PINTO, EDWARD H. "Hand-Made Combs." *Connoisseur* 130 (1952):170-72, 175-76, 221; 17 b&w figs.
    Brief study of comb-making from antiquity through the 18th century with mention of several 15th-16th-century French, Italian, and English carved boxwood and ivory examples and the social conventions associated with them (i.e., as love tokens).

267   WEIXLGÄRTNER, ARPAD. "Ungedruchte Stiche: Materialien und Anregungen aus Grenzgebieten der Kupferstichkunde." *Jahrbuch der kunsthistorischen Sammlungen des allerhöchsten Kaiserhauses* 29 (1911):259-385, 16 b&w pls., 48 b&w figs.
    The art of the engraver as seen not only on printing plates but also in the decoration of rock crystal, metal plaques—often enlivened with enamel and niello—ivory, boxwood, etc., mostly in Gothic and Renaissance Germany, Italy, and Flanders.

6. PERMANENT COLLECTIONS

Berlin

STAATLICHE MUSEEN

268   *Die Bildwerk in Holz, Stein und Tom Kleinplastik.* Catalog by E.F. Bange. Vol. 4 of *Die Bildwerke des deutschen Museums,* edited by Theodor Demmler. Berlin and Leipzig: Walter de Gruyter & Co., 1930. 178 pp, 294 b&w figs.
Catalog of some ninety-seven German, Netherlandish, Flemish, and French small-scale reliefs and sculpture in wood, stone, and clay, produced from the 14th through the 18th century. Most examples are German and date of Renaissance times.

Brussels

MUSÉES ROYAUX D'ART ET D'HISTOIRE

269   *Catalogue* [of the former Musées Royaux des Arts Décoratifs et Industriels] *des ivoires, des objets en nacre, en os gravé et en cire peinte,* by Joseph Destrée. Brussels: Émile Bruylant, 1902. 146 pp., 76 b&w figs.
Catalog of seventy-six ivory, bone, mother-of-pearl, and wax objects in the permanent collection, all illustrated. Nos. 27-32 are 15th-16th-century French, Italian, and German ivories — a casket, a pax, a comb, statuettes; 71-72 are small 15th-16th-century Flemish mother-of-pearl reliefs; 74-75 are 16th-century Italian and Spanish portrait wax reliefs.

Vienna

KUNSTHISTORISCHES MUSEUM

270   *Werke der Kleinplastik in der Skulpturensammlung des A.H. Kaiserhauses.* Vol. 2, *Bildwerke in Holz, Wachs und Elfenbein,* by Julius von Schlosser. Vienna: Anton Schroll & Co., 1910. 17 pp., 55 b&w pls., 8 b&w text figs.
Album of plates preceded by series of useful grouped captions that deal with reliefs and other small sculpture, mostly German, in wood, wax, and ivory. Pls. I-XXIII deal with 16th century carved objects by Flötner, Kels, Polsterer, etc.; pl. XXXII is a wax relief portrait of ca. 1567 representing Archbishop Ferdinand of Tyrol by Francesco Segala; pls. XXXIII-XXXIV reproduce Italian ivory statuettes and a plaquette of the end of the 16th century.

7. EXHIBITION CATALOGS

Frankfurt

LIEBIEGHAUS

271   *Dürers Verwandlung in der Skulptur zwischen Renaissance und Barock.* Exhibition catalog by Herbert Beck, Bernhard Decker, et al. Frankfurt: Liebieghaus Museum alter Plastik, 1981. 404 pp., 24 color pls., 330 b&w figs.
Catalog of 223 small-scale carvings and sculptures, mostly German, produced in the lifetime or in the wake of Albrecht Dürer and reflecting his manifold influences. These relationships are also discussed at length in didactic essays.

VII. Ivory and Bone Carvings

A. MULTI COUNTRY OF ORIGIN

3. SURVEYS AND HISTORIES

272   BEIGBEDER, O. *Ivory.* New York: G.P. Putnam's Sons, 1965. 128 pp., 33 color figs., 103 b&w figs.
      Concise, accessible introduction to the subject. Touches on late Gothic and Renaissance examples.

273   MOLINIER, ÉMILE. *Les Ivoires.* Vol. 1 of *Histoire générale des arts appliqués à l'industrie.* Paris: E. Lévy et Cie [1896]. 245 pp., 24 b&w pls., 104 line drawings.
      Pioneering study on ivory carvings from Roman times to the 18th century. For 15th- and 16th-century French, Italian, Flemish, German, Spanish, and English works, see chap. 5 (pp. 177-210) and 6 (211-20). No index.

274   PHILIPPOVICH, EUGEN VON. *Elfenbein.* 2d ed. Munich: Klinkhardt and Biermann, 1982. 480 pp., 416 b&w figs. (1st ed. 1961.)
      Useful survey of ivory carvings produced in every European country or region, touching each time on 15th-16th century examples. Excellent plates.

275   TARDY [HENRI LENGELLÉ]; BIDAULT, P.; LEVASSEUR, H.; et al. *Les Ivoires: Évolution décorative du Ier siécle à nos jours.* Paris: Tardy, [1966]. 318 pp., 665 b&w figs.
      Pictorial survey with brief captions of secular and religious ivory carvings from the 1st century to the present drawn from European museums. Some 15th-16th-century examples of statuettes, plaques, caskets, and cutlery handles. Concludes with lists of collections, known carvers, and iconographic index.

276   VÖGE, WILHELM. *Die Elfenbeinbildwerke* (Königliche Museen zu Berlin—Beschreibung der Bildwerke der christlichen Epochen). 2d ed. Catalog, Berlin: Georg Reimer, 1911, 100 pp.; portfolio of unbound plates, Berlin: Georg Reimer, 1902, 45 b&w pls.

Ivory from the 4th to the 18th centuries formerly in the Königliche Museum in Berlin some now in the Preussischer Kulturbesitz, Berlin, others in East Berlin and others, whereabouts unknown). Of the 15th century are Italian (cat. nos. 152-53, 155-56), Spanish (154), and Netherlandish (175-77) reliefs and statuettes; of the 16th century are Spanish (159-64), Netherlandish (178-80), and German (182-86) objects.

6. PERMANENT COLLECTIONS

Baltimore

WALTERS ART GALLERY

277 *Masterpieces of Ivory from The Walters Art Gallery.* Catalog by Richard H. Randall, Jr., with texts by five contributors. New York: Hudson Press; Baltimore: Walters Art Gallery, 1985. 338 pp., 100 color pls., 493 b&w figs.

Entries for 493 ivories ranging from antiquity to the twentieth century follow a chronological sequence; each object is illustrated, often in color. Includes a twenty-page introduction on the history of ivory as an artistic medium, and each grouping of entries is preceded by a brief introductory essay. For the 15th-16th centuries see cat. nos. 348-68 comprising ivory mirror cases, combs, caskets, diptychs, plaques, a pax, rosary beads, etc., from Italy, Germany, Flanders, and France.

Berlin

STAATLICHE MUSEEN

278 *Die Elfenbeinbildwerke.* Catalog by W.F. Volbach. Vol. 1 of *Die Bildwerke des deutschen Museums,* edited by Theodor Demmler. Berlin and Leipzig: Walter De Gruyter & Co., 1923. 113 pp., 85 b&w pls., 55 b&w text figs.

Major ivory collection from Byzantine times to the 18th century with twenty-seven 15th-16th-century French, German, Italian, Spanish, and Netherlandish examples (pp. 49, 52, 54-58, 89, 96, 98), partly dispersed during World War II.

Leningrad

HERMITAGE

279 *Westeuropäische Elfenbeinarbeiten aus der Ermitage Leningrad XI.-XIX. Jahrhundert.* Exhibition held in East Berlin at the Kunstgewerbemuseum, Schloss Köpernick. Catalog by Martha Kryjanovskaja and Ljubov Faenson. Berlin: Staatliche Museen, 1974. 88 pp., 141 b&w figs.

137 ivory objects in the collection. Of the 15th-16th century are 4 German, 2 French, 8 Italian, and 3 Portuguese reliefs, statuettes, triptychs, combs, and caskets.

279a *Zachodnioeuropejska rzeźba z kości w latach 1100-1900 ze zbiorów Państwowego Ermitażu w Leningradzie: Katalog wystawy.* Exhibition held in Warsaw at the Muzeum Narodowe. Catalog by Marta Kryżanowskaja and Elena Szlikiewicz. Warsaw: Muzeum Narodowe, Czerwiec, 1981. 34 pp., 49 b&w pls.

Deals with 120 ivory carvings of the period 1100 to 1900 from the Hermitage. Nos. 25-32 date of the 15th century; 33-44, of the 16th, including plaques, statuettes, etc.

London

BRITISH MUSEUM

280   *Catalogue of the Ivory Carvings of the Christian Era with Examples of Mohammedan Art and Carvings in Bone in the Department of British and Mediaeval Antiquities and Ethnography of the British Museum,* by O.M. Dalton. London: Trustees of the British Museum, 1909. 245 pp., 125 b&w pls., 77 b&w text figs.

      Of the 613 items authoritatively cataloged (often with extensive entries), nos. 242-418 are Gothic, while 419-512 include mainly Renaissance examples from England, France, Flanders, Germany, Holland, Italy, Spain, and Portugal.

VICTORIA AND ALBERT MUSEUM

281   *A Description of the Ivories, Ancient and Mediaeval, in the South Kensington Museum.* Preface by William Maskett. London: Chapman & Hall, 1872. 318 pp., 24 b&w pls., 21 woodcut illus.

      A 107-page preface offering a general introduction to the art of ivory-carving from B.C. through medieval times, followed by description of plaques, statuettes, caskets, diptychs, triptychs, panels, book covers, medallions, combs, mirror cases, etc. A thirty-four page appendix presents an overview of the ivories in other English institutions and in the Meyerick Collection.

281a   *Catalogue of Carvings in Ivory* by Margaret H. Longhurst. Part 2. London: Board of Education, 1929. 164 pp., 97 b&w pls., 9 b&w text figs.

      European examples from the 13th to the 20th century: entries on pp. 36-44, 69-71 are for French, English, Flemish 15th-16th-century diptychs, paxes, caskets, plaques, statuettes, chaplet beads; entries on pp. 54-55 are for French 15th-century secular objects: combs, panels from a casket, medallion with a genre scene. Pp. 56-58, 61-69, 71-72, include German, Italian, French, 15th-16th-century chessmen, statuettes, caskets, paxes, diptychs, and Embriachi bone carvings from Venice.

Milan

CIVICHE RACCOLTE D'ARTE

282   *Museo d'Arti Applicate: Gli avori.* Catalog by Oleg Zastrow. Milan: Electa, 1978. 220 pp., 24 color figs., 413 b&w figs.

      Catalog of 435 late antique through 19th-century ivories in the collection of the Castello Sforzesco.

Munich

BAYERISCHES NATIONALMUSEUM

283   *Die Bildwerke in Elfenbein, Knochen, Hirsch-und Steinbockhorn.* Catalog by Rudolf Berliner. Vol. 13, no. 4 of *Kataloge des Bayerischen Nationalmuseums.* Augsburg: Dr. Benno Flilser & Co., 1926. 192 pp., 336 b&w pls.

Ivories dating of the 5th to the 19th century. Of the 15th-16th century are French, German, Italian, and Swiss examples (cat. nos. 59-64, 67-70, 73-113, 782-830): devotional plaques and statuettes, scepter, powder horns, as well as Embriachi carved bone mirror frame and panels in intarsia frames.

Paris

MUSÉE DU LOUVRE

284   *Catalogue des ivoires.* Catalog by Émile Molinier. Paris: Musée du Louvre, 1896. 381 pp., 1 b&w pl., 38 line drawings.
         Catalog of 244 ivories at the Louvre from the 6th to the 19th century: diptychs, polyptychs, plaques, medallions, statuettes, combs, a harp, caskets, and fragments. Entries arranged chronologically (pertaining to 15th-16th centuries are nos. 53-183).

Turin

MUSEO CIVICO D'ARTE ANTICA, PALAZZO MADAMA

See entry 76.

7. EXHIBITION CATALOGS

London

BURLINGTON HOUSE

285   *Catalogue of an Exhibition of Carvings in Ivory.* Exhibition catalog by M.H. Longhurst, with introduction by Eric R.D. Maclagan. London: Burlington Fine Arts Club, 1923. 126 pp., 54 b&w pls.
         Ivories from museums and private collections in Britain and the Brussels Musée du Cinquantenaire with examples ranging from the dawn of history to the 19th century. Fourteen- page introduction traces the history of ivory carving; 252 brief entries of which nos. 155-87 relate to the period 1400-1600. Included are diptychs, paxes, caskets, an altarpiece, many relief panels, a cabinet, medallions, plaques, combs, and statuettes, from all major European countries; ecclesiastical and secular objects. Arranged chronologically.

B. SINGLE COUNTRY OF ORIGIN

BELGIUM (FLEMISH)

3. SURVEYS AND HISTORIES

286   YOUNG, BONNIE. "Scenes in an Ivory Garden." *Metropolitan Museum of Art Bulletin* 14 (1956):252-56, 6 b&w figs.
         Early 16th-century ivory pedestal with carved figures, base for a now lost Vanitas statuette.

BRITISH
(ENGLISH AND SCOTTISH)

3. SURVEYS AND HISTORIES

287 LONGHURST, M.H. *English Ivories.* London: G.P. Putnam's Sons, 1926. 140 pp., 6 color pls., 51 b&w pls., 10 b&w text figs.
Historical introduction (touching on the 15th century) and catalog (see nos. LIX, LXX, LXXII-LXXV): panels of caskets, diptychs, Scottish caskets.

FRENCH

3. SURVEYS AND HISTORIES

288 GRODECKI, LOUIS. *Ivoires français.* Paris: Librairie Larousse, 1947. 157 pp., 48 b&w figs.
Authoritative assessment in paperback of ivory production in France from Carolingian times through the 18th century. Touches on 15th-16th century, pp. 123-31.

289 KOECHLIN, RAYMOND. *Les Ivoires gothiques français.* 3 vols. Paris: August Picard, 1924. 1:549 pp; 2:507 pp.; 3:231 b&w pls.
Standard corpus of French Gothic ivories mostly of the 13th-14th centuries. Vol. 1 is an extensive essay dealing with history, technique, styles, and types of objects; pp. 313-55, 524-30 specifically concern the 15th century. See also pp. 538-40 for mention of 15th-century ivory carvers in contemporary accounts. Vol. 2 is a catalog of 1,328 ivories of which nos. 847-985 are 15th-century religious statuettes, plaques, caskets, paxes; nos. 1223-41 and 1243-47, 1249-59 are 15th-16th-century belt buckles, rosary bead, goblets, horn. See corresponding illustrations in vol. 3.

GERMAN

6. PERMANENT COLLECTIONS

Cologne

SCHNÜTGEN MUSEUM

290 LEGNER, ANTON. "Ein spätgotisches Elfenbeinmedaillon: Eine Neuerwerbung des Schnütgen-Museums." *Museen der Stadt Köln* 1 (1980):1778-79, 1 b&w fig.
A German circular ivory medallion of the Crucifixion dating of the first half of the 15th century and formerly in the Brummer Collection, acquired for the museum.

ITALIAN

3. SURVEYS AND HISTORIES

291 GENGARO, MARIA LUISA. "La bottega degli Embriachi: A proposito di opere ignote o poco note." *Rivista de storia dell'arte* 5(1960):221-28. 8 b&w figs.

While attributing a hitherto unpublished ivory triptych (private collection, Milan) to Baldassare, the author reassigns known works of the early 15th century to different members of the Embriachi Workshop on the basis of Lombard-Tuscan or Venetian stylistic traits.

292   SCHOLOSSER, JULIUS VON. "Die Werkstatt der Embriachi in Venedig." *Jahrbuch der kunsthistorischen Sammlungen des allerhöchsten Kaiserhauses* 20 (1899):220-82, 7 b&w pls., 36 b&w figs.

Fundamental study on the production of caskets with panels of carved bone as principal decoration within frames of inlaid wood. They were principally made in the prolific workshop of the Embriachi family in Venice around 1400. Author gives a checklist of 126 of these describing their courtly and literary subjects. Schlosser also studies those impressive altarpieces made up of such a series of bone carvings produced for the Certosa of Pavia and Jean de Berry.

6. PERMANENT COLLECTIONS

Rome (Vatican)

MUSEO SACRO

293   EGBERT, DONALD DREW. "North Italian Gothic Ivories in the Museo Cristiano of the Vatican Library." In *Art Studies: Medieval, Renaissance and Modern*. Cambridge: Harvard University Press, 1929. Pp. 169-206, 70 b&w figs.

Sixteen pieces including works by the Embriachi and other Venetian, as well as Milanese, workshops of the 14th-15th century. Publication particularly important for the wealth of illustrated comparative material from other institutions.

293a   *Gli oggetti di avorio e di osso.* Catalog by C.R. Morey. Vatican: Biblioteca Apostolica Vaticana, 1936. 113 pp. with 95 b&w text figs., 42 b&w pls.

156 objects, largely devotional, carved out of ivory or bone; nos. 101-16 are mostly North Italian (Venetian) plaques of the 15th century; nos. 117-22, mostly statuettes and memento mori of the 16th century. Within a fifty-page introduction is a study (pp. 42-50) of a 16th-century ivory Michelangesque Deposition.

7. EXHIBITION CATALOGS

Naples

MUSEO DUCA DI MARTINA

294   *Medioevo e produzione artistica di serie: Smalti di Limoges e avori gotici in Campania.* Exhibition catalog by Paolo Giusti and Pierluigi Leone de Castris. Florence: Centro Di, 1981. 143 pp., 11 color pls., 154 b&w figs.

Limoges enamels and Gothic ivories in Campania (mostly in museums in Naples). Primarily concerns the 12th-14th century, but catalog also includes twelve 15th-century caskets by the Embriachi Workshop, and two 15th-century ivory combs and a casket by artists strongly influenced by the Embriachi (cat. nos. II.15- II.27).

NETHERLANDISH

6. PERMANENT COLLECTIONS

Princeton

UNIVERSITY MUSEUM

295   RANDALL, RICHARD H. "Jan van Eyck and the St. George Ivories." *Journal of the Walters Art Gallery* 39 (1981):39- 48, 6 b&w figs.

Author supports the attribution of an ivory diptych (Princeton) to the North Netherlands, probably Utrecht, and proposes a dating of about 1441-70 on the basis of comparison with a now lost panel by Jan van Eyck known from a version by Roger van der Weyden.

VIII. Mother-of-Pearl, Other Shell Carvings, and Coral

A. MULTI COUNTRY OF ORIGIN

3. SURVEYS AND HISTORIES

296   RITCHIE, CARSON I.A. *Shell Carving. History and Techniques.* South Brunswick, N.J. and New York: A.S. Barnes & Co., 1974. 208 pp., 223 b&w illus.
       Survey of the art of shell carving in various cultures. Pertinent to 15th and 16th century Europe are chaps. 7-10 (pp. 119-204) describing the multiple use of carved shells and especially mother-of-pearl in devotional plaques and medallions, jewelry, cups, inlay for boxes and stocks of firearms, powderhorns, furniture, musical instruments, etc.

B. SINGLE COUNTRY OF ORIGIN

GERMAN

3. SURVEYS AND HISTORIES

Book

297   PAZAUREK, GUSTAV E. *Perlmutter.* Berlin: Gebr. Mann, 1937. 79 pp., 64 b&w pls.
       Carved mother-of-pearl medallions or fragments incorporated as decorative elements into objects and furniture. Most examples discussed are German either with devotional scenes (15th century) produced after engravings, or portraits (16th-17th century).

Article

298   FORRER, R. "Muschelmedaillen und Perlmutterplaketten." *Archiv für Medaillen- und Plaketten-Kunde* 1 (1913-14):92-96, 1 b&w pl. comprising 8 figs.

German carver of shell medallions and mother-of-pearl roundels of the late 15th-16th century.

ITALIAN

3. SURVEYS AND HISTORIES

299   SCHEICHER, ELISABETH.   "Korallen in fürstlichen Kunstkammern des 16. Jahrhunderts." *Weltkunst* 52 (1982):3447-50, 3 color figs., 3 b&w figs.
Coloristic objects from German and Italian princely collections of the 16th century that include coral as one of their elements (for figures, trees, decoration). Includes pokals, crucifixion scenes, caskets, and untensils.

6. PERMANENT COLLECTIONS

Dresden

STAATLICHE KUNSTSAMMLUNGEN

300   HACKENBROCH, YVONNE. "A Set of Knife, Fork and Spoon with Coral Handles." *Metropolitan Museum Journal* 15 (1980):183- 84, 1 b&w fig.
This set in the Grünes Gewölbe in Dresden, dates of ca. 1579 and once formed part of the largest known collection of coral-handled cutlery owned by Elector Augustus of Saxony; it is here suggested to have been manufactured in Genoa for the German market.

IX. Box and Other Small Wood Carvings

A. MULTI COUNTRY OF ORIGIN

6. PERMANENT COLLECTIONS

Budapest

IPARMÜVÉSZETI MÚZEUM

301   VADÁSZI, ERZSÉBET. "Peignes du gothique tardif dans notre collection." *Ars Decorativa* 1 (1973):61-71, 16 b&w figs.
   Five 1420-1520 carved boxwood combs in the collection compared to other examples at the Louvre, Musée de Cluny, Victoria and Albert Museum, Royal Scottish Museum, and Historischer Verein, Würzburg.

8. PRIVATE COLLECTION, AUCTION, AND DEALER CATALOGS

See entries. 174, 723d.

B. SINGLE COUNTRY OF ORIGIN

BELGIUM
(BRABANTINE AND FLEMISH)

6. PERMANENT COLLECTIONS

Brussels

MUSÉE DU CINQUANTENAIRE

302   DESTRÉE, JOS[EPH]. "Noix de chapelet." *Bulletin des Musées Royaux d'Art et d'Histoire,* 3d ser. 2 (January 1930):20-22, 4 b&w figs.
       Large boxwood rosary beads — one with minutely carved scenes, another shaped as a skull — are related to large Flemish sculpture of the first third of the 16th century.

Detroit

DETROIT INSTITUTE OF ARTS

303   WIXOM, WILLIAM D. "A Brabantine Boxwood Triptych." *Bulletin of The Detroit Institute of Arts* 61 (1983):38-45, 8 b&w figs.
       Devotional function and iconography of a small triptych dated to ca. 1520 carved with scenes of Christ's infancy; comparisons with related examples.

NETHERLANDISH

6. PERMANENT COLLECTIONS

London

BRITISH MUSEUM

304   BRAUN, E.W. "Ein Holzmodell Michael Hohnauers mit dem Brustibilde des Jan van Leyden im British Museum." *Archiv für Medaillen- und Plaketten-Kunde* 5 (1925-26):133-36, 1 b&w pl.
       Boxwood model of 1534-35 for a medal of Michael Hohenauer by Jan van Leyden.

POLISH

3. SURVEYS AND HISTORIES

305   BRAUN-TROPPAU, EDMUND WILHELM. "Zwei Buchsreliefs vom Joachimsthaler Goldschmied Concz Welcz." *Archiv für Medaillen- und Plaketten-Kunde* 3 (1921-22):128-33, 5 b&w figs.
       Small carved boxwood reliefs dated 1537 of Charles V (Paris, Louvre) and of his brother Ferdinand I (former Thiers Collection, Paris) and medals of 1547 by the goldsmith Concz Welcz.

X. Wax

Does not include waxes intended as models for large-scale sculpture.

A. MULTI COUNTRY OF ORIGIN

2. BIOGRAPHICAL DICTIONARIES

306   PYKE, E.J. *A Biographical Dictionary of Wax Modellers.* Oxford: Clarendon, 1973. 282 pp., 314 b&w figs.
       Comprehensive dictionary preceded by an essay dealing with technique and conservation and a census of private and public collections of waxes. Includes entries for several 16th-century artists such as Abondio, Argenterio, Bandinelli, and Giambologna. Concludes with a twelve-page bibliography and a large index.

3. SURVEYS AND HISTORIES

307   SCHLOSSER, JULIUS VON. "Geschichte der Porträbildnerei in Wachs." *Jahrbuch der kunsthistorischen Sammlungen des allerhöchsten Kaiserhauses* 29 (1911): 171-258, 10 b&w pls., 56 b&w figs.
       Comprehensive study of wax portraiture from ancient Rome through the 19th century. Surveying the techniques used and function of these portraits, the author contends that many effigial sculptures and painted portraits are also based on realistic wax models. Examples of the 15th-16th century are primarily discussed on pp. 203-25.

8. PRIVATE COLLECTION, AUCTION, AND DEALER CATALOGS

PIERPONT MORGAN COLLECTION

See entry 174.

B. SINGLE COUNTRY OF ORIGIN

FRENCH

6. PERMANENT COLLECTIONS

Detroit

DETROIT INSTITUTE OF ARTS

308 PANOFSKY, ERWIN. "A Parisian Goldsmith's Model of the Early Fifteenth Century?" In *Beiträge für Georg Swarzenski zum 11. Januar 1951.* Berlin: Mann; Chicago: Henry Regnery Co., 1951. Pp. 70-84, 16 b&w figs.

A Parisian circular polychromed wax pendant bearing the scene of Christ in Judgment, stolen from this museum in 1935, is suggested to be an example for artists to work from and a model for clients to approve.

Wroclaw (Breslau)

MUZEUM NARODOWE

309 COURAJOD, LOUIS. "Les Médaillons de cire au Musée de Breslau." *Gazette des beaux-arts* 29 (1884):236-41, 1 line drawing.

Series of twenty wax portrait medallions in the museum representing (except for two) 16th-century French personages; that of Catherine de'Medici served as model for the bronze medallion of the queen in the Louvre (or else both were executed after a common model).

ITALIAN

3. SURVEYS AND HISTORIES

310 MASI, GINO. "La ceroplastica in Firenze nei secoli XV-XVI e la famiglia Benintendi." *Rivista d'arte* 9 (1916):124-42.

Publication of documents dating of 1474-96 relating to the Benentendi family known as the primary makers of wax ex-votos in late 15th- and 16th-century Florence.

311 MIDDELDORF, ULRICH. "Two Wax Reliefs by Guglielmo della Porta," *Art Bulletin* 17 (1935):90-97, 7 b&w figs.

Two reliefs of the Crucifixion modeled in wax on slate, one in the Galleria Borghese in Rome, the other with dealers in Stockholm, are attributed, on the basis of drawings in Düsseldorf, to this late 16th-century Roman sculptor.

X. Wax

6. PERMANENT COLLECTIONS

Gotha

MUSEEN DER STADT GOTHA

312   BECHTOLD, A. "Hieronymus Scotus." *Archiv für Medaillen- und Plaketten-Kunde* 4(1923-24):103-18, 2 b&w figs.
   Polychromed wax portrait relief of Girolamo Scotto in the collection; its relationship to medals by Abondio.

London

BRITISH MUSEUM

See entry 1264d.

Milan

AMBROSIANA

See entry 656.

Paris

BIBLIOTHÈQUE NATIONALE

313   BABELON, JEAN. "Un Médaillon de cire du Cabinet des Médailles: Filippo Strozzi et Benedetto da Majano." *Gazette des beaux-arts* 4 (1921):203-10, 5 b&w figs.
   Reassessment of chronology of Benedetto's oeuvre: the marble bust of Filippo Strozzi in the Louvre, the wax (Cabinet des Médailles, Bibliothèque nationale), which is a transposition of the marble, and the medal (also Cabinet des Médailles) for which the wax was a model.

8. PRIVATE COLLECTION, AUCTION, AND DEALER CATALOGS

SCHER COLLECTION

314   SCHER, STEPHEN K. "A Sixteenth Century Wax Model." *Medal* 9 (1986):15-21, 5 b&w figs.
   Wax model, in the collection of the author, produced in the circle of Leoni ca. 1550. It represents Ferrante Loffredo, a general of Emperor Charles V.

See also entry 1268.

XI. Ceramics

A. MULTI COUNTRY OF ORIGIN

1. DICTIONARIES AND ENCYCLOPEDIAS

315   BARBER, EDWIN ATLEE. *The Ceramic Collectors' Glossary.* New York: Walpole Society, 1914. 119 pp., many small line drawings.
    Very useful not only for the field of ceramics but often for terminology of decorative arts in general.

316   HAGGAR, REGINALD G. *The Concise Encyclopedia of Continental Pottery and Porcelain.* 2d ed. London: André Deutsch, 1968. 533 pp., 24 color pls., 160 b&w pls., numerous facsimile makers' marks. (1st ed. 1960.)
    Informative, compendious entries on artists, workshops and factories, materials, and production. Bibliography. Good selection of illustrations.

317   HONEY, WILLIAM BOWYER. *European Ceramic Art from the End of the Middle Ages to about 1815.* Vol. 1, *Illustrated Historical Survey* (1949), 84 pp., 24 color pls., 192 b&w pls.; vol. 2, *A Dictionary of Factories, Artists, Technical Terms, et cetera* (1952), 788 pp., 4 color pls., numerous line drawings. London: Faber & Faber.
    For period 1400-1600 in vol. 1, pp., 19-30, pls. I-V, figs. 1-72. Alphabetically arranged entries in vol. 2 followed by 106-page index with line drawings of potters' marks and other inscriptions.

318   SAVAGE, GEORGE, and NEWMAN, HAROLD. *An Illustrated Dictionary of Ceramics.* With list of principle European factories and marks by John Cushion. London: Thames & Hudson, 1974. 320 pp., 24 color illus., 602 b&w figs.
    Definition of 3,054 terms relating to wares, materials, processes, styles, patterns and shapes from antiquity to the present day. Preceded by an eleven-page list of many European factories, makers, and designers.

3. SURVEY AND HISTORIES

Books

319 CAIGER-SMITH, ALAN. *Lustre Pottery: Technique, Tradition and Innovation in Islam and the Western World.* London and Boston: Faber & Faber, 1985. 246 pp., 43 color figs., 111 b&w figs.

Comprehensive survey of topic beginning with Iraq and Persia to 15th-century Hispano-Moresque ware (pp. 84-126) and 16th-century Italian examples from Deruta and Gubbio (pp. 127-54). Chapters on revival and technique.

319a CAIGER-SMITH, ALAN. *Tin-Glaze Pottery in Europe and the Islamic World.* London: Faber & Faber, 1973. 236 pp., 24 color pls., 189 b&w pls., 9 maps and 33 drawings and diagrams in text.

Earthenware of various cultures geographically and chronologically arranged. Pertinent to 1400-1600 are the chapters on: Moorish Spain and Hispano-Moresque pottery (pp. 56-80, pls. [14 illus., colorplates] E-H, including Malaga, Almeria, Valencia, Paterna, Manises, Barcelona, Muel, etc.); Italy (pp. 81-102, pls. [15 illus., colorplates] I-L, including Florence, Orvieto, Siena, Caffaggiolo, Faenza, Padua, Deruta, Gubbio, Urbino, Venice, Palermo, Castelli, Montelupo); Netherlands (pp. 127-29, map. 6, fig. 102); and Central Europe (mostly Hungary) (pp. 141-43, map. 7, fig. 116). Volume concludes with brief chapters on method, Dutch glaze recipes, and an appendix of practical comments.

320 CHAFFERS, WILLIAM. *Marks and Monograms on European and Oriental Pottery and Porcelain.* 2 vols. 15th enl. and rev. ed. British section edited by Geoffrey A. Godden. European and Oriental sections edited by Frederick Litchfield and R.L. Hobson. London: William Reeves, 1965. 1:643 pp., 56 line drawings, numerous facsimile markers' marks; 2:450 pp., 12 b&w pls., numerous facsimile markers' marks. (1st ed. 1865.)

Standard, readable reference with thorough discussion of every center of ceramic production. The greatest wealth of material is found in the examination of Italian, French, and English wares. Vol. 1: survey of late medieval examples from the British Isles; in-depth study of Continental (primarily with emphasis on Italian and French) productions as well as Oriental. Vol. 2 deals with British examples of the 17th-19th century.

321 CHARLESTON, ROBERT J., ed. *World Ceramics.* Relevant contributions by F.A. Drier, A.W. Frothingham, J. Giacomotti, G. Hurst, G. Liverani, and O. Van Oss. London: Paul Hamlyn, 1968. 352 pp., 64 color figs., 1083 b&w figs.

Geographically and chronologically arranged survey. Chap. 4 (pp. 100-34) deals with lead and salt glaze from Italy, France, England, and Germany (29 illus.); chap. 5 (139-65), tin-glaze in Spain, Italy, Sicily, France, Netherlands, England, and Germany (66 illus.). Includes glossary of terms and marks.

322 DREY, RUDOLPH E.A. *Apothecary Jars: Pharmaceutical Pottery and Porcelain in Europe and the East, 1150-1850.* London: Faber & Faber, 1978. 500 illus., some in color.

Comprehensive survey of subject with many examples dating of the 15th-16th century.

323 EVANS, MARIA MILLINGTON. *Lustre Pottery.* London: Methuen & Co., 1920. 157 pp., 24 b&w pls. with 107 figs.

Origins, manufacture, trade, and cross-influences of Near Eastern, Spanish, Italian, and English lustreware. Relevant to the period 1400-1600 are chaps. 2-4 (pp. 34-139) dealing with Hispano-Moresque and Italian (Gubbio and Deruta) bowls, plates, jars, vases, tiles, etc. Much of the information has subsequently been redefined but the work is still of value for the cited and illustrated examples.

324   HANNOVER, EMIL. *Pottery & Porcelain: A Handbook for Collectors.* Vol. 1, *Europe and the Near East: Earthenware and Stoneware.* Translated and edited by Bernard Rackham. New York: Charles Scribner's Sons, 1925. 589 pp., 684 b&w figs. (1st ed. 1921.)
    Survey of ceramic productions from ancient times to the 18th century. Relevant to the 15th-16th century is the section in chap. 2 pertaining to Hispano-Moresque lustred ware and tiles (pp. 78-91), and chap. 3 (pp. 92-229) focusing on Italian soft-paste and sgraffito wares from major centers, French soft-paste of St.-Porchaire and maiolica by Palissy, German stoneware from Cologne, Siegburg, Raeren, and Nuremberg. Indexes of persons, places, subjects, and techniques.

325   KLEIN, ADALBERT. *Fayencen Europas.* Brunswick: Klinkhardt & Biermann, 1980. 412 pp., 16 color pls., 428 b&w figs.
    Companion volume to Klein's *Deutsche Fayencen* (not in this repertory as deals primarily with later periods). Study of ceramics from other European countries of the 15th-19th century. Geographically arranged by country and subdivided by city/region: 15th- and 16th-century work from Spain (pp. 10-43, 76-78, 52 illus.), Italy (86-164, 98 illus.), France (198-214, 7 illus.), and the Netherlands (283-90, 4 illus.); also mentions Portuguese (80), Bohemian and Hungarian (368, 370), South Tyrolean (379, 3 illus.), and Swedish (389) work. Concludes with technical information.

326   MORLEY-FLETCHER, HUGO, and McILROY, ROGER. *Christie's Pictorial History of European Pottery.* Oxford: Phaidon/Christie's, 1984. Numerous color and b&w illus.
    Lustre-, stone-, sgraffito-, and earthenware, as well as other nonporcelain ceramics from 1400 to 1800. Arranged by country, each section with brief descriptive, historic essay. Profuse (but often small) illustration of nearly two thousand objects available on the art market during the last fifteen years (list of hammer prices with dates of sales included).

Article

327   STRAUSS, KONRAD. "Keramikgefässe, insbesondere Fayencegefässe auf Tafelbildern der deutschen und niederländischen Schule des 15. und 16. Jahrhunderts." *Keramik-Freunde der Schweiz* 84 (1972):3-38, 52 b&w pls.
    Ceramics, especially maiolica, as represented in German and Netherlandish panel paintings of the 15th-16th century; comparison with actual extant examples of the period.

4. BIBLIOGRAPHICAL GUIDES

328   SOLON, M.L. *Ceramic Literature: An Analytical Index.* London: Griffin & Co., 1910. 660 pp.
    Early bibliographical index (often annotated) of books, periodical articles, exhibition and auction catalogs pertaining to ceramics of all nations and centuries; pertinent to 1400-1600 are references presented by country and often subdvided by medium (pp. 559-99), decorative tiles (603-6), stoves (614-15), architectural terra cotta (616-17), biographies of potters (619-22), marks and monograms (627-28).

329 WEINRICH, PETER. *A Bibliographic Guide to Books on Ceramics—Guide bibliographique des oeuvres sur la céramique*. Ottawa: Canadian Crafts Council, 1976. 272 pp.

Lists of books in English, French, German, Italian, Spanish, and Portuguese dealing with ceramics of all nations and periods; pp. 1-36 and 139-246, which deal with European ceramics, include references pertinent to the period 1400-1600.

6. PERMANENT COLLECTIONS

Berlin

STAATLICHE MUSEEN PREUSSISCHER KULTURBESITZ, KUNSTGEWERBEMUSEUM

330 *Majolika spanische und italienische Keramic vom 14. bis zum 18. Jahrhundert*. Catalog by Tjark Hausmann. Berlin: Gebr. Mann, 1972. 423 pp., 29 color illus., 405 b&w figs.

Catalog of the Spanish and Italian maiolica of the 14th-18th centuries. 315 catalog entries including: 15th-16th-century Hispano-Moresque ceramic ware (cat. nos. 1-10, 12-14) and tiles (17-36); 15th-century examples from Florence (66-90); 15th-16th-century examples from Faenza (103-34, 136-37, 139); 16th-century tiles from Albisola (140-41); 16th-century sgraffito ware (37-38, 40-50) and ceramics from Caffaggiolo (91-102), Siena (142-44), Deruta (145-61), Gubbio (162-69), Castel Durante (170-92), Urbino (193-227, 229), Lyon (230-33), and Venice (234-51). Diagram of profile views.

Cambridge

FITZWILLIAM MUSEUM

331 *Catalogue of the Glaischer Collection of Pottery and Porcelain in the Fitzwilliam Museum Cambridge* by Bernard Rackham. 2 vols. Cambridge: University Press, 1935. 1:451 pp., 36 color pls.; 2:15 pp., 266 b&w pls.

Cursory entries of European, Eastern, and Oriental pottery and porcelain; arranged by medium and subdivided by country with wide chronological range. Includes 15th-16th-century lead-glazed earthenware from England (pp. 3-6), Italy (sgraffito ware, 224-26), and France (Palissy ware, 227-28), stoneware from Germany (257-62) and tin-glazed earthenware (maiolica, 279-87) from Italy.

Cleveland

CLEVELAND MUSEUM OF ART

332 *The World of Ceramics: Masterpieces from The Cleveland Museum of Art*. Exhibition catalog edited by Jenifer Neils, pertaining entries by Patrick M. de Winter. Cleveland: Cleveland Museum of Art, 1982. 166 pp., 16 color pls., 171 b&w figs.

Highlights of the collection. For period 1400-1600, see pp. 37-54, nos. 39-56 including Spanish lustreware; Italian examples: oak leaf Medici plate, Buglioni altarpiece, Della Robbia figure, Faenza plate (Master Giorgio), albarelli, pilgrim bottle, relief, Deruta plates, Urbino salts; French wares: St.-Porchaire and Palissy; German tigerware and Bellarmine jugs.

Cologne

KUNSTGEWERBEMUSEUM

333   *Majolika.* Catalog by Brigitte Klesse. Cologne: Kunstgewerbemuseum, 1966. 188 pp., 6 color pls., 20 b&w pls., 426 catalog figs.

Twenty-two-page introduction deals with the history and development of Near Eastern and European ceramics. 360 entries include 15th- and 16th-century Spanish and Portuguese dishes, albarelli, vases, bowls (cat. nos. 156-70); Spanish tiles (188-238); and Italian dishes, flasks, vases, albarelli, basins, etc. (252-324); representative examples from major centers.

Düsseldorf

HETJENS-MUSEUM

334   *Keramic aus 5000 Jahren: 107 Meisterwerke aus dem Hetjens-Museum Düsseldorf. 5000 Years of Ceramics: 107 Masterpieces from the Hetjens-Museum, Düsseldorf,* by Adalbert Klein. 2d rev. and enl. ed. German-English text, translated by Jennifer Frege and Henry Daniel. Düsseldorf: Schwann Düsseldorf, 1979. 300 pp., 108 color pls.

Glossy presentation of major pieces in the museum's collection. Includes, of the period 1400-1600: German stoneware jugs (nos. 17-26), tiles (32), Nuremberg water container (33), stove tiles (34), Spanish/Italian maiolica (58-64), Rouen pharmacy jars (66). Each section preceded by a short introduction.

Faenza

MUSEO INTERNAZIONALE DELLE CERAMICHE

335   *Selezione di opere.* Catalog by Giuseppe Liverani. Faenza: Museo Internazionale delle Ceramiche, 1963.   50 pp., 10 color pls., 170 b&w pls., Italian/French/English/German/Spanish introduction.

Of the 205 ceramics from the museum's collection presented in this catalog, the following date of the 15th-16th centruy: Faenza ware, nos. 15-34; productions of other Italian centers, 52-67; two Rhenish Bellarmine jugs, 130. Twenty-one pages of catalog entries.

London

VICTORIA AND ALBERT MUSEUM

336   *A Descriptive Catalogue of the Maiolica, Hispano-Moresco, Persian, Damascus and Rhodian Wares in the South Kensington Museum.* Catalog by C. Drury E. Fortnum. London: Chapman & Hall, 1873. 699 pp., 12 color pls., 61 b&w figs.

Very comprehensive collection. Pertinent to the years 1400-1600 are the following: Hispano-Moresque tin-glazed wares (pp., 39-67) and Italian pottery (68-639) including maiolica, sgraffito and enameled earthenware of various Italian cities. Catalog entries follow brief discussions of each center and its earthenware; includes marks and monograms and a listing of pieces of uncertain locality of origin. Scanty illustration. Volume superseded, as far as Italian wares are concerned, by B. Rackham's catalog (see entry 414).

337 *A Guide to the Collection of Tiles.* Catalog by Arthur Lane. London: Board of Education, 1939. 75 pp., 49 b&w pls.

Traces history, technique, and style of tiles. Relevant to the 15th and 16th century are: chap. 3 (pp. 22-30), the medieval tile-mosaic and inlaid tiles of Europe; chap. 4 (pp. 32-39), the relief-tiles of Germany and northern Europe; chap. 5 (40-47), painted tiles of the Renaissance; chap. 7 (pp. 57-65), Spanish tiles.

WALLACE COLLECTION

338 *Catalogues of Ceramics 1: Pottery, Maiolica, Faience, Stoneware.* Catalog by A.V.B. Norman. London: Trustees of the Wallace Collection, 1976. 443 pp., 3 color pls., 296 b&w figs., 17 line drawings.

Thirty-seven-page introduction deals with history and defines main points of development for ceramics, primarily European, in the collection. 203 entries including Hispano-Moresque wares (nos. C1-C9), Italian maiolica (C10-C158), French (mostly Palissy—C163-C179), and German wares (C181-C193), representing most shapes and styles. Useful glossary of terms.

8. PRIVATE COLLECTION, AUCTION, AND DEALER CATALOGS

BEIT COLLECTION

339 VALENTINER, W.R.; BRINCKMANN, JUSTUS VON; and RACKHAM, BERNARD. *Catalogue of the Collection of Pottery and Porcelain in the Possession of Mr. Otto Beit.* Parts 1 and 2 edited, with additions and introduction, by A. Van De Put and Bernard Rackham, respectively. London: Privately Printed, 1916. 168 pp., 29 b&w pls., 16 b&w figs.

Outstanding and now dispersed English collection of 374 ceramics spanning the 14th through 18th centuries, the majority dating of 1400-1600. Part 1: Hispano-Moresque pottery—drug jars, dishes, vases; part 2: Italian maiolica—by production centers (Faenza, Florence, Caffaggiolo, Siena, Deruta, Gubbio, Castel Durante, Urbino, Venice); part 3: 18th-century porcelain. Each section preceded by an introduction outlining history, techniques, and stylistic characteristics.

KASSEBAUM COLLECTION

340 KASSEBAUM, JOHN PHILLIP. *The John Philip Kassebaum Collection.* Vol. 1. Kansas City: Lowell Press, 1981. 139 pp., 56 color figs., 69 b&w figs.

Five-page introduction touching on historical developments and techniques followed by 125 good illustrations with catalog captions. Includes 15th-16th-century Spanish, Italian, French, and German albarelli, dishes, bowls, tiles, plaques, etc. Vol. 2 projected on English medieval pottery and English delftware.

KITZINGER COLLECTION

341 *Fayencesammlung Georg Kitzinger München: Vorwiegend deutsche, schweizerische und italienische Erzeugnisse des XVI.-XIX. Jahrhunderts.* Sale held in Munich at Galerie Helbring 7-9 May 1912. Catalog by Georg Lill. 104 pp., 40 b&w pls. with several figs. on each.

Auction of this important ceramic collection of Georg Kitzinger of Munich included 770 lots of German (540), Swiss, Italian, French, and other pieces dating from the 16th to the 19th centuries.

B. SINGLE COUNTRY OF ORIGIN

AUSTRIAN

3. SURVEYS AND HISTORIES

342 FALKE, OTTO VON. "Alpine Keramic." *Pantheon* 6 (1930):501-3, 4 b&w figs.
A large jug in a private Munich collection with incised Gothic designs (dated 1470) compared to a covered vessel in the shape of a pine cone and a stove tile in the shape of a bearded man and proposed to originate in Tyrol or more specifically Salzburg.

BELGIUM (BRABANTINE, FLEMISH, AND LIÉGEOIS)

3. SURVEYS AND HISTORIES

Book

343 RACKHAM, BERNARD. *Early Netherlands Maiolica with Special Reference to the Tiles at the Vyne in Hampshire.* London: Geoffrey Bles, 1926. 36 pp., 12 color pls., 43 b&w pls.
Vessels and tiles primarily of the 16th century: chapters on origin and technique (pp. 1-10); historical and art historical survey of the period (11-21); Netherlandish maiolica in archival records and paintings (23-51); tiles with portraits, human figures, animals, foliage, and geometric designs in the Chapel of Vyne Estate, which Rackham suggests were produced in the Savino workshop (ca. 1520) at Antwerp (53-71); others from Ghent, Limburg, Antwerp, Delft, and Rotterdam (73-93); 16th-century pottery from Antwerp (95-124).

Articles

344 HELBIG, J. "Ancienne céramique de carrelage at de revêtement en Belgique," *Revue belge* 22 (1953):219-40, 16 b&w figs.
Floor tiles with decorative patterns and glazing produced in Flanders, Brabant, and Liège from the 12th to 18th centuries.

345 HYMERSMA, HERBERT-JAN. "Guido di Savino and Other Antwerp Potters of the Sixteenth Century." *Connoisseur* 195 (1977):264-71, 1 color pl., 13 b&w figs.
Biography and works—maiolica floor tiles, plaques, and albarelli—by Guido di Savino (also known as Guido Andries), one of many Italian potters in Antwerp during the first half of the 16th century. Subsequent "Floris style" or "Ferronerie," of purely Flemish inspiration, of the mid-16th century by potters such as de Vries, Cornelis Bos, Pieter Cocke van Aelst, and Cornelis Floris.

346 NICAISE, HENRI. "Les Carreaux en faïence anversoise de l'ancienne abbaye d'Herkenrode." *Bulletin des Musées Royaux d'Art et d'Histoire* 7 (1935):92-104; 117-27, 23 b&w figs.
Examines the series of 16th-century earthenware tiles forming the pavement of the former Herkenrode Abbey, Belgium, which reveal a strong Italian influence in their technique, arrangement, iconography, and style, but also betray marked Flemish characteristics. A contract dated 1532 gives the name of the ceramist "Pierre-Frans van Venedigen," who lived in Antwerp.

6. PERMANENT COLLECTIONS

Sèvres

MUSÉE NATIONAL DE CÉRAMIQUE

347   FOUREST, HENRY PIERRE. "À propos d'une majolique anversoise nouvellement acquise par le Musée national de céramique de Sèvres." *Faenza* 65 (1979):350-52, 2 illus.

    Study of Italian maiolica potters in Antwerp at the beginning of the 16th century and of characteristic maiolica tiles; identification of the maker of an albarello.

7. EXHIBITION CATALOGS

Deurne-Antwerp

PROVINCIAAL MUSEUM VOOR KUNSTAMBACHTEN

348   *Van Antwerps plateel tot Delftse keramiek.* Exhibition catalog by Herta Leemans, H.W. Mauser, and Th. Dobbelmann. Deurne: Drukkerijen C. Govaerts N.V., 1962. 88 pp., 49 b&w figs.

    Twenty-four-page essay on Antwerp tiles, Netherlandish maiolica, and Delft ceramics; 136 pieces of the 16th century to modern times; nos. 1-70 are of the 15th-16th century.

8. PRIVATE COLLECTION, AUCTION, AND DEALER CATALOGS

VECHT COLLECTION

349   VECHT, A. "Un Exceptionnel Carreau de majolique de la première moitié du XVIe siècle." *Cahiers de la céramique du verre et des arts du feu* 6 (1961):110-113, 1 color pl.

    Unusual maiolica tile with a woman in bust length held to be the work of an Italian potter active in Antwerp in the 16th century.

BRITISH (ENGLISH)

3. SURVEYS AND HISTORIES

Books

350   LEWIS, GRISELDA. *A Collector's History of English Pottery.* New York: Viking Press, 1969. 224 pp., 7 color figs., 404 b&w figs.

    Includes discussion of 15th-16th century lead- and tin-glazed earthenware based on types the author considers still available to collectors. Direct and lively descriptions unfortunately marred by often murky illustrations.

351   RACKHAM, BERNARD. *Medieval English Pottery.* 2d ed. rev. by J.G. Hurst. London: Faber & Faber, 1972. 40 pp., 8 color pls., 96 b&w pls. (1st ed. 1948.)

    Originality of early English earthenware (mostly sand-glazed jugs) from the 13th century, including examples from the 15th-16th century from Surrey, East Anglia, York, etc. A pioneering study.

Article

352   RACKHAM, BERNARD. "Early Tudor Pottery." *English Ceramic Circle (Transactions)* 2 (1939-48):15-25. 6 b&w figs.

Green-glazed earthenware decorated with heraldry in the Victoria and Albert, Guildhall, and London Museums; its relationship to contemporary German ware.

6. PERMANENT COLLECTIONS

London

BRITISH MUSEUM

353   *Catalogue of the Collection of English Pottery in the Department of British and Medieval Antiquities and Ethnography of the British Museum.* Catalog by R.L. Hobson. London: British Museum, 1903. 333 pp., 3 color pls., 39 b&w pls., 131 b&w figs.

A brief introduction provides historical background and a description of manufacturing techniques. For 15th-16th-century earthenware see entries A-262 to A-298 dealing with impressed or slip-painted tiles; B-98 to B-287 for jugs, dishes, bottles, stove tiles, etc., mostly glazed.

FRENCH

MULTI REGION

3. SURVEYS AND HISTORIES

354   FOUREST, HENRY-PIERRE. *French Ceramics*. Translated by Robin Charleston. Vol. 6 of *Masterpieces of Western and Near Eastern Ceramics*. Tokyo: Kodansha, 1979. Distributed in U.S.A. by Harper and Row. 294 pp., 120 color pls., 104 b&w figs.

Pictorial survey with cursory text in Japanese and English of French ceramics, 14th-18th century, with examples drawn from French, English, and U.S. collections. Text pp. 20-21 and entries 3-9, 11-12, 14-17, 19-22 deal with period 1400-1600. Valuable for plates.

355   PEYRE, ROGER. *La Céramique française: Fayences, porcelains, biscuits, grès, dates de la fondation des ateliers, caractéristiques, marques et monogrammes*. Paris: Ernest Flammarion, [1910]. 310 pp., 334 line drawings, 876 makers' marks.

Useful early survey of French ceramics from the Middle Ages through the 19th century. Pp. 27-64 deal with 13th-16th century productions of Bernard Palissy, Beauvais, St.-Porchaire, and Rouen.

7. EXHIBITION CATALOGS

Paris

MUSÉE DU LOUVRE

356   *La Faïence française de 1525 à 1820.* Exhibition catalog by Ch. Bernard Metman, assisted by Madeleine David and Mlle. Delarache-Vernet, with historical essays on different production centers by various contributors. Paris: Palais du Louvre, 1923. 515 pp., 20 b&w pls.

    Brief descriptive entries for 3,219 examples of 16th-19th century French faience from public and private French collections, the Musée du Cinquantenaire, Brussels, and the Hamburg museum, grouped by production center in chronological order according to the date of first activity. Of the 15th-16th century are wares by Bernard Palissy and those from St.-Porchaire, Lyon, Nîmes, Rouen, and Nevers.

Strasbourg

MUSÉE ALSACIEN

357   *Grès traditionnels d'Alsace et d'ailleurs...* Exhibition catalog by Jean Favière and Georges Klein. Strasbourg: Musée Alsacien, 1978. 80 pp., 7 color pls., 12 b&w pls.

    Concise and informative study of 14th-19th-century stoneware produced in Alsace and Betschdorf and of analogous wares from nearby centers such as Beauvais and Nevers in France, Siegburg and Cologne in Germany, and Raeren in Belgium. History of each production area, traits common to all these stonewares and characteristics particular to each.

SINGLE CENTER OR TYPE OF PRODUCTION

BEAUVAIS

3. SURVEYS AND HISTORIES

358   CHAMI, ÉMILE. "L'Art céramique du Beauvaisis au XVe et au XVIe siècle." *Cahiers de la céramique, du verre et des arts du feu* 30 (1963):79-116, 3 color pls., 34 b&w figs. English summary.

    Reappraisal of the production of glazed earthenware—generally dishes and vases with relief decoration (often stamped) but also figurines—in Beauvais. The 15th and particularly the 16th century are the periods of major activity.

359   CHAMI, ÉMILE, and FOUREST, HENRY-PIERRE. "La Poterie vernissée au XVIe siècle." *Cahiers de la céramique, du verre et des arts du feu* 53 (1973):28-35, 1 color pl., 9 b&w figs. (Part 4 of "La Céramique du Beauvaisis du Moyen-Age au XVIIIe siècle.")

    16th-century lead-glazed pottery from the Beauvais region with molded, stamped, or applied decoration whose forms were inspired from contemporary goldsmith and metalworks; brief introduction and seventy-three entries for objects in various public and private French collections.

360   FAŸ, ANTOINETTE. "La Poterie vernissée à décor gravé sur engobe au XVIe siècle." *Cahiers de la céramique, du verre et des arts du feu* 53 (1973):37-41, 12 b&w figs. (Part 5 of "La Céramique du Beauvaisis du Moyen-Age au XVIIIe siècle.") English summary.

Technique and characteristics of 16th-century pottery from the Beauvais region with engraved decoration over one or two layers of red slip. While the general configurations of some are Italian (male or female portrait at center with inscription in large Gothic letters around the rim), the style is unmistakeably French. Entries for seventy-one objects from various French public and private collections.

361 MORISSON, HENRY. "Les Grès du XVe au XVIIIe siècle." *Cahiers de la céramique, du verre et des arts du feu* 53 (1973):21-27, 10 b&w figs. (Part 3 of "La Céramique du Beauvaisis du Moyen-Age au XVIIIe siècle.")

Stoneware from the Beauvais region; brief overview of its very limited lifespan as an art form from the 15th to the 18th century and entries for ninety-two objects from various public and private French collections. Blue-hued stoneware of the 16th century, most of it bearing stamped coats of arms (twenty-eight entries).

7. EXHIBITION CATALOGS

Sèvres

MUSÉE NATIONAL DE CÉRAMIQUE

362 *La Céramique du Beauvaisis du moyen-âge au XVIIIe siècle.* Exhibition catalog by Émile Chami, Henry-Pierre Fourest, Claudine and Jean Cartier, Antoinette Faÿ, and Henry Morisson. Sèvres: Société des Amis du Musée national de céramique; Les Cahiers de la céramique du Verre, et des arts du feu, 1973. 52 pp., 34 b&w pls.

Catalog of 397 ceramic objects originating from the vicinity of Beauvais and dating from the 9th to the 18th century. Short, descriptive entries preceded by brief introductory essays to each period and/or pottery type. Of the 15th-16th century are stoneware gourds, pitchers, ewers, etc. (cat. nos. 44-98, 100-10, 136-63) and glazed dishes, gourds, pitchers, statuettes, inkstands, etc. (164-220, 222-307), bearing relief and stamped decorative motifs.

LYON

3. SURVEYS AND HISTORIES

Books

363 DAMIRON, CHARLES. *La Faïence de Lyon. Première époque: Le XVIe siècle.* Paris: Dorbon-Ainé, [1926]. 79 pp., 10 color pls., 13 b&w pls., 20 b&w figs.

Italian potters in 16th-century Lyon; general characteristics of Lyonnais maiolica and particularities of its decoration and production in relation to Italian works. Iconographical sources from engravings published in Lyon; inscriptions; influences on Nevers potters. Eleven-page appendix of documents.

364 RONDOT, M. NATALIS. *Les Potiers de terre italiens à Lyon au seizième siècle.* Lyon: Pitrat Aîné; Paris: Librairie de l'Art, L. Allison & Cie, 1892. 160 pp., 12 b&w pls., 18 line drawings.

Historical study, based on archival records, of Italian potters working in Lyon in the 16th century: those from Faenza, Pesaro, Genoa, those who introduced a superior method of creating a glazed white ware, those who introduced the brightly decorated and historiated maiolica, those responsible for the tiled pavement of the Church of Brou, specific families and their workshops.

365   TABURET, MARJATTA. *La Faïence de Nevers et le miracle lyonnais au XVIe siècle.* *Paris: Les Éditions Sous le Vent, 1981. 187 pp., 41 color figs., 88 b&w figs.*
      Pottery produced in Lyon and Nevers from the 16th century, with the influx of Italian masters, to the 19th: artists and their workshops, evolution of style, commerce, conditions of work, etc. Author presents new evidence, such as the presence of Girolamo della Robbia in Lyon, examines the relationship between local engravers and potters, proposes a new, earlier, dating for historiated faience in Lyon, and explains the filiation that existed between Lyon and Nevers. One-page glossary of technical terms; three pages of makers' marks; eleven pages of transcribed documents.

Article

366   BOULAY, ROBERT. "Le Problème Lyon-Nevers." *Cahiers de la céramique, du verre et des arts du feu* 33 (1964):16-28, 25 b&w figs. English summary.
      Reattribution to 17th-century Nevers, on the basis of inscriptions, of several pieces in the Louvre and the Musée des Arts Décoratifs of Lyon, and attribution to Lyon of pieces frequently attributed to Urbino workshops; their iconography often derives from engravings.

6. PERMANENT COLLECTIONS

Lyon

MUSÉE DES HOSPICES

367   COLLY, MARCEL. "Les Faïences lyonnaises du XVIe siècle au Musée des Hospices." *Bulletin des Musées lyonnais* 1(1951):16-18, 2 b&w figs.
      Glimpses on the ceramic holdings of this medical foundation produced locally in the 16th century.

Paris

MUSÉE DU LOUVRE

368   ENNÉS, PIERRE. "Deux Plats de majolique française." *Revue du Louvre et des Musées de France* 36 (1986):1 (Appendix), 2 color figs.
      Two Lyon maiolica plates depicting the Fall of Manna, Moses and the Daughters of Jethro, after illustrations in the Bible of Jean de Tournes.

MONTPELLIER

3. SURVEYS AND HISTORIES

369   THUILE, JEAN. "Faïences anciennes de Montpellier XVIe-XVIIIe siècle." *Cahiers de la céramique, du verre et des arts du feu* 32 (1963):232-51, 2 color pls., 18 b&w figs. English summary.
      Montpellier, after Nîmes, became the main late 16th-century maiolica production center of Provence with the recorded Pierre Estève and Pierre Ducoin. To the latter is attributed a pitcher with a representation of Henri IV at the Musée national de céramique, Sèvres. Subsequent activity in Montpellier is cursorily discussed.

NEVERS (See LYON)

NÎMES

3. SURVEYS AND HISTORIES

370   VAN DE PUT, ALBERT. "The Nîmes Faience." *Burlington Magazine* 62 (1933): Part 1, 108-14, 4 b&w figs.; part 2, 156-58, 1 b&w pl.; 63 (1933): part 3, 16-21, 4 b&w figs.

    Investigation of the artistic background of the French potter Antoine Sigalon (1524-90) of Nîmes, and of the identification of arms on two pilgrim bottles and a plate by him in the Victoria and Albert Museum and in private collections (former Lambert, Paris, and Morgan, New York). Activity ca. 1600 of Sigalon's nephews, Isaac and Pierre Paris, to whom are ascribed drug vases in the Jacques Sagnier Collections.

PALISSY WARE

3. SURVEYS AND HISTORIES

371   MORLEY, HENRY. *Palissy the Potter: The Life of Bernard Palissy of Saintes.* 2 vols. London: Chapman & Hall, 1852. 1:320 pp.; 2:352 pp.

    Describes Palissy's attempt to develop a French counterpart to Oriental porcelain and the various stages of his ceramic production with applied reliefs and polychromy, glazing. Biographical data related to patronage, especially that of Catherine de' Medici and her sons, and also to Palissy's theories and his writings.

372   SAUZAY, ALEXANDRE DE, and DELANGE, HENRI. *Monographie de l'oeuvre de Bernard Palissy suivie d'un choix de ses continuateurs ou imitateurs.* Paris, Quai Voltaire, no. 5, 1862. 100 color illus, 1 b&w pl.

    Early monograph on the famous French potter: his biography; ceramics attributed to him; his numerous imitators; references on documentation. Large color reproductions of pieces undoubtedly not all by Palissy himself (not included are the fragments of his Tuileries Grotto only excavated in 1878 and now in the Musée Carnavalet). [Readers may also note that small elements related to the Grotto were unearthed in 1985-86 at the nearby Palais du Louvre while excavating was underway for the new glass pyramid by Pei.]

6. PERMANENT COLLECTIONS

New York

METROPOLITAN MUSEUM OF ART

373   DAUTERMAN, CARL CHRISTIAN. "Snakes, Snails, and Creatures with Tails." *Metropolitan Museum of Art Bulletin* 20 (1962):272-85. 18 illus. Reprinted in *Connoisseur* 169 (1968):185-93.

    Presentation of thirty-five additions to the museum's already major collection of Palissy ware. The designs on these dishes are related to contemporary prints.

Paris

MUSÉE DU LOUVRE

374   *La Céramique française: Bernard Palissy et les fabriques du XVIe siècle.* Catalog by M.-J. Ballot. Paris: Albert Morancé, 1924. 39 pp., 25 color pls., 23 b&w pls.
      Brief description of workshops in Rouen, Lyon, Nevers, and St.-Porchaire, as well as that of Palissy and his school, with examples of these in the permanent collection.

8. PRIVATE COLLECTION, AUCTION, AND DEALER CATALOGS

ROTHSCHILD (ÉDOUARD DE) COLLECTION

375   ROTHSCHILD, GERMAINE DE, and GRANDJEAN, SERGE. *Bernard Palissy et son école (Collection Édouard de Rothschild).* Paris: Au Pont des Arts, [1952]. 91 pp., color and b&w pls.
      Biography of the artist (by G. de Rothschild) and catalog (by J. Grandjean) of pieces in the collection.

STRAUSS (ROBERT) COLLECTION

See entry 433.

ZSCHILLE COLLECTION

See entry 434.

ROUEN

3. SURVEYS AND HISTORIES

376   OLIVER, PIERRE. *Masséot Abaquesne et les origines de la faïence de Rouen.* [Rouen]: Le Cerf, 1952. 24 pp., 1 pl.
      Brief account of 15th-century earthenware production in Rouen.

ST.-PORCHAIRE WARE

3. SURVEYS AND HISTORIES

Book

377   DELANGE, CARLE. *Recueil des principales pièces connues de la faïence française dite de Henri II et Diane de Poitiers.* Paris: Leplanquais-Chédeville, 1861. 16 pp., 52 b&w line drawings.
      Early catalog of St.-Porchaire ware. Fifty-one pieces, generally the most important (and at time of publication almost exclusively in private hands) are briefly described with provenance and prices paid when known.

Articles

378   FOUREST, HENRY-PIERRE. "Faïences de Saint-Porchaire." *Cahiers de la céramique, du verre et des arts du feu* 45 (1969):12-25, 1 color pl., 13 b&w figs. English summary.

     The author passes in review all of the many hypothesis as to the origin of St.-Porchaire ware, the main ones being Oiron and St.-Porchaire as place, and Bernard Palissy as the artist.

379   MICHON, LOUIS-MARIE. "Les Faïenceries fines de Saint-Porchaire." *Gazette des beaux-arts* 49 (1957):259-65, 8 b&w figs.

     Problems of technique, localization, dating, and authenticity; author defines three distinct decorative styles of this ware; comparison of motifs with those on bookbindings.

6. PERMANENT COLLECTIONS

Paris

MUSÉE DU LOUVRE.

380   JESTAZ, BERTRAND. "Poteries de Saint-Porchaire." *Revue du Louvre et des Musées de France* 25 (1975):384-96, 1 color fig., 16 b&w figs.

     Problems of localization, complexity of decoration and form, possible models for decorative motifs — including a relationship with metal work — discussed through three exceptional pieces from the Alphonse de Rothschild collection — two ewers and a salt — recently given to the Louvre.

GERMAN

3. SURVEYS AND HISTORIES

Book

381   REINHECKEL, GÜNTER. *German and Austrian Ceramics.* Translated by Eileen Martin. Vol 8 of *Masterpieces of Western and Near Eastern Ceramics.* Tokyo: Kodansha, 1978. Distributed in U.S.A. by Harper & Row. 330 pp., 127 color pls, 115 b&w figs.

     Pictorial survey with cursory text in Japanese and English of German and Austrian ceramics, 5th-19th century, with examples drawn from German and Austrian collection. Color pls. 5-12, 15-45, 54-56 and their corresponding entries on pp. 299-308, 310, deal with 15th-16th century; thirty-one black and white figures of the same period. Valuable for illustrations.

Articles

382   AICHELE, FRIEDER. "Rheinisches Steinzeug." *Weltkunst* 56 (1986):2727-31, 5 color figs., 14 b&w figs.

     Popular presentation of the stoneware, salt-glazed jugs produced in the Rhine Valley from the 16th through the 18th century. Essential characteristics of Siegburg, Cologne, Frechen, Raeren, and Westerland ware. The collecting of such pieces in the 19th century and the present.

383   FALKE, OTTO VON. "Kölnishes Steinzeug." *Jahrbuch der königlich preussischen Kunstsammlungen* 20 (1899):30-53, 1 handcolored fig., 2 b&w figs., 7 line drawings.
       Early attempt at defining the particularities of 16th-century Colognese stoneware jugs within the context of Rhenish production, with emphasis on shapes, relief decoration, and surface finish.

6. PERMANENT COLLECTIONS

Regensburg

MUSEUM DER STADT

384   ENDRES, WERNER, and LOERS, VEIT. *Spätmittelalterliche Keramik aus Regensburg: Neufunde in Prebrunn.* Regensburg: Buchverlag der Mittelbayerischen Zeitung, 1981. 126 pp., numerous b&w figs.
       Stoneware pottery and tiles dating of ca. 1390 to the mid-16th century in the museum's collection excavated from nearby Prebunn.

7. EXHIBITION CATALOGS

Düsseldorf

HETJENS-MUSEUM/DEUTSCH KERAMIKMUSEUM

385   *Deutsches Steinzeug der Renaissance- und Barockzeit.* Exhibition catalog by Ekkart Klinge. Düsseldorf: Hetjens-Museum/Deutsch Keramikmuseum, 1979. 194 pp., 6 color pls., 373 b&w figs.
       379 German stoneware jugs, bottles, flasks, humpen, etc., many of the 16th century, from several European collections. Organized by manufacturing center (Cologne, Frechen, Raeren, Siegburg, Waldenburg, etc.).

8. PRIVATE COLLECTION, AUCTION, AND DEALER CATALOGS

EIGEL COLLECTION

386   GRAUL, RICHARD. "Die Sammlung rheinischen Steinzeugs von Theodor Eigel in Köln." *Pantheon* 8 (1931):374-77, 5 b&w figs.
       16th-century Rhenish stoneware from a private collection in Cologne. Tankards, a vase, jugs from Cologne, Siegburg, and Raeren; style, shape, workshops, and the influence of Cologne on other centers in the region.

HUNGARIAN

3. SURVEYS AND HISTORIES

Book

387   VOIT, PÁL; and HOLL, IMRE. *Old Hungarian Stove Tiles.* Translated by Lili Halapy. Budapest: Corvina Press, 1963. 64 pp., 8 color pls, 40 b&w pls.

Basic development and changing styles of these stove tiles from the 14th century to their heyday in the 16th. Discussion of the tile-making workshops of Matthias Corvinus in Buda Castle and of the guilds, mining towns, and border fortresses.

Article

388   KALMÁR, JANOS. "Parittya âbrâzolâsos kalyhacsempe a XV. szâzadbol." *Archaeol. Er-teseto* 77 (1950):132-33, 1 b&w figs. German summary.
        Stove tile of the 15th century on which figures King Matthias Corvinus, slingshot in hand.

ITALIAN

MULTI REGION

3. SURVEYS AND HISTORIES

Books

389   BALLARDINI, GAETANO. *Corpus della maiolica italiana.* 2 vols. Vol. 1, *Le maioliche datate fino al 1530,* 207 pp., 34 color pls., 360 b&w figs.; vol. 2, *Le maioliche datate dal 1531 al 1535,* 153 pp., 10 color pls., 370 b&w figs. Rome: Libreria dello Stato, 1933-38.
        Pictorial repertory of dated maiolica from all the main Italian centers of production from European and American public and private collections. Vol. 1 treats 255 objects dating of 1466-1530, with brief captions and twenty-eight-page introduction; vol. 2, 219 objects dating of 1531-35, with brief captions and nine-page introduction.

390   CAIROLA, ALDO. *Ceramica italiana dalle origini a oggi.* Rome: Editalia, 1981. 301 pp., 24 color pls., 249 b&w figs.
        Survey of Italian ceramics, chronologically arranged. Includes 15th-16th-century maiolica and porcelain from major centers with emphasis on technical and formal development (pp. 43-82). Illustrates a wide variety of ware mostly in Italian museums and private collections. Includes useful glossary of stylistic and technical terms (219-45) and potters (249-60).

391   CHOMPRET, J. *Répertoire de la majolique italienne.* 2 vols. Paris: Éditions Nomis, 1949. 1:227 pp., 13 color pls.; 2:1100 b&w figs.
        Standard if somewhat dated study on classificaton of 15th-16th-century Italian maiolica. Large number of examples drawn from French collections. Both text and plate volumes alphabetically arranged by production center (forty-two discussed in vol. 1, twenty-six represented in vol. 2).

392   CONTI, GIOVANNI. *L'arte della maiolica in Italia.* Milan: Bramante, 1973. 387 pp., 289 color figs., 409 b&w figs.
        Twenty-two-page introductory essay on technique, function, forgeries, collectors, followed by illustrated anthology of 517 examples of Italian maiolica of the 14th-19th century; nos. 22-305 are of the 15th-16th century. Register lists important events, dated examples, and documents related to maiolica (pp. 108-48 for period 1400-1600). Extensive bibliographical citations.

393   DARCEL, ALFRED, and DELANGE, HENRI. *Recueil de faïences italiennes des XVe,*
       XVIe et XVIIe siècles. Illustrated by Carle Delange and C. Borneman. Paris: [E. Mar-
       tinet], 1869. 39 pp., 100 pls. of hand-tinted line drawings.
          High quality hand-tinted line drawings reproducing important 15th-16th-century ex-
       amples of Italian maiolica drawn from many European collections; preceded by a sixteen-
       page introduction and a twenty-page catalog.

394   FOUREST, HENRY-PIERRE. *Italian Ceramics.* Translated by Jules Young. Vol. 5 of
       Masterpieces of Western and Near Eastern Ceramics. Tokyo: Kodansha, 1980. Distributed
       in U.S.A. by Harper & Row. 304 pp., 124 color illus., 104 b&w figs.
          Pictorial survey with cursory text in Japanese and English of Italian ceramics, 8th-
       18th century, with examples drawn from Italian, French, English, and German collections.
       Text pp. 22-25 and entries 3-5, 7-69, 71-74, 76 deal with periods 1400-1600. Valuable for plates.

395   GARDELLI, GIULIANA. *Ceramiche del medioevo e del Rinascimento.* Ferrara: Bel-
       riguardo, 1986. 316 pp., 119 color pls., 105 b&w figs., line drawings.
          Useful presentation in catalog form, and with good illustration, of 119 quality pieces
       of maiolica produced in major Central Italian kilns and dating from the 13th to the 17th cen-
       tury. These pieces are all in private Italian collections (rarely identified except for their city
       of location) and for the most part are here published for the first time.

396   RACKHAM, BERNARD. *Islamic Pottery and Italian Maiolica: Illustrated Catalogue of a*
       Private Collection. London: Faber & Faber, 1959. 152 pp., 5 color pls., 232 b&w pls.
          Study of influence and relationship of Persian, Syrian, Turkish (Isnik) and Hispano-
       Moresque ware on the major Italian maiolica centers mostly in the 15th-16th century, based
       on the examples in a private collection then in London.

397   TARDY [HENRI LENGELLÉ]. *Les Poteries, les faïences et les porcelaines européennes*
       (France exceptée): caractéristiques, marques. 2 vols. Paris: Tardy Lengellé, 1983. 1,125
       pp., 8,500 makers' marks.
          Relevant to the 15th-16th century are pp. 607-761 dealing with Italian production
       centers of earthenware, maiolica, and Medici porcelain in Florence. Other European
       countries only discussed in terms of later period.

398   WALLIS, HENRY. *Italian Ceramic Art. The Albarello: A Study in Early Renaissance*
       Maiolica. London: Quaritch, 1904. 29 pp., 117 drawings.
          Twenty-one-page introduction on technique, shape and function, ornaments; Eastern
       and Spanish influences on 15th-century Italian albarelli.

398a   WALLIS, HENRY. *Italian Ceramic Art: The Maiolica Pavement Tiles of the Fifteenth*
       Century. London: Quaritch, 1902. 113 pp., 93 illus.
          Sixteen-page introduction describes centers of production and techniques used, and
       points to the relationship between tiles and other Italian maiolica. Location given of few ex-
       tant pieces throughout Italy from Turin to Naples including Perugia, Rome, etc.

Articles

399   FALKE, OTTO VON. "Quattrocento-Majoliken." *Pantheon* 2 (1928):390-91, 4 b&w figs.

Two representative pieces (destroyed in World War II) from the Schlossmuseum, Berlin: a large Faenza basin with the depiction of a bear hunt of ca. 1470 (early example of the use of graphic designs for maiolica painting), and a Florentine basin of ca. 1460 on which is represented a lady with falcon on horseback.

399a HAUSMANN, TJARK. "Maioliche italiane dello 'Schlossmuseum' di Berlino perdute nella seconda guerra mondiale." *Faenza* 60 (1974):24-40. 18 b&w pls. Italian/German text.

Describes the most important examples of the approximately 550 Italian maiolica pieces destroyed when the Berlin Schlossmuseum was bombed in 1944, including Della Robbia reliefs, and examples from Faenza, Siena, Deruta, Gubbio, Castel Durante, Urbino, and Padua.

400 JESTAZ, BERTRAND. "Les Modèles de la maiolique historiée: Bilan d'une enquête." *Gazette des beaux-arts* 79 (1972):215-40, 35 b&w figs.

Presentation of models used for 16th-century historiated maiolica ware: drawings in books of models, bronze medals, Italian engravings (e.g. of Benedetto Montagna, Marcantonio, Marco Dente, Agostino Musi Veneziano, Caraglio), German engravings (e.g., Dürer, Beham, Holbein), and illustrations from Lyon editions (especially the workshop of Bernard Salomon). Also explains how these models were used: faithfulness of copy, suppleness of adaptation, degree of inventiveness.

401 LIVERANI, GIUSEPPE. "La fortuna di Raffaello nella maiolica." *Faenza* 54 (1968):59-77, 3 b&w pls. French/English/German summary.

Evolution of the influence of Raphael on 16th-century maiolica painters such as Zoan Maria Vasaro, Nicola Pellipario, the Monogrammist FR, Orazio Fontana, the Patanazzis, etc., first through the prints of Marcantonio Raimondi and then those of other masters such as Marco Dente, Agostino Musi Veneziano, Caraglio, and Eneus Vico.

402 MÉLY, F. DE. "Les Origines de la céramique italienne." *Gazette des beaux-arts* 29 (1884):111-32, 31 line drawings and signature facsimiles.

Persian elements in early ceramics from Pisa. Earliest dates, signatures, and marks found on wares from Castel Durante, Pesaro, Urbino, Gubbio, Faenza, Caffaggiolo, and Castelli.

403 RACKHAM, BERNARD. "The Sources of Design in Italian Maiolica." *Burlington Magazine* 23 (1913):193-203, 2 b&w pls.

Dependence of maiolica painters on contemporary engravings and woodcut book illustrations. Compositions on Urbino and Gubbio ware (the latter signed by Master Giorgio, 1525) from various private collections traced back to Gabriele Giolito de' Ferrari's set of prints of the *Seven Planets* (1533) and a woodcut by the Master I.B. with the Bird; maiolica painters exhibited varying degrees of understanding of the meaning of their source.

6. PERMANENT COLLECTIONS

Baltimore

WALTERS ART GALLERY

404 *Catalogue of the Italian Majolica in the Walters Art Gallery,* by Joan Prentice von Erdbert and Marvin C. Ross. Baltimore: Walters Art Gallery, 1952. 58 pp., 64 b&w pls.

Eighty-six short entries dealing with maiolica dating ca. 1500 to the late 18th century, chronologically arranged. Seventy-five pieces are 16th-century examples from Faenza, Siena, Deruta, Gubbio, Castel Durante, Urbino, Venice, etc. Includes a few dated examples.

Brunswick

HERZOG ANTON ULRICH-MUSEUM

405 *Italienische Majolika: Katalog der Sammlung*, by Johanna Lessmann. Brunswick: Herzog Anton Ulrich-Museum; Berlin: Wasmuth, 1979. 623 pp., 1015 illus. including 16 color.
Lavish catalog of this important collection of more than nine hundred Italian maiolica pieces including major examples from most centers. Valuable for its scholarship and extensive photographic apparatus.

405a *Italienische Majolika.* Brunswick: Herzog Anton Ulrich-Museum, 1980. 22 pp., 5 color pls., 27 b&w pls.
Booklet (one of a museum series) describes thirty-two outstanding 16th-century Italian maiolica pieces, and is based on Lessmann's catalog (see previous entry).

Faenza

MUSEO INTERNAZIONALE DELLE CERAMICHE IN FAENZA

406 *La donazione Galeazzo Cora: Ceramiche dal medioevo al XIX secolo.* Vol. 1, Catalog by Gian Carlo Bojani, Carmen Ravanelli Guidotti, and Angiolo Fanfani. Milan: Fabbri, 1985. 348 pp., 72 color pls., 867 b&w figs., 152 illus. of date and makers' marks.
A major collection of ceramics formed by Galeazzo Cora and bequeathed to the museum. 849 pieces are Italian dating from the Middle Ages to the 19th century; nos. 850-67 are Oriental. Arranged chronologically with short entries, each illustrated; over half date of the period 1400-1600.

Florence

MUSEO NAZIONALE DEL BARGELLO

407 DEL VITA, ALESSANDRO. "Le maioliche della collezione Carrand." *Bollettino d'arte* 17 (1923-24):433-52, 1 color pl., 17 b&w figs.
Description of outstanding central Italian maiolica of the 15th-16th century from Faenza, Deruta, Gubbio, Urbino, etc. in the Carrand collection acquired by the Bargello.

408 CONTI, GIOVANNI. "La maiolica nel Museo del Bargello: Genesi e fortuna di una raccolta." *Faenza* 50 (1969):58-79, 8 b&w pls. English summary.
Formation of the Bargello's maiolica collection with those formed by the Medici and the Della Rovere as nucleus.

408a *Catalogo delle maioliche*, by Giovanni Conti. Florence: Centro Di, 1971. 154 pp., 29 color pls., 202 b&w pls.
Catalog of 622 Italian maiolica pieces, the majority of the 16th century and often prime examples, from the Medici and Carrand collections. Summary entries, often illustrated.

Hartford

WADSWORTH ATHENEUM

409   *J. Pierpont Morgan, Collector: European Decorative Arts from the Wadsworth Atheneum.*
Edited by Linda Horvath Roth, entries for maiolica by Jörg Rasmussen. Hartford:
Wadsworth Atheneum, 1986. 205 pp., 90 color pls., numerous b&w figs.
          Commerative exhibition highlighting J.P. Morgan's bequest to the museum. Includes
fourteen important Renaissance maiolica plates and jugs. (Florence, Siena, Deruta, Faenza,
Castel Durante, and Urbino). Also goldsmith work, ivories, and porcelain but all of later
periods. Excellent illustration.

Leningrad

HERMITAGE

410   *Italian Majolica XV-XVIII Centuries.* Catalog by A.N. Kube. Edited by O.E. Mikhailova
and E.A. Lapkovskaya. Translated by G.S. Kolokolov. Moscow: Iskusstvo Art
Publishers, 1976. 62 pp., 106 color pls., 42 color figs., 52 b&w figs. Russian-English text.
          Presentation of 106 outstanding items of the collection of over 500 pieces of Italian
maiolica preceded by a sixty-one page bilingual introduction describing salient features and
the work of artists (as represented in the collection) in the major production centers. Large
and high quality illustrations (ninety-five of the 15th-16th-century) with short text entries.

London

BRITISH MUSEUM

411   WILSON, TIMOTHY. "Some Medici Devices on Pottery." *Faenza* 70 (1984):433-40, 1
color pl., 5 b&w pls. Italian/French/German summary.
          Ceramics dating of ca. 1465 to ca. 1521 in the collection bearing the Medici arms and
imprese. Among these are a large Valencian vase and plates and a Caffaggiolo bowl and
plate.

COURTAULD INSTITUTE

412   MALLET, J.V.G. "Italian Maiolica in the Gambier-Parry Collection." *Burlington
Magazine* 109 (1967):144-51, 1 color illus., 10 b&w figs.
          Representative examples from an important bequest of wares from Faenza, Castel
Durante, Deruta, Gubbio, and Siena, including dishes, albarelli, ewers, jugs, a vase, and ton-
dino.

VICTORIA AND ALBERT MUSEUM

413   SHAPIRO, MAURICE L. "A Renaissance Birth Plate." *Art Bulletin* 49 (1967):236-43, 3
b&w figs.
          Study of the complex iconographical program replete with symbolism of an Italian
maiolica plate of ca. 1530 now in the museum's collection. It is composed of a birth scene at
center adapted from an illustration of the Birth of Hercules in an incunabula of Ovid's
Metamorphoses printed in Venice in 1497, and concentric rings with the planets, theological
and cardinal virtues, the goddess Fortune, and putti.

414   *Catalog of Italian Maiolica,* by Bernard Rackham. 2 vols. 2d ed., with amendments by J.V.G. Mallet. London: Victoria and Albert Museum, 1977. 1:525 pp.; 2:222 b&w pls. (1st ed. 1940.)

Standard reference and principal research tool for the vast collection of 1,442 items with representative and generally outstanding examples of all shapes and from all centers. Vol. 1, divided in fifteen chapters, subdivided according to origin, type, technique and/or decoration with introduction followed by catalog entries; vol. 2, plates with figures (small) for each piece.

Modena

GALLERIA ESTENSE

415   *Le Maioliche della Galleria Estense di Modena,* by Francesco Liverani. Faenza: Faenza Editrice, 1979. 142 pp., 43 color pls., numerous b&w figs.

Presentation of major collection of Italian Renaissance maiolica.

New York

METROPOLITAN MUSEUM OF ART

416   RAGGIO, OLGA. "The Lehman Collection of Italian Maiolica." *Metropolitan Museum of Art Bulletin* 14 (1956):186-97, 17 b&w figs.

Presentation of twelve important examples from kilns in Florence, Deruta, Castel Durante, Caffaggiolo, Gubbio, and Faenza.

Paris

MUSÉE DE CLUNY

417   ERDBERG, JOAN PRENTICE VON. "Maiolica by Known Artists in the Collection of the Musée de Cluny." *Burlington Magazine* 92 (1950):283-87, 8 b&w figs.

Author attributes a number of plates in the collection of the museum to particular artists among whom the Master C.I. and Baldassare Manara of Faenza, Giovanni Maria of Castel Durante, Nicola Pellipario, and Guido Duranti of Urbino, etc., based on Bernard Rackham's catalog of the Victoria and Albert collection (see entry 414).

MUSÉE DU LOUVRE, ETC.

418   *Catalogue des majoliques des musées nationaux—Musées du Louvre et de Cluny, Musée national de céramique à Sèvres, Musée Adrien-Dubouché à Limoges,* by Jeanne Giacomotti, with introduction by Pierre Verlet. Paris: Éditions des Musées Nationaux, 1974. 517 pp., 1 color pl., 1,448 b&w figs.

Catalog of Italian maiolica pieces of the 14th-19th centuries in four national French museums. Twelve-page introduction deals with the formation and holdings of these collections and prior publications; 1,448 entries divided according to date, color used, decorative patterns or subjects, types, or glazes. Pertinent to the years 1400-1600 are: part 1—severe style (archaic, Oriental, or Gothic floral) (nos. 1-163); part 2—Renaissance style of the first third of the 16th century including pieces from Faenza of ca. 1500-25 (164-294) and 1520-30 (295-350), wares by Della Robbia and studio (351-70), pieces from Siena (371-413), Siena or Deruta (414-22), Ravenna (423-27), and Montelupo and Caffaggiolo (428-50); part 3—Renaissance style of the first half of the 16th century including examples from Deruta (451-670), Gubbio (671-746), Castel Durante (747-828), Urbino (829-906), Forle (907-8), Rimini (909-12), Pesaro (913-14), Montelupo (915); part 4 — centers of the second half of the 16th century including Deruta (916-23), Faenza (924-70), Castel Durante (971-92), Urbino (993-1121), Lyon and Nevers (1122-74); part 5 — diffusion of the ornamental style and white faience pieces from Faenza (1175-214), Venice and Padua (1215-58), Deruta and Rome (1259-99), Montelupo (1300-18) and Sicily (1319-34).

Prague

UMELECKOPRUMYSLOVÉ MUZEUM

419   *Italská Majolika.* Catalog by *Jirina Vydrová. Prague: Umeleckoprumyslové Muzeum, 1955. 66 pp., 48 b&w pls., 4 pages of line drawings. Czech text, captions also in Russian and English.*
          Summary catalog of 244 ceramics of the 15th-18th century including examples from Città di Castello, Deruta, Faenza, Caffaggiolo, Gubbio, Siena, Castel Durante, Urbino, Pesaro, and Palermo. One-page bibliography; drawings of shapes; reproduction of marks.

Ravenna

MUSEO NAZIONALE

420   *Le maioliche del museo nazionale di Ravenna.* Catalog by Francesco Liverani and Giovanni L. Reggi. Modena: Paolo Toschi & C., 1976. 159 pp., 16 color pls., 2 b&w pls. of line drawings, 177 b&w figs.
          Ninety-three entries (some comprising several pieces) describing the museum's permanent collection of maiolica dating from the 13th-19th century and classified according to production center: Romagna (the majority), Deruta, Urbino, Abruzzo, Lyon, Manises, and miscellaneous (in appendix). Brief overview and bibliographical references for each section; description of pieces, mention of similar ware; illustration of print or drawing that inspired historiated scenes.

420a   *Ceramiche dalle collezioni del museo nazionale di Ravenna.* Exhibition catalog edited by Anna Maria Iannucci, with essays and entries by Giancarlo Bojani, Rino Casadio, Marzia Faietti, Luciana Martini, and Giovanni Reggi. Bologna: University Press, 1982. 142 pp., 32 color pls., 244 b&w figs.
          Four essays trace history of the collection and of ceramic production in Ravenna. Catalog of 248 items from the museum's collection dating of the 14th to the 18th century representative of ceramic production in Ravenna, Faenza, Deruta, Urbino, Forli, and Manises. Besides individual entries for each object, providing description and relevant data, there is a running commentary on general characteristics of particular types of wares, description of techniques, examination of iconographic sources, and historical notes (see no. catalog of same collection.)

CORCORAN GALLERY OF ART

421   *Italian Renaissance Maiolica from the William A. Clark Collection.* Exhibition catalog by Wendy M. Watson. London: Scala Books, 1986. 191 pp., 62 color pls., numerous b&w figs.

118 pieces of the 15th-16th century forming the holdings of the Clark Collection, bequeathed to the museum in 1926. Includes examples from Faenza, Pesaro, Caffaggiolo, Naples, Siena, Gubbio, Castel Durante, Urbino, Pesaro, Venice, including works by Fontana, Francesco Xanto Avelli, Francesco Durantino, Patanazzi, etc. Well-illustrated. Exhibition traveled to Mount Holyoke College Art Museum, South Hadley, Massachusetts; the Mary and Leigh Block Gallery, Evanston, Illinois; the Elvehjem Museum of Art, Madison, Wisconsin; Bowdoin College Museum of Art, Brunswick, Maine; Los Angeles County Museum of Art; The Saint Louis Art Museum; Gardiner Museum of Ceramic Art, Toronto; Museum of Fine Arts, Boston; Dayton Art Institute; University Art Museum, University of Minnesota, Minneapolis.

7. EXHIBITION CATALOGS

Bassano

PALAZZO STRUM

422   *Immagini architettoniche nella maiolica italiana del Cinquecento.* Exhibition catalog by Carla Bernardi. Milan: Electa, 1980. 71 pp., 12 color pls., 74 b&w illus.

Eighty-six short catalog entries of outstanding maiolica plates of the 16th century including architectural representations from various European museums.

Bloomington

INDIANA UNIVERSITY ART MUSEUM

423   *Italian Maiolica from Midwestern Collections.* Exhibition catalog by Bruce Cole. Bloomington: Indiana University Art Museum, 1977. 101 pp., 51 b&w figs.

Informative seven-page introduction related to function, styles, and production centers; fifty-one short catalog entries of pieces of 1400-1570 from Urbino, Deruta, Faenza, Orvieto, Florence, Caffaggiolo, Siena, Gubbio, Castel Durante, Emilia(?); all illustrated.

423a   COLE, BRUCE. "Italian Maiolica from Mid-Western Collections." *Apollo* 107 (1978):38-43, 4 color figs., 11 b&w figs.

Highlights from the exhibition.

London

BURLINGTON HOUSE

424   RACKHAM, BERNARD. "The Italian Exhibition. III-Maiolica." *Burlington Magazine* 56 (1930):16-22, 2 b&w figs.

Outstanding maiolica from British private collections (Beit, Harris, Oppenheimer, Courtauld, etc.) exhibited at Burlington House, including oak leaf jars from Florence and dishes from Faenza, Caffaggiolo, Siena, Deruta, Gubbio, Castel Durante, and Urbino.

8. PRIVATE COLLECTION, AUCTION, AND DEALER CATALOGS

BEIT COLLECTION

425   RACKHAM, BERNARD. "La raccolta Beit di maioliche italiane." *Bollettino d'arte* 25 (1932):341-49, 14 b&w figs.
    Highlights from the collection of Italian maiolica owned by Alfred and Otto Beit, London, featuring oak leaf drug jars, plates, albarelli (Florence, Caffaggiolo, Faenza, Deruta, etc.) and examples by Pellipario and Francesco Xanto.

See also entry 339.

DAMIRON COLLECTION

426   RACKHAM, BERNARD. "The Damiron Collection of Italian Maiolica." *Apollo* 26 (1937). Part 1, 61-67, 10 b&w figs.; part 2, 251-57, 10 b&w figs.
    Brief history of the evolution of the art—major centers, techniques, stylistic characteristics—as exemplified from the collection of Charles Damiron of Lyon.

DAMIRON; FLANNERY; WALLRAF, ETC. COLLECTIONS

427   *Important Italian Maiolica and Continental Pottery and Porcelain: The Property of P. Damiron, from the Thomas J. Flannery, Jr. Coll., of the Late Paul Wallraf, and of Various Owners.* Sale held in London at Sotheby's 22 November, 1983. 104 pp., 21 color figs., 111 b&w figs.
    Includes important group of 16th-century Italian maiolica (lots 160-213), some pieces being unique, produced in various centers; also a few Rhenish stoneware pieces (139-43); a rare Hungarian stove tile (154) and other miscellanea.

HARRIS COLLECTION

428   BORENIUS, TANCRED. "Italian Maiolica in the Collection of the Right Hon. F. Leverton Harris." *Apollo* 1(1925). Part 1, 266-72, 1 color pl., 8 b&w figs.; part 2, 320-23, 8 b&w figs.
    Impressive for the quality of its holdings: oak leaf jar, Orvieto ware; examples from Pesaro, Faenza, Urbino (lustred at Gubbio) by Fra Xanto, Orazio Fontana.

HEARST COLLECTION

429   COMSTOCK, HELEN. "Sources of Design on Some Italian Maiolica." *Connoisseur* 109 (1942):69-73, 10 b&w figs.
    Scenes on five Urbino, Castel Durante, and Gubbio dishes and plates from the Hearst Collection, derived from engravings of Campagnola, Marcantonio Raimondi, the Flemish Master of the Die, and Dürer.

PRINGSHEIM COLLECTION

430   FALKE, OTTO VON. *Die Majolikasammlung Alfred Pringsheim im München.* 2 vols.
[Leiden]: A.W. Sijthoff's Uitgevers- Maatschappij, [1914]. 1:49 pp. with 8 b&w text figs.,
143 hand-colored figs.; 2:36 pp. with 3 b&w text figs., 152 hand-colored figs.
      Catalog of erstwhile famous Alfred Pringsheim Colletion of Italian maiolica in
Munich. Vol. 1: text deals with formation of the collection, 14th-16th-century maiolica,
Oriental and Spanish influences, wares from Siena and Deruta; vol. 2: text refers primarily to
16th-century maiolica from Caffaggiolo and wares by Nicola Pellipario; illustrations of 16th-
century pieces from Deruta, Caffaggiolo, Faenza, Forli, Castel Durante, Siena, Venice, Gubbio, and Urbino.

430a   *Catalogue of the Renowned Collection of Italian Maiolica: the Property of Dr. Alfred
Pringsheim of Munich.* Sale held in London at Sotheby's. Part 1 (7-8 July, 1939), 59 pp.,
36 b&w pls.; part 2 (19-20 July, 1939), 124 pp., 32 b&w pls.
      Four hundred lots including major examples of oak leaf and other Florentine types;
Deruta, Faenza, and Siena wares; Urbino and Castel Durante pieces signed by Fra Xanto
Avelli, Nicola Pellipario, Fontana; lustred ware from Gubbio by Master Giorgio, etc.

SCHIFF COLLECTION

431   DE RICCI, SEYMOUR. *A Catalogue of Early Italian Majolica in the Collection of Mortimer L. Schiff.* New York: Privately Printed, 1927. 116 pp., 134 b&w pls.
      110 generally outstanding maiolica pieces of ca. 1400-1530, and one Medici porcelain
plate. Entries are chronoligically arranged according to region/city (Tusany, Florence, Siena,
Deruta, Lombardy, Veneto, North Italy, Facnza, Gubbio, Urbino), each with an illustration,
many also of back or side views.

STOWE MANOR COLLECTION

See entry 118.

STRAUSS (ROBERT) COLLECTION

432   *The Robert Strauss Collection of Italian Maiolica.* Sale held in London at Christie's 21
June 1976. 104 pp., 58 color figs., 14 b&w pls.
      Sixty-five lots including many highly important pieces dating of 1450-1550 from all the
major centers of maiolica production in Italy. Also some Hispano-Moresque lustreware (lots
1-5), an historiated dish from Lyon (57), and some Palissy ware dishes (59-65).

ZSCHILLE COLLECTION

433   FALKE, OTTO VON. *Sammlung Richard Zschille. Katalog der italienischen Majoliken.*
Leipzig: Karl W. Hiersmann, 1899. 40 pp., 190 figs. on 35 b&w pls.
      Sixteen-page historical introduction and 229 brief entries describe late-15th to 18th-
century maiolica, mostly from Italy (Faenza, Caffaggiolo, Siena, Castel Durante, Venice,
Deruta, Gubbio, Urbino, Castelli). Nos. 172-86 are Spanish lustreware; 187-97 are Palissy or
Nevers, while 198-229 are from the Orient.

Milan

GALLERIA ANTIQUARIA DI CARLA SILVESTRI

434   *Una collezione di maioliche del Rinascimento.* Exhibition catalog by Giovanni Conti. Milan: Galleria Carla Silvestri, 1984. 50 color pls, 50 b&w pls.

Fifty maiolica albarelli, dishes, bowls, vases, and salts, many signed and/or dated, from major production centers (Deruta, Siena, Gubbio, Venice, Castel Durante, Urbino, Forli, Caffaggiolo, and mainly Faenza) on the market. Particularly useful for excellent illustrations with a view also of the reverse of each object.

REGIONAL CENTERS OF PRODUCTION

EMILIA

3. SURVEYS AND HISTORIES

435   MAZZUCATO, OTTO. "Ceramiche emiliane a Roma." *Musei ferraresi, Bollettino annuale,* 7 (1977):97-108, 23 b&w figs.

Presentation in catalog form of twenty-three ceramics produced in Emilian centers from ca. 1489 to ca. 1600, now housed in public and private collections in Rome.

6. PERMANENT COLLECTIONS

Bologna

MUSEO CIVICO MEDIEVALE

436   *Ceramiche occidentali del Museo Civico Medievale di Bologna.* Catalog by Carmen Ravanelli Guidotti. Bologna: Grafis Edizioni, 1985. 347 pp., 19 color pls., 448 b&w figs.

Collection of 294 15th-17th-century ceramics, the great majority being Italian. Special emphasis on Emilia Romagna kilns; includes major examples of sgraffito, Faenza, Venice, Castel Durante, and Urbino wares by known masters. Entries discuss and often illustrate the engraving or other source at the base of the composition. Nos. 271-83 are Spanish lustreware; 284-94, German Rhenishware. Introduction with a short history on the formation of the collection.

ROMAGNA

3. SURVEYS AND HISTORIES

437   REGGI, GIOVANNI L. "Trovamenti ceramici nella Rocca Sforzesca di Imola." *Musei ferraresi, Bolletino annuale* 5/6 (1975/76):77-98, 71 b&w figs.

Essay and catalog dealing with seventy-one maiolica dishes and jugs excavated at the castle of Imola and subsequently restored. They date of the 14th-18th century but most are of the 15th, and are the work of kilns in Faenza, Imola, or the surrounding region of Romagna.

SICILY

3. SURVEYS AND HISTORIES

438   RAGONA, NINO. "Note sulla maiolica siciliana dei secoli XVI e XVII." *Faenza* 43 (1957):12-15, 2 b&w pls., French/English/German summary.
        Evidence of the little-documented Sicilian maiolica production with examples, one dated 1578, found at Castelgirone near Trapani.

TUSCANY

6. PERMANENT COLLECTIONS

Rotterdam

BOYMANS-VAN-BEUNINGEN MUSEUM

439   KUYKEN, D. "Enige opmerkingen bij twee fragmenten van Italiaanse tegelvloeren uit het einde van de vijftiende eeuw." *Bulletin Museum Boymans-van Beuningen* 15 (1964):53-62, 12 b&w figs.
        Two large fragments of historiated maiolica floor tiles in the museum's collection are held to be Tuscan and dating to ca. 1470; their decoration and relationship with other maioloca.

UMBRIA

7. EXHIBITION CATALOGS

Spoleto

REGIONE DELL'UMBRIA

440   *Ceramiche medioevali dell'Umbria: Assisi, Orvieto, Todi.* Exhibition catalog, with essays by Gian Carlo Bojani, Hugo Blake, Alberto Satolli, and Ticiana Biganti. Florence: Amministrazione Provinciale di Perugia, 1981. 201 pp., 209 color figs., numerous b&w illus. and line drawings.
        165 glazed earthenware dishes and pitchers of the 14th-16th century from Assisi, Orvieto, Todi, in public and private collections of the region. The specific emphasis is on shapes and painting style.

VENETO

7. EXHIBITION CATALOGS

Montagnana

441   *Ceramica dal XIV al XVII secolo a Montagnana.* Exhibition catalog edited by Giovanbattista Siviero and L. Munari. Montagnana: Palazzo degli Uffici, 1974. 83 pp., illus.
        Colorful earthenware produced in this town, between Padua and Mantua, and the surrounding region.

SINGLE CENTERS OF PRODUCTION

BERGAMO

7. EXHIBITION CATALOGS

Bergamo

TEATRO SOCIALE

442   *Ceramica a Bergamo, secoli XV-XVII e persistenze.* Exhibition catalog by Renzo Mangili. Bergamo: Edizioni Bolis, 1985. 170 pp., 34 b&w pls., 102 figs., many in color.
Ceramics produced in Bergamo from the 15th-17th century and now mostly in the archeological museum of that city and in private collections. Forty-three-page introduction discusses workshops, documented producers and merchants, and stylistic and technical evolution. Following is a catalog of numerous fragments and some bowls and plates recently excavated as well as Venetian and other Lombard examples introduced for comparison. Eleven pages of document transcriptions; bibliography; index of excavation sites.

BOLOGNA

3. SURVEYS AND HISTORIES

443   BERGONZONI, F. "Ceramiche rinascimentali dal sottosuolo della Piazza Maggiore alla mostra del Museo Civico." *Culta bononia* 5 (1973):101-3, 1pl.
Bolognese sgraffito ware of the Renaissance.

444   HONEY, W.B. "Bologna Pottery of the Renaissance Period." *Burlington Magazine* 48 (1926):224-35, 1 color pl., 5 b&w figs.
Characteristics of a coherent group of wares produced in the sgraffito technique: heavy incising on light red pottery through white slip and colored lead glazes of brownish-yellow, amber, or green.

6. PERMANENT COLLECTIONS

Bologna

MUSEO CIVICO MEDIEVALE

445   REGGI, GIOVANNI L. "Una fornace del Rinascimento in Piazza Maggiore a Bologna." *Faenza* 59 (1973):59-63, 4 b&w pls.
Fragments of Bolognese sgraffito ware of the late 15th and early 16th century from a dig in Piazza Maggiore, now in the museum's collection.

CAFFAGGIOLO

6. PERMANAENT COLLECTIONS

Nuremberg

GERMANISCHES NATIONALMUSEUM

446   SCHIEDLAUSKY, GÜNTHER. "Die Taufgarnitur des Dr. Christophe Scheurl." *Keramik-Freunde der Schweiz* 85 (1973):3-16, 1 color pl., 9 b&w pls.

Baptismal maiolica dish and pitcher in the museum's collection made in Caffaggiolo ca. 1535, bearing the polychromed arms of Dr. Christophe Scheurl of Nuremberg.

CASTEL DURANTE [URBANIA]

3. SURVEYS AND HISTORIES

447   RACKHAM, BERNARD. "Nicola Pellipario and Bramante." *Burlington Magazine* 86 (1945):144-49, 8 b&w figs.
    Examines the architecture, often reminiscent of Bramante's Tempietto, so prominent in the works of this maiolica painter from Castel Durante, also birthplace of the famed architect.

448   SERRA, VALENTE. "Maioliche di Nicolò Pellipario." *Antichità viva* 2, no. 9 (1963):86-89, 1 color fig., 4 b&w figs.
    Points to the wide repertory of the maiolica painter Nicola Pellipario active first in Castel Durante and then Urbino.

6. PERMANENT COLLECTIONS

London

VICTORIA AND ALBERT MUSEUM

449   RACKHAM, BERNARD. "A Maiolica Plate by Giovanni Maria." *Burlington Magazine* 56 (1930):31-37, 1 color pl., 1 b&w fig.
    A maiolica plate in the museum's collection bearing the image of Cupid bound is assigned to Giovanni Maria of Castel Durante and dated ca. 1510.

8. PRIVATE COLLECTION, AUCTION, AND DEALER CATALOGS

HEARST COLLECTION

450   RACKHAM, BERNARD. "Der Majolikamaler Giovanni Maria von Castel Durante." *Pantheon* 2 (1928):434-45, 17 b&w figs.
    A signed maiolica dish dated 1508 in the Hearst Collection by Giovanni Maria of Castel Durante made for Pope Julius II, is related to several others by the same artist.

DERUTA
3. SURVEYS AND HISTORIES

Book

451   DE-MAURI, L., [E. SARASINO]. *Le maioliche di Deruta: Una pagina di storia dell'arte umbra.* Milan: Bottega di Poesia, 1924. 61 pp., 10 color pls., 47 b&w pls.
    Maiolica produced in Deruta from the 13th century to modern times with emphasis on the period 1400-1600. Includes references to documentary sources and analysis of Deruta lustre glaze.

Articles

452   FALKE, OTTO VON. "Siena oder Deruta?" *Pantheon* 4 (1929):363-68, 1 color pl., 11 b&w figs.
    Dependence of early 16th-century Deruta ware on Sienese examples as illustrated by major pieces in public and private collections.

453   RACKHAM, BERNARD. "A New Chapter in the History of Italian Maiolica." *Burlington Magazine* 27 (1915). Part 1, Deruta, 28-35, 8 b&w figs.; Part 2, Siena, 49-55, 7 b&w figs.

New considerations on the subject ignited by von Falke's catalog of the Pringsheim Collection in Munich (see entry 431). Part 1: relationship between a group of maiolica wares frequently characterized by a petallike pattern painted on their reverse, and by their colors, and the lustred wares of Deruta; close relationship between maiolica of Siena and Deruta, those from the latter probably being derivatives; ascription of the petal-back group to Siena by von Falke. Part 2: refutal of several of von Falke's attributions of Sienese wares to Maestro Benedetto and of his connection between Pellipario of Castel Durante and pieces with the initials "F.R."

454   SERRA, DOMENICO. "Le maioliche di Deruta." *Antichità viva* 6, no. 2 (1967):17-21, 1 color fig., 5 b&w figs.

Characteristics of large Deruta plates and vessels produced between 1505 and 1525.

6. PERMANENT COLLECTIONS

New York

METROPOLITAN MUSEUM OF ART

455   SZABO, GEORGE. "Pollaiuolo and Maiolica: Three Plates with the Labors of Hercules." *American Ceramic Circle Bulletin* 5 (1986):42-65, front cover in color, 23 b&w figs.

Large highly decorative Deruta dishes of ca. 1500-25 in the Lehman Collection with scenes based on Antonio Pollaiuolo's compositions.

Ravenna

MUSEO NAZIONALE

456   BALLARDINI, GAETANO. "Eine Deruta-Schüssel mit der Passion Christi." *Pantheon* 6 (1930):464-68, 5 b&w figs.

Description of an early 16th-century Deruta dish in the museum's collection, with an involved decorative program of the Passion.

7. EXHIBITION CATALOGS

Deruta

MUSEO REGIONALE DELLA CERAMICA UMBRA

457   *Antiche maioliche di Deruta.* Exhibition catalog edited by Grazietta Guaitini. Perugia: Provincia di Perugia, 1980. 160 pp., 137 color figs., 17 b&w figs., line drawings.

Five essays on the social, economic, and technical aspects of maiolica production in Deruta and surrounding area from the 14th-20th century including pavements and ex-votos. Reproduction of 121 objects from public and private regional collections (less than half of the 16th century, several of which are dated), with short captions.

ESTE

7. EXHIBITION CATALOGS

Este

PALAZZO DEL MUNICIPIO

458   *Ceramica dal XII al XVIII secolo da collezioni pubbliche e private in Este.* Exhibition catalog by G.B. Siviero. Este: Museo Nazionale Atestino-Club Ignoranti, 1975. 124 pp., numerous figs., some in color.

Sgraffito ware and maiolica, often in fragmentary condition, mostly produced in Este from the 13th through the 18th century from the Este Museum and local private collections.

FAENZA
3. SURVEYS AND HISTORIES

459   FALKE, OTTO VON. "Der Majolikamaler TB von Faenza." *Pantheon* 13 (1934):18-22, 7 b&w figs.

Works of the monogramist TB (active 1503-20s) in various public and private collections; his combination of Gothic and Renaissance elements; his fusing of an individual style with a dependence on the prototypes of others; the eventual mass production characteristics of his workshop.

460   LIVERANI, GIUSEPPE. "Bianco di Faenza: The Development of White Maiolica." *Connoisseur* 140 (1957):160-63, 10 b&w figs.

Invented in the mid-16th century to enhance the new "sketchy" style, this hard milky glaze was used during two centuries by many Faenza workshops (e.g., those of Francesco Mezzarisa, Virgiliotto Calamelli, and Francesco Risino in the Cinquecento), and adopted by other Italian cities and in France and Central Europe.

461   LIVERANI, GIUSEPPE. "Di un boccale cinquecentesco faentino e di altre cose." *Faenza* 61 (1975):140-43, 1 color pl., 7 b&w pls. French/English/German summary.

A large Faenza-produced pitcher in a private collection, Florence, of the second half of the 16th century bears the monogram of Virgiliotto Calamelli and perhaps of his wife Isabetta.

462   LIVERANI, GIUSEPPE. "Una sconosciuta bottega maiolicara del primo Cinquecento a Faenza," *Faenza* 43 (1957):3-11, 6 b&w pls. French/English summary.

Workshop of Maestro Francesco Torelo, active in Faenza in 1522 as documented by a signed maiolica plate in an English private collection; further pieces attributed by the author.

463   MALLET, JOHN V.G. "Alcune maioliche faentine in raccolte inglesi." *Faenza* 60 (1974):3-23, 19 b&w pls. Italian/English text.

Italian maiolica ware in English collections: two reliefs of the Virgin and Child of ca. 1480-1520 (Hever Castle) said to be from Faenza; Neapolitan maiolica (Robert Strauss Collection), historiated Faenza plates from the museum of Stoke-on-Trent, Victoria and Albert Museum, etc.

464   PUGLIESE, JOSEPH. "The Matthias Corvinus Maiolica Service." *Connoisseur* 155 (1964):151-53, 4 b&w figs.

Describes four maiolica plates (dispersed among the Victoria and Albert Museum, The Metropolitan Museum, and the University of California, Berkeley) from the service commissioned from a Faentine workshop by the king of Hungary in 1476. These are particularly important since they are the first known maiolica wares with Renaissance decorative motives.

465 RACKHAM, BERNARD, and BALLARDINI, GAETANO. "Il pittore di maiolica 'F.R.'" *Bollettino d'arte* 26 (1933):393-407, 1 color pl., 20 b&w figs.

Attribution of twenty one pieces from various public and private European collections to the Faenza maiolica master "F.R." on the basis of stylistic compositions and the initials inscribed on some plates; four very distinctive groupings are proposed.

6. PERMANENT COLLECTIONS

Bologna

MUSEO CIVICO MEDIEVALE

466 GENNARI, GUALBERTO. "Un calamaio quattrocentesco faentino al Museo Civico di Bologna." *Faenza* 43 (1957):29-31, 1 b&w pl. French/English summary.

Unusual inkwell in the collection made in Faenza in 1487 with statuettes of four protecting saints supporting a city.

Budapest

IPARMÜVÉSZETI MÚZEUM

467 CSEREY, EVA S. "Di un calamaio in maiolica del Rinascimento al Museo delle Arti Applicate di Budapest." *Faenza* 61 (1975):86-93, 4 b&w pls. French/English/German summary.

Maiolica inkstand with a scene of the Nativity in the collection compared to similar Faenza-produced objects of ca. 1500.

Faenza

MUSEO DELLE CERAMICHE

468 CORBARA, ANTONIO. "Le plastiche fiammingheggianti del tardo Quattrocento e la 'Linea' Faenza-Ferrara—Un presepe a Zattaglia." *Faenza* 59 (1973):64-72, 4 b&w pls. French/English/German summary.

Faenza relief of the Nativity from Zattaglia now in the museum's collection and related reliefs in a "Flemish influenced style" also prevailing in Ferrara at the end of the 15th century.

Paris

MUSÉE DE CLUNY

469 LIVERANI, GIUSEPPE. "Di un calamaio quattrocentesco al Museo di Cluny." *Faenza* 61 (1975):7-12, 6 b&w pls. French/English/German summary.

Faenza maiolica inkstand of 1482 with an equestrian figure and the arms of Galeotto Manfredi, Lord of Faenza, and those of his wife Francesca Bentivoglio, now in the museum's collection.

FERRARA

3. SURVEYS AND HISTORIES

Book

470 MAGNANI, ROMOLO. *La ceramica ferrarese tra Medioevo e Rinascimento.* 2 vols. Ferrara: Belriguardo, 1981. 1:239 pp., 16 color pls., 44 b&w pls., 87 b&w figs., line drawings; 2:273 pp., 17 color pls., 48 b&w pls., 180 b&w figs., line drawings.

Comprehensive study of sgraffito ware produced in 15th-16th-century Ferrara for the Este court and their circle. Stylistic characteristics and relationship of composition to those of contemporary painting and sculpture.

Article

471   SIVIERO, GIOVANBATTISTA. "Considerazioni differenziali su alcuni motivi ornamentali della ceramica graffita emiliana et veneta." *Musei ferraresi, Bollettino annuale* 2 (1972):241-47, 12 b&w figs.
Figural representations on sgraffito ware of the Renaissance produced in and around Ferrara influenced by medals cast in the region, while other motifs bear relationship to contemporary paintings of the Veneto.

FLORENCE

3. SURVEYS AND HISTORIES

Books

472   CORA, GALEAZZO. *Storia della maiolica di Firenze e del Contado.* 2 vols. Florence: Sansoni, 1973. 1:505 pp.; 2:68 color pls., 365 b&w pls.
Exhaustive compilation of 14th-15th-century maiolica produced in Florence and vicinity. Jars, plates, reliefs, and tiles painted with designs in copper green, manganese purple (oak leaf), or cobalt blue and eventually polychromed, classified by styles and workshops. Vol. 1, text divided into twenty-one chapters with an apparatus of documents and chronological tables. Vol. 2, pls. 1-336, maiolica ware; 337-54, particularly useful reproduction of potters' marks; 355-65, documents.

473   DAVILLIER, CHARLES. *Les Origines de la porcelaine en Europe: Les Fabriques italiennes du XVe au XVIIe siècle avec une étude spéciale sur les porcelaines des Médicis.* Paris: J. Rouam; London: Remington & Co., 1882. 140 pp., 24 line drawings.
Fundamental study of Italian and especially Medici porcelain produced in 16th-century Florence; pp. 91-121 include a catalog of thirty-six pieces; 125-35, inventories.

Articles

474   LESSMANN, JOHANNA. "Polychromes Medici-Porzellan." *Pantheon* 34 (1976):280-87, 1 color fig., 11 b&w figs.
The only two known jugs (Herzog Anton Ulrich-Museum, Brunswick, and British Museum, London) of polychromed Medici porcelain produced from 1575 to the beginning of the 17th century.

475   MIDDELDORF, ULRICH. "Medals in Clay and Other Odd Materials." *Faenza* 65 (1979):269-78, 6 b&w figs. French/English/German summary. Reprinted in *Raccolta di scritti, that is, Collected Writings. II. 1974-1979.* Florence: Studio per Edizioni Scelte, 1981, pp. 271-78, figs. 222-27.
Known medals made of unusual materials: two of clay made in Florence in 1581, another of porcelain representing Francesco I de' Medici of 1585, etc.

6. PERMANENT COLLECTIONS

Boston

MUSEUM OF FINE ARTS

476 LANE, ARTHUR. "A Rediscovered Cruet of Medici Porcelain." *Bulletin of the Museum of Fine Arts* 56 (1958):77-83, 8 b&w figs.
Cruet with a decor of swimming fish, frog, and crustaceous fauna, produced—as are others now in Vienna, Chatsworth, and the Victoria and Albert Museum—in Florence under the reign of Francesco I of Tuscany (1574-87).

Brunswick

HERZOG ANTON ULRICH-MUSEUM

477 LESSMANN, JOHANNA, and KILB, LOTHAR. "Neue Untersuchungen zum Medici-Porzellan." *Faenza* 66 (1980):165-69, 12 b&w figs. German/Italian text. English summary.
An amphora-shaped vase in the collection painted in the style of Urbino maiolica, is confirmed, on scientific examination, to be Medici porcelain.

Detroit

DETROIT INSTITUTE OF ARTS

478 MIDDLEDORF, ULRICH. "Medici Pottery of the Fifteenth Century." *Bulletin of The Detroit Institute of Arts* 16 (1937):91-96, 3 b&w figs. (plus cover).
Maiolica vase in the collection shaped as a piece of Hispano-Moresque ware and bearing the Medici-Orsini arms, produced in Florence between 1469 and 1487.

GROSSETO

7. EXHIBITION CATALOGS

Valentano

COMMUNE

479 *Antiche maioliche di scavo della Rocca Farnese in Valentano e altre sparse dal Ducato di Castro, Sec. XIII-XVII.* Exhibition catalog by Romualdo Luzi and Mario Romagnoli. Valentano: Commune di Valentano, 1981. 96 pp., 4 color figs., 62 b&w figs.
110 maiolica pieces, often restored, uncovered in 1980 in the former Duchy of Castro at proximity of Grosseto (between Florence and Rome). Produced by local kilns, they date from the 15th to the 18th century in styles often reflective of those of more important centers.

GUBBIO

3. SURVEYS AND HISTORIES

480 FALKE, OTTO VON. "Der Majolikamaler Giorgio Andreoli von Gubbio." *Pantheon* 14 (1934):328-33, 10 b&w figs.

Examining a group of lustred bowls and plates of 1518-19 and a series of historiated works of 1520-25 by Master Giorgio in various European museums, author pinpoints the characteristics of the artist's work — ornamental motifs, figure style, landscapes, method of execution.

481   MALLET, JOHN V.G. "Francesco Urbini in Gubbio and Deruta." *Faenza* 65 (1979):279-95, 12 b&w figs. French/English/German summary.
       Several pieces of maiolica in various collections made, painted, and lustred at Gubbio ca. 1531-36, attributed to Francesco Urbini.

482   SERRA, DOMENICO. "Maioliche di Gubbio." *Antichità viva* 6, no. 5 (1967):54-58, b&w figs.
       Characteristics of Gubbio maiolica ca. 1500-30; the workshop of Master Giorgio Andreoli.

IMOLA

3. SURVEYS AND HISTORIES

Book

483   REGGI, GIOVANNI L. *La ceramica in Imola dal XIV al XIX secolo.* Imola: Grafiche Galeati, 1973. 134 pp., 21 color figs., 153 b&w figs.
       173 plates, jugs, votive plaques, etc. from public and private Italian collections produced in Imola from the 14th through the 18th century, with many examples dated to the Renaissance.

Articles

484   LIVERANI, GIUSEPPE. "La ceramica in Imola." *Faenza* 42 (1956):3-11, 4 b&w pls. French/English summary.
       Imola, on a smaller scale than its neighbors Faenza and Rimini, was a production center for maiolica jugs, plates, and votive plaques in the 15th-16th century.

485   REGGI, GIOVANNI L. "Studi ceramici. Notizie dall'Emilia Romagna." *Musei ferraresi, Bollettino annuale* 4 (1974):161-64, 5 illus. 14th-15th-century ceramic pitchers found in a well at Rocca Sforzesca, Imola.

LORETO

6. PERMANENT COLLECTIONS

Loreto

MUSEO DEL PALAZZO APOSTOLICO DELLA SANTA CASA

486   SANTUCCI, ENNIO; GRIMALDE, FLORIANO; and BERNINI, DANTE. *Le ceramiche da farmacia della Santa Casa di Loreto.* Rome: Tesori d'Arte sul Cammino delle Autostrade, 1979. 51 pp., 92 color pls., some b&w.
       Important collection of albarelli produced locally.

MANTUA

6. PERMANENT COLLECTIONS

Mantua

PALAZZO DUCALE

487   *Ceramiche nel Palazzo Ducale di Mantova.* Exhibition catalog by Giovanbattista Siviero. Mantua: Soprintendenza per i Bene Artistici e Storici per le Provincie di Brescia, Cremona, Mantova, 1981. 104 pp., 48 b&w figs., line drawings.
   Catalog of 180 sgraffito and maiolica wares of the 14th-17th century in the ducal palace, with short entries dealing mostly with 15th-16th-century pitchers, dishes, and plaques, many of which are said to have been fired right in Mantua.

MILAN

3. SURVEYS AND HISTORIES

488   BARONI, COSTANTINO. *Maioliche di Milano.* Milan: Libreria Lombarda, 1940. 71 pp., 98 b&w figs.
   Milanese maiolica of the 14th-18th centuries. Chap. 1 deals with Renaissance pieces (pp. 9-24, figs. 4-12); majority of the works discussed are in the Castello Sforzesco.

MODENA

3. SURVEYS AND HISTORIES

489   RIGHI, LIDIA. "La ceramica graffita a Modena dal XV al XVII secolo." *Faenza* 60 (1974):91-106, 7 b&w pls., French/English/German summary.
   Modena-produced sgraffito maiolica of the 15th-17th century studied mostly through examples (generally fragments) in the Museo Civico of that city and from mentions of local potters in the archival sources.

MONTELUPO

3. SURVEYS AND HISTORIES

490   CORA, GALEAZZO. "Boccale di Montelupo datato 1435 (1455?)." *Faenza* 65 (1979):260-61, 2 b&w figs. French/English/German summary.
   A jug in a fragmentary state in a private collection bearing the design of a bell and the date 1435 (or 55), may have been produced at Montelupo. The early date would suggest that it was made to commemorate the dedication of a church bell.

7. EXHIBITION CATALOGS

Pontedera; Pisa

MANIFATTURA PASQUINUCCIO PASQUINUCCI (Pontedera); PALAZZO
LANFRANCHI (Pisa)

491   *Antiche maioliche di Montelupo secoli XIV-XVIII.* Exhibition catalog essay by Fausto
Berti, with entries by Gianna Pasquinelli. Pontedera: Bandecchi & Vivaldi, 1984. 112
pp., 10 color pls., 58 b&w figs.
    Group of damaged or fragmentary maiolica — now restored — of the 14th-17th century
discovered in Montelupo Fiorentino during excavations made in 1973 in the residential section called "Il Castello." Includes some important additions to Galeazzo Cora's *Storia della
maiolica di Firenze e del Contado* (see entry 472), and thus further illustrates the activity of
the Montelupo kilns.

NAPLES

3. SURVEYS AND HISTORIES

Book

492   MOSCA, LUIGI. *Napoli e l'arte ceramica dal XII al XX secolo con marche e piante di antiche fabbriche.* 2d rev. ed. Naples: Fausto Fiorentino, [1963]. 257 pp., illus., several
color pls. (1st ed. Naples: R. Ricciardi, 1908.)
    Survey of ceramic production in and around Naples from the 12th to 20th century.
Many 15th-16th-century examples discussed.

Article

493   DONATONE, GUIDO. "Contributo alla conoscenza della maiolica napoletana del
secolo XV: Albarelli dalla Spezieria de Castelnuovo.: *Faenza* 60 (1969):38-44, 3 b&w
pls. English summary.
    Reattributes albarelli in public and private European collections to the royal chemist
shop at Castelnuovo (Naples), recorded in 1493 and already in existence during the reign of
Alfonso of Aragon.

ORVIETO

7. EXHIBITION CATALOGS

Orvieto

PALAZZO PAPALE

494   *La ceramica orvietana del medioevo: I 'butti' di Palazzetto Faina: Un intervento di ar-
cheologia urbana.* Exhibition catalog by Luana Cenciaiolo and Giuseppe M. Della Fina,
with essays by five contributors. Florence: Centro Di, 1985. 98 pp., 10 color pls., 150
b&w figs., line drawings.

Ninety-seven restored maiolica vessels and plates from fragments excavated at the Palazzetto Faina of Orvieto. Most examples date of the 15th century and were produced in Orvieto; the rest brought from other kilns of the region.

PESARO

3. SURVEYS AND HISTORIES

Book

495   BERARDI, PARIDE. *L'antica maiolica di Pesaro dal XIV al XVII secolo.* Florence: G.C. Sansoni, 1984. 356 pp., 86 color figs., 42 b&w figs. and line drawings.
Comprehensive study of Pesaro maiolica production: its history; socio-economic aspects of market and production; cross influences of other centers; technical examination of glazing, polychromy, etc.; style; dating; iconography; and detailed classification by technical and stylistic types. Majority of examples—from public and private European and American collections—date of the 15th-16th centuries and include plates, bowls, ewers, bottles, vases, and tiles. Index of Pesarese potters.

Articles

496   MALLET, J.V.G. "Istoriato-painting at Pesaro." *Faenza* 66 (1980): 153-59, 25 b&w figs.
Attribution of some Pesaro historiated maiolica of the first half of the 16th century to an anonymous artist here named "The Argus Painter" (after a dish at the British Museum) who is said to have worked with Nicola (Pellipario) da Urbino and Francesco Xanto Avelli da Rovigo.

497   UGOLINI, GRAZIA BISCONTINI. "Di alcuni piatti pesaresi della bottega dei Lanfranco delle Gabicce." *Faenza* 64 (1978):27-32, 26 b&w figs. French/English/German summary.
Attribution to the workshop of the Lanfranco delle Gabicce family of Pesaro of maiolica plates of ca. 1540-45, in a private collection, the Wallace Collection, the Hermitage, on the basis of a signed fragment at the Castello Sforzesco, Milan.

498   UGOLINI, GRAZIA BISCONTINI. "Sforza di Marcantonio, figulo pesarese cinquecentesco." *Faenza* 65 (1979): 7-10, 2 b&w figs. French/English/German summary.
Activity in Pesaro of the mid-16th century potter, Sforza di Marcantonio; maiolica votive plaques painted by him in the Museo Civico Medievale, Bologna, and British Museum.

6. PERMANENT COLLECTIONS

Pesaro

MUSEI CIVICI

499   POLIDORI, GIAN CARLO. "Orazio Fontana e le sue maioliche nei Musei Civici di Pesaro." *Bollettino d'arte* 44 (1959): 141-50, 19 b&w figs.
Attribution of a group of eighteen historiated maiolica dishes to Fontana (1510-71) on the basis of stylistic comparison with a signed and dated plate in the Chigi-Saracini Collection, Siena.

XI. Ceramics

PISA

3. SURVEYS AND HISTORIES

500   BERTI, GRAZIELLA, and TONGIORGI, LIANA. "Ceramica decorata a 'occhio de penna di pavone' nella produzione di una fabbrica pisana." *Faenza* 65 (1979):263-68, 3 b&w figs. of line drawings. French/English/German summary.
    Analysis of the pottery found at the waste dump of Lungarno Simonelli, Pisa, illustrates the characterisitic of a local production of plates and vessels. One particular pattern, in the sgraffito technique, is defined as polychromed "eye of peacock's feather." It is repeated in triple rows around the rim of the plate while at the center is an apple, a pear, or a fish motif.

RIMINI

3. SURVEYS AND HISTORIES

501   GARDELLI, GIULIANA. *5 Secoli di maiolica a Rimini dal '200 al '600.* Ferrara: Belriguardo, 1982. 148 pp., 76 color figs., 103 b&w figs.
    Published in the wake of the *XX Mostra di Ceramica nella città dei Malatesti* in Rimini (8 August-6 September 1981). Survey of maiolica production in Rimini from the 13th century to 1600, often exemplified by objects from the Cucci Collection , Rimini. Relevant to the period 1400-1600 are chaps. 2-3 (pp. 37-105) mostly dealing with pitchers and plates, the 16th century examples being historiated, and some three-dimensional pieces; also includes documents (chap. 6, pp. 117-32).

6. PERMANENT COLLECTIONS

Rimini

MUSEO CIVICO

502   GARDELLI, GIULIANA. "Un complesso devozionale in maiolica nei Musei Communali de Rimini. *Faenza* 65 (1979):353-66, 1 color fig., 2 b&w figs. French/English/German summary.
    Devotional maiolica plaque (dated 25 May 1599) of the Virgin and Child with St. Francis and the youthful John the Baptist in a double frame, produced by a Riminese workshop.

SIENA

3. SURVEYS AND HISTORIES

503   FRANCOVICH, RICCARDO. *La ceramica medievale a Siena e nella Toscana meridionale(secc. XIV-XV).* Florence: All'Insegna del Giglio, 1982. 332 pp., 5 color figs., 290 b&w figs.
    Sienese and other South Tuscan ceramics: documentary sources; types (technical characteristics, forms, colors, motifs); archaeological sites; mineralogical and chemical analysis of works from a Sienese kiln.

6. PERMANENT COLLECTIONS

Grosseto

FORTEZZA MEDICEA

504   *La ceramica della Fortezza Medicea di Grosseto.* Exhibition catalog by Riccardo Francovich and Sauro Gelichi. Rome: De Luca Editore, 1980. 169 pp., 274 b&w figs.
Selection of 170 pieces, many isolated fragments, some reconstructed plates, bowls, jugs, albarelli, mostly of Sienese type, discovered in 1975-76 excavations in-situ and dating from the early medieval period to the 19th century (see pp. 49-101, nos. 30-90 for 15th-16th-century examples).

Rouen

MUSÉE DES ANTIQUITÉS

505   LUCCARELLI, MARIO. "Contributo alla conoscenza della maiolica senese: Di un piatto nel Musée des Antiquités di Rouen." *Faenza* 61 (1975):83-85, 2 color pls., 3 b&w pls. French/English/German summary.
Maiolica plate in the museum decorated with the scene of a procession before a cityscape (Siena?) attributed to a late-15th-century Sienese workshop.

TREVISO

3. SURVEYS AND HISTORIES

506   COMINESI, IRENO RAIMONDI. "Frammenti di un grande piatto quattrocentesco trovati a Treviso." *Faenza* 52 (1966):49-50, 1 b&w pl. French/German/English summary.
Partial reconstruction of a large historiated 15th-century sgraffito platter, probably made for a wedding, from fragments found during demolition of a rampart in Treviso; attributed to a workshop active near the convent of S. Paolo in Treviso.

URBINO

3. SURVEYS AND HISTORIES

507   CASTELLI, PATRIZIA. "'Atteon converso in cervo,' un episodio delle 'Metamorfosi' di Ovidio nelle ceramiche cinquencentesche." *Faenza* 65 (1979):312-32, 9 b&w figs. French/English/German summary.
Representation of the Ovidian theme of Acteon transformed into a stag as he surprises Diana, on 16th-century Urbino and Faenza maiolica.

508   FLOCCIA, FRANCESCO. "Orazio Fontana: Considerazioni sull'esistenza di un compendiario urbinale e non solo faentino." *Storia dell'arte 36/37 (1979): 157-64, 12 b&w figs.*
Oeuvre of the maiolica painter Orazio Fontana whose spontaneous decorative style mirrors the late 16th-century Urbino trend away from traditional historiated ceramics.

509   GERE, J.A. "Taddeo Zuccaro as a Designer for Maiolica." *Burlington Magazine* 105 (1963):306-15, 22 b&w figs.

Author traces various elements of a maiolica service produced by the Fontana Workshop after the designs of Zuccaro on commission of Guidobaldo II, duke of Urbino, who presented the set to Philip II of Spain. Elements are localized in Pesaro, Paris, Narford Hall, London, Florence, and New York.

509a LASKIN, MYRON JR. "Taddeo Zuccaro's Maiolica Designs for the Duke of Urbino." In *Essays Presented to Myron P. Gilmore*. Vol. 2. Florence: La Nuova Italia, 1978. Pp. 281-84, 2 b&w figs.
　　An Urbino maiolica dish in Toronto of the Banquet in a Piazza is also part of the service for Philip II. The model for its decoration is a drawing by Zuccaro in the Louvre.

510 LIVERANI, GIUSEPPE. "Un piatto a Montpellier marcato da Orazio Fontana ed altri ancora." *Faenza* 43 (1957):131-34, 4 b&w pls. French/English summary.
　　Plates dated 1541-44 and bearing the monogram of Orazio Fontana of Urbino in various European museums; one newly discovered representing the Rape of Helen of Troy is in the Musée Fabre in Montpellier.

511 POLIDORI, CARLO. "Nicolò Pellipario, con particolare cenno ad una sua fase stilistica." *Pantheon* 20 (1962):348-55, 1 color pl., 7 b&w figs.
　　Author distinguishes stylistic characteristics marking the five phases of the work of this maiolica painter (also known as Nicola or Nicolò da Urbino), with particular attention on the third stage best represented by a plate dated 1528 with the Martyrdom of Saint Cecilia in the Museo Nazionale, Florence.

512 RACKHAM, BERNARD. "Xanto and 'F.R.': An Insoluble Problem?" *Faenza* 43 (1957):99-111, 8 b&w figs.
　　Observation of distinctive characteristics helping to define the oeuvre of each master, with examples from the Victoria and Albert Museum, Fitzwilliam Museum, Faenza, and elsewhere.

513 SPALLANZANI, MARCO. "Maioliche di Urbino nelle collezioni di Cosimo I, del Cardinale Ferdinando e di Francesco I de' Medici." *Faenza* 65 (1979):111-26, 13 b&w figs. French/English/German summary.
　　Urbino maiolica in the collections of Cosimo I, Cardinal Ferdinando, and Francesco I de' Medici, including no fewer than forty pieces from the workshop of Flaminio Fontana, several of which are now in the Bargello, the Victoria and Albert Museum, and the Bayerisches Nationalmuseum.

6. PERMANENT COLLECTIONS

Baltimore

WALTERS ART GALLERY

514 ERDBERG, JOAN PRENTICE VON. "Early Work by Fra Xanto Avelli da Rovigo in the Walters Art Gallery." *Journal of the Walters Art Gallery* 13 (1950):30-37, 75; 10 b&w figs.
　　A maiolica plate representing Perseus and Andromeda here suggested to be a work of 1528 by Fra Xanto active in Urbino; reattribution to the artist of other pieces, all datable 1528-30, formerly held to be the work of the Faenza painter F.R.

Detroit

DETROIT INSTITUTE OF ARTS

515   WETHEY, ALICE SUNDERLAND. "A Historiated Majolica Serving Platter." *Bulletin of The Detroit Institute of Arts* 58 (1980):36-45, 12 b&w figs.
Urbino plate of ca. 1470 painted with an adaptation of Raphael's Fire in the Borgo, here meant to represent the Burning of Troy; the Detroit plate and another at the Victoria and Albert bear the escutcheon of Guidobaldo II della Rovere, duke of Urbino: inscriptions on the reverse indicate that they were gifts to a certain Fra Andrea da Volterra.

Hanover

KESTNER MUSEUM

516   LESSMANN, JOHANNA. "Majoliken aus der Werkstatt der Fontana." *Faenza* 65 (1979):333-49, 12 b&w figs. French/English summary.
Attribution to the Fontana workshop of Urbino of a maiolica fragment of ca. 1540-50 in the museum; its relationship to other pieces in London, Cambridge, Modena, and Faenza by the same painters.

London

WALLACE COLLECTION

517   NORMAN, A.V.B. "Sources for the Design on a Majolica Dish." *Apollo* 81 (1965):460-63, 4 b&w figs.
The Triumph of Venus on a maiolica dish painted in Urbino by Francesco Xanto Avelli in 1533 and now in the museum's collection, is an eclectic work deriving from many engravings, among which are those of Marco Dente da Ravenna after Raphael and Baccio Bandinelli, and those of Giovanni Giacomo Caraglio after Il Rosso.

Roccavaldina (Messina)

S. SALVATORE

518   LIVERANI, GIUSEPPE. "Il corredo in maiolica di una farmacia cinquecentesca." *Faenza* 53 (1967):35-43, 7 b&w pls. French/German/English summary.
A large and important collection in the pharmacy of this institution, consisting of 238 albarelli, flasks, and amphoras made by several hands in the Urbino workshop of Antonio Patanazzi in 1580 for Cesare Candia whose arms they bear. Description of this Raphaelesque style; examination, and identification of historiated scenes.

Washington

NATIONAL GALLERY OF ART

519   WALLEN, BURR. "A Maiolica Panel in the Widener Collection." *Report and Studies in the History of Art* 2 (1968):94-105, 12 b&w figs.

Plaque of the Adoration of the Magi formerly in the Spitzer and Maurice Kahn collections and bearing the monogram of Nicolò (probably not Pellipario) da Urbino compared to other works by the same painter.

7. EXHIBITION CATALOGS

Urbania

PALAZZO DUCALE

520   *La ceramica rinascimentale metaurense.* Exhibition catalog by Corrado Leonardi. Rome: Paleani, 1982. 142 pp., 36 color illus., 116 b&w illus.
Ceramics from private collections produced in the Duchy of Urbino (Marches) in the 15th and 16th centuries. All 151 items are given a short entry and are illustrated. Nine-page introduction.

VENICE

3. SURVEYS AND HISTORIES

Book

521   BORTOLOTTO, ANGELICA ALVERÀ. *Storia della ceramica a Venezia dagli albori alla fine della Repubblica.* Florence: Sansoni, 1981. 430 pp., 62 color pls., 162 b&w text figs.
Survey of Venetian ceramics. Brief chapters provide valuable references to 15th- and 16th century literary and documentary sources, as well as recently discovered pieces of the period; include technical and iconographical analysis of 15th- and 16th-century terra cotta and glazed objects. Chap. 4 (pp. 51-84) deals with 15th- to mid-16th-century maiolica potters, patrons, and styles; chap. 5 (pp. 85-105) includes mid- and late 16th-century maiolica potters, styles, and techniques. Many plates illustrate 15th- and 16th-century prime examples. Several documentary sources of the period given in appendix (pp. 366-78, doc. nos. 6-30).

Articles

522   BORTOLOTTO, ANGELICA ALVERÀ. "Una nuova coppa istoriata di Maestro Domenico al Museo Correr di Venezia." *Faenza* 65 (1979):38-40, 1 color fig., 5 b&w figs. French/English/German summary.
Maiolica plates of ca. 1550-60 (Venice, Museo Correr, and Brunswick, Herzog Anton Ulrich-Museum) representing the death of Lucretia modeled after an engraving here attributed to Master Domenico of Venice.

523   CONCINA, ENNIO. "Un contributo alla definizione della cronologia ed all'ambiente di Maestro Domenico da Venezia." *Faenza* 61 (1975):136-39, 2 b&w pls. French/English summary.
Documents relating to the mid-16th-century Venetian maiolica painter who signed "domenego da urnecia" and whose workshop was adjacent to the Campo San Paolo.

VITERBO

3. SURVEYS AND HISTORIES

524   MAZZA, GUIDO. *La ceramica medioevale di Viterbo e dell'Alto Lazio.* Viterbo: Edizione Libri d'Arte, 1983. 167 pp., 79 color illus., 133 b&w figs.
Catalog of 212 pieces with bold designs produced at Viterbo, in Lower Tuscany, and in the region of Lazio, above Rome, from the 13th to mostly the 15th century, particularly exemplified in the Miralli Collection, Bagnaia, and in a private but unspecified collection in Viterbo.

NETHERLANDISH

3. SURVEYS AND HISTORIES

Books

525   KORF, DINGEMAN. *Nederlandse majolica.* Haarlem: De Haan, 1981. 257 pp., 24 color pls., 759 b&w text figs.
Study of Dutch maiolica mostly of the 16th and 17th century. Discussed are technique, dating, schools, styles, subjects, motifs, and decorative patterns. Examples include bowls, shallow dishes, albarelli, and tiles. Numerous small illustrations including line drawings.

526   NEURDENBURG, ELISABETH. *Old Dutch Pottery and Tiles.* Translated and with annotations by Bernard Rackham. New York: Himebaugh & Browne, 1923. 170 pp., 8 color pls., 104 b&w figs.
Survey of 16th-18th-century examples. Particularly relevant for the 16th century are chaps. 1-4 dealing with maiolica and the early manufacture of tiles in Delft and elsewhere. Also discussed are manufacturing techniques and centers of production. Examples cited are mostly from the Rijksmuseum.

Articles

527   KORF, DINGEMAN. "Het a foglie-ornament op Nederlandse majolica." *Antiek* 9 (1975):693-711, 36 b&w figs.
Polychromed foliated ornaments on Dutch tiles and maiolica of the late 16th century derived from Venetian examples.

528   VAN GANGELEN, H. "Een bijzondere schotel van slib-aardewerk met de voorstelling van een veldheer (ca. 1570-1580)." *Antiek* 20 (1986):594-98, 1 color fig., 6 b&w figs.
Sgrafitto earthenware plate with the representation of a nobleman made in Friesland ca. 1570-80, now in a private collection.

See also entry 343.

POLISH

6. PERMANENT COLLECTIONS

Kraków

ZAMEK KRÓLEWSKI NA WAWELU

529   PIATKIEWICZ-DERONIOWA, MARIA. "Les Poêles Renaissance au Château de Wawel." *Cahiers de la céramique, du verre et des arts du feu* 54 (1974):8-19, 14 b&w figs. English summary.
Polish stoves made of brick and ceramic tiles — description from extant remains and account books and reconstruction of several types from fragments found in the Castle of Wawel.

SPANISH

MULTI REGION

3. SURVEYS AND HISTORIES

Books

530   FROTHINGAM, ALICE WILSON. *Lustreware of Spain.* New York: Hispanic Society of America, 1951. 1 color pl., 220 b&w figs.
Standard work tracing the origin, development, and evolution of lustre pottery in Spain from the 10th to the 17th centuries; chap. 1 (pp. 1-78) includes discussion of 15th-century examples produced in Andalusia; chap. 2 (79-209) contains analysis of 15th- and 16th-century pieces from Valencia; chap. 3 (210-78) includes 15th- and 16th-century pottery from Aragon, Catalonia, and Seville.

531   FROTHINGHAM, ALICE WILSON. *Tile Panels of Spain: 1500-1650.* New York: Hispanic Society of America, 1969. 106 pp., 6 color illus., 98 b&w illus.
The decoration of tile panels produced mostly in Seville and Talavera de la Reina; their manufacture and glazing. Tile panels of the New World also discussed.

Articles

532   BUCKMASTER, MARTIN A. "Hispano-Moresque Pottery of the 15th and 16th Centuries." *Old Furniture* 3 (1928) Part 1, 131-38, 1 color pl., 10 b&w figs.; part 2, 203-8, 9 b&w figs.
Discusses the processes and techniques of turning, firing, painting, and lustring Hispano-Moresque ware; also examines form and decorative styles. Many examples illustrated from private collections: bowls, plates, vases, jugs, a ewer, salt, etc.

533   BUNT, CYRIL G.E. "Hispano-Moresque Pottery." *Connoisseur* 110 (1942):52-57, 12 b&w figs.
Investigation into the origins of lustreware, description of the varied types and centers of production; examples drawn mostly from the Victoria and Albert Museum.

534 MIGEON, GASTON. "Les Faiences Hispano-Moresques." *Revue de l'art* 19 (1906):291-307, 8 b&w figs.
Introduction to Spanish lustreware of the 12th-15th century. Of the later period are ceramics from Valencia with lustres of six main decorative motifs, and tiles from Seville. Examples are drawn from French, Spanish, and Russian collections.

6. PERMANENT COLLECTIONS

Detroit

DETROIT INSTITUTE OF ARTS

535 SPALLANZANI, MARCO. "Il vaso Medici-Orsini di Detroit in un documento d'archivio." *Faenza* 60 (1974):88-90, 1 b&w pl. French/English summary.
Hispano-Moresque maiolica urn of ca. 1487 bearing the Medici-Orsini arms in the museum listed in a Medici inventory of the Villa Poggio a Caiano.

Madrid

INSTITUTO DE VALENCIA DE DON JUAN

536 *Ceramica español en el Instituto Valencia de Don Juan.* Catalog by Balbina Marinez Caviro. Madrid: Instituto de Valencia de Don Juan, 1978. 200 pp., 8 color figs., 320 b&w figs.
Catalog of 307 pieces from Paterna, Aragon, Catalina, Cuerda Seca, Talavera de la Reina, Alcora, Manises, primarily dating of the 14th-16th century.

New York

HISPANIC SOCIETY OF AMERICA

537 *Hispano-Moresque Pottery in the Collection of the Hispanic Society of America.* Catalog by Edwin Atlee Barber. New York: Hispanic Society of America, 1915. 278 pp., 1 color pl., 88 b&w pls.
Catalog of 132 lustred plates, dishes, jars, bowls, tazze, etc., mostly of the 15th-16th century. Thirty-four-page historical, technical, and descriptive introduction.

538 *Catalogue of Hispano-Moresque Pottery in the Collection of the Hispanic Society of America,* by Alice Wilson Frothingham. New York: Hispanic Society of America, 1936. 291 pp., 48 b&w pls.
Sixty-five-page introduction on origins and development of Hispano-Moresque pottery in an historical context: chapter 1 (pp. 9-14) includes 15th-16th century non-lustre tiles and pottery from Andalusia and Toledo (seventeen catalog entries); chap. 2 (43-48) includes non-lustre pottery from Paterna, Manises, and Teruel (five entries); chap. 3 (63-70) discusses Gothic tiles of the 15th and 16th century (twenty-three entires); chap. 4 (95-98) includes 15th- and 16th-century socarrats (painted, unglazed tiles) (three entries); chap. 5 (105-15) deals with gold-lustre pottery from Granada (three entries); chap. 6 (123-35) deals with gold-lustre pottery from Aragon (124 entries).

538a FROTHINGHAM, ALICE WILSON. "Formed of Earth and Fire." *Apollo* 95 (1972):272-82, 3 color pls., 13 b&w figs.

Worthy examples of Hispano-Moresque ware (plates, jars, and tiles) from Manises, Malaga, Seville; baptismal font from Toledo; glass from Barcelona, all in the society's collection.

Tentudía

MONASTERIO DE SANTA MARIA

539   FROTHINGHAM, ALICE WILSON. "Tile Altars by Niculoso Pisano and Others at Tentudía, Spain." *Connoisseur* 155 (1964):28-36, 14 b&w figs.
Description and tracing of iconographic sources of the high altar of the Monastery of Santa Maria depicting scenes from the life of the Virgin and of the Order of Santiago produced in 1518 by Niculoso, an Italian very likely trained in Faenza who introduced the technique of Italian maiolica painting to Spanish wall tiles. Mention of two subsidiary altars by his imitators dating of the 1570s.

8. PRIVATE COLLECTION, AUCTION, AND DEALER CATALOGS

HARDY COLLECTION

540   HARDY, JOHN P. "Early Hispano-Moresque Lustre Pottery." *Connoisseur* 126 (1950):108-13, 14 b&w figs.
Fifteenth-century lustreware from Andalusia, Valencia, and Aragon: plates, dishes, albarelli.

STRAUSS (ROBERT) COLLECTION

See entry 433.

ZSCHILLE COLLECTION

See entry 434.

REGIONAL CENTERS OF PRODUCTION

ANDALUSIA

3. SURVEYS AND HISTORIES

541   MORALES, ALFREDO J. *Francisco Niculoso Pisano.* Seville: Excma Diputación Provincial de Sevilla, 1977. 129 pp., 8 color pls., 8 b&w figs.
Brief study of eighteen church altars and portals with a tile decoration by this Italian who brought a new technique and a new repertory of forms to the early 16th-century ceramics of Seville. Glimpses on his life, style, technique, workshop; corporations and confraternities.

6. PERMANENT COLLECTIONS

Valsequillo (Canary Islands)

EGLESIA DE VALSEQUILLO

542   HERNÁNDEZ PERERA, J.   "Una pila bautismal de cerámica vidriada sevillana en Gran Canaria." *Archivo español de arte* 25 (1952):292-93, 1 b&w fig.

    Glazed earthenware baptismal font produced in Seville at the end of the 15th century and preserved in the church of Valsequillo on the island of Gran Canaria.

Seville

CASA DE PILATOS

543   CORBACHO, ANTONIO SANCHO.   *La ceramica Andaluza: Azulejos sevillanos del siglo XVI, de Cuenca, Casa de Pilatos.*   Seville: Laboratorio de Arte, Universidad de Sevilla, 1953. 40 pp., 100 b&w pls.

    Highly decorative and richly worked panels of glazed tiles with patterns in relief — inspired from 15th-century Mudejar carpets — forming the ceiling and wall decoration of this dwelling and dating of the first half of the 16th century.

CASTILE

3. SURVEYS AND HISTORIES

544   FEIT, CHRISTIAN.   "Talavera." *Keramos* 134 (1979):99-118, 2 color illus., 30 b&w figs.

    Survey of Spanish faience made in Talavera de la Reina from the 16th to 19th century in its characteristic forms and patterns — the "butterfly" family, the "blue-green" family, the "blue-white" family.

VALENCIA

3. SURVEYS AND HISTORIES

Books

545   VAN DE PUT, A.   *Hispano-Moresque Ware of the XV Century: A Contribution to Its History and Chronology Based upon Armorial Specimens.*   London: Chapman & Hall, 1904. 105 pp., 3 color pls., 31 b&w pls., 17 b&w figs.

    Evidence of the renown of Valencian lustreware of the late Middle Ages are thirty-four plates and bowls decorated with prominent heraldic devices of various Spanish, French, and Italian families and individuals.

545a   VAN DE PUT, ALBERT.   *Hispano-Moresque Ware of the Fifteenth Century. Supplementary Studies and Some Later Examples.*   London: Art Worker's Quarterly, 1911. 108 pp., 35 b&w illus.

    Sequel to the preceding work presenting subsequent research on the history of lustre decoration and maiolica, on productions from Manises, and on the Buyls family, prominent patrons of Valencian potters. Includes detailed study of six 15th-century and seven 16th-17th-century examples.

Articles

546   ALMARCHE, FRANCISCO. "Marcas alfareras de Paterna." *Archivo de arte valenciano*
4 (1918):35-47, 39 b&w figs.
    Various incised or stamped potters' marks found on Paterna tin-glazed earthenware
of the 14th through 16th century.

547   HUSBAND, TIMOTHY. "Valencian Lustreware of the Fifteenth Century: Notes and
Documents." *Metropolitan Museum of Art Bulletin* 29 (1970-71):11-19, 13 b&w figs.
    Describes the historical background and technique, and examines extant documen-
tary evidence and the representation of lustreware objects in paintings.

6. PERMANENT COLLECTIONS

Naples

CASTEL DELL'OVO

548   MIDDIONE, ROBERTO. "Importazioni di 'azulejos' valenzani a Napoli negli anni di Alfonso il Magnanimo." *Faenza* 65 (1979):71-77, 4 b&w figs. French/English/German summary.
    Valencian azulejos from the period of Alfonso the Magnanimous. This 15th-century
king wished to foster the prosperity of Manises workshops by having all his Neapolitan
residences fitted with these colorful emblem-bearing floor tiles.

New York

METROPOLITAN MUSEUM OF ART – CLOISTERS

549   HUSBAND, TIMOTHY. "Valencian Lustreware of the Fifteenth Century: An Exhibition at the Cloisters." *Metropolitan Museum of Art Bulletin* 29 (1970-71):20-32, 22 b&w
figs.
    Highlights several bowls, plates, deep dishes, albarelli, a pitcher, and a pharmacy jug
from the museum's collection, to illustrate the range and scope of Valencian production.

Venice

MUSEO CORRER

550   CONCINA, ENNIO. "Documenti ed appunti per la pavimentazione Giustinian ad
azulejos valenzani." *Faenza* 61 (1975):80-82, 1 b&w pl. French/English summary.
    Valencian tiles (azulejos) of the second half of the 15th century from the Olivetan
Monastery of S. Elena, Venice, now in the museum.

SWISS

6. PERMANENT COLLECTIONS

Zurich

SCHWEIZERISCHES LANDESMUSEUM

551   FREI, KARL. "Ein Scherztrinkgefäss des Winterthurer Hafners Ludwig I Pfau und andere Arbeiten seiner Werkstatt." *Jahresbericht der Schweizerisches Landesmuseum Zürich* (1951):65-73, 4 b&w figs.

Book-shaped drinking vessel produced in 1584 by the Zurich potter Ludwig Pfau, better known for his stove tiles.

XII. Glass

A. MULTI COUNTRY OF ORIGIN

1. DICTIONARIES AND ENCYCLOPEDIAS

552 *The Encyclopedia of Glass.* Edited by Phoebe Phillips. Several contributors. New York: Crown Publishers, 1981. 320 pp., 65 color pls., numerous b&w figs.

Part 1: historical survey chronologically arranged, from ancient Egypt to modern times. Part 2: developments of technique; ten-page glossary; lists of glass museums and glass periodicals; seventeen-page bibliography presented by country and type of glass; index.

553 NEWMAN, HAROLD. *An Illustrated Dictionary of Glass.* London: Thames & Hudson, 1977. 351 pp., 16 color pls., 609 b&w figs.

2,442 concise, informative entries on definition of wares, materials, processes, forms, styles, principal glassmakers and designers, from antiquity to the present. Some bibliographical references.

3. SURVEYS AND HISTORIES

Books

554 BUCKLEY, WILFRED. *European Glass: A Brief Outline of the History of Glass Making, with Notes on Various Methods of Glass Decoration Illustrated by Examples in the Collection of the Author.* London: Ernest Benn, 1926. 96 pp., 104 b&w pls.

General history and overview of decoration. Parts of chap. 3 (pp. 34-39, 43-45, 47, 49-55, 81-83) include entries for 15th-16th-century Italian, French, German, and English pieces in author's collection. Valuable illustrations.

555 *The History of Glass.* Edited by Dan Klein and Lloyd Ward. London: Orbis, 1984. 288 pp., numerous color and b&w illus.

History of styles, techniques, shapes, centers, markets, etc., from ancient to modern times; chap. 3, by Perran Wood (pp. 66-91, including 7 b&w figs. and 24 color illus.), deals with 15th-16th-century Venetian, Spanish, German, Austrian, and Bohemian glassware.

556   KÄMPFER, FRITZ, and BEYER, KLAUS G. *Glass: A World History, The Story of 4000 Years of Fine Glass-Making.* Translated and revised by Edmund Launert. Greenwich, Conn.: New York Graphic Society, 1966. 315 pp., 40 color illus., 203 b&w illus.

Pictorial history of glassmaking from origins to the present, featuring specimens from each period, style, and nationality. Relevant to period 1400-1600 are plates and entry nos. 66-78, 84-89, 91, 94-105, 107-11, 113-14, 117-21, 125-26, including Venetian, German, Austrian, and Spanish jugs, ewers, goblets, tankards, bottles of various shapes, beakers, etc. Useful twenty-page glossary of glassmaking terms.

557   SCHLOSSER, I. *Das alte Glas.* Brunswick: Klinkhardt & Biermann, 1977. 452 pp., 24 color pls., 362 b&w illus.

Handbook of glassware emphasizing styles and techniques. For 15th-16th-century examples see pp. 70-80, 93-134, 144-66, 176-80, 185.

558   SCHMIDT, ROBERT. *Das Glas.* Berlin: Georg Reimer, 1912. 402 pp., 218 b&w figs.

Early authoritative history of glassmaking, discussing techniques and production centers. The book's present value is in featuring major prewar holdings — many of which have since been lost — of German museums.

559   VÁVRA, JAROSLAV R. *5000 Years of Glass-Making: The History of Glass.* Translated by I.R. Gottheiner. Prague: Artia, 1954. 226 pp., 32 color pls., 585 b&w illus.

Survey of glassmaking from ancient times to the present; organized both chronologically and according to country with discussion of glass-blowing, cutting, painting, gilding, enameling, etc. Relevant to 1400-1600: Middle Ages (pp. 90-96); Venice (99-111); Early Bohemian (119-20, 124-34); diagrams, line drawings, woodcuts, monochrome photographs, and color plates with details.

Article

560   MURRAY, MARIA D. "Reverse-Painted and Gilded Glass through the Ages," *Connoisseur* 180 (1972):201-11, 3 color figs., 15 b&w figs.

Presentation of some major examples of Hinterglass or verre églomisé in U.S. public collections, some being of the late medieval-Renaissance periods.

4. BIBLIOGRAPHICAL GUIDES

561   CORNING, THE CORNING MUSEUM OF GLASS. *The History and Art of Glass: Index of Periodical Articles, 1956-1979.* Compiled by Louise K. Bush and Paul N. Perrot. Edited by Gail P. Bardhan. Boston: G.K. Hall, 1982. 883 pp.

Articles on art, history, archaeology, and early manufacture of glass from over five hundred international periodicals, conference proceedings, and chapters in annals. Arranged into three categories (general, technology, history), the latter then in broad chronological sections and subsequently by country. Some entries cursorily annotated.

561a   CORNING, THE CORNING MUSEUM OF GLASS. *The History and Art of Glass: Index of Periodical Articles, 1980-1982.* Compiled by Louise K. Bush. Edited by Gail P. Bardhan. Boston: G.K. Hall, 1984. 310 pp.

Supplement to above.

6. PERMANENT COLLECTIONS

Directories

562   *Répertoire international des musées et collections du verre; International Repertory of Glass Museums and Glass Collections.* Sponsored by International Council of Museums, Comité International pour les Musées et Collections du Verre, Paris. Liège: Musée du Verre, 1966. 216 pp.

Directory alphabetically arranged by continent, then country, city, and museum. Each entry provides address of museum, director's and curators' names, departments with glass collections, origins, size, and nature of collections, periods and geographical regions represented, and brief bibliography.

563   "Glas in der Deutschen Demokratischen Republik." Edited by Fritz Kämpfer with entries for different museums by respective contributors. *Bulletin de l'Association Internationale pour l'Histoire du Verre* 7 (1973-76):13-149, 173 b&w figs.

Alphabetical repertory of museums in East Germany that have glass collections, with an overview of their holdings, which include many 16th-century pieces, with bibliographical references.

Cologne

KUNSTGEWERBEMUSEUM DER STADT KÖLN

564   *Glas.* Catalog essays by Brigitte Klesse and Gisela Rieneking-von Bock. Cologne: Kunstgewerbemuseum, 1973. 370 pp., 7 color pls., 32 b&w pls., 736 b&w figs.

History of glassmaking as demonstrated by examples in the permanent collection dating from antiquity to the present. Several 15th-16th-century Venetian and German pieces. Glossary; diagrams of different types of glasses.

Corning, N.Y.

CORNING MUSEUM OF GLASS

565   CHARLESTON, ROBERT J. *Masterpieces of Glass: A World History from the Corning Museum of Glass.* New York: Harry N. Abrams, 1980. 239 pp., 103 color pls., 2 b&w figs.

102 of the museum's most noteworthy and representative examples illustrated in particularly good plates with a comprehensive one-page commentary. Nos. 34-41 are 16th-century Venetian, "façon de Venise", German, and English pieces; 43- 47, Spanish and Bohemian pieces.

Düsseldorf

KUNSTMUSEUM

566   *Kataloge des Kunstmuseums Düsseldorf.* Vol. 1, *Glas.* Catalog edited by Elfriede Heinemeyer. Düsseldorf Kunstmuseum, 1966. 188 pp., 610 b&w illus.

Among the 581 items cataloged (short entry and small photograph for each) of the 15th-16th century, are German bottles, bowls and beakers (nos. 85-120, 126); German enameled glass (153-61); Venetian glass (214-34); Venetian, German, Austrian, and Bohemian cut glass (280-86).

MUSEUM FÜR KUNSTHANDWERK

567 *Europäisches und aussereuropäisches Glas.* Catalog by Annaliese Ohm. Frankfurt: Museum für Kunsthandwerk, 1973. 295 pp., 13 color pls., 629 b&w figs.

629 glass objects in the museum's permanent collection (each illustrated) of ancient, Islamic, European, and Chinese origin spanning the 6th century B.C. through the 20th century. Of the 15th-16th century are Venetian, German, Tyrolean, and Bohemian examples: beakers, goblets, dishes, bowls, etc., many with enameled decoration (pp. 60-80, 96-107, 111-13, 117, 131-39, 150, 155-56).

Hanover

KESTNER-MUSEUM

568 *Die Glas—Sammlung.* Catalog by Irmgard Woldering. Edited by Christel Mosel. Hanover: Kestner-Museums, 1957. 108 pp., 72 b&w pls.

Catalog of 280 enameled humpen, tumblers, beakers, bowls, cups and goblets in the permanent glass collection ranging from the 15th to 20th century. Forty-page introduction describes materials and techniques, distinguishes among various forms, discusses the trade and its commerce, and presents a historical overview of glass with mention of the various production centers represented in the collection: Thuringia, Saxony, Bohemia, Silesia, Venice, etc.

London

BRITISH MUSEUM

569 *Masterpieces of Glass.* Exhibition catalog by D.B. Harden, K.S. Painter, R.H. Punder-Wilson, and Hugh Tait. London: British Museum, 1968. 199 pp., 4 color pls., 269 b&w figs.

269 outstanding examples from the museum's permanent collection ranging from the 15th century B.C. to the 18th century A.D. Of the period 1400-1600 are: German and Netherlandish clear glass objects of the 15th-16th century (nos. 170-87); Italian and South Netherlandish 16th-century glass with gold decoration (193-99); Venetian, French, German, Spanish, South Netherlandish, and Bohemian 15th-16th-century glass with enameled decoration (206-20, 222-23); Venetian, German, English 16th-century glass decorated with diamond point (230-33); Venetian, Austrian, Netherlandish 16th-century colored glass (251-53); Venetian opaque-white glass of the 16th century (260). All objects are illustrated and studied in a comprehensive entry.

COURTAULD INSTITUTE

570 CHARLESTON, R.J. "Glass in the Gambier-Parry Collection." *Burlington Magazine* 109 (1967):162-66, 8 b&w figs.

16th-century Venetian, German, and Bohemian glass dishes, cups, and bowls illustrating various techniques, bequeathed to the Courtauld Institute.

VICTORIA AND ALBERT MUSEUM

571   *A Descriptive Catalogue of the Glass Vessels in the South Kensington Museum.* Introduction by Alexander Nesbitt. London: South Kensington Museum, 1878. 378 pp., 9 color pls., 12 monochrome pls.

160-page introduction outlines technical processes, shapes, styles, history, and production centers, followed by a 194-page catalog of glassware from ancient times to the 19th century and including many 15th-16th-century examples (Venetian, Spanish, German, Bohemian, etc.).

572   *Glass. A Handbook for the Study of Glass Vessels of All Periods and Countries & a Guide to the Museum Collection.* Catalog by W.B. Honey. London: Ministry of Education, 1946. 169 pp., 72 b&w pls.

From B.C. to 1935; short chapters by country of origin. Of the 15th-16th century are Venetian glass (pp. 55-71); German and Bohemian works (72-77); English (95-97), and Spanish (144) examples.

WALLACE COLLECTION

573   GAYNOR, SUZANNE. "Glass in the Wallace Collection." *Apollo* 116 (1982):312-15, 10 b&w figs.

Highlights including Venetian examples—a "calcedonio" goblet of ca. 1500, an enameled pilgrim's flask (1523-26), a 16th-century tazza and ewer—and outstanding vessels from France, Austria, Spain, and Bohemia.

Turin

MUSEO CIVICO D'ARTE ANTICA

574   *I vetri dorati graffiti e i vetri dipinti.* Catalog by Silvana Pettenati. Turin: Museo Civico, 1978. 183 pp., 19 color pls., 260 b&w figs.

Catalog of famous collection of 184 reverse-painted and gilded glass (verre églomisé); includes major 15th-16th- century Italian, French, Flemish, and German examples (nos. 10- 94), the majority with religious scenes and some with mythological subjects.

Weimar

STAATLICHE KUNSTSAMMLUNGEN

575   *Glaser vom XIV. bis zum XIX. Jahrhundert; aus dem Bestand der Kunstsammlungen zu Weimar.* Exhibition catalog by Jutta Horning. Weimar: Staatliche Kunstsammlungen, 1979. 110 pp., 6 color figs., 139 b&w figs.

Catalog of the museum's permanent collection of 145 glass pieces; includes 16th-century Venetian and German examples, some with enameling.

8. PRIVATE COLLECTION, AUCTION, AND DEALER CATALOGS

BREMEN COLLECTION

576   *Glas, Form und Farbe: Die alten Gläser und Glasgemälde der Sammlung [Walther] Bremen in Krefeld.* Exhibition held in Bonn at the Rheinisches Landesmuseum. Catalog by H. von Petrikovits, J.M. Fritz, et al. Düsseldorf: Rheinland-Verlag, 1964. 28 pp., 10 color pls., 81 b&w pls.

    Short guide to the collection (usually housed in Krefeld), consisting of 254 glass objects (beakers, goblets, bowls, ewers, humpen, etc., mostly German, Venetian, and Flemish) out of which fifty-nine are illustrated with a short caption, and eighty-six stained glass pieces (twenty-one illustrated). The majority of examples are of the period 1400-1600.

KRUG COLLECTION

577   KLESSE, BRIGITTE. *Glassammlung Helfried Krug.* 2 vols. Vol. 1, Munich: Lambert Müller, 1965, 364 pp., 431 b&w figs. Vol. 2, Bonn: Rudolf Habelt, 1973, 316 pp., 4 color pls., 421 b&w figs.

    Catalog of the outstanding Helfried and Jopie Krug Collection in Mülheim/Ruhr comprised of 762 glass items (several with enamel) that originate from all countries and periods, though Germany is best represented. Pertaining to the 15th-16th centuries are catalog nos. 34-39, 449, 519 (German); 74-79, 81, 84, 472-81, 483 (Venetian); 120, 518, 520 (Bohemian); and 482 (Tyrolian). Entries, preceded by short essays on the different schools, include bibliography. Publication particularly important for the scope of the material covered and for the quality of its reproductions.

B. SINGLE COUNTRY OF ORIGIN

BELGIUM

3. SURVEYS AND HISTORIES

578   CHAMBON, RAYMOND. *L'Histoire de la verrerie en Belgique du IIme siècle à nos jours.* Brussels: Éditions de la Librairie Encyclopédique, 1955. 331 pp., 77 b&w pls.

    The making of glass objects in the territory of today's Belgium from the time of the Roman invasions to the 20th century. 15th-century production (see pp. 61-73) is dominated by the Colinet family active in Hainaut, Liège, and Flanders. Under the Spanish regime from 1482 until 1602 (pp. 79-102), Antwerp is the most important of several local centers influenced by Venetian glass.

BRITISH (ENGLISH)

3. SURVEYS AND HISTORIES

Books

579 BUCKLEY, WILFRED. *Diamond Engraved Glasses of the Sixteenth Century with Particular Reference to Five Attributed to Giacomo Verzelini.* London: Ernest Benn, 1929. 25 pp., 33 b&w pls.

Five glasses, all dated, in the British Museum, Musée de Cluny, and two private English collections attributed to a Venetian working in London, city which the monopoly of making glasses "à la façon de Venise" from 1575 until 1602. Repertory of all other dated 16th-century diamond-engraved glasses known to the author (nineteen), and seven undated, with classification of the various types.

580 CHARLESTON, R.J. *English Glass and the Glass Used in England, Circa 400-1940.* London: George Allen & Unwin, 1984. 318 pp., 24 line drawings, 64 b&w pls.

Historical survey of glass manufacture and trade in England; examines the rise of production centers, techniques, forms and colors, designs, demand, foreign influence, etc. Chaps. 2-3 (pp. 17-108; pls. 7-14) deal with the late medieval and Tudor glass industries.

581 THORPE, W.A. *English Glass.* 2d rev. and enl. ed. London: A. & C. Black, 1961. 320 pp., 23 b&w pls., b&w text figs. (1st ed. 1935.)

Comprehensive study of glassmaking in England from the 2d to the 20th century. The period 1400-1600 is dealt with in chaps. 2-4: development in relation to production on the Continent; attributions to the masters and their workshops; study of techniques.

Articles

582 CHARLESTON, ROBERT J. "New Light on Renaissance Glass in England." *Journal of Glass Studies* 25 (1983):129-33, 6 b&w figs. and line drawings.

Addition of several glasses to a group from the London glasshouse of Giacomo Verzelini with diamond-point decoration attributable to the engraver Anthony de Lisley; a lattimo group with London hallmarked mounts suggested to be Murano productions expressly made for export to England; fragments of many Venetian imports excavated in Southampton.

583 CHARLESTON, R.J. "16th to 17th Century English Glass." *Bulletin de l'Association Internationale pour l'Histoire du Verre* 8 (1977-80):77-99, 8 b&w figs.

English market in the 16th century for Venetian glass; early attempts to have foreign artisans manufacture same in England.

584 RACKHAM, BERNARD. "Three Elizabethan Glasses." *Burlington Magazine* 24 (1913-14):23-27, 3 b&w figs.

Goblets bearing the dates 1581, 1586 in the British Museum and a private collection made in England in the Venetian style.

585 THORPE, W.A. "The Lisley Group of Elizabethan Glasses." *Connoisseur* 122 (1948):110-17, 8 b&w figs.

Ascription of the diamond engraving and gilding of a group of eight stemmed glasses now in various collections to Anthony de Lisley, a French-born engraver of pewter and glass working in London after 1582.

6. PERMANENT COLLECTIONS

London

GUILDHALL MUSEUM

586 HUME, NOËL. "Tudor and Early Stuart Glasses Found in London." *Connoisseur* 150 (1962):269-73, 12 b&w figs., 2 line drawings.
Fragments of late 16th-century ale glasses recovered from postwar London sites.

CZECHOSLOVAKIA (BOHEMIAN)

3. SURVEYS AND HISTORIES

587 HEJDOVÁ, DAGMAR. "Types of Medieval Glass Vessels in Bohemia." *Journal of Glass Studies* 17 (1975):142-50, 11 b&w figs., line drawings.
Forty-two differently shaped glass vessels produced in Bohemia between 1350 and 1450, as known from archeological finds and illustrations in illuminated manuscripts.

FRENCH

3. SURVEYS AND HISTORIES

588 BARRELET, JAMES. *La Verrerie en France de l'époque gallo-romane à nos jours.* Paris: Librairie Larousse, 1953. 206 pp., 72 b&w pls.
Concise history of glassmaking in France from Gallo-Roman until modern times. Useful since literature is generally scarce on French medieval/Renaissance glass. For the centers active during the 15th century, see pp. 54-63; for those of the 16th, see 64-73.

GERMAN

3. SURVEYS AND HISTORIES

589 RADEMACHER, FRANZ. *Die deutschen Gläser des Mittelalters.* Berlin: Verlag für Kunstwissenschaft, 1933. 151 pp., 64 b&w pls.
Survey of use, form, technique, and development of glassware in medieval Germany. Includes numerous examples of 15th-16th-century flasks, beakers, ewers, and lamps—many illustrated in contemporary engravings, illuminated manuscripts, and panel painting.

6. PERMANENT COLLECTIONS

Corning, N.Y.

CORNING MUSEUM OF GLASS

590 *German Enameled Glass: The Edwin J. Beinecke Collection and Related Pieces.* Catalog by Axel von Saldern. Corning, N.Y.: Corning Museum of Glass, 1965. 474 pp., 38 color pls., 591 b&w illus.

Comprehensive catalog of Central European glass presented by themes (portraits, biblical, mythological, armorial, ornamental, etc.) and regions; 167 catalog entries, all illustrated (of the 16th century are the South German stange, no. 1; and the Bohemian goblets, mugs, humpens, and stanges, nos. 3, 5-16, 31-33, 42A, 47-48, 50, 63, 70-73).

8. PRIVATE COLLECTION, AUCTION, AND DEALER CATALOGS

SELIGMANN COLLECTION

591   RADEMACHER, F. "Die gotischen Gläser der Sammlung Seligmann-Köln." *Pantheon* 8 (1931):290-94, 15 b&w figs.
       German 15th-16th-century tumblers, goblets, bowls, and flasks (the latter suggested to be of middle-Rhine production); description of color, shape, form.

ITALIAN

MULTI REGION

3. SURVEYS AND HISTORIES

592   MARIACHER, GIOVANNI. *Italian Blown Glass from Ancient Rome to Venice.* Translated by Michael Bullock and Johanna Capra. London: Thames & Hudson, 1961. 247 pp., 85 color pls., 59 b&w figs. (English translation of *Il vetro soffiato da Roma antica a Venezia.* [Milan]: Electa, [1960]. 243 pp., 84 color pls., 59 b&w text figs.)
       Well-illustrated survey of blown glass from ancient Rome to Venetian productions of the 14th-19th century. The emphasis is on formal and technical evolution. Pls. 21-55, 58-59 are of 15th-16th-century examples. Useful general bibliography.

592a   MARIACHER, GIOVANNI. *Vetri italiani del Cinquecento.* Milan: Antonio Vallardi, 1959. 91 pp., 7 color pls., 140 b&w figs.
       16th-century glassmaking in Italy: production centers; characteristics and types of ware; techniques; originals and imitations; comparative material from paintings and prints of the period.

6. PERMANENT COLLECTIONS

Florence

MUSEO NAZIONALE DEL BARGELLO

593   *Vetri rinascimentali* by Silvana Pettenati. Florence: Museo Nazionale del Bargello, 1986. 30 pp., 8 color figs., 13 b&w figs.
       Selected examples of reverse-painted and gilded glass (verre églomisé) in the collection include two outstanding 16th-century examples formerly owned by Carrand.

7. EXHIBITION CATALOGS

London

BURLINGTON HOUSE

594 BUCKLEY, WILFRED. "The Italian Exhibition. IV-Glass." *Burlington Magazine* 56 (1930):22, 31; 5 b&w figs.
Outstanding examples of 15th- and 16th-century vetro di Trino, eis-glas, verre églomisé, and enameled, engraved, and marble glass in British private collections.

SINGLE CENTERS OF PRODUCTION

FLORENCE

3. SURVEYS AND HISTORIES

595 HEIKAMP, DETLEF. "Studien zur mediceischen Glaskunst: Archivalien, Entwurfszeich-nungen, Gläser und Scherben." *Mitteilungen des kunsthistorischen Institutes in Florenz* 30 (1986):12-423, 1 color pl., 210 b&w figs. Italian summary.
Ground-breaking, scholarly, and thorough study in book-length format of the glass production in Florence in the 16th to early 18th century. Well documented.

VENICE

3. SURVEYS AND HISTORIES

Books

596 GASPARETTO, ASTONE. *Il vetro di Murano dalle origini ad oggi.* Venice: Neri Pozza, 1958. 289 pp., 16 color pls., 196 b&w figs.
History of glassmaking in Murano from its origins (for 15th-16th century, pp. 63-69, 74-113, 155-56, 162-64, 184-88): technical discoveries; influences; types and styles; migration of artists to other centers; dishes and receptacles, window panes, mirrors, beads.

597 MENTASTI, ROSA BAROVIER. *Il vetro veneziano.* Milan: Electa, 1982. 346 pp., 34 color figs., 305 b&w figs.
Survey of the Venetian production of glass from medieval times to present day. Pp. 33-66 deal with the 15th century and 67-108 with the 16th. Author outlines main types, decoration, and techniques.

Articles

598 CHARLESTON, R.J. "The Import of Venetian Glass into the Near-East, 15th-16th Century." *Annales du 3ᵉ Congrès International d'Étude Historique du Verre* (1964):158-68, 5 b&w figs.
Venetian lamps, beakers, goblets imported to Syria after the destruction of Syrian glass centers in 1400, and nine hundred lamps ordered by Grand Vizier Mohammed Pasha of Turkey for a mosque under construction.

598a   CHARLESTON, R.J. "The Import of Western Glass into Turkey: Sixteenth-Eighteenth Centuries." *Connoisseur* 162 (1966):18-26, 15 b&w figs.
Import of Venetian blown glass mosque-lamps into Turkey and Egypt after Tamerlane disrupted the glassmaking centers of Syria in 1400.

599   CLARKE, TIMOTHY H. "Lattimo—A Group of Venetian Glass Enameled on an Opaque-White Ground." *Journal of Glass Studies* 16 (1974):22-56, 63 b&w figs.
Documentary sources suggest that enameled milk glass was readily produced around 1500 in imitation of Chinese porcelain then available in Venice. Fourteen surviving pieces are studied for their decoration, including compositions after Carpaccio, Mocetto, and Mantegna.

600   MARIACHER, GIOVANNI. "La scoperta di due bottiglie veneziane del secolo XV." *Journal of Glass Studies* 6 (1964):70-74, 4 b&w figs.
Two Venetian blown glass bottles for oil and wine recently discovered in a niche in the Church of San Sigismondo, Cremona, here dated to 1463.

601   SCHMIDT, ROBERT. "Die venezianischen Emailgläser des XV. und XVI. Jahrhunderts," *Jahrbuch der königlich preussischen Kunstsammlungen* 32 (1911):249-86, 1 b&w pl., 21 b&w figs.
Enameled glass produced in Venice from the late 15th century through the 16th century; method of production, craftsmen, types of decoration.

602   TAIT, HUGH. "Continental Glass of the Renaissance and the Seventeenth Century." *Bulletin de l'Association Internationale pour l'Histoire du Verre* 8 (1977-1980):101-12, 6 b&w figs.
Mention of certain aspects of Venetian glass—enameled decoration, "calcedonio" (imitation of semiprecious stones), "cristallo" (pure colorless glass), represented in the British Museum and Victoria and Albert Museum.

6. PERMANENT COLLECTIONS

Baltimore

WALTERS ART GALLERY

603   PERROT, PAUL N. "A Venetian Pilgrim Flask." *Apollo* 84 (1966):492, 1 color pl.
Brief history of Venetian lattimo glass on the basis of an example in the collection that the author places at the end of the series of such still extant pieces (ca. 1525).

London

BRITISH MUSEUM

604   TAIT, HUGH. *The Golden Age of Venetian Glass.* London: British Museum, 1979. 139 pp., 16 color pls., 257 b&w figs.
Critical attempt to distinguish Murano glass from "façon de Venise" examples and from productions from Syria and other centers, as exemplified by the outstanding Slade Collection in the museum. 236 entries for enameled and gold glasses, "cristallo" and "filigrana," and others, most of which are of the period 1400-1600.

Murano

MUSEO VETRARIO

604a   DORIGATO, ATTILIA. *Il Museo Vetrario di Murano*. Milan: Electa SpA, 1986. 95 pp., 23 color figs., 114 b&w figs.

Good overview of the formation of the principal holdings of this major public Venetian collection of glass produced in situ. Useful biography to other local publications.

Turin

MUSEO CIVICO D'ART ANTICA, PALAZZO MADAMA

See entry 76a.

7. EXHIBITION CATALOGS

Corning, N.Y.

CORNING MUSEUM OF GLASS

605   *Three Great Centuries of Venetian Glass*. Exhibition catalog by Paul N. Perrot. Corning, N.Y.: Corning Museum of Glass, 1958. 119 pp., 7 color pls., 124 b&w figs.

Concise eighteen-page history of Venetian glassmaking from the 11th to the 17th century followed by a catalog of 128 objects from several public and private American collections and from the Victoria and Albert Museum, dating of the 15th, 16th, and 17th century (all illustrated). Entries describe different techniques, types, and styles, trace sources, and mention other similar pieces.

Venice

BIENNALE

606   MARIACHER, GIOVANNI. "La mostra storica del vetro di Murano alla XXVI Biennale." *Arte Veneta* 7 (1953):200-204, 10 b&w figs.

Assessment of an exhibition (for which no catalog was published) of Murano glass held in conjunction with the 26th Biennale at Venice. Author discusses several prime examples of Venetian enameled glassware of ca. 1500 mainly drawn from Italian public collections for the exhibit.

PALAZZO DUCALE and MUSEO CORRER

607   *Mille anni di arte del vetro a Venezia*. Exhibition catalog edited by Attilia Dorigato, with contributions on 15th- 16th-century objects by Astone Gasparetto, Patrick M. de Winter, Hugh Tait, et al. Venice: Albrizzi, 1982. 325 pp., 58 color illus., 632 b&w figs.

Catalog of an international exhibition comprising 665 entries (all illustrated) of glassmaking in Venice from the earliest age to the present. Pertaining to the 15th-16th century are entry nos. 52 to 163 for often outstanding examples.

SPANISH

3. SURVEYS AND HISTORIES

608 FROTHINGHAM, ALICE WILSON. *Barcelona Glass in Venetian Style.* New York: Hispanic Society of America, 1956. 49 pp., 38 b&w figs.

16th-century vases, goblets, decanters, bowls, etc. "a la manera de Venecia": their design, iconography, shape, technique, workshops, and market.

609 FROTHINGHAM, ALICE WILSON. *Spanish Glass.* London: Faber & Faber, 1963. 96 pp., 4 color pls., 130 b&w figs.

Authoritative study of glassmaking in Spain from the 11th through the 19th century (for 15th-16th century, see in particular pp. 23-45, 57-61): styles; influences (Islamic and Venetian); technique; workshops, etc., discussed on a regional basis. Several examples from the 15th-16th century are reproduced.

610 GUDIOL, RICART JOSÉ, and DE ARTÍÑANO, P.M. *Vidre. Resum de la història del vidre. Catàleg de la collecció Alfons Macaya.* Barcelona: Tipografia Casuelleras, 1935. 271 pp., 25 b&w pls., 304 b&w figs.

First half of the volume presents a history of glass in Europe, and specifically in Spain, from antiquity to present, with examples from public and private Spanish collections. Second half is a catalog of 304 entries from the Alfons Macaya Collection, Barcelona; nos. 122-26, 130 are 16th-century Catalonian productions.

6. PERMANENT COLLECTIONS

New York

HISPANIC SOCIETY OF AMERICA

611 FROTHINGHAM, ALICE WILSON. *Hispanic Glass with Examples in the Collection of the Hispanic Society of America.* New York: Hispanic Society of America, 1941. 204 pp., 124 b&w illus.

History of glassmaking in Spain: styles; types; techniques; examples from contemporary paintings and references to Renaissance literature. For the 15th century see pp. 6-29. For 16th-century Catalonian, Andalusian, and Castilian glass see 33-58, 71, and 83-87, respectively. Chap. 7 is a catalog of Spanish glass in the Hispanic Society's collection, with four 16th-century examples (131-35, 141).

XIII. Gems and Semiprecious Stones Including Rock Crystal and Amber

A. MULTI COUNTRY OF ORIGIN

2. BIOGRAPHICAL DICTIONARIES

See entry 1189

3. SURVEYS AND HISTORIES

Books

612   EVANS, JOAN. *Magical Jewels of the Middle Ages and the Renaissance Particularly in England.* 2d ed. New York: Dover, 1976. 264 pp., 4 b&w pls. (1st ed. Oxford: Clarendon Press, 1922.)
       Four-page introduction on magical virtues of amulets, talismans, and precious stones. Chap. 4 (pp. 51-94) mentions 15th-century popular, ecclesiastical, and scientific lapidary treatises; chap. 6 (110-38) includes magical jewels (precious stones, engraved gems, inscribed jewels, and reliquary pendants) of the 15th century; chap. 7 (140-66) lapidary treatises of the 16th century; chap. 8 (167-83) includes magical jewels of the Renaissance. Seven appendixes with excerpts from Latin lapidary treatises.

613   FALK, FRITZ. *Edelsteinschliff und Fassungsformen im späten mittelalter und im 16. Jahrhundert: Studien zur Geschichte der Edelsteine und des Schmuckes.* Ulm: Wilhelm Kempter KG, 1975. 150 pp., 82 b&w figs.
       Detailed study of 14th- to 16th-century jewelry forms, stone cutting, polishing, and metal mounts, as exemplified by extant pieces as well as contemporary miniatures, panels, and inventories (e.g., those of Jean de Berry, Margaret of Flanders, and Charles the Bold).

614   HAHNLOSER, HANS R, and BRUGGER-KOCH, SUSANNE. *Corpus der Hartsteinschliffe des 12.-15. Jahrhunderts.* Berlin: Deutscher Verlag für Kunstwissenshaft, 1985. 295 pp., 32 color pls., 466 b&w pls, 11 figs. and line drawings.

Corpus of polished hard stones (mostly rock crystal) in mounts from the 12th to the 15th centuries. Seventy-five-page introduction describes stones, techniques of cutting and polishing, and purpose. Catalog of 573 entries arranged by type of objects. Relevant for the period 1400-1600 are rock crystal cylinders for monstrances and pyxes, game boards, altar crosses, standing cups, tankards, candlesticks, spoons, handles of utensils, etc.

615   OSBORNE, DUFFIELD. *Engraved Gems, Signets, Talismans and Ornamental Intaglios, Ancient and Modern.* New York: Henry Holt & Co. 1912. 424 pp., 32 b&w pls., some text figs.

Scholarly history of gem engraving dealing with the characteristics and developments in each period from ancient to modern times. Also studies iconography—generally pagan themes—techniques, and materials used. Chap. 10 specifically discusses medieval examples (pp. 155-69), chap. 11 (170-80) those of the Renaissance.

Articles

616   ALCOUFFE, DANIEL. "Le collezioni francesi di gemme del XVI secolo." *Arte illustrata* 59 (1974):264-78. 22 illus.

Presentation of the collection of objects (bowls, cups, aquamanile, vases) carved out of rock crystal or other hard stones now in the Louvre, Prado, or in Siena, etc., and in the 16th century owned by the kings of France, of Navarre, and by the Guise family.

617   FALKE, OTTO VON. "Gotisch oder fatimidisch?" *Pantheon* 5 (1930):120-29, 18 b&w figs.

A group of vessels in German, Austrian, U.S. museums, most of faceted rock crystal with mounts discussed in terms of their style.

617a   FOCK, C. WILLEMIJN. "Pietre Dure Work at the Court of Prague: Some Relations with Florence." *Leids kunsthistorisch jaarboek* 1 (1982):259-69, 7 b&w figs.

Activity of late-16th-century gem cutters in Milan and the courts of Florence and Prague: the Miseronis, the Caronis, Giorgio Gaffuri, etc.

618   HACKENBROCH, YVONNE. "A Royal Gift." *Connoisseur* 173 (1970):152-57, 2 color figs., 3 b&w figs.

A late 16th-century Milanese pendant (Paris, private collection) with a female profile portrait in the commesso technique bears a likeness of Jahangir, emperor of India, on the reverse, which is here attributed to Renold Elstrack (1571-after 1625) of London after an Indian miniature, and is suggested to have been a gift from King James I to the emperor presented throught the English ambassador to India, Sir Thomas Roe.

619   MASSON, GEORGINA. "Two Thousand Years of Cameo Jewels." *Apollo* 103 (1976):196-201, 8 b&w figs.

Cameos as fashionable objects; their often prominent owners since antiquity; some 16th-century actual examples and others as illustrated in paintings.

620   NEVEROV, OLEG. "Gems in the Collection of Rubens." *Burlington Magazine* 121 (1979):424-32, 33 b&w figs.

Account of the formation, history, and dispersal of this important collection as relayed through correspondence betweeen Rubens and Peiresc. Author identifies—through inventory listings, descriptions, and engravings—cameos and intaglios (mostly Italian) once belonging to the artist and now in Paris, Boston, London, Leningrad, and Berlin.

621 TONNOCHY, A.B. "Some Examples of Engraved Gems as Armorial Signets." *Old Furniture* 2 (1927):59-62, 11 b&w figs.
Description of of several signet rings in fashion among members of the 15th-16th-century nobility.

6. PERMANENT COLLECTIONS

Amsterdam

RIJKSMUSEUM

622 *Uit de schatkamer—The Treasures.* Vol. 1. Catalog by Th. M. Duyvené de Wit-Klinkhamer. Amsterdam: Rijksmuseum, 1955. 6 pp., 34 b&w pls.
Brief overview of thirty-four rock-crystal receptacles and other 16th-century objects of precious stones with goldsmith mounts (including jewels) produced in France, Italy, and Germany. Six-page-introduction in Dutch and English followed by illustrations with captions.

Leningrad

HERMITAGE

623 *Western European Cameos in the Hermitage Collection.* Catalog by Ju. Kagan. Leningrad: Aurora Art Publishers, 1973. 96 pp., 103 color figs., 71 b&w figs. English/Russian text.
Twenty-three-page historical introduction in English (followed by Russian) outlines the art of glyptics and its practioners; catalog of 103 cameos ranging from the 13th to the 19th century including religious, classical, mythological, animal subjects as well as individual portraits. Cat. nos. 12-64 deal with 15th-16th-century French, Italian, German, English, Polish, and Austrian examples.

London

BRITISH MUSEUM

624 DALTON, O.M. "Medieval and Later Engraved Gems in the British Museum." *Burlington Magazine,* Part 1, 23 (1913):128-36, 1 b&w pl.; part 2, 24 (1913-14):28-32, 1 b&w pl.
Part 1: evolution of the gem engraver's art from the 13th to the 16th century illustrated with representative examples of the collection such as the sapphire engraved with a seated prince—Jean de Berry—and the cameo belonging to Lorenzo de' Medici of Noah Entering the Ark; characteristics that distinguish the work of the Renaissance from the antique; technical innovations. Part 2: Renaissance gems with portraits (e.g. onyx of René d'Anjou dating of 1475-80, perhaps by Thomas Peigne; onyx portrait of Sigismund Malatesta; double-sided cameo with portraits of Francis I and Eleonora of Portugal; Renaissance gems with classical and ideal heads).

624a *Catalogue of the Engraved Gems of the Post-Classical Periods in the Department of British and Medieval Antiquities and Ethnography in the British Museum.* Catalog by O.M. Dalton. London: Trustees of the British Museum, 1915. 257 pp. with 79 text figs., 37 b&w pls., with several illus. on each.

Seventy pages of the history of the collection and of gem carvings and engravings in Europe. Catalog of 1,112 cameos, carved shells, and engraved gems arranged by subject: religious, mythological and legendary; allegoric and heraldic; portraits. Includes many important examples dating of the 16th century including works by artists such as Belli and Giovanni Bernardi.

Madrid

MUSEO DEL PRADO

625   *Catálogo de las alhajas del Delfín.* Catalog by Diego Angulo Iñiguez. 2d. ed. Madrid: Museo del Prado, 1954-55. 146 pp., 24 b&w pls. (1st ed. 1944.)
        Collection of 120 French and Italian objects of rock crystal, agate, jasper, lapis lazuli, and cameos and goldsmith works of 16th and 17th centuries amassed by the elder son of Lousi XIV, which he gave to his son who had become king of Spain.

Paris

BIBLIOTHÈQUE NATIONALE

626   *Catalogue des camées antiques et modernes de la Bibliothèque nationale.* 2 vols. Catalog by Ernest Babelon. Paris: Ernest Leroux, 1897. 1:642 pp.; 2:76 b&w pls.
        179-page introduction clarifies terminology and describes various gems and techniques (pp. I-XXVI), discusses the antique gems and those of later periods in the library (see pp. LVIII-XCV for the 15th-16th centuries), and traces the formation of the collection. Catalog of 1,050 cameos: nos. 1-386, ancient, and nos. 387-1050, of the 15th-18th centuries, arranged by subject (religious, mythological, allegorical, antique revival, portraits); many date of the 15th and especially 16th century.

Vienna

KUNSTHISTORISCHES MUSEUM

627   *Die Kameen im Kunsthistorischen Museum.* Catalog by Fritz Eichler and Ernst Kris. Vienna: Anton Schroll, 1927. 256 pp., 84 b&w pls., 83 b&w figs.
        726 entries for cameos dating from classical times throughout the 19th century. Of the 15th-16th centuries are nos. 144 (Netherlandish), 145-387, 413 (Italian), 388-412, 414 (French, German, Netherlandish).

Windsor

WINDSOR CASTLE

628   FORTNUM, C. DRURY E. "Notes on Some of the Antique and Renaissance Gems and Jewels in Her Majesty's Collection at Windsor Castle." *Archaeologia* 45 (1877):1-28, 4 b&w pls., 3 line drawings.
        Several 16th-century cameos and intaglios with historiated subjects or portrait busts included in this repertory.

8. PRIVATE COLLECTION, AUCTION, AND DEALER CATALOGS

See entries 174, 721b, 723d, 726.

B. SINGLE COUNTRY OF ORIGIN

CZECHOSLOVAKIA (BOHEMIAN)

6. PERMANENT COLLECTIONS

Prague

SVATOVÍTSKÉHO POKLADU

629　BUKOVINSKÁ, BEKET. "Rudolfínská Kamej ze Svatovítského Pokladu." *Uměni* 22 (1974):58-64, 5 b&w figs.
Study of the lapis lazuli cameo with bust of Christ and of the Virgin set in enameled gold mount in the Treasury of St. Vit. Product of the workshop founded in Prague at the end of the 16th century by Rudolph II.

FRENCH

3. SURVEYS AND HISTORIES

630　FALKE, OTTO VON. "Gotische Kristallgefässe in Istanbul." *Pantheon* 14 (1934):208-10, 5 b&w figs.
Among 14th-15th century rock-crystal vessels found in the treasures of the sultans in the Old Seraglio, Istanbul, are four (one now in the Hermitage, Leningrad, the other in the Istanbul Museum) 15th century Franco-Burgundian ewers characterized by vertical facets and an angularly shaped handle. Three bear added Turkish or German goldsmith works.

6. PERMANENT COLLECTIONS

Cleveland

CLEVELAND MUSEUM OF ART

631　VERDIER, PHILIPPE. "A French Royal Cameo and Its Historical Background." *Bulletin of The Cleveland Museum of Art* 67 (1980):150-55. 9 b&w figs.
Agate cameo bust-length portrait of Charles VIII of France (1470-1498) closely related to a gold medal struck in 1494 by Louis Lapère and Niccolò Fiorentino in Lyon.

Florence

MUSEO DEGLI ARGENTI

632　HACKENBROCH, YVONNE. "A French Perfume Bottle in the Medici Collections in Florence," *Münchner Jahrbuch der bildenden Kunst* 36 (1985):72-80, 10 b&w figs.

This object is made of agate, rubies, and diamonds in an enamel gold mount with figures of youths, and dates of ca. 1525.

Vienna

KUNSTHISTORISCHES MUSEUM

633   LEITHE-JASPER, MANFRED. "Der Bergkristallpokal Herzog Philipps des Guten von Burgund–das 'Vierte Stück' der Geschenke König Karls IX. von Frankreich an Erzherzog Ferdinand II." *Jahrbuch der kunsthistorischen Sammlungen in Wien* 30 (1970):227-42, 14 b&w figs.

    Rock-crystal cup in gold mounts recorded in the 1467 inventory of Duke Philip the Good of Burgundy, gift of the French king Charles IX to Archduke Ferdinand II in 1570.

GERMAN

3. SURVEYS AND HISTORIES

634   REINEKING-VON BOCK, GISELA. *Bernstein: Das Gold der Ostsee.* Munich: Callwey, 1981. 185 pp., 21 color figs., 278 b&w figs., 14 text figs.

    Amber, extracted on the shores of the Baltic Sea, was a much favored material in North Germany, especially in the 16th-17th centuries, for the ornamentation of a variety of decorative arts objects. Volume presents its use from Roman times until the present day. Many examples of Renaissance cups, plates, candlesticks, knives and forks, necklaces, caskets, game boards are discussed and well illustrated.

635   ROHDE, ALFRED. *Bernstein, ein deutscher Wekstoff: Sein künstlerische Verarbeitung vom Mittelalter bis zum 18. Jahrhundert.* Berlin: Deutscher Verein für Kunstwissenschaft, 1937. 83 pp., 118 b&w pls. comprising 317 figs.

    Clear account of the diversity of uses of amber. The illustrations, however, are not of adequate quality to render the particular appeal of the medium often referred to as "the gold of the Baltic Sea."

6. PERMANENT COLLECTIONS

Baltimore

WALTERS ART GALLERY

636   SCARISBRICK, DIANA. "Forever Adamant: A Renaissance Diamond Ring." *Journal of the Walters Art Gallery* 40 (1982):57-64, 16 b& figs.

    Ring in the collection said to have been produced in Augsburg/Nuremberg ca. 1546 leads to a study of the use and purposes of diamonds in the 15th-16th centuries: cuttings, settings, mystical interpretations, symbolism, heraldic device.

Berlin

STAATLICHE MUSEEN PREUSSISCHER KULTURBESITZ, KUNSTGEWERBEMUSEUM

637   APPUHN, HORST. "Bürgereidkristall und Schwurlade." *Wallraf-Richartz Jahrbuch* 40 (1978):13-21, 15 b&w figs.

Deals with a silver and rock-crystal reliquary of 1443 used in oath-taking, formerly in the town hall in Lüneburg, relating it to similar receptacles.

ITALIAN

2. BIOGRAPHICAL DICTIONARIES

See entry 997.

3. SURVEYS AND HISTORIES

Book

638   KRIS, ERNST. *Meister und Meisterwerke der Steinschneidekunst in der italienischen Renaissance.* 2 vols. Vienna: Anton Schroll & Co., 1929. 1:202 pp.; 2:658 b&w figs.

Standard corpus of rock crystal and other semiprecious stones cut mostly by artists of Renaissance Italy. Important essay (148 pages) and catalog (forty-six pages) of 658 items including iconographic sources; all illustrated.

Articles

639   BEARD, CHARLES R. "Rock Crystals of the Renaissance." *Connoisseur* 107 (1941):186-93, 1 color pl., 11 b&w figs.

Cups, bowls, and intricate vessels in various public and private Eurpean collections carved from rock crystal and set in enameled gold mounts, often with the addition of gems, many from the Milanese workshop of the Saracchis, who worked for the German market. Also includes a rock-crystal crucifix and candlestick (Victoria and Albert Museum) generally attributed to Valerio Belli but here proposed to be by Giovanni Bernardi.

640   DISTELBERGER, RUDOLF. "Beobachtungen zu den Steinschneidewerkstätten der Miseroni in Mailand und Prag." *Jahrbuch der kunsthistorischen Sammlungen in Wien* 74 (1978):79-152, 88 b&w figs.

The oeuvre of Gasparo Miseroni and his workshop from ca. 1550-70; productions of the workshop in Milan ca. 1600 as known from the 1607-11 inventory of Emperor Rudolph II; its activity in Prague and its stylistic evolution.

641   DISTELBERGER, RUDOLF. "Die Sarachi-Werkstatt und Annibale Fontana." *Jahrbuch der kunsthistorischen Sammlungen in Wien,* n.s. 35 (1975):95-164, 72 b&w figs.

Etched rock-crystal cups, platters, and vases of the late 16th century produced in Milan, several of which were cut by the Saracchi Workshop after designs of Annibale Fontana.

642   FOCK, C. WILLEMIJN. "Vases en lapis-lazuli des collections médicéennes du seizième siècle." *Münchner Jahrbuch der bildenden Kunst* 27 (1976):119-54, 29 b&w figs.

Gold mounts on lapis lazuli vessels produced in the Medici Workshop from ca. 1567 until 1600 by the Florentine G.G. Cervi and the Dutch or German goldsmith Domes.

643 HACKENBROCH, YVONNE. "Commessi." *Antichità viva* 5, no. 3 (1966): 13-26, 2 color figs., 30 b&w figs.; *Metropolitan Museum of Art Bulletin* 24 (1966):212-24, 2 color figs., 29 b&w figs.

Large commessi of 1547-59, now in various collections, said to be due to the patronage of the court of the French king Henri II and produced by Italian arists such as Matteo da Nassero di Verona.

644 HOLZHAUSEN, WALTER. "Florentinisches Halbedelstein- Gefässe im Palazzo Pitti: Ein Kapitel aus dem Manierismus," *Pantheon* 3 (1929):16-24, 11 b&w figs.

To a large lapis lazuli vase of 1583 in enameled gold mounts (Museo degli Argenti, Florence) made by Jacopo Bylivelt on the design of Buontalenti for Francesco de' Medici, can be associated eight other vessels in the same institution and the Kunsthistorisches Museum, Vienna.

645 JESTAZ, BERTRAND. "Polo da Monte Cristaller: Cristal de roche et orfèvrerie à Venise au XVe siècle," *Arte veneta* 36 (1982):239-53.

Analysis of uncovered documents relating to the career of the Venetian carver of rock crystal Polo da Monte (active 1432, died 1494), producing cups, vases, necklaces, etc., for which he commissioned mounts from goldsmiths.

646 KRIS, ERNST. "Notes on Renaissance Cameos and Intaglios." *Metropolitan Museum Studies* 3 (1930-31):1-13, 27 b&w figs.

Renaissance carved gems at the Metropolitan Museum and elsewhere by Gian Giacomo Caraglio, Leone Leoni, Alessandro Masnago, and others.

647 KRIS ERNST. "Zur mailänder Glyptik der Renaissance." *Pantheon* 6 (1930):548-54, 10 b&w figs.

A carved rock-crystal pitcher in the Palazzo Pitti, Florence, is attributed to Giulio Taverna (active ca. 1540) of Milan; three carved rock-crystal plaques depicting the Labors of Hercules (formerly a series of twelve cut for a casket) all attributed to the Milanese sculptor Annibale Fontana (1540-87).

648 MC CRORY, MARTHA. "Some Gems from the Medici Cabinet of the Cinquecento." *Burlington Magazine* 21 (1979):511-14, 15 b&w figs.

Brief synopsis of gem collecting by the Medicis during the Renaissance: examines cameos and intaglios documented to have been in the Medici cabinet during the 16th century.

649 MIDDELDORF, ULRICH. "A Renaissance Jewel in a Baroque Setting." *Burlington Magazine* 118 (1976):157-58. Reprinted in *Raccolta di scritti, that is Collected Writings. III. 1974-1979.* Florence: Studio per Edizioni Scelte, 1981, pp. 43-48, figs. 45-48.

A small gold relief of the Virgin Mourning over the Body of Chirst set in a late 17th-century jewel now in a private collection, attributed to Guglielmo della Porta.

650 SLOMANN, VILHELM. "Rock-Crystals by Giovanni Bernardi." *Burlington Magazine* 48 (1926):9-23, 3 b&w pls. comprising 20 figs.

Giovanni's intaglios after drawings by Michelangelo; a crystal in the Pierpont Morgan Collection intended for, but never used in, the silver Farnese Casket in the Naples Museum; attribution to Giovanni of a rock-crystal jewel depicting the Entry into the Ark in the Bargello, Florence; four crystals carved for Cardinal Farnese traced to a silver casket in the Danske Nationalmuseet in Copenhagen.

651   ZORZI, GIANGIORGIO. "Alcuni rilievi sulla vita e le opere di Valerio Belli detto Vicentino." *L'arte* 23 (1920):181-94, 9 b&w figs.

Career of Valerio Belli, carver of gems and goldsmith in Rome and Vicenza of the 16th century, and description of his major works.

See also entries 998-1025 passim.

6. PERMANENT COLLECTIONS

Florence

MUSEO DEGLI ARGENTI

652   HOLZHAUSEN, WALTER. "Studien zum Schatz des Lorenzo il Magnifico im Palazzo Pitti," *Mitteilungen des kunsthistorischen Institutes in Florenz* 3 (1919-32):104-31, 25 b&w figs.

Study of the famed collection amassed by Lorenzo the Magnificent of vessels carved out of semiprecious stones and set in gold mounts and bearing his mark of ownership LAVR.MED now in the museum's collection.

MUSEO NAZIONALE

653   POGGI, GIOVANNI. "Di un cammeo di Giovan Antonio De' Rossi nel R. Museo Nazionale di Firenze." *Rivista d'arte* 9 (1916):41-45, 2 b&w pls.

Famed large cameo of 1556 with the portraits of Cosimo I de' Medici, Eleonora of Toledo, and their four sons.

Leningrad

HERMITAGE

654   KRASNOWA, NATALIE. "Rock-Crystals by Giovanni Bernardi in the Hermitage Museum." *Burlington Magazine* 56 (1930):37- 38, 3 b&w figs.

The author proposes that the three oval intaglios in the collection representing the Rape of Deianira, Venus and Adonis, and Dedalus and Icarus formed part of a series with three others (known from their casts) depicting the Rape of Ganymede, Tityus, and the Fall of Phaeton, executed in sketches by Perino del Vaga, to adorn a casket for Pier Luigi Farnese.

Madrid

MUSEO LÁZARO GALDIANO

655   SANZ, MARIA JESUS. "Vasos renacentistas de cristal de roca en el Museo Lázaro Galdiano." *Goya* 152 (1979):66-77, 16 b&w figs.

Outstanding 16th-century fanciful rock-crystal covered cups, ewers and plates with enameled gold mounts. Examples by Belli, the Saracchi, and others elsewhere.

XIII. Gems and Semiprecious Stones Including Rock Crystal and Amber

Milan

AMBROSIANA

656 KRIS, ERNST. "Di alcune opere inedite dell'Ambrosiana." *Dedalo* 9 (1928-29):387-99, 11 b&w illus.

Carved semiprecious stones by Caraglio, Girolamo Miseroni, wax portraits by Antonio Abondio among treasures of the collection.

Munich

STAATLICHE MÜNZSAMMLUNG

657 MIDDELDORF, ULRICH. "Un cammeo di Gian Giacomo Caraglio." *Vita veronese* 29 (1976):6-8. Reprinted in *Raccolta di scritti, that is Collected Writings. III. 1974-1979.* Florence: Studio per Edizioni Scelte, 1981, pp. 59-62, fig. 59.

Cameo of ca. 1550 representing Barbara Radziwill, queen of Poland, attributed to Gian Giacomo Caraglio.

Naples

MUSEO DUCA DI MARTINA

658 DE RINALDIS, ALDO. "Il cofanetto farnesiano del Museo di Napoli." *Bollettino d' arte* 17 (1923-24):143-65. 17 b&w figs.

Mannerist silver casket 49 cm. high fashioned (ca. 1544-61) by the Florentine goldsmith Manno (assistant of Cellini) with rock-crystal reliefs of classical scenes carved by Giovanni Bernardi after drawings of Perino del Vaga and others, for Cardinal Alessandro Farnese.

New York

METROPOLITAN MUSEUM OF ART

659 HACKENBROCH, YVONNE. "Goldsmiths' Work from Milan." *Metropolitan Museum of Art Bulletin* 23 (1965):258-64, 12 b&w figs.

A hat jewel from the former Pierpont Morgan Collection suggested as Milanese is the occasion for a brief discussion of the Sforza inventories.

660 LANGEDIJK, KARLA. "A Lapis Lazuli Medallion of Cosimo I de' Medici." *Metropolitan Museum Journal* 13 (1978):75-78. 6 b&w figs.

A gem portrait of Duke Cosimo I based on a portrait medal by Pietropaolo Galeotti, is here dated ca. 1567-88 by comparing it to similar dated and undated gems and medals bearing the duke's likeness.

Rome (Vatican)

MUSEO CRISTIANO

661 COTTON, A.G., and WALKER, R.M. "Minor Arts of the Renaissance in the Museo Cristiano." *Art Bulletin* 17 (1935):119-62.

Most important among objects discussed is the rock-crystal cross by Valerio Belli for Clement VII, the candlesticks and cross attributed to Antonio Gentile, and bronze plaques by Riccio and Leone Leoni.

662   KRIS, ERNST. "Di alcune opere ignote di Giovanni dei Bernardi nel Tesoro di San Pietro." *Dedalo* 9 (1928-29):97- 111, 26 b&w figs.

Gilt-silver cross and candlesticks (completed 1582) by Antonio Gentile with sixteen rock crystals on lapis lazuli by Giovanni Bernardi and Muzio Grandio on commission of Cardinal Alessandro Farnese for the high altar of St. Peter. Another and related series of rock crystals by Bernardi in Copenhagen.

Vienna

KUNSTHISTORISCHES MUSEUM

663   KRIS, E. "Zur italienischen Glyptik der Renaissance." *Pantheon* 13 (1934):116-19, 7 b&w figs.

A 16th-century Milanese rock-crystal goblet with engraved figures of the cardinal virtues copied from Peter Flötner, is connected to the Saracchi Workshop.

See also entries 1026-43 passim.

7. EXHIBITION CATALOGS

Florence

PALAZZO MEDICI RICCARDI

664   *Il Tesoro di Lorenzo il Magnifico.* 2 vols. Florence: Sansoni. Vol. 1, *Le gemme* (1973), by Nicole Dacos, Antonio Giuliano and Ulrico Pannuti, 167 pp., 15 color illus, 99 b&w illus.; Vol. 2, *I vasi* (1974), by Detlef Heikamp and Andreas Grote, 231 pp., 8 color illus., 109 b&w illus.

Exhibition catalogs of precious gems and vases owned by Lorenzo de' Medici (the Magnificent). Vol. 1: collection of sixty-two cameos and carnelians of classical times and the Renaissance period (pp. 65-66, nos. 40-42; pp. 78-79, 80-81, nos. 56-57, 60-62); vol. 2: sixty-one vases of rock crystal and other hard stones, most with gold mounts (pp. 129-59, nos. 28-61 of 15th-16th century). Imported apparatus of inventory and other documentary evidence.

See also entries 1044-49 passim.

8. PRIVATE COLLECTION, AUCTION, AND DEALER CATALOGS

WEIL COLLECTION

665   KRIS, ERNST. *Catalogue of Postclassical Cameos in the Milton Weil Collection.* Vienna: Anton Schroll & Co., 1923. 49 pp., 40 b&w pls.

Largely unpublished collection on long-term loan to the Metropolitan Museum at the time of publication. Includes 126 pieces, 36 of which are of the 16th century and mostly Italian with devotional subjects, others after the antique, as well as a portrait of Charles V by Leone Leoni.

WELLINGTON COLLECTION

666 WELLINGTON, DUKE OF. "The Scaffold George of Charles I." *Antiquaries Journal* 33 (1953):159-68, 2 b&w figs.

Onyx cameo with depiction of St. George Vanquishing the Dragon by Pier Maria Serbaldi da Pescia (ca. 1455-ca. 1522), active in Rome, held to have been worn by Charles I of England on the day of his beheading.

XIV. Metalwork — Introduction

A. MULTI COUNTRY OF ORIGIN

3. SURVEYS AND HISTORIES

Books

667 MARYON, HERBERT. *Metalwork and Enamelling: A Practical Treatise on Gold and Silversmiths' Work and their Allied Crafts.* 5th rev. ed. New York: Dover, [1971]. 347 pp., 29 b&w pls., 333 line drawings. (1st ed. 1912.)
Technical manual useful to laymen for understanding techniques and differentiating between those that are closely related (e.g. repoussé work and chasing, champlevé enamel and bassetaille). Also brief history of techniques; materials and tools used.

668 MICHAELIS, RONALD F. *Old Domestic Base-Metal Candlesticks from the 13th to 19th Century, Produced in Bronze, Brass, Paktong, and Pewter.* Woodbridge, Suffolk: Antique Collectors' Club, 1978. 139 pp., 203 b&w figs.
Types of alloys, manufacturing processes, candlestick types, centers of manufacture (Venice, Holland, Germany, England, Scandinavia) dealing mainly with later periods but including 15th-16th-century pricket candle holders (pp. 34-37), socket candlesticks (38-47), candlesticks with conical bases (49-57).

669 SELING, HELMUT, and DOMDEY-KNÖDLER, HELGA. *Europäische Stadtmarken die sie nicht verwechseln sollten: Typologie alter Goldschmiedemarken.* Munich: C.H. Beck/Weltkunst Verlag, 1984. 190 pp., facsimile town marks. English/French summaries.
Handy compilation of town marks arranged in typological order for most European countries based on standard published repertories such as Rosenberg, *Der Goldschmiede Merkzeichen* (entry 758). Very useful as an introduction to the field.

670 STEINGRÄBER, ERICH, ed. *Royal Treasures.* Ten contributors. Translated by Stefan de Haan. New York: Macmillan & Co., 1968. 100 pp., 92 color figs., line drawings.
Ten outstanding secular treasures belonging to princes in Florence, Paris, Madrid, Vienna, Munich, Dresden, Moscow, London, Copenhagen, and Stockllholm. Selections range from the 10th to the 19th century with many representing the period 1400-1600. Includes

jewels (crowns, scepters, orbs, imperial swords, etc.); plate (salts, ewers, goblets, etc.); enameled and bejeweled objects (pendants, salts, mirror frames, vessels, candlesticks); carved gems and rock crystals (intaglios, cameos, vessels).

671   SUTHERLAND, C.H.V. *Gold: Its Beauty, Power and Allure.* London: Thames & Hudson, 1959. 196 pp., 15 color pls., 54 b&w figs., 4 line drawings.
        Introductory survey of gold from antiquity to the 20th century: demand, trade, sources. Relevant to the 16th century is chap. 7 (pp. 128-45) mostly dealing with gold found in the New World.

Article

672   RASMUSSEN, JÖRG. "Mittelalterliche Nautilusgefässe." In *Studien zum europäischen Kunsthandwerk: Festschrift Yvonne Hackenbroch.* Munich: Klinkhardt & Biermann, 1983. Pp. 45-61, 11 b&w figs.
        Some of the sources for 15th-16th-century boat-shaped receptacles in France and Germany.

6. PERMANENT COLLECTIONS

Amsterdam

RIJKSMUSEUM

673   *Het goud-en zilverwerk in het Nederlandsch Museum voor gechiedenis en kunst te Amsterdam,* by A. Pit. Amsterdam: Gebroeders van Rijkom, [1901]. 42 pp., 34 b&w pls.
        Examples of Netherlandish, Flemish, French, Spanish, English, gold- and silversmith works of the 13th through 17th century in the museum's permanent collection. Includes several 15th-16th-century pyxes, drinking horns, necklaces, ewers, plates, cups, tazze, etc.

Leningrad

HERMITAGE

674   *Applied Art of the Middle Ages in the Collection of the State Hermitage: Artistic Metalwork,* by E.A. Lapkovskaya. English translation by L. Sorokina. Moscow: Iskusstvo, 1971. 39 pp., 87 color pls., 46 b&w figs. Text in Russian/English/German/French.
        Twenty-eight-page introduction tracing the history of the collection; presentation of eighty-four objects, with very brief captions, including some of the 15th-16th century: candelabra, aquamanile, mortar, horns, door-knocker, ciborium, monstrances, reliquary, chalices, crozier, plaque (nos. 46, 49-52, 72-73, 75- 84).

London

BRITISH MUSEUM

675   *Nielli, Chiefly Italian of the XV Century: Plates, Sulphur Casts and Prints Preserved in the British Museum,* Catalog by A.M. Hind. London: British Museum, 1936. 71 pp., 57 b&w figs.

Catalog of important nielli collection. Fifteen-page introduction deals with technique, types of niello work, and problems of attribution; reproduces excerpts from Theophilus and Vasari relating to the process, accounts by Maso Finiguerra, and notes pertaining to the early history of niello in Vasari and Cellini. Catalog with 324 entries of niello plates (nos. 1-133), and their presevation in sulphur casts (134-52), and prints (153-324). Includes concordance of numbers from previous studies by Duschene and Passavant dealing with nielli prints. A few German examples and modern forgeries.

VICTORIA AND ALBERT MUSEUM

676 *Catalogue of Chalices & Other Communion Vessels.* Catalog by W.W. Watts. London: His Majesty's Stationery Office, 1922. 84 pp., 28 b&w pls.

Forty-six-page introduction mostly discusses the metals from which chalices were wrought and the form and evolution of these vessels from the early days of the Church to the 18th century. Eighty-six catalog entries with several Italian, Flemish, English, Spanish, Hungarian, German, Dutch, and French 15th-16th-century examples.

New York

METROPOLITAN MUSEUM OF ART

677 HACKENBROCH, YVONNE. *Bronzes, Other Metalwork and Sculpture in the Irwin Untermyer Collection.* London: Thames & Hudson, 1962. 129 pp., 201 b&w pls., 27 b&w figs.

A fifty-seven-page introductory essay discusses the collection by place of origin (Venice, Milan, Padua, Florence, Rome; Flanders and Germany; Holland and Germany; England and France). This is followed by a repertory of 201 bronze statuettes, mortars, inkstands, brass chandeliers, iron firedogs, firetools, a fire back, etc., largely of the 15th-16th century, since bequeathed to the museum.

Paris

MUSÉE DES ARTS DÉCORATIFS

678 *Le Métal.* Vol. 2, *Le Bronze — le cuivre — l'étain — le plomb. Premier album: Du Moyen Age au milieu de XVIIIe sièle.* Catalog by Louis Metman and J.-L. Vaudoyer. Paris: Ateliers Photomécaniques D.A. Longuet, n.d. 24 pp., 777 figs. on 80 pls.

Nos. 49-174 (pls. II-XVI), mostly, cover the 15th-16th century: Flemish, Italian, and French keys, mortars, candleholders, door-knockers, relief sculpture, caskets, plates, appliqués, statuettes, liturgical objects, etc.

Toledo, Ohio

TOLEDO MUSEUM OF ART

679 RIEFSTAHL, RUDOLF M. "European Jeweled Arts." *Museum News* 13 (1970):50-70, 2 color illus. (cover), 42 b&w figs.

Brief history of Renaissance metalwork with emphasis on jewelry as seen through paintings and actual examples (a rosary, pendants, rings; flasks, bowls, cameos in gold, enameled and jeweled mounts, etc.), from the museum's collections.

See also entry 625.

7. EXHIBITION CATALOGS

Berlin

KUNSTGEWERBEMUSEUM, SCHLOSS KÖPENICK

680   *Metall im Kunsthandwerk.* Essays by nine contributors. Berlin: Staatliche Museen zu Berlin, 1967. 336 pp., many unnumbered b&w figs.
      Loan exhibition of German art objects wrought out of metal from various public collections of West and East Germany, Czechoslovakia, and Poland commemorating the centennial of the Museum of Decorative Arts of Berlin. Pertaining to the 15th-16th century are pp. 95-190, including bronze candlesticks, ewers, cups, pitchers, jewels, medals, plate; 273-312, arms, armor, and ironworks.

8. PRIVATE COLLECTION, AUCTION, AND DEALER CATALOGS

LEE COLLECTION

681   WATTS, W.W. "Treasures of Silversmiths' Work, The Collection of Viscount Lee of Fareham." *Country Life,* September 1928, 353-56, 390-93, 15 b&w figs.
      Overview of major pieces produced in Augsburg, Nuremberg, London, etc., mostly during the 16th century.

681a   WATTS, WILLIAM W. *Works of Art in Silver and Other Metals Belonging to Viscount and Viscountess Lee of Fareham.* London: Privately Printed, 1936. 26 pp., 118 pls.
      Catalog of 118 mostly European objects, all illustrated and accompanied by a descriptive entry. Eighteen-page introduction deals with the scope, character, and highlights of the collection; sec. 1 (nos. 1-35) deals with British silver including 15th- and 16th-century cups, tankards, mazers, tazze, goblets, salts, etc.; sec. 2 (36-67), German silver, including 15th- and 16th-century cups, beakers, tankards, aquamanile, salts, wine jug, etc.; sec. 3 includes an assortment of pieces from other countries including 15th- and 16th- century medals, plaquettes, small bronze figures, chalices, ciborium, cups, crucifix, spoons, candlesticks, etc.

ROTHSCHILD (JAMES) COLLECTION

682   JONES, E. ALFRED. *A Catalogue of the Collection of the Baroness James de Rothschild.* London: Constable & Co., 1912. 200 pp., 101 b&w pls.
      Outstanding collection including some 16th-century German (primarily) and Spanish tankards, cups, caskets, flasks, chalices, small shields, pyxes, statuettes, reliquaries, and Limoges enamels. Short catalog entries; useful primarily for illustration.

RECENT MULTI OWNER AUCTIONS

683   *Collection de médaillons et plaques en bronze peint ou doré et en plomb. Italie, Allemagne, Flandres, XVe-XVIIe siècle.* Sale held in Paris at Hôtel Drouot 31 October 1984. Paris: Maîtres Couturier et Nicolay Commissaires-Priseurs Associés, 1984. 31 pp., 2 color figs., 17 b&w figs.

Sale includes important plaque of Christ before Pilate by Léonard Limosin (lot 25); other Limoges (24); about forty Italian, German, French, and Flemish plaquettes and/or medals (several aftercasts).

684   *European Sculpture and Works of Art.* Sale held in London at Christie's 3 July 1985. 97 pp., 30 color figs., 90 b&w figs.
Among the 258 lots of the 15th century are a brass mount (lot 28) and a French crozier (29); of the 16th century are two wood caskets (51, 54), and several Italian, German, and Netherlandish bronzes (plaquettes, medallions, sandbox, mortar, reliefs, statuettes, etc.. — 97-98, 102-5, 107, 110-13, 116-17).

B. SINGLE COUNTRY OF ORIGIN

BELGIUM

3. SURVEYS AND HISTORIES

685   COLLON-GEVAERT, SUZANNE. *Histoire des arts du métal en Belgique.* Académie royale de Belgique, Classe des Beaux-Arts, Mémoires, vol. 7. 2 parts. Brussels: Palais des Académies, 1951. 1:476 pp.; 2:109 b&w figs.
The most comprehensive survey of metalwork produced in the geographical area that is now Belgium; bronze, goldsmith and ironwork, pewter and lead. Candlesticks, mortars, lecterns, chalices, plate, etc., of the 15th-16th century from the Meuse Valley, Flanders, and Brabant are discussed within chaps. 8-12 (pp. 248-418). Includes six-page glossary.

BRITISH (SCOTTISH)

3. SURVEYS AND HISTORIES

686   HOW, G.E.P. "Canongate Goldsmiths and Jewellers." *Burlington Magazine* 74 (1939):282-88, 8 b&w figs.
Brief history of goldsmithing in Canongate, once a separate district of Edinburgh, from the 16th through 19th century; presents examples of gold/silversmith works, including a mazer of 1557 and a spoon of 1589. Repertory of goldsmiths.

FRENCH

3. SURVEYS AND HISTORIES

687   HAVARD, HENRY. *Histoire de l'orfèvrerie française.* Paris: May & Metteroz, 1896. 473 pp., 5 hand-colored pls., 332 line drawings.
Early important study of French gold- and silversmith works from antiquity through the 19th century; relevant to the years 1400-1600 are chaps. 8-9 (pp. 143-86) dealing with the formation and the role of the goldsmith associations; chap. 12 (219-82) on 15th-century productions; chap. 13 (283-308) including 15th- and 16th-century enamels; chap. 14 (309-54)

on 16th-century works; chap. 15 (355-96) including 16th-century jewelry. Covers a wide assortment of secular and ecclesiastical objects with reference to documentary source. Lacks, however, adequate illustration and index.

4. BIBLIOGRAPHICAL GUIDES

688 MARQUET DE VASSELOT, JEAN JOSEPH. *Bibliographie de l'orfèvrerie et de l'émaillerie françaises.* Société Française de Bibliographie. Paris: August Picard, 1925. 305 pp.

A bibliography of more than twenty-seven hundred books and articles from the 18th century to the time of publication on the history of French goldsmithing and enamels. Classifications are: techniques, trades, marks, models, subjects, periods, geographical locations, museums, exhibitions, private collections, church treasuries, artists, specific objects. Index of authors, persons, and places.

ITALIAN

3. SURVEYS AND HISTORIES

689 PLON, EUGÈNE. *Benvenuto Cellini, orfèvre, médailleur, sculpteur: Recherche sur sa vie, sur son oeuvre et sur les pièces qui lui sont attribuées.* Paris: E. Plon, 1883. 414 pp., 82 b&w pls.

Well-documented if dated biography (pp. 1-134) of the famed 16th-century Florentine goldsmith and sculptor; essay on his known works (135-243) and on attributions (244-377); includes appendixes with quotations from inventories.

690 POPE-HENNESY, JOHN. *Cellini.* London: Macmillan & Co., 1985. 324 pp., 54 color pls., 101 b&w pls., 103 b&w figs.

Sumptuous and comprehensive biography of the famed autobiographer and his work in Florence, Rome, Ferrara, and Paris. Detailed study of the Saltcellar of Francis I (chap. 5), the Nymph of Fontainebleau (4), the Perseus of the Loggia dei Lanzi (7), and the marble Crucifix at the Escorial (9).

SPANISH

3. SURVEYS AND HISTORIES

691 DAVILLIER, CH. *Recherches sur l'orfèvrerie en Espagne au Moyen Age et à la Renaissance (documents inédits tirés des archives espagnoles).* Paris: A. Quantin, 1879. 292 pp., 53 line drawings.

Part 1; history of ecclesiastical and secular Spanish metalwork: liturgical implements, arms, statuettes, medals, table plate, personal jewelry; Moorish, French, Italian influences; confraternities and regulations, styles, excerpts from inventories, etc. Part 2, chronological listing of principal Spanish metalworkers from the 10th to the 17th century (pp. 163-254 of the 15th-16th century); indexes of subjects and names.

7. EXHIBITION CATALOGS

Madrid

SOCIEDAD ESPAÑOLA DE AMIGOS DEL ARTE

692   *Orfebrería civil española.* Exhibition catalog by Pedro Mg. de Artíñaño. Madrid: Mateu, Artes e Industrias Gráficas, 1925. 163 pp., 41 b&w pls., facsimile town marks.

      1,231 pieces of secular goldsmith work of Spain dating from Neolithic times until the 19th century. Includes many examples of jewels, armor, plate, mounted stones, maces, and plaques dating of the 15th-16th century mostly drawn from private collections. Preceding is a seventy-five-page essay and a thirteen-page table of town marks.

U.S.S.R. (RUSSIAN AND GEORGIAN)

3. SURVEYS AND HISTORIES

693   GOLDBERG, T.; MICHOUKOV, F.; PLATONOVA, N.; and POSTNIKOVA-LOSSEVA, M. *Russkoe zolotoe i serebriãnoe delo XV- XX bekob. L'Orfèvrerie et la bijouterie russes aux XV- XX siècles.)* Moscow: Nauka, 1967. 307 pp., 5 color pls., 104 b&w figs., line drawings, facsimile town and makers' marks. Text in Russian, with nine-page-summary, captions, and list of illustrations in French.

      Principal centers (Novgorod, Moscow, etc.), style and ornaments (in 15th century filigree combined, in the 16th century, with enamel), variety of metals and stones used, types of objects, goldsmith corporations, marks (17th-20th century).

694   PISSARSKAIA, L; PLATONOVA, N.; OULIANOVA, B.; and POSTNIKOVA-LOSSEVA, M. *Russkie emali XI-XIX VV. iz sobranij gosudarstvennyj muzeev Moskovskovskogo Kremlja, Gosudarstvennogo Istoriceskogo Muzeja, Gosudarstvennogo Ermitaza (Les Émaux russes XIe-XIXe siècle. Collections des musées: Musées du Kremlin de Moscou, Musée Historique d'État, L'Ermitage.)* Moscow: Iskusstvo, 1974. 240 pp., 121 color pls. Text in Russian, with three-page summary and entries in French (translated by A. Nekrassov).

      Presentation of 121 major Russian goldsmith works of the 11th through the 19th century produced for liturgical or court ceremonial use and now mostly housed in the State Kremlin Museum, the Historical Museum, and the Hermitage: no. 12 is a gospel book binding dated 1499; 13-29 are 16th-century cups, crosses, icons, and a pendant.

7. EXHIBITION CATALOGS

Paris

GALERIES NATIONALES DU GRAND PALAIS

695   *Au Pays de la Toison d'or: Art ancien de Géorgie soviétique.* Exhibition catalog by Ioulon Gagochidze, Gouran Abramishvili, Nana Bourtchouladze, et al., introduction by Danielle Gaborit-Chopin, essay by Tamaz Sanikidze and Ioulon Gagochidze. Paris: Association Française d'Action Artistique, 1982. 224 pp., 19 color figs., 156 b&w figs.

Exhibition of 122 masterpieces of Georgian art—mostly metalwork—dating from about 2200 B.C. to the 17th century from the collections of three Georgian museums. Chronologically arranged entries provide technical description and bibliography. Glossary.

YUGOSLAVIAN

7. EXHIBITION CATALOGS

Belgrade

MUZEJ PRIMENJENE UMETNOSTI

696   *Umetnička Obrada Metala Naroda Jugoslavije kroz Vekove.* 2 vols. Exhibition catalog by Juan Bach, Bojana Radojković, and Durdica Comisso. Belgrade: Muzej Primenjene Umetnosti, 1956. 1:30 pp., 125 b&w figs.; 2:110 pp.

Vol. 1: historical introduction, bibliography, illustrations; vol. 2: brief catalog entries for 1,252 objects of Yugoslav metalwork (mostly gold and silver) ranging from the 7th to the 20th century with many examples of the 15th and 16th century; includes chalices, censers, reliquaries, monstrances, croziers, crucifixes, ewers, standing cups, bowls, salts, jewelry, etc.

XV. Jewelry

A. MULTI COUNTRY OF ORIGIN

1. DICTIONARIES AND ENCYCLOPEDIAS

697 NEWMAN, HAROLD. *An Illustrated Dictionary of Jewelry.* London: Thames & Hudson, 1981. 335 pp., 16 color pls., 669 b&w figs.
"2,530 entries, including [informative and concise] definitions of jewels, gemstones, materials, processes, and styles, and entries on principal designers and makers, from antiquity to the present day" (from title page). Historical background included in entries; short bibliographical references in some; many cross references.

3. SURVEYS AND HISTORIES

Books

698 BATTKE, HEINZ. *Geschichte des Ringes in Beschreibung und Bildern.* Pforzheim: Meyle & Müller Graphische Kunstanstalt, 1953. 111 pp., 29 pls. comprising 205 figs., some in color.
Short history of rings by types and period. Each plate (mediocre reproductions) illustrates several examples for which there are long captions in the text. For the period 1400-1600, see pp. 57-66, pls. XIII-XVIII.

699 EVANS, JOAN. *A History of Jewellery 1100-1870.* London: Faber & Faber, [1953]. 240 pp., with 35 text figs., 10 color pls., 176 b&w pls.
Historical survey written mostly from the standpoint of patronage and fashion. Period 1400-1600 covered on pp. 71-136.

700 GREGORIETTI, GUIDO. *Jewelry through the Ages.* Translated by Helen Lawrence. New York: American Heritage, 1969. 319 pp., 400 illus., more than half in color. *From Il gioiello nei secoli.* Milan: Arnoldo Mondadori, 1969.
Broad, well-illustrated introduction to jewelry from prehistoric to modern times; goldsmiths, patrons, types of jewelry, and styles as seen from painted portraits as well as extant pieces. For the period 1400-1600, see pp. 173-208. Five- page table of precious stones.

701   HACKENBROCH, YVONNE. *Renaissance Jewellery.* London: Sotheby Parke Bernet, 1979. 124 pp., 45 color pls., 927 b&w figs. with details.

Comprehensive survey of Renaissance jewelry. Five-page introduction deals with patronage, styles, goldsmiths, designs and techniques; separate chapters deal with jewelry and jeweled objects from Italy (pp. 2-52), France (54-104), Germany (106-222), the Netherlands (224-64), England (266-306), and Portugal and Spain (308-43). Well illustrated including comparative material in paintings, drawings, engravings, etc. Twenty-seven pages of extracts from contemporary documents.

702   LANLLIER, JEAN, and PINI, MARIE-ANNE. *Cinq siècles de joallerie en Occident.* Fribourg: Office du Livre, 1971. 336 pp., 273 figs., many in color.

Broad survey of European jewelry from the 16th to the 20th century with quality illustration. Pp. 41-76 deal with the Renaissance period primarily in France and England.

703   PUIFORCAT. *L'Orfèvrerie française et étrangère.* Paris: Garnier Frères, 1981. 191 pp., 30 color pls., 129 b&w figs.

Basic information on different metals and technical processes (pp. 6-21), confraternities, regulations, hallmarks (22-31), followed by a very general historic/artistic survey of jewelry from Egyptian times to the 20th century (48-57, 141-42, 166-71, 173-74, 179-81, 183-85 are relevant to the 15th-16th centuries).

704   SMITH, H. CLIFFORD. *Jewellery* London: Methuen, 1908. 457 pp., 4 color pls., 50 b&w pls., 33 b&w text figs.

From Egyptian times to the 19th century; early introduction to the subject illustrated by examples mostly in the Victoria and Albert Museum.

705   STEINGRÄBER, ERICH. *Alter Schmuck: Die Kunst des europäischen Schmuckes.* Munich: Hermann Rinn, 1956. 191 pp., 7 color figs., 333 b&w figs.

General history of secular jewelry from the 9th through the 19th century. A chapter deals with the so-called Burgundian-style jewels of the 15th century, another with brooches, buckles, medals, and pendants made for the German burghers; others with the courts of Florence, Spain, and Prague.

706   TWINING, EDWARD FRANCIS. *European Regalia.* London: B.T. Batsford, 1967. 351 pp., 96 b&w pls. with several illus. on each, 8 line drawings.

Origin, development and meaning attributed to the principal royal ornaments—crowns, scepters, orbs, swords, annointing vessels—and to some lesser ones—lances, bracelets, spurs, rings, keys of state—from earliest origins to the present day. Chapter on royal obsequies with an appendix of royal tombs that have been opened and found to contain regalia. Companion volume to following entry.

706a   TWINING, EDWARD FRANCIS. *A History of the Crown Jewels of Europe.* London: B.T. Batsfrod, 1960. 747 pp., 230 b&w pls. with several illus. on each.

Comprehensive work dealing with the crown jewels and regalia of all of the kingdoms of Christian Europe from the 3d to the 20th century. Historical background for each realm, description of ceremonies, traditions, ornaments as known from inventories, chronicles, as well as extant pieces.

707   WARD, ANNE; CHERRY, JOHN; GERE, CHARLOTTE; and CARTLIDGE, BARBARA. *Rings through the Ages.* New York: Rizzoli, 1981. 214 pp., 46 color figs., 359 b&w figs.

General survey. On the 15th century, pp. 51-86: inscriptions, materials, shapes, and types, followed by a catalog (nos. 153-203); on the 16th century, pp. 89-133: documentary sources, drawings, etc., cutting of gemstones, catalog (nos. 205-18).

Articles

708   BEARD, CHARLES R. "Cap-Brooches of the Renaissance." *Connoisseur* 104 (1939):287-93, 1 color pl., 14 b&w figs.
       French, Italian, German, English hat jewels of the 15th-16th century; their representation in paintings of the time.

709   FOCK, C. WILLEMIJN. "Les Orfèvres-joailliers étrangers à la cour des Médicis" in *Firenze e la Toscana dei Medici nell'Europa del '500.* Vol. 3, *Relazioni artistiche, il linguaggio architettonico europeo.* Florence: Leo S. Olschki, 1983. Pp. 831-59, 4 b&w figs.
       Useful synthesis of the activity of non-Italian goldsmiths at the Medici court in the second half of the 16th century. Addenda with archival documents.

6. PERMANENT COLLECTIONS

Baltimore

WALTERS ART GALLERY

710   *Jewelry: Ancient to Modern.* Catalog edited by Anne Garsicle, with various contributors. New York: Viking Press; Baltimore: Walters Art Gallery, 1980. 256 pp., 116 color figs., 528 b&w figs.
       Catalog of 715 pieces from the permanent collection. Includes (pp. 171-211) 15th- and 16th-century European rings, pendants, hat badges, rosary beads, crucifixes, amulets, belts, engraved gems, etc., in a variety of precious and semiprecious materials with brief catalog entries. Pertinent to the period 1400-1600 are brief essays and catalog entries by Richard H. Randall, Jr., and Diana Scarisbrick.

Berlin

STAATLICHE MUSEEN PREUSSISCHER KULTURBESITZ, KUNSTGEWEBEMUSEUM

711   *Die Ringsammlung des Berliner Schlossmuseums zugleich eine Kunst- und Kulturgeschichte des Ringes.* Catalog by Heinz Battke. Berlin: Leonhard Preiss, 1938. 114 pp., 16 b&w pls.
       Collection of 245 rings from all periods and places; nos. 58-73 are 15th-century Italian and German; 74-90 are 16th-century Italian, French, and German. Includes forty-seven-page introduction.

Cologne

KUNSTGEWERBEMUSEUM DER STADT KÖLN

712 *Schmuck.* Catalog by Anna Beatriz Chadour and Rüdiger Joppien. 2 vols. Cologne: Kunstegewerbemuseum der Stadt Köln, 1985. Vol. 1, *Hals-, Ohr-, Arm- und Gewandschmuck,* 596 pp., 24 color pls., numerous b&w figs.; vol. 2, *Fingerringe,* 373 pp., 4 color pls., numerous b&w figs.

Collection catalog of 910 jewelry pieces from the earliest times until the present day and from all countries (major holdings are the Clemens, Sieversen, and the Treshow Collections). Material organized by types, often includes lengthy descriptions and comments on style and construction. Examples of the 15th-16th century are found throughout. Includes ten pages of diagrams defining elements of jewelry; a twenty-page glossary and a fifty-two-page bibliography.

London

BRITISH MUSEUM

713 *Franks Bequest: Catalogue of the Finger Rings, Early Christian, Byzantine, Teutonic, Medieval and Later.* Catalog by O.M. Dalton. 378 pp., 30 b&w pls., 17 text figs.

Introduction (pp. xiii-lvii) deals with the provenance of the collection, classifications, uses, dating, components and types of rings. 2,532 catalog entries follow including many European examples of 1400-1600: signet rings (set with antique and Renaissance gems, crystal, and engraved with heraldic monograms), devotional and ecclesiastical rings, amulet rings, inscribed rings, love and marriage rings, memorial and official rings.

VICTORIA AND ALBERT MUSEUM

714 *Catalogue of Rings,* by C.C. Oman. London: Victoria and Albert Museum, 1930. 170 pp., 40 b&w pls.

Introduction (pp. 1-43) on the manner of wearing rings and their various types. Catalog including 15th- and 16th-century European rings of all types: decorative (nos. 263-314); signet (482-92, 513-28, 535-65, 583-610); betrothal, wedding, and love (624a-62); religious and magical (717-40a, 760-73); commemorative (783); papal (917-33); and fancy (939-40).

715 COCKS, ANNA SOMERS. *An Introduction to Courtly Jewellery.* Warminster: Compton Press; London: Victoria and Albert Museum, Pitman House, 1980. 48 pp., 40 color figs., 5 line drawings.

History of English and Continental jewelry from the 15th to the 17th century as represented in the museum's collection: importance and function of jewelry in courtly life (exchange in diplomatic encounters, reward for services, symbol of office, heraldic, religious, and amorous insignias, etc.); types, forms, designs.

716 *Jewellery Gallery Summary Catalog,* by Shirley Bury. London: Victoria and Albert Museum, 1982. 252 pp., numerous b&w fig.

Summary catalog of major holdings formed by the Evans, Cory, Townshend collections and other bequests. The objects are succinctly described in the order they are exhibited; those pertaining to the 15th-16th century are watches, rings, brooches, pendants, enamels, livery collars, hat badges, lockets, reliquary crosses, pomanders, etc., from most European countries.

717   *An Introduction to Rings,* by Shirley Bury. London: Her Majesty's Stationery Office, 1984. 48 pp., 27 color figs., 21 b&w figs.

Useful, appealing introduction to the history of ring-making and wearing as seals or symbols of love and marriage based on examples in the museum's collection. Includes several 15th-16th century rings with good color illustrations.

Milan

MUSEO POLDI PEZZOLI

See entry 72.

Oxford

ASHMOLEAN MUSEUM

718   *Finger Rings from Ancient Egypt to the Present Day.* Exhibition held in London at Goldsmith's Hall and at Oxford, Ashmolean Museum. Catalog by Gerald Taylor and Diana Scarisbrick. London: Lund Humphries, 1978. 100 pp., 8 color pls., 191 b&w figs., line drawings.

1,006 examples in the Ashmolean from the collections of C.D.E. Fortnum and John Evans. Nine-page essay on the two English connoisseurs and their collections; two-page introduction to rings and their wearing followed by seven pages of diagrams on the typology and parts of rings and brief descriptions of types. Several 15th-16th-century examples.

718a   SCARISBRICK, DIANA. "Rings in the Fortnum Collection." *Connoisseur* 199 (1978):114-20, 18 color figs., 15 b&w figs.

Highlights of European finger rings, 13th-17th century, from the permanent holdings; deals with both ecclesiastical and secular types, illustrating many 15th- and 16th-century examples.

7. EXHIBITION CATALOGS

Chicago

LOYOLA UNIVERSITY, MARTIN D'ARCY GALLERY OF ART

719   *The Art of Jewelry 1450-1650: A Special Exhibition of Jewels and Jeweled Objects from Chicago Collections.* Exhibition catalog by Donald F. Rowe. Chicago: Loyola University of Chicago, 1975. 72 pp., 90 b&w figs.

Fifty-two catalog entries include pendants, badges, rings, beakers, medallions, necklaces, crowns, etc., from major European countries; pieces are generally secular. Includes many hitherto unknown objects from private collections [ex-Thomas Flannery, etc.]

London

VICTORIA AND ALBERT MUSEUM

720   *Princely Magnificence: Court Jewels of the Renaissance, 1500-1630.* Exhibition catalog entries and essays by fifteen authors. London: Debrett's Peerage, 1980. 140 pp., many color and b&w illus.

Catalog of exhibit drawn from various European collections: contains brief essays on the status and making of jewelry (pp. 3-7); social implications of jewels (8-11); sources of gemstones (12-19); cuttings and settings (20-26); dress in Western Europe (27-30), and English jewels (31-40). Descriptive catalog entries for 127 objects including pendants, rings, prayer book covers, miniature case, lockets, hat jewels, necklaces, reliquary crosses, crowns, orbs, sceptres, etc., of all European nations; twenty-nine additional catalog entries of portraits with sitters wearing jewelry; fifty further entries of graphic designs for jewelry. Comprehensive treatment of subject.

8. PRIVATE COLLECTION, AUCTION, AND DEALER CATALOGS

DESMONI COLLECTION

721   D'OTRANGE-MASTAI, M.L. "A Collection of Renaissance Jewels." *Connoiseur* 139 (1957):126-32, 2 color pls., 28 b&w figs.

The Martin J. Desmoni Collection, New York, comprising above all, many enameled pendants. Useful for illustrations.

721a   *Exhibition of Renaisance Jewels Selected from the Collection of Martin J. Desmoni.* Exhibition held in San Francisco at the M.H. De Young Memorial Museum. Catalog by Yvonne Hackenbroch. New York: Privately Printed, 1958. 56 pp., 4 color pls., 16 b&w pls.

Brief entry and illustration for sixty-six secular and thirty-eight devotional pendants, medals, rings, nearly all dating of the 16th-17th century from Italy, Spain, Hungary, Germany, and France.

721b   *Catalogue of the Well-Known Collection of Renaissance Jewellery the Property of Martin J. Desmoni, Esq., of New York City.* Sale held in London at Sotheby's 17 May 1960. 47 pp., 4 color pls., 21 b&w pls.

125 lots including an enameled gold armlet attributed to Cellini, Venetian pendant formed as a nef, German pendant in the shape of a mermaid, cameos, intaglios, rings, crosses, rock- crystal and agate goblets and vases with enameled gold mounts.

GUILHOU COLLECTION

722   DE RICCI, SEYMOUR. *Catalogue of a Collection of Ancient Rings Formed by the Late E. Guilhou.* Paris: Privately Printed, 1912. 194 pp., 24 b&w pls. Reprint. Somerset, England: Hillmann Printers (Fromme), n.d.

Largest collection ever gathered in France of rings and including the celebrated ring of the Black Prince. 1,636 entries with cursory descriptions and small illustrations. Nos. 1093-1197 are medieval examples; 1208-1319 are armorial rings of the 14th-16th century; 1332-1570 are of Renaissance times.

XV. Jewelry

GUTMAN COLLECTION

723   D'OTRANGE, M.L. "A Collection of Renaissance Jewels at the Art Institute of
Chicago." *Connoisseur* 130 (1952):66- 74, 1 color pl., 12 b&w figs.
       A selection of outstanding, and mainly 16th-century, pieces on loan from the Melvin
Gutman Collection: enameled and bejeweled pendants, necklaces, cameos, vessels of semi-
precious stones, etc.

723a   D'OTRANGE, M.L. "Jewels of the XVth and XVIth Centuries." *Connoisseur* 132
(1953):126-33, 1 color pl., 16 b&w figs.
       Pendants and brooches for devotional and sentimental purposes, produced in
Flanders, Italy, and Germany, and at the time of writing part of the Gutman Collection,
reflecting the evolution of taste in 15th-16th-century design.

723b   NORFOLK, NORFOLK MUSEUM OF ARTS AND SCIENCES. *The Melvin Gutman
Collection of Antique Jewelry.* Norfolk: Norfolk Museum of Arts and Sciences, 1966. 51
pp., 17 color pls., 56 b&w figs.
       Catalog of 150 brief entries for objects from this collection on long-term loan to the
museum. Items range from antiquity to the 19th century and include 15th-16th-century
cameos, pendants, crucifixes, boxes, a mirror, earrings, necklaces, etc. (See also following
entry.)

723c   BALTIMORE, BALTIMORE MUSEUM OF ART. *Renaissance Jewels and Jeweled
Objects from the Melvin Gutman Collection.* Catalog by Parker Lesley. Baltimore: Baltimore Museum of Art, 1968. 194 pp., 5 color pls., 146 b&w figs.
       Seventy outstanding objects from this well-known collection, nearly all dating 1400-
1600 and most being of Italian, German, or Spanish origin: crosses, pendants, necklaces, a
pomander.

723d   *Medieval and Renaissance Jewelry and Vessels of Rock Crystal and Other Semi-Precious
Stones. The Melvin Gutman Collection.* Sale held in New York at Parke-Bernet. Part 1:
24 April 1969, 88 pp., 4 color pls., 100 b&w figs.; Part 2: 17 October 1969, 96 pp., 4 color
pls., 103 b&w figs.
       A total of 290 lots of secular and devotional jewelry from most major European
countries: jeweled and enameled pendants, cameos, necklaces, mirrors, pectoral crosses,
paxes, plaques, vessels fashioned from carved rock crystal and other semiprecious stones,
carved boxwood nuts, a rosary, etc. Many of the 145 lots from the second part of the sale
date of the 17th and 19th centuries and a few are Byzantine.

LOVE COLLECTION

724   *Important Gold Boxes and Renaissance Jewellery Including Property Sold by the Order of
the Audrey B. Love Foundation from the Collection of C. Ruxton Love.* Sale held in
Geneva at Christie's 13 November 1984. 62 pp., 35 color pls.
       Sale included a few (lots 42, 45-48) but very select 16th- century jewels: a rock-crystal
cross (circle of Belli), a highly important Paris brooch of ca. 1540 with Hercules, and large
Italian pearl pendants.

OATES COLLECTION

725   OATES, F.A. HARMAN. *Catalogue of Finger Rings Brought Together by F.A. Harman Oates, F.S.A.* London: Privately Printed, 1917. Reprint. London: Thomas Heneage, 1981. 14 pp., 5 b&w pls.
      Collection of 101 gold, silver, bronze, iron, lead, latten, and solid carnelian rings formed between 1911-17 described in brief entries. Most of the thirty-one dating of the 15th-16th century are English, the others being Italian, French, and Turkish.

PIERPONT MORGAN COLLECTION

See entry 174.

THYSSEN-BORNEMISZA COLLECTION

726   COCKS, ANNA SOMERS, and TRUMAN, CHARLES. *The Thyssen-Bornemisza Collection: Renaissance Jewels, Gold Boxes and Objets de Vertu.* London: Philip Wilson for Sotheby Publications, 1984. 384 pp., 143 color illus., numerous b&w figs.
      Catalog of 139 objects from this outstanding private collection ranging from the 16th through 20th century; profusely illustrated, often with comparative material. For 16th-century items, see cat. nos. 1-26, 35-36, 40, 42 (pendants, cameos, necklaces, rock-crystal and semiprecious stone vessels), and introduction (pp. 10-61) dealing with collecting, production, acquisition, and technique. Index of makers' marks.

WERNHER COLLECTION

727   SMITH, H. CLIFFORD. "Renaissance Jewellery in the Wernher Collection at Luton Hoo." *Connoisseur* 125 (1950):76-81, 132; 22 b&w figs.
      Private collection of some seventy 16th-century cameos, intaglios, rings, cap badges, etc., produced in Italy, Germany, or Spain.

B. SINGLE COUNTRY OF ORIGIN

BRITISH (ENGLISH AND SCOTTISH)

3. SURVEYS AND HISTORIES

Books

728   EVANS, JOAN. *English Jewellery from the Fifth Century A.D. to 1800.* London: Methuen & Co., 1921. 168 pp., 2 color pls., 32 b&w pls.
      Jewelry intended for ceremonial use by the crown princes and the clergy and also for personal adornment. Pertinent to the years 1400-1600 are: pp. 46-67 (late Middle Ages); 68-86 (early Renaissance); 87-109, Elizabethan cameo and portrait jewels.

729   OMAN, CHARLES. *British Rings 800-1914.* London: B.T. Batsford, 1974. 146 pp., 4 color pls., 96 b&w pls., all with several figs.

Concise study of English and Scottish rings. Chaps. 1-2 deal with the wearing of rings and their makers, materials, and marking. Chaps. 3-11 are headed according to use: decorative, signet, love, political and portrait, religious, scientific, magical, medicinal, and mourning rings, rings with miscellaneous inscriptions. Catalog listings complement the illustrations of 518 pieces, which include many 15th-16th-century examples.

Articles

730   JENKINS, C.K. "Collars of SS: A Quest." *Apollo* 49 (1949):60-63, 1 color pl., 5 b&w figs.
        Motif common on royal heraldry and in English collars is a stylized swan or more probably a peacock famous as a regal symbol since Jacques de Longuyon's *Vows of the Peacock* of 1310.

731   JONES, E. ALFRED. "The Gold Collar of SS." *Connoisseur* 109 (1942):14-18, 8 b&w figs.
        Collars seemingly devised by Henry IV depicted on portraits and effigies of English monarchs, noblemen, judges, and officers of the colleges of arms; four extant examples date of the 16th and 19th century; the Founder's Cup at Oriel College, Oxford, with the same motif.

732   JONES, E. ALFRED. "Some Notes on Nicholas Hilliard Miniaturist and Goldsmith c. 1547-1617." *Connoisseur* 112 (1943):3-6, 1 color pl., 10 b&w figs.
        Hilliard as goldsmith of Elizabeth I designing seals and the Armada Jewel (Victoria and Albert Museum).

733   TAIT, HUGH. "Historiated Tudor Jewellery." *Antiquaries Journal* 42 (1962):226-46, 41 b&w figs.
        English enameled goldsmith works of ca. 1525-75 — pendants, hat jewels, book-covers — compared to Italian prototypes.

6. PERMANENT COLLECTIONS

London

LONDON MUSEUM

734   *The Cheapside Hoard of Elizabethan and Jacobean Jewellery.* Catalog by R.E. Mortimer Wheeler. London: London Museum, 1928. 35 pp., 4 color pls., 11 b&w pls., 6 line drawings.
        Catalog of mostly 16th-century English jewelry from the Cheapside hoard discovered in London in 1912, distinguished by size and range. Describes history and discovery of hoard with detailed entries including chains (pp. 14-15), bracelets (16), pendants and earrings (18-23), hat ornaments (24), crystal and glass objects (26), and gems (intaglios, cameos, etc., 27-32). Appendix lists small portion of the hoard deposited among the Guildhall, British, and Victoria and Albert museums.

8. PRIVATE COLLECTION, AUCTION, AND DEALER CATALOGS

EVANS COLLECTION

735   EVANS, JOAN. "Un Bijou magique dessiné par Hans Holbein," *Gazette des beaux-arts* 14 (1926):357-61, 5 b&w figs.

Gold pendant belonging to the author with inscription said to be magical and mounted with a hyacinth, sapphire, and olivine, gems noted for their beneficial qualities, proposed to be after drawings of 1532-43 by Holbein the Younger.

FRENCH

3. SURVEYS AND HISTORIES

Book

736   WINTER, PATRICK M. DE *La Bibliothèque de Philippe le Hardi, duc de Bourgogne (1364-1404): Étude sur les manuscrits à peintures d'une collection princière à l'époque du "Style Gothique International."* Paris: Centre National de la Recherche Scientifique, 1985. 475 pp., 272 b&w figs.
        Emphasizes (pp. 86-111) the often close relationship between the miniature painting and goldsmith work produced in Paris in the early 15th century and points out that the Limbourg brothers and other contemporary painters were trained as goldsmiths.

Article

737   HACKENBROCH, YVONNE. "New Knowledge on Jewels and Designs after Étienne Delaune." *Connoisseur* 162(1966):83-89, 4 color figs., 16 b&w figs.
        Pendant jewels related in their style and iconography to Delaune's armor decoration for Henri II.

7. EXHIBITION CATALOGS

Paris

MUSÉE DU LOUVRE

738   *Dix siècles de joaillerie française.* Exhibition catalog by Daniel Alcouffe, Bertrand Jestaz, Colombe Verlet, and Irène Bizot. Paris: Ministère d'État-Affaires Culturelles, 1962. 155 pp., 13 color figs.
        249 French jewels spanning the 10th to the mid-20th century most of which are in goldsmith mounts and of historical importance. Nos. 28-37, 48-52 are of the 15th-16th-century.

GERMAN

3. SURVEYS AND HISTORIES

Book

739   EGGER, GERHART. *Bürgerlicher Schmuck: 15. bis 20. Jahrhundert.* Munich: Georg D.W. Callwey, 1984. 222 pp., 52 color illus., 413 b&w figs.
        Pictorial presentation of jewelry made for the upper middle class from the 15th to the 20th century. Of the 15th-16th-century are some examples (mostly German, some Italian) from major museums (mostly in Germany) and in contemporary portraits: rings, pendants, necklaces, bracelets, chains, and brooches (see illus. 1-26, 28-37, 39, 41-43).

XV. Jewelry

Articles

740 HACKENBROCH, YVONNE. "Jewellery of the Court of Albrecht V at Munich." *Connoisseur* 165 (1967):74-82, 1 color fig., 30 b&w figs.

Author brings together a group of jewels made in Augsburg after designs by Mathias Zeundt—a pax in the Munich Schatzkammer, a prayer book binding in a private collection, Paris, a morse dated 1562 in the Basilica of S. Barbara, Mantua—on the basis of Zeundt's engraved designs and illustrations from Hans Mielich's illustrated inventory of the jewelry in Anna of Austria's collection. Also includes extant pieces that can be linked to Mielich's illustrations: a pendant in the Kunstgewerbemuseum, Cologne, a pendant in the Melvin Gutman Collection, New York, and one in the Gruenes Gewölbe in Dresden.

741 HACKENBROCH, YVONNE. "Renaissance Pendants after Designs by Jost Amman." *Connoiseur* 160 (1965):58-65, 25 b&w figs.

Jewels in the Historisches Museum and Gruenes Gewölbe, Dresden, in the British Museum, the Louvre, the Rijksmuseum, the Wernher Collection, Luton Hoo, the Robert Lehman Collection, New York, and an anonymous New York private collection, matched with woodcuts by the Zurich-born artist from his *New Book of Animals, Book of Art and Teaching,* and *Artist and Craftsman,* published in Frankfurt in 1569, 1578, and 1568, respectively.

742 WATZDORF, ERNA V. "Fürstlicher Schmuck der Renaissance aus dem Besitz der Kurfürstin Anna von Sachsen." *Münchner Jahrbuch der bildenden Kunst* 11 (1934):50-64, 12 b&w figs.

16th-century enameled gold jewelry set with rubies, emeralds, and diamonds formerly owned by Duchess Anna of Saxony and now in the Dresden Grünes Gewölbe and Munich Residenz Treasury—a necklace, pendants, a ring. Similar examples illustrated in contemporary paintings.

6. PERMANENT COLLECTIONS

Mantua

S. BARBARA

743 HACKENBROCH, YVONNE. "Un gioiello della corte di Monaco ora in Santa Barbara a Mantova." *Antichità viva* 6, no. 3 (1967):51-58, 12 b&w figs.

Gold and diamond brooch dated 1562 probably made in Augsburg or Munich for the Bavarian court of Albrecht V of Wittelsbach and Anna of Austria.

8. PRIVATE COLLECTION, AUCTION, AND DEALER CATALOGS

WADDESDON COLLECTION

744 DEFRATES, JOANNA. "Late Renaissance Jewellery from the Waddesdon Collection." *Connoiseur* 190 (1975):272-77. 15 b&w figs.

Examples of northern pendants, a toothpick, and a hat- badge related to designs by Erasmus Hornick, active in Augsburg and Nuremburg in the mid-16th century.

HUNGARIAN

3. SURVEYS AND HISTORIES

745   HÉJJ-DÉTÁRI, ANGÉLA. *Hungarian Jewellery of the Past.* 2d enl. and rev. ed. Translation revised by Mary S. Newton. Budapest: Corvina Press, 1976. 60 pp., 8 color pls., 40 b&w pls., 26 line drawings.
Forty-six-page introduction traces the history of Hungarian goldsmith and jewelry production, patronage, and stylistic evolution from the 9th to the 18th century; followed by presentation of forty-nine objects from Hungarian museums: brooches, pendants, rings, clasps, crowns, buckles, ecclesiastical jewels, etc. (all illustrated with detailed captions), many dating of the 15th-16th centuries.

ITALIAN

3. SURVEYS AND HISTORIES

Book

746   ROSSI, FILIPPO. *Italian Jeweled Arts.* Translated by Elisabeth Mann Borgese. Milan: Electa; New York: Harry N. Abrams, 1954. 56 pp., 83 color pls., 7 color figs., 42 b&w figs.
Somewhat useful as an introductory pictorial overview even though many color plates of generally important goldsmith works (12th-17th century) including stones, are garish.

Articles

747   BUNT, CYRIL G.E. "The Medici Crown." *Connoisseur* 107 (1941):115-18, 6 b&w figs.
Probably wrought by the goldsmith Santini for the coronation of Cosimo I as grand duke in 1569, the crown is known today only through engravings, tapestries, and mostly Bronzino's portrait of Cosimo I. The author here suggests that the crown was altered by Jaques Bylivelt of Delft, court jeweler to Francesco, for the latter ca. 1576 and was eventually placed in the tomb of Cosimo III in 1723.

748   FOCK, C. WILLEMIJIN. "The Medici Crown: Work of the Delft Goldsmith Jaques Bylivelt." Translated by Patricia Wardle and Allan Griffiths. *Oud Holland* 85 (1970):197-209, 8 b&w figs.
Replacement crown for the grand duke produced in 1577-83 as documented by the Delft goldsmith's account book.

749   HACKENBROCH, YVONNE. "Un gioiello mediceo inedito." *Antichità viva* 14 (1975):31-34, 2 color illus.
Two miniatures of ca.1585 painted on silver and set in gold to form a pendant (location unknown), attributed to Alessandro Allori; portrait on obverse identified as that of Virginia de' Medici, daughter of Cosimo I.

750   HACKENBROCH, YVONNE. "Jewels by Giovanni Battista Scolari." *Connoisseur* 159 (1965):200-205, 2 color figs., 10 b&w figs.

Attribution to Scolari of a group of jeweled pendants with amorous figures, musicians within a gondola (at Metropolitan Museum, Waddesdon Manor, Palazzo Pitti, Bayerisches Nationalmuseum, etc.), produced in Munich shortly after 1568 and inspired by the artist's experiences as an actor with a Venetian troupe performing at the court of Bavaria.

751   HACKENBROCH, YVONNE. "Some Florentine Jewels: Buontalenti and the Dragon Theme." *Connoisseur* 169 (1968):137-43, 4 color figs., 8 b&w figs.
       Describes a group of four pendant jewels and associates these with some of the drawings of Bernardo Buontalenti, Francesco de' Medici's chief architect, here suggested to have designed jewelry.

NETHERLANDISH

3. SURVEYS AND HISTORIES

752   GANS, M.H. *Juwelen en mensen: De geschiedenis van het bijou van 1400 tot 1900, voornamenlijk naar Nederlandse bronnen.* Amsterdam: J.H. de Bussy, 1961. 479 pp., 16 color pls., 202 b&w figs., numerous line drawings.
       Jewelry as personal adornment in Holland from ca. 1420 until 1900 as seen mostly through paintings. Styles, influences, and fashions are discussed. Chaps. 1 and 2 deal with the 15th- 16th century.

SCANDINAVIA
(DANISH AND NORWEGIAN)

3. SURVEYS AND HISTORIES

753   BEARD, CHARLES R. "The 'Lion' Jewel: A Work of Corvinianus Saur in the Possession of Lord Fairhaven." *Connoisseur* 101 (1938):72-77, 2 color illus., 5 b&w figs.
       A pendant of ca. 1595 of enameled gold, pearls, and precious stones fashioned as a lion's head, is attributed to the court goldsmith of King Christian IV of Denmark by comparing it to works by the artist in the Danish Royal Collection; the emblematic significance of the lion is elucidated.

6. PERMANENT COLLECTIONS

Stavanger

STAVANGER MUSEUM

754   LEXOW, JAN HENDRICH. "En magisk ring." *Stavanger Museum Årbok* (1954):77-84, 10 b&w figs.
       Norwegian 15th-century ring bearing a magical inscription.

SPANISH

3. SURVEYS AND HISTORIES

755 MULLER, PRISCILLA. *Jewels in Spain 1500-1800.* New York: Hispanic Society of America, 1972. 195 pp., 9 color pls., 257 b&w text figs.

Jewels, jewelers, and patrons; stylistic and iconographic aspects of religious and secular jewels (excluding crown jewels and those of chivalric orders) as seen in contemporary manuscripts, paintings, inventories, and designs, many previously unpublished, that were submitted to the goldsmith's guild (now in Barcelona, Museo de Artes Decorativas) as well as extant pieces. Chap. 1 (pp. 7-26) deals with jeweled collars, necklaces, crowns, chains, pendants, rings, and bracelets produced during the reign of Ferdinand and Isabel; chap. 2 (27-38) deals with stylistic and technical influences of the New World; chap. 3 (39-103) deals with 16th-century portrait medallions, pendants, necklaces, crosses, rosary beads, rings, etc.

6. PERMANENT COLLECTIONS

Madrid

INSTITUTO DE VALENCIA DE DON JUAN

756 *Catálogo de azabaches compostelanos precedido de apuntes sobre los amuletos contra il aojo, las imágenes del apóstol-Romero y la Cofradía de los azabacheros de Santiago,* by G[uillermo] J[oaquin] Osma [y Scull]. Madrid: 1916. 247 pp., 82 b&w figs.

Study of amulets related to the cult of St. James of Compostella and their makers from 1402 until ca. 1800. Catalog of eighty such pieces (nos. 4-39, figurines of the saint, limbs, shells, etc., date of the 15th-16th century) in the collection.

8. PRIVATE COLLECTION, AUCTION, AND DEALER CATALOGS

REGORDOSA COLLECTION

757 "Exposició de la Collecció Regordosa." *Butlletí dels museus d'art de Barcelona* 5 (1935):234- 42, 13 b&w figs.

Overview of this collection of medieval and Renaissance art exhibited at the Museu de los Arts Decoratives, Barcelona, in June 1933. Includes several important 16th-century Spanish jewels, five of which are illustrated.

XVI. Gold and/or Silver Secular Plate and Ecclesiastical/Devotional Objects

A. Multi Country of Origin

1. DICTIONARIES AND ENCYCLOPEDIAS

758   ROSENBERG, MARC. *Der Goldschmiede Merkzeichen.* 4 vols. Frankfurt: Frankfurter Verlags-Anstalt, 1922-28. 1: 373 pp., 30 b&w pls., 9 b&w figs.; 2: 405 pp., 39 b&w pls.; 3: 429 pp., 38 b&w pls.; 4: 740 pp., 22 b&w pls., 328 b&w figs.; facsimile town and makers' marks throughout.
　　　Standard and indispensable reference for the identification of town and makers' marks throughout Europe with greatest emphasis on German marks; follows alphabetical arrangement by town then goldsmith, providing brief biographical data, listing of works, and bibliography. Vols. 1-3 cover Germany; vol. 4, the rest of Europe. Numerous entries for 15th-16th-century marks.

3. SURVEYS AND HISTORIES

Books

759   BAILEY, C.T.P. *Knives and Forks.* London and Boston: Medici Society, 1927. 16 pp., 3 color pls., 72 b&w figs.
　　　Knives and forks as works of art and collectibles. Includes an historical essay dealing with table manners, such as the use of forks, etc. A second essay studies dates (many of the 15th-16th centuries), nationalities, and methods of decoration, most examples being drawn from the Victoria and Albert Museum.

760   BENKER, GERTRUD. *Alte Bestecke: Ein Beitrag zur Geschichte der Tischkultur.* Munich: Georg D.W. Callwey, 1978. 184 pp., 379 b&w figs., 28 text figs.
　　　Old flatware; essay on the history of table manners from Neolithic times until the present. Pp. 15-20 and figs. 27-82 deal with a variety of 15th-16th-century spoons, knives, saws, and toothpicks produced by goldsmiths.

761   BRAUN, JOSEPH. *Die Reliquiare des christlichen Kultes und ihre Entwicklung.* Freiburg im Breisgau: Herder & Co., 1940. 743 pp., 157 pls. comprising 602 b&w figs.

The standard study on Christian reliquaries: cults, patronage, materials, techniques, shapes, iconography, inscriptions, from the 10th to 16th century.

762 CAME, RICHARD. *Silver.* New York: G.P. Putnam's Sons, 1961. 128 pp., 32 color figs., 92 b&w figs.
Broad introduction to European silver. Chaps. 1 and 2 deal with the late medieval and Renaissance periods.

763 DAWSON, NELSON. *Goldsmiths' and Silversmiths' Work.* New York: G.P. Putnam's Sons; London: Methuen & Co., 1907. 127 b&w figs.
General overview, somewhat dated, of goldsmith work from antiquity to 18th century. Part 1 (pp. 1-24) discusses technique, production centers, and practical and decorative uses; part 3 (130-238), gold and silver pieces (domestic and liturgical) of 1400-1600 in England, Germany, France, and Italy; part 4 (239-44), hallmarking.

764 EMERY, JOHN. *European Spoons before 1700.* Edinburgh: John Donald, 1976. 205 pp., 131 b&w figs.
Survey of spoons from antiquity. Pp. 4-14 deal with classification, function, technical manufacture, hallmarking, fakes and forgeries. Specifically pertinent to 1400-1600 are pp. 37-39, 15th- and 16th-century Italian spoons; 61-66, northern European utensils; 82-84, English ficulate pattern spoons; 86-87, various types of Scottish spoons; 105, Scandinavian silver spoons; 109, German, Polish, and Austrian spoons; 110-11, French silver spoons; 145-49, pre-1600 Netherlandish utensils and their classification. The volume concludes with appendixes on the making of a diamond-point spoon and brass foundry work in medieval Italy.

765 FRITZ, JOHANN MICHAEL. *Goldschmiedekunst der Gotik in Mitteleuropa.* Munich: C.H. Beck, 1982. 377 pp., 16 color pls., 975 b&w figs.
Comprehensive study of German and Netherlandish goldsmith work dating mostly of ca. 1350-1500. Deals with all aspects of the field including function, existing documentation, lost works, guild regulations, major centers, etc. Both ecclesiastical and secular objects are well-illustrated; each color plate and many black and white figures are accompanied by lengthy notes. Includes appendixes listing major centers and pieces bearing special inscriptions and signatures.

766 GRIMME, ERNST GÜNTHER. *Goldschmiedekunst im Mittelalter: Form und Bedeutung des Reliquiars von 800 bis 1500.* Cologne: M. DuMont Schauberg, 1972. 190 pp., 67 b&w figs.
Form and meaning of reliquaries from 800 to 1500. Broad essay, useful complement to Braun's standard work (see entry 761). Cites many 15th-century (mostly German and French) examples.

767 HAYWARD, J.F. *Virtuoso Goldsmiths and the Triumph of Mannerism 1540-1620.* London: Sotheby Parke Bernet, 1976. 751 pp., 24 color pls., 739 b&w figs.
Milestone study of European goldsmiths active 1540-1620. Separate chapters deal with such topics as methodology for the study of silver, patrons, goldsmiths and guilds, working methods; other sections conveniently arranged by country, region and/or city, deal with productions from Italy (pp. 133-70), France (171- 87), Spain and Portugal (189-99), South Germany (201-42), Erasmus Hornick (243-51), North and Western Germany, Switzerland and Saxony (253-66), Hungary and Poland (267-79), the Netherlands (281-98), England (299-311). An illustrated catalog with useful descriptive notes follows; extensive bibliographies of early and later literature.

768   HERNMARCK, CARL. *The Art of the European Silversmith 1430-1830.* 2 vols. London and New York: Sotheby Parke Bernet, 1977. 1: 411 pp., 134 b&w figs.; 2: 1001 b&w figs. on 386 pls.

Vol. 1: part 1 (pp. 1-39) consists of an historical essay dealing with works in each major country; part 2 (41-51) deals with stylistic influences in the late Gothic and Renaissance; part 3 (75-290) studies secular silver (drinking vessels, tableware, household articles, etc.) many produced 1400-1600; part 4 (305-57), church silver (liturgical implements and church furnishings) many of the 15th-16th century. Concludes with a chapter (362-74) on decorative techniques (engraving, flat chasing, etched moresques, filigree, style rustique).

769   HONOUR, HUGH. *Goldsmiths and Silversmiths.* London: Weidenfeld & Nicholson, 1971. 320 pp., 31 color pls., 225 b&w figs.

Brief essays on gold- and silversmiths from the 9th to the 20th century; of the years 1400-1600 are seven masters including Pollaiuolo, Sebastian Lindenast, Enrique de Arfe, Ludwig Krug, Cellini, Jamnizer, and Antonio Gentile.

770   LINK, EVA M. *The Book of Silver.* Translated by Francisca Garvie. 2d ed. New York: Praeger, 1973. 301 pp., 16 color figs., 145 b&w figs., line drawings. (1st ed. Frankfurt, Berlin, and Vienna: Ullstein, 1968.)

A well-documented and reliable introduction to the history of European silver- and goldsmith work from classical times to the present. Pp. 47-112 deal with the 15th-16th century. Concludes with tables of major assay and makers' marks.

771   McNAB, JESSIE. *Silver.* New York: Cooper-Hewitt Museum, 1981. 128 pp., 25 color pls., 100 b&w figs.

General survey of silver from antiquity to the 20th century. Chap. 2 (pp. 11-21) deals with technique; chap. 4 (29- 39), with European silver of the 7th-16th century, touching upon 15th-16th-century centers and illustrating some fine examples.

772   MOLINIER, ÉMILE. *Histoire générale des arts appliqués à l'industrie.* Vol. 4, *L'Orfèvrerie religieuse et civile du Ve à la fin du XVe siècle.* Paris: E. Lévy, n.d. 297 pp., 21 b&w pls., 110 text figs.

Pioneering study on sacred and secular goldsmith works from the 5th to the end of the 15th century. Of this last period are pp. 219-31 (French works), 254-72 (Italian), 276-83 (German), and 286-89 (Spanish and Portuguese objects). Examples drawn from many public and private collections. No index.

773   OMAN, CHARLES. *Medieval Silver Nefs.* London: Her Majesty's Stationery Office, 1963. 31 pp., 25 b&w pls., 15 b&w figs.

The nef originating as a drinking vessel and evolving into an important ornamental table piece marking the place of the host; its design and iconography, and its varying reliability as source of information on the appearance of actual ships, as seen through nine surviving Spanish, Italian, French, and German examples mostly of the 15th-16th century today in European museums and churches.

774   PAATZ, WALTER. *Sceptrum universitatis: Die europäischen Universitätsszepter.* Heidelberg: Carl Winter-Universitätsverlag, 1953. 152 pp., 39 b&w pls., 7 line drawings.

University maces of gilt-silver, and often including enamels, from the 15th to the 18th century in Europe. Purpose, significance, iconographic program. Extant examples (some of the 15th-16th century) and their representation in paintings, etc., from a total of fifty-four universities.

775 RICHTER, ERNST-LUDWIG. *Altes Silber: Imitiert-kopiert- gefälscht.* Munich: Keyser, 1983. 255 pp., 240 b&w figs.

Gothic and Renaissance goldsmith works and 19th-century copies or versions. Connoisseurship and technical elements for differentiating one from the other. Tools and techniques are also discussed.

776 SCHEFFLER, WOLFGANG. *Gemalte Goldschmiedearbeiten: Kostbare Gefässe auf den Dreikönigsbildern in den Niederlanden und in Deutschland 1400-1530. Ein typologischer Beitrag zur Goldschmiedekunst.* Berlin and New York: Walter de Gruyter & Co., 1985. 306 pp., 249 b&w figs.

Important goldsmith objects, mostly cups, chalices, pyxes, and shrines, as represented in German and Netherlandish panel paintings depicting the Adoration of the Magi in the period 1400-1530.

Articles

777 BUNT, CYRIL G.E. "The Silver Nef." *Connoisseur* 111 (1943):90-95, 10 b&w figs.

Serving both an ecclesiastical purpose (ex-voto, reliquary) and a secular use (ceremonial, table plate), these boat-shaped gilt-silver objects were wrought (especially in France and Germany) from at least the 14th century to the 19th, the 16th century representing their heyday.

778 GRIMWADE, A.G. "Silver and Glass Cups. A Comparison of Sixteenth-Century Examples." *Connoisseur* 131 (1953):86-87, 6 b&w figs.

The style of a group of mid-16th-century English and Dutch silver cups; their relationship to 15th-century Venetian examples.

779 LIGHTBOWN, R.W. "Ex-Votos in Gold and Silver: A Forgotten Art." *Burlington Magazine* 121 (1979):352-59, 7 b&w figs.

Examples from the Middle Ages to the 18th century. Mentions several of the 15th-16th century and describes some, such as the gilded and silvered copper model of Soissons (1560) and the kneeling gold figure of Charles the Bold in Liège (1467-71).

780 STEINGRABER, ERICH. "Nachträge und Marginalien zur französische-niederländischen Goldschmiedekunst des frühen 15. Jahrhunderts." *Anzeiger des germanischen Nationalmuseums* (1969):29-39, 14 b&w figs.

Attribution of enameled devotional goldsmith works and rock-crystal cups to Paris or the Netherlands of the early 15th century; a crucifix in Lisbon; small altars in the Metropolitan Museum, the Rijksmuseum, and the church of S. Tomà in Venice; rock crystal in Milan, Florence, etc.

781 WIRTH, KARL-AUGUST. "Von silbernen und silbermontierten Eulengefässen." *Anzeiger des Germanischen Nationalmuseums* (1968):42-83, 90 b&w figs.

Study of owl-shaped receptacles of silver, often incorporating a coconut or carved maple insets, produced in the late 16th century mostly in Germany and Switzerland. Concludes with catalog of eighty-three such pieces.

6. PERMANENT COLLECTIONS

Amsterdam

RIJKSMUSEUM

782   *Uit de schatkamer—The Treasures.* Vol. 2.   Catalog by Th. M. Duyvené de Wit-Klinkhamer. Amsterdam: Rijksmuseum, 1957. 5 pp., 37 b&w pls.

Brief overview of thirty-seven Renaissance goldsmith masterpieces in the collection by Dutch, German, and French artists. Five-page introduction in Dutch and English followed by illustrations with captions.

Glasgow

GLASGOW MUSEUMS AND ART GALLERIES – BURRELL COLLECTION

783   FINLAY, IAN.   "Silver in the Collection of Sir William Burrell." *Connoisseur* 101 (1938):242-46, 12 b&w figs.

Presentation of outstanding objects, several of the 15th- 16th century, from this collection.   Includes a South German parcel-gilt hanap with architectural elements; an English chalice of ca. 1420; a maplewood mazer with gilt-silver mount; Elizabethan communion cups; a South German pyx; three tigerware jugs with Elizabethan mounts.

Kraków

MUZEUM NARODOWE

784   *Stare Srebra.* Catalog by Jadwiga Bujánska. Kraków: Muzeum Narodowe, 1972. 139 pp., 45 b&w pls. including 2 pls. of makers' marks, 4 b&w text figs.

Forty-five silversmith works in the National Museum—most from the well-known Czartoryski Collection—ranging from the 1st century A.D. to the 19th century. Cat. nos. 4-12 are of 15th- and 16th-century objects: Polish processional and altar crosses, including one of rock crystal (no. 5), a tankard (Nuremberg), pokal, standing cup with cover, and a nautilus cup with mounts and cover in the shape of a peacock.

Lincoln

CATHEDRAL

785   OMAN, CHARLES.   "Lincoln Cathedral Treasury." *Connoisseur* 145 (1960):241-44, 12 b&w figs.

Briefly lists the holdings, which include two chalices with patens of 1560 and 1569, a gilt-silver beaker with cover of 1577 (London hallmark), and a gilt tazza embossed with a scene of Esther before Ahasuerus of 1600 (Christoph Lencker, Augsburg mark).

XVI. Gold and/or Silver Secular Plate and Ecclesiastical/Devotional Objects

London

BRITISH MUSEUM

786   *Catalogue of the Silver Plate, Mediaeval and Later, Bequeathed to the British Museum by Sir Augustus Wollaston Franks, with Selected Examples from Other Sources.* Catalog by Hercules Read and A.B. Tonnochy. London: British Museum, 1928. 96 pp., 62 b&w pls., 28 b&w figs., numerous town, maker, and date marks, and line drawings.

Silver objects and silver-mounted receptacles (rock crystal, tigerware, maple, etc.), the majority secular. Of the 105 pieces cataloged, many are 15th- and 16th-century German, English, French, Italian, Dutch, Swiss, Danish, Swedish, and Portuguese examples (see nos. 1-7, 9, 14, 16, 18-32, 49, 52-56, 66, 70-75, 89, 95, and 100-104), often with extensive descriptions and including town and makers' marks.

VICTORIA AND ALBERT MUSEUM

787   *Ancient and Modern Gold and Silver Smiths' Work in the South Kensington Museum.* Catalog by John Hungerford Pollen. London: G.E. Eyre and W. Spottiswoode, 1878. 614 pp., 1 color pl., 14 b&w pls. (etchings), 47 line drawings.

Gold-and silversmith works of the 15th-16th century in the permanent collection (chalices, reliquaries, monstrances, spoons, knives, cups, salvers, bookcovers, daggers, etc.) described on pp. 79-173; plaster casts after famous originals (crosses, candlesticks, altar fronts, etc.) elsewhere (churches, museums, etc.) of the same period (pp. 322-39). Includes a 194- page introduction.

Milan

MUSEO POLDI PEZZOLI

See entry 72.

Vienna

KUNSTHISTORISCHES MUSEUM

788   *Goldschmiedearbeiten des Mittelalters der Renaissance und des Barock: Arbeiten in Gold und Silber.* Catalog by Ernst Kris. Vienna: Anton Schroll, 1932. 89 pp., 250 b&w figs. on 88 pls.

135 detailed entries for 14th-18th-century gold and silver secular (mostly) and religious objects in the permanent collection. Of the 15th-16th century are nos. 6-93: German (mostly), Portuguese, Spanish, French, Italian, and Swiss beakers, drinking horns, standing cups, pokals, monstrance, salt, medals, salvers, etc.

Windsor

ETON COLLEGE

789   *The Plate of Eton College.* Catalog by E. Alfred Jones, assisted by Arthur Cochrane and J.H.B. Noble. London: Saint Catherine Press, 1938. 92 pp., 32 b&w pls.

Thirteen-page introduction; catalog of primarily post-1600 silver but includes major English examples of the late 15th and 16th century: a coconut cup, seal dated 1474, chalices and patens, flagons of 1598-99, rosewater ewer and basin. Also an important 16th-century Spanish/Portuguese tazza.

7. EXHIBITION CATALOGS

London

BURLINGTON HOUSE

790   *Exhibition of a Collection of Silversmiths' Work of European Origin.* Exhibition catalog by J. Starkie Gardner. London: Burlington Fine Arts Club, 1901. 242 pp., 120 b&w pls.
    Thirty-five page introduction deals with technique, hallmarks; 622 short entries (not chronologically arranged) include 15th- and 16th-century European statuettes, cups, chalices, ciboria, monstrances, patens, spoons, ewers, tazze, tankards, knives, salts, etc., drawn from British collections. Principally useful for plates.

8. PRIVATE COLLECTION, AUCTION, AND DEALER CATALOGS

BUCCLEUCH COLLECTION

791   JONES, E. ALFRED. "Old Silver in the Possession of the Duke of Buccleuch, K.T." Parts 2 and 3, *Old Furniture* 7 (1929):93-99, 12 b&w figs.; 130-38, 14 b&w figs. Part 1 deals with 17th-century objects.
    Part 2: a set of twelve silver plates engraved with scenes from the Life of the Prodigal Son in the style of Virgil Solis and bearing the mark of an unknown maker and the London date-letter for 1568-69 and 1569-70. Part 3: a shell-shaped box presented to Elizabeth I by the Worshipful Company of Goldsmiths in celebration of the defeat of the Armada in 1588; a coconut cup of ca. 1590 bearing the arms of the queen; two late 16th-century German standing cups, one by Michel Flindt of Nuremberg and the other by Nikolas Rapp of Ulm.

NERESHEIMER COLLECTION

792   FRITZ, ROLF. *Sammlung August Neresheimer.* Hamburg-Altona: Carl W. Dingwort, 1974. 203 pp., 20 color figs., 123 b&w figs.
    Catalog of this Zurich collection of 139 generally outstanding goldsmith works. Includes 15th-century French, Italian, and German ecclesiastical plate (nos. 15-16, 19-20, 24- 25, 27, 30), 16th-century pokals from Nuremberg and Lübeck (55, 57, 70, 84, 89, 94, 107, 115), German rock-crystal monstrance (129), Spanish monstrance, reliquary, chalice, dish (85, 96, 123, 128), Milanese rock-crystal cup (87), Limoges salt and plaques (110, 122).

PIERPONT MORGAN COLLECTION

793   JONES, E. ALFRED. *Illustrated Catalogue of the Collection of Old Plate of J. Pierpont Morgan, Esquire.* London: Bemrose & Sons, 1908. 162 pp., 98 b&w pls.
    Fifty-four-page introduction; catalog of 108 primarily English silver and gilt-silver plate ranging from the 16th through 19th century of which eleven pieces date before 1600 (a small bowl, complete set of thirteen Apostle spoons, tazza, tankard, cups, etc., see pls. I-VIII, pp. 2-10); also includes a selection of Continental silver (chalices, statuette, beakers, cups,

rock-crystal cup with gilt-silver mounts, tazze — among which is the Vespasian Tazza commissioned by Cardinal Aldobrandini, p. 84, pl. LXXV — coconut cup, ewer, etc.) of which thirty items date of 1400-1600 (pp. 66, 68-96, pls. LIX- LXXXVI).

RÜTSCHI COLLECTION

794   *Der Sammlung Alfred Rütschi: Alte Goldschmiedewerke im Zürcher Kunsthaus*. Part 1. Catalog by Otto von Falke. Sale held in Lucerne at the Galerie Fischer 5 September 1931. 28 pp., 66 b&w pls. (An abridged French version of this catalog with a one-line description of each lot was published concurrently.)

Sale of the Alfred Rütschi Collection of mostly liturgical metalwork, which had been on permanent exhibition at the Zurich Kunsthaus. Many of the 120 lots date of the 15th- 16th century and are French, Italian, German reliquaries, monstrances, chalices, caskets, bookcovers, processional crosses, an enameled vessel with playful monkeys in grisaille. Also French and Flemish leather boxes and a few German Renaissance jewels.

SCHRÖDER COLLECTION

795   WATTS, W.W. "Continental Silver in the Collection of Baron and Baroness Bruno Schröder." *Old Furniture* 2 (1927):2-14, 86-95, 21 b&w figs.

Well-known 16th-century specimens, mostly German (some Swiss and Dutch); fanciful cups — nautilus, coconut, owl — tankards, beaker, an enameled gilt-silver salt, folding spoon and fork, etc.

795a   *The Art of the European Goldsmith: Silver from the Schroder Collection*. Exhibition held in New York at the American Federation of Arts. Catalog and essay by Timothy B. Schroder, with another essay by J.F. Hayward. New York: American Federation of Arts, 1983. 208 pp., 19 color pls., numerous b&w figs. and makers' marks.

Seventy-nine outstanding objects in this private English collection ranging from the 12th to 19th centuries (the appendix includes fifteen additional entries not in the exhibition). Introductory essays on the history of the collection (pp. 10-13) and the art of the European goldsmith (pp. 15-29). For the 15th- 16th centuries, see cat. nos. 2-36, 38-40, 44-45, and appendix nos. 2-11 comprising standing cups, coconut and nautilus cups, an Aldobrandini tazza (no. 16), tankards, beakers, animal-shaped cups, ceramic jugs with mounts, salts, etc.

SMITH COLLECTION

796   HAYWARD, J.F. "The Howard E. Smith Collection of Cutlery." *Connoisseur* 134 (1954):164-73, 70 b&w figs.

European knives and forks, some damascened, some with sheaths, handles of ivory, amber, horn, hardstone or silvered, gilt or blued iron, etc. 16th-century examples are illustrated figs. 1-24.

THYSSSEN-BORNEMISZA COLLECTION

797   MÜLLER, HANNELORE. *The Thyssen-Bornemisza Collection: European Silver*. Translated by P.S. Falla and Anna Somers Cocks. London: Philip Wilson for Sotheby Publications, 1986. 312 pp., 16 color pls., 231 b&w figs., numerous assay, date, and makers' marks.

Catalog of ninety-five, often outstanding, pieces from nearly all major centers. Includes several 16th-century tazze and cups from England, France, Germany, Hungary, and the Netherlands. Excellent illustration and reproduction of marks.

UNTERMYER COLLECTION

798   HACKENBROCH, YVONNE. *English and Other Silver in the Irwin Untermyer Collection.* London: Thames & Hudson, 1963. 126 pp., 201 b&w pls., 12 b&w figs., numerous reproductions of makers' marks.
      Includes several 16th-century pieces produced in London: coconut cup with mounts, covered cups, tazza, tigerware jug, flagons, tankard, beakers, salts, bottles. Also a 15th-century French parcel gilt olearium, a pyx of Toledo, a Viterbo bust reliquary, a Portuguese 16th-century dish, a nautilus cup from Nuremberg, German and Italian 16th-century spoons, forks, and knives.

B. SINGLE COUNTRY OF ORIGIN

AUSTRIAN

3. SURVEYS AND HISTORIES

799   ROSSACHER, KURT. *Der Schatz des Erzstiftes Salzburg: Ein Jahrtausend deutscher Goldschmiedekunst.* Salzburg: Residenz Verlag, 1966. 235 pp., 39 color pls., 238 b&w figs.
      Goldsmith works produced for the prince-bishops of Salzburg from the 11th century until 1803. Includes twenty-seven-page historical essay, glossary, catalog of 238 pieces of which nos. 16-131 are crosses, cups, pokals, capsulae, candlestick, croziers, ewers and basins, platters, dating of the 15th-16th century.

6. PERMANENT COLLECTIONS

Florence

MUSEO DEGLI ARGENTI

800   ROSSACHER, KURT. "Il tesoro nel tesoro." *Antichità viva* 3, no. 1 (1964):49-59, 2 color figs., 12 b&w figs.
      Important goldsmith work produced in Salzburg ca. 1600 and until 1805 in the Archbishop's Palace and then brought to Florence by Ferdinand III of Tuscany.

7. EXHIBITION CATALOGS

Innsbruck

VEREIN KUNSTAUSSTELLUNGEN HOFBURG

801   *Gold und Silber: Kunstschätz aus Tirol.* Exhibition catalog by Magdalena Weingartner. Innsbruck: Verlagsanstalt Tyrolia, 1961. 138 pp., 64 b&w figs.

275 goldsmith works produced in the Tyrol or owned by local institutions. Nos. 9-108 mostly date of the 15th-16th century and include chalices and cups, 'monstrances and reliquaries, paxes, croziers, a bookbinding, clocks, etc.

Salzburg

SALZBURGER DOMKAPITEL

802   *Salzburg alte Schatzkammer.* Exhibition catalog by Kurt Rossacher et al. Salzburg: Salzburger Domkapitel, 1967. 99 pp., 8 color pls., 32 b&w figs.
       121 ecclesiastical goldsmith works produced in Salzburg from the 8th to the 19th century. Nos. 18-29 are of the 15th century; 30-61, of the 16th century, including reliquaries, crosses, chalices, drinking horn, croziers, etc. Particularly important are the enameled objects produced for the Erzbischof Wolf Dietrich von Raitenau, ca. 1600.

Vienna

ÖSTERREICHISCHES MUSEUM FÜR ANGEWANDTE KUNST

803   *Gold- und Silberschätz in Kopien des Historismus.* Exhibition catalog by Gerhart Egger. Vienna: Österreichisches Museum für Angewandte Kunst, 1972. 40 pp., 37 b&w pls.
       186 objects of goldsmith work in Gothic and Renaissance styles but actually 19th-century revival productions made in Austria. For many, the name of the craftsman is actually known.

BELGIUM

1. DICTIONARIES AND ENCYCLOPEDIAS

804   STUYCK, R. *Belgische Zilvermerken/Poinçons d'argenterie belges.* Antwerp/Brussels: Erasme, 1984. 314 pp., numerous b&w line drawings, makers' marks. Dutch/French text.
       Repertory of 5,408 Belgian town and makers' marks from the 15th to the 19th century with a cross-referenced list of silversmiths alphabetically arranged by localities.

3. SURVEYS AND HISTORIES

Books

805   COLMAN, PIERRE. *L'Orfèvrerie religieuse liégeoise du XVe siècle à la Révolution.* 2 vols. Liège: Université de Liège, 1966. 1:298 pp.; 2:111 pp., 244 b&w pls.
       A comprehensive study of religious objects wrought uniquely in silver and gilt-silver, produced in the city of Liège from the 15th to the 18th century. Vol. 1: repertory of over nine hundred pieces, most of which bear hallmarks, in churches, convents, museums, and private collections throughout the world; twenty-three date of the 15th-16th century. Twelve chapters thoroughly deal with all aspects: apprenticeship, rights and obligations, hallmarks, patrons, iconographic themes, subjects, styles, techniques, models, analysis of corpus of objects by types (e.g. bust reliquaries, reliquary crosses, patens, etc.), biographies of documented masters (two of the 16th century). Vol. 2: appendixes: chronological, by type of object, by makers' mark, iconographic; indexes by names of persons and places.

806   POSKIN, G., and STOKART, PH. *Orfèvres namurois.* Namur: Société Archéologique de Namur, 1982. 417 pp., 47 b&w pls.
       Goldsmiths and minting in the town of Namur and the surrounding Meuse region from the 11th through the 18th century. Valuable for defining the activity during the reigns of Philip the Good and Charles the Bold of Burgundy and for focusing on the flowering of the 16th century. Historical essays, lists of goldsmiths, documents, bibliography, and glossary.

Articles

807   HAYWARD, J.F. "The Mannerist Goldsmiths: 3. Antwerp, Part I." *Connoisseur* 156 (1964):92-96, 10 b&w figs.
       Activity of Antwerp masters: Hans of Antwerp, Jan Vermeyen the Elder, Bartolomäus Spranger, and especially Erasmus Hornick, who brought Italian mannerism to northern Europe.

807a   HAYWARD, J.F. "The Mannerist Goldsmiths: 3. Antwerp, Part II." *Connoisseur* 156 (1964):165-70, 11 b&w figs.
       Drawings by Hornick paralleled to the design of Antwerp-produced goldsmith works: a tazza at Emmanuel College, Cambridge, a standing cup in the collection of the Marquess of Exeter, a ewer in the Louvre commemorating Charles V's expedition against Tunis.

807b   HAYWARD, J.F. "The Mannerist Goldsmiths: 3. Antwerp, Part III." *Connoisseur* 156 (1964):251-54, 10 b&w figs.
       Ewers with strapwork decoration in the style of Cornelius Bos, Cornelius Floris, and Erasmus Hornick; later tazze, etc., more restrained in form and degree of decoration.

807c   HAYWARD, J.F. "The Mannerist Goldsmiths: 3. Antwerp, Part IV: Italian Influence in the Designs of Erasmus Hornick." *Connoisseur* 158 (1965):144-49, 12 b&w figs.
       Author suggests Hornick traveled to Italy in the 1550s. Some of his drawings (in the Victoria and Albert Museum) indicate he knew the works of artists such as Salviati, Giulio Romano, Eneo Vico, and Agostino Musi Veneziano.

808   LEFEVRE, PLAC. "Les Travaux de l'orfèvre anversois Renier de Jaesveld pour l'abbaye d'Averbode durant la second moitié du XVIe siècle." *Revue belge d'archéologie et d'histoire de l'art* 2 (1932):289-308, 2 b&w figs.
       Works commissioned in 1551-65 by Abbot Mathieu S'Volders of Averbode Abbey from the Antwerp goldsmith Renier de Jaesveld (transcription of accounts supplement the few pieces that are actually extant) — chalices, cruets, reliquaries, pastoral and pectoral crosses, holy water vessel, etc. The same goldsmith also restored works produced two centuries before by Herman of Lübeck.

809   PHILLIPE, JOSEPH. "The Art of the Goldsmith in Sixteenth-Century Belgium." *Apollo* 82 (1965):294-301, 10 b&w figs.
       Guillaume van der Mont, Jérôme Mamacker, N. Vyrgers, and other goldsmiths active in Liège, Antwerp, Bruges, Brussels, etc., and producing Renaissance-style tazze, reliquaries, chalices, ewers, and bookcovers.

810   VAN MOLLE, FRANS. "Een zeldzame Brusselse kelk geschonken door Maximiliaan Oostenrijk (ca. 1480)." *Revue belge d'archéologie et d'histoire de l'art* 38 (1969):3-17, 8 b&w figs.

Gilt-silver chalice (now in a chapel near Trent) commissioned by Archduke Maximilian of Austria between 1477 and 1486 bears a Brussels mark and is related to a cup in the Historisches Museum in Bern.

6. PERMANENT COLLECTIONS

Antwerp

PROVINCIALE MUSEA

811   *Catalogus edelsmeedkunst.*   Catalog by A.M. Claessens-Peré.   Antwerp: Provinciale Musea, 1983. 111 pp., 242 b&w figs., reproductions of makers' marks.
242 mostly Flemish silver objects: catalog nos. 1-5 date of the 16th century: a chalice, medallion, coconut pokal, two tazze.

Bern

BERNISCHES HISTORISCHES MUSEUM

812   THOMAS, [BRUNO]. "Die silbervergoldete Schale mit dem österreichisch-burgundischen Wappen im Bernischen Historischen Museum." *Jahrbuch des Bernischen historischen Museums* 31 (1951):92-96, 2 figs.
Gilt-silver cup bearing the combined arms of Burgundy and Austria, proposed to have been made on the occasion of Maximilian I's wedding with Mary of Burgundy in 1477, or at a slightly later date.

Bruges

MUSÉE COMMUNAL

813   *Orfèvrerie d'art à Bruges.* Introduction by M. English. Translated by L. Fraeijs Veubeke. Brussels: Éditions de la Connaissance, 1950. 48 pp., 31 b&w pls.
Goldsmith works in Bruges, 13th-18th century. 468 short catalog entries of ecclesiastical, guild, and domestic implements. Useful to suggest character of local production.

Hal

ÉGLISE NOTRE-DAME

814   CRÖY, FERNAND. *Les Orfèvreries anciennes conservées au Trésor de Hal.* Brussels: G. Van Oest & Cie, 1910. 59 pp., 23 b&w pls.
Monograph on this particularly wealthy treasure among Belgian churches and to which major 15th-16th-century historical figures made gifts: ostensories of Henry VIII and Louis XI, mace, staffs, candlesticks, bejeweled crown.

London

WALLACE COLLECTION

815   MANN, JAMES. "The Horn of Saint Hubert." *Burlington Magazine* 92 (1950):161-65, 3 b&w figs.

History of a late 15th-century Flemish cow's horn (Wallace Collection) formerly decorated with a gesso relief of which only fragments remain and two silver enameled bands given by Louis de Bourbon, Prince Bishop of Liège, to Duke Charles the Bold of Burgundy who founded a chapel in his castle of Chauvirey to house the purported relic.

BRITISH
(ENGLISH, SCOTTISH, AND IRISH)

1. DICTIONARIES AND ENCYCLOPEDIAS

816   CHAFFERS, WILLIAM. *Hall Marks on Gold & Silver Plate Illustrated with Revised Tables of Annual Date Letters Employed by the Assay Offices of England, Scotland and Ireland.* 10th ed. rev. and enl. by C.A. Markham. London: Reeves & Turner, 1922. 454 pp., 4 b&w pls., 13 line drawings. (1st ed. 1863).

    Enlarged edition of the classic work that lists and illustrates marks employed in the assay offices of England, Scotland, and Ireland. Included are also the marks from Chaffers's early *Gilda aurifabrorum* (1899).

817   CLAYTON, MICHAEL. *The Collector's Dictionary of the Silver and Gold of Great Britain and North America.* 2d ed. Woodbridge, Suffolk: Antique Collectors' Club, 1985. 481 pp., 77 color pls., 730 b&w figs. (1st ed. 1971.)

    Useful guide for terminology, definition of types, and main examples, which are dispersed among many collections. Includes a fair percentage of 15th-16th-century English examples (eg. ewers, mazers, salts, spoons, etc.).

818   *English Silver Hall Marks Including the Marks of Origin on Scottish & Irish Silver Plate, Gold, Platinum & Sheffield Plate.* Edited by Judith Banister. 2d ed. London: W. Foulsham & Co., 1983. 118 pp. (1st ed. 1970.)

    Convenient pocket guide to English and Scottish (some Irish) town and makers' marks; eighteen-page historical introduction; over five hundred marks (the earliest dating of 1544) reproduced in facsimile and arranged by city and/or alphabetically by maker's name.

2. BIOGRAPHICAL DICTIONARIES

819   HEAL, AMBROSE. *The London Goldsmiths 1200-1800: A Record of the Names and Addresses of the Craftsmen, Their Shop-Signs and Trade-Cards.* Cambridge: University Press, 1935. 280 pp., 80 engraved pls.

    Supplement to Jackson's *English Goldsmiths and Their Marks* (see entry 827) providing an alphabetical list with 3,600 additional goldsmiths and jewelers as well as 350 pawnbrokers.

820   KENT, TIMOTHY ARTHUR. *London Silver Spoonmakers 1500 to 1697.* London: Silver Society, 1981. 56 pp., 74 b&w figs.

    Biographical directory of craftsmen arranged chronologically, giving pertinent facts and reproducing examples of some of their work and their marks.

3. SURVEYS AND HISTORIES

Books

821   BENTON, G. MONTAGU; GALPIN, F.W.; and PRESSEY, W.J., *The Church Plate of the County of Essex.* Colchester: Benham & Co., 1926. 345 pp., 27 b&w pls.
Standard and comprehensive survey of ecclesiastical plate in this English county arranged by town (Colchester, Ramsey, Hatfield, etc. — and then by parish); mostly 17th-19th-century pieces with some however dating of ca. 1480-1600: chalices, standing cups, patens, mazers, etc.; a few objects are also Spanish or Dutch. Ten-page introduction and four appendixes.

822   CARRINGTON, JOHN BODMAN, and HUGHES, GEORGE RAVENSWORTH. *The Plate of the Worshipful Company of Goldsmiths.* Oxford: University Press, 1926. 158 pp., 83 b&w pls.
Includes prime Tudor and Elizabethan examples among the drinking cups, mazer, tazza, tankards, dishes and ewers, salts, communion cups and patens, standing cups in the collection. Most pieces bear a London mark.

823   CRIPPS, WILFRED JOSEPH. *Old English Plate. Ecclesiastical, Decorative, and Domestic: Its Makers and Marks.* 10th ed. London: John Murray, 1914. 6 b&w pls., numerous line drawings, makers' and town marks. (1st ed. 1878.)
Standard reference from 1878 until Jackson's *English Goldsmiths* (see entry 827). Deals with production from medieval times to the 18th century in the British Isles. Relevant to the 15th-16th century are chaps. 1-4, 6-7, 9-10. Includes appendixes with London date-letters and marks of goldsmiths active in other centers in England, Scotland, and Ireland.

824   HAYDEN, ARTHUR. *Chats on Old Silver.* Rev. and enl. ed. New York: Dover, 1969. 371 pp., 133 b&w figs. (1st ed. 1915; rev. ed. 1949 by Cyril G.E. Bunt.)
Easy introduction to the field of English and American plate. Touches on some of the major Renaissance pieces. Tables of London hallmarks and date-letters.

825   HOWARD, MONTAGUE. *Old English Silver: Its History, Its Makers and Its Marks.* New York: Charles Scribner's Sons; London: B.T. Batsford, 1903. 421 pp., 6 silver-gilt pls, 130 b&w figs.
Short history of English secular plate (pp. 1-51), evolution of different types (53-199): spoons, knives, forks, salts, cups, tankard, salvers, candlesticks, etc.; alphabetical listing of makers' initial marks; chronological table of London hallmarks. Largely superseded by Jack-. son's (entry 827) and Chaffer's (entry 816) repertories.

826   HUGHES, BERNARD and THERLE. *Three Centuries of English Domestic Silver 1500-1820.* New York: Wilfred Funk, 1952. 248 pp., 47 b&w pls.
Overall survey discussing, in twenty-three short chapters, hallmarks by type of objects. Pertinent to the period 1400-1600 are chapters on pomanders, candlesticks and tapesticks, standishes and inkstands, spoons, knives, forks, salts, casters and cruets, various dishes and platters, tankards.

827   JACKSON, CHARLES JAMES. *English Goldsmiths and Their Marks: A History of the Goldsmiths and Plate Workers of England, Scotland and Ireland.* 2d. rev. and enl. ed. London: Macmillan & Co., 1921. 763 pp., 8 b&w illus. (1st ed. 1905.)

Standard, comprehensive work on subject: history of goldsmiths, legislation, gold and silver standards, explanation of marks, chronological tables of marks, chronological list of goldsmiths' names; London and provincial centers, Scotland, Ireland. Over thirteen thousand marks (maker, town, assay, year).

828   JACKSON, CHARLES JAMES. *An Illustrated History of English Plate Ecclesiastical and Secular in Which the Development of Form and Decoration in the Silver and Gold Work of the British Isles. . . ,* 2 vols. London: Country Life and B.T. Batsford, 1911. 1064 pp., 77 photogravure pls, 1507 b&w text figs.

Standard, comprehensive survey of English, Irish, and Scottish plate, arranged chronologically, with chapters on Gothic (1:94-161) and Renaissance (1:162-203) products, and typologically with various chapters including 15th- and 16th-century ecclesiastical (1) and secular (2) pieces; covers a wide range of objects including chalices, ciboria, monstrances, communion cups, ewers, spoons, saltcellars, rosewater dishes, mazers, cups, candlesticks, andirons, etc.

829   JONES, E. ALFRED. *The Old Church Plate of the Isle of Man.* London: Bemrose & Sons, 1907. 65 pp., 20 b&w pls.

Thirty-two page introduction including a brief outline of the evolution of the form of the chalice; repertory of fifty-eight mostly silver objects of English manufacture surviving in Manx churches of which three (pls. I-III) date of the 16th century: a parcel-gilt chalice (1521-22), a silver paten (ca. 1525), and a silver beaker (1591-92).

830   LOWES, E.L. *Chats on Old Silver.* London: T. Fisher Unwin; New York: A. Stokes Co., 1909. 329 pp., 1 color pl., 54 b&w figs., numerous line drawings.

Chatty, somewhat dated text though a still useful introduction for the collector to the art of the silversmith. The emphasis is predominantly on English works; numerous references to the 16th century.

831   MARKHAM, CHRISTOPHER A. *The Church Plate of the County of Northampton.* London: Simpkin, Marshall, Hamilton, Kent & Co.; Northampton: Joseph Tebbutt, 1894. 368 pp., 1 b&w pl., 27 line drawings.

Description of plate including dimensions, inscriptions, etc., in parishes of Northamptonshire in alphabetical order of locality. Includes many 16th-century examples.

832   OMAN, CHARLES. *English Church Plate 597-1830.* London: Oxford University Press, 1957. 356 pp., 200 b&w pls.

Comprehensive study of English church (Anglican and Roman Catholic) plate; traces history and evolution, uses, form, iconography, craftsmen, patrons, etc.; illustrates a wide assortment of late medieval and post-Reformation chalices, patens, cruets, paxes, pyxes, flagon, communion cups and bowls (pls. 11-23, 27-37, 40-41, 44, 48-73, 107).

833   OMAN, CHARLES. *English Domestic Silver.* 7th ed. London: Black, 1968. 252 pp., 32 b&w pls. (1st ed. 1934.)

Standard concise history, particularly useful to collectors. Discussion of hallmarks, heraldic engraving, forgeries. Bibliography.

834   OMAN, CHARLES. *English Engraved Silver 1150 to 1900.* London and Boston: Faber & Faber, 1978. 158 pp., 159 b&w figs.

Survey dealing with technique, sources and Continental influence, iconography, and ornamental motifs. Examples of the period 1400-1600 (chaps. 1-2, pp. 21-54) include patens, paxes, cups, chalices, goblets, and mazers, plates and ewers, livery-pots, and tankards.

835   RUPERT, CHARLES G. *Apostle Spoons: Their Evolution from Earlier Types, and the Emblems Used by the Silversmiths for the Apostles.* Oxford: Oxford University Press; London; Humphrey Milford, 1929. 47 pp., 23 b&w pls.
Description of five complete sets in British collections, noting the attributes given to each Apostle.

836   TAYLOR, GERALD. *Silver.* 2d ed. Baltimore: Penguin Books, 1963. 302 pp., 64 b&w pls., line drawings. (1st ed. 1956.)
Concise and lucid outline in paperback edition of British plate (mostly domestic) from the 14th to the 20th century. Pp. 57-107 deal with the late Middle Ages and Renaissance periods. Concludes with useful tables of date-letters punched at British assay offices, glossary, tables of weight, and select bibliography.

837   WATTS, W.W. *Old English Silver.* New York: Charles Scribner's Sons, 1924. 179 pp., 134 b&w pls.
English plate from late medieval times to the 19th century. Guilds, styles, and social history surveyed on the basis of primary examples in public English collections. Useful classic reference work.

Articles

838   BEARD, CHARLES R. "The King's Lynn Plate." *Connoisseur* 107 (1941):148-53, 13 b&w figs.
Collection of English silver in the county of Norfolk (England) that includes a 15th-century sword and a seal of the Guild of St. George, and a gilt-silver mayor's collar of the 16th century.

839   BLAIR, CLAUDE. "A Drawing of an English Medieval Royal Gold Cup." *Burlington Magazine* 121 (1979):370-73, 3 b&w figs.
A sketch (City of London Letter Book K, f. 70, Public Record Office) recording a gold cup given to Lord Mayor William Estfield after the coronation of Henry VI in 1429.

840   BUNT, CYRIL G.E. "The Romantic Marriage of an English Covered Cup of 1514." *Connoisseur* 118 (1946):105-8, 7 b&w figs.
The discovery and subsequent reuniting of a gilt-silver Tudor communion cup of 1514 (in a private collection) to its foot.

841   COOPER, JOHN K.D. "An Assessment of Tudor Plate Design, 1530-1560." *Burlington Magazine* 121 (1979):360-64, 13 b&w figs.
Examines the accelerated transition from the Gothic to the Renaissance style in English plate. Mention of the first known two-handled cups in the history of English plate, a little-known secular cup of 1535-36 at St. Finn Barre's Cathedral, Cork, the well-known Bowes Cup, suggested as being the earliest surviving example of an English nautilus cup.

842   COOPER, JOHN K.D. "A Re-assessment of Some English Late Gothic and Early 'Renaissance' Plate." *Burlington Magazine* 119 (1977):408-12, 473-78, 18 b&w figs.

On the basis of stylistic details, some English late 15th- and early 16th-century gilt-silver objects now in London, Oxford, and Bristol, are classified into several categories with proposals for more precise datings.

843   FINLAY, IAN. "Old Scots Silver in Scottish Churches." *Connoisseur* 104 (1939):64-70, 12 b&w figs.
Engraved silver communion cups mostly produced in Edinburgh from the mid-16th century and now in parish churches.

844   GASK, NORMAN. "Maidenhead Spoons." *Old Furniture* 3 (1928):45-48, 6 b&w figs.
15th-16th-century silver and pewter English spoons with a maiden's bust as finial.

845   GASK, NORMAN. "Medieval English Silver Spoons." *Apollo* 21 (1935):135-38, 12 b&w figs.
Six types of 15th-century spoons are described and illustrated: Apostle, diamond-point, acorn-head, lion sejant guardant, maidenhead, wrythen-knop.

846   GASK, NORMAN. "Rare English Spoons." *Collector* 11 (1930):193-97, 9 b&w figs.
A spoon surmounted by St. Nicholas and bearing the London hallmark and date-letter for 1528-29. Among others are the 15th- century examples with a wild man, with a Moor's head, and a set of twelve Apostle spoons dating to 1592-93.

847   GLANVILLE, PHILIPPA. "Chinese Porcelain and English Goldsmiths c. 1560 to c. 1660." *V&A Album* 3 (1984):246-56, 12 color figs.
Oriental bowls, dishes, cups and ewers in various collections set in gilt-silver mounts bearing a London hallmark.

848   GLANVILLE, PHILIPPA. "Tudor Drinking Vessels." In *The Burlington House Fair Handbook.* (Incorporated in *Burlington Magazine* 127 [1985]:19-22, 10 b&w figs.)
Changing tastes in 16th-century English vessels (e.g., drinking "pots," serpentine bowls, silver-mounted stoneware jugs, tankards) as gleaned through inventories of the Tudor Jewel House as well as from extant pieces.

849   GRIMWADE, A.G. "Period Ornament on English Silver. I—Elizabeth I and James I." *Apollo* 56 (1952):74-78, 12 b&w figs.
Chief decorative techniques (engraving, chasing, repoussé, stamping) and patterns (strapwork, egg and dart, etc.) found on late 16th- and early 17th-century English silver; examples from the Victoria and Albert Museum and various English societies and guilds.

850   HAYWARD, J.F. "The Mannerist Goldsmiths: 4. England, Part I. The Holbein Designs." *Connoisseur* 159 (1965):80-84, 7 b&w figs.
Introduction and spread of mannerist ornament in England with Holbein and his associate, Hans von Antwerpen, mainly through the patronage of King Henry VIII.

850a   HAYWARD, J.F. "The Mannerist Goldsmiths: 4. England, Part II." *Connoisseur* 162 (1966):90-95, 7 b&w figs.
Holbein's designs for a clock presented to Henry VIII in 1545; importance of this artist and royal patronage for English silver; influx of Continental goldsmiths in the years 1575-1600.

850b   HAYWARD, J.F. "The Mannerist Goldsmiths: 4. England, Part III." *Connoisseur* 164 (1967):19-25, 12 b&w figs.

Involved standing salts, pelican, nautilus and standing cups as well as ewers, bearing London marks and reflecting Continental or indigenous models or elements of decoration.

851   HOW, G.E.P. "Early Scottish Spoons." *Connoisseur* 98 (1936):341-46, 8 b&w figs.

Examines two types of Scottish spoons—the "seal top" and the forerunner of the "Death's head"—very distinct in their form from any contemporary English examples; their marks, dating, and owners. Includes several late 16th-century examples.

852   JONES, E. ALFRED. "Viscount Rothermere's Gifts of Plate to the Middle Temple." *Apollo* 22 (1935):121-26, 6 b&w figs.

Includes descriptions of three Elizabethan gilt-silver vessels: a tazza-shaped cup (1572-73), a standing salt with a finial figure (1565-66), and a rosewater basin with embossed relief work (1596-97).

853   OMAN, CHARLES. "The Civic Plate and Insignia of the City of Norwich." *Connoisseur* Part 1, "The Insignia", 155 (1964):238-43, 1 color pl., 6 b&w figs.; part 2, "The Civic Plate", 156 (1964):6-14, 1 color pl., 15 b&w figs.

Highlights from the civic collection—some dating of 1400-1600: the Norwich city seal of 1404 (from an engraving and 1686 re-cast), a "waits" collar (1553), the Chamberlain's mace (1549), the Reade Salt (1568-69), and two gilt-silver communion cups of 1567 and 1561-62, the latter bearing a London hallmark.

854   OMAN, CHARLES. "The Civic Plate and Insignia of the City of Portsmouth." *Connoisseur* 160 (1965):216-24, 4 color figs., 20 b&w figs.

Pieces dating of the end of the 16th to the end of the 17th century. Of the earlier period are a gilt-silver mace with the arms of Charles II, a silver mace with the arms of James I, the Bodlein Cup bearing a London hallmark of 1525, the Lee Cup with a London hallmark of 1590, and three sealtop spoons with a London hallmark of 1558.

855   OMAN, CHARLES. "The False Plate of Medieval England." *Apollo* 55 (1952):74-75. 3 b&w figs.

A 15th-century drinking horn and a 16th-century mazer and cup (in Västergulands Muscum, Skara, Sweden; Church of St. Giles, Cripplegate; and Victoria and Albert Museum) with mounts of gilded base metal.

856   OMAN, C.C. "Some Plate in the West of England." *Connoisseur* 100 (1937):171-74, 7 b&w pls.

Seven silver pieces of English production—covered cups, bowl, salt, candlesticks, small casket—dating from the 15th to the 18th century and belonging to English churches and private collections.

857   VEITCH, HENRY NEWTON. "English Domestic Spoons—I." *Connoisseur* 20 (1911-12):153-61, 1 b&w pl., 10 line drawings.

Evolution of types and styles from Roman times to the 16th century; examples mostly from private collections.

858   WENHAM, EDWARD. Part 1, "Silver-Mounted Porcelain," *Connoisseur* 97 (1936):189-94, 10 b&w figs.; part 2, "Silver-Mounted Pottery," *Connoisseur* 97 (1936):251-56, 13 b&w figs.

First part: 16th-century English (mostly London produced) silver and gilt-silver mounts on Chinese porcelain bowls, jars, cups, jugs, and ewers. Second part: mounts on Near Eastern, German, and English pottery and jugs. All examples are drawn from British collections.

6. PERMANENT COLLECTIONS

Boston

MUSEUM OF FINE ARTS

859   BUHLER, KATHERYN C. "English Silver in the Bemis Collection." *Connoisseur* 130 (1952):226-31, 14 b&w figs.
      Highlights several pieces from this former private collection including some dating of the 16th century: a communion cup, a wine cup, coconut cup, the covered Westbury Cup, and a pomander.

Edinburgh

NATIONAL MUSEUM OF ANTIQUITIES OF SCOTLAND

860   VEITCH, HENRY NEWTON. "Early Scottish Spoons in the National Museum of Antiquities, Edinburgh." *Connoisseur* 22 (1912-13):331-37, 1 b&w pl.
      Nine silver spoons dating of the 16th to the 18th centuries; of the earlier period are two with characteristically Scottish details but fig-shaped bowl similar to the English type.

Hartford

WADSWORTH ATHENEUM

861   HOW, G.E.P. "The Plunkett St. Christopher and Apostle Spoons Initialled and Dated C.P., I.P., 1518 & I.P., K.L., 1538." *Connoisseur* 112 (1943):13-17, 11 b&w figs.
      Identification of the original owners in Dunshoughlin, Ireland, of this complete set of London-made spoons until the early 1940s in a private collection, Dublin.

862   *The Elizabeth B. Miles Collection: English Silver.*   Catalog by Elizabeth B. Miles. Hartford: Wadsworth Atheneum, 1976. 145 pp., 2 color pls., 174 b&w figs.
      Catalog of this private collection spanning the 16th to 19th century on permanent loan at the Wadsworth Atheneum of which twelve objects (cat. nos. 4-15) date of the 16th century: Apostle, seal-top, maidenhead, and acorn-knop spoons, and an Elizabeth I wine cup.

London

BRITISH MUSEUM

863   TAIT, HUGH. "The 'Stonyhurst' Salt." *Apollo* 79 (1964):270-78, 20 b&w figs.
      Secular goldsmith work bearing London hallmarks for 1577 and maker's mark I.R., enlivened with stones and mounts from earlier reliquaries melted down at the time of the Reformation.

864   "The Rochester Cathedral Tazzas." *Burlington Magazine* 114 (1972):31-32, 2 b&w illus.

Two Henry VIII gilt-silver tazze, one with cover bearing marks dating from 1528-33, purchased from the Cathedral of Rochester.

VICTORIA AND ALBERT MUSEUM

865 *Catalogue of English Silversmiths' Work (with Scottish and Irish) Civil and Domestic.* Introduction by W.W. Watts, with catalog entries by H.P. Mitchell. London: His Majesty's Stationery Office, 1920. 75 pp., 65 b&w pls.

Twenty-four-page introduction surveys the history and development of silversmithing; 230 catalog entries for objects of the 14th through the 18th century; relevant to the period 1400-1600 are cat. nos. 3-32 (pls. 2-14) including a mazer, tigerware jugs with gilt-silver mounts, a Chinese porcelain jug with English mounts of 1585-86; cups, goblets, salts, ewers, a tazza, etc.

866 BUNT, CYRIL, G.E. "Der Howard-Grace-Becher." *Pantheon* 8 (1931):417-19, 2 b&w figs.

History of a gilt-silver English standing cup of ca. 1525 with ivory bowl, cover with finial representing St. George and the Dragon, and bearing both late Gothic as well as Renaissance elements.

867 PENZER, N.M. "The Howard Grace Cup and the Early Date-Letter Cycles." *Connoisseur* 117 (1946):87-91, 11 b&w figs.

Unique gilt-silver English cup of ca. 1525 studded with gems and with an ivory bowl.

868 OMAN, CHARLES, and MAYNE, JONATHAN. "Six Elizabethan Silver-Gilt Plates." *Burlington Magazine* 89 (1947):182, 184-87; 8 b&w figs.

Hypothesis on commission and identity of the goldsmith whose monogram FR appears with the London hallmark for 1573-74 on these plates; sources for the engraved scenes.

869 OMAN, CHARLES. *English Silversmiths' Work Civil and Domestic: An Introduction.* London: Her Majesty's Stationery Office, 1965. 15 pp., 192 b&w pls.

Survey of English silver through examples provided by the museum's collection as of 1961. Includes eighteen well-illustrated pieces of the 15th-16th century: bowls, cups, snuffer, plates, ewer, salts, and a horn.

Los Angeles

LOS ANGELES COUNTY MUSEUM OF ART

870 NORMAN-WILCOX, GREGOR. "The Methuen Cup." *Los Angeles County Museum Bulletin* 13 (1961):11-15, 1 color pl. (cover), 3 b&w figs.

Rare Scottish gilt-silver covered cup of ca. 1525-50, bearing the maker's mark Vh in a shield, gift of the Hearst Foundation.

Moscow

KREMLIN

871 JONES, E. ALFRED. *The Old English Plate of the Emperor of Russia.* London: Privately Printed, 1909. 115 pp., 50 b&w pls.

Gifts of the sovereigns of England and of Christian IV of Denmark to the court of Russia from 1557 until 1663 in the Treasury of the Kremlin and the Antchkoff Palace, Leningrad. Most pieces (cups, bottles, salts, tankards) bear London marks.

872 OMAN, CHARLES. *The English Silver in the Kremlin 1557-1663.* London: Methuen & Co., 1961. 112 pp., 55 b&w pls.

Outstanding examples, many of which date of the 16th century. Visiting embassies, gifts, etc. are traced as sources of the collection. Included are standing cups, basins, livery-pots, flagons, and salts.

Munich

RESIDENZ

873 HAYWARD, J.F. "A Rock-crystal Bowl from the Treasury of Henry VIII." *Burlington Magazine* 100 (1958):120-24, 7 b&w figs.

Covered drinking bowl in enameled-gold mount in the Schatzkammer attributable to Hans Holbein's design.

Oxford

MAGDELEN COLLEGE

874 HAYWARD, JOHN. "The Tudor Plate of Magdelen College, Oxford." *Burlington Magazine* 125 (1983):260-65, 8 b&w figs.

The recent discovery of documents leads the author to new speculations on the "Founder's Cup" of 1601 bearing a 16th-century Magdalene finial, and to a new attribution (English rather than German) for a rare early 16th-century covered flagon.

ORIEL COLLEGE

875 *Catalogue of the Plate of Oriel College Oxford,* by E. Alfred Jones. Oxford: Oxford University Press; London: Humphrey Milford, 1944. 131 pp., 21 b&w pls.

Mostly post-1600 silversmith works but includes three outstanding 15th-century pieces: the Founders Cup (French, ca. 1462-70), a maplewood mazer with gilt-silver mounts, and a coconut cup, both English of ca. 1470-85. Ten-page introduction; transcription (pp. 89-94) of an inventory (1596) of Oriel College plate.

Paris

MUSÉE DU LOUVRE

876 KOVÁKS, ÉVA. "Le Reliquaire de l'Ordre du Saint-Esprit: La 'Dot' d'Anne de Bretagne." *Revue du Louvre et des musées de France* 31 (1981):246-51, 1 color fig., 8 b&w figs.

Painted enamel reliquary of the Trinity, property in the late 15th century of Anne de Bretagne, here dated to ca. 1410 and suggested to have been produced in London, on the basis of its traditional composition and its comparatively inferior workmanship.

Reims

CATHÉDRALE

877 EVANS, JOAN. "A Note on the Rheims Resurrection 'Reliquary'." *Antiquaries Journal* 35 (1955):52-54, 4 b&w figs.

A late medieval gilt-silver monstrance-reliquary in the Treasury, gift of Henri II of France (with his initials added) on the occasion of his coronation in 1547, suggested as having perhaps been made in England.

San Marino, Calif.

HENRY E. HUNTINGTON LIBRARY AND ART GALLERY

878 *British Silver in the Huntington Collection.* Catalog by Robert R. Wark. San Marino, Calif.: Huntington Library, 1978. 191 pp., 391 b&w figs.

375 entries for objects ranging from the 15th to the 19th century. Of the 15th-16th century are nos. 1-4 (pp. 308-9): a mazer, communion cup, tigerware jug with gilt-silver mounts, a coconut cup, spoons.

7. EXHIBITION CATALOGS

Cambridge

FITZWILLIAM MUSEUM

879 *Cambridge Plate: An Exhibition of Silver, Silver-Gilt and Gold Plate Arranged as Part of the Cambridge Festival 1975, Drawn from the Holdings of the City of Cambridge, the University of Cambridge, the Colleges, the National Trust (Anglesey Abbey), and the Cambridge Beefsteak Club.* Exhibition catalog by R.A. Crighton. Cambridge: Fitzwilliam Museum, 1975. 95 pp., 153 b&w figs.

211 objects of the 12th through the 20th century mostly produced in England. Includes several pieces dating of 1400-1600 such as a sceptre, chalice, mazers, coconut cup, tankards, nautilus cup, Isnik jug in 16th-century English mounts, "ostrich egg" mounted as a standing cup, various other cups as well as tazze, some with lids, ewers and basins, etc. Entries are arranged typologically.

London

GOLDSMITHS' HALL

880 *Catalogue of the Historic Plate of the City of London Exhibited at Goldsmiths' Hall.* Exhibition catalog by J.F. Hayward. 2 vols. Vol. 1, catalog, 89 pp.; vol. 2, illustrations, 77 b&w pls. London: Goldsmiths' Hall, 1951.

With its 276 objects dating from the 15th through the 18th century and drawn mostly from livery companies, this is the most comprehensive catalog of secular silver objects from the City. For the period 1400-1600, see cat. nos. 1-64 including salts, standing and other cups, mazers, tankards, flagons, basins, tigerware jugs with silver mounts, etc.

881   *Corporation Plate of England and Wales.* Exhibition catalog by J.F. Hayward, assisted by
      A.G. Grimwade. 2 parts. Part 1, catalog, 62 pp.; part 2, illustrations, 46 b&w pls. compris-
      ing 249 figs. London: Goldsmiths' Hall, 1952.
         249 works spanning the 14th to the 18th century by former members of the Worship-
      ful Company of the Goldsmiths of London and those of provincial centers of York, New-
      castle, Chester, Hull, etc. Drawing from 102 civic collections, the exhibit includes 15th-16th-
      century cups, ewer, basins, swords of state, and maces.

881a OMAN, CHARLES. "Corporation Plate of England and Wales at Goldsmiths' Hall,
      Until 30th August." *Connoisseur* 130 (1952):27-31, 11 b&w figs.
         Author highlights examples from the exhibition (see previous entry), discussing
      several 1400-1600 examples: gilt-silver maces (insignias of office), a sword and scabbard with
      silver and gilt mounts (London, 1554), the Bodkin Cup (1525), the Reade Standing Salt
      (1568), etc.

ST. JAMES'S COURT

882   *Old Silver-Work Chiefly English from the XVth to the XVIIIth Centuries: A Catalogue of the
      Unique Loan Collection Exhibited in 1902 at St. James's Court, London, in Aid of the
      Children's Hospital, St. Ormond Street, Supplemented by Some Further Specimens from the
      Collections of the Dukes of Devonshire and Rutland, Earl Cowper, and Others,* by J. Starkie
      Gardner. London: B.T.Batsford, 1903. 212 pp., 121 b&w pls.
         Important gathering of silversmith works mostly from private collections and includ-
      ing those of J.P. Morgan and Henry Walker. Ninety-four-page introduction describes some
      406 objects by types (drinking vessels, flagons, ewers, candlesticks, spoons, salts, vases, etc.),
      some of which are of the 16th century, followed by catalog organized according to the layout
      of the exhibition. Principally useful for plates.

New York

ROYAL OAK FOUNDATION

883   *Heritage of England: Silver through Ten Reigns.* Exhibition catalog by James Charles. Lon-
      don: Asprey & Co., 1983. 125 pp., 55 b&w pls.
         Thirty-seven masterpieces of English silversmithing from British public and private
      collections and ranging from the 16th to 18th century; pertinent to the 16th century are nos. 1-
      9, including cups, a bowl, caster, tazza, plates, tankard, and flagons.

Oxford

ASHMOLEAN MUSEUM

884   *Catalogue of a Loan Exhibition of Silver Plate Belonging to the Colleges of the University of
      Oxford.* Exhibition catalog introduction by W.W. Watts. Oxford: Clarendon, 1928. 93
      pp., 74 b&w figs.
         Ten-page introduction; 435 entries of almost exclusively English ecclesiastical and
      secular silver ranging from late 14th to 20th century; includes chalices, mazers, beakers,
      coconut cups, salts, rosewater dishes, tankards, several of which are outstanding examples.
      For 15th-16th-century items, see nos. 1-10, 60-87a, 421, 425.

884a   WATTS, W.W. "Exhibition of Oxford College Plate at the Ashmolean Museum." *Old Furniture* 5 (1928):170-77, 12 b&w figs.

Illustrates and briefly describes a few exceptional English pieces of 1400-1600: a mazer, a covered cup, a coconut cup, and a covered beaker.

8. PRIVATE COLLECTION, AUCTION, AND DEALER CATALOGS

ELLIS COLLECTION

885   ELLIS, H.D. "Some Steps in the Evolution of the Apostle Spoon." *Burlington Magazine* 23 (1913):283-87, 1 b&w pl.

Two spoons in the author's collection here dated of ca. 1460-75 on the basis of the position of the crowning figure's halo and nimbus, thereby antedating the hitherto earliest known Apostle spoons (1490).

885a   *Catalogue of a Remarkable Collection of 16th & 17th Century Provincial Silver Spoons Incorporating Practically the Entire Collection Left by the Late H.D. Ellis, Esq. at His Death, the Property of Lt.-Col. Claude Beddington.* Sale held in London at Sotheby's 15-16 April, 1937. 58 pp., 16 b&w pls.

252 lots comprised of thirty-nine different groups (i.e. York, fleur-de-lys, "London forgery" groups), a fourth of which date of the 16th century. Indexes of groups, makers' names, initials, marks and ornaments, Apostles. (Based on the fuller catalog compiled by G.E.P. How for a Sotheby sale planned for 13-14 November 1935, but that actually did not take place.)

HARRIS COLLECTION

886   HARRIS, WILFRED. "The Education of a Spoon Collector." *Connoisseur* 125 (1950):28-34, 50; 28 b&w figs.

English silver Apostle, maidenhead, wrythen-knop, acorn-top spoons made mostly between 1400-1600 in the author's collection.

LEE COLLECTION

887   BEARD, CHARLES R. "Early Silver in the Collection of Viscount and Viscountess Lee of Fareham." *Connoisseur* 99 (1937):63-70, 13 b&w figs.

Author re-examines dating of several pieces inventoried by Watts in his folio catalog of 1936 (see entry 681a), and proposes different early ownerships.

PIERPONT MORGAN COLLECTION

888   JONES, E. ALFRED. "A Mazer Bowl of 1501-2." *Connoisseur* 110 (1942):13, 1 b&w fig.

Drinking vessel then in the Pierpont Morgan Collection, perhaps the earliest bearing a London date-letter on its silver mount.

SCHRÖDER COLLECTION

889   WATTS, W.W. "English Silver, Chiefly of the Tudor Period, in the Collection of Baron and Baroness Bruno Schröder." *Old Furniture* 1 (1927):245-56, 15 b&w figs.

Gilt-silver cups and salts, and coconut, crystal, Chinese porcelain cups with gilt-silver mounts; also stoneware, tankards, and a ewer bearing 16th-century London hallmarks.

CZECHOSLOVAKIA

3. SURVEYS AND HISTORIES

890   TORANOVÁ, EVA. *Goldschmiedekunst in der Slowakei*. Hanau: Werner Dausien, 1982. 261 pp., 84 color figs., 346 b&w figs., makers' marks.
The art of the goldsmith in Slovakia from Gothic times until the 19th century. Includes a forty-seven-page introduction and a catalog of 292 ecclesiastical and secular pieces, nos. 3-210 dating of the period 1400-1600.

6. PERMANENT COLLECTIONS

Prague

UMĚLECKOPRŮMYSLOVÉ MUZEUM

891   *Nože, lžíce, vidličky: Ze sbírek uměleckoprůmyslového Musea v Praze*. Catalog by Vera Vokácova. Prague: Uměleckoprůmyslové Muzeum, [1981]. 220 pp., 4 color pls., 306 b&w figs., facsimile makers' marks.
310 knives, spoons, and forks produced in Prague and elsewhere in Central Europe from the 14th to 19th century. Nos. 1-50 are 15th-16th-century examples. Eight pages of marks; bibliography.

FRENCH

1. DICTIONARIES AND ENCYCLOPEDIAS

892   BEUQUE, ÉMILE. *Dictionaire des poinçons officiels, français et étrangers, anciens et modernes de leur création (XIVᵉ siècle) à nos jours*. 2 vols. Paris: F. de Nobele, 1976. 1:375 pp., 3181 line drawings; 2:310 pp., 2612 line drawings. (Reprint of 1925 [1] and 1927 [2] eds.)
5,793 control marks on platinum, gold, and silver from all over the world and dating from the 14th to the 20th century, classified by figure and object type, and by letters, numbers, and signs, each reproduced in a line drawing, with annotation, date of inception and termination, and the nature of its guarantee. Vol. 1 includes 43 marks of the 15th century and 245 of the 16th century; vol. 2, 11 of the 15th and 72 of the 16th century.

893   BEUQUE, E., and FRAPSAUCE, M. [F.] *Dictionnaire des poinçons de maîtres-orfèvres français du XIVᵉ siècle à 1838*. Paris: E. Beuque et F. Frapsauce, 1929. 355 pp., numerous facsimile makers' marks. Reprint. Paris: F. de Nobele, 1964.
Early repertory of three thousand marks of French master goldsmiths of the 14th century to 1838. Arranged alphabetically by initials, then by signs and symbols.

894   CARRÉ, LOUIS. *Les Poinçons de l'orfèvrerie française du quatorzième siècle jusqu'au début du dix-neuvième siècle*. Paris: Louis Carré, 1928. 355 pp., 12 b&w pls., numerous town and makers' marks. Reprint. New York: Burt Franklin, 1968.
French marks from the 14th to the early 19th century. Part 1 is an historical essay; part 2 studies marks of master goldsmiths, of control, and of confraternities, and assay marks of cities and state officials; part 3 lists Paris marks followed by those of other centers in alphabetical order. Indexes of marks. Useful for its readability.

894a   CARRÉ, LOUIS. *A Guide to Old French Plate.* Translated from the French with a foreward by Maurice Bouvier-Ajam. London: Eyre & Spottiswoode, [1971]. 298 pp., 32 b&w pls.

      Well-rounded handbook of French gold and silver plate and their marks. Part 1 (the only one relevant to the period 1400-1600): marks on French plate from the 13th through the 19th century; this is an abridged version of the above entry.

2. BIOGRAPHICAL DICTIONARIES

895   BOIVIN, JEAN. *Les Anciens Orfèvres français et leurs poinçons.* Paris: J. Boivin, [1925]. 401 pp., numerous facsimile makers' marks.

      Recorded French goldsmiths and their work; first Parisian masters followed by those of other cities in alphabetical order from the 7th century through the First Empire. The marks they used, when known, are reproduced in line drawings. Also, town and assay marks. This study underlines that goldsmithing was a prosperous trade in many French centers by the 15th-16th century.

896   BRAULT-LERCH, SOLANGE. *Les Orfèvres de Franche-Comté et de la Principauté de Montbéliard du Moyen Age au XIXe siècle.* Vol. 1 of *Dictionnaire des poinçons de l'orfèvrerie provinciale française.* Geneva: Droz, 1976. 1,088 pp., 1 color pl., 96 b&w pls.

      Comprehensive four-part study of goldsmiths from Franche-Comté and the principality of Montbéliard from the 12th-19th century. Part 1 (pp. 3-78): history of goldsmithing in Franche-Comté (8-30 on the 15th-16th century); part 2 (79-142): master goldsmiths of Besançon (their neighborhoods, shops, social conditions, regulations, etc.) from the 13th century; part 3 (143-750): repertory of 16th-19th-century master goldsmiths of Franche-Comté, arranged first by location and then alphabetically—biographical data, description of their work, bibliography; part 4 (751-860): goldsmiths of the principality of Montbéliard—historical background and alphabetical listing. Over a hundred document extracts: inventories, accounts, ordinances and regulations, of the 16th-18th century. Table of letter marks, alphabetically listed; subject and name index.

897   BRAULT-LERCH, SOLANGE. *Les Orfèvres de Troyes en Champagne.* Vol. 4 of *Dictionnaire des poinçons de l'orfèvrerie provinciale française.* Geneva: Droz, 1986. 356 pp., 40 b&w pls., makers' marks.

      Repertory of goldsmith/silversmiths active in the city of Troyes in Champagne from the 14th through the 18th century. Includes several of the late Gothic and Renaissance periods with some of their works illustrated. Historical essay, archival data, town and makers' marks.

898   CASSAN, CLAUDE-GÉRARD, *Les Orfèvres de la Normandie du XVIe au XIXe siècle et leur poinçons.* Paris: F. De Nobele, 1980. 276 pp., 3 color pls., 68 b&w figs., numerous makers' marks.

      Repetory of goldsmiths/silversmiths active in Normandy alphabetically arranged by town and individuals; includes historical data and chronology for each city and biographical information for each maker, with archival references; town and makers' marks.

899   GODEFROY, GISÈLE. *Les Orfèvres de Lyon (1306- 1791) et de Trévoux (1700-1785): Répertoire biographique—poinçons—oeuvres.* Paris: Éditions A. et J. Picard, 1965. 398 pp., 35 b&w pls., 312 marks.

First part of book (only one relevant to period 1400-1600) deals with goldsmiths of Lyon from the 14th to the 18th century (pp. 1-325): overview of goldsmithing seen in historical and artistic context of each century; the various aspects of the trade: the neighborhood of the goldsmiths, confraternity chapel, shield, acceptance into the trade, numbers, traditions, regulations, marks, etc.; alphabetical repertory of masters with biographical data, descriptions of marks (some illustrated), documentary references; table of marks; catalog of 114 religious and secular goldsmith objects made in Lyon and now in American and European public and private collections.

900   GODEFROY, GISÈLE, and GIRARD, RAYMOND. *Les Orfèvres du Dauphiné du Moyen Age au XIXe siècle*. Vol. 3 of *Dictionnaire des poinçons de l'orfèvrerie provinciale française*. Geneva: Droz, 1985. 606 pp., 66 b&w pls., numerous makers' marks.
       Thorough study of goldsmiths working in the region of Dauphiné from Carolingian times until the 19th century. Part 1, chronological survey of goldsmithing, chaps. 3 and 4 (pp. 23-49) dealing with the 15th-16th century: evolution, religious and secular commissions, regulations; part 2 (87-309), master goldsmiths of Grenoble: guilds, social conditions, relationship with other trades, assay marks, repertory of recorded masters (see passim for period 1400-1600); part 3 (313-465), goldsmiths of the Dauphiné region: Vienne, Bourgoin, Saint-Marcellin, Valence, Romans, Montélimar, etc. Appendixes include transcriptions of regulations and inventories, marks, indexes of names of persons and places.

901   JOURDAN-BARRY, RAYMOND. *Les Orfèvres de la généralité d'Aix-en-Provence du XIVe siècle au début du XIXe siècle*. Paris: F. De Nobele, 1974. 496 pp., 66 b&w pls., facsimile makers' marks.
       Biographical repertory, alphabetically arranged, of goldsmiths of the Aix-en-Provence region from the 14th century to the beginning of the 19th. A fourteen-page essay reviews apprenticeship, guilds, rights of widows, etc. Transcription of various documents; indexes of master goldsmiths alphabetically arranged by initials, of cities, makers' marks, goldsmiths' works presented by type of object.

902   NOCQ, HENRY. *Le Poinçon de Paris: Répertoire des Maîtres-orfèvres de la jurisdiction de Paris depuis le moyen-âge jusqu'à la fin du XVIIIe siècle*. 5 vols. Paris: H. Floury, 1926-31. 1:342 pp., 1 hand-painted pl., 11 b&w pls., 152 line drawings, makers' marks and signature facsimiles; 2:379 pp., 2 hand-painted pls., 13 b&w pls., 178 line drawings, makers' marks, and signature facsimiles; 3:450 pp., 14 b&w pls., 229 line drawings, makers' marks, and signature facsimiles; 4:301 pp., 2 hand-painted pls., 9 b&w pls., 143 line drawings and makers' marks; 5:97 pp., 1 b&w pl., 47 line drawings and makers' marks. Reprint. Paris: Laget, 1967.
       Vast alphabetical repertory of 5,511 Parisian master-goldsmiths from the 13th to the 18th century: biographical notices and description of their marks (876 reproduced); illustration of 240 goldsmith works. Vol. 1: A-C; 2: D-K; 3: L-R; 4: S-Z. Seventy-page historial essay: chronological repertory of 16th-18th-century assayors, with year letter; chronological listing of farmer-generals, description of their marks, and extracts from documents; assayors' itineraries within the city; general notes on goldsmiths in Paris and surroundings; bibliography. Vol. 5: errata and addenda; table of masters arranged alphabetically by their initials; table of symbols.

903   THUILE, JEAN. *Histoire de l'orfèvrerie du Languedoc, généralités de Montpellier et de Toulouse: Répertoire des orfèvres depuis le moyen age jusqu'au début du XIXe siècle*. 3 vols. Vol. 1 (1964), 547 pp., 28 b&w pls. comprising 83 figs., 239 makers' marks; vol. 2

(1966), 473 pp., 50 b&w pls. comprising 186 figs., 313 makers marks; vol. 3 (1969), 496 pp., 65 b&w pls. comprising 182 figs., 362 makers' marks. Montrouge: Théo & Florence Schmied.

Repertory of gold- and silversmiths who fashioned ecclesiastical and secular plate in the region of Toulouse-Montpellier from the Middle Ages to the 19th century. Biographical sketches as gleaned from archival records with mention of their works when known. Vol. 1: A-C; 2: D-L; 3: M-Z. Each volume comprises indexes of names of persons, places, and marks.

904   VERLET-REAUBOURG, NICOLE. *Les Orfèvres du ressort de la Monnaie de Bourges.* Vol. 2 of *Dictionnaire des poinçons de l'orfèvrerie provinciale française.* Geneva: Droz, 1977. 501 p., 15 b&w pls., 119 makers' marks on 6 additional pls.

Detailed study of goldsmithing and goldsmiths in Bourges to the 19th century. First half of book examines the trade — apprenticeship, marks, registers — princely patrons, religious and municipal commissions, competition, and assessment of goldsmiths' own wealth; extracts from 16th-18th-century documents. Second half of book is a repertory of 14th-19th-century masters from Bourges and surroundings listed first by location and then alphabetically — biographical data, description of their mark, bibliography. Tables of letter marks; subject and name index.

3. SURVEYS AND HISTORIES

Books

905   AUZAS, PIERRE-MARIE. *L'Orfèvrerie religieuse bretonne.* Paris: A.&J. Picard & Cie., 1955. 157 pp., 28 b&w pls., 106 marks.

Religious goldsmith works produced in Brittany from the 12th to the 18th century: description of the main types of objects (chalices, processional crosses, reliquaries, etc.); lists of 359 extant pieces (31 of the 15th and 54 of the 16th century) repertoried by regions (départements); list of master goldsmiths (684 names) with biographical data and descriptions of marks, list of same by location; list of apprentice goldsmiths; description of 41 objects bearing marks from Brittany.

906   CARTIER, NICOLE. *Orfèvrerie de la Jurande d'Arras (Arras, Bapaume, Béthune, Hesdin).* [Arras?]: Commission Départementale d'Histoire et d'Archéologie, 1983. 317 pp., 242 b&w figs.

Goldsmith work of the wardship of Arras in Artois (Arras, Bapaume, Béthune, and Hesdin) from Renaissance times until the Revolution. Four-page introduction touches on the medieval period; chap. 1 deals with Arras goldsmiths of the 16-17th century; subsequent chapters concerned with other towns of the wardship often touch on the period preceding 1710. Concludes with list of known Arras goldsmiths, table of town, makers', and control marks.

907   CRIPPS, WILIFRED JOSEPH. *Old French Plate: Its Makers and Marks. A Handbook for the Collector.* 3d ed. London: John Murray, 1920. 125 pp., line drawings of marks. (1st ed. 1880.)

Overview of production from the 7th to the 19th century. Relevant to the 15th-16th century are the sections on Parisian guilds, ordinances, and marks (pp. 19-25), list of some well-known 16th-century goldsmiths (25), table of alphabetical date-letters used in Paris from 1461/2 to 1600 (41-43), plate in the provinces (53-54), and table of description of arms of French towns where plate was produced before 1783 (60-65).

908 HAUG, HANS. *L'Orfèvrerie de Strasbourg dans les collections publiques françaises.* Vol. 22 of *Inventaire des collections publiques françaises.* Paris: Éditions des Musées Nationaux, 1978. 222 pp., 239 b&w figs.

221 goldsmith and silversmith works produced in Strasbourg from the 15th through the 18th century and now in French national museums. Nos. 1-21 are cups, chalices, coconut vessels, enameled pyx and pax, processional cross, of the 15th-16th century, some bearing marks of Georg Kobenhaupt, Dibolt Krug, Abraham Berner, Lienhart Bauer, Wilhelm V. Meie, Paulus Grasseck, Dietrich Brey, Steffen Vesuch, Adam Kurn, Melchen Hartum, and Nikolas Rapp, etc. Includes reproduction of marks and master seals.

909 LIGHTBOWN, R.W. *Secular Goldsmiths' Work in Medieval France: A History.* London: Society of Antiquaries, 1978. 150 pp., 7 color pls., 74 b&w pls.

Though dealing primarily with 14th-century examples, the depth of this study provides valuable perspectives on early 15th-century techniques and style.

Articles

910 HAYWARD, J.F. "The Mannerist Goldsmiths: 2. France and the School of Fontainebleau." *Connoisseur.* Part 1, 152 (1963): 240-45, 7 b&w figs.; part 2, 153 (1963):11-15, 15 b&w figs.

Plate for Francis I by Rosso (as shown from engravings by René Boyvin) and Cellini; stylish elements and designs of the Italian mannerists; slow acceptance of the imported mode by the French goldsmiths as seen in extant pieces from major European collections and mostly from designs by Jacques and Androuet Du Cerceau, Boyvin, Étienne Delaune, and the engraver signing CC who maintained close inspirational ties with the North.

911 HEROLD, MICHEL, and PLOUVIER, MARTINE. "L'Orfèvrerie amiénoise au XVIe siècle: Jehan de Graval et la châsse de sainte Godeberthe de Noyon." *Revue de l'art* 67 (1985):77-84, 7 b&w figs.

Reproduction of the 1499 contract between Jehan de Graval and the Cathedral of Noyon for the making of a reliquary casket and of the artist's preliminary drawing of this church-shaped receptacle. Examination of the careers of the goldsmith and his contemporaries in Amiens, and of the reliquary.

912 KOVÁKS, ÉVA. "Problèmes de style autour de 1400: I, L'Orfèvrerie parisienne et ses sources." *Revue de l'art* 28 (1975):25-33. 15 illus.

Identification of late 14th- to early 15th-century Parisian goldsmith works from royal inventories as well as those of dukes Philip the Bold and Jean de Berry; dating of earliest examples of enameling of gold modeled in the round.

913 TOESCA, ILARIA. "Silver in the Time of François I: A New Identification." *Apollo* 90 (1969):292-97, 13 b&w figs.

A rare gilt-silver Parisian casket with mother-of-pearl, precious and semiprecious stones (bearing the date-letter for 1533-34 and the Master's initial 'B') in the Mantua Cathedral Treasury linked to three other objects the author attributes to the same master: a ciborium in the Louvre, a clock-salt in London (Worshipful Company of Goldsmiths), and a casket in a private collection (formerly in the Randolph Hearst Collection). All pieces are strongly characterized by the distinctive Francis I style coupling the flamboyant with Italianate elements.

6. PERMANENT COLLECTIONS

Altötting

PFARRKIRCHE

914   BLAIR, CLAUDE, and CAMPBELL, MARIAN. "Das goldene Rössl von Altötting."
Weltkunst 52 (1982):2902-7, 6 color figs.
High quality color photography of the gold and enamel shrine given to Charles VI of
France in 1404 by Isabeau of Bavaria.

Esztergom, Hungary

FÖSZÉKESEGYHÁZI KINCSTÁR

915   KOVÁKS, ÉVA. *Der goldene Kalvarienberg des Königs Matthias Corvinus in der
Domschatzkammer zu Esztergom.* German translation by Anikó Harmath. Budapest:
Helikon Kiadó/Corvina Kiadó, 1984. 56 pp., 19 color figs.
Gold and enamel reliquary of the Calvary produced in Paris about 1402 and later
owned by King Matthias Corvinus of Hungary, connected by the author to the Order of the
Passion devised by Phillipe de Mezières.

London

VICTORIA AND ALBERT MUSEUM

916   *French Silver.* Catalog by R.W. Lightbown. London: Her Majesty's Stationery Office,
1978. 127 pp., 197 b&w figs.
Catalog of 119 objects of French silversmith work from the 12th through the 19th century in the permanent collection. Pertinent to 1400-1600 are catalog nos. 14-29: beaker,
spoons, chalices, standing cup, bowls, processional crosses, salt. All are illustrated, some with
details. Valuable particularly in view of the scarcity of pre-Revolutionary French silver.

New York

METROPOLITAN MUSEUM OF ART

917   YOUNG, BONNIE. "A Jewel of St. Catherine." *Metropolitan Museum of Art Bulletin* 24
(1966):316-24, 10 b&w figs.
Gold enameled statuette with jewels, French (probably Parisian), of ca. 1400-10, representative of the International Style.

Vienna

KUNSTHISTORISCHES MUSEUM

918   SALET, FRANCIS. "La 'Croix du serment' de l'Ordre de la Toison d'or." *Journal des
savants,* 1974:73-94, 9 figs.
A 14th-century gold cross in the Schatzkammer once owned by Jean de Berry and to
which were made several 15th-century additions when it passed into the possession of Duke
Philip the Good of Burgundy.

See also entry 47.

7. EXHIBITION CATALOGS

Narbonne

MUSÉE DES BEAUX-ARTS DE NARBONNE

919 *Trésors d'orfèvrerie des églises du Roussilon et du Languedoc méditeranéen.* Exhibition catalog by Jean Thuile. Narbonne: Musée des Beaux-Arts de Narbonne, 1954. 97 pp., 100 b&w pls.

    Ninety-six goldsmith works drawn from churches in Rousillon and South Languedoc. Included are several 15th-century processional crosses, reliquaries, statuettes, and chalices produced in Toulouse, Carcassone, Montpellier, Avignon, and arranged alphabetically by present whereabouts.

GERMAN

2. BIOGRAPHICAL DICTIONARIES

920 SCHEFFLER, WOLFGANG. *Berliner Goldschmiede: Daten, Werke, Zeichen.* Berlin: Bruno Hessling, 1968. 647 pp., 137 b&w figs., numerous facsimile makers' marks.

    Berlin goldsmiths, their dates, works, and marks. Lists of three of the 15th century and seventy-three of the 16th century (pp. 1-10).

920a SCHEFFLER, WOLFGANG. *Goldschmiede Hessens: Daten, Werke, Zeichen.* Berlin and New York: Walter de Gruyter, 1976. 848 pp., 32 b&w pls., makers' marks.

    Goldsmiths working in Hesse: biographical data, their known works and marks. Alphabetical arrangement by town and then chronologically; several from the period 1400-1600.

920b SCHEFFLER, WOLFGANG. *Goldschmiede an Main und Neckar: Daten, Werke, Zeichen.* Hanover: Verlag Kunst und Antiquitäten, 1977. 119 pp., makers' marks.

    Goldsmiths working in the Main and Neckar region: biographical data, their known works and marks. Alphabetical arrangement by town and then chronologically; several from the period 1400-1600.

920c SCHEFFLER, WOLFGANG. *Goldschmiede Mittel- und Nordostdeutschlands von Wernigerode bis Lauenburg in Pommern: Daten, Werke, Zeichen.* Berlin and New York: Walter de Gruyter, 1980. 666 pp., 24 b&w pls.

    Goldsmiths working in middle and northeast Germany from Wernigerode to Lauenburg in Pomerania: biographical data, their known works and marks. Alphabetical arrangement by town and then chronologically; several from the period 1400-1600.

920d SCHEFFLER, WOLFGANG. *Goldschmiede Niedersachsens: Date, Werke, Zeichen.* 2 vols. Berlin: Walter de Gruyter & Co., 1965. 1:681 pp., makers' marks; 2:575 pp., 12 b&w pls., makers' marks.

    Goldsmiths working in Lower Saxony: biographical data, their known works and marks. Alphabetical arrangement by town and then chronologically; several from the period 1400-1600.

920e   SCHEFFLER, WOLFGANG. Goldschmiede Ostpreussens: Daten, Werke, Zeichen. Berlin and New York: Walter de Gruyter, 1983. 346 pp., 24 b&w pls., makers' marks.

Goldsmiths working in East Prussia: biographical data, their known works and marks. Alphabetical arrangement by town and then chronologically; several from the period 1400-1600.

920f   SCHEFFLER, WOLFGANG. *Goldschmiede Rheinland-Westfalens: Daten, Werke, Zeichen.* 2 vols. Berlin and New York: Walter de Gruyter, 1973. 1:686 pp., makers' marks; 2:471 pp., 48 b&w pls., makers' marks.

Goldsmiths working in Rheinland-Westphalia: biographical data, their known works and marks. Alphabetical arrangement by town and then chronologically; several from the period 1400-1600.

3. SURVEYS AND HISTORIES

Books

921   BÖHM, ERNST. *Hans Petzolt, ein deutscher Goldschmied.* Munich: F. Bruckmann, 1939. 90 pp., 29 b&w pls., 4 b&w text figs.

Monograph on the Nuremberg goldsmith Hans Petzolt (1551-1633); his creations and his influence.

922   BÖSKEN, SIGRID. *Die Mainzer Goldschmiedezunft: Ihre Meister und deren Werke vom Ende des 15. bis zum ausgehenden 18. Jahrhundert.* Dissertation of the Johann-Gutenberg-Univerität zu Mainz series. (Beiträge zum Geschichte der Stadt Mainz, vol. 21.) Mainz: 1970. 140 pp., 125 b&w figs.

The goldsmiths' guild in Mainz; activity of its members from the end of the 15th until the 18th century. Includes essay, catalog of 189 pieces, documents, bibliography, and indexes.

923   FRANKENBURGER, MAX. *Die alt-Münchner Goldschmiede und ihre Kunst.* Munich: F. Bruckmann A.-G., [1912]. 558 pp., 132 b&w figs., numerous facsimile makers' marks.

Munich goldsmiths and their art from 1292 until 1805. Includes a 255-page essay, a 166-page chronological biographical listing, transcription of archival documents, lists of marks, and indexes.

924   FRITZ, ROLF. *Die Gefässe aus Kokosnuss in Mitteleuropa 1250-1800.* Mainz: Philipp von Zabern, 1983. 146 pp., 16 color pls., 135 b&w ps., 32 b&w figs.

Comprehensive, well-illustrated study of the various forms of delicately carved coconut vessels: beakers, double pokals, chalices, jugs, flasks, ciboria, reliquaries,. etc., in involved silver-gilt mounts, produced essentially in Germany. Includes a catalog of 252 examples in European and North American museums and private collections, the majority dating of the 16th century.

925   GRIMME, ERNST GÜNTHER. *Aachener Goldschmiedekunst im Mittelalter von Karl dem Grossen bis zu Karl V.* Cologne: E.A. Seemann, 1957. 211 pp., 6 color pls., 63 b&w pls., 54 b&w figs.

The art of Aachen goldsmiths from Charlemagne until Charles V. The activity of late 15th- and 16th-century practitioners (reigns of Maximilian and Charles V) is discussed on pp. 89-132. Most cited examples are in the treasury of the cathedral or in other local churches.

926   GÜNDEL, CHRISTIAN. *Die Goldschmiedekunst in Breslau.* Berlin: Steiniger-Verlag, [ca. 1940]. 38 pp., 100 b&w pls.
      Pictorial survey of goldsmithwork in Breslau following a thirty-two-page introductory essay; pls. 6-14 are 15th-century examples (reliquaries, chalices); pls. 15-39 date of the 16th century (chalices, reliquaries, pokals, goblets, ewers).

927   KOHLHAUSSEN, HEINRICH. *Nürnberger Goldschmiedekunst des Mittelalters und der Dürerzeit 1240 bis 1540.* Berlin: Deutscher Verlag für Kunstwissenschaft Berlin, 1968. 590 pp., 5 color pls., 738 b&w figs.
      Essays on various aspects of Nuremberg goldsmithwork of the late Gothic-Renaissance period: seals, reliquaries, bookcovers, chalices, mazers, pokals, paxes, monstrances, medals, jewelry; Paulus Müllner, Sebastien Lindenast the Elder, Dürer and his designs for table fountains, Dürer and the Krug Workshop, Melchior Bauer the Elder, Peter Flötner, Master ME. Repertory of 501 Nuremberg-produced objects now in European and American museums and collections.

928   *Paul Flindt's des berühmten Nurnberger Kupferstechere und Goldschmiedes der Hoch-Renaissance—Meister Entwürfe zu Gefässen und Motiven für Goldschmiedearbeiten.* Leipzig: Karl W. Hiersemann, 1905. 33 b&w pls.
      Reproductions of original punch engravings by the Nuremberg goldsmith active 1601-died 1618: thirty-three goldsmiths' designs for cups, goblets, tazze, candelabra, and ornamental motifs.

929   PAZAUREK, GUSTAV E. *Alte Goldschmiedearbeiten aus schwäbischen Kirchenschätzen.* Leipzig: Karl W. Hiersemann, 1912. 52 pp., 80 b&w pls.
      Goldsmith works of the 11th through the 18th century in the treasuries of the churches of Horb, Mergenheim, Ulm, Tubingen, etc., in Swabia. Includes a nineteen-page introduction followed by large captions for a series of plates, nos. X-XXXIX dealing with 15th-16th-century ecclesiastical implements.

930   PERPEET-FRECH, LOTTE. *Die gotischen Monstranzen in Rheinland.* Düsseldorf: Rheinland-Velag, 1964. 232 pp., 285 b&w figs.
      The making of Corpus Christi monstrances during the 15th- 16th centuries in Cologne and the Rhine Valley. Very useful for illustrations and the short catalog descriptions provided for each.

931   ROHDE, ALFRED. *Goldschmiedekunst in Königsberg.* Stuttgart: W. Kohlhammer, 1959. 160 pp., 161 b&w illus., facsimile makers' marks. (Text written ca. 1932, edited by Ulla Stöver.)
      Goldsmith work in Königsberg (Kaliningrad, RSFSR); includes a few 15th- and 16th-century examples by known and unknown masters (Jobst Freudener, Caspar Hille, Paul Hoffmann, Cornelius Vorwed, Hieronymus Kösler, Gerhard Lentz, Gaspar Blauhut, Elias Rasser, Michael Thöber, etc.).

932   ROSENBERG, MARC. *Jamnitzer, alle erhaltenen Goldschmiedearbeiten, verlorene Werke, Handzeichnungen.* Frankfurt: Joseph Baer & Co., 1920. 22 pp., with 2 b&w text figs.
      Early monograph on the German mannerist goldsmith family; eight-page introduction followed by family hallmarks and family tree. No bibliography.

933   SELING, HELMUT.   *Die Kunst der Augsburger Goldschmiede 1529-1868: Meister, Marken, Werke.* 3 vols. Munich: C.H. Beck, 1980. 1:419 pp., 32 color pls., 32 b&w figs.; 2:1,099 b&w figs.; 3:552 pp.

Comprehensive, essential study of Augsburg goldsmith works form 1529 to 1868. Examination of the historical circumstances of the 16th century, patronage, and ecclesiastical and secular objects (pp. 21-91). Catalog of 1,099 objects including chalices, ciboria, monstrances, candlesticks, altar vases, reliefs, tankards, beakers, pokals, bowls, etc., of the 16th century, all illustrated in vol. 2. Vol. 3 is an essential compilation of masters' and town marks.

934   SOLIS, VIRGIL.   *Drinking-Cups, Vases, Ewers, and Ornaments Designed for the Use of Gold and Silversmiths — Twenty-One Facsimiles of Extremely Rare Etchings by Virgil Solis.* London: James Rimell, 1862. 1 p., 21 b&w pls.

Line drawings after the goldsmith's designs by the influential German engraver Virgil Solis (1514-62).

935   WARNCKE, JOHS.   *Die Edelschmiedekunst in Lübeck und ihre Meister* (Veröffentlichungen zur Geschichte der Freien und Hansestadt Lübeck; Herausgegeben vom Staatsarchiv zu Lübeck, vol. 8.) Lübeck: Max Schmidt-Römhild, 1927. 368 pp., 61 b&w pls.

Over 665 goldsmiths active in Lübeck from the 13th through the 18th century (many of the 15th-16th century): biographical information, then works and marks; well indexed. Ninety-six-page introduction provides solid background information on regulations, trends, etc.

936   WINTER, PATRICK M. DE.   *Der Welfenschatz: Zeugnis sakraler Kunst des deutschen Mittelalters.* Translated by Liesselott Baustian. Hanover: Touristbuch Verlag, 1986. 184 pp., 48 color pls., 166 b&w figs.

Explores historical significance and artistic importance of the Guelph Treasure housed in the Cathedral of Brunswick until the 17th century. Includes several German eccelesiastical goldsmith works — monstrances, reliquaries, capsulae, caskets, mother-of-pearl carving, etc. — of the 15th century. Notes, indexes, and tables.

Articles

937   ANDERSON, A.   "Ängsöbägaren beställd för Erland Pedersson Bååt?" *Fornvännen tidskrift för svensk antikvarisle forskning* [Stockholm] 79 (1984):108-9, 1 b&w fig. English summary.

Silver drinking cup of Ängsö was produced before 1490 in Lübeck by F. Burmeister on commission of E.P. Bååt.

938   ANGERER, MARTIN.   "Ein neuentdecker Goldschmiedeentwurf Peter Flötners." *Anzeiger des Germanischen Nationalmuseums* (1986):51-54, 8 b&w figs.

Relationship of Peter Flötner's designs to those of Dürer's followers, Matthias Zündt, Hans Pflaum, etc.

939   BEARD, CHARLES R.   "The Airthrey Gold Cup: Discovery of a Unique Renaissance Treasure." *Connoisseur* 98 (1936):3-8, 1 color pl., 12 b&w figs.

A Renaissance cup with its bowl fashioned as a terrestrial globe and made for a member of the House of Bavaria, bears the makers' initials IP, and is here ascribed to Nuremberg with a date of circa 1560-65.

940   DELMÁR, EMIL.   "Zwei Goldschmiedewerke von Ludwig Krug." *Zeitschrift für Kunstwissenschaft* 4 (1950):49-67, 17 b&w figs.

Two standing cups, one in the Hearst Collection, New York, a second in the Bruno Schroder Collection, England, produced in the 1520's by the Nuremberg goldsmith Ludwig Krug.

941   FALKE, OTTO VON. "Silberarbeiten von Ludwig Krug." *Pantheon* 11 (1933):189-94, 8 b&w figs.
      Additions and chronological order proposed for the oeuvre of Ludwig Krug, a 16th-century Nuremberg goldsmith.

942   FALKE, OTTO VON. "Die zwei Georgsstatuetten aus Elbring." *Pantheon* 3 (1929):263-66, 4 b&w figs.
      Reassigns the place of origin of two late 15th-century St. George silver statuettes in Berlin from Elbring to Lübeck; traces form of an apple-shaped silver pokal of ca. 1520 bearing a Nuremberg mark (Germanisches Nationalmuseum, Nuremberg) and of a pear goblet by the Lübeck goldsmith Heyno Schroeder to designs by Dürer.

943   HACKENBROCH, YVONNE. "The Emperor Tazzas." *Metropolitan Museum of Art Bulletin* 8(1950):189-97, 14 b&w illus.
      Gilt-silver Aldobrandini tazze, each with a statuette of a Roman emperor, are discussed with particular references to the example in the Metropolitan Museum. The author suggests they were produced in Augsburg, ca. 1580.

944   HAYWARD, JOHN. "Fontainebleau nell'interpretazione degli orafi di Norimberga." *Antichità viva* 7, no. 4 (1968):17-25, 10 b&w figs.
      Adaptations of the designs and compositions of Primaticcio, Rosso Fiorentino and their French followers such as René Boyvin, and by Wenzel Jamnitzer, Elias Lancker, Erasmus Hornick, and other goldsmiths active in 16th-century Nuremberg.

945   HAYWARD, J.F. "The Mannerist Goldsmiths: 5. Germany. Part I. Nürnberg." *Connoisseur* 164 (1967):78-84, 11 b&w figs.
      Overwhelming importance of Nuremberg with Wenzel Jamnitzer; the demands placed by the guilds on aspiring masters when producing their trial pieces; elaborate new style influenced by Florentine designs.

945a   HAYWARD, J.F. "The Mannerist Goldsmths: 5. Germany. Part II. Wenzel Jamnitzer of Nurenberg." *Connoisseur* 164 (1967):148-54, 9 b&w figs.
      Activity of the foremost German goldsmith active ca. 1534-85: commissions from the city of Nuremberg, emperors, princes, etc.; his crowning achievements—the Merckelsche Tafelaufsatz, the Kaiserbecker, his works cast directly from nature, etc.

945b   HAYWARD, J.F. "The Mannerist Goldsmiths: 5. Germany. Part III. Erasmus Hornick and the Goldsmiths of Augsburg." *Connoisseur* 164 (1967):216-22, 10 b&w figs.
      Author discovered that Hornick worked in Augsburg prior to settling in Nuremberg in 1559. The influence of his mannerist designs is readily felt on Master Hans, Elias Gnoss, and other goldsmiths active at the time in Augsburg.

945c   HAYWARD, J.F. "The Mannerist Goldsmiths: 5. Germany. Part IV. The Followers of Wenzel Jamnitzer." *Connoisseur* 165 (1967):162-67, 8 b&w figs.

After Jamnitzer's death in 1585, other members of his family, mainly his two sons Hans and Abraham, continued to produce goldsmith works in Nuremberg in his manner including small casts from nature and pattern casting. Among principal followers were Jonas Silber and Hans Petzolt.

945d   HAYWARD, J.F. "The Mannerist Goldsmiths: 5. Germany. Part V. The Later Mannerist Masters." *Connoisseur* 168 (1968):15-19, 8 b&w figs.

Vessels by Hans Beutmuller, Pieter Schliech, and Christoph Jamnitzer in which vertical movement has replaced the horizontal structure of the Renaissance.

945e   HAYWARD, J.F. "The Mannerist Goldsmiths: 5. Christoph Jamnitzer and His Contemporaries." *Connoisseur* 168 (1968):161-66, 11 b&w figs.

Late 16th-century extravagantly shaped vessels by Christoph Jamnitzer, at times based on designs by Erasmus Hornick; translucent enamel decoration by David Altenstetter of Augsburg and by Hans Lencker the Elder of Nuremberg.

945f   HAYWARD, J.F. "The Mannerist Goldsmiths: 5. Northern Germany. Part VII." *Connoisseur* 175 (1970):22-30, 11 b&w figs.

Silver from Lübeck, Lüneburg, and subsequently Hamburg and Riga. Most important evidence is the Ratsschatz (silver treasure of the city council) of Lüneburg. Goldsmiths such as Luleff Meyer, Dirich Utermarke, and their creations.

946   HOOS, HILDEGARD. "'Neugotik' in der Nürnberger Goldschmiedekunst um 1600?" *Städel-Jahrbuch* 9 (1983):115-30, 13 b&w figs.

Return to Gothic forms in late 16th-century Nuremberg goldsmith works as exemplified by standing cups of Hans Petzolt, Christoph Jamnitzer and others.

947   KRIS, ERNST. "Zum Werke Peter Flötners und zur Geschichte der Nürnberger Goldschmiedekunst." *Pantheon.* Part 1, "Ein Kokonussbecher," 8 (1931):496-99, 6 b&w figs.; part 2, "Ein Pokal von Jacob Fröhlich," 9 (1932):28-32, 6 b&w figs.; part 3, "Zum Werke Peter Flötners und zur Geschichte der Nürnberger Golschmiedekunst," 9 (1932):95-98, 6 b&w figs.

Part 1: study of the relationship of Nuremberg artists in the 16th century through a carved coconut cup with silver mounts in the Kunsthistorisches Museum, Vienna. The reliefs of the shell are attributed to Peter Flötner; the goldsmith work is suggested to be by Melchior Bayr; part 2: the style of gilt-silver pokal of the 16th century by Jacob Fröhlich of Nuremberg is discussed in relation to Flötner's designs; part 3: the influence of Flötner on "Astronomia" by Wenzel Jamnitzer (London, Henry Oppenheimer Collection) dated 1537.

948   KRIS, ERNST, and FALKE, OTTO VON. "Beiträge zu den Werken Christoph und Hans Jamnitzers." *Jahrbuch der preuszischen Kunstsammlungen* 47 (1926):185-207, 25 b&w figs.

Definition of an oeuvre for the Nuremberg goldsmiths Christoph and Hans Jamnitzer citing objects in Berlin, Munich, and Dresden museums and in various private collections.

949   PAATZ, WALTER. "Bildschnitzer und Goldschmiede in Lübeck: Benedikt Dreyer und Heyno Schröder-Bernt Heynemann und Henning V.D. Heide." *Pantheon* 3 (1929):258-62, 7 b&w figs.

The collaboration of goldsmiths and sculptors in 16th-century Lübeck as reflected in a covered cup of ca. 1525 (private collection) produced by Heyno Schroeder after a model of Benedikt Dreyer, and a silver St. George reliquary (Treasury, Riga) completed in 1507 by Bernt Heynemann and based on the model of Henning von der Heide.

950   PECHSTEIN, KLAUS. "Beiträge zur Jamnitzerforschung." *Anzeiger des Germanischen Nationalmuseums* (1984):71-76, 13 b&w figs.
       Plaques and medals of Wenzel Jamnitzer and of his circle in Nuremberg.

951   PECHSTEIN, KLAUS. "Hans Epischofer – Der Monogrammist HSE." *Anzeiger des Germanischen Nationalmuseums* (1970):96-102, 14 b&w figs.
       Activity of the Nuremberg goldsmith Master HSE (Hans Epischofer) in the second half of the 16th century: his signed and dated globe of 1566 (Germanisches Nationalmuseum) and various other pieces attributed to him including scales in Berlin and Cleveland.

952   PECHSTEIN, KLAUS. "Jamnitzer-Studien." *Jahrbuch der Berliner Museen* 8 (1966):237-83, 65 b&w figs. English summary.
       Pattern books of Wenzel and Christoph Jamnitzer: relationship to extant works in Amersterdam, Basel, Berlin, and Munich, and especially to a large reliquary box signed and dated to 1570 in the Descalzas Reales, Madrid.

953   PECHSTEIN, KLAUS. "The 'Welcome' Cup: Renaissance Drinking Vessels by Nuremberg Goldsmiths." Translated by Nicholas Fry. *Connoisseur* 199 (1978):180-87, 6 color figs., 8 b&w figs.
       Elaborate gilt-silver ceremonial cups; development of this form, tradition, design, and their market in the 16th and early 17th century.

954   PECHSTEIN, KLAUS. "Wenzel Jamnitzers Silverglocken mit Naturabgüssen." *Anzeiger des Germanischen Nationalmuseums* (1967):36-43, 8 b&w figs.
       Silver bells by Wenzel Jamnitzer in the British Museum, Residenz Museum, and other insitutions, ornamented with casts after small plants, lizards, shells, etc.

955   PECHSTEIN, KLAUS. "Zeichnungen von Wenzel Jamnitzer." *Anzeiger des Germanischen Nationalmuseum* (1969):81-95, 18 b&w figs.
       Drawings by Wenzel Jamnitzer for known or lost goldsmith works — mostly pokals — produced by the master or his workshop in Nuremberg.

956   RASMUSSEN, JÖRG. "Figürliche Goldschmiedearbeiten nach Modellen von Daniel Mauch." *Münchner Jahrbuch der bildenden Kunst* 36 (1985):81-94, 14 b&w figs.
       Early 16th-century figural goldsmith work (bookcover and statuettes) by L. von Bommerrshoven and others reflecting the style of the wood sculptor Daniel Mauch.

957   SCHMIDT, ROBERT. "Der Musikbecher von Reutlingen." *Münchner Jahrbuch der bildenden Kunst* 13 (1938):138-41, 3 b&w figs.
       Standing silver cup with musical motifs produced by Christoph Gretzinger about 1600.

958   STEINGRÄBER, ERICH. "Modelli e campionari nell'arte orafa tedesca." *Antichità viva* 7, no. 6 (1968):43-49, 13 b&w figs.
       Drawings, prints, lead or wood models used for goldsmith works by Dürer, Flötner, Wenzel Jamnitzer, and other German artists of the 16th century.

959 STEINGRÄBER, ERICH. "Süddeutsche Goldemailpastik der Frührenaissance." In *Studien zur Geschichte der europäischen Plastik: Festschrift Theodor Müller zum 19. April 1965.* Munich: Hirmer, 1965. Pp. 223-33, 20 b&w figs.

Small shrines and medallions of enameled goldsmith work produced in South Germany during the early Renaissance. Cited examples are in the Victoria and Albert Museum; Cabinet des Médailles, Paris; Cathedral Treasury, Cologne; and Baltimore Museum of Art.

960 SZCZEPKOWSKA-NALIWAJEK, KINGA. "Spätgotische Goldschmiedeplastik im königlichen Preussen." *Niederdeutsche Beiträge zur Kunstgeschichte* 24 (1985):49-72, 28 b&w figs.

Reliquaries of the late 15th century created by North German goldsmiths working in the style of the sculptor Bernt Notke.

6. PERMANENT COLLECTIONS

Berlin

STAATLICHE MUSEEN PREUSSISCHER KULTURBESITZ, KUNSTGEWERBEMUSEUM

961 SCHÖNBERGER, ARNO. "Die 'Weltallschale' Kaiser Rudolfs II." In *Studien zur Geschichte der europäischen Plastik: Festschrift Theodor Müller zum 19. April 1965.* Munich: Hirmer, 1965. Pp. 253-62, 12 b&w figs.

Large piece of goldsmith work made by Jonas Silber of Nuremberg of Christ reigning over the heavens (a covered dish) on a foot representing the aristocratic abode of Emperor Rudolf II (who paid for the commission) with Adam and Eve and the animal world on the base.

962 *Goldschmiedewerke des Renaissance.* Catalog by Klaus Pechstein. Berlin: Kunstgewerbemuseum, 1971. Unpaginated, 8 color pls., 165 b&w figs., 73 b&w illus. of makers' marks.

165 generally outstanding examples of goldsmith work from all principal centers of the German realm in the Renaissance; includes pokals, (buchel, coconut, nautilus, etc.), beakers, tumblers, dishes, salts, caskets, clock cases, jewelry, etc.; each illustrated and with comprehensive entry.

Cleveland

CLEVELAND MUSEUM OF ART

963 VERDIER, PHILLIPPE. "A Mid-Sixteenth Century Nuremberg Standing Cup in the Cleveland Museum of Art." In *Studien zum europäischen Kunsthandwerk: Festschrift Yvonne Hackenbroch.* Munich: Klinkhardt & Biermann, 1983. Pp. 129- 36, 11 b&w figs.

Gilt-silver pokal produced ca. 1550 in the workshop of Wenzel Jamnitzer after designs by Matthias Zündt.

Cologne

DOM

964   *Der Kölner Domschatz.* Catalog by Walter Schultern. Cologne: Greven, 1980. 155 pp., numerous color and b&w pls.
   Catalog of the cathedral treasury. Includes some fine examples of 15th-16th-century ecclesiastical goldsmith work — chalices, monstrances, pyxes, candlesticks — for which the city of Cologne was then famous.

SCHNÜTGEN-MUSEUM

965   *Die liturgischen Geräte und andere Werke der Metallkunst in der Sammlung Schnütgen in Cöln zugleich mit einer Geschichte des liturgischen Gerätes.* Catalog by Fritz Witte. Berlin: Verlag für Kunstwissenschaft, 1913. 119 pp., 6 text figs., 90 b&w pls.
   Catalog of liturgical objects in the Schnütgen Collection (since a museum), mostly of German origin; some of the period 1400-1600. Informative essays on the history and development of portable altars, chalices, ciboria, monstrances, tabernacles, altar and processional crosses, altar candle receptacles, censers, water vessels and basins, reliquaries, pyxes, plaquettes, etc.

966   CLASEN, CARL-WILHELM. "Ein Bebenhausener Abtsstab und eine Münstereifeler Strahlenmontranz im Schnütgen-Museum," *Wallraf-Richartz-Jahrbuch* 43 (1982):107-14, 4 b&w figs.
   The unusual mid-16th-century crozier of Sebastian Lutz, abbot of Bebenhausen, with Christ on the cross comforting Bernard of Clairvaux. Also discussed is an 18th-century monstrance by Joseph Elbertz.

Darmstadt

LANDESMUSEUM

967   DEGEN, KURT. "Bicchieri decorativi a Darmstadt." *Antichità viva* 2, no. 8 (1963):34-50, 1 color figs., 12 b&w figs.
   Major examples of goldsmith work vessels produced in Nuremberg, Augsburg, and Strasbourg in the 16th-17th century.

Dortmund

MUSEUM FÜR KUNST UND KULTURGESCHICHTE

968   *Gold und Silber.* Catalog by Rolf Fritz. Dortmund: Museum für Kunst und Kulturgeschichte, 1965. 225 pp., 5 color pls., 128 b&w figs., 52 illus. of makers' marks.
   133 goldsmith works (mostly German) in the permanent collection ranging from the 12th through the 18th century. Representing the period 1400-1600 are nos. 11-47, both ecclesiastical and secular items, including: chalices, monstrances, cups, beakers, pokals, relief plaquette, a powder horn, spoons, censer, ets.; concludes with a list of town and makers' marks (several reproduced).

XVI. Gold and/or Silver Secular Plate and Ecclesiastical/Devotional Objects

Göteborg

RÖHSSKA KONSTLÖJDMUSEET

969   AXEL-NILSSON, GÖRAN. "Ein Doppelbecher von 1585. Falk Simons Donation 1954."
Röhsska Kontstslöjdmuseet (1955):49-68, 1 color pl., 5 b&w figs.
Double mazer carved out of maple and with engraved silver mounts held to have
been produced in Ravensburg (Württemberg) in 1585.

Hamburg

MUSEUM FÜR KUNST UND GEWERBE

970   *Goldschmiedearbeiten Renaissance und Barock.* Catalog by Renate Schalz. Hamburg:
Museum für Kunst und Gewerbe, 1974. 106 pp., 61 b&w figs., numerous illus. of makers'
marks.
Forty-six goldsmith works of the 16th-18th century from the collection preceded by a
sixteen-page introduction on design, use, and manufacturing. Nos. 1-10 are 16th-century cups
and plates from Augsburg, Riga, Rostock, Nuremberg, and other centers.

London

VICTORIA AND ALBERT MUSEUM

971   *German and Swiss Domestic Silver of the Gothic Period.* London: Her Majesty's
Stationery Office, 1960. 29 pp., 27 b&w pls.
Two-page introduction; twenty-five of the twenty-seven examples (cups, bowls,
mazers, beakers, bowls) date from 1400-1521. Useful for illustrations.

Lübeck

MUSEEN FÜR KUNST UND KULTURGESCHICHTE – ST. ANNEN- MUSEUM

972   SUADICANI, ERNA. "Das Dolchbesteck des Lübecker St.-Annen-Museums." *Pantheon* 14 (1934):204-7, 6 b&w figs.
Author ascribes the nielloed engravings of St. George on a silver scabbard of ca.
1500 found in the St. Jürgen Chapel at Lübeck to the Master of the Lübeck Bible of 1494.

Münster

WESTFÄLISCHES LANDESMUSEUM FÜR KUNST UND KULTERGESCHICHTE

973   JÁSZAI, GÉZA. *Der Martinus-Pokal: Gestalt und Bildprogramm.* Münster:
Landschaftsverband Westfalen-Lippe/Westfälisches Landesmuseum für Kunst und Kulturgeschichte, 1980. 62 pp., 4 color pls., 11 b&w pls., 24 b&w figs.
Parcel-gilt cup bearing the arms of Provost Johann II Torik, made in 1597 by the
goldsmith Johannes Schown of Münster.

Nuremberg

GERMANISCHES NATIONALMUSEUM

974 KOHLHAUSSEN, HEINRICH. "Der Veit Holszchuher-Pokal von Elias Lencker in Germanischen National-Museum." *Münchner Jahrbuch der bildenden Kunst* 13 (1938):114-20, 6 b&w figs.
Standing cups produced by Nuremberg goldsmith Elias Lencker in the third quarter of the 16th century.

Osnabrück

DOM

975 *Der Domschatz zu Osnabrück.* Catalog by Fritz Witte. Berlin: Verlag für Kunstwissenschaft, [1925]. 66 pp., 40 b&w pls.
Catalog of forty goldsmith works in the cathedral treasury of Osnabrück. Nos. 25-36 date of the period 1400- 1600 and include a reliquary cross, pyxes, plates, chasse, silver statuettes (by Dalhoff, Master L., Hofsleger, etc.).

976 FELDWISCH-DRENTRUP, HEINRICH, and JUNG, ANDREAS. *Dom und Domschatz in Osnabrück.* Königstein im Taunus: Karl Robert Langewiesche Nachfolge Hans Köster, 1980. 80 pp., numerous color and b&w figs.
The cathedral treasury includes some notable 15th-16th-century goldsmith works: the Shrine of St. Cordula of 1446/47, a gilt-silver statuette of St. Peter of 1480-90, a processional cross of ca. 1525, a silver seated Virgin of ca. 1450 attributed to Johannes Dalhoff, chalices of 1468 and 1536. Also bronze lavabo, candlesticks, and embroideries for ecclesiastical vestments.

Weiner Neustadt

STADTMUSEUM

977 KLUSH, H. "Der 'Corvinusbecker.'" *Forschnungen zur Volks- und Landeskunde* [Bucharest] 28 (1985):59-64, 1 b&w fig.
A mid-15th-century gilt-silver chalice with enameling attributed to Wolfgang Zulinger, a pupil of the Transylvanian goldsmith Sigmund Langenauer.

7. EXHIBITION CATALOGS

Arnsberg

ALTES RATHAUS

978 *Goldschmiedekunst im kurkölnischen Sauerland aus 8 Jahrhunderten.* Exhibition catalog by Karl Bernd Heppe, Helmut Knirim, et al. Arnsberg: Rathaus, 1977. 109 pp., 6 color pls., 90 b&w figs.
Catalog of 202 goldsmith works from the late Middle Ages until the mid-19th century in regional public and private collections. Of the 15th-16th century are a chalice, ciborium, monstrances, a chased holy water receptacle, and a bookcover, all produced in the Rhine region of Westphalia.

Bonn

RHEINISCHES LANDESMUSEUM

979 *Rheinische Goldschmiedekunst der Renaissance- und Barockzeit.* Exhibition catalog by Carl-Wilhelm Clasen, Walter Schulten, and Hans Küpper. Bonn: Rheinland-Verlag, 1975. 195 pp., 199 b&w figs., 157 town and makers' marks.

Ecclesiastical and secular goldsmith work of the Rhine Valley from the Renaissance and Baroque periods geographically arranged (Cologne, Aachen, Bonn, Dülken, Düsseldorf, Kalkar, Kleve, Krefeld, Neuss, Wesel) and in chronological order. Includes a twenty-four-page introduction.

Bremen

BREMER LANDESMUSEUM FÜR KUNST UND KULTURGESCHICHTE (FOCKE-MUSEUM)

980 *Bremer Silber.* Exhibition catalog by Alfred Löhr. Bremen: Bremer Landesmuseum, 1982. 251 pp., 8 color figs., numerous b&w figs.

360 silver objects made in the Hanseatic city of Bremen from ca. 1380 until the Art Nouveau period, arranged by shapes. Incudes several late Gothic and Renaissance examples. Two essays, one of which is a reprint of Gerd Dettmann and Albert Schröder's "Die Bremischen Gold-und Silberschmiede" of 1931 (*Veroffentlichungen aus dem Staatsarchiv der Freien Hansestadt Bremen* 7:11-32, 47-59), trace the activity and the development of the trade in the town.

Kassel

PFARRKIRCHE

981 HILGER, HANS PETER. "Ein Kelch des Israhel van Meckenem." *Anzeiger des Germanischen Nationalmuseums* (1967):7-26, 22 b&w figs.

Silver chalice in the parish church with engraved ornaments that the author considers closely related to the prints of Israhel van Meckenem.

Kleve

STÄDTISCHES MUSEUM HAUS KOEKKOEK

982 *Klevisches Silber 15.-19. Jahrhundert.* Exhibition catalog by Guido de Werd, with the assistance of Ellen Ihne. Cleves: Städtisches Museum Haus Koekkoek, 1978. 136 pp., 8 color pls., 188 b&w figs.

Objects now mostly in German and Dutch collections wrought out of silver made in the region of Cleves from the 15th to the 19th century. Nine-page introduction precedes 122 catalog entries of which the first 16 deal with 1400-1600 chalices, collars of the Brotherhood of St. Anthony and of St. George, a monstrance, altar cross, plaques and devotional figures. Identification of marks. Includes photographic reproduction of makers' marks.

XVI. Gold and/or Silver Secular Plate and Ecclesiastical/Devotional Objects

Lübeck

MUSEEN FÜR KUNST UND KULTURGESCHICHTE

983   *Lübecker Silber 1480-1800.* Exhibition catalog by Max Hesse. Lübeck: Museen für Kunst und Kulturgeschichte, 1965. 100 pp., 43 b&w figs., 23 makers' marks.

196 pieces of Lübeck silver dating from 1480 until 1800. Of the 15th-16th century are reliquaries, chalices, and other ecclesiastical implements (nos. 1-23) and secular beakers, pokals, etc. (66-71).

Nuremberg

GERMANISHES NATIONALMUSEUM

984   *Wenzel Jamnitzer und die Nürnberger Goldschmiedekunst 1500-1700:   Golschmiedear-beiten — Entwürfe, Modelle, Medaillen, Ornamentstiche, Schmuck, Porträts.* Exhibition catalog by Klaus Pechstein et al. Munich: Klinkhardt & Biermann, 1985. 531 pp., 20 color pls., 773 b&w figs.

Eight hundred goldsmith works produced in Nuremberg from 1500 to 1700 with emphasis on the major practitioner Wenzel Jamnitzer and his large workshop, which exercised a wide-ranging influence. Represented are tankards, cups, statuettes, jewelry, plaques and plaquettes, medals, as well as drawings and ornamental prints, drawn almost entirely from German collections. The catalog is preceded by thirteen essays, each by a different author, on 206 pages dealing with various aspects and phases of Nuremberg goldsmithing.

Regensburg

DIÖZESANMUSEUM

985   *Kostbarkeiten aus kirchlichen Schatzkammern: Goldschmiedekunst im Bistum Regensburg.* Exhibition held in the Diözesanmuseum. Catalog by Achim Hubel, with essay by Paul Mai. Munich: Schnell & Steiner, 1979. 184 pp., 6 color pls., 239 b&w figs.

Catalog of 432 works of the 10th-19th century from the treasury of the bishop's palace; twenty-one-page introductory essay deals with materials and techniques, significance and stylistic development of liturgical implements, brief history of the museum; while dealing predominantly with later centuries, of interest to the years 1400-1600 are entries 81-97, 106-20, which include South German and Regensburgian crucifixes, chalices, reliquaries, monstrances, ciboria, portable altars, statuettes, etc.

Tiefenbronn

PFARRKIRCHE

986   WEBER, INGRID. "Die Tiefenbronner Monstranz und ihr küstlerischer Umkreis." *Anzeiger des Germanischen Nationalmuseums* (1966):7-87, 85 b&w figs.

Mid-16th-century elaborate Corpus Christi monstrance in the parish church porposed to reflect the styles of Jörg Seld of Augsburg and Jörg Schweiger of Basel.

8. PRIVATE COLLECTION, AUCTION, AND DEALER CATALOGS

ERNST COLLECTION

987   *Eine Weisbadener Privatsammlung: Gold- und Silberschmiedearbeiten vom 15-19 Jahrhundert.* Exhibtion held in Weisbaden at the Städtischen Museum. Catalog by Otto F. Ernst. Weisbaden: Städtischen Museum, 1969. 58 pp., 17 color pls., 63 b&w pls.
        Catalog of gold-and silversmith work of the 15th-19th century from this private collection; 426 short entries with a few 15th- and 16th-century examples including tableware and liturgical objects, mostly German.

PIERPONT MORGAN COLLECTION

988   JONES, E. ALFRED. *Catalogue of the Gutmann Collection of Plate Now the Property of J. Pierpont Morgan, Esquire.* London: Bemrose & Sons, 1907, 75 pp., 53 b&w pls.
        Seventy-three, mostly German, pieces, each illustrated and accompanied by a brief caption; on pl. I is a German 15th-century Gothic horn, on pls. II-XVIII are Nuremberg, Augsburg, etc. 16th-century tankards, covered cups, double cups, mounted shells, group of Diana and Stag, and an Annunciation triptych. The objects are not included in Jones's subsequent catalog (1908) of old plate in the Pierpont Morgan Collection (see entry 793).

THYSSEN-BORNEMISZA COLLECTION

989   MÜLLER, HANNELORE. "Notes on Sixteenth-Century German Silverware." Translated by P.S. Falla. *Apollo* 118 (1983):49-53, 63 b&w figs.
        Key examples of standing cups, double cups, and a tankard representing the work of Veit Moringer, Matin Rehlein, and the circle of Wenzel Jamnitzer.

HUNGARIAN

1. DICTIONARIES AND ENCYCLOPEDIAS

990   KÖSZEGHY, ELEMÉR. *Magyarországi ötvösjegyek a középkortól 1867-ig. Merkzeichen der Goldschmiede ungarns vom Mittelalter bis 1867.* Budapest: Királyi Magyar Egyetemi Nyomda, 1936. 432 pp., 30 b&w pls., makers' marks. Hungarian/German text.
        Goldsmith and town marks from medieval times until 1867 within the boundaries of the former kingdom of Hungary. The material is arranged alphabetically by locality.

3. SURVEYS AND HISTORIES

Book

991   KOLBA, JUDIT H., and NÉMETH, ANNAMÁRIA T. *Goldsmith's Work.* Translated by Elisabeth Hoch and revised by Elisabeth West. Budapest: Corvina-Magyar Helikon, 1973. 46 pp., 5 color pls., 72 b&w figs.
        Selection of seventy-two often highly ornamented Hungarian objects dating from the 11th to the 19th century. Includes chalices, cups, and jewels of the period 1400-1600.

992   *Article*

GEREVICH, LÁSZLO. "Középkori budai kelyhek." *Budapest régiségei* 14 (1945):335-77, 7 b&w figs. French summary.

Chalices produced in Buda from the 14th through the 16th century; characteristics of base, enamel, filigree work; influences from Italy.

6. PERMANENT COLLECTIONS

Budapest

MAGYAR NEMZETI MÚZEUM

993   *The Treasures of the Hungarian National Museum. Goldsmiths Work.* Catalog by Judit H. Kolba and Annamária T. Németh. Translated by Elisabeth Hoch. Budapest: Corvina-Magyar Helikon, 1973. 46 pp., 5 color pls., 72 b&w figs.

Presentation of seventy-two gold and silver pieces including 15th-16th century monstrances, reliquaries, chalices, clasps, necklace, cups (cat. nos. 16-35), produced locally in an ornate Nuremberg-type style for churches, the royalty, and the Magyars.

994   KOLBA, JUDIT H. "Der Nyári-Kelch." *Acta archaeologica* [Budapest] 32 (1980):373-402, 31 b&w figs.

Silver chalice with figures of angels in relief and engraved medallion of saints held to date of ca. 1460 and be the work of a goldsmith of Kolozsár (Cluj).

7. EXHIBITION CATALOGS

Budapest

IPARMÜVÉZETI MÜZEUM

995   *A Magyar történeti ötvösmü-Kiállitá lajstroma.* Exhibition catalog. Budapest: Franklin-Társulat Könyvnomdája, 1884. 532 pp., numerous line drawings.

Hungarian goldsmith and silversmith works from antiquity until the 18th century. Valuable for the quality of objects published.

Brussels

PALAIS DES BEAUX-ARTS

996   *Trésors de l'orfèvrerie hongroise du Xe au XIXe siècle.* Exhibition catalog introduction by Ferenc Fülep. Brussels: Musées Royaux des Beaux-Arts de Belgique, 1970. 99 pp., 4 color pls., 30 b&w figs. French/Dutch text.

Catalog of 223 silversmith works of Hungarian origin drawn from the national collections in Budapest; many outstanding, chiefly liturgical, examples for period 1400-1600 (cat. nos. 38- 83): monstrances, chalices, reliquaries, beakers, standing cups, etc.

ITALIAN

2. BIOGRAPHICAL DICTIONARIES

997 BULGARI, COSTANTINO G. *Argentieri, gemmari e orafi d'Italia: Notizie storiche e raccolta dei loro contrassegni.* 5 vols. Part 1 (2 vols.), *Roma,* Rome: Lorenzo del Turco, 1958-59, 1:608 pp., 15 color pls., 21 b&w pls., line drawings, 769 makers' and assay marks; 2:633 pp., 7 color pls., 27 b&w pls., 609 makers' marks. Part 2, *Roma; Lazio-Umbria,* Rome: Lorenzo del Turco, 1966, 465 pp., 17 color pls., 15 b&w pls., 352 makers' marks. Part 3, *Marche-Romagna,* Rome: Ugo Bozzi, 1969, 495 pp., 19 color pls., 21 b&w pls., 29 line drawings, 856 makers' marks. Part 4, *Emilia.* Rome: Fratelli Palombi, 1974, 491 pp., 38 color pls., 40 line drawings, 389 makers' marks.

Comprehensive reference work on silver- and goldsmiths and gem engravers working in Rome (parts 1 and 2), Lazio and Umbria (part 2), the Marches-Romagna (part 3), and Emilia (part 4) from the 14th to the 19th century. In each part arrangement by location with first, a chronological survey of important events and legislation relating to the trade, followed by an alphabetical repertory of artists with biographical data and documentary references. Table of marks; indexes of names and places.

3. SURVEYS AND HISTORIES

Books

998 ACCASCINA, MARIA. *I marchi delle argenterie e oreficerie siciliane.* Busto Arsizio: Bramante, 1976. 244 pp., 16 color pls., 190 b&w figs., numerous makers' marks.

Sicilian silver- and goldsmith makers', town, and assay marks—general characteristics, laws, nature of guarantee—as gleaned from archival documents. Arranged geographically (Palermo, Messina, Catania, Syracuse, Trapani, Acireale) and then chronologically. Description of many objects, both ecclesistical and secular, from public and private collections, with identification of their marks.

999 ACCASCINA, MARIA. *Oreficeria di Sicilia dal XII al XIX secolo.* Palermo: S.F. Flaccovio, 1974. 507 pp., 89 color figs., 273 b&w figs.

Comprehensive study of devotional and liturgical goldsmith work produced in Sicily from the 12th to the 19th century. Dealing with the period 1400-1600 are pp. 139-236 in which are presented works the author can securely authenticate either from their marks or documentation. Examination of artists, workshops, and specific works in relation to the artistic ambience of the time.

1000 BUNT, CYRIL G.E. *The Goldsmiths of Italy, Some Account of Their Guilds, Statutes, and Work.* Compiled from the pubished papers, notes, and other materials collected by Sidney J.A. Churchill. London: Martin Hopkinson & Co., 1926. 197 pp., 1 color pl., 21 b&w pls.

Italian gold- and silversmith works from the 14th to the 19th century with emphasis on the Renaissance; chap. 1 (pp. 1-12) deals with statutes; chap. 2 (13-24) relates to papal patronage; chap. 3 (25-30) deals with archival documents concerning Cellini, Caradosso, and others; chap. 4 (31-43), Tuscan goldsmiths and Sienese and Florentine guild requirements and laws; chap. 5 (44-61), Pistoiese, Sienese, and Arentine goldsmiths; chap. 6 (62-70), Florentine goldsmiths with reference to the Medici wardrobe account books; chap. 7 (71-88), Perugian and Bolognese goldsmiths; chap. 8 (89-109), artists from Milan, Turin, and Bergamo; chap. 9

(110-31), statutes of Naples, the Abruzzi, and Aquila; chap. 10 (132-43), Venetian goldsmiths; chap. 11 (144-60), sumptuary laws and peasant jewelry; volume concludes with five appendixes of primary and secondary sources.

1001   CATELLO, ELIO and CORRADO. *Argenti napoletani dal XVI al XIX secolo.* Naples: Edizioni d'Arte Giannini, 1973. 452 pp., 5 color pls., 85 b&w pls., 217 marks.

      Important study of Neapolitan silversmithing from the 16th to the 19th century: corporations and their legislation, organization, foreign influences, assay marks, alphabetical repertory of identified masters and their marks, entries for ninety objects bearing marks from public and private collections in the south of Italy. Indexes of names of people and places, and of their works.

1002   CATELLO, ELIO and CORRADO. *L'oreficeria a Napoli nel XV secolo.* Naples: Di Mauro, 1975. 166 pp., 30 color pls., 28 b&w pls.

      Historical circumstances, patronage, and archival documentation relating to Neopolitan goldsmith work (pp. 21-45) for the Quattrocento: ecclesiastical pieces including reliquaries, monstrances, chalices, crosses, candlesticks, and paxes with reference to secular items such as plaquettes, jewelry, medals, and caskets (49-92); hallmakrs (75-92); individual masters with an alphabetical listing (95-124).

1003   FORNARI, SALVATORE. *Gli argenti romani.* Rome: Edizioni del Tritone, 1968. 316 pp., illus.

      Thorough survey of Roman goldsmith works from antiquity through the 19th century. Patricularly relevant to the period 1400-1600 are chaps. 2 (history of guilds and gold- and silversmith colleges), 3, (little-known masterpieces of the 15th and 16th century and master goldsmiths of the Renaissance), and 4 (Roman silversmithing in the 15th and 16th century, Roman works in Lisbon). Well illustrated.

1004   ZASTROW, OLEG. *L'oreficeria in Lombardia.* Milan: Electa, 1978. 237 pp., 64 color illus., 251 b&w illus.

      Goldsmith work in treasuries and museums of Lombardy. The 15th and 16th centuries are dealt with on pp., 152-202 with altar and processional crosses, monstrances, reliquaries, chalices, pyxes, statuettes, jewels, ewer, cutlery, produced mostly in the region. Particularly useful illustration.

Articles

1005   BUNT, CYRIL G.E. "Details of Italian Goldsmiths' Work." *Connoisseur* 116 (1945):76-81, 13 b&w figs.

      Examines the sculptural characteristics and modeling of some highly individualistic and outstanding Italian goldsmiths' work, the majority of which date of the 15th-16th century. Includes the Bust Reliquary of St. Lussore the Martyr (style of Donatello); Cross of the Fratelli Rocchi (ca. 1515); and the Salt of Francis I by Cellini (1543), etc.

1006   DEL VITA, ALESSANDRO. "L'urna dei Santi Lorentino e Pergentino nel Museo d'Arezzo." *Dedalo* 6 (1925):365-77, 9 b&w figs.

      A gold reliquary chest executed 1498-99 in Arezzo by the goldsmith Nicolò di Giovanni to preserve the relics of the two martyrs. The pyramid-shaped lid is surmounted by a statuette of the Madonna of Mercy; on the sides are scenes in relief of the saints' martyrdom.

1007   FOCK, C. WILLEMIJN. "Francesco I e Ferdinando I, mecenati di orefici e intagliatori di pietre dure." In *Le arti del principato mediceo*. Florence: Studio per Edizioni Scelte, 1980. Pp. 317-63, 25 b&w figs.

Mannerist gold mounts of 1575-1600 on vessels of semiprecious stones and a commesso, at the Musei degli Argenti, Florence, and the Kunsthistorisches Museum, Vienna, by Jaques Bylivelt, Giovannbattista Domes, and Battista Cervi on commission of Grand Dukes Francesco I and Ferdinando I.

1008   FOCK, C. WILLEMIJN. "Der Goldschmied Jaques Bylivelt aus Delft und sein Wirken in der mediceischen Hofwerkstatt in Florenz." *Jahrhbuch der kunsthistorischen Sammlungen in Wien* 70 (1974):89-178, 35 b&w figs.

Activity from 1573 unti 1603 of the Dutch goldsmith Jaques Bylivelt in the workshop at the service of the court in Florence. The author suggests Bylivelt produced not only a bejeweled ducal crown but also several mounts for rock-crystal and other semiprecious stone vessels.

1009   FOCK, C. W[ILLEMIJN]. "Goldsmiths at the Court of Cosimo II de' Medici." *Burlington Magazine* 114 (1972):11-17, 5 b&wfigs.

Chronology of goldsmiths at the service of Ferdinand I and Cosimo II in the late 16th and early 17th centuries (Bylivelt, Vallet, Zaerles, Mola, Dinello, Falchi, Merlini, etc.).

1010   FRITZ, JOHANN MICHAEL. "Zwei toskanische Kelche berühmter Kardinäle des Quattrocento." *Mitteilungen des kunsthistorischen Institutes in Florenz*. 13 (1967-68):273-88, 9 b&w figs.

Stylistic comparison of two hitherto unpublished chalices with enamels — one made for Cardinal Juan de Torquemada probably in Florence ca. 1440-43 (Museum für Kunst und Kulturgeschichte, Dortmund), the other for Cardinal Nikolaus von Cues (1401-64), founder of the Hospital of Cues on the Moselle, where the object, said to date of the 14th century, is housed today.

1011   HAYWARD, JOHN. "The Aldobrandini Tazzas." *Burlington Magazine* 112 (1970):669-74, 13 b&w figs.

History and present whereabouts of the twelve celebrated gilt-silver dishes made ca. 1570-80 by a German goldsmith in Italy. Alterations made to six of them ca. 1891 by Spitzer are assessed.

1012   HAYWARD, J.F. "The Mannerist Goldsmiths: 1. (Italian Sources) And Some Drawings and Designs." *Connoisseur* 149 (1962):156-65, 1 color pl., 10 b&w figs.

Introduction to a series of fourteen articles: significant features of mannerist goldsmith work; the preeminence of Italian artists as suppliers of designs to goldsmiths — Pollaiuolo, Salviati, Guilio Romano, Perino del Vaga, Zoan Andrea, etc.

1013   HAYWARD, J.F. "Roman Drawings for Goldsmiths' Work in the Victoria and Albert Museum." *Burlington Magazine* 119 (1977):412-20, 13 b&w figs.

Eleven drawings for secular and ecclesiastical plate by a Roman artist who had easy access to the Cassetta Farnese of 1541 by Manno Fiorentino (Sebastiano di Sbarri) and the altar cross and candlesticks of 1581 (in St. Peter's) by Antonio Gentile da Faenza, both produced for Cardinal Alessandro Farnese.

1014   HAYWARD, J.F. "Some Spurious Antique Vase Designs of the Sixteenth Century." *Burlington Magazine* 114 (1972):378-86, 15 b&w figs.

Twenty-four hitherto unpublished pen and wash drawings in the Berlin Kunstbibliothek, with annotations, attributed to the goldsmith Jacopo Strada, court antiquary of Emperor Rudolph II at Prague.

1015   JACOBSEN, MICHAEL A. "Lautizio da Perugia and the Seal of Cardinal Giulio de' Medici." *Apollo* 108 (1978):120-21, 4 b&w figs.
        Examines a gilt-bronze model of ca. 1513 for a seal attributed to Lautizio da Perugia and depicting the Adoration of the Christ Child, now in a private collection, Cleveland.

1016   LAZZARESCHI, EUGENIO. "Gli orafi Cola Spinelli e Bartolomeo Stefani." *Rivista d'arte* 1 (1929):254-61, 2 b&w figs.
        Activity of the goldsmiths Cola Spinelli, Bartolomeo Stefani, and others in early 15th-century Lucca.

1017   LISCIA BEMPORAD, DORA. "Appunti sulla bottega orafa di Antonio del Pollaiolo e di alcuni suoi allievi." *Antichità viva* 19, no. 3 (1980);47-53, 8 b&w figs. English summary.
        Antonio Pollaiuolo directed the most important silversmith workshop in Florence in the second half of the 15th century. There were trained Francesco di Giovanni, Antonio di Salvi, Bernardo di Paolo di Giovanni Pieri, Andrea di Leonardo di Paolo, Amerigo di Giovanni, and probably many others.

1018   MACHETTI, IPPOLITO. "Orafi senesi." *Diana* 4 (1929):5-110, 73 figs.
        Principal account of Sienese goldsmithing of the 13th to the 15th century: artists, their work. Archival documents.

1019   MIDDELDORF, ULRICH. "In the Wake of Guglielmo della Porta." *Connoisseur* 194 (1977):75-84. Reprinted in *Raccolta di Scritti, that is, Collected Writings. III. 1974-1979.* Florence: Studio per Edizioni Scelte, 1981, pp. 93-102, figs. 91-105.
        Attribution to Cesare Taragone of a gold relief of ca. 1580 (private collection) of the Dead Christ and the Mourning Virgin and attribution of a gilt terra cotta relief of the Deposition (Rome, Galleria Spada) to Teodoro della Porta, son of Guglielmo. Other reliefs and statuettes placed in this Roman circle.

1020   MIDDELDORF, ULRICH. "Zur Goldschmiedekunst der toskanischen Frührenaissance." *Pantheon* 16 (1935):279-82, 5 b&w figs. English summary. Reprinted in *Raccolta di scritti, that is, Collected Writings. I. 1924-38.* Florence: Studio per Edizioni Scelte, 1979, pp. 211-15, figs. 158-62.
        Author points out that Vasari wrote that many sculptors, painters, and architects of Renaissance Italy were apprenticed to goldsmiths and may have continued to practice this art as well as their other, yet the goldsmith works they produced remain by and large unknown. Attributed examples brought into context: a reliquary at Città di Castello (Ghiberti), others in the Duomo of Prato (Maso di Bartolommeo), in the former Harris Collection (now in the Metropolitan Museum), etc.

1021   MITCHELL, H.P. "An Altar Cross and Candlesticks Said to Have Been Made by Valerio Belli for King Francis I." *Burlington Magazine* 9 (1906):124-29, 2 b&w pls.
        Identification of a hexagonal chiseled and enameled gilt-silver vessel in the Victoria and Albert Museum as an element of the stem of a rock-crystal altar cross in the same museum by Valerio Belli while two candlesticks forming a set with it are traced to the Léopold de Rothschild Collection.

1022　SANGIORGIO, GIORGIO. "Opere di Antonio Gentili, orefice faentino." *Bollettino d'arte* 26 (1932):220-29, 8 b&w figs.

Works of Antonio Gentile, goldsmith from Faenza, active in Rome during the second half of the 15th century: a gilt-silver cross and two candlesticks made for Cardinal Farnese in 1581 (treasury of St. Peter's), a silver knife, fork and spoon set—all of these at one point attributed to Cellini—and a bronze Venus (formerly Lederer Collection).

1023　SCALABRONI, LUISA. "Oreficeria viterbesi tra Gotico e Rinascimento." In *Il Quattrocento a Viterbo,* edited by Roberto Cannatà and Claudio Strinati and published in connection with an exhibition in the Museo Civico of Viterbo. Rome: De Luca, 1983. Pp. 361-98, 76 b&w figs.

Chalices and reliquaries with chiseling and enamels produced in the 15th century by goldsmiths active in Viterbo: Archimanno Battista da Viterbo, Pietro di Giovanni, Anastasio da Vitale, and others.

1024　STEINGRÄBER, ERICH. "Studien zur florentiner Goldschmiedekunst I[1]." *Mitteilungen des kunsthistorischen Institutes in Florenz* 7 (1953-56):87-110, 31 b&w pls.

An engraved and enameled gilt-silver reliquary cross (1476-83) made by Pollaiuolo for the Convent of San Gaggio, Florence (now in the Museo Nazionale), with extracts from accounts documenting it; a reliquary of 1476 with gems by the Florentine Vittorio Ghiberti (Florence, Museo dell'Opera del Duomo); the activity of Antonio di Salvi, another Florentine goldsmith who produced the relief for the silver altar of the Baptistry (now in the Museo del Duomo), and to whom the author attributes the making of reliquaries, crosses, and a pax.

1025　STEINGRÄBER, ERICH. "Studien zur venezianischen Goldschmiedekunst des 15. Jahrhunderts." *Mitteilungen des kunsthistorischen Institutes in Florenz* 10 (1961-63):147-92, 58 b&w figs.

Survey of the activity of Venetian goldsmiths in the 15th century through specific objects such as the processional cross in the Cathedral of Venzone produced by Bernardo in 1421. Author emphasizes the close stylistic affinity to Venetian works with those of Westphalia and those produced for the court of Burgundy.

6. PERMANENT COLLECTIONS

Amsterdam

RIJKSMUSEUM

1026　LUTTERVELT, R. VAN. "Het zogenaamde keteltje van Maximiliaan van Buren." *Bulletin van het Rijksmuseum* 2 (1954):3-8, 5 b&w figs. English summary.

Italian silver basin of ca. 1400 probably looted by the Turks near Naples in 1534 and brought to Tunis from where Maximiliaan van Buren, a Dutch captain, appropriated it in 1535 and added his arms to it.

Baltimore

WALTERS ART GALLERY

1027　GABHART, ANN. "A Sixteenth-Century Gold Relief." *Journal of the Walters Art Gallery* 31-32 (1968-69):29-39, 11 b&w figs.

Gold repoussé Entombment relief set in a ground of red agate at the Walters is linked to compositions of Guglielmo della Porta and suggested to be a work of Antonio Gentile of the late 16th century as would be a series of plaques in Berlin and in the Metropolitan Museum.

1028   VERDIER, PHILIPPE. "Nielles de la Renaissance italienne à Walters Art Gallery." In *Arte in Europa: Scritti di storia dell'arte in onore di Edoardo Arslan.* 2 vols. [Milan: Confalonieri, 1966.] Pp. 465-69, 11 b&w figs.

Mid-15th-century Florentine niello paxes, perhaps designed by Donato di Leonardo and chiseled by Antonio di Salvi; other examples produced in Venice ca. 1500.

Florence

MUSEO DELL'OPERA DEL DUOMO

1029   MACKOWSKY, HANS. "Das Silberkreuz für Johannisalter im Museo di S. Maria del Fiore zu Florenz." *Jahrbuch der königlich preussischen Kunstsammlungen* 23 (1902):235-46, 19 b&w figs.

Silver altar cross by Antonio Pollaiuolo, Miliano di Domenico Dei, and Betto di Francesco Betti. Author discusses the commission and attribution of work to each artist.

1030   POGGI, GIOVANNI. "Il reliquario 'del libretto' nel Battistero fiorentino." *Rivista d'arte* 9 (1916):238-49, 5 b&w pls.

Parcel gilt tabernacle-shaped reliquary on foot, work of 1500-1501 by Paolo Sogliani, made on the commission of the Arte dei Mercatanti. It incorporates relics given by Charles V of France to Louis I of Anjou.

MUSEO NAZIONALE DEL BARGELLO

1031   *Calici italiani.* Text and catalog by Marco Collareta. Florence: Museo Nazionale del Bargello, 1983. 33 pp., 2 color figs., 30 b&w figs.

Brief survey of Italian chalices of the 13th-16th century through examples in the collection, which are mostly Tuscan, are engraved, and generally bear enamels.

1032   BERTELÀ, GIOVANNA GAETA; MORIGI, GIOVANNI; and COLLARETA, MARCO. "Firenze, Museo del Bargello, il restaura della croce del Pollaiolo e di tre paci." *Bollettino d'arte* 69 (1984):89-104, 18 color figs., 23 b&w figs.

Discussion of conservation and restoration of the reliquary cross by Pollaiuolo and three paxes by Maso Finiguera, Matteo Dei, etc. Re-appraisal of goldsmithing and enameling techniques in Florence of the first half of the 15th century.

London

VICTORIA AND ALBERT MUSEUM

1033   OMAN, CHARLES. "Argenti italiani al Victoria and Albert Museum." *Antichità viva* 6, no. 5 (1967):43-53, 14 b&w figs.

Ecclesiastical and domestic silver objects made in Italy (Venice, Siena, Florence, Rome, Milan) from the 14th to the 18th century, most dating of the period 1400-1600.

Mazara del Vallo, Sicily

DUOMO

1034 ACCASCINA, MARIA. "La croce di Mazara." *Dedalo* 11 (1931):1074-81, 6 b&w figs.
Gilt-silver processional cross produced in the first half of the 15th century by Palermo goldsmiths influenced by Spanish models.

Milan

S. MARIA PRESSO S. CELSO

1035 REGGIORI, FERDINANDO. *Il Santuario di Santa Maria presso San Celso e i suoi tesori.* Milan: Banca Popolare di Milano, 1968. 55 pp., 18 color pls., 84 b&w pls., 26 b&w figs.
Description of the interior of this famed Milanese Counter-Reformation church, which includes a rich treasury with several Italian goldsmith works of the 16th century and later times.

1036 VALERIO, ANNA PATRIZIA. "Annibale Fontana e il paliotto dell'altare della Vergine dei Miracoli in Santa Maria presso San Celso." *Paragone* 279 (1973):32-53, 13 b&w pls.
Drawings by Martino Bassi (Milan, Biblioteca Ambrosiana) of 1583 for the altar of the Virgin of this church, the hitherto unpublished small terra cotta bozzetti (also Ambrosiana) for the altar frontal by Annibale Fontana (1540-87), and the actual reliefs in silver.

Minneapolis

MINNEAPOLIS INSTITUTE OF ARTS

1037 MC FADDEN, DAVID REVERE. "An Aldobrandini Tazza: A Preliminary Study." *Minneapolis Institute of Arts Bulletin* 63 (1976-77):42-55, 12 b&w figs.
A gilt-silver tazza crowned by the figure of Emperor Augustus from the famed series of twelve dating of ca. 1570-80 and owned by Cardinal Ippolito Aldobrandini, perhaps produced in Rome by an Augsburg master.

New York

METROPOLITAN MUSEUM OF ART

1038 AVERY, C. LOUISE. "Sculptured Silver of the Renaissance." *Metropolitan Museum of Art Bulletin* 5 (1947):252-54, 4 b&w figs.
Description of late 16th-century Italian ceremonial knife, fork, and spoon of silver with handles in the shape of satyrs and a nymph believed to be creations of Antonio Gentile da Faenza.

1039 RORIMER, JAMES J. "A Reliquary Bust Made for Poggio Bracciolini." *Metropolitan Museum of Art Bulletin* 14 (1956):246-51, 9 b&w figs.
Gilt-silver enameled reliquary shaped as a bust of a bishop and intended to house a bone of St. Lawrence, made ca. 1440 by an unidentified goldsmith, perhaps Florentine or Ferrarese.

Padua

BASILICA DEL SANTO

1040   SARTORI, ANTONIO. "Il reliquario della lingua di S. Antonio di Giuliano da Firenze."
        Rivista d'arte 34 (1959):123-49, 1 b&w fig.
            Gothic reliquary monstrance of the tongue of St. Anthony of Padua, in the treasury
of the Santo, produced in 1437 by Giuliano da Firenze.

Prato

MUSEO DELL'OPERA DEL DUOMO

1041   GIOVANNINI, ANNA LANDOLFI. "Il busto reliquario di Sant'Anna nel Museo
        dell'Opera del Duomo a Prato." *Antichità viva* 22, no. 1 (1983):29-37, 19 b&w figs.
        English summary.
            On the basis of documents, attributions of silver bust reliquary of St. Ann to the
Florentine goldsmith Antonio di Salvi. Formerly held to be of the 18th-19th century, the reliquary can now be dated 1489-90.

Rome (Vatican)

MUSEO D'ARTE SACRA

1042   CHADOUR, ANNA BEATRIZ. "Der Altersatz des Antonio Gentili in St.Peter zu
        Rom." *Wallraf-Richartz-Jahrbuch* 43 (1982):133-93, 80 b&w figs.
            The style and iconography of an altar cross and two matching candlesticks produced
by the goldsmith Antonio Gentile (1519/25-1609) bearing the arms of Alessandro Farnese and
of Pope Paul III.

Venice

S. MARCO

1043   OMAN, C.C. "Über die Kandelaber von San Marco und ihren Meister." *Pantheon* 6
        (1930):471-75, 6 b&w figs.
            Two elaborately decorated gilt-silver candlesticks in the treasury bearing the arms of
Doge Cristoforo Moro (1462-71) compared to a reliquary base (also S. Marco), a monstrance
(treasury of the cathedral of Capodistria), and two chalices (Capodistria, Victoria and Albert
Museum), which the author proposes to be by the same Venetian goldsmith.

7. EXHIBITION CATALOGS

Florence

1044   *L'oreficeria nella Firenze del Quattrocento.* Exhibition catalog by Maria Grazia Ciardi
        Dupré, Roberto Lunardi, Alessandro Guidotti, et al. Florence: Studio per Edizioni
        Scelte, 1977. 441 pp., over 270 b&w figs.
            Catalog of a didactic exhibition dealing with the art of goldsmiths in fifteenth-century
Florence (pp. 3-392). The subject is divided into themes using reproductions of famous monuments, paintings, prints, as well as actual works or artifacts in present Florentine collections.

XVI. Gold and/or Silver Secular Plate and Ecclesiastical/Devotional Objects

Milan

MUSEO POLDI PEZZOLI

1045   *Argenti italiani dal XVI al XVIII secolo.* Exhibition catalog by Renata Cipriani. Milan: Museo Poldi Pezzoli, 1959. 103 pp., 237 b&w pls.

   333 Italian silver objects dating from the 16th to the 18th centuries from public and private collections; nos. 1-19 (rock-crystal crosses, reliquary, knives, paxes, ewer, plate, ciborium, chalice, binding, candlesticks) are of the 16th century.

Pordenone

CENTRO CULTURALE ODORICO

1046   *Oreficeria sacra del Friuli Occidentale sec. XI-XIX.* Exhibition catalog by Giovanni Mariacher, with essay by Paolo Goi. 104 pp., 101 b&w pls.

   Catalog of 111 pieces of goldsmith works from churches in the region of Pordenone in the Friuli. Items 10-38: reliquaries, chalices, altar crosses, pyxes in Venetian style, are said to date of the 15th-16th century. Includes seven-page essay outlining the activity of goldsmiths in the region.

Udine

MUSEO DIOCESANO D'ARTE SACRA

1047   *Oreficeria sacra in Friuli.* Exhibition catalog by Pietro Bertolla and Gian Carlo Menis. Udine: Museo Diosesano d'Arte Sacra, 1963. 94 pp., 120 b&w figs.

   120 religious goldsmith works in churches and other institutions of the Friuli region, principally Cividale, Pordenone, and Udine. Many date of the 15th-16th century and reveal a dependence on Venetian examples for their general style.

Venice

CA' VENDRAMIN CALERGI

1048   *Oro di Venezia. Antichi argenti veneti.* 5ª Mostra dell'Oreficeria, Gioielleria, Argenteria. Exhibition catalog by Elena Bassi, et al. Venice: Società Orafa Veneziana, 1981. 207 pp., 102 b&w illus.

   Includes illustration and description of many reliquaries and other pieces of goldsmith work, some little known, in S. Maria dei Servi and other Venetian churches (unfortunately not specified to avoid theft), dating of the period 1400-1600 and produced locally (see especially pp. 142-76).

1049   *Oro di Venezia. Collezione di antiche filigrane.* 6ª Mostra dell'Oreficeria, Gioielleria, Argenteria. Exhibition catalog by Pietro Pazzi, et al. Venice: Società Orafa Veneziana, 1983. 234 pp., 6 color figs., many b&w illus.

   Includes short descriptions of fourteen monstrances, reliquaries, paxes of 1400-1600 in the diocesan museum, all illustrated.

NETHERLANDISH

1. DICTIONARIES AND ENCYCLOPEDIAS

1050   CITROEN, KAREL A. *Amsterdam Silversmiths and Their Marks*. North-Holland Studies in Silver, vol. 1. Amsterdam: North-Holland; New York: American Elsevier, 1975. 280 pp., facsimile makers' marks.

Repertory of 1,253 makers' marks produced in Amsterdam between 1550 and 1800 with biographical and professional data on each identified master. Introductory text in English; repertory in Dutch; Dutch/English two-page glossary. Twelve-page index of makers' marks.

1051   VOET, ELIAS, JR. *Nedelandse goud- en zilvermerken 1445-1951*. The Hague: Martinus Nijhoff, 1951. 73 pp., facsimile assay marks.

Assay marks on gold- and silversmith pieces produced in forty-three (alphabetically presented) urban centers of the Netherlands in the period 1445-1951. Pertinent for the 15th-16th century are Den Bosch, Breda, Delft, Haarlem, Leiden, Middelburg, Nijmegen, Utrecht, Zierikzer, Zutphen, and Zwolle.

2. BIOGRAPHICAL DICTIONARIES

1052   VOET, ELIAS, JR. *Haarlemsche goud-en zilversmeden en hunne merken*. Haarlem: De Erven F. Bihn, 1928. 361 pp., 6 b&w figs.

Gold- and silversmiths active in Haarlem from about 1550 until 1814; biographical data, quotes from archival documents, lists of marks.

1052a   VOET, ELIAS, JR. *Merken van Amsterdamsche goud- en zilversmeden*. The Hague: Martinus Nijhoff, 1966. 170 pp., 1,473 facsimile makers' marks.

Master gold- and silversmiths active in the city of Amsterdam from 1509 until 1813. Pp. 19-20 list nineteen for the 16th century with reproduction of marks.

1052b   VOET, ELIAS, JR. *Merken van Friesche goud- en zilversmeden*. The Hague: Martinus Nijhoff, 1931. 340 pp., 8 b&w pls., numerous facsimile maker's marks.

Biographical sketch and other data, such as marks and production, of Dutch gold- and silversmiths from the 16th to the 18th century. Relevant to the 16th century are pp. 5-30, 135-40, 237, 250, 269, 291.

3. SURVEYS AND HISTORIES

Book

1053   FREDERIKS, J.W. *Dutch Silver*. 4 vols. Vol. 1, *Embossed Plaquettes, Tazze and Dishes from the Renaissance until the End of the Eighteenth Century* (1952), 538 pp., about 382 b&w figs.; vol. 2, *Wrought Plate of the North and South-Holland from the Renaissance until the End of the Eighteenth Century* (1958), 246 pp., 313 b&w pls.; vol. 3, *Wrought Plate of the Central Northern and Southern Provinces from the Renaissance until the End of the Eighteenth Century* (1960), 169 pp., 332 b&w pls.; vol. 4, *Embossed Ecclesiastical and Secular Plate from the Renaissance until the End of the Eighteenth Century*. (1961), 215 pp., 334 b&w pls. The Hague: Martinus Nijhoff.

In-depth catalog of silver representative of various provinces, towns, workshops, and styles in European and American public and private collections. Vol. 1: twelve-page introduction to shape, technique, and decoration, followed by entries arranged according to periods and subdivided into main geographical areas (pp. 3-55, cat. nos. 1-33 for the Renaissance); vols. 2-3: thirty-two page introduction deals with the various categories of objects (plaques, medals, boxes, bookcovers, knives, spoons, tazze, beakers, tankards, cups, church plate, etc.), the techniques of their decoration (stamping, engraving), ornaments, followed by chronological lists of print engravers and their works and then entries of silver work arranged by geographical origin (several of the 16th century); vol. 4: twenty-nine-page introduction deals with monstrances, ciboria, incense-burners, cups, salts, etc., their manufacture, ornaments, foreign influence, followed by entries arranged as in vol. 1 (pp. 1-29, cat. nos. 1-54, for the Renaissance); includes addenda (embossed plaquettes, tazze and dishes), indexes of masters, design sources, and object type in each volume and in vol. 4, indexes of makers' marks and of owners.

Articles

1054   BANGS, JEREMY D. "The Central Organization of Goldsmiths' Guilds and Marks from 3 June 1466." *Oud Holland* 94 (1980):287.
          Transcription of the decree issued by Philip the Good, duke of Burgundy, ruling that all goldsmith works be provided with stamps indicating names of city and maker and that guilds be established in all cities of Holland and Zeeland.

1055   HACKENBROCH, YVONNE, and CITROEN, KAREL. "A Chalice of Jacoba of Bavaria in Gouda." *Nederlands kunsthistorisches jaarboek* 31 (1980). Part 1, "The Chalice's Origin and Style," by Hackenbroch, pp. 1-6, 9 b&w figs.; part 2, "The Chalice's History since the Reformation," by Citroen, pp. 6-15, 3 b&w figs.
          Gilt-silver chalice and paten with enamel plaques of the Passion and armorial shields wrought in Gouda in 1427-28; copies made after it in the 19th century.

6. PERMANENT COLLECTIONS

Amsterdam

RIJKSMUSEUM

1056   *Catalogus van goud en zilverwerken: Benevens zilveren, loden en bronzen plaquetten.* Catalog by C.J. Hudig and Th. M. Duyvené de Wit-Klinkhamer. Amsterdam: Rijksmuseum, 1952. 212 pp., 55 b&w figs.
          Twenty-four-page historical survey—first in Dutch then in English—provides introduction to Netherlandish gold- and silversmith works from the 11th to the 18th century: evolution of styles, forms, motifs; notes on marks. Catalog of 398 often detailed entries for gold and silver works of the 11th- 18th century and 70 entries for silver, lead, and bronze plaquettes of the 16th-17th century.

1057   DUYVENÉ DE WIT-KLINKHAMER, TH. M. "Een Hollandse nautilusbeker." *Bulletin van het Rijksmuseum* 1 (1953):25- 30, 5 b&w figs. English summary.
          Nautilus cup of the end of the 16th century in mannerist mounts held to have been produced in Delft or Rotterdam.

Lawrence, Kansas

SPENCER MUSEUM OF ART

1058   WURFBAIN, M.L. "A Sixteenth-Century Coconut Cup Made in Leiden." *Register of the Museum of Art* 5 (1975):4-17, 9 b&w figs.
        Author attributes the cup's silver mounts to Gysbrecht Arentsz van Griecken in 1546; the nut shell, carved with scenes of Pyramus and Thisbe (after Aldegrever), a Dionysian scene and the Battle of Centaurs and Lapiths, is suggested to have come from Cologne.

7. EXHIBITION CATALOGS

Amsterdam

RIJKSMUSEUM

1059   *Nederlands Zilver/Dutch Silver 1580-1830.*   Traveling exhibition catalog by A.L. den Blaauwen, with contributions by J.H. Leopold, J.R. ter Molen, and B. ter Molen-den Outer. Dutch/English text. Translation by Patricia Wardle. Amsterdam: Rijksmuseum, 1979. 390 pp., 239 b&w figs.
        Sixteen-page essay by J. Verbeek with historic overview and characteristics of major production centers; twenty-two-page essay by J.H. Leopold on silversmiths and hallmarks. 168 catalog entries on pieces from Dutch museums (mostly Rijksmuseum) and private collections, including a few 16th-century cups, tazze, beakers (nos. 1-7). Essays and catalog entries in both Dutch and English. This exhibition also traveled in 1980 to the Toledo Museum of Art, Toledo, Ohio, and the Museum of Fine Arts, Boston.

Groningen

GRONINGER MUSEUM

1060   *Groninger Zilver.* Exhibition catalog by W.A. Hofman and J.H. Leopold. Groningen: Groninger Museum, 1975. 158 pp., 336 b&w figs.
        Catalog of 436 silver objects produced in Groningen. Nos. 2-17 date of the 15th-16th century and include rings, a figurine of a bishop, maces, a chalice, seals, a beaker, and a binding.

The Hague

GEMEENTEMUSEUM

1061   OMAN, CHARLES. "Four Centuries of Dutch Silver Exhibited at The Hague." *Connoisseur* 130 (1952):163-66, 221; 8 b&w figs.
        Highlights of the exhibition drawn from private (mostly Dutch) collections, small Dutch museums, and major European and U.S. museums, of examples from the 15th to the 18th century illustrating the diverse character of Dutch silversmithing resulting from its many production centers. Some examples of the 16th century include a covered tazza of 1575 commemorating the Battle of Zuiderzee and a communion cup dated 1599.

1062   *Haags zilver uit vijf eewen.*   Exhibition catalog by Beatrice Jansen, et al.   The Hague: Haags Gemeentemuseum, 1967. 372 pp., 463 b&w figs.

Eight centuries of silver objects produced in The Hague. Catalog of 387 pieces, nos. 1-7 dating of the 15th-16th century (cruets, crown, brooch, dish, and seal).

's-Hertogenbosch

NORDBRABANTS MUSEUM

1063   *Zilver uit 's-Hertogenbosch van bourgondisch tot biedermeier.* Exhibition catalog by A.M. Koldeweij, J. van Cauteren, T. Graas, and T. Klip-Martin. 's-Hertogenbosch: Noordbrabants Museum, 1985. 301 pp., 2 color pls., numerous b&w figs. and makers' and town marks.

249 representative objects of the silver production in the town of 's-Hertogenbosch from the late 15th through the early 19th century. Nos. 4-44 are 15th-16th century chalices, monstrances, pyxes, pokals, ornaments, brooches, drawn from Dutch church treasuries and public collections, while a coconut cup of 1509-10 (17) is a loan from the Metropolitan Museum of Art. The catalog is preceded by eleven essays which study in detail the organiza-tion of the guild and provides a thorough illustrated listing of makers' (better known for the period 1490-1600 are Jan Marien, Frans Vueechs, Jan Willensem, Geffert Wyllemsen, Jan van Amsterdam, Aert Joerdens, Erasmus van Houwelingen, Lambert van der Don, Willem Geverts, Adriaan de Groet) as well as town marks.

Leewarden

FRIES MUSEUM

1064   *Fries Zilver.* Leeuwarden: Fries Museum, 1968. 442 pp., over 750 b&w figs.

Over 750 silver objects produced in Friesland from 1397 until the 19th century. In-cludes some 16th-century goblets, drinking horn, mounted coconut, etc. An English transla-tion of the Dutch introduction is provided on pp. XX-XXXII.

POLISH

3. SURVEYS AND HISTORIES

1065   BOCHNAK, ADAM.   "Zabytki zlonictwa poznogotyckiego związane z Kard. Fryderykiem Jagiellonczykiem." *Prace Komisji Historii Sztuki* 9 (1948):1-26, 19 b&w figs. French summary.

Goldsmith works of the late 15th, early 16th century owned or commissioned by Frederick Jagellon, Cardinal of Kraków. Most important are the reliquary of St. Stanislas, university mace, and the large Gniezno Cross (all three held to be works of Martin Marciniec).

PORTUGUESE

1. DICTIONARIES AND ENCYCLOPEDIAS

1066   VIDAL, MANUEL GONÇALVES. *Marcas de contrastes e ourives portugueses.* Vol. 1, *Século XV a 1887,* with the collaboration of Fernando Moitinho de Almeida. Lisbon: Im-prensa Nacional-Casa da Moeda, 1974. 352 pp., facsimile makers' marks.

Marks on Portuguese goldsmith works from the 15th century to 1887 arranged alphabetically.

3. SURVEYS AND HISTORIES

1067   COUTO, JOAÕ, and GONÇALVES, ANTÓNIO M. *A ourivesaria em Portugal.* Lisbon: Livros Horizonte, 1960. 186 pp., 7 color pls., 148 b&w pls., 27 line drawings.
      Portuguese goldsmith work up to the 18th century. Chap. 1 surveys regulations, methods, marks; chaps. 3-4 contain a repertory of 15th-16th-century mostly ecclesiastical objects in museums in Portugal and elsewhere in the world; ornamentation and motifs.

6. PERMANENT COLLECTIONS

Lisbon

MUSEU NACIONAL DE ARTE ANTIGA

1068   *Roteiro da ourivesaria.* Catalog by João Couto. Lisbon: Museu Nacional de Arte Antiga, 1959. 125 pp., 6 b&w figs.
      Short guide to goldsmith works (mostly Portuguese and French) from the 12th to the 18th century from the permanent collection as well as long-term loans. Includes several 15th-16th-century examples.

1068a   *Roteiro de ourivesaria.* Catalog edited by Natália Correia Cuedes et al., after the work of Cuoto (previous entry). Lisbon: Museu Nacional de Arte Antiga, 1975. 74 pp., 38 b&w figs., facsimile town and makers' marks. Summary in French.
      Catalog of 303 goldsmith works, mostly Portuguese, in the permanent collection of this museum. Nos. 1-95 are church implements but include some secular jewels of the period 1400- 1600.

London

VICTORIA AND ALBERT MUSEUM

See entry 1103.

7. EXHIBITION CATAGLOGS

Paris

MUSÉE DES ARTS DÉCORATIFS

1069   *Les Trésors de l'orfèvrerie du Portugal.* Paris: Musée des Arts Décoratifs, 1954. 96 pp., 193 b&w pls.
      Exhibition catalog of Portuguese and French goldsmith work of the 12th through the 19th century drawn from various public and private collections mostly in Portugal. Includes introduction (by Reynaldo Dos Santos, pp. 15-20) and essay dealing with and reproducing Portuguese town marks (by Irène Quilho, pp. 21-28). Short captions for 491 pieces of which nos. 12-90 are of the 15th-16th century: processional crosses, reliquaries, chalice, croziers, statuettes, dishes, spoons, ewers, salts, a nef, etc.

U.S.S.R. (RUSSIAN AND GEORGIAN)

3. SURVEYS AND HISTORIES

1070   POSTNIKOVA-LOSEVA, M.M. *Russian Gold- and Silversmithing: Its Centers and Masters of the 16th-19th Centuries.* Moscow: Izdatel'stvo Nauka, 1974. 372 pp., 115 b&w figs., facsimile town and makers' marks.
        Scholarly study includes notes and bibliography. All marks postdate 1613.

1071   SVIRIN, A.N. *Early Russian Jewelry Work in the XI-XVII Centuries.* Moscow: Iskusstvo Publishing House, 1972. 188 pp., 36 color pls., 42 b&w pls. Russian text with captions translated in English/French/German.
        Seventy-eight plates reproducing examples from the 4th century B.C. until 1689 from various U.S.S.R. institutions; nos. 33-53, 65 are dated of the 15th-16th century including silver frames, ladle, chalice, icons, boar-spears, dish, candelbrum.

1072   TSCHUBINASCHWILI, G.N. *Georgian Repoussé Work VIIIth to XVIIIth Centuries.* Academy of Sciences of the Georgian SSR. Institute of History of Georgian Art. Tiflis: Gosudarstvennoe Isdatel'stvo Gruzinskoi SSR, 1957. 5 text fascicles, each 20 pp., in English/Georgian/Russian/German/French, 200 b&w pls.
        Exhaustive study of the field of icons, portable altars, and crosses in silver repoussé work in the Tbilisi Museum and churches; thirteen-page introductory essay and six pages of captions. Much of the material might date of the 15th-16th century but few actual dates are offered by the author.

6. PERMANENT COLLECTIONS

Moscow

KREMLIN

1073   *Russian Silver of the Fourteenth to Early Twentieth Centuries from the Moscow Kremlin Reserves.* Catalog by S. Kovarskaia, I.D. Kostina, and E.V. Shakurova. Moscow: Sovetskaia Rossiia, 1984. 249 pp., 193 color pls., 23 b&w figs.
        193 pieces include 15th-16th-century ecclesiastical plate and jewels. Excellent reproductions.

Tbilisi

GOSUDARSTVENNYI MUSEJ ISKUSSTV

1074   *Orfèvrerie géorgienne du VIIe au XIXe siècle.* Exhibition held in Geneva at the Musée d'Art et d'Histoire. Catalog by T. Sanikidzé and G. Abramishvili. Geneva: Musée d'Art et d'Histoire, 1979. 97 unnumbered pp., 80 color pls. French/German/English text.
        Seventy-three goldsmith works of the 7th to the 19th century on loan from the Tbilisi State Art Museum of Georgia. Includes icons, cross, shrine, flabellums of the 15th-16th century (see nos. 45-54, 59, 61-67).

SCANDINAVIA
(DANISH, FINNISH, NORWEGIAN, AND SWEDISH)

2. BIOGRAPHICAL DICTIONARIES

1075   BOJE, CHR. A. *Danske guld og søln smedemaerker før 1870.* Copenhagen: Nordisk Forlag Arnold Busck, 1946. 590 pp., 3,073 marks. (Compact editions with introductory
material also in English published in 1954, 1962, 1969 by Politikens, Copenhagen.)
Comprehensive repertory of Danish gold- and silversmiths from the 14th to the 19th
century. Arranged by location (first Copenhagen, then other centers alphabetically), and then
chronologically; very brief entries for each.

3. SURVEYS AND HISTORIES

1076   BOESEN, GUDMUND, and BØJE, CHR. A. *Old Danish Silver.* Translated by Ronald
Kay. Copenhagen: Alfred G. Hassing, 1949. 43 pp., 498 b&w figs.
Pictorial survey of table plate from 1550 to 1840 arranged by types of vessels. Introductory text deals with table silver, goldsmiths and their technique; indexes of marks and
owners; bibliography; list of goldsmiths.

1077   BORG, TYRA. *Guld-och silversmeder I Finland deras stämplar och arbeten 1373-1873.*
Helsinki: AB. F. Tilgmann OY., 1935. 528 pp., 308 b&w illus., 2,574 maker, town and
year marks.
Catalog of Finnish metalwork in gold and silver arranged by city and artists'
workshop. Applying to the 15th-16h century are pp. 29-39, 110-12. 130-31, 159-60, 198-200,
325-26, 433-37, 476-78, and part of introduction.

1078   GRANDT-NIELSEN, FINN. *Fynsk kirkesølv.* Odense: Loaklhistorisk, 1983. 200 pp., 6
color pls., 4 color figs., 444 b&w figs. English/German summary.
Church silver from the Island of Fyn (Denmark) dating from 1520 to the 20th century
and made in Copenhagen, towns in Jutland, etc. Comprehensive for the period 1520-1660.

1079   KÄLLSTRÖM, OLLE; HERNMARCK, CARL; ANDRÉN, ERIK; HELLNER,
BRYNOLF; and HOLMQUIST, KERSTI. *Svenskt silversmide 1520-1850.* 4 vols. Vol. 1,
Renässans och barock. 1520-1700 (1943), by Källstrom and Hernmarck, 248 pp., 542 b&w
figs., line drawings; vol. 2 (1700-1780); vol. 3 (1780-1850); vol.4, *Guld-och silverstämplar*
(1963), by Andrén, Hellner, Hernmarck, and Holmquist, 791 pp., facsimile control, town
and makers' marks; English summary (pp. 682-85). Stockholm: Nordisk Rotogravyr.
Most complete study of Swedish silver from 1520 until 1850 superseding Gustaf Up-
mark's *Guld-och silversmeder i Sverige 1520-1850.* Vol. 1 deals with the period 1520-1700: pp.
19-20 discuss the Gothic background; 43-136, the period 1520-1600. Vol. 4 is comprised of a
biographical repertory of 3,211 masters grouped by towns, reproduction of 9,092 marks, and
various indexes; bibliography, pp. 667-81.

1080   KIELLAND, THOR. *Norsk guldsmedkunst i middelalderen.* Oslo: Steenske, [1927]. 511
pp., 340 b&w figs.
Extensive and somewhat dated study of Norwegian goldsmith works of the Middle
Ages (7th century to 1500); several 15th-16th- century chalices, pokals, plates, drinking horns,
spoons, reliquaries, monstrances, discussed in terms of their stylistic dependence as well as
originality.

1081 KROHN-HANSEN, THV., and KLOSTER, ROBERT. *Bergens gullsmed kunst fra laugstiden.* 2 vols. Bergen: Utgitt av Gullsmedlauget i Bergen og Vestlandske Kunstindustrimuseum, 1957. 1:385 pp., several b&w figs. and makers' marks; 2:256 b&w pls. English summary.
A history of the activity of goldsmiths in Bergen (Norway) during the guild period (1568-1840). Partially relevant to the 16th century are pp. 1-77.

1082 MUNTHE, GUSTAF. *Falk Simons silversamling.* Stockholm: P.A. Norstedt & Sömer, 1938. 329 pp., 238 b&w pls. English summary (pp. 72-76).
The Falk Simon Collection of silver including parts given to Röhsska Konstlöjdmuseet, Göteborg, as well as to the Kulturhistoriska Museet of Lund. Includes a drinking bowl by a 16th-century Stockholm silversmith, several Renaissance goblets and spoons. Cat. nos. 1-555 are Swedish, 556-790 foreign, a few of the latter being of the 15th-16th century.

1083 OLRIK, JØRGEN. *Danske sølvarbejder fra Renaissancen til vore dage.* Copenhagen: G.E.C. Gad, 1915. 144 pp., 228 b&w illus.
Catalog of Danish silversmith works from the 16th to the 19th century. Includes five pre-1600 objects (pp. 3-6, nos. 1- 5)(pokal, tankards, spoons). Two-page introduction, appendixes of maker and town marks.

1084 POLAK, ADA. *Norwegian Silver.* Oslo: Dreyers Forlag B.A. Butenschon A/S & Co., 1972. 155 pp., 186 b&w figs., a few town and makers' marks.
Brief survey that touches on examples from Bergen dating of the late 16th century and points to their dependence on German models.

1085 SCHOUBYE, SIGURD. *Guldsmede-håndvaerket i Tonder og på Tonder-egnen 1550-1900.* [Copenhagen]: Danske Boghandleres Kommissionsanstalt, [1961]. 359 pp., 4 color pls., 357 b&w figs., 227 marks.
Silversmithing in the Danish region of Tonder from 1550 to about 1900. 16th-century examples mostly known from epitaph panel portraits.

1086 UGGLAS, CARL R. AF. *Senmedeltida profant silversmide i Sverige.* Vol. 1. Stockholm: Wahlström & Widstrand, 1942. 168 pp., 40 b&w pls. German summary.
Iconographic study of 15th-century silver drinking cups in Castle Angsö and Castle Stjärnorp, Sweden.

6. PERMANENT COLLECTIONS

London

VICTORIA AND ALBERT MUSEUM

1087 *Catalogue of Scandanavian and Baltic Silver.* Catalog by R.W. Lightbown. London: Her Majesty's Stationery Office, 1975. 255 pp., 162 b&w figs.
One of few books in English on Scandanavian secular plate. 133 detailed catalog entries, only eleven of which are of the 15th-16th century.

SPANISH

1. DICTIONARIES AND ENCYCLOPEDIAS

1088 FERNÁNDEZ, ALEJANDRO; MUNOA, RAFAEL; and RABASCO, JORGE. *Enciclopedia de la plata española y Virreinal americana.* San Sebastián: Rafael Munoa, 1984. 566 pp., numerous b&w figs., facsimile makers' and town marks.
Encyclopedia of silver in Spain and in the American Viceroyalty. Part 1 (pp. 1-96): history of Spanish silver; part 2 (97-496): repertories of marks; part 3 (497-536): Spanish-dominated Mexico, California, Florida, Peru, Brazil, Paraguay, and Chile. This volume is to date the most comprehensive of its kind.

1089 ORTIZ JUAREZ, DIONISIO. *Punzones de platería cordobesa.* Cordoba: Monte de Piedad y Caja de Ahorros de Cordoba, 1980. 214 pp., numerous reproductions of makers' marks.
Marks of silversmith work from Cordoba, 15th-19th century; town marks (variations of lion rampant); dictionary of makers with reproduction of their marks.

1090 RABASCO CAMPO, JORGE. *Los plateros españoles y sus punzones.* [Vitoria: 1975]. Unpaginated, 14 b&w figs., town and makers' marks.
Pocket-size guide of Spanish marks. Part 1: town marks; part 2: principal goldsmiths of the 16th-18th century.

3. SURVEYS AND HISTORIES

Books

1091 ARNÁEZ, ESMERALDA. *Orfebrería religiosa en la provincia de Segovia hasta 1700.* 3 vols. Madrid: Gráficas Cóndor, S.A., 1983. 1:342 pp., 157 b&w figs.; 2:378 pp., 191 b&w figs.; 3:395 pp.
Religious goldsmith work produced in the province of Segovia until 1700, most cited examples still being in churches and convents. Emphasis is placed on style and the oeuvre of individual goldsmiths. Vol. 1 deals with the late Gothic and the early Renaissance period in Segovia and defines the Plateresque style. Vol. 2 deals partly with the Plateresque style and partly with the late 16th century. Vol. 3 studies provincial goldsmiths.

1092 BRASAS EGIDO, JOSÉ CARLOS. *La platería vallisoletana y su difusión.* Valladolid: Institucion Cultural Simancas, 1980. 371 pp., 521 b&w figs.
Detailed study on ecclesiastical goldsmith work from Valladolid; author deals with confraternity, workshop practices, production, patronage, marks. For the Gothic period, see pp. 101-31; for the Renaissance, 135-241.

1093 CRUZ VALDOVINOS, J.M., and GARCÍA Y LOPEZ, J.M.[a] *Platería religiosa en Úbeda y Baeza.* Jaén: Instituto de Estudios Giennenses, Excma. Diputación Provincial, 1979. 217 pp., 209 b&w figs.
Ecclesiastical silver in churches of the cities of Úbeda and Baeza (Province of Jaén). Includes a few 15th- and several 16th-century chalices, monstrances, crosses, etc.

1094 ESTERAS MARTÍN, CRISTINA. *Orfebrería de Teruel y su provincia siglos XIII al XX.* 2 vols. Teruel: Instituto de Estudios Turolenses de la Excma. Diputación Provincial de Teruel, 1980. 1:319 pp., 237 b&w figs.; 2:501 pp., line drawings of makers' marks.

Goldsmith work produced in Teruel and the surrounding Aragonese region from the 13th to 20th century. Vol. 1 comprises an essay (medieval-Renaissance period studied pp. 11-254); Vol. 2 includes a biographical dictionary of goldsmiths, a list of marks, a catalog of 453 objects (nos. 6-41 date of the 15th century and nos. 42-203 of the 16th), excerpts from archival documents, and an extensive bibliography.

1095   HEREDIA MORENO, MARIA DEL CARMEN. *La Orfebrería en la Provincia de Huelva.* 2 vols. [Huelva?]: Excma. Diputación Provincial de Huelva, 1980. 1:492 pp., 349 b&w figs.; 2:292 pp., makers' marks.
Goldsmith works in the province of Huelva from the 15th to the 18th century, primarily ecclesiastical plate in religious institutions. Pp. 37-599 deal with the late Gothic style, 61-136 with the Renaissance. Vol. 2 includes a catalog of marks and one of objects geographically arranged; appendix with documents; bibliography and indexes.

1096   JOHNSON, ADA MARSHALL. *Hispanic Silverwork.* New York: Hispanic Society of America, 1944. 328 pp., 266 b&w figs.
Covers works of the 14th-19th century from various centers, chap. 2 (pp. 36-57) dealing with 15th-century Gothic silverwork, and chap. 3 (58-99) with 16th-century pieces. Includes monstrances, chalices, reliquaries, jewelry, processional shrines, maces, chests, urns, ewers, etc., with emphasis on the role of princely patronage and Italian and Flemish influences, and mentions of inventories and individual masters. Chap. 6 (147-283) is a catalog of pieces in the collection of the Hispanic Society of America including many fine 15th-16th-century examples on pp. 158-215.

1097   TEMBOURY ALVAREZ, JUAN. *La orfebrería religiosa en Malaga: Ensayo de catalogacion.* Malaga: Excmo. Ayuntamiento de Malaga-Delegación de Cultura, 1948. 403 pp., numerous b&w unnumbered figs.
Ecclesiastical goldsmith work of Malaga. Chap. 1 (pp. 9- 61) describes the organization of the guild; chap. 2 (65-89) is a catalog of eight 15th-century pieces; chap. 3 (91-161) is a catalog of twenty-nine objects dating to the 16th century. Concludes with indexes of goldsmiths, etc.

Articles

1098   ARNÁEZ, ESMERALDA. "Cruces procesionales de Hernando de Olmedo." *Archivo español de arte* 51 (1978):63-80, 29 b&w figs.
Large processional silver crosses bearing the mark of Hernando de Olmedo produced in Segovia during the second part of the 16th century when Spain had a very large supply of metal from the New World.

1099   MARTIN, FERNANDO A. "El punzon de Cuenca." *Goya* 151 (1979):12-18, 13 b&w figs.
Evolution of hallmarks of the city of Cuenca on goldsmith works of the 15th-16th century.

1100   VALDOVINOS, JOSÉ MANUEL CRUZ. "Tras el IV centenario de Francisco Becerril." *Goya* 125 (1975):281-90, 1 color illus., 18 b&w figs.
Biographical outline of this Spanish goldsmith active ca. 1530-77; chronology of his major works: chalices, crowns, reliquaries, paxes, processional crosses, a ewer, etc., for the cathedral of Cuenca and other institutions.

6. PERMANENT COLLECTIONS

Chera

MUSEO DIOCESANO

1101   MORALES SAN MARTIN, B. "Hostiario gótico encontràdo en Chera." *Archivo de arte valenciano* 5 (1919):101-2, 2 line drawings.
Wafer-box of 1490 with host-shaped engraved scenes of the Passion.

Córdoba

CATEDRAL

1102   MARTÍN RIBES, J. *Custodia procesional de Arfe.* Córdoba: Caja Provincial de Ahorros, 1983. 117 pp., 1 b&w figs.
Silver Gothic ostensory, a work of 1517 by the goldsmith Enrique de Arfe, in the cathedral treasury.

London

VICTORIA AND ALBERT MUSEUM

1103   *The Golden Age of Hispanic Silver 1400-1665.* Catalog by Charles Oman. London: Her Majesty's Stationery Office, 1968. 118 pp., 279 b&w figs.
Thirty-four-page introduction; 179 catalog entries of Spanish and Portuguese silver of both ecclesiastical and secular origin, the majority of pieces (altar plate, reliquaries, ewers, salts, dishes, plaques, statuettes, etc.) dating of the 15th-16th century (cat. nos. 1, 5-132). Reproductions of makers' and town marks; index of goldsmiths' names.

Madrid

MUSEO ARQUEOLÓGICO NACIONAL

1104   CANO CUESTA, MARINA. "Marcas de orfebres en tres calices, del Museo Arqueológico Nacional." *Goya* 153 (1979):156-59, 7 b&w figs.
Hallmarks on three 16th century Spanish chalices identified as those of the goldsmiths Pedro Eslaba, Corcuera, and possibly Francisco de San Román.

New York

HISPANIC SOCIETY OF AMERICA

1105   MULLER, PRISCILLA E. "Spain's Golden Age in Silver." *Apollo* 95 (1972):264-71, 1 color pl., 14 b&w figs.
Altar and processional crosses, chalices, custodia, pyx, ewer, paxes, and devotional jewels of the early 15th to the late 16th century.

SWISS

2. BIOGRAPHICAL DICTIONARIES

1106 LÖSEL, EVA-MARIA, with contributions by Jürg A. Meier and Dietrich W.H. Schwartz. *Zürcher Goldschmiedekunst vom 13. bis zum 19. Jahrhundert.* Zurich: Buchverlag Berichthaus, 1983. 503 pp., 12 color illus., many b&w figs. and facsimile city and makers' marks.

Goldsmiths active in Zurich from the 13th to the 19th century (chap. 1-5 [pp.11-53], 9-12 [pp. 86-121] deal with 1400-1600 period). Repertory of over 693 artists—nearly half of the 15th-16th centuries—on 203 pages with abbreviated biographies and listing of their works. Valuable illustration of seals, liturgical and secular plate, jewelry, medals, and arms.

3. SURVEYS AND HISTORIES

1107 GRANDJEAN, MARCEL. "L'Orfèvrerie lausannoise au XVIe siècle et les coupes de 1584." *Unsere Kunstdenkmäler* 12 (1961):74-75, 1 b&w fig.

Career of Simon Leclerc who specialized in the making of chalices and activity of twenty-one other goldsmiths (many of French origin), in Lausanne at the end of the 16th century.

1108 LÖSEL, EVA MARIA. "Practical Luxury in Zwingli's City: Silverware Produced by Zurich Goldsmiths for the Guilds and Bourgeoisie." *Apollo* 110 (1979):260-67, 19 b&w figs.

Brief historical account of 16th-18th century goldsmithing in Zurich; deals with patronage, guild regulations, the major masters (Abraham Gessner, Ulrich Oeri, Felix Keller, etc.) and their work.

6. PERMANENT COLLECTIONS

London

VICTORIA AND ALBERT MUSEUM

See entry 971.

Zurich

KUNSTHAUS

1109 *Alte Goldschmiedewerk im Zürcher Kunsthaus.* Catalog by Otto von Falke. Zurich and Leipzig: Rascher & Co., 1928. 159 pp., 124 b&w pls.

Catalog of 1,258 ecclesiastical and secular goldsmith and enamel works ranging from the 12th through the 18th century. Of the period 1400-1600 are liturgical vessels and implements (chalices, crucifixes, reliquaries, monstrances, paxes); enamel plaques, plates, caskets, and other vessels; secular vessels of gold and gilt-silver (cups, beakers, goblets, coconut and nautilus cups, etc., mazers)., some jeweled objects (pendants, necklaces).

SCHWEIZERISCHES LANDESMUSEUM

1110   *Weltiches Silber.* Catalog by Alain Gruber, with the collaboration of Anna Rapp. Zurich: Berichthaus, 1977. 344 pp., over 600 b&w figs. Summaries in French/Italian/English.

   Catalog of permanent collection (and some loans) of 583 pieces of silver plate from the mid-14th century until 1925 (excluding cutlery as well as pieces not exhibited) from some thirty-five centers but mainly Basel, Geneva, Zurich, Bern, Lausanne, and Lucerne, all illustrated. Reproduction of marks.

YUGOSLAVIA (SERBIAN)

7. EXHIBITION CATALOGS

London

VICTORIA AND ALBERT MUSEUM

1111   *Masterpieces of Serbian Goldsmiths' Work: 13th-18th Century.* Exhibition catalog by Dušan Milovanivić. Introduction by Bojana Radojković. Translated by Aleksander Saša Petrović. London: Victoria and Albert Museum, 1981. 68 pp., 58 b&w figs.

   Fifteen-page historical introduction; 111 detailed catalog entries for secular and ecclesiastical objects of gold, silver, and gilt-silver—often decorated with niello, filigree, enamel, embossing, and gems—from Yugoslav museums, churches, and monasteries. Of the 15th-16th century are rings, earrings, necklaces, bowls, buckles, censers, chalices, incense boat, jug, crosses, reliquaries, etc.

XVII. Enamels

A. MULTI COUNTRY OF ORIGIN

3. SURVEYS AND HISTORIES

Books

1112   BENJAMIN, SUSAN. *Enamels*. New York: Cooper-Hewitt Museum, 1983. 128 pp., 33 color pls., 100 b&w figs.

    Brief introductory survey of the art of enameling through the ages. Includes chapter on enameling techniques, others arranged by origin. Illustrates examples in several U.S. and European public collections dating from the 15th-16th century.

1113   BURGER, WILLY. *Abendländische Schmelzarbeiten*. Berlin: Richard Carl Schmidt & Co., 1930. 229 pp., 8 color pls., 136 b&w figs.

    Enamel work from antiquity to the 16th century with examples drawn from public and private European collections. Pp. 146-72 deal with French and Italian 15th-16th-century enameled objects, and 173-202 specifically with 16th-century Limoges works.

1114   CUNYNGHAME, HENRY H. *European Enamels*. London: Methuen & Co., 1906. 188 pp., 4 color pls., 49 b&w pls.

    Standard but now dated survey with emphasis on technique and style. Still useful for 16th-century painted enameling as it touches on other centers besides Limoges.

Article

1115   MIDDELDORF, ULRICH. "On the Origins of 'Email sur ronde-bosse.'" *Gazette des beaux-arts* 55 (1960):233-44. Reprinted in *Raccolta di scritti, that is, Collected Writings. II. 1939-1973*. Florence: Studio per Edizioni Scelte, 1980, pp. 257-74, figs. 99-101.

    Frequent mention in 14th- and 15th-century inventories of colorfully enameled jewels, figures, and objects typified by the Pace di Siena (Arezzo), the Goldenes Rössl (Altötting), and a silver ewer (Copenhagen).

6. PERMANENT COLLECTIONS

Baltimore

WALTERS ART GALLERY

1116   *Catalogue of the Painted Enamels of the Renaissance,* by Philippe Verdier. Baltimore: Trustees of the Walters Art Gallery, 1967. 423 pp., 8 color pls., 306 b&w figs.

Standard reference on Limoges enamel painting of the 16th-17th century with detailed entries of two hundred items (often outstanding examples by the Master of the Orléans Triptych, Pénicaud, the Aeneid Master, Reymond, Couly Nouailher, Limosin, etc.); also includes one Netherlandish and thirteen Italian pieces.

Paris

MUSÉE DU LOUVRE

1117   *Notice des émaux exposés dans les galeries du Musée du Louvre,* by [A.] de Laborde. 2 vols. Vol. 1, *Histoire et descriptions,,* 348 pp.; vol. 2, *Documents et glossaire,* 552 pp. Paris: Vinchon, 1852-53.

Standard if outdated reference on enamel works from the 12th to the 18th century based on the collection of the Louvre. Vol. 1: pp. 1-20, deals with 158 pieces of cloisonné and champlevé; 121-343 with 405 Italian and Limoges painted enamels. Vol. 2 includes the inventory of Louis d'Anjou (ca. 1368) and a 532-page glossary held to be a lasting contribution to the field.

Turin

MUSEO CIVICO D'ARTE ANTICA, PALAZZO MADAMA

See entry 76.

7. EXHIBITION CATALOGS

Chicago

MARTIN D'ARCY GALLERY OF ART

1118   *Enamels: The XII to the XVI Century.* Exhibition catalog by Donald F. Rowe. Chicago: Loyola University of Chicago, 1970. Unpaginated, 1 color pl., 65 b&w figs.

Forty-one enameled objects from various public and private collections (liturgical vessels, crosses, plaques, jewels, and rock-crystal mounts), mostly dating of 1400-1600 (see especially nos. 17-41).

London

BURLINGTON HOUSE

1119   *Catalogue of a Collection of European Enamels from the Earliest Date to the End of the XVII Century.* Exhibition catalog by J. Starkie Gardner, with essay on painted enamels by Alfred Higgins. London: Burlington Fine Arts Club, 1897. 113 pp., 3 color pls., 69 b&w pls.

        Thirty-one-page text at beginning on technique, origins, and development of enameling, and major painters in enamel. 282 entries dating from the 13th to the 17th century of often major pieces in British collections; includes 15th- and 16th-century medallions, crucifixes, plaques, caskets, dishes, tazze and covers, candlesticks, ewers, jewels, etc. from various centers. Adequate illustrations often lacking.

Milan

MUSEO D'ARTI APPLICATE

1119a   *Museo d'Arti Applicate—Smalti.* Catalog by Oleg Zastrow. Edited by Carlo Pirovano. Milan: Electa, 1985. 191 pp., 59 color figs., 172 b&w figs.

        Ninety-eight entries describing with good illustrations enamel work from the 13th to the 20th century, including several 15th-16th-century examples from Limoges (works by Pierre Reymond, etc.) Venice, and Lombardy.

B. SINGLE COUNTRY OF ORIGIN

FRENCH

2. BIOGRAPHICAL DICTIONARIES

1120   MOLINIER, ÉMILE. *Dictionnaire des émailleurs depuis le Moyen Age jusqu'à la fin du XVIIIe siècle.* Paris: Jules Rouam, 1885. 113 pp.

        Small biographical dictionary consisting of mostly French enamelers (many of period 1400-1600) with sixty-seven facsimile signatures and marks. Includes lists of principal public and private collections of enamels.

3. SURVEYS AND HISTORIES

Books

1121   BOURDERY, LOUIS. *Les Émaux peints.* Limoges: Ve H. Ducourtieux, 1888. 235 pp., 5 line drawings.

        Earliest large-scale classification after Laborde (see entry 1117) of Limoges painted enamels based on an exhibition held in Limoges in 1886 that included seven hundred examples dating from the late 15th to the 18th century. Arrangement by workshop families (Pénicaud, Limosin, Pierre Courteys, Suzanne Court), etc.

1122   BOURDERY, L., and LACHENAUD, E. *L'Oeuvre des peintres émailleurs de Limoges: Léonard Limosin, peintre de portraits.* Paris: L.-H. May, 1897. 425 pp., 25 b&w pls., 132 line drawings (mostly of monochrome signatures and dates, and of coats of arms).

   Catalog raisonné of the oeuvre of Léonard Limosin, author of over 132 painted enamel portraits of the French aristocracy of the 16th century. Arranged by sitters. Very useful also for the wealth of information provided, such as variants, collectors, prices fetched, etc.

1123   GAUTHIER, MARIE-MADELEINE, and MARCHEIX, MADELEINE. *Limoges Enamels.* London: Paul Hamlyn, 1962. 40 pp., 27 color pls., 30 b&w pls.

   Deals with the appearance at Limoges of painting in enamel in the 15th century; the technical process and the enamelers' sources of inspiration such as model books and engravings. All enamels reproduced belong to the Louvre and represent the following workshops: Pseudo-Monvaerni, High Foreheads, Aeneid, Triptych of Louis XII, Jean Ier Pénicaud.

1124   LAVEDAN, PIERRE. *Léonard Limosin et les émailleurs français.* Paris: Henri Laurens, 1913. 127 pp., 24 b&w pls.

   Biographical essay on France's most famous Renaissance enameler sketched in the context of the artist's predecessors and peers.

1125   MARQUET DE VASSELOT, J.-J. *Les Émaux limousins de la fin du XVe siècle et de la première partie du XVIe: Étude sur Nardon Pénicaud et ses contemporains.* 2 vols. Paris: Auguste Picard, 1921. 1:412 pp.; 2:85 b&w pls.

   Classic study of Limoges enamelers' workshops. Includes 220 descriptive entries of objects in European museums. Appendixes include reproductions of contemporary documents and a list of enamelers.

   Articles

1126   HACKENBROCH, YVONNE. "A Limoges Enamel Hunting Horn." *Connoisseur* 133 (1954):249-51, 7 b&w figs.

   Horn in a private New York collection with brilliantly colored enamels depicting hunting scenes and St. Hubert, as well as a grisaille medallion. Signed by Léonard Limosin and dated 1536 (period during which artist was under direct impact of Italian forms), it was very likely commissioned by Francis I.

1127   MITCHELL, H.P. "Some Limoges Enamels of the Primitive School." *Burlington Magazine* 30 (1917):219-25, 5 b&w figs.

   Author distinguishes the work of four distinct enamelers in examples of the latter half of the 15th century as represented in the Taft Collection, Cincinnati (the Odiot Triptych bearing the inscription "Monvaerni"), the Victoria and Albert Museum, the Glasgow Museum, and in the Musée Communal, Verviers, and suggests abandoning the nomenclature "Monvaerni" when referring to early enamels.

1128   MITCHELL, H.P. "Who Was the Limoges Enameller 'Kip'?" *Burlington Magazine* 14 (1908-9):278-90, 14 b&w figs.

   Mid-16th-century grisaille enameler "Kip" can be identified with the goldsmith Poillevé on the basis of a Greek inscription borne by a plaque in the Pierpont Morgan Collection [now in the Metropolitan Museum]. Examination of style, techniques, marks, and signatures on fourteen plaques, medallions, and a vase.

1129 MÜLLER, THEODOR, and STEINGRÄBER, ERICH. "Die französische Gol-
demailplastik um 1400." *Münchner Jahrbuch der bildenden Kunst*, 3d ser., 5 (1954):29-79,
69 b&w figs.
Catalog of thirty-eight objects of goldsmith works in the International Style of ca.
1400 drawn from various collections, preceded by an essay in which the author gives reasons
for assigning to France such often famous objects as the Goldenes Rössl, now in Altötting, or
the so-called "White Lady" in Cleveland.

6. PERMANENT COLLECTIONS

Baltimore

WALTERS ART GALLERY

1130 ROSS, MARVIN CHAUNCEY. "Six Enamels by the Master 'KIP.'" *Connoisseur* 102
(1938):182-84, 214, 6 b&w figs.
On the basis of examples from the collection, the author lends support to the
hypothesis of H.P. Mitchell (see entry 1128) that the signature "KIP" or "KI" found on many
16th-century enamels is the pseudonym of the Limoges enameler Jean Poillevé.

1131 ROSS, MARVIN CHAUNCEY. "Notes on Enamels by Pierre Reymond." *Journal of the
Walters Art Gallery* 2 (1939):77- 103. 44 b&w figs.
Discusses a group of mid-16th-century tazze, plates, salts, ewers and stands by one of
Limoges's famous enamelers and the relationship of their scenes with engravings of Lucas van
Leyden, those of the Bible of Jacques de Tournes, etc.

1132 ROSS, MARVIN CHAUNCEY. "The Master of the Orléans Triptych: Enameller and
Painter." *Journal of the Walters Art Gallery* 4 (1941):9-25, 20 b&w figs.
Description of five pieces by this 16th-century Limoges enameler and their relation-
ship to contemporary miniature painting of western France.

1133 VERDIER, PHILIPPE. "A Limoges Enamel Plaque of the School of Fontainebleau."
Apollo 84 (1966):491, 1 b&w fig.
Briefly examines the style and subject of a large plaque depicting six intertwined
acrobatic figures copied from an engraving by Juste de Juste, a Florentine mannerist established in Tours who worked in the gallery of Francis I at Fontainebleau. The style and
technique of the plaque are likened to four other Limoges plaques in the Musée de Cluny
and the Louvre.

Bern

ABEGG-STIFTUNG

1134 FAŸ, ANTOINETTE. *Un Chandelier émaillé de Pierre Reymond.* Bern: Abegg-Stiftung,
1971. 39 pp., 1 color pl., 37 b&w figs.
A copper enameled candlestick in the foundation's collection bearing the date 1577
and the initials PR and depicting the labors of Hercules, was probably influenced by earlier
works of Master IC.

Cincinnati

TAFT MUSEUM

1135   MITCHELL, H.P. "Good-bye to 'Monvaerni'?" *Connoisseur* 17 (1910):37-39, 1 b&w pl.
Author reads inscription on a Crucifixion triptych not as the name of the artist, but of Jean Barton de Montbas, archbishop of Nazareth, a patron of the Limoges ateliers.

Limoges

MUSÉE MUNICIPAL

1136   MARCHEIX, MADELEINE. "Une Crucifixion de Léonard Limosin." *Revue du Louvre et des musées de France* 36 (1986):264-67, 1 color fig., 4 b&w figs.
Oval enamel Limoges plaque with the Crucifixion and bearing the monogram of Léonard Limosin and the date 1556, acquired by the museum in 1985.

London

COURTAULD INSTITUTE

1137   MARCHEIX, MADELEINE. "The Painted Limoges Enamels in the Gambier-Parry Collection." *Burlington Magazine* 109 (1967):157-61, 8 b&w figs.
Six Limoges painted enamels of the 15th-16th century bequeathed to the institute and attributed to Monvaerni, Pénicaud, Pierre Reymond, and Léonard Limosin.

VICTORIA AND ALBERT MUSEUM

1138   PHILLIPS, CLAUDE. "Two Limoges Plaques and the Maître de Moulins." *Burlington Magazine* 12 (1907-8):26-32, 2 b&w pls.
An Annunciation and an Adoration of the Shepherds enamel plaques here suggested to date of 1500 and to be after designs executed by the Master of Moulins or by a close follower. The Annunciation was subsequently copied by Nardon Pénicaud and others.

1139   MITCHELL, H.P. "The Limoges Enamels in the Salting Collection." *Burlington Magazine* 20 (1911-12):77-89, 3 b&w pls.
The most notable pieces among the ninety enamels in the collection: works by Nardon Pénicaud, Jean I and Jean II Pénicaud, Jean Poillevé, Léonard Limosin, Pierre Courteys, Jean Court dit Vergier, etc.

1140   PINKHAM, ROGER. "Attributions to the Aeneid Master." *Apollo* 95 (1972):370-75, 13 b&w figs.
Three 16th-century Limoges enamels formerly attributed to Jean I Pénicaud, here reassigned.

Madrid

MUSEO LÁZARO GALDIANO

1141   TORRALBA, FEDERIGO. "Esmaltes en el Museo Lázaro Galdiano." *Goya* 55
(1963):14-29, 19 b&w figs.
Important collection of Limoges enamels in the museum: a triptych with scenes of
the Passion by Nardon Pénicaud, another by Jean I Pénicaud, a Crucifixion of the early
enamel primitive school, four medallions by Jean II Pénicaud, a plate with a bust of Anna
d'Este (1595) by Jean Reymond, a pax with the Virgin and Child and St. John inscribed KIP,
etc.

New York

FRICK COLLECTION

1142   VERDIER, PHILIPPE. "Limoges Painted Enamels: Sixteenth and Seventeenth Centuries," assisted by Joseph Focarino. In *The Frick Collection: An Illustrated Guide.* Vol. 8,
Enamels, Rugs, and Silver. New York: Frick Collection, 1977. 354 pp., 9 color pls., 145
b&w figs.
Presentation of forty-two objects representative of seventeen enamelers: Jean I
Pénicaud, Léonard Limosin, Pierre Reymond, Jean de Court, Jean II Limosin, etc. The emphasis is on physical description of enamel including condition and source of composition; includes biographical summary for each artist.

8. PRIVATE COLLECTION, AUCTION, AND DEALER CATALOGS

WELD-BLUNDELL COLLECTION

1143   READ, HERBERT. "A Pénicaud Masterpiece." *Burlington Magazine* 57 (1930):278-84, 1
color pl., 2 b&w figs.
A Limoges enamel triptych depicting Christ's Passion is assigned to the workshop of
Jean I Pénicaud on the basis of related works.

HUNGARIAN

3. SURVEYS AND HISTORIES

1144   MIHALIK, SÁNDOR. *Old Hungarian Enamels.* Budapest: Corvina Press, 1961. 39 pp.,
8 color figs., 40 b&w figs.
Popularized presentation of goldsmith works with enamel decoration either
produced in Hungary or in Hungarian institutions. Includes a brief discussion and illustration
of ronde bosse and filigree examples of the 15th-16th century.

NETHERLANDISH

3. SURVEYS AND HISTORIES

1145 KOHLHAUSSEN, HEINRICH. "Niederländisch Schmelzwerk." *Jahrbuch der preuszischen Kunstsammlungen* 52 (1931):153-69, 16 b&w figs.
   15th-16th-century goldsmith production with enamel attributed to Netherlandish shops: cups, spoons, reliquaries, monstrance, brooches, in German, Austrian, Italian, and Swiss collections.

6. PERMANENT COLLECTIONS

Baltimore

WALTERS ART GALLERY

1146 VERDIER, PHILIPPE. "A Medallion of the 'Ara Coeli' and the Netherlandish Enamels of the Fifteenth Century." *Journal of the Walters Art Gallery* 24 (1961):9-37, 26 b&w figs.
   Enamel medallion linked to medals owned by Jean de Berry in the early 15th century and to manuscript illuminations commissioned by this prince from the Limbourgs, is proposed to be the work of Arnould de Limbourg, goldsmith and younger brother to the famed Pol, Herman, and Jan. Netherlandish localization and approximate dating of ca. 1420 suggested from stylistic comparisons.

SPANISH

3. SURVEYS AND HISTORIES

Book

1147 JUARISTI, VICTORIANO. *Esmaltes con especial mención de los españoles.* Barcelona and Buenos Aires: Editorial Labor, S.A., 1933. 286 pp., 51 b&w pls.
   General history of enameling with particular emphasis on examples produced in Spain. The Spanish Gothic and Renaissance periods are discussed on pp. 218-55.

Article

1148 SANCHIS Y SIVERA, JOSÉ. "La esmaltería valenciana en la Edad Media." *Archivo de arte valenciano* 7 (1921):3-42, 24 b&w figs.
   Valencian enameling of the 14th-15th century principally preserved on highly ornamented altar crosses. Appendix with transcriptions of cathedral, royal, and other inventories.

XVIII. Seals

A. MULTI COUNTRY OF ORIGIN

3. SURVEYS AND HISTORIES

1149 BIRCH, WALTER DE GRAY. *Seals.* London: Methuen & Co., 1907. 355 pp., 52 b&w pls.
  Comprehensive, if somewhat rambling, history of seals; conception, purpose, of various offices, designs. Deals primarily with material of Great Britain.

6. PERMANENT COLLECTIONS

Rome (Vatican)

ARCHIVIO VATICANO

1150 *Le bolle d'oro dell'Archivio Vaticano,* by Pietro Sella. Inventari dell'Archivio Segreto Vaticano. Vatican City: Biblioteca Apostolica Vaticana, 1934. 69 pp., 37 b&w pls.
  Series of forty-two gold seals in the Vatican archives dating from the 12th through the 18th century. Essay and catalog nos. 22-29 are seals of European rulers and of a Byzantine emperor. All are illustrated.

1151 *I sigilli dell'Archivio Vaticano,* by Pietro Sella. Inventari dell'Archivio Segreto Vaticano. 3 vols. of text, 3 vols. of pls. Vatican City: Biblioteca Apostolica Vaticana, 1937-64. 1:475 pp.; 2:406 pp.; 3:475 pp.; 1:100 b&w pls.; 2:112 b&w pls.; 3:85 b&w pls.
  Catalog of a major collection of seals comprised of 3,609 impressions dating from the 11th to the early 20th century. Classification is in hierarchical order (first ecclesiastical — popes, cardinals, etc. — then secular — emperors, princes, etc.), chronological, and by country within each division. Each seal impression receives a short entry providing date, brief description, measurements, and inventory number. Text volumes conclude with a detailed index.

1151a   *Il sigillo nella storia della civiltà attraverso i documenti dell'Archivio Segreto Vaticano.* Exhibition catalog by Aldo Martini, Stefania Ricci, Bruno Becchetti, and Eugenia Bolognesi. Vatican: Archivio Vaticano, 1985. 163 pp., numerous illus., some in color. French/English/German/Spanish summaries.

Catalog of a didactic exhibition including 210 seals from the Vatican secret archives from the early Middle Ages through the 18th century.

B. SINGLE COUNTRY OF ORIGIN

BRITISH

6. PERMANENT COLLECTIONS

London

BRITISH MUSEUM

1152   BIRCH, WALTER DE GRAY. *Catalogue of Seals in the Department of Manuscripts in the British Museum.* 6 vols. London: Trustees of the British Museum, 1887-1900.

Most complete repertory of British seals, many dating of the 15th, and some of the 16th century.

See entry 732.

GERMAN

3. SURVEYS AND HISTORIES

Book

1153   KITTEL, ERICH. *Siegel.* Brunswick: Klinkhardt & Biermann, 1970. 531 pp., 8 color pls., 400 b&w figs.

Well-documented, thorough survey with good illustrations of the sigillary arts from ancient times to the 20th century with all postclassical examples drawn from Germanic lands. The material is discussed primarily on the basis of social status or offices of owners and includes many examples of the 15th-16th century.

Articles

1154   GESSERT, OSKAR. "Augustin Adelmann andere Heidelberger Meister." *Archiv für Medaillen- und Plaketten-Kunde* 3 (1921-22):53-62, 3 b&w figs.

The seals produced by Augustin Adelmann and other masters of Heidelberg in the mid-16th century.

1155   GESSERT, OSKAR. "Benedikt Braunskorn der Ältere zu Nürnberg." *Archiv für Medaillen- und Plaketten- Kunde* 5 (1925-26):161-63, 1 b&w pl.

Seal of Cardinal Albrecht of Brandenburg in Halle, produced by Benedikt Braunskorn in 1532.

1156   HABICH, GEORG. "Heinrich Aldegrever als Siegelstecher." *Jahrbuch der preuszischen Kunstsammlungen* 52 (1931):81-90, 23 b&w figs.
Heinrich Aldegrever as maker of seals with an involved decoration in the mid-16th century, mostly for the House of Cleves. His sources of inspiration were chiefly Dürer and Hans Baldung.

ITALIAN

3. SURVEYS AND HISTORIES

1157   WEISS, ROBERTO. "La bolla plumbea di Papa Paolo II (1464-1471)." *Numismatica* 2 (1961):129-35, 11 b&w figs.
Lead seal of Pope Paul II attributed to Emiliano Orfini, mint engraver at Rome.

6. PERMANENT COLLECTIONS

Turin

MUSEO CIVICO

1158   FAVA, ANNA SERENA. "Tipari ossia matrici di sigilli religiosi italiani nelle raccolte numismatiche torinesi." In *Studi e ricerche di storia dell'arte in memoria di Luigi Mallé,* ed. Luciano Tamburini et al. Turin: Associazione Amici dei Musei Civici di Torino, 1981. Pp. 61-74, 41 b&w figs.
Description of twenty seals of Italian prelates from the 13th to the 15th century in the numismatic collection of the museum. Nos. 1, 5-8, 11, 17, 19 are of the 15th century.

7. EXHIBITION CATALOGS

Venice

MUSEO CORRER

1159   *Il sigillo nella storia e nella cultura.* Exhibition catalog edited by Stefania Ricci, with sections by Ricci and six other contributors. Rome: Società Editoriale Jouvence, 1985. 264 pp., 8 color pls., numerous b&w figs.
Important contribution to the history of seals from the 13th through the 19th century. Catalog of 246 seal impressions. Well-documented entries study mostly Italian examples and predominantly those of the Veneto region. Many examples owned by doges, clerics, institutions, officials, and private individuals date of the 15th-16th century.

SPANISH

6. PERMANENT COLLECTIONS

Valencia

ARCHIVO CATEDRAL DE VALENCIA

1160   DE LA TORRE, ANTONIO. "La colección sigilográfica del Archivo Catedral de Valencia." *Archivo de arte valenciano.* Parts 1-3: vol. 1 (1915):103-10, 7 b&w figs.; 142-51, 11 b&w figs.; vol. 2 (1916):19-29, 23 b&w figs.; vol. 3 (1917):11-25, 24 b&w figs.; vol. 4 (1918):81-115, 64 b&w figs. Parts 4-5: vol. 5 (1919): 50-64, 30 b&w figs.; vol. 6 (1920):52-64, 48 b&w figs.; vol. 7 (1921):72-103, 68 b&w figs.; vol. 8 (1922):112-36, 49 b&w figs.

Rich collection of seals dating from the late 13th to the 17th century. Includes ecclesiastical seals (Parts 1-3) of bishops and archbishops of the chapter, deans and canons, of parishes, orders, abbeys and monasteries and of other Spanish sees. Also includes secular seals (parts 4-5): regal seals, those of various communities, cities, and individuals. Concludes with useful alphabetical table.

XIX. Bronze — General

A. MULTI COUNTRY OF ORIGIN

3. SURVEYS AND HISTORIES

1161   SAVAGE, GEORGE. *A Concise History of Bronzes.* New York: Praeger, 1969. 264 pp., 16 color pls., 193 b&w figs. (1st ed., 1968.)
      Introductory survey (ancient times through the 20th century) that briefly discusses casting techniques, chasing, artists, workshops, and major works. See chap. 3 (pp. 81-105) for a few late Gothic examples and chap. 5 (137-94) for Renaissance bronzes — statuettes, reliefs, candelabra, etc. — from Italy, Germany, and France.

1162   SCHOTTMÜLLER, FRIDA. *Bronze Statuetten und Geräte.* 2d ed. Berlin: Richard Carl Schmidt & Co., 1921. 204 pp., 142 b&w figs. (1st ed. 1918.)
      Brief history of small bronzes from Egyptian times through the 18th century. Chapters on Gothic and Renaissance period discuss lecterns, mortars, jugs, plaques, reliquaries, statuettes, bells, the majority of examples being drawn from Berlin collections.

6. PERMANENT COLLECTIONS

Berlin

STAATLICHE MUSEEN PREUSSISCHER KULTURBESITZ,
KUNSTGEWERBEMUSEUM

1163   *Bronzen und Plaketten vom ausgehenden 15. Jahrhundert bis zur Mitte des 17. Jahrhunderts.* Catalog by Klaus Pechstein. Berlin: Kunstgewerbemuseum, 1968. 263 pp., 292 b&w figs.
      Useful catalog of small bronzes, plaquettes, and metal goldsmith models in the Berlin decorative arts museum. Includes several major critical revisions of attributions; traces the history of the collection (4 pp.), and lists objects destroyed in 1940-45 (6 pp.). 286 catalog entries, typologically arranged, include 15th-16th-century German, Austrian, French, Netherlandish, and Italian products; objects include statuettes, mortars, small ornaments, ink stands,

door-knockers, bells, candlesticks, oil lamps, goldsmith models, appliqués, medals, reliefs, and plaquettes. Valuable for the wide range of the holdings, the detailed catalog entries, and the useful bibliographies.

Budapest

SZÉPMÜVÉZETI MÚZEUM

1164   *Katalog der ausländischen Bildwerke des Museums der bildenden Künst in Budapest IV.-XVIII. Jahrhundert.* Catalog by Jolán Balogh. 2 vols. Budapest: Akadémiai Kiadó, 1975. 1:308 pp.; 2:499 b&w figs.
    Catalog of non-Hungarian sculptural objects in the museum. Of the 443 entries, nos. 197-203, 207, 217-18, 230, 233-40, 260-81, are Italian Renaissance bronze statuettes, plaques, door-knockers; 457-83 are medals and plaquettes.

London

VICTORIA AND ALBERT MUSEUM

1165   *A Descriptive Catalogue of the Bronzes of European Origin in the South Kensington Museum.* Catalog by C. Drury E. Fortnum. London: Her Majesty's Stationery Office, 1876. 458 pp., 30 b&w pls. and line drawings.
    Several hundred objects of this collection, well known by 1876, cataloged by categories: busts, statuettes, plaques and plaquettes, bells, book mounts, caskets, candlesticks, ewers, andirons, inkstands, door-knockers, mortars, salts, salvers, stirrups, vases, etc.; over half date of the period 1400-1600. Also includes a 210-page historical essay dealing with various bronze-casting centers from earliest times. Dated but still useful since not superseded.

Munich

BAYERISCHES NATIONALMUSEUM

1166   *Bronzeplastik Erwerbungen von 1956-1973.* Catalog by Lenz Kriss-Rettenbeck. Munich: Bayerisches Nationalmuseum, 1974. 83 pp., 67 b&w figs.
    Short guide highlighting fifty-five acquisitions made in 1956-1973. Includes small bronzes dating from the 12th to the 19th century; nos. 5-31 are 15th-16th-century statuettes, door-knockers, plaques, etc., by Multscher, Riccio, Giambologna, Sansovino, Roccatagliata, van der Schardt, etc.

New York

FRICK COLLECTION

1167   *The Frick Collection: An Illustrated Catalogue.* Vol. 3, *Sculpture*, by John Pope-Hennessy, assisted by Anthony F. Radcliffe. New York: Frick Collection, 1970. 254 pp., 7 color pls., 115 b&w figs.
    Exemplary catalog, each entry comprising a lucid essay on mostly small and generally important Renaissance bronzes (statuettes, casket, bell, candlesticks) by Antonio Pollaiuolo, Bertoldo, Francesco da Sangallo, Bellano, Riccio, Severo da Ravenna, Grandi, Aspetti, Bandini, Federico Brandani, Soldani, etc.

ROYAL ONTARIO MUSEUM

1168   *European Bronzes in the Royal Ontario Museum.* Catalog by K. Corey Keeble. Toronto:
Royal Ontario Museum, 1982. 255 pp., 9 color pls., 216 b&w figs.

107 detailed catalog entries with iconographic description, biographical data, relationship to similar examples, and précis of former literature and controversies, from Roman to modern times; of the 15th-16th century are Italian (mostly), German, French, and Netherlandish plaquettes, medals, statuettes, corpus, inkwell, etc. (pp. 11-22, 28-48, 52-54, 56-59).

Vienna

KUNSTHISTORISCHES MUSEUM

1169   *Die Bronzeplastiken: Statuetten, Reliefs, Geräte und Plaquetten.* Catalog by Leo Planiscig.
Vienna: Anton Schroll & Co., 1924. 278 pp., 495 b&w figs.

Catalog of small bronzes, plaquettes, and busts. 495 entries, chronologically arranged, include 15th-16th-century Italian, German, Austrian, and Netherlandish objects—statuettes, inkstands, mortars, bells, oil lamps—by Filarete, Bertoldo, Riccio, the Master of the Dragon [Severo], Antico, Moderno, Belli, Giambologna, Jamnitzer, Vischer, etc., as well as numerous pieces with a geographical ascription.

Washington

NATIONAL GALLERY OF ART

1170   *Renaissance Bronzes from the Samuel H. Kress Collection: Reliefs, Plaquettes, Statuettes, Utensils and Mortars.* Catalog by John Pope-Hennessy. London: Phaidon, 1965. 341 pp., 616 b&w figs.

Catalog of this famous collection of 589 items and a standard reference in the field. It includes mostly Italian 15th-16th-century objects with some German, a few French and Netherlandish, and one Spanish example of the same period. Each is illustrated.

1171   *Renaissance Small Bronze Sculpture and Associated Decorative Arts at the National Gallery of Art.* Compiled by Carolyn C. Wilson. Washington: National Gallery of Art, 1983. 231 pp., several illus.

Handbook of mostly Italian 16th-century small bronzes (sculpture, plaquettes, medals) of the Kress Collection, and some maiolica, jewelry, rock crystals, and Limoges enamels in the gallery's new 1983 installation.

7. EXHIBITION CATALOGS

Buffalo

ALBRIGHT ART GALLERY

1172   *Master Bronzes Selected from Museums and Collections in America.* Exhibition catalog edited by Gordon Bailey Washburn with introductions to various sections by Arthur Upham Pope et al. Buffalo: Buffalo Fine Arts Academy, 1937. Unpaginated. 173 b&w figs.

Nine-page technical introduction, short essays preceding each section, and 173 brief catalog entries of objects drawn from public and private U.S. collections and representing all periods and cultures. Of the 15th-16th century are cat. nos. 119-43 including aquamanile and statuettes by Verrochio, Luca della Robbia, Bertoldo di Giovanni, Bellano, Riccio, Giambologna, etc.

Cleveland

CLEVELAND MUSEUM OF ART

1173 *Renaissance Bronzes from Ohio Collections.* Exhibition catalog by William D. Wixom. Cleveland: Cleveland Museum of Art, 1975. 184 pp., 5 color pls., 272 b&w figs.

236 detailed entries include small-scale figures, plaquettes and medals, mostly Italian and several German, all illustrated, in the Cleveland, Toledo, and Oberlin museums, as well as local private collections.

Dortmund

MUSEUM FÜR KUNST UND KULTURGESCHICHTE

1174 *Deutsche Bronzen des Mittelalters und der Renaissance: Medaillen und Goldschmiedearbeiten.* Exhibition catalog by Johannes Jantzen, et al. Dortmund: Museum für Kunst und Kulturgeschichte, 1960. 54 pp., 26 b&w figs.

Features 145 Renaissance bronzes (statuettes, mortars, pitchers, bells, medals, plaquettes, etc.) mostly German (followed by Italian), from the museum's holdings. Also includes forty-five rings of all periods, as well as earlier fibulae, etc.

Ferrara

PALAZZINA DI MARFISA D'ESTE

1175 *Placchette e bronzi nelle Civiche Collezioni.* Exhibition (1974) catalog by Ranieri Varese. Florence: Centro Di, 1975. 247 pp., 561 b&w figs.

Catalog of 210 small bronzes (and also some lead objects) dating from the 15th century until 1927 in the city museums of Ferrara; nos. 1-47 are 15th-16th-century plaquettes from North Italian centers, Germany, Flanders (by Giuseppe de Levis, Riccio, Moderno, Belli, IO.F.F., Flötner); 82-160, statuettes bearing attributions to Campagna, Vittoria, Olivieri, Riccio, Giambologna, Pietro da Barga, etc. Informative and well illustrated.

Münster

WESTFÄLISCHES LANDESMUSEUM FÜR KUNST UND KULTURGESCHICHTE

1176 *Bronzen von der Antike bis zur Gegenwart.* Exhibition catalog edited by Peter Bloch and Marie-Theres Suermann, with entries by numerous contributors. Berlin: Stiftung Preussischer Kulturbesitz, 1983. 311 pp., 6 color pls., 218 b&w figs.

Comprised of 153 bronze objects dating from antiquity to the present from Berlin State Museum collections. Cat. nos. 50-61 are 15th-century statuettes, plaques, aquamanile, from Italy, Germany, and France; 62-93 are statuettes, plaquettes, mortar from Padua, Venice, Nuremberg, Augsburg, each illustrated and with informative entry. Exhibition also traveled to the Saarland-Museum, Saarbrücken, and the Kestner-Museum, Hanover.

8. PRIVATE COLLECTION, AUCTION, AND DEALER CATALOGS

CASTIGLIONI COLLECTION

1177   *Sammlung Camillo Castiglioni. Bronzestatuetten und Geräte.* Edited by Leo Planiscig.
Vienna: Kunstverlag Anton Schroll & Co., 1923. 55 pp. with 2 b&w text figs., 115 b&w
pls.
Catalog of famed Viennese collection of 115 bronzes, mostly aquamanile, statuettes,
mortars and plaques, from antiquity to Clodion. Nos. 7-111 are of the 15th-16th century and
mostly North Italian of ca. 1500.

PIERPONT MORGAN COLLECTION

1178   BODE, WILHELM. *Collection of J. Pierpont Morgan—Bronzes of the Renaissance and
Subsequent Periods.* 2 vols. Paris: Librairie Centrale des Beaux-Arts, 1910. 1:30 pp. with
18 text figs.; 2:45 pp. with 17 text figs.; 1 and 2: 162 b&w tinted pls., numbered consecutively.
Elaborate catalog printed in 150 copies. Forty-two-page introduction highlights
major pieces. Catalog of 225 often outstanding examples with lengthy descriptions; all illustrated in lavish plates; majority of pieces (small scale sculptures and plaques) are of the
Italian Renaissance with a few French and German examples. Ambitious undertaking of connoisseurship, though many of the attributions have since been revised. Collection has subsequently been dispersed, many pieces having gone to the Frick Collection.

STRAUSS COLLECTION

1179   *The Robert Strauss Collection of Renaissance and Other Bronzes.* Sale held in London at
Christie's 3 May 1977. 144 pp., 13 color pls., 97 b&w figs.
Dispersal of a collection of mostly Italian bronze plaquettes (lots 25-43), statuettes
and objects (bells, andirons, oil lamps, inkstands, ewers, mortars, etc.) of the Paduan school
(Moderno, IO.F.F., Riccio, Desiderio da Firenze, Severo da Ravenna) and Venice (Roccatagliata, DeLevis, etc.); also some German-Netherlandish examples (Peter Vischer, Duquesnoy, etc.).

B. SINGLE COUNTRY OF ORIGIN

GERMAN

3. SURVEYS AND HISTORIES

1180   HEADLAM, CECIL. *Peter Vischer and the Bronze Founders of Nuremberg.* London:
George Bell & Sons, 1901. 144 pp., 28 b&w figs.
15th-century bronze sculptor of Nuremberg who also produced plaquettes and inkstands; for these see pp. 86-100.

1181   SCHÄDLER, ALFRED. "Bronzebildwerke von Hans Multscher." In *Intuition und
Kunstwissenschaft: Festschrift für Hanns Swarzenski zum 70. Geburtstag am 30. August
1973.* Berlin: Gebr. Mann, 1973. Pp. 391-408, 17 b&w figs.

Bronze statuettes, reliquaries, and plaques attributable to Hans Multscher; their relationship to the artist's large-scale stone and wood sculptures.

ITALIAN

3. SURVEYS AND HISTORIES

Book

1182   PLANISCIG, LEO. *Andrea Riccio.* Vienna: Anton Schroll & Co., 1927. 504 pp., 586 b&w figs.
   The major study on the bronzes of Andrea Riccio and of his contemporaries in Padua. If the author has been criticized for attributing too many pieces to Riccio, the presentation of the vast body of material he discusses is yet to be surpassed. It includes statuettes, plaques and plaquettes, perfume burners, candlesticks, inkstands and other desk artifacts, door-knockers, casts of reptiles and shells, as well as other bibelots.

Articles

1183   CESSI, FRANCESCO. "Andrea Briosco detto il Riccio, scultore (1470-1532)." In *Collana artisti trentini,* edited by Riccardo Maroni, vol. 45. Trent: 1965. Reprinted in *Collana artisti trentini,* vol. 2. Trent: Arti Grafiche Saturnia, 1977, pp. 4-110, 63 b&w figs.
   Biographical essay on Riccio, a native of Trent, who became the principal sculptor of small bronzes in Padua in the early 16th century, and a critical discussion of some of his works.

1184   DRAPER, JAMES. "Andrea Riccio and His Colleagues in the Untermyer Collection: Speculations on the Chronology of His Statuettes and on Attributions to Franceso di Sant'Agata and Moderno." *Apollo* 107 (1978):170-80, 21 b&w figs.
   As he presents Paduan bronzes given to the Metropolitan Museum, the author proposes that Riccio's plaques of the Descent into Limbo and Resurrection at the Louvre are part of Trombetta's tomb (1524) in the Santo, that the Deposition plaque in Washington was meant for the artist's own funerary monument at S. Giovanni di Verdara; he attributes three statuettes (Budapest, Frick Collection, and Padua) to the goldsmith Francesco di Sant'Agata and a Ricciesque Horse and Rider at the Metropolitan Museum and a gilt Venus in Cleveland to Moderno.

1185   MIDDELDORF, ULRICH. "Filarete?" *Mitteilungen des kunsthistorischen Institutes in Florenz* 17 (1973):75-86. Reprinted in *Raccolta di scritti, that is, Collected Writings. II. 1939-1973.* Florence: Studio per Edizioni Scelte, 1980, pp. 369-76, figs. 207-20.
   Various bronze plaques, a tabernacle door at Impruneta, and some paxes proposed to be Filarete's.

6. PERMANENT COLLECTIONS

Ravenna

MUSEO NAZIONALE

1186   *Piccoli bronzi e placchette del Museo Nazionale di Ravenna.* Exhibition catalog by Luciana Martini, assisted by Giovanni Curatola, Marzia Faietti, Anna Maria Iannucci, Giovanni Morigi, Marco Spallanzani. Ravenna: Cassa di Risparmio di Ravenna, 1986. 127 pp., 27 color illus., numerous b&w figs.

Catalog of this little-known collection of bronzes (until 1977 in the municipal Collezione Classense). It consists of eighty-three three-dimensional bronze objects, mostly statuettes, and eighty-six plaquettes. Nearly all are Italian and of the Renaissance period. Introductory essays by Maria Grazia Ciardi Dupré Dal Pogetto and Carmen Ravanelli Guidotti provide history and art historical context. Short entries with few attributions conclude with a bibliography. Includes works by Girolamo Campagna, Riccio, Moderno, Severo da Ravenna, Gianfrancesco Enzola, Fra Antonio da Brescia, IO.F.F., Caradosso, Belli, and Bernardi.

Venice

MUSEO CORRER

1187   *Venetian Bronzes from the Collections of the Correr Museum, Venice.* Exhibition held in Austin at the University of Texas; Dayton Art Institute; William Rockhill Nelson Gallery of Art, Kansas City; Toledo Museum of Art; Santa Barbara Museum of Art; Dallas Museum of Fine Arts. Catalog by Giovanni Mariacher. Washington: Smithsonian Institution, 1968. 47 pp., 36 b&w figs.

Six-page introduction addresses the major sculptors and centers of the 15th-16th century. Catalog of thirty-five entries with descriptions and bibliographies spans works from Bellano through Roccatagliata; mostly statuettes but includes a few plaquettes and busts. Important publication as it remains to date the only one relating to the important collection.

Vienna

KUNSTHISTORISCHES MUSEUM

1188   *Skulpturen und Plastiken des Mittelalters und der Renaissance.* Vol. 1 of *Die estensische Kunstsammlung* Catalog by Leo Planiscig. Vienna: Anton Schroll & Co., 1919. 215 pp., 37 b&w pls., 251 b&w figs.

Part of collection of the dukes of Este, removed to Vienna in 1859. Includes (nos. 181-243) mostly small Italian Renaissance bronze statuettes, plaques, inkstands, andirons, candlesticks by Donatello, Antico, Vittoria, Campagna, Aspetti, Roccatagliata and others. Also plaquettes (252-434) by Moderno, Riccio, IO.F.F., Caradosso, Lombardi, Bernardi, Belli, Abondio and others; two French examples (440-41) of ca. 1500, and German plaquettes (447-60) including several by Flötner.

1188a   *Renaissance Master Bronzes from the Collection of the Kunsthistorisches Museum, Vienna.* Exhibition held in Washington at the National Gallery of Art; Los Angeles County Museum of Art; and The Art Institute of Chicago. Catalog by Manfred Leithe-Jasper. London: Scala Publications; Washington: Smithsonian Institution Traveling Exhibition Service, 1986. 304 pp., 10 b&w text figs., 75 color pls., several with b&w details.

Selection of seventy-five bronze statuettes, plaques and plaquettes from this prestigious collection. Scholarly, often lengthy, entries include bibliographies. Most examples are 16th- century Italian. All are reproduced in color.

XX. Medals

MULTI COUNTRY OF ORIGIN

2. BIOGRAPHICAL DICTIONARIES

1189   FORRER, L[EONARD]. *Biographical Dictionary of Medallists, Coin-, Gem-, and Seal-Engravers, Mint-Masters, etc., Ancient and Modern, with References to Their Works B.C. 500–A.D. 1900.* 8 vols. Vol. 1, A-D (1904), 691 pp.; vol. 2, E-H (1904), 588 pp.; vol. 3, I-MAZ (1907), 649 pp.; vol. 4, M- Q (1909), 725 pp.; vol. 5, R-S (1912), 738 pp.; vol. 6, T-Z (1916), 738 pp.; vol. 7, Supplement, A-L (1923), 567 pp.; vol. 8, Supplement, M-Z (1930), 461 pp. Numerous b&w figs. and line drawings throughout. London: Spink & Son. Reprint. New York: B. Franklin, 1970.

   Comprehensive dictionary, useful for handy quick reference but needs to be supplemented by later publications.

3. SURVEYS AND HISTORIES

Books

1190   BABELON, JEAN. *Great Coins and Medals.* Translated by Stuart Hood. London: Thames & Hudson, 1959. 37 pp., 167 b&w pls. (1st ed., 1958.)

   Largely pictorial survey of portraiture on coins and medals from antiquity through the Renaissance. For European medals of 1400-1600 (including a few boxwood medallions), see pp. 29-39 and pl. nos. 93-167 with examples by Pisanello, Melioli, della Robbia, Matteo di Pasti, Antico, Nicholas Hilliard, Reinhart, Hagenauer, Vischer, Pilon, etc.

1191   BERNHART, MAX. *Die Bildnismedaillen Karls des Fünften.* Munich: Helbing, 1919. 97 pp., 22 b&w figs.

   Series of German and Italian medals with portraits of Emperor Charles V. Study is supplemented by the author's article "Bildnismedaillen Karls V (Nachtrag)," *Archiv für Medaillen- und Plaketten-Kunde* 5 (1925-26):137-43, 1 b&w pl. comprising 9 figs.

1192   GOLDSCHNEIDER, LUDWIG. *Unknown Renaissance Portraits: Medals of Famous Men and Women of the XV & XVI Centuries.* London: Phaidon, 1952. 14 pp., 66 b&w pls., 4 b&w figs.

Sixty-six select examples from European public and private collections with captions providing data on both artist and sitter. Plates are enlargements showing details of modeling and technique.

1193   HILL, GEORGE. *Medals of the Renaissance.* 2d ed. rev. and enl. by Graham Pollard. London: British Museum Publications, 1978. 230 pp., 32 b&w pls. (1st ed. 1920.)

Survey of the field based on lectures delivered in 1915. Ten-page introduction traces origins and development of commemorative medals during the Renaissance; chap. 1 (pp. 23-35) deals with technique; chap. 2 (36-66) surveys 15th-century North Italian medals and medalists; chap. 3 (67-82), 15th-century Roman and Florentine pieces; chap. 4 (83-100), 16th-century Italian products; chap. 5 (101-16), German medals; chap. 6 (117-29), Netherlandish medals; chap. 7 (130-42), French medals; chap. 8 (143-67), English and Scottish medals. New notes and revised bibliography.

1194   JONES, MARK. *The Art of the Medal.* London: British Museum Publications, 1979. 192 pp., 8 color pls., 484 b&w figs.

Survey from the early Renaissance to modern day: concept, purpose, popularity and diffusion, models, medalists. Relevant to 15th-16th century are chaps. 2-8 (pp. 12-74) dealing with Italy, France, Germany, the Netherlands, and England. Well illustrated with examples mainly from the British Museum.

Article

1195   BERNHART, MAX. "Die Granvella-Medaillen des XVI. Jahrhunderts." *Archiv für Medaillen- und Plaketten-Kunde* 2 (1920-21):101-20, 40 b&w figs.

Lead, silver, and bronze medals of Cardinal Antoine Perrenot de Granvelle, chancellor of Charles V, by Joachim Deschler, Leone Leoni, Jacques Jonghelinck and others. Essay followed by catalog of twenty-six items.

6. PERMANENT COLLECTIONS

Boston

MUSEUM OF FINE ARTS

1196   MARINCOLA, MICHELE D.; POULET, ANNE L.; and SCHER, STEPHEN K. "Gothic, Renaissance, and Baroque Medals from the Museum of Fine Arts, Boston." *Medal* 9 (1986):79-105, 14 b&w figs.

Presentation, in the form of catalog entries, of the fourteen most important medals in the collection. Included are those of Constantine and Heraclius attributed to Michelet Saulmon, Leonello d'Este by Pisanello, Guido Pepoli by Sperandio, self-portrait by Boldù.

XX. Medals

Brunswick, Me.

BOWDOIN COLLEGE MUSEUM OF ART

1197   *Medals and Plaquettes from the Molinari Collection at Bowdoin College.* Exhibition
catalog by Andrea S. Norris, Graham Pollard, Ingrid Weber, and David P. Becker.
Brunswick, Me.: Bowdoin College, 1976. 303 pp., 812 b&w figs.
     The majority of the 357 medals and 69 plaquettes in this collection are Italian with ex-
amples dating of the 15th and mostly 16th century. Among artists represented are Pisanello,
Laurana, de' Pasti, Antico, Candida, Cavino, Sansovino, Spinelli, and Moderno. Includes also
some French and German casts of the same period, notably by Delaune, Dupré, and Flötner.
All examples are illustrated.

London

BRITISH MUSEUM

1198   HILL, G.F. "The Whitcombe Greene Plaquettes." *Burlington Magazine* 30 (1917):103-10,
10 b&w figs.
     Plaquettes by Moderno and Riccio, a Donatellesque example bearing the name and
arms of Marino Tomacelli, Bishop of Cassano (1485-94), a 16th-century plaquette of the
Spanish school, and others, from this bequest, lead to author's differentiation between the
original plaquette and its subsequent derivates (lead impressions made from matrix, bronze
casts from seal impressions), as well as on identification and characteristics of Moderno's and
Riccio's plaquettes.

Santa Barbara, Calif.

UNIVERSITY ART MUSEUM

1199   MIDDELDORF, ULRICH, and GOETZ, OSWALD. *Medals and Plaquettes from the
Sigmund Morgenroth Collection.* Chicago: Art Institute of Chicago, 1944. 78 pp., 32 b&w
pls.
     Publication related to a special exhibit of the collection (since given to Santa Bar-
bara) at the Art Institute of Chicago. Includes 436 informative catalog entries for mostly
Italian Renaissance examples, a number of German, and some French and Netherlandish
ones.

Washington

NATIONAL GALLERY OF ART

1200   *Renaissance Medals from the Samuel H. Kress Collection at the National Gallery of Art,* by
George Francis Hill. Revised and enlarged by Graham Pollard. London: Phaidon Press,
[1967]. 307 pp., 140 b&w pls.
     Standard reference, particularly valuable when used in conjunction with Hill's *Corpus*
of 1930 (entry 1236). Extensive collection, largely comprised of medals formerly belonging to
Gustave Dreyfus, Paris (when originally cataloged by Hill). 640 entries deal with 15th- and
16th-century Italian (mostly), French, German, and Netherlandish medals, 27 with Renaissance coins. All items are illustrated, many with both obverse and reverse. Cross-reference
indexes and concordances.

8. PRIVATE COLLECTION, AUCTION, AND DEALER CATALOGS

CIECHANOWIECKI COLLECTION

1201   *Sculpture in Miniature: The Andrew S. Ciechanowiecki Collection of Gilt & Gold Medals and Plaquettes.* Exhibition held in Louisville at the J.B. Speed Art Museum. Catalog by Jacques Fischer, in collaboration with Gay Seagrim. Louisville: J.B. Speed Art Museum, 1969. 222 pp., 460 b&w figs., often with obverse and reverse representation.

Private collection of a well-known London art dealer consisting of 414 European and American medals and forty-six plaquettes from the 15th to 19th century including 15th- and 16th-century Austrian (cat. nos. 3-28), German (48-59), French (147-54), Italian (230-47, 284-97), Netherlandish (331-43), and Spanish (378-80) examples, among which portrait and commemorative medals, and plaquettes with mythological or devotional subjects, often by well-known bronzists.

RECENT MULTI OWNER AUCTION

1202   *A Collection of Renaissance and Later Medals.* Sale held in Zurich at Sotheby's 27 May 1974. 55 pp., 32 b&w pls. with several illus. on each.

Major sale of 272 lots including examples by most important medalists: Antico, Giovanni Candida, Giovanni dal Cavino, Guillaume Dupré, Enzola, Fiorentino, Bertoldo, Cristoforo di Geremia, Leoni, Mola, Matteo de' Pasti, Pisanello, Poggini, Sperandio and others. Outstanding is the series of papal medals (nos. 214-72).

B. SINGLE COUNTRY OF ORIGIN

AUSTRIAN

3. SURVEYS AND HISTORIES

1203   DWORSCHAK, FRITZ. "Die Renaissancemedaille in Österreich (mit einen Exkurs über Hubert Gerhard als Medailleur)." *Jahrbuch der kunsthistorischen Sammlungen in Wien* 1 (1926):213-44, 9 b&w pls., with several figs. on each, 13 b&w figs.

Important survey of medals in the Austrian realm during the Renaissance, particularly in Vienna and Prague. Works of Italians such as Adriano Fiorentino, Antonio Abondio, Raphael Ranghieri, and of local artists such as Hans Kels, Konrad Osterer, Ludwig Neufahrer, Johan Descher, Lorenz Rosenbaum, Michael Fuchs, Hans Wild, and Severin Brachmann. Discussed in greater detail is Hubert Gerhard's oeuvre as a medalist.

BELGIUM (FLEMISH)

3. SURVEYS AND HISTORIES

1204   ALVIN, FR. "Rectification à propos d'une médaille de J. Zagar et oeuvre nouvelle de cet artiste." *Gazette numismatique* 13 (1908-9):149-61.

Jacques Zagar, Flemish medalist and lawyer, had been a student at the university of Bourges ca. 1550 when he produced medals of faculty members Eguinaire Baron and François Baudouin.

1205 DAVIS, CHARLES. "Medals of Marco Mantova Benavides by Jacob Zagar and Giovanni dal Cavino." *Studies in the History of Art* [National Gallery of Art, Washington] 6 (1974):97-103, 9 b&w figs.

Author theorizes on a sojourn by the Flemish medalist Zagar at the university of Padua where he produced a medal (stone model in Berlin) of the well-known jurist-professor Marco Mantova Benavides. Since Tomasini, this medal has been incorrectly ascribed to Giovanni dal Cavino.

1206 TOURNEUR, VICTOR. "Jacob Zagar und die Everard Back- Medaille." *Archiv für Medaillen- und Plaketten-Kunde* 1 (1913-14):14-20, 1 b&w fig.

Medal dated 1578 by Jacques Zagar of Everard Back, prior of the Convent St. Sauveur in Antwerp.

6. PERMANENT COLLECTIONS

Brussels

BIBLIOTHÈQUE ROYALE ALBERT I

1207 TOURNEUR, VICTOR. "Jacques Zagar et la médaille de Liévin Kaarsemaker." *Archiv für Medaillen- und Plaketten-Kunde* 1 (1913-14):200-204, 1 b&w fig.

Lead medal of 1550 by the Fleming Jacques Zagar representing a fellow student.

BRITISH (ENGLISH)

3. SURVEYS AND HISTORIES

1208 BUNT, CYRIL G.E. "British War Medals." *Connoisseur* 107 (1941):23-27, 41, 15 b&w figs.

Two medals of Elizabeth I commemorating the defeat of the Armada (1588-89), one cast in gold recalling the design of the enameled Armada jewel (Victoria and Albert Museum).

FRENCH

3. SURVEYS AND HISTORIES

Books

1209 MAZEROLLE, F. *Les Médailleurs français du XVe siècle au milieu du XVIIe*. 3 vols. Vol. 1: *Introduction et documents,* 808 pp.; vol. 2, *Catalogue des médailles et des jetons,* 267 pp.; vol. 3, *Album,* 6 pp., 42 b&w pls. often with many illus. on each. Paris: Imprimerie Nationale, 1902-4.

Vol. 1: 178-page introduction describes production method of medals, examines the history and general characteristics of medals from the 15th to the middle of the 17th century, and provides entries for the documentary references (Leclerc, Lepère, Marende, Gauvain, de Laune, Pilon, Jacques Primavera, etc.). Followed by chronologically arranged transcription of relevant documents. Vol. 2: catalog of 1,021 medals, mostly from the Cabinet de France des Médailles, Bibliothèque nationale, chronologically arranged; alphabetical index and index of mottos. Vol. 3: plates (objects reproduced from plaster casts).

1210   RONDOT, NATALIS. *Jacques Gauvain, orfèvre, graveur et médailleur à Lyon au seizième siècle.* Lyon: Imprimerie Pitrat Aîné, 1887. 73 pp., 5 b&w pls, 2 line drawings.
        The medals produced by Jacques Gauvain of Picardy, master goldsmith in Lyon from ca. 1520-47—most important are one of Margaret of Austria and another presented to the Dauphin in 1533 by the city of Lyon.

Article

1211   BODE, WILHELM VON. "Die Medaille von Johann Duc de Berry und ihr mutmasslicher Künstler Michelet Saulmon." *Archiv für Medaillen- und Plaketten-Kunde* 3 (1921-22):1-10, 5 b&w figs.
        Author discusses the medals of Constantine, Hercules, etc. owned by Jean, duc de Berry, and their attribution to the putative Michelet Saulmon.

GERMAN

3. SURVEYS AND HISTORIES

Books

1212   BERNHART, MAX. *Medaillen und Plaketten.* Bibliothek für Kunst- und Antiquitätenfreunde, vol. 1. 2d ed. Munich: Klinkhardt & Biermann, 1984. 245 pp., 2 color pls., 246 b&w figs. (1st ed. 1966.)
        Well-rounded introduction to the history of medals up to the present. Supplemented with some plaquettes bearing portraits. Useful list, alphabetically arranged, of artists' monograms and signatures.

1213   HABICH, GEORG. *Die deutschen Medailleure des XVI. Jahrhunderts.* Halle: A. Riechmann & Co., 1916. 292 pp., 12 b&w pls., 18 b&w text figs.
        Short biography of German medalists of the Renaissance and list of their known works. Arranged alphabetically. A preliminary version of the author's definitive *Deutschen Schaumünzen* (next entry). Well illustrated; indexes.

1214   HABICH, GEORG. *Die deutschen Schaumünzen des XVI. Jahrhunderts.* 3 vols. in 5 parts. Vol. 1, part 1 (1929), part 2 (1931); vol. 2, part 1 (1932), part 2 (1934); 132 pp. of introduction with 169 text figs.; 557 pp. of catalog with 664 text figs., 334 b&w pls. Vol. 3 (1934), 48 pp. Munich: F. Bruckmann.
        Monumental standard reference on medals made in Germany and/or by German medalists during the 16th century, with nearly four thousand entries. Vol. 1: introduction (pp. v-xxxv) deals mostly with technique; detailed catalog entries (mostly illustrated) for the early masters (Vischer, Dürer, Burgkmair, Cranach, Krug, etc.) followed by the first half of the 16th century medalists of Augsburg; Germans in the Netherlands; Nuremberg; medals produced in stone and wood; Tyrol; Switzerland; Franconia; Austria; Poland, Bohemia and South Germany. Vol. 2: mid-to late-16th-century medalists in Rhineland, Saxony, and other

North German areas; late South German medals including the work of Italian (especially Antonio Abondio), French, and Netherlandish artists active on Germanic lands. Vol. 3: indexes of artists, sitters, inscriptions, and subjects.

1215 MENDE, MATTHIAS. *Dürer-Medaillen: Münzen, Medaillen, Plaketten von Dürer, auf Dürer, nach Dürer.* Nuremberg: Hans Carl, 1983. 559 pp., 8 color pls., 625 b&w figs.

Coins, medals, and plaquettes designed by Dürer, depicting him, or deriving from his compositions. Author develops and constructively criticizes the worth of Habich's *Deutschen Schaumünzen* (see previous entry).

Articles

1216 BERNHART, MAX. "Der Meister mit dem Krüglein (Hans Krug d.J.?)." *Archiv für Medaillen- und Plaketten-Kunde* 2 (1920-21):34-41, 1 b&w pl. comprising 14 figs., and HABICH, GEORG. "Hans Schenck, der 'Meister mit dem Krüglein.'" *Archiv für Medaillen- und Plaketten-Kunde* 5 (1925-26):46-57, 2 b&w pls. comprising 17 figs.

Activity of the medalist Hans Schenck (not Krug) from ca. 1524 to 1548 at the court of Duke Albrecht of Prussia.

1217 BERNHART, MAX. "Deutsche Medaillen aus der Frühzeit der Renaissance." *Pantheon* 14 (1934):257-61, 21 b&w figs.

German medals of the early Renaissance by Peter Vischer, Dürer, and Matthias Gebel of Nuremberg, Hans Schwarz and Friedrich Hagenauer of Augsburg, and Martin Schalfrer of Ulm, etc.; designs for coins and medals by Dürer, Lucas Cranach, Hans Burgkmair, and Albrecht Altdorfer.

1218 DWORSCHAK, FRITZ. "Bemerkungen und Nachträge zum Meister des Heidegger und zum Monogrammisten S.B. (Severin Brachmann)" and "Die drei Monogrammisten WV, DR und R.R." *Archiv für Medaillen- und Plaketten-Kunde* 4 (1923-24):63-79, 80-81, 2 b&w pls. comprising 39 figs.

Additions to Habich, *Die deutschen Medailleure des XVI. Jahrhunderts* (see entry 1213), dealing with the oeuvre of late 16th-century medalists: the Master of the Mint, Severin Brachmann, Wolf Verdross, David Rottlius, and Raphael Ranghieri.

1219 DWORSCHAK, FRITZ. "Loy Hering als Medailleur." *Archiv für Medaillen- und Plaketten-Kunde* 5 (1925-26):148-57, 1 b&w pl. comprising 11 figs.

Medals of Bishop Philipp of Freising and other sitters produced by the sculptor Loy Hering in the first decades of the 16th century.

1220 HABICH, GEORG. "Beiträge zu Hans Kels." *Archiv für Medaillen- und Plaketten-Kunde* 1 (1913-14):35-41, 1 b&w pl. comprising 4 figs.

Medals, a boxwood, and two hone models of the 1530s by Hans Kels.

1221 HABICH, GEORG. "Dietrich Schro, der Monogrammist DS." *Archiv für Medaillen- und Plaketten-Kunde* 2 (1920- 21):29-33, 5 b&w figs.

Medals of the Saxon counts von Solms produced by Dietrich Schro in 1542-45.

1222 HABICH, GEORG. "Peter Flötner oder Hieronymus Magdeburger?" *Archiv für Medaillen- und Plaketten-Kunde* 5 (1925-26):26-45, 47 b&w figs.

Reattribution of medals of the 1530s to Peter Flötner of Nuremberg and Hieronymus of Magdeburg.

1223 HABICH, GEORG. "Sixtus and Felicitas Forster." *Archiv für Medaillen- und Plaketten-Kunde* 1 (1913-14):152-60, 1 b&w fig.

Unique example of a silver medal dated 1527 in the Berlin Münzkabinett representing the elderly Sixtus and Felicitas Forster, burghers of Augsburg.

1224 HABICH, GEORG. "Studien zur Augsburger Medaillenkunst am Ende des XVI. Jahrhunderts." *Archiv für Medaillen- und Plaketten-Kunde* 1 (1913-14):175-99, 3 b&w pls comprising 43 figs.

The activity of several medalists in Augsburg during the years 1572-1620.

1225 MYLIUS, GEORG. "Die Medaillen auf Georg Mylius. Augsburg-Wittenberg 1548-1607." *Archiv für Medaillen- und Plaketten-Kunde* 5 (1925-26):91-104, 1 b&w pl. comprising 11 figs.

Medals of Georg Müller of Augsburg including his self-portraits, as studied by one of his descendants.

1226 ZINK, FRITZ. "Die frühesten Stadtansichten auf deutschen Medaillen und Münzen." *Anzeiger des Germanischen Nationalmuseums* (1954-59):192-221, 37 b&w figs.

German medals and coins of the 16th and 17th centuries with representations of specific cities: Leipzig, Nuremberg, Graz, Strasbourg, Munich, Frankfurt, and others. Concludes with a catalog of fifty-four such pieces.

ITALIAN

3. SURVEYS AND HISTORIES

Books

1227 ARMAND, ALFRED. *Les Médailleurs italiens des quinzième et seizième siècles.* 3 vols., 2d ed. Vol. 1 (1883), 308 pp.; vol. 2 (1883), 368 pp.; vol. 3 (1887), 356 pp. Paris: E. Plon et Cie. (1st ed. 1879.)

Somewhat dated mine of information on medals with often lengthy entries including biographical facts on artists, descriptions, and transcription of inscriptions. Vol. 1: known Italian artists of the mid-15th to the end of the 16th century (chronologically arranged). Vol. 2: earlier medals, those produced by Italians outside Italy, anonymous works, tables. Vol. 3: addition of eight hundred ninety-nine attributions made for medals published in vols. 1 and 2 with tables. Index of artists and subjects.

1228 CALABI, A., and CORNAGGIA, G. *Matteo dei Pasti: La sua opera medaglistica distinta da quella degli anonimi riminesi del XV secolo in relazione al medaglioni malatestiani aggiunte le falsificazioni.* Milan: Guido Modiano, [1926]. 145 pp., 83 b&w figs.

The medals of Matteo de' Pasti; redefinition of the artist's oeuvre leads the author to reattribute many medals traditionally given to the artist to anonymous Riminese artists of the 15th century. Later falsifications are also discussed.

1229 CALABI, A., and CORNAGGIA, G. *Pisanello.* Milan: Guido Mondadori, 1928. 253 pp., including 75 b&w pls.

XX. Medals

Thirty-two-page essay (in Italian and then in English) pointing out the salient characteristics of Pisanello's style in his paintings, drawings, and mostly in his medals, followed by a catalog of medals unquestionably by Pisanello (three), and of those close to and/or made in direct imitation, arranged chronologically from contemporaneous examples to those made in the 17th century (thirty-six pieces); six large marble medallions of the 15th-17th century.

1230   CESSI, FRANCESCO. *Alessandro Vittoria, medaglista (1525-1608)*. In *Collana artisti trentini,* edited by Riccardo Maroni, vol. 23. Trent: 1960. Reprint. *Collana artisti trentini,* vol. 1. Trent: Arti Grafiche Saturnia, 1977, pp. 23-130, 49 b&w figs.

Activity of Vittoria in Trent, Venice, Vicenza; attribution to him of medals representing contemporaries (Aretino, Rangone, etc.), and also of the silver binding of the Grimani Breviary.

1231   DWORSCHAK, FRITZ. *Antonio Abondio, medaglista e ceroplasta (1538-1591)*. In *Collana artisti trentini,* edited by Riccardo Maroni, vol. 19. Trent: 1958. Reprint. *Collana artisti trentini,* vol. 2. Trent: Arti Grafiche Saturnia, 1977, pp. 131-217, 86 b&w figs.

Antonio Abondio (Riva di Garda 1538—Vienna 1591), maker of medals and of medallion wax portraits; his activity in Italy and Spain, and for Rudolf II in Vienna and Prague as court medalist. Includes hand list of his works (revising Habich's catalog).

1232   FABRICZY, CORNELIUS VON. *Italian Medals.* Translated by Mrs. Gustavius W. Hamilton. New York: E.P. Dutton & Co.; London: Duckworth & Co., 1904. 224 pp., 41 b&w pls. (From the German *Medaillen der italienischen Renaissance.* Leipzig: H. Seemann [1903], 108 pp., 181 figs.)

Well-known if somewhat dated study. Twenty-two-page introduction deals with form, execution, and subject of the Renaissance commemorative medal. Separate chapters deal with Pisano and other North Italians (pp. 27-68), Venetian and Bolognese medalists (71-99), Florentine medals (103-50), Roman medalists (153-73), the medals of the Medicean court (177-85), the Papal mint (186-96), and Paduan, Milanese artists (196-211); approach is attribution oriented. Useful for reference to early publications.

1233   FRIEDLAENDER, JULIUS. *Die italienischen Schaumünzen des fünfzehnten Jahrhunderts (1430-1530): Ein Beitrag zur Kunstgeschichte.* Berlin: Weidmannsche Buchhandlung, 1882. 223 pp., 42 b&w pls.

Early study, not superseded until Hill (see entry 1236), of Italian and some French Renaissance medals. Material arranged chronologically.

1234   HABICH, GEORG. *Die Medaillen der italienischen Renaissance.* Stuttgart and Berlin: Deutsche Verlags-Anstalt, [1924]. 168 pp. with 45 b&w text figs., 100 b&w pls.

Informative if somewhat dated study of Italian Renaissance medals and medalists; emphasis on identification and attribution of medals to a wide range of major and minor artists from Pisanello to the late mannerists.

1235   HEISS, ALOÏS. *Les Médailleurs de la Renaissance.* 9 parts. Part 1, *Vittore Pisano* (1881), 48 pp. with 63 text figs., 11 b&w pls.; part 2, *Francesco Laurana, Pietro da Milano* (1882), 56 pp. with 60 text figs., 5 b&w pls.; part 3, *Niccolò, Amadio da Milano, Marescotti, Lixignolo, Petrecino, Baldassare Estense, Corradini, anonymes travaillant à Ferrare au XVe siècle* (1883), 60 pp. with 130 text figs., 8 b&w pls.; part 4, *Léon-Baptiste Alberti, Matteo de' Pasti, et anonyme de Pandolphe IV Malatesta* (1883), 60 pp. with 100 text figs., 8 b&w pls.; part 5, *Niccoló Spinelli, Antonio del Pollaiuolo, Giovanni delle Corniole, les Della Robbia, Bertoldo, Gentile Bellini, Costanzo, et anonymes d'Alphonse 1er d'Este, de*

Charles VIII, d'Anne de Bretagne, de Lucrèce Borgia, de Laurent-le- Magnifique et de Mahomet II (1885), 88 pp. with 100 text figs., 11 b&w pls.; part 6, *Sperandio de Mantoue et les médailleurs anonymes des Bentivoglio, seigneurs de Bologne* (1886), 84 pp. with 160 text figs., 16 b&w pls.; part 7, *Venise et les vénitiens du XVe au XVIIe siècle; histoire, institutions, moeurs, coutumes, monuments, biographies* (1887), 215 pp. with 450 text figs., 17 b&w pls.; part 8, sec. 1, *Florence et les Florentins du XVe au XVIIIe siècle: Histoire — Institutions — Moeurs — Monuments — Biographies* (1891), 188 pp. with 225 text figs., 27 b&w pls.; part 8, sec. 2, Florence et la Toscane sous les Médicis (1892), 304 pp. with 331 text figs., 30 b&w pls. Paris: J. Rothschild.

Foundation stone for modern studies of Italian Renaissance medals and coins; if now dated, includes still valuable information.

1236   HILL, GEORGE FRANCIS. *A Corpus of Italian Medals of the Renaissance before Cellini*. 2 vols. London: British Museum, 1930. 1: 371 pp., 8 b&w figs.; 2:1333 b&w figs. on 201 pls.

Standard reference work with its 1,333 entries of medals produced between 1390-1530; arranged by cities of origin; extensive bibliographies of early literature. Still unmatched for the wealth of its information and for its reproduction of the obverse and reverse of each medal to scale but note, from plaster casts.

1237   HILL, G.F. *Portrait Medals of Italian Artists of the Renaissance*. London: Philip Lee Warner, 1912. 109 pp., 1 color pl., 32 b&w pls.

Chronological description of over sixty contemporary medals representing Italian artists (Alberti, Pisanello, Filarete, Candida, Bellini, Bandinelli, Clovio, Michelangelo, Sansovino, Vasari, Titian, Vittoria, and others).

1238   MIDDELDORF, ULRICH, and STIEBRAL, DAGMAR. *Renaissance Medals and Plaquettes*. Florence: Studio per Edizioni Scelte, 1983. 208 pp. (unpaginated) including 97 b&w pls., 1 color pl.

Catalog of eighty-nine medals and eight plaquettes, all mostly Italian in a private collection (anonymous). Particularly useful for its assessment of the former literature and of attributions. Includes medals by Fiorentino, Amadio da Milano, Bertoldo, Giovanni Candida, Cristoforo di Geremia, Enzola, Lysippus, Matteo de' Pasti, Pisanello, Sperandio, Belli, Caradosso, Giovanni dal Cavino, Leone Leoni and by many other medalists. Plaquettes by Alvise de' Rizzardi and Moderno.

1239   ROSATI, FRANCO PANVINI. *Medaglia e placchette italiane dal Rinascimento al XVIII secolo*. Rome: De Luca, [1968]. 75 pp., 360 b&w figs. (Expanded version of the German language catalog *Italienische Medaillen und Plaketten von der Frührenaissance bis zum Ende des Barock* of the 1966 exhibition held at the Hamburg Kunsthalle [published in Cologne], with added notes and bibliography.)

Includes 253 medals and thirty-three plaquettes from Italian public collections by major artists of the Peninsula and dating from the late-14th until the 18th century. The majority are Renaissance examples.

Articles

1240   ALLISON, ANN HERSEY. "Antico's Medals for the Gonzaga." *Medal* 9 (1986):9-13, 8 b&w figs.

Chronology of Antico's medals of Gianfrancesco Gonzaga, Antonia del Balza, and Giulia Gonzaga Colonna through iconography and style.

1241   AVERY, CHARLES.   "Medicean Medals."   In *Firenze e la Toscana dei Medici nell'Europa del '500.* Vol. 3, *Relazioni artistiche, il linguaggio architettonico europeo.* Florence: Leo S. Olschki, 1983. Pp. 885-97, 36 b&w figs.
Medals of the various members of the Medici dynasty by Bertoldo, Fiorentino, Cellini, Francesco del Prato, Bernardi, Poggini, Galleotti, Pastorino, and Mola. Others suggested to perhaps be the work of Donatello, Orsino Ceraiolo, Camelio, and Domenico di Polo.

1242   BERNHART, MAX. "Nachträge zu Armand." *Archiv für Medaillen- und Plaketten-Kunde* 5 (1925-26):69-90, 2 b&w figs.
Supplement of 142 Italian medals to Armand's (entry 1227) and Hill's (entry 1236) repertories.

1243   BERNHART, MAX, and HABICH, GEORG. "Beiträge zu Antonio Abondio." *Archiv für Medaillen- und Plaketten- Kunde* 1 (1913-14):97-109, 161, 22 b&w figs.
Reassessment of the artistic personality and oeuvre of Antonio Abondio.

1244   FORRER, LEONARD. "A Uniface Portrait Medal of Anne, duc de Joyeuse, Admiral of France." *Archiv für Medaillen- und Plaketten-Kunde* 1 (1913-14):141-44, 1 b&w pl.
Author suggests that medal was produced in 1584-86 by Rolando Gastaldo, engraver of dies and mint-master at Desana.

1245   FOVILLE, JEAN DE. "L'Élève vénitien de Riccio." *Archiv für Medaillen- und Plaketten- Kunde* 1 (1913-14):73-81, 2 b&w pls. comprising 23 figs.
Attribution of medals representing Andrea Riccio, the Cornaro and Podocatharo familes, Elisabetha Quirini, Francesco Comendore, Caterina and Adria Aretino, to a Venetian pupil of Riccio. (Argument disputed by G.F. Hill [see entry 1251].)

1246   FOVILLE, JEAN DE. "Une Médaille de l'Amiral de Coligny." *Archiv für Medaillen- und Plaketten-Kunde* 1 (1913-14):7-13, 1 b&w pl. comprising 6 figs.
Medals of the French admiral Gaspar de Coligny and of his wife Jacqueline d'Entremonts by an Italian artist bearing the initials AR, which the author holds are not those of Alfonso Ruspagiari.

1247   FRIEDLÄNDER, JULIUS.   "Die italienischen Schaumünzen des fünfzehnten Jahrhunderts, 1430-1530." *Jahrbuch der königlich preussischer Kunstsammlung* 1 (1880):3-11, 78-112, 263-70, 8 b&w pls.; 2 (1881):24-54, 4 b&w pls.; 92-110, 5 b&w pls.; 157-86, 5 b&w pls.; 225-54, 7 b&w pls.; 3 (1882):29-46, 4 b&w pls.; 136-49, 2 b&w pls.; 190-210, 6 b&w pls.
Earliest scholarly catalog of Italian medals by Pisanello, Matteo de' Pasti; the Ferrarese: Amadeo, Niccòlo, Antonio Morescotto, Jacopo Lixignolo, Petrecino, Sperandio, Baldassare Estense, Corradino, Mea; the Paduans and Venetians: Jacopo Vellano (*sic*), Riccio, Boldù, Bellini, Gambello, Agrippa; the Veronese: Pomedello, Giulio della Torre, Caroto, Enzola; the Mantuese: Cristoforo di Geremia, Meliolo, Lysippus, Ruberto, Talpa; the Florentines: Guazzalotti, Niccòlo Fiorentino, Antonio Pollaiuolo, Bertoldo, Filippino Lippi, Francesco da San Gallo; the Romans: Caradosso; also Pietro Domo Fani, Paolo da Ragusa, the Genoese: Battista Elias, Pietro da Milano, Laurana, and French medalists of Lyon, etc.

1248   GAETTENS, RICHARD. "Christophoro Colombo: His Portrait from Life Sculptured by Guido Mazzoni (d. 1518)." *Connoisseur* 156 (1964):175-81, 12 b&w figs.
Attribution to Guido Mazzoni, who the author suggests traveled to Spain ca. 1504-7, of bronze medals depicting Christopher Columbus.

1249   GALSTER, GEORG. "Die Schaumünzen Christierns I." *Archiv für Medaillen- und Plaketten-Kunde* 3 (1921- 22):85-90, 1 b&w pl. comprising 6 figs.
Medal of Christian I of Denmark of 1484 by Bartolomeo Melioli; other works by the artist for the court of Mantua.

1250   HILL, G.F. "Classical Influence on the Italian Medal." *Burlington Magazine* 18 (1910-11):259-68, 2 b&w pls.
Examines the role of Roman coins, cameos, and intaglios as direct or indirect models for 15th-century Italian medalists: Camillo Mariani, Pisanello, Bertoldo di Giovanni, Andrea da Viterbo, Cristoforo di Geremia, Alessandro Cesati, etc.

1251   HILL, G.F. "A Group of Venetian Medals." *Archiv für Medaillen- und Plaketten-Kunde* 1 (1913-14):122-26.
Disputes Foville's argument in "L'Élève vénitien de Riccio" (see entry 1245) on grounds of relief style.

HILL, G.F. "Notes on Italian Medals," parts I, II, and III, see entries 1264-1264a, 1259.

1252   HILL, G.F. "Notes on Italian Medals," part IV. "The Medallist Lysippus." *Burlington Magazine* 13 (1908):274-86, 8 b&w pls.
Nephew of Cristoforo di Geremia, active in Rome in the late 15th century, author of a medal of Sixtus IV and of some twenty others; author discusses attributions.

HILL, G.F. "Notes on Italian Medals," parts V and VI, see entries 1264b, 1268.

1252a   HILL, G.F. "Notes on Italian Medals—VII." *Burlington Magazine* 15 (1909):94-98, 1 b&w pl.
Three medals by Enzola and two ascribed to Giulio della Torre.

1252b   HILL, G.F. "Notes on Italian Medals—VIII." *Burlington Magazine* 16 (1909-10):24-31, 2 b&w pls.
Preparatory pen sketches in Oppenheimer and Gay collections by Sperandio of Mantua for medals; medal of Alfonso of Aragon by Paolo da Ragusa; medal of the late 15th-century cleric Raffaelo Maffei da Volterra; medal of Gianfrancesco de' Rangoni by Lysippus(?); medal of the Paduan Girolamo Pesaro; forgeries of the late 16th century.

1252c   HILL, G.F. "Notes on Italian Medals—IX." *Burlington Magazine* 17 (1910):143-46, 1 b&w pl.
Portrait medal of Federico da Montefeltro of Urbino of ca. 1475 possibly the first commission of the duke from the Sienese Francesco di Giorgio.

1252d   HILL, G.F. "Notes on Italian Medals—X." *Burlington Magazine* 18 (1910-11):13-21, 2 b&w pls.
Medals of ca. 1534-40 representing Ercole II, Clement VII, Jean de Lorraine, Pietro Piantanida by, or attributed to, Cellini; activity of Antonello della Moneta at the Venetian mint, medals by him of Doges Francesco Foscari (1423-57) and Cristoforo Moro (1462-71); Milanese medal dated 1508 of the monument of Gian Giacomo Trivulzio.

1252e   HILL, G.F. "Notes on Italian Medals—XI." *Burlington Magazine* 19 (1911):138-44, 2 b&w pls.

Medal with features and impressa of Leonello d'Este after Pisanello by the otherwise unknown medalist Nicholaus; notes on Sperandio and a new medal of ca. 1473 (Giustianino Cavatelli of Cremona) added to his oeuvre; a medal of ca. 1495 representing Bernardo Nasi by an unknown Bolognese; a medal of Angela Brenzoni by the Veronese Giovanni Maria Pomedelli (1478-ca. 1537).

1252f   HILL, G.F. "Notes on Italian Medals—XII." *Burlington Magazine* 20 (1911-12):200-208, 2 b&w pls.

Federico of Montefeltro by Enzola; impressions of medals on bookbindings; medals of Maximilian I and Frederick III by Gian Marco Cavalli; those of Giulio della Torre representing members of his family; Lalio Torelli as cast by Francesco da Sangallo; medals by Giovanbattista Capocaccia.

1252g   HILL, G.F. "Notes on Italian Medals—XIII." *Burlington Magazine* 22 (1912-13):131-38, 2 b&w pls.

Late 15th-century medals produced in Florence of various Italian and French sitters; medals of Girolamo Panico (ca. 1538) and Pompeo Ludovisi (1537) by Cavino; of Bishop Girolamo Vida (ca. 1533) by Tegniza (or Tegnizzi).

1252h   HILL, G.F. "Notes on Italian Medals—XIV: Lodovico Scarampi by Cristoforo di Geremia." *Burlington Magazine* 23 (1913):17-22, 1 b&w pl.

Medal of Cardinal Scarampi by Cristoforo di Geremia; another of Ippolito d'Este attributed to Niccolò Fiorentino; medal of the Milanese soldier Pietro Monti and of several Venetian sitters of the 16th century.

HILL, G.F. "Notes on Italian Medals," parts XV and XVI, see entries 1264c-1264d.

1252i   HILL, G.F. "Notes on Italian Medals—XVII: Constantinus Cominatus." *Burlington Magazine* 25 (1914):221-27, 1 b&w pl.

Late 15th-century medals of the Macedonian prince Constantinus Cominatus (by Lysippus?), another of Condottiere Roberto da Sanseverino (by Fiorentino?).

1252j   HILL, G.F. "Notes on Italian Medals—XVIII: Giovanni Zacchi and the Bolognese School." *Burlington Magazine* 25 (1914):335-41, 2 b&w pls.

Mid-16th-century examples of various ecclesiastics by Giovanni Zacchi and other Bolognese medalists.

HILL, G.F. "Notes on Italian Medals," part XIX, see entry 1264e.

1252k   HILL, G.F. "Notes on Italian Medals—XX: Some Anonymous Medals." *Burlington Magazine* 27 (1915):235-42, 2 b&w pls.

Anonymous examples of the 15th-16th century from Florence, Mantua, etc., in the Victoria and Albert Museum and private collections.

1252l   HILL, G.F. "Notes on Italian Medals—XXI. "*Burlington Magazine* 29 (1916):56-59, 1 b&w pl.

Various medals of 1550-60 by an artist working under the influence of 15th-century imitators of the antique.

1252m   HILL, G.F. "Notes on Italian Medals—XXII." *Burlington Magazine* 29 (1916):251-55, 1 b&w pl.

Further attribution to the medalist "P" (active mid-16th century) perhaps Tommaso Perugino: a medal representing the Florentine Antonio Pucci, another of Ippolito d'Este, Giulio de' Medici; others to Bombarda (unknown lady) and Ruspagiari (Camilla Ruggieri).

1252n HILL, G.F. "Notes on Italian Medals—XXIII." *Burlington Magazine* 30 (1917):190-98, 2 b&w pls.

Problems of connoisseurship, of attribution and identification of sitters in late 15th-early 16th-century examples produced mostly in Florence in the circle of Bertoldo, Francesco de' Bonsi, Niccolò Fiorentino, Giulio della Torre, Camillo Bossetti, and others who remain anonymous as primarily exemplified by the Victoria and Albert and British museum collections.

1252o HILL, G.F. "Notes on Italian Medals—XXIV." *Burlington Magazine* 31 (1917):99-105, 2 b&w pls.

Late 15th-century medal by Niccolò Fiorentino of Maria, wife to Angelo Poliziano, and others attributed to him; a reverse with Marcus Curtius attributed to Maffeo Olivieri; a medal of Andrea Caraffa attributed to Girolamo Santacroce; a medal with a portrait of Gianfrancesco Gratt and his wife Franceschina suggested to be the work of a Bolognese artist of the transition between Francia and Zacchi.

1252p HILL, G.F. "Notes on Italian Medals—XXV & XXVI." *Burlington Magazine* 31 (1917):178-83,211-17, 2 b&w pls.

Techniques of Renaissance medals: cast in molds or struck with engraved dies; the making and composition of molds and casting methods; particularities of late casts. Struck examples using minting techniques with new refinements by Gian Francesco Enzola, Cellini Caradosso, and the various means of patination, gilding, and silvering.

1253 JOHNSON, VELIA. "La medaglia italiana in Europa durante i secoli XV e XVI." *Medaglia* (1974):6-22, 24 illus.

The prominent role of the Italian medal, especially between 1450-1520, as disseminator of Renaissance modes outside of Italy, seen through the work of Giovanni da Candida, Niccolò Spinelli, Francesco Laurana, Pietro da Milano, Gian Marco Cavalli, Adriano de' Maestri, and Giovanni Maria Pomedelli.

1254 KUBLER, GEORGE. "A Medal by G.P. Poggini Depicting Peru and Predicting Australia." *Mitteilungen des kunsthistorischen Institutes in Florenz* 11 (1963-65):149-52, 2 b&w figs.

Documentary evidence dealing with this medal of Philip II dating of 1561-62 and alluding to hopes of territorial expansion on the part of the Hapsburgs.

1255 LEITHE-JASPER, MANFRED. "Eine Medaille auf Papst Pius IV. von Guglielmo Della Porta?" *Mitteilungen des kunsthistorischen Institutes in Florenz* 16 (1972):329-35, 8 b&w figs.

Attribution of a medal of Pope Pius IV dedicated by the city of Bologna (Vienna, private collection) to Guglielmo Della Porta on the basis of stylistic comparison with known works by the artist: a series of plaquettes with scenes from Ovid's *Metamorphoses,* drawings of the same and especially of a tomb project for Pius IV (London, Victoria and Albert Museum).

1256 LOGUS, GEORG. "Zwei Medaillen auf den schlesischen Dichter." *Archiv für Medaillen-und Plaketten-Kunde* 5 (1925-26):144-47, 2 b&w figs.

Two medals of the Silesian poet Georg von Logau by the Modenese medalist Nicolò Cavallerino dating of 1535-40.

1257 MAURI MORI, GUISEPPE. "Una Medaglia per Alfonso d'Aragona." *Antologia di belle arti* 21 (1984):7-9, 3 b&w figs.

Rare medal of Alfonso of Aragon in a private collection, Naples, signed by Paolo da Ragusa and held to have been cast in 1451-52.

1258 MIDDELDORF, ULRICH. "On the Dilettante Sculptor." *Apollo* 107 (1978):310-22. Reprinted in *Raccolta di scritti, that is Collected Writings. III. 1974-79.* Florence: Studio per Edizioni Scelte, 1981, pp. 173-202, figs. 157-69.

Occasional casters, principally of medals, in the Renaissance: Giovanni Candida, Baldassare d'Este, Fra Antonio da Brescia, Giulio della Torre, Franceso Revesla of Novara, Alfonso Ruspagiari, Bertoldo, and Matteo de' Pasti, the latter seen as designer of the Tempio Malatesta.

1258a MIDDELDORF, ULRICH. "Una proposta per Alfonso Lombardi." *La Medaglia d'Arte. Atti del primo convegno internazionale di studi*, Udine, 10-12 October 1970. Udine: 1973, pp. 20-28. Reprinted in *Raccolta di scritti, that is Collected Writings. II. 1939-73.* Florence: Studio per Edizioni Scelte, 1980, pp. 361-68, figs. 202-6.

Alfonso's medals (first half of 16th century) in stucco, wax, and bronze, mostly as recorded by Vasari.

1259 ROSENHEIM, MAX, and HILL, G.F. ["Notes on Italian Medals," part III]. "Notes on Some Italian Medals." *Burlington Magazine* 12 (1907-8):141-54, 4 b&w pls.

Redefining the oeuvre of Antonio Abondio, the authors propose that the medalist who signs AA is another artist, medals signed AR are probably by Alessandro Ardenti; those of Niccolò III d'Este attributed to Amadeo da Milano; medal of doge Pasquale Malipiero (1457-62); large round medal of Pope Paul II with tiara; medal of Guglielmo Batonatti associated with Lysippus; others of Galeotto dal Ferro influenced by Pisanello; the Venetian medalist Giovanni Falier; medal of ca. 1527 of Andrea Magno attributed to Giovanni Maria Pomedelli; Paduan medal (ca. 1555) of the English humanist John Cheke.

1260 WEISS, ROBERTO. "The Medals of Pope Julius II (1503-1513)." *Journal of the Warburg and Courtauld Institutes* 28 (1965):163-82, 5 b&w pls. with 40 figs.

Foundation and commemorative medals produced from 1483 until ca. 1508 by Caradosso, Camelio, Giancristoforo Romano, Pier Maria Serbaldi, and Francesco Francia.

See also entry 475.

6. PERMANENT COLLECTIONS

Florence

MUSEO NAZIONALE DEL BARGELLO

1261 *Medaglie di Pisanello e della sua cerchia.* Exhibition catalog by Giovanna de Lorenzi. Florence: Museo Nazionale del Bargello, 1983. 109 pp., 128 b&w figs.

Exhibition of medals by Pisanello and contemporaries (Pietro da Milano, Matteo de' Pasti, Gianfrancesco Enzola, Sperandio, Bertoldo di Giovanni, etc.) from the Bargello's own vast collection. Sixty-three detailed entries with bibliographical references.

1262   *Medaglie italiane dell'alto Rinascimento,* by J. Graham Pollard. Florence: S.P.E.S., 1983. 32 pp., 41 b&w figs.
Presentation of eighteen outstanding medals in the collection of the Bargello. Brief essay (pp. 3-23) in Italian and English on the evolution of the struck medal used as a form of propoganda in the 16th century. Short catalog entries on five pages in Italian only.

1262a   *Medaglie italiane del Rinascimento,* by J. Graham Pollard. Florence: S.P.E.S., 1983. 30 pp., 34 b&w figs.
Presentation of eighteen outstanding medals in the collection of the Bargello. Brief essay (pp. 3-25) in Italian and English on the evolution of the cast medal in the 15th century. Short catalog entries on five pages in Italian only.

1263   *Italian Renaissance Medals in the Museo Nazionale of Bargello.* Catalog by J. Graham Pollard. 3 vols. Vol. 1 (1984), 651 pp., 8 color pls., numerous b&w figs.; vol. 2 (1985), 576 pp., 8 color pls., numerous b&w figs.; vol. 3 (1985), 421 pp., 4 color pls, numerous b&w figs. Florence: Associazione Amici del Bargello.
Exemplary catalog of one of the largest holdings of Italian medals. Vol. 1 deals with the period 1400-1530 (308 entries); vols. 2 and 3 deal with the period 1513-1640 (comprise entry nos. 309-886). Text (in Italian and English) is informative yet concise. The recto and verso of each medal is reproduced to scale. All centers and most major artists are represented. Exhaustive bibliographies and useful indexes.

London

BRITISH MUSEUM

1264   HILL, G.F. ["Notes on Italian Medals," part I]. "Some Medals by Pastorino da Siena." *Burlington Magazine* 9 (1906):408-12, 1 b&w pl.
Chronology of artist's known oeuvre, reproducing the features of notable Italian contemporaries, from 1540 until 1579, as exemplified in the museum's collection.

1264a   HILL, G.F. ["Notes on Italian Medals," part II]. "Some Italian Medals in the British Museum." *Burlington Magazine* 10 (1906-07):384-87, 1 b&w pl.
F. Parkes Weber bequest includes works of Pisanello and the 16th-century Pastorino and Giovanni Zacchi.

1264b   HILL, G.F. ["Notes on Italian Medals," part V]. "Eight Italian Medals." *Burlington Magazine* 14 (1908-09):210-17, 2 b&w pls.
Late 15th- to late 16th-century medals in the collection: identification of sitters (e.g. Dom Baltasar, Abbot of Vallombrosa); medalists (e.g. Pietro Paolo Galeotti); dating; interpretation of symbolism on reverse, and some interesting features on casting methods (e.g., detachability of outer inscription ring, process of casting a mold hollow).

1264c   HILL, G.F. "Notes on Italian Medals—XV." *Burlington Magazine* 24 (1913-14):36-40, 1 b&w pl.
Seven medals from the T. Whitcombe Greene Collection, two with allegorical subjects, others with sitters: Ottaviano Pallavicini, Ottavio Farnese (by Pastorino), Giulio della Rovere, Niccolò Madruzzo (by Abondio).

1264d   HILL, G.F. "Notes on Italian Medals—XVI: Raphael Martinus Gothalanus." *Burlington Magazine* 24 (1913-14):211-12, 217, 1 b&w pl.

A portrait medal in the T. Whitcombe Greene Collection of Raphael Martin, possibly a Spaniard living in Florence, of the late 15th-century Niccolò Fiorentino type, with the Three Graces on its reverse from the same model as that on the medals of Pico della Mirandola and Giovanni Albuzzi; a medal of Bartolommeo Cepola (same collection) with many similar characteristics as that of Bartolomeo Bellano by Antonio Roselli; a medal of Francesco Fermi in the British Museum signed by Leone Leoni; two 16th-century wax models for medals of Ferdinand I de' Medici and Sigismund III of Poland (Greene Collection); and new theories on casting methods.

1264e   HILL, G.F. "Notes on Italian Medals—XIX: Scipione Clusona." *Burlington Magazine* 27 (1915):65-66, 2 b&w pls.
　　　　Mid-16th-century medal of Scipione Clusona of Verona (T. Whitcombe Greene Collection) in the style of Maffeo Olivieri.

Milan

MUSEO ARCHEOLOGICO - PINACOTECA DI BRERA

1265   *Le medaglie del Rinascimento.* Exhibition handlist by Pietro Florio et al. Milan: Comune di Milano, 1973. 28 pp.
　　　　List of 179 important 15th-16th century medals in the collection including works by Pisanello, de'Pasti, Laurana, Amadio da Milano, Marescotti, Antico, Melioli, Enzola, Francesco di Giorgio, Sperandio, Boldù, Olivieri, Caradosso, Bertoldo. This publication is supplemented by the exhibition catalogs edited by Giulia Bologna: *Milano e gli Sforza. Francesco e Galeazzo Maria (1450-1476)* and *Milano e gli Sforza: Gian Galeazzo Maria e Ludovico il Moro (1476-1499)* held in 1981 and 1983 at the Castello Sforzesco, Milan (Milan: Rizzoli, 1981, 1983) which include portrait medals of the dukes of Milan from the Brera.

New York

METROPOLITAN MUSEUM OF ART

1266   PHILLIPS, JOHN GOLDSMITH. "Medals of the Renaissance." *Metropolitan Museum of Art Bulletin* 9 (1950):77-82, 10 b&w figs.
　　　　Selected examples from the permanent collection by Pisanello, Niccolò Fiorentino, and Sangallo.

Paris

MUSÉE DU LOUVRE

1267   JESTAZ, BERTRAND. "De nouveaux bronzes italiens: Reliefs et médailles." *Revue du Louvre* 24 (1974):91-100, 8 b&w figs.
　　　　Two Italian bronze plaquettes, one of the Virgin and Child of the 16th century and four 15th-16th-century portrait medals of Lucretia Borgia, Mohammed II (by Bertoldo di Giovanni), Mary Tudor (by Jacopo da Trezzo), and Tommaso da Ravenna.

8. PRIVATE COLLECTION, AUCTION, AND DEALER CATALOGS

OPPENHEIMER COLLECTION

1268　HILL, G.F. "Notes on Italian Medals—VI: Three Wax Models." *Burlington Magazine* 15 (1909):31-35, 1 b&w pl.

Rare wax models for medals of Commander Giacomo Negroboni (died 1527), Barbara Romana, and Antonio Galateo, the last two of ca. 1550-75.

SALTING COLLECTION

1269　HILL, G.F. "The Italian Medals in the Salting Collection" *Burlington Magazine* 20 (1911-12):18-24, 2 b&w pls.

Particularly fine gathering of late 15th- or early 16th-century examples including works by Pietro da Milano, Pisanello, Giovanni Boldù, Bertoldo Guazzalotti, Enzola, Lysippus, Sperandio, Lorenzo Ciglamocchi, Giovanni Candida, Antico, Giancristoforo Romano, Adriano Fiorentino, the "Medallist of 1523" (suggested to be Fra Antonio da Brescia?), and others of figures generally in the limelight of the time.

WEISS COLLECTION, ETC.

1270　*Spink Coin Auction—Sales Catalog 18/1981.* Sale held in London at Spink & Son 18-19 November 1981. 87 pp., 61 b&w pls.

Pp. 1-26 concisely describe and pls. 1-32 provide good illustrations of two collections of medals slated for dispersal. The first and more important (lots 1-62) is of Italian Renaissance examples by Pisanello, de' Pasti, Sperandio, Enzola, Caradosso, Cristoforo di Geremia, Bertoldo, etc., formed by Roberto Weiss (died 1969); the second (anonymous) is of mostly Italian Renaissance and Baroque pieces with some German, French, British, and Netherlandish examples (lots 63-193).

NETHERLANDISH

3. SURVEYS AND HISTORIES

1271　HILL, G.F. "Stephen H., Medallist and Painter." *Burlington Magazine* 12 (1907-08):355-63, 2 b&w pls.

Also referred to as "Stephen of Holland," this artist was a Dutchman active (ca. 1558-ca. 1572) in both Holland and England recording the features of the gentry in medals and paintings.

SPANISH

3. SURVEYS AND HISTORIES

1272　CARUANA Y REIG., JOSÉ. "Medallero Valenciano o sea catalogo de medallas." *Archivo de arte valenciano* 19 (1933):53-76, 41 b&w figs.; 20 (1934):51-80, 69 b&w figs.; 21 (1935):69-96, 21 b&w figs.

Historical, personal, and commemorative medals of individuals or events connected with the city of Valencia between the mid-15th century and 1833. Sitters include Alfonso V of Aragon, Calixtus III, Juan Paloman, Ferdinand of Aragon, Alexander VI Borgia, Cardinal Casanova, Charles V, and various courtiers, for the period ending 1600.

XXI. Plaquettes

A. MULTI COUNTRY OF ORIGIN

3. SURVEYS AND HISTORIES

1273   MOLINIER, ÉMILE. *Les Bronzes de la Renaissance — Les Plaquettes: Catalogue raisonné.* 2 vols. Vol. 1, Paris: Jules Rouam, 1886, 216 pp., 82 b&w figs. Vol. 2, Paris: Jules Rouam; London: Gilbert Wood & Co., 1886, 240 pp., 26 b&w figs.

Classic repertory of over 750 different Renaissance plaquettes in various museums. Still a standard work for Italian examples (over 684), each described and attributed often for the first time. The important forty-page introduction suggests origins and points to influence of plaquettes on other works.

1274   WEBER, INGRID. *Deutsche, niederländische und französische Renaissanceplaketten 1500-1650: Modelle für Reliefs an Kult-, Prunk-, und Gebrauchsgegenständen.* 2 vols. Munich: Bruckmann, 1975. 1:443 pp., 56 b&w figs., 17 line drawings; 2:302 b&w pls.

Catalog of 1,062 plaquettes, mostly German 16th-century (Nuremburg [Krug, Vischer, Flötner, Jamnitzer, etc.], Augsburg [Daucher, Forster, Lencher, etc.]) in the Bayerischen Nationalmuseum and Staatlichen Münzsammlung, and other Munich institutions. Also some Swiss, Netherlandish, Austrian, and French examples. Important for scholarly apparatus and body of illustration.

6. PERMANENT COLLECTIONS

Brescia

MUSEO CIVICO, PINACOTECA TOSIO-MARTINENGO

1275   *Placchette sec. XV-XIX.* Catalog by Francesco Rossi. Brescia: Neri Pozza, 1974. 194 pp., 272 b&w figs.

Standard catalog of the 272 plaquettes on the collection. Includes important 15th-century Italian examples (nos. 12-76) and 16th-century Italian (87-222), German (242-60), Flemish (261-68), and French (271-72) ones.

Brunswick, Maine

BOWDOIN COLLEGE MUSEUM OF ART

1276   *The Salton Collection: Renaissance & Baroque Medals & Plaquettes.* Exhibition catalog by Marvin S. Sadik. Brunswick, Me.: Bowdoin College Museum of Art, 1965. 77 pp., 81 b&w figs.

Nine-page introduction with broad outline; concise entries for 187 mostly 15th-16th-century plaquette and medals representative of most Italian centers, and also including German, Netherlandish, French, English, Danish, Swedish, and Spanish examples. Indexes of artists, inscriptions, and sitters.

Poznan

MUZEUM NARODOWE

1277   *Katalog. Plakieta Renesansowa jej zwiazek z grafica i zastoswanie w rzemiośle artystycznym,* by Aleksandra Wasilkowska. Poznan: Muzeum Narodowe, 1962. 35 pp., 28 b&w figs.

Catalog of 167 Renaissance plaquettes, mostly Italian and German, dating of the 16th century, in the collection. Includes works of Belli, Riccio, Moderno, Leoni, Flötner, François Briot.

Venice

MUSEO CORRER

1278   JACOBSEN, EMIL. "Plaketten im Museo Correr zu Venedig." *Repertorium für Kunstwissenschaft* 16 (1893):54-75.

Checklist of an important, still little-known because practically never exhibited, collection of plaquettes. If the majority are Italian (Moderno, IO.F.F., Ulocrino, Belli, Enzola, etc.), also includes examples from the French, German, and Netherlandish schools.

See also entries 673, 1197, 1199, 1305.

8. PRIVATE COLLECTION, AUCTION, AND DEALER CATALOGS

See entry 1201.

B. SINGLE COUNTRY OF ORIGIN

BELGIUM (FLEMISH)

3. SURVEYS AND HISTORIES

1279   AVERY, CHARLES. "Antwerp, August 1577, the 'Spanish Fury' and the Liberation of the Citadel: A Series of Bronze Plaquettes after Martin de Vos." *Connoisseur* 195 (1977):252-63, 22 b&w figs.

XXI. Plaquettes

Seven circular bronze plaquettes dating of no later that 1596 deriving from a series of engravings of 1577 by the Wierix brothers depicting political events and made after designs by the mannerist painter Marten de Vos.

GERMAN

3. SURVEYS AND HISTORIES

1280   BANGE, E.F. "Zur Datierung von Peter Flötners Plakettenwerk." *Archiv für Medaillen- und Plaketten- Kunde* 3 (1921-22):45-52, 4 b&w pls. comprising 11 figs.
Dating of Flötner's plaquettes to 1534-43 on the basis of compositional elements and style.

1281   BRAUN, EDUARD WILHELM. "Eine figurale Plakette des Nürnberger Goldschmiedes Paul Flindt." *Archiv fur Medaillen- und Plaketten-Kunde* 4 (1923-24):154-56, 1 b&w fig.
Oval plaquette of Venus and Adonis attributed to the Nuremberg goldsmith Paul Flindt and dated to ca. 1580.

1282   BRAUN-TROPPAU, EDMUND WILHELM. "Hans Peissers Plaketten und der Nürnberger Kleinmeister IB." *Archiv für Medaillen- und Plaketten-Kunde* 3 (1921-22):104-14, 2 b&w pls.
Small reliefs of Hans Peisser; their relationship to Master IB, the engraver active in Nuremburg in the 1520s-40s.

1283   BRAUN-TROPPAU, E.W. "Plaketten von Paul Flind." *Archiv für Medaillen- und Plaketten-Kunde* 1 (1913-14):21-26, 7 b&w figs.
Large round plaquettes with mythological subjects attributed to the late 16th-century designer of goldsmith models, Paul Flind[t].

1284   MIDDELDORF, ULRICH. "Su alcune placchette tedesche." *Musei Ferraresi. Bollettino Annuale* 4 (1974):144-46. Reprinted in *Raccolta di scritti, that is Collected Writings. III. 1974-1979.* Florence: Studio per Edizioni Scelte, 1981, pp. 21-23, figs. 23- 26.
Unpublished South German bronze and lead plaquettes of the late 15th century in the Museo Civico, Ferrara, and in a private collection, Florence.

1285   WEBER, INGRID. "Bemerkungen zum Plakettenwerk von Peter Flötner." *Pantheon* 28 (1970):521-25, 18 b&w figs.
Plaquettes with symbolic subjects produced by Peter Flötner and his workshop in the 1530s.

1286   WEBER, INGRID. "Fragen zum Oeuvre des Meister H.G." *Münchner Jahrbuch der bildenden Kunst* 22 (1971):133-45, 15 b&w figs.
Study of a group of Nuremburg bronze and lead plaquettes of mythological or biblical subjects signed and proposed by Otto von Falke as the work of Hans Jamnitzer II; Weber discusses the attribution and shows their use as models for reliefs on silver bowls.

6. PERMANENT COLLECTIONS

London

BRITISH MUSEUM

1287   BERLINER, RUDOLF. "Plakette nach einer Dürerzeichnung." *Archiv für Medaillen-und Plaketten- Kunde* 5 (1925-26):158-60, 2 b&w figs.
The composition of a 16th-century circular plaquette of Hercules and Cerberus based on a drawing of Dürer.

Munich

BAYERISCHES NATIONALMUSEUM

1288   KRIS, ERNST. "Eine Modellplakette Wenzel Jamnitzers: Zur Motivverwendung in der Werkstatt der Spätrenaissance." *Archiv für Medaillen- und Plaketten-Kunde* 3 (1921-22):136-43, 2 b&w pls.
Plaquette with friezes and architectural elements attributed to the Nuremberg goldsmith Wenzel Jamnitzer (1508-85).

8. PRIVATE COLLECTION, AUCTION, AND DEALER CATALOGS

MOLTHEIN COLLECTION

1289   BRAUN, EDMUND WILHELM. *Die deutschen Rennaissanceplaketten der Sammlung Alfred Walcher Ritter von Molthein in Wien.* Vienna: Kunstverlag Anton Schroll & Co., 1918. 75 pp. with 13 b&w text figs., 73 b&w pls.
Collection of 242 late Gothic to early Baroque plaquettes (bronze or lead) from Augsburg, Nuremberg, Lüneberg, as well as some late Dutch and Austrian examples; some incorporated in objects, in the collection of Alfred Walcher von Molthein, Vienna.

ITALIAN

3. SURVEYS AND HISTORIES

1290   MIDDELDORF, ULRICH. "Una miscellanea di placchette." In *Scritti di storia dell'arte in onore di Ugo Procacci.* Milan: 1977, pp., 326-30. Reprinted in *Raccolta di scritti, that is, Collected Writings. III. 1974-1979.* Florence: Studio per Edizioni Scelte, 1981, pp. 103-8, figs. 106-9.
Attribution of an oval-shaped plaquette with the scene of the Resurrected Christ within a border of cherub heads (private collection) to Alvise de' Rizzaldi, a member of the workshop of Giuseppe De Levis.

1291   POPE-HENNESSY, JOHN. "The Italian Plaquette." In *Proceedings of the British Academy* 50 (1964):63-85, 35 b&w figs. Reprinted in *The Study and Criticism of Italian Sculpture.* New York: Metropolitan Museum of Art; Princeton: Princeton University Press, 1980. Pp. 192-222, 35 b&w figs.

Author shifts the development of bronze plaquettes from Donatello and Padua, as generally held, to the Roman milieu, while particularly discussing works attributed to Moderno, Caradosso, Riccio, and Belli.

1292   ROSSI, FRANCESCO. "Maffeo Olivieri e la bronzistica bresciana del '500." *Arte lombarda* 47/48 (1977):115-34, 28 b&w figs.

        Overview of the activity in Brescia during the late 15th and early 16th centuries of masters (IO.F.F., Fra Antonio, Abondio, and particularly Maffeo Olivieri) producing plaquettes, medals, and small scale sculpture.

See also entries 1238-39, 1267.

6. PERMANENT COLLECTIONS

Berlin

KAISER-FRIEDERICH-MUSEUM

1293   BANGE, E.F. *Die italienischen Bronzen der Renaissance und des Barock.* Vol. 2, part 2. Berlin and Leipzig: Walter De Gruyter & Co., 1922. 140 pp., 85 b&w pls.

        Epoch-making census for its classifications of what was probably the major collection of Italian Renaissance plaquettes with 1,060 items representing all regional schools and often in particularly fine examples; each illustrated. Indexes. Much of the collection was lost, dispersed, or segregated at the end of World War II.

Florence

CHIESA DELLA BADIA

1294   MIDDELDORF, ULRICH. "Un rame inciso del Quattrocento." In *Scritti di storia dell'arte in onore di Mario Salmi.* Rome: 1962, pp. 273-89. Reprinted in *Raccolta de scritti, that is, Collected Writings. II. 1939-1973.* Florence: Studio per Edizioni Scelte, 1980, pp. 275-85, figs. 102-14.

        Copper plaque of about 1436 engraved with the figure of Christ Holding the Cross, on a small tabernacle in the chapel of S. Mauro, studied in relationship with similar plaques.

Leningrad

HERMITAGE

1295   RAKINT, V. "Une plaquette du Filarete au Musée de L'Ermitage." *Gazette des beaux-arts* 10 (1924)157-66, 2 b&w figs.

        Signed bronze plaquette of ca. 1466-70 by Filarete with a bull confronting a lion, an oak tree, and a bee, considered by author to be papal emblems.

London

VICTORIA AND ALBERT MUSEUM

1296   *Catalogue of Italian Plaquettes,* by Eric Maclagan. London: Board of Education, 1924. 87 pp., 17 b&w pls.

Some 250 plaquettes alphabetically arranged by artist. Most well-known practitioners are represented and a short biography is given for each. Objects are briefly described, often informatively; a list is provided with the location of other casts known to the author.

New York

METROPOLITAN MUSEUM OF ART

1297 HACKENBROCH, YVONNE. "The Triumph of Neptune." *Connoisseur* 149 (1962):18-23, 12 b&w figs.
A bronze roundel attributed to a master—perhaps Venetian—working in Padua ca. 1520 and strongly influenced both by Mantegna and Riccio.

Rome

MUSEO DI PALAZZO VENEZIA

1298 *Rilievi e placchette dal XV al XVIII secolo.* Exhibition catalog by Pietro Cannatà. Rome: De Luca, 1982. 92 pp., 193 b&w figs.
Informative twenty-one-page introduction reassessing Roman plaquette workshops; excerpts of 15th-century inventories of Pietro Barbo, and Piero, and Lorenzo de' Medici. 109 detailed entries of objects drawn entirely from the museum's own collection providing iconographic analysis, comparative material, and state of research.

8. PRIVATE COLLECTION, AUCTION, AND DEALER CATALOGS

LEDERER COLLECTION

1299 AVERY, CHARLES. *Plaquettes, Medals and Reliefs from the Collection 'L'.* London: Christie's, 1985. 120pp., 1 col. pl., 64 b&w figs.
Brief catalog of the fifty-seven best plaquettes, property of Mrs. Adolf Lederer now dispersed (the majority are in the Metropolitan Museum of Art). Most are 15th-16th-century Italian examples including works by Riccio, Enzola, IO.F.F., Master of Coriolanus, Moderno, Belli, Domenico De' Vetri, and Roccatagliata.

SPANISH

3. SURVEYS AND HISTORIES

1300 BRAUN-TROPPAU, EDMUND WILHELM. "Über eine Gruppe spanischer Spätrenaissance-Plaketten." *Archiv für Medaillen- und Plaketten-Kunde* 3 (1921-22):15-22, 2 b&w pls. comprising 8 figs.
Group of twenty late 16th-century rectangular plaquettes with devotional subjects, held to be Spanish.

XXII. Bronze Statuettes, Mortars, Hand Bells, Aquamanile, Candlesticks, Etc.

A. MULTI COUNTRY OF ORIGIN

3. SURVEYS AND HISTORIES

Books

1301   LIST, CLAUDIA. *Kleinbronzen Europas vom Mittelalter bis zur Gegenwart.* Munich: Keysersche Verlagsbuchhandlung, 1983. 275 pp., 1 color pl., 192 b&w figs.
        The bronze statuette from late medieval times until the present. A useful, well-illustrated survey for the German and Italian schools.

1302   RADCLIFFE, ANTHONY. *European Bronze Statuettes.* London: Connoisseur and Michael Joseph, 1966. 120 pp., 8 color pls., 76 b&w figs.
        Accessible survey of bronze statuettes of the 15th-19th century; concerned mainly with Italian and German Renaissance examples of major artists (Bellano, Riccio, Pollaiuolo, Bertoldo, Antico, Severo, the Vischers, Bandinelli, Giambologna, Melchior Bayr, etc.).

1303   WEIHRAUCH, HANS R. *Europäische Bronzestatuetten, 15.-18. Jahrhundert.* Brunswick: Klinkhardt & Biermann, 1967. 539 pp., 576 b&w figs.
        The most extensive study to date on the wide development of bronze statuette-making from the 15th to 18th century in Italy, Germany, the Netherlands, and France. Discussion of forms, styles, attributions, iconography, and collecting. Good illustration.

1304   WITTOP KONING, DIRK ARNOLD. *Bronzemörser.* Frankfurt: Govi-Verlag, 1975. 66 pp., 2 color pls., 25 b&w pls.
        Brief pictorial survey of bronze mortars from 12th- century Persia until the present. Includes Italian, German, Flemish, Austrian, and Swiss examples of the 15th-16th century in various museums.

6. PERMANENT COLLECTIONS

Munich

BAYERISCHES NATIONALMUSEUM

1305   *Die Bildwerke in Bronze und in anderen Metallen.* Catalog by Hans R. Weihrauch. *Kataloge des bayerischen Nationalmuseums,* Vol. 13, no. 5. Munich: F. Bruckmann, 1956. 239 pp., 287 b&w figs.
Catalog of 264 small objects of bronze or other metal in the collection and an appendix of thirty-one bronzes in the Residenzmuseums, Munich; nos. 14-77 are German 15th-16th-century examples (by Vischer, Jamnitzer, Leinberger, Muscat, and others); 82-169, 265-70 are Italian (Bellano, Riccio, Antico, Fr. di S. Agata, Tullio Lombardo, De' Rossi, Giambologna, and others); 171- 73, 181, 202, 204-5, 271-72 are 16th-century Netherlandish and Flemish bronzes.

8. PRIVATE COLLECTION, AUCTION, AND DEALER CATALOGS

DANIELS COLLECTION

1306   *Sculpture from the David Daniels Collection.* Exhibition held in Minneapolis at the Minneapolis Institute of Arts. Minneapolis: Minneapolis Insitute of Arts, 1979. 168 pp., 4 color pls., 73 b&w figs.
Seventy-three examples from this private collection ranging from ca. 1400 B.C. to A.D. 1969 and including 15th- and 16th-century Italian bronze statuettes (cat. nos. 1, 5-6), 16th-century French, German statuettes, busts, and a medal (2-4, 11).

New York

PAUL ROSENBERG & CO.

1307   *Renaissance Bronzes and Later Sculpture.* Introduction and notes by Alexandre P. Rosenberg. New York: Paul Rosenberg & Co., 1984. 92 pp., 8 color pls., 31 b&w pls.
Thirty-nine entries, all but ten of the 15th-16th century, for objects by Severo da Ravenna, Riccio, Maffeo Olivieri, Camelio, Baccio Bandinelli, Ponce Jacquiot, Girolamo Campagna, Tiziano Aspetti, Giambologna, Christopher Jamnitzer, and anonymous artists.

ROSENBERG & STIEBEL

1308   *A Bronze Bestiary.* Exhibition catalog by Penelope Hunter-Stiebel. New York: Rosenberg & Stiebel, 1985. 88 pp., 76 b&w figs.
Seven-page introduction outlining place of birds and beasts in Renaissance life and thought is followed by seventy entries dealing with Italian, German, French, and Dutch 16th- and a few 17th-century small-scale bronze sculptures of realistic and fantastic animals from various U.S. dealers and collectors.

B. SINGLE COUNTRY OF ORIGIN

AUSTRIAN

6. PERMANENT COLLECTIONS

New York

METROPOLITAN MUSEUM OF ART

1309   HACKENBROCH, YVONNE. "A Group of XVth-Century Bronze Mortars." *Connoisseur* 132 (1953):171-73, 6 b&w figs.
    Iconogaphic motifs of a cast bronze mortar dated 1451 from the Untermyer Collection points to its having been produced in Salzburg for the Bavarian family Froeschl von Martzoll.

BELGIUM (FLEMISH)

6. PERMANENT COLLECTIONS

Rotterdam

MUSEUM BOYMANS-VAN BEUNINGEN

1310   DUBOIS-VAN VEEN, R.J. "Koperen en bronzen voorwerpen uit de collectie Mr. J.W. Frederiks." *Bulletin Museum Boymans-van Beuningen* 21 (1971):38-105, 68 b&w figs.
    Copper and bronze objects, primarily candlesticks, aquamanile, figurines, ewers, and platters, dating mostly of the late Gothic period and made in Flanders, from the J.W. Fredericks Collection.

FRENCH

3. SURVEYS AND HISTORIES

1311   GIBBON, ALAN. *Bronzes de Fontainebleau.* [Paris]: Frédéric Birr, 1985. 94 pp., 22 color figs., 71 b&w figs.
    Discusses many bronze statuettes by French, Italian, and Flemish 16th-century artists (Pierre Biard, Bontemps, Cellini, Ponce Jacquiot, Prieur, Pilon, Mathieu Jacquet) who in some way were connected with the School of Fontainebleau.

GERMAN

3. SURVEYS AND HISTORIES

Book

1312 BANGE, E.F. *Die deutschen Bronzestatuetten des 16. Jahrhunderts.* Berlin: Deutscher-
verein für Kunstwissenschaft, 1949. 166 pp., 153 b&w pls., 72 b&w text figs.

German 16th century bronze statuettes: main centers of production (Nuremberg, Innsbruck, Landshut, Augsburg, and also the Netherlands) and masters (the Vischers, Peter
Flötner, Veit Arnberg, Conrad Meit, etc.)(pp. 11-110); descriptive catalog of 203 pieces from
public and private European and American Collections (113-50).

Articles

1313 JANTZEN, JOHANNES. "Bronzemörser." *Anzeiger des Germanischen Nationalmuseums* (1968):27-34, 16 b&w figs.

Group of mostly German mortars of the 16th century in a private collection in
Bremen.

1314 MENDE, URSULA. "Nürnburger Aquamanilien und verwandte Gussarbeiten um 1400."
Anzeiger des Germanischen Nationalmuseums (1974):8-25, 12 b&w figs.

Lion- and horse-shaped aquamanile produced around 1400 in Nuremberg.

1315 WEIHRAUCH, HANS R. "Italienische Bronzen als Vorbilder deutscher
Goldsmiedekunst" In *Studien zur Geschichte der europäischen Plastik: Festschrift Theodor
Müller zum 19. April 1965.* Munich: Hirmer, 1965. Pp. 263-80, 22 b&w figs.

Italian bronze statuettes by Jacopo Sansovino and others serving as models for German goldsmiths such as Christoph Jamnitzer, Hans Ludwig Kienle, Hans Keller, in multiple
aspects of their production.

8. PRIVATE COLLECTION, AUCTION, AND DEALER CATALOGS

AXEL-NILSSON COLLECTION

1316 AXEL-NILSSON, GÖRAN. "Grand Art en petit format." *Antologia di belle arte* 29-30
(1986):45, 2 b&w figs.

Solid cast bronze statuette probably representing St. Elizabeth of Thuringia held to
have been produced in the 15th century. It was excavated at the foot Cologne Cathedral.

ITALIAN

3. SURVEYS AND HISTORIES

Books

1317 BODE, WILHELM. *The Italian Bronze Statuettes of the Renaissance.* 2d rev. ed. by
James David Draper. New York: M.A.S. De Reinis, 1980. 129 pp. with 102 b&w text
figs., 266 b&w pls.

Edited and revised edition of Bode's (assisted by Murray Marks) monumental three-volume English edition of 1907-8/1912 with additional and corrected information on location of pieces and reattributions.

1318 CESSI, FRANCESCO. *Alessandro Vittoria, bronzista (1525-1608)*. *Collana artisti trentini,* edited by Riccardo Maroni, vol. 26. Trent: 1960. Reprint *Collana artisti trentini,* vol. 1. Trent: Arti Grafiche Saturna, 1977. Pp. 132-238, 59 b&w figs.
    Biographical elements of Vittoria's mature years in Venice, his mannerist handling of small bronzes (some new attributions) of classically posed figures, and of candelabra.

1319 CESSI, FRANCESCO. *Vincenzo e Gian Gerolamo Grandi scultori (secolo XVI).* *Collana artisti trentini,* edited by Riccardo Maroni, vol. 51. Trent: 1967. Reprint. *Collana artisti trentini,* vol. 2. Trent: Arti Grafiche Saturnia. 1977. Pp. 336-446, 47 b&w figs.
    Activity of Vincenzo and Gian Gerolamo Grandi and their workshop in 16th-century Trent and Padua, producing small bronzes: mortars, bells, door-knockers, bookcovers, etc.

1320 CIARDI DUPRÉ, MARIA GRAZIA. *Small Renaissance Bronzes.* Translated by Betty Ross. London: Hamlyn Publishing Group, 1970. 67 color illus. (From the Italian *I Bronzetti del Rinascimento* [Milan: Fratelli Fabri, 1966].)
    Brief survey: major schools, main points of development, artists, designs, casting methods, chasing, etc.

1321 GIBBON, ALAN, AND BANKS, GIL. *Bronzes de la Renaissance.* Paris: Frédéric Birr, 1982. 117 pp., 17 color figs., 83 b&w figs.
    Useful only as pictorial introduction to Florentine, Venetian, Sienese, and Paduan Renaissance statuettes from public and private collections.

1322 NICODEMI, GIORGIO. *Bronzi minori del Rinascimento italiano.* Milan: Luigi Filippo Bolaffio, 1933. 235 pp., 138 b&w figs.
    Broad survey of small Italian Renaissance bronzes from Ghiberti to Giambologna dealing, in progression, with 15th- century Florence, the Paduan School, the Venetian, and Tuscan masters.

1323 PLANISCIG, LEO. *Piccoli bronzi italiani del Rinascimento.* Milan: Fratelli Treves, 1930. 66 pp., 383 b&w figs. on 226 pls.
    Important early survey of small-scale Italian bronze examples from various museums and private collections throughout Europe and the U.S. Fifty-page text is followed by illustrations for 383 bronze objects — mostly statuettes — representing the work of nearly all major schools and artists: Bellano, Riccio, Cellini, Cattaneo, Severo da Ravenna ("Maestro del Drago"), Antico, Giambologna, Susini, etc. While some whereabouts and attributions have changed since publication, it remains a useful source for illustration and provenance. No notes or bibliography.

Articles

1324 AVERY, CHARLES H.F. "Giuseppe De Levis of Verona — a Bronze Founder and Sculptor of the Late Sixteenth Century: 1 — Bells and Mortars." *Connoiseur* 181 (1972):179-88, 17 b&w figs.
    Corpus of works by the artist, several bearing signature, date, and coat of arms of owner, in public and private European collections. Manner by which these objects were manufactured; function they fulfilled.

1325 CIARDI DUPRÉ, MARIA GRAZIA. "I bronzetti toscani del Quattrocento." *Antichità viva* 18, no. 2 (1979):28-35, 10 b&w figs. English summary.

Small bronzes in the Medici collection at the death of Lorenzo the Magnificent in 1492; antique ones forming a collection on their own, and contemporary ones by Filarete, Bertoldo, Pollaiuolo, Vecchietta, etc., used for decorative purposes in the household.

1326 CUST, ROBERT. "A Bronze Crucifix." *Connoisseur* 17 (1910):299-300, 1 b&w fig.

A Florentine 16th-century gilt-bronze Corpus Christi owned by Baron Szàszvaros of the imperial Austrian court, attributed to Benvenuto Cellini.

1327 LEITHE-JASPER, MANFRED. "Beiträge zum Werk des Agostino Zoppo." *Jahrbuch des Stiftes Klosterneuburg,* n.s. 9 (1979):109-38, 27 b&w figs.

Attribution of small bronzes, including four perfume burners entitled Mount of Hell, formerly said to be works of Riccio or Bellano, to Zoppo primarily on the basis of the Contarini monument in the Basilica of the Santo, Padua.

1328 MC CURDY, EDWARD. "Leonardo's Bronze Statuette at Burlington House." *Burlington Magazine* 56 (1930):141, 4 b&w figs.

Leonardo's drawing of a rearing horse in the *Codice atlantico* connected with the genesis of a bronze representing a Warrior on Horseback (on loan from the Museum of Fine Arts, Budapest) is grounds for the author to question the often voiced opinion that it is a study for the Trivulzio monument.

1329 MIDDELDORF, ULRICH. "Eine Kleinbronze von Valerio Belli." *Pantheon* 34 (1976):115. Reprinted in *Raccolta di scritti, that is, Collected Writings. II. 1974-1979.* Florence: Studio per Edizioni Scelte, 1981, pp. 49-51, figs. 49-52.

A small bronze of the Enthroned Madonna and Child known in a single cast and in a private collection, bears on its back the inscription VALERIVS F.

1330 MIDDELDORF, ULRICH. "Eine seltene Bronze der Spätrenaissance." In *Giessner Beiträge zur Kunstgeschichte, Festschrift Günther Fiensch zum 60. Geburtstag.* Vol. 1. Giessen: 1970, pp. 78-86. Reprinted in *Raccolta di scritti, that is, Collected Writings. II. 1939-1973.* Florence: Studio per Edizioni Scelte, 1980, pp. 303-8, figs. 135-42.

Group of academic bronze statuettes of the second half of the 16th century produced in Rome.

1331 PLANISCIG, LEO. "Gasparo, fonditore Veneziano." *Bollettino d'arte* 26 (1933):345-51, 6 b&w pls.

An eclectic bronze candlestick in an anonymous collection signed 'Gaspar' and dated 1551; companion with works by Riccio and other bronzes by the Venetian Gasparo.

1332 RADCLIFFE, ANTHONY. "Bronze Oil Lamps by Riccio." *Victoria and Albert Museum Yearbook* 3 (1972):29-58, 34 b&w figs.

Detailed study of the style, iconography, and chronology of these objects by Riccio now in various public and private collections—the Cadogan Lamp (Victoria and Albert Museum); the Fortnum Lamp (Ashmolean Museum); the Louvre Lamp; the Rothschild Lamp (private collection); the Frick Lamp, etc.—produced for the Paduan humanist circle and subsequently considered to have been actual pieces form antiquity.

1333   VOLBACH, WOLFGANG FRITZ. "Antonio Gentili da Faenza and the Large Candle-
sticks in the Treasury of St. Peter's." *Burlington Magazine* 90 (1948):281-86. 7 b&w figs.
        Author examines two large 16th-century candlesticks with a stem in the style of
Andrea Riccio and added portions by Gentile, relating them to an earlier candlestick in The
Cleveland Museum of Art, and attributes several watercolor drawings in Chigi codex (Vatican
Library) to this eclectic goldsmith.

6. PERMANENT COLLECTIONS

Berlin

STAATLICHE MUSEEN PREUSSISCHER KULTURBESITZ,
KUNSTGEWERBEMUSEUM

1334   VALENTINER, W.R.   "Verrocchio's Lost Candlestick."   *Burlington Magazine* 62
(1933):228-32, 3 b&w figs.
        Identification of a bronze candelabrum in the museum as the one documented to
have been produced by Verrocchio in 1468 for the Audience Chamber of the Palazzo Vecchio, Florence.

London

WALLACE COLLECTION

1335   TERNI DE GREGORY, W. "Giovanni da Crema and His 'Seated Goddess.'"   *Burlington Magazine* 92 (1950):158-61, 12 b&w figs.
        Master IO.F.F., who produced distinctive plaquettes for sword pommels, is identified
as Giovanni Fonduli da Crema, a bronze sculptor active in Padua who signed a parcel gilt
statuette of a seated woman at the Wallace.

Munich

BAYERISCHES NATIONALMUSEUM

1336   WEIHRAUCH, HANS R. "Ein unbekanntes Frühwerk von Andrea Riccio." *Pantheon*
18 (1960):222-32, 15 b&w figs.
        A bronze writing casket formerly in the collection of Christian August of Waldeck is
attributed to Andrea Riccio from the style of its rich relief work depicting sea deities and is
dated to ca. 1506.

Oxford

ASHMOLEAN MUSEUM

1337   SPENCER, JOHN R. "Two Bronzes by Filarete." *Burlington Magazine* 100 (1958):392,
394-5, 397, 10 b&w figs.
        Attribution to Filarete of two statuettes on the basis of a signed silver processional
cross dated of 1449 in S. Maria del Colle, Bassano del Grappa.

XXII. Bronze Statuettes, Mortars, Hand Bells, Aquamanile, Candlesticks, Etc.

Paris

BIBLIOTHÈQUE NATIONALE

1338   FOVILLE, JEAN DE. "Les Bronzes de la Renaissance de la Bibliothèque nationale: Bronzes italiens du XVe siècle." *Revue de l'art ancien et moderne* 35 (1914):223-36, 1 b&w pl., 11 b&w figs.
    Little-known Italian bronze figurines of the 15th century in the Cabinet des Médailles attributed to the schools of Donatello, Pollaiuolo, Venice, etc.

MUSÉE DU LOUVRE

1339   PLANISCIG, LEO. "Der 'Zwerg auf der Schnecke' als repräsentant einer bisher un-beachteten naturalistischen Richtung des venezianischen Cinquecento." *Jahrbuch der kunstistorischen Sammlungen in Wien* n.s. 13 (1944):243-54, 7 b&w figs.
    A statuette of a dwarf riding a large snail related to other 16th century bronzes and seen as expression of naturalistic elements in Venetian sculpture.

1340   JESTAZ, BERTRAND. "Une Statuette de bronze: Le Saint Christophe de Severo da Ravenna." *La Revue du Louvre et des musées de France* 22 (1972):67-78, 17 b&w figs.
    Attribution to Severo of a Paduan bronze statuette of St. Christopher (formerly known as Atlas) of about 1500 at the Louvre and of the blessing Christ Child it complements in the National Gallery, Washington, formerly given to Bellano.

Richmond

VIRGINIA MUSEUM OF FINE ARTS

1341   BLISS, JOSEPH R. "A Renaissance Bronze Statuette of a Dancing Putto." *Arts in Virginia* 26 (1986):3-17, 1 color pl., 16 b&w figs.
    Based on antique figures of the child Eros and influenced by the works of Donatello, it is proposed to have been cast in Mantua ca. 1475-1500.

7. EXHIBITION CATALOGS

Amsterdam

RIJKSMUSEUM

1342   *Meesters van het brons der Italiaanse renaissance.* Exhibition catalog by A. van Schendel, with introduction by John Pope-Hennessey. Amsterdam: Rijksmuseum, 1961. 95 pp. (unpaginated), 96 b&w figs.
    Summary catalog of a major exhibition of Italian bronzes of the 15th-18th century first held at the Victoria and Albert Museum (see entry 1345). Some differences in attribution from London catalog, and many more pieces illustrated. While some items from English private collections did not travel to Amsterdam, to the exhibit were added seventy-nine medals and plaquettes recorded in checklist form.

XXII. Bronze Statuettes, Mortars, Hand Bells, Aquamanile, Candlesticks, Etc.

Edinburgh

ROYAL SCOTTISH MUSEUM

1343   *Giambologna 1529-1608, Sculptor to the Medici.* Exhibition organized by the Arts Council of Great Britain and the Kunsthistorisches Museum, Vienna, in association with the Edinburgh Festival Society, the Royal Scottish Museum, and the Victoria and Albert Museum. Catalog edited by Charles Avery and Anthony Radcliffe, with essays and entries by Avery, Radcliffe, Anthea Brook, Herbert Keutner, Manfred Leithe-Jasper, Lars Olof Larsson, and Katherine Watson. London: Arts Council of Great Britain, 1978. 239 pp., 21 color figs., 265 b&w figs. Exhibition also held in London at the Victoria and Albert Museum, and in Vienna at the Kunsthistorisches Museum.

International exhibiton highlighting the genius of Giambologna and distinguishing between his own work and that of assistants, pupils, followers, and copyists. Six essays examining his workshop and specific productions are followed by a catalog of 249 entries arranged by types: female, male figures, groups, Labors of Hercules, religious iconography, equestrian statuettes and horses, etc.

Laarne, Belgium

KASTEEL LAARNE

1344   *Bronzen uit de Renaissance van Donatello tot Frans Duquesnoy behorend tot Belgische privé verzamelingen.* Exhibition catalog by J. de Ghellinck d'Elseghem. Brussels: Koninklijke Vereniging der Historische Woonsteden van België, 1967. 172 pp. including 134 b&w figs. Flemish/French text.

Exhibition of Renaissance bronzes in private Belgian collections. Includes 113 entries out of which about 80 are of the 15th-16th century. The Paduan, Florentine, and Venetian schools are best represented with bronzes attributed to Bellano, Riccio, Cellini, Sangallo, Giambologna, Tribolo, Vittoria, Sansovino, Roccatagliata, etc.

London

VICTORIA AND ALBERT MUSEUM

1345   *Italian Bronze Statuettes.* Exhibition organized by the Arts Council of Great Britain. Catalog by Antonio Santangelo and John Pope-Hennessey. London: Arts Council of Great Britain, 1961. 47 pp. (unpaginated), 32 b&w pls.

Summary catalog of important exhibition of 203 works drawn from European public and private collections and illustrating the full range and diversity of 15th-18th-century Italian bronze statuettes. Includes well-known examples of Riccio, Antico, Sansovino, Pollaiuolo, Tullio Lombardo, Giambologna, etc. Five-page introduction. (See also entry 1342.)

1345a   POPE-HENNESSEY, JOHN. "An Exhibition of Italian Bronze Statuettes." *Burlington Magazine* 105 (1963):14-23, 58-71, 50 b&w figs. Reprinted in *Essays on Italian Sculpture.* London and New York: Phaidon Press, 1968. Pp. 172-98.

Reappraisal of variously attributed small Italian bronzes in light of the 1961 London, Amsterdam (see entries 1345, 1342), and Florence exhibitions. Author reassigns statuettes to Francesco di Giorgio, Desiderio da Firenze, Severo da Ravenna, Paolo Savin, and Camelio.

317

Northampton, Mass.

SMITH COLLEGE MUSEUM OF ART

1346   *Renaissance Bronzes in American Collections.* Exhibition catalog prepared by David Brooke et al., with basic entries provided by lenders. Introduction by John Pope-Hennessey. Northampton: Smith College Museum of Art, 1964. 73 pp., 28 b&w pls.

Twenty-eight bronzes—mostly statuettes—from workshops of Florence, Siena, Padua, Mantua, Venice, Milan, Rome, and one from Nuremberg. Includes works by Riccio, Severo da Ravenna, Cellini, Tullio Lombardo, Antico, Giambologna, Bellano, etc. All illustrated and with short catalog entries.

8. PRIVATE COLLECTION, AUCTION, AND DEALER CATALOGS

BLUMKA COLLECTION

1347   PLANISCIG, LEO. "Severo da Ravenna (der 'Meister des Drachens')." *Jahrbuch der kunsthistorisches Sammlungen in Wien* 9 (1935):75-86, 21 b&w figs.

The discovery of a signature on a bronze permits the attribution of a group of statuettes to Severo da Ravenna, a Paduan sculptor active ca. 1490-ca. 1537.

CORSI COLLECTION

1348   MIDDELDORF, ULRICH. *Fifty Mortars: A Catalogue.* Florence: S.P.E.S., 1981. 195 pp., 91 b&w illus.

Bronze mortars in the Giorgio Corsi Collection studied in catalog form. Most examples are Italian and date of the 15th-16th century. Useful, groundbreaking publication that includes good descriptions, measurements, patina, comparative examples, and provides the best bibliography to date on the subject.

NETTLEFOLD COLLECTION

1349   FORRER, R. *The Collection of Bronzes and Castings in Brass and Ormolu Formed by M.J. Nettlefold.* London: Privately Printed, 1934. 214 pp., 66 b&w pls.

Prestigious collection formed over twenty years that included Renaissance casts by Giambologna and school, Girolamo Campagna, Severo da Ravenna, Danese Cattaneo, and the school of Riccio.

SALTING COLLECTION

1350   HILL, G.F. "The Salting Collection—I: The Italian Bronze Statuettes." *Burlington Magazine* 16 (1909-10):311- 18, 2 b&w pls.

Renaissance bronze statuettes and plaques by or attributed to Bertoldo, Antico, Giambologna, Poggini, and Riccio.

XXIII. Brass and Copper: Dinanderie, Church Bells, Lecterns, Fonts, Effigy Tablets

A. MULTI COUNTRY OF ORIGIN

7. SURVEYS AND HISTORIES

Books

1351   BOUQUET, A.C., and WARING, MICHAEL. *European Brasses*. New York: Praeger, 1967. 78 pp., 32 b&w pls.
    Nine-page introduction deals with technique, development of brass effigy tablets during the Middle Ages. Thirty-two plates reproduce rubbings; of the 15th and 16th century are those given between pp. 35 and 75.

1352   MACKLIN, HERBERT W. *Monumental Brasses*. 7th ed. rev. by Charles Oman. London: Allen & Unwin, 1953. 196 pp., 34 b&w illus. (1st ed. London: Swan Sonnerschein, 1890.)(Also published in rev. and extensively rewritten ed. by John Page-Phillips as *Macklin's Monumental Brasses*.   New York and Washington: Praeger, 1969.)
    Classic survey of incised brass effigies of late medieval Europe and especially England. Discusses various centers of production, costumes, heraldic elements, and general iconography found on brasses.   List of examples and exhaustive bibliography for those in England, Ireland, Scotland, and Wales, arranged by countries.

1353   NORRIS, MALCOLM. *Monumental Brasses: The Craft*. London and Boston: Faber & Faber, 1978. 148 pp., 269 b&w figs.
    The manufacture of brasses and their design; geographical distribution, mostly in 15th-16th-century British Isles, also France, Netherlands, Germany, and Poland; the purchaser, his social status, interests, and motives; engravers and their sources. Companion volume to *Monumental Brasses: The Memorials* (see following entry).

1353a   NORRIS MALCOLM. *Monumental Brasses: The Memorials.* 2 vols. London: Phillips & Page, 1977. 1:287 pp.; 2:309 b&w figs.

    Chronological study of French, Flemish, German, Silesian, Polish, and mostly English engraving centers; workshops and stylistic characteristics; subjects: armed figures, ecclesiatics, civilians such as women, children, academics. Companion volume to *Monumental Brasses: The Craft* (see preceding entry) with reference to its illustrations.

1354   TAVENOR-PERRY, J. *Dinanderie: A History and Description of Medieval Work in Copper, Brass, and Bronze.* London: George Allen & Sons, 1910. 250 pp., 48 b&w pls., 71 line drawings.

    Comprehensive introduction to the art of coppersmithing in Germany, the Netherlands, France, England, Italy, and Spain: origins, materials, processes, various schools, specific objects (portable altars, pyxes, reliquaries, etc.).

1355   TENNENHAUS, RUTH AND MICHAEL. *Das unsterbliche Bildnis: Europäische gravierte Metallgrabplatten vom 12. bis zum 17. Jahrhundert.* Leipzig: Edition Leipzig, 1977. 4 color pls., 42 b&w figs.

    Survey of monumental brass tombs in Europe from the 12th to the 17th century with discussion of makers, production, inscriptions, and records documenting costumes, arms, etc.

6. PERMANENT COLLECTIONS

London

VICTORIA AND ALBERT MUSEUM

1356   TURNER, ERIC. *An Introduction to Brass.* London: Her Majesty's Stationery Office, 1982. 48 pp., 30 color pls., 2 b&w figs.

    Sixteen-page introduction dealing with history, technique and ornamentation; catalog of thirty European brass objects in the collection dating of the 14th through the 20th century. For the period 1400-1600, see pls. 2-13 illustrating cauldrons, dishes, mortars, holy water buckets, ewers, a lavabo, weights, and candlesticks, accompanied by detailed entries.

B. SINGLE COUNTRY OF ORIGIN

BELGIUM (FLEMISH)

3. SURVEYS AND HISTORIES

1357   MOLLE, F. VAN. "Koperen koppenen vuisten in het oude Vlaamse strafrecht." *Antiek* 9 (1974):141-66, 26 b&w illus.

    Brass heads, fists, and inscribed plaques of the late 15th-16th century now in the town hall of Veurne made on order of Flemish courts of justice as means of atonement for offenses.

BRITISH

3. SURVEYS AND HISTORIES

Book

1358   STEPHENSON, MILL. *A List of Monumental Brasses in the British Isles.* London: Headley Bros., 1926. Supplement by Ralph Griffin and M.S. Giuseppi, 1938. 718 pp.
Lists all the brasses known at the time in Great Britain.

Article

1359   SMITH, M.Q. "Medieval Chandeliers in Britain and Their Symbolism. *Connoisseur* 190 (1975):266-71
Six little-known and generally undocumented brass and pewter examples of the 15th and 16th century in British churches are discussed for their involved decoration often including small figures.

6. PERMANENT COLLECTIONS

Florence

SS. ANNUNZIATA

1360   LOTZ, WOLFGANG. "Due leggii nella Chiesa della SS. Annunziata." *Rivista d'arte* 14 (1942):49-59, 5 b&w figs.
Two brass lecterns crowned with eagles in this church held to be English works of the early 16th century.

London

VICTORIA AND ALBERT MUSEUM

1361   *Catalogue of Rubbings of Brasses and Incised Slabs,* by Muriel Clayton. 2d rev. and enl. ed. London: Board of Education, 1929. Reprint. London: Her Majesty's Stationery Office, 1968. 250 pp., 72 b&w pls. (1st ed., *List of Rubbings of Brasses,* 1915.)
Particularly useful to gain knowledge of the whereabouts of brasses and the history of costume, arms and armor, and heraldry. Includes chronological tables, indexes of names and places.

GERMAN

1. DICTIONARIES AND ENCYCLOPEDIAS

1362   LOCKNER, HERMANN P. *Die Merkzeichen der Nürnberger Rotschmiede.* Munich: Deutscher Kunstverlag, 1981. 329 pp., facsimile makers' marks.
Repertory of 1,972 coppersmiths of Nuremberg, their marks and brief outline of their activity. Includes 485 practitioners active in the 16th century, chronological and subject indexes of marks.

3. SURVEYS AND HISTORIES

1363   THURM, SIGRID. *Deutscher Glockenatlas: Bayerisch- Schwaben.* Edited by Franz
Dambeck and Günther Grundmann. Munich and Berlin: Deutscher Kunstverlag, 1967.
611 pp., 357 b&w figs.
Census of church bells in Bavaria-Swabia (main city: Augsburg). Pp. 20-50 of the introduction discuss examples of the 15th-16th century. Descriptive catalog of 1,818 bells
geographically arranged. Indexes of founders, coats of arms, and other iconographic motifs
appearing on these specific bells.

1363a   THURM, SIGRID. *Deutscher Glockenatlas: Mittlefranken.* Edited by Franz Dambeck.
Munich and Berlin: Deutscher Kunstverlag, 1973. 497 pp., 276 b&w figs.
Census of church bells in Middle Franconia (main city: Nuremberg). Pp. 5-51 of the
introduction discuss examples of the 15th-16th century. Descriptive catalog of 1,395 bells
geographically arranged. Indexes of founders, coats of arms, and other iconographic motifs
appearing on these specific bells.

1363b   THURM, SIGRID. *Deutscher Glockenatlas: Württemberg und Hohenzollern.* Edited by
Günther Grundmann. Munich and Berlin: Deutscher Kunstverlag, 1959. 715 pp., 422
b&w figs.
Census of church bells in Württemberg and Hohenzollern (main towns: Boblingen,
Freudenstadt, Ravensburg, Schwäbich Hall, Tübingen). Pp. 17-52 of the introduction discuss
examples of the 15th-16th century. Descriptive catalog of two thousand bells geographically
arranged. Indexes of founders, coats of arms, and other iconographic motifs appearing on
these specific bells.

6. PERMANENT COLLECTIONS

Boston

MUSEUM OF FINE ARTS

1364   COMSTOCK, HELEN. "A Baptismal Font by Gottfried Klinghe, 1483." *Connoisseur*
109 (1942):67, 2 b&w figs.
Brief description of cast bronze font from North Germany with figural reliefs and
coats of arms.

ITALIAN

7. EXHIBITION CATALOGS

Verona

MUSEO DI CASTELVECCHIO

1365   *Fonditori di campane a Verona dal XI al XX secolo.* Exhibition catalog by Lanfranco
Franzoni. Verona: Museo di Castelvecchio, 1979. 134 pp., 1 color fig., 80 b&w figs.
The history of bronze bell-making in Verona—biographies of casters, technical infor-
mation, and a chronology of bronze bells produced in the city during the period 1081-1850.

NETHERLANDISH

3. SURVEYS AND HISTORIES

Book

1366   VERSTER, A.J.G. *Koper en brons van voorheen: Oude koperen en bronzen gebruiksvoor-werpen.* Amsterdam: J.H. de Bussy, 1966. 115 pp., 103 b&w pls. (1st ed., *Brons in den tijd,* 1956.)
        Deals primarily with copper and bronze objects (bells, candlesticks, door-knockers, lavabos, mortars, censers, chalices, etc.) produced in the 15th-17th-century Netherlands.

Article

1367   KOLDEWEIJ, A.M. "De Utrechtse geschut- en klokkengieter Antoni de Borch ($\pm$1520-1576)" *Antiek* 16 (1982):601-19, 3 color figs, 9 b&w figs.
        Bells and mortars produced by the bronze founder Antoni van der Borch in mid-16th-century Munster, Alkemaar, etc.

6. PERMANENT COLLECTIONS

Amsterdam

RIJKSMUSEUM

1368   TER KUILE, O. "Onderdelen van een kerkkroon en van twee kandelaars uit de St. Jacobskerk te Den Haag." *Bulletin van het Rijksmuseum* 28 (1980):125-33, 11 b&w figs. English summary.
        Elements of a brass chandelier and of two candlesticks of the 15th century produced in the area of Dordrecht and formerly in the St. Jacobskerk in The Hague.

New York

METROPOLITAN MUSEUM OF ART

1369   HACKENBROCH, YVONNE. "Two Dinanderie Figures by Aert Van Tricht." *Connois-seur* 139 (1957):219-21, 5 b&w figs.
        A pair of late Gothic candlesticks in the form of dancing jesters formerly in the Un-termyer Collection made in Maastricht by this Dutch artist also responsible for the baptismal font (1492) in Xanten and candleholders in the Bargello and Victoria and Albert Museum, among other works.

XXIV. Pewter, Tin, Lead, and Latten

A. MULTI COUNTRY OF ORIGIN

3. SURVEYS AND HISTORIES

1370 BOUCAUD, PHILLIPE, and FREGNAC, CLAUDE. *Les Étains. Des Origines au début de XIXe siècle.* Fribourg: Office du Livre, 1978. 339 pp., 400 b&w figs.
The making of tin and pewter objects in Europe from antiquity until the early 19th century. Thirteen-page introduction describes alloys, manufacturing techniques and craftsmen's corporations. Relevant to period 1400-1600 are chap. 2 (pp. 13-57), religious implements; chap. 3 (58-71), items for domestic use; chap. 4 (73-83), Germanic ceremonial cups; chap. 5 (85-108), profusely decorated Edelzinn of 1550-1650. Appendix of hallmarks used in the various countries.

1371 BRETT, VANESSA. *Phaidon Guide to Pewter.* Oxford: Phaidon Press, 1981. 256pp., 115 color figs., numerous b&w figs. and line drawings.
Very useful introduction to the history and collecting of mostly secular pewtersmithing from medieval times until the present. Short chapters give essential characteristics by countries with subdivision by type of object (tankards, measures, plates, etc.). Illustrates a few 15th-16th-century examples. Includes appendixes of pewter marks and glossary.

1372 COTTERELL, HOWARD HERSCHEL. *Pewter down the Ages, from Medieval Times to the Present Day with Notes on Evolution.* Boston and New York: Houghton Mifflin Co., 1932. 237 pp., 160 b&w figs.
European pewter from the Middle Ages to the 20th century. Chaps. 2 (pp. 37-64) and 3 (65-91) are relevant to the period 1400-1600 and deal with evolution of form, style, and decoration of mostly northern and eastern European examples (cups, measuring vessels, chalices, bowls, slats, fonts, candlesticks, pilgrim bottles, see pls. 9-51) and their representation in paintings of the period. Useful glossary and twenty-three-page index of marks on British pewter (18th century onward).

1373 HAEDEKE, HANNS-ULRICH. *Zinn: Ein Handbuch für Sammler und Liebhaber.* Bibliothek für Kunst- und Antiquitätenfreunde. Vol. 16. Brunswick: Klinkhardt & Biermann, 1973. 368 pp., 1 color pl., 498 b&w figs. (1st ed. 1963.)

Comprehensive survey of European ecclesiastical and domestic pewter from the dawn of time until World War I. Chaps. 5 and 6 deals with the Middle Ages and Renaissance periods. Well illustrated.

1374 MASSÉ, H.J.L.J. *Pewter Plate: A Historical and Descriptive Handbook.* 2d rev. ed. London: George Bell & Sons, 1910. 352 pp., 108 b&w figs. (1st ed. 1904)

Early survey of the pewterer's art: general history, technical aspects of production, decoration, regulations and marks; often deals with and illustrates 15th-16th-century examples. Includes lists of pewterers and marks, many of which are reproduced.

1375 MORY, LUDWIG. *Schönes Zinn: Geschichte Formen und Probleme.* Munich: F. Bruckmann KG, 1972. 336 pp., 10 color pls., 334 b&w figs., numerous line drawings, facsimile town marks, map. (1st ed. 1961.)

European pewter-making centers and their products (tankards, flasks, cups, plates, bowls, ewers, caskets, candlesticks, medals, plaquettes, etc.) from the Middle Ages through the present with emphasis on techniques, functions, and style.

1376 WACHA, GEORGE. *Zinn und Zinngiesser in den Länden Mitteleuropas.* Munich: Keyersche Verlagssbuchhandlung, 1983. 150 pp., 135 b&w figs., numerous facsimile town marks.

Useful overview of the activity of pewterers from Central Europe (Germany, Poland, Czechoslovakia, Hungary, Rumania, Austria, and Yugoslavia) from the 15th century to the present.

4. BIBLIOGRAPHICAL GUIDES

1377 DENMAN, CAROLYN. "A Bibliography of Pewter." *The Pewter Collectors' Club of America* 15 (October 1945):1-21 (entire issue).

Useful starting point for the earlier literature, both periodicals and books. Subdivided in General, American, English, Continental, Asiatic, and Modern. Also short lists of exhibitions and sales catalogs, and of museums with pewter collections.

6. PERMANENT COLLECTIONS

Düsseldorf

KUNSTMUSEUM

1378 *Zinn.* Catalog by Wolfgang Schepers. Düsseldorf: Kunstmuseums. 1981. 87 pp., 213 b&w figs.

Permanent collection of badges, bottles, ewers, tankards, caskets, etc. made of pewter in the 14th-19th century and including French, German, Austian examples of the 15th-16th century (pp. 19-28, nos. 5-23; p. 30, no. 25; pp. 32-36, nos. 28- 34), all reproduced with their marks. Brief essay on technique; glossary.

Rotterdam

MUSEUM BOYMANS-VAN BEUNINGEN

1379 *Tin.* Catalog by A.J.G. Verster. Rotterdam: Boymans Museum, 1954. 70 pp., 24 b&w pls.

Catalog of 253 vases, pitchers, chalices and paten, cups, candlesticks, plates, and pilgrim badges wrought out of pewter, many of which date of the 15th-16th century and originate from the Netherlands, France, Germany, and Switzerland, and more specifically from the towns of Leyden, Gouda, Rotterdam, Hamburg, Malines, Rouen, and Toulouse.

7. EXHIBITION CATALOGS

Kraków

MUZEUM NARODOWE

1380   *Cyna w dawnych wiekach: Katalog wystawy.* Exhibiton catalog by Janina Michalska. Kraków: Muzeum Narodowe, 1973. 160 pp., 78 b&w pls., facsimile makers' and town marks.
      250 pieces of Polish, French, and German pewter in Polish museums and produced from the 15th through the 19th century. Entries 1-13 deal with the 15th-16th century: jug, tankards, plates, candlestick.

B. SINGLE COUNTRY OF ORIGIN

BRITISH
(ENGLISH, IRISH, AND SCOTTISH)

3. SURVEYS AND HISTORIES

Books

1381   COTTERELL, HOWARD HERSCHEL. *Old Pewter, its Makers and Marks in England, Scotland, and Ireland: An Account of the Old Pewterer & His Craft.* New York: Charles Scribner's Sons; London: B.T. Batsford, 1929. 447 pp., 82 b&w pls., numerous facsimile makers' marks. Reprint. Rutland, Vt.: Tuttle, 1963.
      Standard reference work on subject: history of pewter-making as compiled from accounts; alphabetical list of pewterers with illustrations of their marks; alphabetical list of marks with their owners' initials; unidentified marks. Indexes of devices and hallmarks.

1382   MARKHAM, C.A. *The New Pewter Marks and Old Pewter Ware.* 2d rev. and enl. ed. London: Reeves & Turner; New York: Charles Scribner's Sons, 1928. 355 pp., 9 b&w pls., 118 b&w figs., line drawings, numerous reproductions of makers' marks. (1st ed. 1909.)
      To date the most complete study of the pewterer's craft in England from the late 15th to the 18th century with emphasis on the London production of plate, candlesticks, and maces. Indexes of touches (marks) and pewterers; chapter on cleaning and repairing pewter ware.

1383   MASSÉ, H.J.L.J. *Chats on Old Pewter.* 2d ed. London: T. Fisher Unwin, 1919. 422 pp., 91 b&w figs. (1st ed. 1911.)
      Practical history, geared to the collector, of the pewterer's craft in England from 1550 until 1824. It includes chapters on care, marks, as well as lists of pewterers.

1384   WEAVER, LAWRENCE. *English Leadwork: Its Art & History*. London: B.T. Batsford, 1909. 268 pp., 1 b&w pl., 441 b&w figs.
    Useful study that surveys lead fonts, gutter pipe heads, cisterns, church spires and steeples, domes, lanterns, statues, vases and flower pots, funerary urns, coffins, and house ornaments, including some medieval and Renaissance examples.

Articles

1385   GASK, NORMAN. "Old Base-Metal Spoons." *Old Furniture* 5 (1928):101-4, 8 b&w figs.
    Introduction to the rather rare English pewter and latten (alloy of copper and zinc) spoons of the 14th-16th century whose shapes and period styles are generally similar to their silver counterparts.

1385a   GASK, NORMAN. "Old Base-Metal Spoons." *Connoisseur* 100 (1937):253-56, 6 b&w figs.
    Author pursues his study of English pewter and latten spoons dating of Roman times to the 17th century and found in London in the course of excavations: types (e.g., diamond-point, acorn-, wrythen-, or ball-knop, maiden-head, etc.), makers' marks. Mostly, illustrated with examples in the author's collection.

1386   PEAL, CHRISTOPHER A. "English Knopped Latten Spoons." *Connoisseur* Part 1, 173 (1970):254-57, 15 b&w figs.; Part 2, 174 (1970):196-200, 22 b&w figs.
    Part 1: latten spoons from the 12th century, the evolution of the shape of their bowls and handles, and of the motif of their knops. Part 2: 16th-17th-century latten spoon-makers and their marks; Apostle knops.

6. PERMANENT COLLECTIONS

London

VICTORIA AND ALBERT MUSEUM

1387   *British Pewter*. London: Her Majesty's Stationery Office, 1960. 3 pp., 28 b&w pls.
    Picture book presentation of fifty-seven mostly English examples of plate preceded by a three-page introduction. Five date of the 15th century, two of the 16th.

8. PRIVATE COLLECTION, AUCTION, AND DEALER CATALOGS

SUTHERLAND-GRAEME COLLECTION

1388   SUTHERLAND-GRAEME, A.V. "Latten Spoons—An Appreciation." *Connoisseur* 130 (1952):120-21, 4 b&w figs.
    Made from an alloy of copper, zinc, and iron, many of these spoons, popular in 15th-16th-century England, were produced by pewterers who used the same molds (acorn type, seal, Apostle, etc.) and struck their marks on them.

GERMAN

2. BIOGRAPHICAL DICTIONARIES

1389   HINTZE, ERWIN. *Die deutschen Zinngiesser und ihre Marken.* 7 vols. Vol. 1, *Sächsische Zinngiesser* (1921), 345 pp., 1531 pewter marks; vol. 2, *Nürnberger Zinngiesser* (1921), 175 pp., 341 marks; vol. 3, *Norddeutsche Zinngiesser* (1923), 544 pp., 1652 marks; vol. 4, *Schlesische Zinngiesser*, part 1, Aalen-Kronach (1927), 339 pp., 803 marks; part 2, Künzelsau-Sulzbah (1928), 320 pp., 786 marks; part 3: Tauberbischofsheim-Zweisel [with appendix for Alsace, Austria, Switzerland, and Hungary] (1931), 507 pp., 1693 marks. Leipzig: Karl W. Hiersemmann. Reprint. Aalen: Otto Zeller Verlagsbuchandlung, 1964-65.
    German pewtersmiths: biographical data, their known works and marks. Alphabetically arranged by town and then chronologically; several for the period 1400-1600. Vol. 1: Saxony; 2: Nuremberg; 3: North Germany; 4: Schleswig; 5-7: South Germany.

1390   WISWE, MECHTHILD. *Historische Zinngiesserei im südöstlichen Niedersachsen: Meister-Marken-Erzeugnisse.* Brunswick: Braunschweigisches Landesmuseum, 1981. 186 pp., numerous b&w unnumbered figs.
    Documented pewterers active in the southern part of Lower Saxony based on examples in the extensive collection of the Braunschweigisches Landesmuseum in Brunswick; their marks and specific works from 1319 until 1916 arranged by town of activity; 15th- and 16th-century pewterers are recorded at Brunswick, Helmstedt, and Wolfenbüttel.

3. SURVEYS AND HISTORIES

Books

1391   FREUDENBERG, ELISA ZU, and MONDFELD, WOLFRAM ZU. *Altes Zinn aus Niederbayern.* 2 vols. Regensburg: Friederich Pustet, 1982. 1:262 pp., 160 b&w figs., line drawings; 2:269 pp., 226 b&w figs., facsimile makers' marks.
    Plate made out of pewter in Lower Bavaria from the 14th to 19th century. Primary centers of activity discussed for the 15th-16th century are Landshut, Cham, and the Danube Valley with Staubing, Regensberg, and Passau. Includes catalog and reproduction of makers' marks geographically arranged.

1392   HINTZE, ERWIN. *Nürnberger Zinn.* Leipzig: Klinkhardt & Biermann, 1921. 22 pp. with 2 text figs., 143 b&w pls.
    Survey of tin objects produced in Nuremberg from the 15th to the 19th century; introduction traces historical development; illustration of tankards, plates, basins, etc.

Article

1393   KÖSTER, K. "Die Pilgerzeichen der Neusser Quirinus-Wallfahrt im Spätmittelalter. Originale Fundstücke, Abgüsse auf Glocken, Bildzeugnisse." *Neusser Jahrbuch für Kunst, Kulturgesichte und Heimatkunde* (1984):11-29, 18 b&w figs.
    Molds of pilgrimage badges cast out of lead or pewter also used for the decoration of 15th- early 16th-century church bells in the Rheinland, Slovenia, and Scandinavia.

6. PERMANENT COLLECTIONS

Cologne

KUNSTGEWERBEMUSEUM DER STADT KÖLN

1394   *Zinn.* Vol. 3 of *Kataloge des Kunstgewerbemuseums Köln.* Catalog by Fritz Bertram, with
introduction by Hanns-Ulrich Haedeke. Cologne: Kunstgewerbemuseum der Stadt
Köln, 1968. 174 pp., 321 b&w figs.

Catalog of 275 objects made of pewter (pilgrim badges, plate, and statuettes), mostly
German, in the permanent collection of the museum of decorative arts. Includes several 15th-
16th-century examples reproduced with their marks.

Dresden

MUSEUM FÜR KUNSTHANDWERK

1395   *Nürnberger Zinn.* Catalog by Günter Reinheckel. Dresden: Staatliche Kunstsammlungen, 1971. 71 pp., numerous b&w figs.

Catalog of 109 pewter objects (dishes, tankards, ewer) made in Nuremberg and in
the museum's permanent collection. A twenty-five-page essay is followed by short descriptive
entries (nos. 1-34 are 16th-century examples) including reproduction of marks.

7. EXHIBITION CATALOGS

Dortmund

MUSEUM FÜR KUNST UND KULTURGESCHICHTE

1396   *Ausstellung der Sammlungen Kirsch und Gläntzer.* Exhibition catalog by Rolf Fritz, Lily
Kirsch, Herrn Eibelshäuser, and Heinrich Gläntzer. Dortmund: Museum für Kunst und
Kulturgeschichte, 1961. 51 pp., 25 b&w figs., several figs and line drawings of makers'
marks.

Deals with 131 German pewter vessels and plates described in brief entries and with
illustration of marks. Nos. 1-3 are 15th-century examples; 4-17, 16th-century.

HUNGARIAN

1. DICTIONARIES AND ENCYCLOPEDIAS

1397   WEINER, PIROSKA. *Zinngiessermarken in Ungarn 16.-19. Jahrhundert.* Budapest:
Akadémiai Kiadó, 1978. 107 pp., 11 b&w pls., numerous facsimile makers' and town
marks.

Census of makers' and town marks on Hungarian pewter from the 16th through 19th
century arranged by towns. Includes several of the 16th century.

NETHERLANDISH

3. SURVEYS AND HISTORIES

1398   DUBBE, B. *Tin en tinnegieters in Nederland.* Lochem: De Tijdstroon BV, 1978. 470 pp., 222 b&w illus., 630 facsimile makers' marks.

Comprehensive study of the manufacture in the Netherlands of pewter objects and those in other tin-lead alloys from the 12th through the 20th century: trade, guilds, technique, tools, alloys, makers'-town-owners' marks, assaying. Dutch text with English summary (pp. 446-70).

7. EXHIBITION CATALOGS

Amsterdam

MUSEUM WILLEL-HOLTHUYSEN

1399   *Keur van tin uit de Havensteden Amsterdam, Antwerpen en Rotterdam.* Exhibition catalog entries by Claessens-Peré, F. van Erpers Royaards, and B.R.M. de Neeve, with essays by B. Dubbe, J. Van Deun, J.W.M. de Jong, M.L. Caron, G. Thand and H.C. Pieck. Antwerp: Provinciaal Museum Sterckshof; Amsterdam: Museum Willel-Holthuysen; Rotterdam: Museum Boysmans-van Beuningen, 1979. 350 pp., numerous b&w figs. and makers' marks. Summary of essays in English.

Pewter tankards, dishes, cups, etc. produced in the three large port cities of Amsterdam, Antwerp, and Rotterdam. Catalog of 329 pieces illustrating the predominance of Antwerp in the 15th to mid-16th century including the making there of "Spanish plates." Amsterdam and Rotterdam, though not without earlier activity, only rose to importance in the 17th century. This exhibition also traveled to the Provinciaal Museum Sterckshof, Antwerp, and the Museum Boymans-van Beuningen, Rotterdam.

Lakenhal

STEDELIJK MUSEUM

1400   *Tin ten toon.* Exhibition catalog introduction by M.L. Wurfbain, with essay by W.L. Moerman. Lakenhal: Stedelijk Museum, 1972. 46 pp., 19 pls.

Netherlandish tinware from the 16th to the 19th century. 105 examples from the Leiden area and some from the Rotterdam Historisch Museum: plates, tankards, spoons, candlesticks, etc., each accompanied by a brief entry with marks and bibliography.

SWISS

2. BIOGRAPHICAL DICTIONARIES

1401   BOSSARD, GUSTAV. *Die Zinngiesser der Schweiz und ihr Werk.* 2 vols. Zug: 1920 (vol.1), 1934 (vol.2). 1:103 pp., 43 pls. of line drawings; 2:260 pp., line drawings throughout, 48 b&w pls., town and makers' marks. Reprint (2 vols. in 1). Osnabrück: Otto Zeller, 1978.

Pewterers of Switzerland: their work from the 14th to the 19th century. Vol. 1: line drawings of 866 makers' marks arranged geographically. Vol. 2: local styles, particularities, town marks, biographical data on pewtersmiths, and their specific works (mostly tankards and plates).

1402   SCHNEIDER, HUGO, and KNEUSS, PAUL. *Zinn: Die Zinngiesser der Schweiz und ihre Marken.* Olten and Freiburg im Breisgau: Walter Verlag, 1983. 382 pp., numerous b&w figs. and line drawings of makers' marks.

Pewtersmiths of Switzerland: biographical data, their marks. Alphabetized arrangement by town and then chronologically; many for the period 1400-1600. Iconographic repertory of marks.

3. SURVEYS AND HISTORIES

1403   FALKE, OTTO VON. "Schweizer Zinn." *Pantheon* 17 (1936):64-68, 11 b&w figs.

General features and main types of Swiss pewterware including a few 16th-century examples of "town jugs."

6. PERMANENT COLLECTIONS

Fribourg

MUSÉE D'ART ET D'HISTOIRE

1404   *Étains fribourgeois: Contribution à l'histoire des potiers d'étains fribourgeois.* Exhibition held in the Château de Gruyères. Catalog by Yvonne Lehnherr. Fribourg: Museé d'Art et d'Histoire, 1972. 103 pp., 15 b&w pls., makers' marks. French/German text.

The activity of pewterers in the town of Fribourg, Switzerland, from the early 15th through the 18th century. Includes introduction, dictionary of craftsmen and their marks, catalog of forty-nine pieces in the permanent collection.

XXV. Ironworks

A. MULTI COUNTRY OF ORIGIN

3. SURVEYS AND HISTORIES

1405 AYRTON, MAXWELL, and SILCOCK, ARNOLD. *Wrought Iron and Its Decorative Use.* London: Country Life; New York: Charles Scribner's Sons, 1929. 196 pp., 240 b&w figs., line drawings.

History of wrought iron in England from the 12th through the 19th century: methods of manufacture, branches of ironwork, designs, smiths, and conditions of the day. Some examples of the 15th-16th century on pp. 34-45, including grilles, screens, gates, door-hinges, locks, etc., often in situ in well-known buildings.

1406 BAUR-HEINHOLD, MARGARETE. *Geschmiedetes Eisen vom Mittelalter bis um 1900.* Königstein im Taunus: Karl Robert Langewiesche, 1963. 112 pp., 96 b&w pls., 8 b&w figs.

Selected examples of wrought iron doors, gates, screens, and knobs in Germany, Austria, and Switzerland from the 12th to the 19th century. Photographic survey with a ten-page introduction and captions.

1407 FFOULKES, CHARLES. *Decorative Ironwork from the XIth to the XVIIIth Century.* London: Methuen & Co., 1913. 148 pp., 32 b&w pls., 80 line drawings.

Hinges, door ornaments, grilles, railings and gates, well covers, furniture, locks, keys and bolts, handles, knockers, chests and caskets, clocks, mirrors, and jewelry, arranged by country of origin; includes representative examples dating 1400-1600; names of smiths and ironworkers.

1408 HÖVER, OTTO. *Wrought Iron: Encyclopedia of Ironwork.* Translated by Ann C. Weaver. 2d ed. New York: Universe Books, 1969. 34 pp. with 11 b&w text figs., 320 b&w pls. (1st ed. New York: E. Weyhe, 1927.)

Introductory essays discuss evolution of style and technique in European decorative ironwork including Gothic and Renaissance periods (pp. 15-28). Pls. 17-124 are of the 15th-16th century: doors, grilles, door-handles, door-knockers, fire-irons and chandeliers.

6. PERMANENT COLLECTIONS

Frankfurt

MUSEUM FÜR KUNSTHANDWERK

1409   *Schmiedeeiserne, Schlösser und Beschläge.* Exhibition catalog. Frankfurt: Museum für Kunsthandwerk, 1978. 28 pp., 9 b&w figs.

Selection of sixty-five locks and other metal fittings from the permanent collection of the museum of decorative arts. Eleven-page essay follwed by catalog. Nos. 14, 16-41 date of the period 1400-1600.

London

VICTORIA AND ALBERT MUSEUM

1410   *Ironwork,* by J. Starkie Gardner. 2 vols. Vol. 1, *From the Earliest Times to the End of the Mediaeval Period,* 4th ed., rev. by W.W. Watts, London: Board of Education, 1927, 157 pp., 63 b&w pls., 31 b&w figs. (1st ed. 1892). Vol. 2, *Continental Ironwork of the Renaissance and Later Periods,* 2d ed., rev. and enl. by W.W. Watts, London: Board of Education, 1930, 136 pp., 44 b&w pls. (1st ed. 1896).

Comprehensive and lucid history of ironwork from biblical times through the rococo period as illustrated by the museum's collection, one of the most extensive. Vol. 1 (pp. 112-38) covers the 15th century; vol. 2 (1-89) deals in separate chapters with the Renaissance period in Italy, Germany, the Netherlands, Spain, and France. Topographical and makers indexes.

New York

METROPOLITAN MUSEUM OF ART – CLOISTERS

1411   HOFFELD, JEFFREY M. "The Art of the Medieval Blacksmith." *Metropolitan Museum of Art Bulletin* 28 (1969):160-73, 16 b&w figs.

Ironwork from the collection: locks, hinges, keys, purse clasp, etc., many bearing figural representations and all dating of the 15th-16th century.

Rouen

MUSÉE LE SECQ DES TOURNELLES

1412   *Ferronnerie ancienne.* Edited by H.R. d'Allemagne. 2 vols. Vol. 1, *Serrurerie monumentale,* 28 pp. with 4 text figs., 206 b&w pls. with many objects illustrated on each; vol. 2, *Menus ouvrages en fer et en acier,* 31 pp. with 2 text figs., 208 b&w pls. with many objects illustrated on each. Paris: J. Schemit, 1924.

4,525 objects of European ironwork of the 12th-18th century grouped by type: vol. 1, largest pieces such as grilles, locks, keys, door-knockers, signs; vol. 2, jewelry, small boxes and caskets, religious implements (crosses, waterfonts, etc.) watches, purse clasps, thimbles, scissors, knives, forks. Valuable pictorial compendium with cursory captions.

7. EXHIBITION CATALOGS

Houston

UNIVERSITY OF ST. THOMAS ART DEPARTMENT

1413   *Made of Iron.* Exhibition catalog by Dominique de Menil. Introduction by Stephen V. Grancsay. Essay by Cyril Stanley Smith. Houston: University of St. Thomas, 1966. 288 pp., 314 b&w illus.

Two essays introduce the history and the technical and decorative characteristics of iron; catalog of 515 objects typographically and chronologically arranged from many U.S. and European public and private collections provide multifarious examples of decorative and functional ironwork of different civilizations from antiquity to the 20th century. Includes 15th-16th-century figurines, plaques, caskets, grilles, door-knockers, keys, locks, table utensils, tools, arms and armor, and purse frames displaying various techniques (chiseling, embossing, gilding, damascening, etc.).

London

BURLINGTON HOUSE

1414   *Exhibition of Chased and Embossed Steel and Iron Work of European Origin.* Catalog by J. Starkie Gardner et al. London: Burlington Fine Arts Club, 1900. 103 pp., 70 b&w pls.

325 objects, primarily French, Flemish, Italian, and mostly of the 15th-16th century, from public and private British collections: keys, locks, door-knockers, andirons, caskets, arms and armor, plaques, purse mounts, horse trappings, etc., decorated by chasing, chiseling, piercing, embossing, as well as gilding.

B. SINGLE COUNTRY OF ORIGIN

AUSTRIAN

3. SURVEYS AND HISTORIES

1415   KASTNER, OTFRIED. *Handgeschmiedet Eisenkunst in Österreich aus der Zeit der Landnahme, Romanik und Gotik.* Linz: J. Wimmer, 1967. 308 pp., 16 color pls., 120 b&w pls.

Handwrought ironwork of medieval times in Austria: on doors, window gratings, frames of religious and secular buildings throughout the country, most examples dating of the early 16th century.

BELGIUM

3. SURVEYS AND HISTORIES

1416   FFOULKES, CHARLES. "Belgian Ironwork." *Connoisseur* 41 (1915):143-53, 18 b&w figs.

Doors with ironwork fittings of the 14th-17th century in Liège, Hal, Brussels, Bruges, and Louvain. Also series of iron landiers in the Musée du Cinquantenaire, Brussels.

1417   MOLLE, F. VAN. "Notities bij de oude 'vuurwagen' in Vlaanderen en Brabant." *Antiek* 16 (1982):533-39, 1 color fig., 5 b&w figs.
Flemish brazier cast of iron in Flanders studied through paintings and an actual example of 1571 in the Provinciaal Museum, Bruges.

BRITISH

3. SURVEYS AND HISTORIES

1418   BLAIR, CLAUDE. "The Most Superb of All Royal Locks." *Apollo* 84 (1966):493-94, 4 b&w figs.
Author attributes two highly decorative cast iron and chiseled door-locks (Walters Art Gallery and Victoria and Albert Museum) as well as two andirons (Knole, Sevenoaks, Kent) to Henry Romayne (active in London ca. 1528-53).

1419   HUGHES, G.B. "Old English Fire-Dogs." *Old Furniture* 8 (1929):189-97, 29 b&w figs.
Illustrates and briefly describes several Gothic and Elizabethan cast and wrought iron andirons.

1420   STRANGE, E.F. "Fire-Dogs and Screen at Knole." *Old Furniture* 3 (1928):168-70, 2 b&w figs.
An Italianate wrought iron fire screen dated 1599 with decorative dragons and female head; two English firedogs of steel and brass bearing the arms and initials of Henry VIII and an initial of Ann Boleyn dating of ca. 1533-36.

FRENCH

6. PERMANENT COLLECTIONS

New York

METROPOLITAN MUSEUM OF ART

1421   RANDALL, RICHARD H. "A Gothic Bird Cage." *Metropolitan Museum of Art Bulletin* 11 (1953):286-92, 5 b&w figs.
Study of a southern French iron bird cage of the 15th century—an object commonly represented in medieval illuminations and tapestries.

7. EXHIBITION CATALOGS

Bordeaux

MUSÉE DES ARTS DÉCORATIFS

1422   *La Clef et la serrure.* Exhibition catalog by Jacqueline de Pasquier (1st part) and the Société Bricard, Paris (2d part). Bordeaux: Musée des Arts Décoratifs, 1973. 95 pp., 35 b&w figs.

Locks and keys, door-knockers, and small locking metal caskets from the 12th to the 18th century in the museum and from private collections (mostly Bricard, a lock manufacturer) in Bordeaux and Paris. Four-page glossary and labeled drawings showing the different parts of locks and keys.

GERMAN

3. SURVEYS AND HISTORIES

1423   SCHMITZ, WILHELM. *Die mittelalterlichen Metall- und Holtz- Türen Deutschlands: Ihr Bildwerk und ihre Technik.* Trier: Druck und Verlag der Kunst- und Verlags-Anstalt Schaar & Dethe; Leipzig: Karl W. Hiersemann, 1905. 39 pp., 73 b&w pls., 65 text figs.

Medieval doors of German churches; study of their ironwork reinforcements. Thirty-five-page introduction and plates, most of which reproduce line drawing details of the ironworks on specific doors. Pls. 31-67 deal with 15th-century examples, 68-73 with others of the 16th century.

ITALIAN

3. SURVEYS AND HISTORIES

1424   FERRARI, GIULIO. *Il ferro nell'arte italiana.* 3d enl. ed. Milan: Ulrico Hoepli, [1910]. 18 pp., 170 b&w pls.

Thirteen-page introduction followed by pictorial survey of 368 Italian wrought iron works from Romanesque times until the 19th century; some 15th-century examples and many of Renaissance times.

1425   PEDRINI, AUGUSTO. *Il ferro battuto, sbalzato e cesellato nell'arte italiana dal secolo undicesimo al secolo diciottesimo.* Preface by Corrado Ricci. Milan: Ulrico Hoepli, 1929. 31 pp., 316 pls.

Pictorial survey of about six hundred Italian wrought iron works, mainly gates, screens, doors, with some form of chiseling (as decoration or inscription). Includes many examples of the 15th-16th century.

SPANISH

3. SURVEYS AND HISTORIES

Books

1426   BYNE, ARTHUR, and STAPLEY, MILDRED. *Spanish Ironwork.* New York: Hispanic Society of America, 1915. 143 pp., 159 b&w figs.
Decorative ironwork in Spain from the 13th to the 19th century. Chapters deal with Gothic screens and pulpits (pp. 20- 44), fittings and domestic utensils, (45-68), development of Renaissance rejas (69-79), those within churches (80-101), windows, door-mountings and fittings (102-19); includes a checklist of ironwork in the collection of the Hispanic Society in New York.

1427   GALLEGO DE MIGUEL, AMELIA. *Rejería castellana Segovia.* Segovia: Caja de Ahorros y Monte de Piedad, 1974. 230 pp., 95 b&w figs.
Iron screens, balconies, railings, gratings, pulpits, etc. in the region of Segovia. Pp. 27-111 discuss those in the Gothic and more ornate Plateresque style (choir screens of the monastery of Santa Isabel and those of Segovia's cathedral are the most important.).

1427a   GALLEGO DE MIGUEL, AMELIA. *Rejería castellana Valladolid.* Valladolid: Institucion Cultural Simancas, 1982. 348 pp., 204 b&w figs.
Iron grilles, church choir screens, window gratings, balustrades, pulpits, and locks in Valladolid from Romanesque times through the 18th century. Cites and illustrates many 16th-century examples in situ, although a famed one, the choir screen (1596) of the cathedral, is now in the Metropolitan Museum, New York. Includes alphabetical repertory of artists.

1428   LABARTA, LOUIS. *Hierros artisticos. Fers artistiques.* 2 vols. [Barcelona: F. Seix, 1901]. 1:116 pp., 100 b&w pls.; 2:100 pp., 100 b&w pls. Spanish/French text.
Survey, through line drawings with long captions, of mostly Spanish wrought iron works. Of interest for it illustrates many unusual objects. The author, however, generally does not cite the place of conservation of these pieces.

Article

1429   SANCHIS Y SIVERA, JOSÉ. "Contribución al estudio de la ferretería valenciana en los siglos XIV y XV." *Archivo de arte valenciano* 8 (1922):72-103, 29 b&w figs.
Contribution to the study of wrought iron in Valencia of the 14th and 15th century discussing screens in local and other cathedrals, the doors of the Valencia Lonja, door-knocker, keys, etc.

6. PERMANENT COLLECTIONS

Toledo

CATEDRAL

1430   OLAGUER-FELIU ALONSO, FERNANDO DE. *Las rejas de la Catedral de Toledo.* Toledo: Disputacion Provincial, 1980. 302 pp., 66 b&w figs., line drawings.

XXV. Ironworks

Wrought iron screens for the choir and chapels of the cathedral produced by Master Pablo, Juan Francés, Juan Piñas, Masters Domingo, Céspedes, Benito, etc., mostly from the late 15th to mid-16th century.

XXVI. Scales, Weights, Tools, and Utensils

A. MULTI COUNTRY OF ORIGIN

3. SURVEYS AND HISTORIES

1431   KISCH, BRUNO. *Scales and Weights: A Historical Outline.* 3d ed. New Haven and London: Yale University Press, 1975. 318 pp., 98 b&w figs., 10 charts, 14 tables. (1st ed. 1965.)
        Useful, well-documented history of this little-studied field of metallurgy; includes many 15th-16th-century examples, elucidating their national and local characteristics.

7. EXHIBITION CATALOGS

Paris

MUSÉE DES ARTS DÉCORATIFS

1432   *Exposition des instruments et outils d'autrefois.* Paris: Musée des Arts Décoratifs, 1936. 130 pp., 8 b&w pls.
        Deals with 1,202 scientific instruments and tools dating from the 16th to the 20th century drawn from many public and private collections. Includes 16th-century spheres, sundials, astrolabes, astronomical lenses, topographical tools (no. 327 signed by Wentzel Jamnitzer), draftsmens' tools, linear and liquid measuring devices, carpenters' tools, hair curling iron, pastry tins, clocks, garden tools (no. 828 bearing Medici arms), goldsmiths' tools, shop signs, automatons.

Pontoise

MUSÉE TAVET-DELACOURT

1433   *Les Fers à repasser et leur histoire.* Exhibition catalog. Pontoise: Musée, 1981. 96 pp., 20 b&w figs.

The history of the iron as implement to press textiles. Includes ninety-nine entries; nos. 5-12 deal with examples presumably dating of the 16th century.

B. SINGLE COUNTRY OF ORIGIN

BRITISH (ENGLISH)

3. SURVEYS AND HISTORIES

1434   DENT, HERBERT. "The Bronze Wool-Weights of England." *Apollo* 10 (1929):25-33, 12 b&w figs.
A selection of shield-shaped standards used in the weighing of wool, with the arms of the reigning monarch, particularly those of Henry VII (1485-1509) and Elizabeth I (1558-1603).

6. PERMANENT COLLECTIONS

Skipton, England

CRAVEN MUSEUM

1435   GILKS, J.A. "A Fifteenth-Century Bronze Skillet from Near Pately Bridge." *Yorkshire Archaeological Journal* 51 (1979):147-50, 1 b&w fig.
Bronze globular-shaped and three-legged skillet of the late 14th-15th century.

ITALIAN

3. SURVEYS AND HISTORIES

1436   HILDBURGH, W.L. "Italian Wafering-Irons of the Fifteenth and Sixteenth Centuries." *Proceedings of the Society of Antiquaries* 2d ser. 27 (1915):161-201, b&w illus.
Series of cialde (molds) for the confection of biscuits and with elaborate stamped decoration, which the author proposes were made in Umbria, probably in Perugia.

XXVII. Clocks, Watches, Sundials, Automatons, and Scientific Instruments

A. MULTI COUNTRY OF ORIGIN

1. DICTIONARIES AND ENCYCLOPEDIAS

1437   LLOYD, H. ALAN. *The Collector's Dictionary of Clocks.* South Brunswick, N.J.: A.S. Barnes & Co., 1965. 214 pp., 1 color fig., 509 b&w figs.
Particularly useful for its clear explanation of technical facts.

1438   SMITH, ALAN, ed. *The Country Life International Dictionary of Clocks,* by eighteen contributors. London, New York, Sydney, Toronto: Hamlyn Publishing Group for Country Life Books, 1979. 351 pp., 63 color pls., numerous b&w figs.
Provides basic information on styles, types, mechanical movements, tools, materials, workshop methods, brief history of clockmaking by country, clockmaking workshops, biographical data on some lesser-known clockmakers; nineteen pages dedicated to sundials and astronomical instruments.

2. BIOGRAPHICAL DICTIONARIES

1439   BAILLIE, G.H. *Watchmakers and Clockmakers of the World.* 3d ed. London: N.A.G. Press, 1951. Reprint. 1974. 421 pp. (1st ed. London: Methuen & Co., 1929.)
Alphabetical listing of about thirty-five thousand names of makers (last name, first name, place of activity, date[s], specialty and/or posts) from medieval times until shortly after 1825.

3. SURVEYS AND HISTORIES

Books

1440   BAILLIE, G.H. *Watches: Their History, Decoration and Mechanism.* London: Methuen & Co., 1929. 383 pp., 1 color pl., 65 b&w pls.
Standard history of watchmaking—movements, decoration of casements, national and regional characteristics—from Peter Henlein's creations of 1510 in Nuremberg until the 19th century. Author cites many goldsmith-watchmakers of the 16th century.

1441   BASSERMANN-JORDAN, ERNST VON. *Uhren.* Bibliothek für Kunst - und Antiquitätenfreunde, vol. 7. Brunswick: Klinkhardt & Biermann, 1961. 518 pp., 20 color pls.,
388 b&w figs.
Comprehensive survey of watches and clocks and earlier time devices; pp. 27-94 deal
in large part with the 16th century.

1442   BRITTEN, FREDERICK JAMES. *Britten's Old Clocks and Watches and Their Makers:
A History of Styles in Clocks and Watches and Their Mechanisms,* edited by G.H. Baillie,
Courtenay Ilbert, and Cecil Clutton. 9th ed. rev. and enl. by Cecil Clutton. London:
Methuen in association with E. & F.N. Spor, 1982. 727 pp., 9 color pls., 348 b&w figs.
(1st ed. 1899.)
Indispensibele early reference on the history of clock and watch styles from earliest
times to the 20th century. All the important events in horological history are reviewed and
technical explanation clearly presented for the layman (for a more detailed study of
mechanisms including description of each part, functions of tools and machinery, etc., see Britten's *Watch and Clock Maker's Handbook: Dictionary and Guide* of 1878 [16th ed., edited by
R. Good, 1978]). For the period 1400-1600, see chaps. 1-2 (pp. 1-70). Appendix 1 presents a
chronologically arranged biography of famous makers; appendix 2 is an alphabetical list of
recorded clock and watch makers. Twelve-page glossary.

1443   BRUSA, GIUSEPPE. *L'arte dell'orologeria in Europa: Sette secoli di orologi meccanici.*
Busto Arsizio: Bramante, 1978. 491 pp. including 112 color figs., 849 b&w figs.
Comprehensive study of mechanical clocks and watches in Europe from the 14th to
the 20th century with emphasis on scientific and technical aspects. Major developments,
description of timepieces in contemporary documents and representations in miniatures;
detailed entries for all illustrations of examples which are in European collections. Twenty-
two-page glossary.

1444   BRUTON, ERIC. *The History of Clocks and Watches.* New York: Rizzoli, 1979. 288
pp., 120 color figs. 283 b&w figs.
General survey; pertinent to the years 1400-1600 are sand glass (p. 29), medieval and
Renaissance turret clocks (38-42), astronomical clocks (45), spring-driven domestic clocks (47-
50), personal portable time keepers (54-58), clockmaking centers (61- 63), early watches (109-
10), astronomical instruments and timepieces (211-20).

1445   CHAPUIS, ALFRED. *De Horologiis in arte: L'Horloge et la montre à travers les âges,
d'après les documents du temps.* Lausanne: Scriptar S.A., 1954. 154 pp., 1 color pl., 212
b&w pls.
Instruments for measuring time as seen in paintings, miniatures, and sculpture from
antiquity to the present: development of technique, evolution of style. For the 15th-16th century see pp. 3-5, 10-48, 152-53.

1446   CLUTTON, CECIL, and DANIELS, GEORGE. *Watches: A Complete History of the
Technical and Decorative Development of the Watch.* 3d rev. and enl. ed. London:
Sotheby Parke Bernet, 1979. 312 pp., 16 color pls., 120 b&w pls. (1st ed. London: B.T.
Batsford, 1965.)
Movements and decoration from the 14th to the 20th century. Mostly on later
watches but for the period 1400-1600, see pp. 29-35, 81-84, 99. Eleven-page glossary.

1447   GARCÍA FRANCO, SALVADOR. *Catálogo crítico de astrolabios existentes en España.* Madrid: Instituto Histórico de Marina, 1945. 446 pp., 57 b&w figs., numerous line drawings.

Study of the evolution of the astrolabe as a scientific instrument and as a manifestation of progress based on twenty examples in Spanish public collections. Nine date of the 16th century.

1448   GUNTHER, ROBERT T. *The Astrolabes of the World.* 2 vols. in 1. London: Holland Press, 1976. 609 pp., 153 b&w pls. (1st ed. 1932.)

Comprehensive study of history, usage, application, and design, with primary emphasis on technical aspects. Vol. 1: Eastern astrolabes; vol. 2: Western astrolabes dating up to the 17th century, including many of 1400-1600. Catalog of representative examples from the Lewis Evans Collection, Ashmolean Museum, Oxford, the British Museum, and other public and private collections. Many reprints of early treatises, essays, and technical observations. Twenty-three pages of bibliography listing many primary sources.

1449   JAGGER, CEDRIC. *Royal Clocks: The British Monarchy and Its Timekeepers 1300-1900.* London: Robert Hale, 1983. 340 pp., 394 color and b&w figs.

Briefly discussed in the first chapter are Henry VIII's astrolabe of ca. 1545, the Royal Tudor Clock (a German work of ca. 1540), and some less important 16th century examples, as well as others mentioned in royal inventories.

1450   LLOYD, H. ALAN. *Some Outstanding Clocks over Seven Hundred Years 1250-1950.* 2d ed. Woodbridge, Suffolk: Antique Collectors Club, 1981. 333 pp. with 42 b&w text figs. (1st ed. London: Leonard Hill [Books], 1958.)

Pertinent to the period 1400-1600 in this survey are pp. 2-69 with early spring-driven clocks, carillons, minute hands, fusee chains, of Nuremberg, Strasbourg; Eberhart Baldewin's astronomical (1561) and plantary clocks; also Jobst Burgi table clocks of the end of the 16th century.

1451   MEIS, REINHARD.   *Die alte Uhr: Geschichte--Technik--Stil.* 2 vols.   Brunswick: Klinkhardt & Biermann, 1978. 1:336 pp., 16 color pls., 474 b&w figs.; 2: 306 pp., 16 color pls., 579 b&w figs.

Clocks and watches from medieval to modern times. Vol. 1 deals with technology in all countries; vol. 2 with casements and their decoration. The period 1400-1650 is covered on pp. 1-42 with examples from Swiss and German collections.

1452   MICHEL, HENRI. *Scientific Instruments in Art and History.* Translated by R.E.W. and Francis R. Maddison. London: Barrie & Rockliff, 1967. 208 pp., 103 color pls., line drawings.

Form and function of instruments used for physical measurement, drawing, calculating, and to measure the earth, the heavens, and time seen in historical context and in terms of aesthetic value; technical explanations; detailed entries to accompany plates. Includes representative examples of the 15th-16th century: measures, standards of weight, drawing instruments, rule, water level, miner's compass, geometrical measures, astrolabes, sundials, astronomical rings, armillary spheres, celestial globe, equatorium. Index of makers, designers, and collectors.

1453   TARDY, [HENRI LENGELLÉ]. *La Pendule française: La Pendule dans le monde.* Part 4, *Europe du nord, centrale, orientale et méditerranéenne, Japon.* 5th rev. and enl. ed. Paris: Tardy, 1985. 615 pp., 147 color pls., numerous b&w figs. (1st ed. 1949.)

History of clockmaking outside France; especially valuable for the quantity and selection of its illustrations showing examples from public and private collections with captions both in French and English. Included are 15th-16th century Swiss, German, Austrian, Czech, Polish, Danish, Italian, and Spanish mechanisms generally in ornamented casements.

Articles

1454 BORN, WOLFGANG. "Early European Automatons." *Connoisseur* 100 (1937): Part 1, 123-29, 10 b&w figs.; part 2, 246-52, 14 b&w figs.
Part 1: evolution of clocks with movable figures from Egyptian times (water-clocks) to the late 16th century when Augsburg became the clockmaking center of Europe: increased technical sophistication, main clockmakers and patrons, examples in the British Museum (by Nuremberg maker Isaak Habrecht), Technisches Museum, Vienna (of 1555 by Philippus Imss of Tubingen on order of Charles V), Kunsthistorisches Museum, Vienna (Augsburg, ca. 1590, presented to Archduke Ferdinand of Tyrol by Duke Ferdinand of Bavaria), etc.; part 2: intricate moving table automatons, some incorporating clocks, favored by Renaissance princes to delight their guests. Involved examples in the shape of Diana riding a centaur, elephant, chariot, ships, made in Augsburg in the late 16th-century, many after Oriental models; their popularity until the 18th century.

1455 CULVER, HENRY B. "Early Scientific Instruments." *Connoisseur* 97 (1936):147-151, 10 b&w figs.
Among objects of the 16th-17th century that combined artistic qualitites and usefulness, are discussed a signed Italian bronze astrolabe dated 1592, a signed German miniature armillary Ptolemaic sphere of 1593, two late 16th-century surveyor's instruments, and a gunner's level. Most of these are in private English collections.

1456 STURM, FABIENNE XAVIÈRE. "Montres de la Renaissance, Suisse et Allemagne 1560-1620." *Musées de Genève* 21 (1980):2-5, 4 b&w figs.
Swiss and German clocks and watches dating 1560-1620 in a private Basel collection.

4. BIBLIOGRAPHICAL GUIDES

1457 BAILLIE, G.H. *Clocks and Watches: An Historical Bibliography*. London: N.A.G. Press, 1951. 427 pp., 118 b&w line drawings. Reprint. London: Holland Press, 1978.
Comprehensively annotated bibliography of all books on horology up to 1800.

6. PERMANENT COLLECTIONS

Basel

HISTORISCHES MUSEUM

1458 *Die Uhrensammlung Nathan-Rupp im Historischen Museum Basel*. Catalog by Hans Christoph Ackermann. Munich: George D.W. Callwey, 1984. 333 pp., 53 color pls., numerous b&w figs.
The Nathan-Rupp bequest, an exceptional collection of 242 clocks and watches including 16th century examples (nos. 18-20, 32-35, 43-44, 46-52, 90-92, 94-96, 105, 107, 221-23), which are mostly South German and some French. Good color plates.

Brussels

MUSÉES ROYAUX D'ART ET D'HISTOIRE

1459 MICHEL, HENRI. "Les Instruments anciens de mathématiques des Musées d'Art et d'Histoire." *Bulletin des Musées Royaux d'Art et d'Histoire* 7(1935):26-34, 13 b&w figs.
Objects used for astronomy, topography, and to measure time and space, among which some 16th-century sundials and astrolabes.

London

BRITISH MUSEUM

1460 TAIT, HUGH. *Clocks and Watches.* London: British Museum Publications, 1983. 72 pp., 36 color figs., 40 b&w figs.
Short monograph outlining main developments of mechanical clocks and watchmaking harnessing the power of the falling weight and the unwinding spring from the Middle Ages to the 19th century as illustrated by numerous examples in the British Museum — clockmakers, movements, types of escapement, case design, etc.

Milan

MUSEO D'ARTI APPLICATE

1461 *Museo d'Arti Applicate: Strumenti scientifici-orologi.* Catalog by Tullio Tomba and Giuseppe Brusa. Milan: Electa, 1983. 164 pp., 39 color figs., 136 b&w figs.
Catalog of thirty-three scientific instruments, among which are three 15th- and 16th-century astrolabes and a 16th-century sundial, and sixty-two clocks and watches including two German watches of the late 16th century.

MUSEO POLDI PEZZOLI

1462 *Gli orologi.* Catalog by Giuseppe Brusa. Milan: Museo Poldi Pezzoli, 1974. 84 pp., 71 b&w pls.
The Bruno Falck collection of watches — the largest on public view in Italy — including four 16th-century scientific instruments and fourteen 16th-century German and French clocks (one in the form of a breviary, another shaped as an ostensory).

See also entry 72.

7. EXHIBITION CATALOGS

Berlin

STAATLICHE MUSEEN PREUSSISCHER KULTURBESITZ, KUNSTGEWERBEMUSEUM

1463 *Winkelmessinstruments vom 16. bis zum frühen 19. Jahrhundert.* Exhibition catalog by Franz Adrian Dreier. Berlin: Staatliche Museen Preussischer Kulturbesitz, 1980. 168 pp., 8 color figs., 94 b&w figs.

Thirty-one chapters deal with the history and use of scientific instruments such as astronomical, geodetic, and nautical from the 16th-19th century; chronological tables, glossary of astronomical terms. Detailed entries for sixty-eight objects, each reproduced.

New York

METROPOLITAN MUSEUM OF ART

1464   *Northern European Clocks in New York Collections.* Exhibition catalog by Clare Vincent. New York: Metropolitan Museum of Art, 1972. 25 pp., 27 b&w figs.
Thirteen-page introductory essay deals with the power sources, types, and designs of the European domestic clock of the 14th-18th century; cat. nos. 1-6, 10-11, 13-18, 25-27, pertain to 16th-century French, German, Austrian, and English spring-driven table clocks.

Pforzheim

SCHMUCKMUSEUM

1465   *Die Uhr: Zeitmesser und Schmuck in fünf Jahrhunderten.* Exhibition catalog by Alfred Leiter and Alma Helfrich-Dörner. Kornwestheim: Alfred Reichert KG, 1967. 359 pp., 17 color pls., numerous b&w pls., line drawings.
Timepieces in goldsmith work dating from 1530 to 1870. Pp. 22-101 illustrate and briefly describe German, French Czech, Italian watches, clocks lent from public and private German and Swiss collections.

8. PRIVATE COLLECTION, AUCTION, AND DEALER CATALOGS

BILLMEIR COLLECTION

1466   JOSTEN, C.H. "Scientific Instruments from the Thirteenth to the Nineteenth Century." *Connoisseur* 134 (1954):85-91, 25 b&w figs.
Includes 16th-century European astrolabes, an armillary sphere, astronomical ring, sundials, a nocturnal, and topological instruments, many signed and dated, from this London collection.

PIERPONT MORGAN COLLECTION

1467   WILLIAMSON, G.C. *Catalogue of the Collection of Watches the Property of J. Pierpont Morgan.* London: Privately Printed at the Chiswick Press, 1912. 305 pp., 92 photogravure pls., 3 b&w pls.
Extraordinary collection of 242 outstanding watches of the 16th-18th century (many of the 16th) made in France (Paris, Azen, Autun, Blois, Lyon, Rouen, etc.—85 pieces), Germany and Austria (mostly Augsburg—39 pieces), London (93 pieces), Holland and Flanders (9 pieces), Russia (one 16th-century example), and Switzerland and Italy (15 pieces), preceded by a clear thirty-six page exposition on the development of the watch, changes in shape (e.g., cross-shaped, as a ring, pocket watches), types of decoration (engraved, enamel, etc.), historiated subjects, use as gifts.

SARASIN-VONDER MÜHLL COLLECTION

1468   *Uhren-Sammlung Ernst Sarasin-Vonder Mühll, Basel.* Sale held in Lucerne at the Galerie Fischer 18 November 1948. 53 pp., 32 b&w pls.
Dispersal of famed Basel collection of 197 timepieces, lots 1-24 being German, Hungarian, French, and Dutch 16th-century watches encased in goldsmith work.

B. SINGLE COUNTRY OF ORIGIN

BRITISH
(ENGLISH AND SCOTTISH)

3. SURVEYS AND HISTORIES

1469   DAWSON, PERCY G.; DROVER, C.B.; and PARKES, D.W. *Early English Clocks: A Discussion of Domestic Clocks up to the Beginning of the Eighteenth Century.* [London]: Antique Collectors' Club, 1982. 550 pp., 35 color figs., 800 b&w figs.
Domestic clockmaking: types, mechanisms, and casing (many richly decorated); for 16th-century examples, see chap. 1, pp. 13-41. Makers' index.

1470   SMITH, JOHN. *Old Scottish Clockmakers from 1453 to 1850.* 2d rev. and enl. ed. Edinburgh: Oliver & Boyd, 1921. 452 pp., 25 pls. (1st ed. Edinburgh, 1903.)
Includes some examples of the 15th-16th century.

FRENCH

2. BIOGRAPHICAL DICTIONARIES

1471   TARDY; assisted by BRATEAU, PAUL; DAUMAS, M.; and ARDIGNAC, ROBERT. *Dictionnaire des horlogers français.* Paris: Tardy, 1972. 760 pp., numerous b&w figs. and line drawings.
Dictionary of some twenty-three thousand French clock- and watchmakers from 1292 to the 20th century. Entries vary considerable in length but are generally more useful than Baillie, *Watchmakers and Clockmakers* (see entry 1439).

3. SURVEYS AND HISTORIES

1472   BASSERMANN-JORDAN, ERNST VON. *The Clock of Philip the Good of Burgundy.* Leipzig: Wilhelm Diebener, n.d. 43 pp., 1 color pl., 40 b&w figs.
Provenance and description of double-spired cathedral-shaped timepiece of ca. 1430 held to be oldest wheel-clock preserved, the oldest spring-actuated clock, and the oldest clock with a fusee.

1473   DEVELLE, E. *Les Horlogers blésois au XVIe et au XVIIe siécle.* Nogent-le-Roi: Librairie des Arts et Métiers-Éditions, 1917. 2d ed. 459 pp., 30 b&w pls. Reprint. 1978. (1st ed. 1912.)

History of watch and clockmaking in Blois in the 16th-17th century: recruitment of craftsmen, apprenticeship, work conditions, production time, statutes, contracts, specialities, abuses, etc. Twenty-seven-page catalog of extant signed watches and clocks produced in Blois in various public and private European collections. 239-page repertory of Blois workshops, chronologically arranged.

1474   EDEY, WINTHROP. *French Clocks.* New York: Walker & Co., [1967]. 83 pp., 2 color pls., 40 b&w figs.
    Brief survey from the Renaissance through the 18th century. Chap. 2 gives essential characteristics of 16th-century examples.

1475   SCHOPPIG, RENÉ. *L'Horloge française à poids. Sa période artisanale du XVIe siècle au début du XIXe siècle.* Part 1. Paris: Tardy, 1984. 271 pp., 32 color illus., numerous b&w figs. and technical drawings.
    Technical study of large domestic and civic French clocks designed to aid collectors in tracing the origins of a piece and to recognize its restoration. Detailed descriptions of exterior shape and decoration and of interior functioning of mechanisms. Mostly later examples but includes several dating of the 16th century (see especially pp. 30-34 and 65-79).

1476   TARDY. *La Pendule française dans le monde.* Part 1, *Des Origines à la transition Louis XV-Louis XVI.* 5th rev. and enl. ed. Paris: Tardy, 1981. 356 pp., 46 color pls., numerous b&w figs. (1st ed. 1949.)
    French clocks from ca. 1400 through the mid-eighteenth century with emphasis on their shape, casements, and dial decoration; includes abundant comparative material drawn from prints, paintings, and illuminated manuscripts. Pertinent to the period 1400-1600 are pp. 28-116. While the text is in French, the captions are French/English.

1476a   TARDY. *La Pendule française des origines à nos jours.* Rev. ed. Paris: Tardy, 1974. Part 1, *De L'Horloge gothique à la pendule Louis XV;* part 2, *De Louis XVI à nos jours;* part 3, *Les Provinces françaises, horloges et pendules étrangères.* 893 pp., many b&w figs. (1st ed. 1949.)
    History of French clockmaking from the 14th to the 20th century presented by and large from an aesthetic point of view. For the 15th-16th century, see part 1, pp. 6-21, and part 3, which deals with clocks of all periods whose provenance is in French clockmaking centers other than Paris and with clocks from other countries, passim.

6. PERMANENT COLLECTIONS

Paris

MUSÉE DE CLUNY

1477   UNGERER, THÉODORE. "Une Horloge de table d' Isaac Habrecht (vers 1580)." *Archives alsaciennes d'histoire de l'art* 8 (1929):125-28, 1 b&w fig.; "Une Horloge astronomique disparue d'Isaac Habrecht (1583)." *Archives alsaciennes d'histoire de l'art* 9 (1930):101-11, 2 b&w figs.
    Atronomical table clock in the museum attributed to the Strasbourg clockmaker Isaac Habrecht and dated to ca. 1580. Records dealing with a large astronomical clock produced by the same craftsman ca. 1583 for Hans Fugger of Augsburg.

GERMAN

3. SURVEYS AND HISTORIES

Book

1478   MAURICE, KLAUS. *Die deutsche Räderuhr. Zur Kunst und Technik des mechanischen Zeitmessers in deutschen Sprachraum.* 2 vols. Munich: C.H. Beck, 1976. 1:322 pp., 18 color pls., 166 b&w figs.; 2:125 pp., 1,443 b&w figs.

     Comprehensive study of German clocks (14th-early 20th century). Vol. 1, chap. 1 (pp. 5-16) introduces the symbolic significance of the clock as an analogy and metaphor; chap. 2 (17-34) deals with chronological (calendar, astronomy, daily and hourly) clocks; chap. 3 (35-69), monumental astronomical clocks; chap. 4 (70-126) is concerned with all varieties of weight and spring-driven clocks of the 16th century; chap. 5 (127-93), production centers and individual makers in Vienna, Dresden, Innsbruck, Munich, Strasbourg, Nuremberg, Kassel, Prague, and Augsburg. Vol. 2: 1,184 catalog entries and plates.

Articles

1479   ECKHARDT, WOLFGANG. "Erasmus Habermel—zur Biographie des Instrumentenmachers Kaiser Rudolfs II." *Jahrbuch der hamburger Kunstsammlungen* 21 (1976):55-92, 24 b&w figs.

     Spheres, compasses, and other scientific instruments produced in the late 16th century by Erasmus Habermel for Emperor Rudolf II at his court of Prague.

1480   HAYWARD, J.F. "The Celestial Globes of Georg Roll and Johannes Reinhold." *Connoisseur* 126 (1950):167-72, 220; 7 b&w figs.

     Six astronomical clocks of engraved gilt-bronze made between 1584-89 at the court of Rudolph II in Prague by Roll and Reinhold, now in Vienna, London, Paris, Dresden, and Naples.

6. PERMANENT COLLECTIONS

Leningrad

HERMITAGE

1481   MATVEEV, V. "Sixteenth-Century Sundials." *Soobscenija, Hermitage* 44 (1979):27-29, 5 b&w figs.

     16th-century portable sundials, four made in Augsburg in 1584 by J. Reinhold and G. Roll, and two in Nuremberg, one of these by P. Reinmann.

London

SOCIETY OF ANTIQUARIES

1482   HOLIŃSKI ALFRED. "Jacob Zech and a Royal Fusee Clock." *Connoisseur* 152 (1963):183-87, 14 b&w figs.

     Description and historical background of the oldest dated (1525) and signed (Jacob Zech of Prague) astronomical clock known, purported to have been made for the Polish king Sigismund I and formerly housed in Wawel Castle, Kraków.

Nuremberg

GERMANISCHES NATIONALMUSEUM

1483   *Schätze der Astronomie: Arabische und deutsche Instrumente aus dem Germanischen Nationalmuseum.* Exhibition catalog by Johannes Willers and Karin Holzamer, edited by Gerhard Bott. Nuremberg: Germanisches Nationalmuseum, 1983. 140 pp., 8 color pls., 38 b&w figs. German/English/Arabic text.

    Forty-one Arabic and German astronomical instruments and related objects from the permanent collection ranging from the 11th through 18th century. Includes several examples of 1400-1600: celestial globes, folding and table sundials, astrolabes, torquetum, clock, pocket calendar, telemeter, compasses, etc. Catalog entries are preceded by four-page history of astronomy in Islamic and European countries and followed by four-page glossary.

Vienna

KUNSTHISTORISCHES MUSEUM

1484   BERTELE, H. VON. "Jost Burgis Beitrag zur Formentwicklung der Uhren." *Jahrbuch der kunsthistorischen Sammlungen in Wien* n.s. 15 (1955):169-88, 22 b&w figs.

    Clocks by Jost Burgis, active 1579-1639 at the courts of Kassel and Prague; one of his major productions of 1594 encased in rock crystal in the collection of this museum.

1485   NEUMANN, ERWIN. "Die Tischuhr des Jeremias Metzker von 1564 und ihre nächsten Verwandten. Bemerkungen zur Formengeschichte einer Gruppe süddeutscher Stutzuhren der Renaissance." *Jahrbuch der kunsthistorishen Sammlungen in Wien* 57 (1961):89-122, 34 b&w figs.

    A gilt-silver table clock of 1564 by the Augsburg clockmaker Jeremias Metzker, now in this collection, is examined in relation to a group of similar South German clocks from various European and U.S. collections featuring highly ornate casements, dials (both astrological and horological), and decorative finials.

Waddesdon

WADDESDON MANOR

1486   WARD, F.A.B. "An Outstanding Domestic Clock Rediscovered—at Waddesdon." *Connoisseur* 160 (1965):34- 35, 1 b&w fig.

    A signed clock by Jeremias Metzker of Augsburg dated 1563, very similar to the clock by the same clockmaker dated of a year later in the Kunsthistorisches Museum, Vienna.

Wuppertal

WUPPERTALER UHRENMUSEUM

1487   *Das Wuppertaler Uhrenmuseum* by Jürgen Abeler. Berlin and New York: Walter de Gruyter, 1971. 86 pp., 4 color pls., 48 b&w figs., line drawings.

    Overview of the museum's main holdings including an astronomical pocket watch of 1568 by Nicolas Rensberger, an automat clock of the Calvary (Augsburg/Nuremberg) of ca. 1580, and several other South German timepieces of the late 16th century.

7. EXHIBITION CATALOGS

Washington

SMITHSONIAN INSTITUTION

1488   *The Clockwork Universe: German Clocks and Automata 1550-1650.* Exhibition catalog edited by Klaus Maurice and Otto Mayr. New York: Neale Watson Academic Publications, 1980. 321 pp., 32 color pls., 213 b&w figs.
   Fourteen essays by various contributors discuss in depth mechanical clocks as technical, intellectual, social, and artistic expressions of German-speaking Central Europe. 120 catalog entries illustrate exceptional pieces from European and American Museums and private collections; including many unique automatons — musical clocks, mechanical theatres, and celestial pieces. Catalog arranged thematically with sixty-eight entries of pieces dating of 1600 or earlier. Many technical diagrams and useful glossary.

NETHERLANDISH

3. SURVEYS AND HISTORIES

1489   MORPURGO, ENRICO. *Nedelandse klokken- en horlogemakers vanaf 1300.* Amsterdam: Scheltema & Holkema nv, 1970. 152 pp.
   Dictionary of Dutch clock- and watchmakers from 1300 through the 19th century.

SCANDINAVIA (NORWEGIAN)

3. SURVEYS AND HISTORIES

1490   INGSTAD, OLAV. *Urmakerkunst: Norge fra midten av 1500- arene til laugstidens slutt.* Oslo: Gyldendal, 1980. 464 pp., illus.
   The art of watchmaking in Norway from the mid-16th century until the abolition of the guild system. Some early examples are discussed.

SWISS

3. SURVEYS AND HISTORIES

1491   TARDY. *Les Plus Belles Pendules suisses.* Paris: Tardy, 1984. 127 pp., 78 color plates, numerous b&w figs.
   In this pictorial survey, the first clocks discussed date of 1564-99 and were made by the Liechti family of Winterthur, and Joachim Halbrecht of Schaffhausen.

XXVIII. Arms and Armor

A. MULTI COUNTRY OF ORIGIN

Works Dealing with Both Arms and Armor

1. DICTIONARIES AND ENCYCLOPEDIAS

1492   *The Complete Encyclopedia of Arms and Weapons.* Edited by Leonid Tarassuk and Claude Blair. Translated by Sylvia Milcahy, Simon Pleasance, and Hugh Young. New York: Simon & Schuster, 1982. 544 pp., 90 color pls., 469 b&w figs. of line drawings. (Originally published as *Enciclopedia ragionata delle armi* [Milan: Mondadori, 1979].)

      Comprehensive corpus dealing with all periods and countries. Alphabetically arranged by individual arms and armor type, their component parts, style and decoration; principal evolutions traced from origin.

1493   GYNGELL, DUDLEY S. HAWTREY. *Armourers Marks Being a Compilation of Known Marks of Armourers, Swordsmiths and Gunsmiths.* London: Thorsons Publishers, 1959. 131 pp., numerous facsimile armourers' marks.

      Reproduction by means of sketches of over two thousand marks. Useful for tracing and identifying armor, arms, and guns to armorers and gunmakers from the 14th to the 18th century in Austro-Hungary, Belgium, Britain, France, Germany, Holland, Italy , Spain, and Switzerland.

1494   STONE, GEORGE CAMERON. *A Glossary of the Construction, Decoration and Use of Arms and Armor in All Countries and in All Times, Together with Some Closely Related Subjects.* Portland, Me.: Southworth Press, 1934. 694 pp., 876 b&w figs.

      Description of different types of arms and armor and of their component parts, of methods of constructing, decorating, and using them. Entries for development of types and of styles of decoration and for main armorers. Eight-page bibliography.

3. SURVEYS AND HISTORIES

1495   CLEPHAM, ROBERT COLTMAN. *The Defensive Armour and the Weapons and Engines of War of Medieval Times and of the "Renaissance."* London: Walter Scott, 1900. 237 pp., 51 b&w illus.

Early study of the history of arms and armor with emphasis on defensive armor and weapons; deals with wide variety of mail, helms, plate armor, swords, daggers, crossbows, etc. Includes a brief chapter on tournaments and mentions important European collections.

1496   DEMMIN, AUGUSTE. *Guide des amateurs d'armes et armures anciennes par ordre chronologique depuis le temps les plus reculés jusqu'à nos jours.* Paris: Ve Jules Renouard, 1869. 628 pp., 1,700 line drawings, 200 makers' marks.

Arms and armor from earliest times (B.C.) to the 19th century; chronological framework with description of complete suits and then of component parts by types. Thirty pages of monograms, initials, and names of German, Italian, Spanish, Portuguese, French, English, Swiss, Flemish, and Dutch armorers. Line drawings after engravings, manuscripts, and reliefs, as well as from extant examples in public and private collections.

1497   LAKING, GUY FRANCIS. *A Record of European Armour and Arms through Seven Centuries.* Introduction by Baron [C.A.] de Cosson, prefaces and appendixes by Francis Henry Cripps-Day. Vol. 1 (1920), 286 pp.; vol. 2 (1920), 347 pp.; vol. 3 (1920), 358 pp.; vol. 4 (1921), 353 pp.; vol. 5 (1922), 383 pp.; total of 1,805 b&w figs. numbered consecutively throughout 5 vols. London: G. Bell & Sons.

Comprehensive survey of European arms and armor of the 11th to the 17th century. Pertinent to 1400-1600 are: vol 1, general history of 15th century armor (pp. 160-224), 15th-century basinet (225-65); vol. 2, salade (1-56), war hats (57-70), armet head pieces (71-98), 15th-century helms (99-166), chain mail and interlined textile defenses (167-202), gauntlets (203-22), 15th-century shields (253-50) and swords (251-310), 15th- and 16th-century British ceremonial swords (311-47); vol. 3, daggers (1-80), hafted weapons (81-126), crossbows (127-46), equestrian mountings (147-208), 16th-century Landsknecht armor (272-301), Spanish and French imports and manufacturing (302-58); vol. 4, English "Greenwich" School (1-76), Pisan armors (77-86), 16th-century close helmets (87-124), burgonet helmets (125-92), morions and cabassets (193-217), pageant shields (218-59), 16th-century swords and rapiers (260-329) and hafted weapons (330-53); vol. 5, appendixes: notes on forgeries (111-48), list of pieces preserved in British churches (151-273).

1498   MEYRICK, SAMUEL RUSH. *A Critical Inquiry into Antient Armour as it Existed in Europe, but Particularly in England from the Norman Conquest to the Reign of King Charles II, with a Glossary of Military Terms of the Middle Ages.* 3 vols. London: Robert Jennings, 1824. 1:282 pp., 30 handcolored pls. and line drawings; vol. 2:297 pp., 36 handcolored pls. and line drawings; 3:283 pp., 14 handcolored pls. and line drawings.

Study in the spirit of the Romantic age on the history of English, Norman, Welsh, Danish, etc., armors, discussed by and large chronologically by English reigns. For the 15th century, see vol. 2, pp., 56-240; for the 16th century, vol. 2, 241-97, and vol. 3, 1-72.

1499   NORMAN, VESEY. *Arms and Armor.* New York: G. P. Putnam's Sons, 1964. 128 pp., 33 color figs., 96 b&w figs.

Introduction to the history of arms and armor. Chap. 3 (pp. 39-57) deals with development of 15th-century German and Italian armor for war and tournaments; chap. 4 (59-80) deals with Italian, German, Spanish, and French 16th-century armor; chap. 6 (95-109) traces development of the sword and dagger; chap. 7 (111-28) deals with other weapons including infantry spears, maces, war hammers, bows. Frequent reference to the depiction of arms and armor in painting, illumination, and relief sculpture of the period. No footnotes or bibliography.

1500   THOMAS, BRUNO; GAMBER, ORTWIN; and SCHEDELMANN, HANS. *Arms and Armor of the Western World.* Translated by Ilse Bloom and William Reid. New York: McGraw-Hill Book Co., 1964. 251 pp., 46 color pls., 52 b&w pls.

Twenty-three-page introduction deals with weapons through history—their aesthetic appeal and use, manufacture, collectors and collections. Ninety-seven catalog entries discuss and illustrate choice pieces from the 13th to the 19th century; includes many examples of swords, maces, helmets, crossbows, battleaxes and full suits of armor of the 15th and 16th century (cat. nos. 4-62).

5. GENERAL REFERENCES TO AUCTION CATALOGS

1501   CRIPPS-DAY, FRANCIS HENRY. *A Record of Armour Sales 1881-1924.* London: G. Bell & Sons, 1925. 395 pp., 210 b&w figs.

Compendium of abridged entries of arms and armor from sales catalogs of major auctions in Great Britain, France, Germany, and Italy; includes price fetched for each lot number; arranged chronologically. Forty-eight-page essay discusses the formation and dispersal of collections. Extensive indexes of arms and armor elements, of names, and of inscriptions and armorers' marks.

6. PERMANENT COLLECTIONS

Budapest

MAGYAR NEMZETI MÚZEUM

1502   *The Treasures of the Hungarian National Museum: Arms and Armor.* Catalog by Ferenc Temesváry. Translated by R.D.C. Sturgess. Budapest: Helikon Kiado/Corvina Kiado, 1982. 71 pp., 16 color pls., 36 b&w pls.

Highlights of holdings. Includes thirty pieces of the 15th-16th century from Hungary, Transylvania, Augsburg (by Wilhelm von Worms), Nuremberg, Italy, Flanders; particularly outstanding are the arms of Ferdinand of Tyrol, armor of Louis II, a papal sword, also a Rhenish ivory saddle.

Churburg

BURG/RÜSTKAMMER

1503   TRAPP, OSWALD. *The Armoury of the Castle of Churburg.* Translated with a preface by James Gow Mann. London: Methuen & Co., 1929. 370 pp., 72 b&w pls.

Catalog of 369 detailed entries inventorying the important arms and armor collection of the Tyrolean castle of Churburg, stronghold of the lords of Matsch. Collection is significant since it has remained intact from its inception thus preserving marks of ownership as well as homogeneous suits. Includes a twenty-eight-page translator's preface and a fifty- three-page historical introduction with background information on the collection. The most important pieces of German and Italian origin are illustrated in black and white plates, as well as diagrams and details of armorers' marks. The majority of objects in the collection are of the period 1400-1600; included are mail and brigandine (nos. 1-12), Gothic armor (nos. 18-68), Maximilian armor (nos. 69-96), miscellaneous suits and components of the 16th century (nos. 97-269), shields (nos. 270-71), weapons, including swords, maces, pole arms, crossbows, and parts of firearms (nos. 272-363). Valuable table of armorers' marks (pp. 301-10).

Cleveland

CLEVELAND MUSEUM OF ART

1504 *Catalogue of the Severance Collection of Arms and Armor in The Cleveland Museum of Art.* Permanent collection catalog by Helen Ives Gilchrist. Cleveland: Cleveland Museum of Art, 1924. 52 b&w pls.

565 short entries of 15th-18th-century European examples in the museum at the time of publication; majority of pieces date from 1400-1600 including suits of armor, component pieces, helmets, swords, guns, pole arms, daggers, riding equipment, maces, shields, etc. Volume concludes with list of armorers' names and marks.

Dresden

HISTORISCHES MUSEUM

1505 *Princely Arms and Armour: A Selection from the Dresden Collection,* by Johannes Schöbel. Translated by M.O.A. Stanton. London: Barrie & Jenkins, 1975. 255 pp., 52 color figs., 131 b&w figs.

183 entries of 16th-18th-century parade arms and armor originally from the armory of the electors and kings of Saxony. Majority of pieces are of German origin and date from the 15th- 16th century with representative examples from France, Italy, Hungary, Spain, and Flanders. Entries are typologically arranged (including defensive arms, edged weapons, firearms, and hunting weapons) with five/six page essay preceding each section.

Edinburgh

ROYAL SCOTTISH MUSEUM

1506 LAKING, GUY. "The Nöel Paton Collection of Arms and Armour Now in the Royal Scottish Museum, Edinburgh—I." *Burlington Magazine* 17 (1910):148-58, 2 b&w pls.

Author distinguishes between important authentic French, English, Scottish, Hungarian pieces in the collection and forgeries.

Florence

MUSEO STIBBERT

1507 BUTTIN, CH. "Le Musée Stibbert à Florence." *Les Arts* 105 (1910):2-32, 39 b&w figs.

Description of some of the principle arms and armor in this museum—complete suits, jousting armor, horse armor, helmets, swords—mostly of the 15th-16th century and of German and Italian origin.

See also entry 69

Glasgow

GLASGOW MUSEUMS AND ART GALLERIES—KELVINGROVE MUSEUM

1508   MILWARD, CLEMENT. "The R.L. Scott Collection of Arms and Armour." *Apollo* 32 (1940):139-43, 9 b&w figs.
         Collection of many outstanding examples of European armors bequeathed to the museum. Includes a suit of ca. 1440 by the Missaglias of Milan acquired from the Count von Trapp at Castle Churburg, Tyrol; Maximilian suits; part of a gilt and etched Nuremburg suit (ca. 1545); and an English tilting helm of ca. 1480.

1509   BEARD, CHARLES S. "The Scott Collection of Arms and Armour, a Gift to the City of Glasgow." *Connoisseur* 107 (1941):8-14, 12 b&w figs.
         Notable examples from this collection include many of the 15th-16th century, such as the Missaglia armor from St. Donat's Castle, two Greenwich harnesses from Pembroke armory, a rare Bavarian crested three-quarter field armor of ca. 1530, a half armor of ca. 1545 by Kunz Lochner of Nuremberg, the 'Lindsay Helm' (a 15th-century English jousting helmet), and the rare German or Burgundian early 15th-century saddle with engraved polished staghorn.

London

TOWER OF LONDON

1510   *Inventory and Survey of the Armouries of the Tower of London.* 2 vols. Catalog by Charles J. Ffoulkes. London: His Majesty's Stationery Office, 1915. 1:231 pp., 1 color pl., 25 b&w pls., many b&w figs.; 2:278 pp., 38 b&w pls., many b&w figs.
         Repertory of this vast collection from all countries and periods of time. Vol. 1—inventory of defensive armor: 128 complete suits and 898 component parts (typologically arranged), 343 helmets and parts of, 78 shields, and 316 elements of horse armor. First half of volume traces the history of the armories, presents extracts of related documents by royal and distinguished visitors and lists earlier inventories. Vol. 2—short descriptions of nearly five thousand offensive arms arranged by type.

1511   MANN, JAMES G. "The Norton Hall Arms & Armour for the Tower." *Connoisseur* 111 (1943):3-11, 76; 20 b&w figs.
         Highlights of this collection of over five hundred items ranging from the 15th to the 19th century including an early armor by Anton Peffenhauser, a Milanese armor with the two-towered castle mark mostly appearing on pieces in Mantua, and an etched sword by Ercole de' Fideli.

1512   DUFTY, A.R.; and KENNARD, A.N. "Arms and Armour from the Hearst Collection Acquired for the Tower of London Armouries." *Connoisseur* 131 (1953):23-30, 23 b&w figs.

Brief outline of the armor collections in the Tower and descriptions of select pieces from the William Randolph Hearst Collection; suits, components, helmets, swords, horse armor, and firearms, many of which came from the imperial collection in Vienna.

1513   BLAIR, CLAUDE. "Arms and Armour from Spain." *Connoisseur* 146 (1960):16-20, 10 b&w figs.
     Describes several major pieces from the 1960 exhibition "Spanish Royal Armor at the Tower of London" (actually, arms and armor owned by the Spanish royalty), including a Flemish half armor of Philip I, a complete field garniture of Emperor Charles V of ca. 1518 by Kolman Helmschmied of Augsburg, an equestrian garniture of Philip II of 1551 made by Wolfgang Grosschedel of Landshut, etc.

1514   *Treasures from the Tower of London.* Exhibition held in Norwich at the Sainsbury Centre for Visual Arts, University of East Anglia; Cincinnati, Cincinnati Art Museum; Toronto, Royal Ontario Museum. Catalog by A.V.B. Norman and G.M. Wilson. London: Lund Humphries Publishers, 1982. 131 pp., 23 color pls., 118 b&w pls.
     111 entries of major pieces: European suits, individual elements, shields, swords, daggers, spears, pistols, etc., the majority of the period 1400-1600. The emphasis is on aesthetic and historical significance; includes essays on the history of the armories of the Tower.

VICTORIA AND ALBERT MUSEUM

1515   BAILEY, C.T.P. "The Farquharson Collection of Arms & Armor." *Old Furniture* 1 (1927) Part 1, "Firearms," 172-81, 8 b&w figs.; part 2, "Armour," 266-71, 13 b&w figs.
     Selection of items from this private collection (since bequeathed to the museum) including a 16th-century Italian match-lock arquebus, several South German wheel-locks, a 15th-century English sallet, a three-quarter German armor of ca. 1580, and various helmets, components, and horse armor dating of the 16th century.

1516   MILWARD, CLEMENT. "The Ramsbottom Collection of Arms and Armour." *Apollo* 32 (1940):36-40, 11 b&w figs.
     The collection, bequeathed to the museum, is particularly noteworthy for its extensive series of swords, among which are some 16th-century German, Italian, and English examples; also some 16th-century Italian helmets and a German breastplate.

WALLACE COLLECTION

1517   *European Arms and Armour.* Catalog by James Mann. 6th ed. 2 vols. Vol. 1, *Armour,* 292 pp., 1 color pl., 104 b&w pls.; vol. 2, *Arms,* 443 pp., 103 b&w pls., facsimile armorers' marks. London: Trustees of the Wallace Collection, 1962. (1st ed. 1900, compiled by Guy Laking.)
     A detailed yet concise description of an outstanding collection of often richly embossed and etched examples. Vol. 1: introduction dealing with formation of collection and historical development of types; extensive glossary; catalog, typologically arranged, describing chain mail, full armors, components, helmets, shields, and horse armor from Germany, Italy, France, and England with reproduction of their marks (most date of 1400-1600). Vol. 2: catalog of swords, daggers, pommels, pole arms, firearms, cannons, crossbows, powder flasks, primers, keys, steel embossed plaques, and carving and table knives; concludes with comprehensive bibliography, general index, and index of inscriptions and marks.

Munich

MÜNCHNER STADTMUSEUM

1518   *Das münchner Zeughaus.* Edited with catalog entries by Rudolf H. Wackernagel [et al.]. Munich- Zurich: Schnell & Steiner, 1982. 190 pp., 26 line drawings, 4 color pls., 42 b&w pls., 52 facsimile makers' marks.
       Essays by seven authors on the history of the Munich arsenal and its collections of mostly German arms and armor but including some exceptional North Italian and French pieces, dating of the 15th-16th century: types and components; armorers' marks; catalog of 98 items (full suits, component pieces, swords, pole arms, wheel-lock and flint-lock pistols).

New York

METROPOLITAN MUSEUM OF ART

1519   KIENBUSCH, CARL OTTO VON, and GRANCSAY, STEPHEN V. *The Bashford Dean Collection of Arms and Armor in the Metropolitan Museum of Art.* Portland, Me: Southworth Press, 1933. 270 pp., 64 b&w pls.
       Forty-page biographical outline of Bashford Dean and the collection he formed, followed by 197 often detailed entries of European arms and armor of the 15th-18th-century. Majority of pieces (some of major importance) date from the 15th and 16th century and are of Italian or German manufacture. Examples include complete suits of armor, individual pieces, shields, swords, daggers, firearms, and equestrian trappings. Concludes with tables of weights and measurements and armorers' marks.

1520   *Loan Exhibition of Medieval and Renaissance Arms and Armor from the Metropolitan Museum of Art.* Exhibition held in Los Angeles at the Los Angeles County Museum of Art. Catalog by Stephen V. Grancsay. Los Angeles County Museum of Art, 1953. 34 pp., 50 b&w pls.
       144 entries of representative examples from major European centers; full suits and components. Equestrian trappings and a variety of weapons. No bibliography.

1521   *The Art of Chivalry: European Arms and Armor from the Metropolitan Museum of Art.* Exhibition held in Seattle at the Seattle Art Museum. Catalog by Helmut Nickel, Stuart W. Pyhr, and Leonid Tarassuk. New York: American Federation of Arts, 1982. 179 pp., 7 color pls., 120 b&w illus.
       Selection of 120 pieces from the Metropolitan Museum collection of arms and armor, the largest in the Western hemisphere: late medieval and Renaissance parade armor, swords, daggers, halberds, crossbows, generally chiseled and often inlaid. Exhibition also traveled to: Denver Art Museum, Witte Museum in San Antonio; Minneapolis Institute of Arts; Detroit Institute of Arts.

Paris

MUSÉE DE L'ARMÉE

1522   *Armes et armures anciennes et souvenirs historiques les plus précieux.* 2 vols. Paris: Hôtel des Invalides. Vol. 1 (1917), edited by Général Niox, 142 pp., 56 b&w pls.; vol. 2 (1927), edited by Général Mariaux and Colonel Payard, 249 pp., 66 b&w pls.

Selection of the most important items from France's war museum, including pieces from the royal armory. Descriptive analysis including hallmarks, provenance, and bibliography for each illustration. Vol. 1: French, Italian, German defensive arms and armor of the Renaissance: entire suits, horse armor, helmets, shields; vol. 2: offensive French, Spanish, Italian, German, English, Swiss arms from the 15th to the 18th century, mostly of the 16th.

Philadelphia

PHILADELPHIA MUSEUM OF ART

1523   KIENBUSCH, CARL OTTO VON. *The Kretzschmar von Kienbusch Collection of Armor and Arms.* Princeton: Princeton University Library, 1963. 365 pp., 165 b&w pls. comprising 762 figs.

Catalog of private collection, since bequeathed to the museum, compiled by owner. Nine-page introduction followed by 762 entries, typologically arranged, for objects mostly dating of the period 1400-1600 (Italian and German): complete and partial suits; horse armor (plus saddles, spurs, and stirrups); shields, swords, daggers, hunting arms, pole arms, crossbows, guns, pistols; miscellaneous items (banners, tools, flasks, etc.); unique pieces such as superbly painted pageant shields with historiated scenes (cat. nos. 299-300). Features list of inscriptions (pp. 337-38); list of sources of collection (pp. 343-57). Each entry is adequately illustrated. (For the bequeathal, see D. Dodge Thompson in the *Bulletin, Philadelphia Museum of Art* 73 [1977]:2.)

Solothurn, Switzerland

1524   VITAL, NICOLO. *Das alte Zeughaus Solothurn.* Solothurn: Vogt-Schildt AG, 1980. 183 pp., 30 color pls., 167 b&w figs.

Glossy overview of important collection of arms and armor ranging from the 15th century to present. Includes historical introduction, illustrations with legends (in German/French/English) of 15th century swords (pp. 76-82), crossbow (87), wheel-lock guns (88-89, 94-95), armor (118-25, 130-33, 136-39, 144-47); embroidered banners (150-51, 154-55), and a gold necklace of ca. 1410 (152-53).

Vác, Hungary

BOTTYÁN MÚZEUM

1525   TEMESVÁRY, FERENC. *A váci Vak Bottyán Múzeum fegyvergyüjteménye.* Vác: Vak Bottyán Múzeum, 1984. 207 pp., numerous line drawings.

Catalog of approximately 450 firearms, edged weapons, and elements of armor in this Hungarian museum. One-page summary and one-page table of contents in German. Includes many examples from late medieval and Renaissance times.

Valetta, Malta

PALACE OF THE GRAND MASTERS – ARMOURY

1526   *A Catalogue of the Armour and Arms in the Armoury of the Knights of St. John of Jerusalem, Now in the Palace, Valetta, Malta.* London: Bradbury, Agnew & Co., n.d. 52 pp., 32 b&w pls.

Brief introduction to the collection; catalog of 464 choice pieces from a total of over 5,000. Includes a few complete suits, several component pieces, helmets, shields, pole arms, swords, and firearms dating of the 16th century and after, and being mostly of Italian, German, French, or English origin.

Vienna

KUNSTHISTORISCHES MUSEUM – WAFFENSAMMLUNG

1527 BOEHEIM, WENDELIN. *Album hervorragender Gegenstände aus der Waffensammlung des allerhöchsten Kaiserhauses.* 2 vols. Vol. 1 (1894), 29 pp., 50 b&w pls.; vol. 2 (1898), 19 pp., 50 b&w pls. Vienna: J. Löwy, K.U.K. Hofphotograph.

Selection of the major examples of arms and armor in the collection. Useful for plates, each reproducing several pieces. The text consists of captions grouped after a short introduction.

1528 *Katalog der Waffensammlung in der Neuen Burg.* Catalog by August Grosz and Bruno Thomas. Vienna: Kunsthistorisches Museum, 1936. 291 pp., 24 b&w pls.

Slightly dated, chronologically arranged summary catalog of the outstanding imperial collection of arms and armor in the museum, which consists of German and Italian specimens (a few Polish, Hungarian, Turkish, and Persian pieces) ranging from the 6th to the 18th century but with the great majority belonging to the 15th-16th century. Includes field and parade armors, jousting helmets, shields, swords, and early firearms. Scanty illustration.

1529 *Katalog der Leibrüstkammer.* Vol. 1. *Der Zeitraum von 500 bis 1530.* Führer durch das Kunsthistorisches Museum, no. 13. Vienna: Anton Schroll & Co., 1976. 264 pp., 132 b&w figs., 142 photographs of marks and monograms. [No subsequent volumes published as of January 1987].

Catalog of renowned collection of arms and armor of the Leibrüstkammer of the museum. Includes provenance of each object. Entries arranged chronologically and by gallery location. Examples from all countries with emphasis on courtly German and Austrian armor. Pertinent to the years 1400-1600 are European weapons, equestrian mountings, suits of armor, individual pieces, shields, etc. (pp. 59-245).

Waddesdon, England

WADDESDON MANOR

1530 BLAIR, CLAUDE. *Arms, Armour and Base-Metalwork.* Vol. 5 of *The James A. de Rothschild Collection at Waddesdon Manor,* edited by Anthony Blunt. London: National Trust for Places of Historic Interest or Natural Beauty; Fribourg: Office du Livre, 1974. 531 pp., 231 figs., many in color, plus several small details, 5 pp., of illus. of marks and signatures.

Famed collection – particularly important for some specific pieces of high quality such as Emperor Charles V's burgonet (by Caremolo Modrone of Mantua) and cowters (by Filippo Negroli), rather than for the breadth of its representative examples – formed by Alice de Rothschild (1847-1922) and bequeathed to the National Trust in 1957. Emphasis is on works bearing decoration and specifically 16th-17th-century arms – with some of earlier and later dates. Also some armor and cutlery. 237 detailed entries with bibliography. Eight-page glossary.

Warwick, England

WARWICK CASTLE

1531   MANN, JAMES G. "Die alten Rüstkammerbestände auf Warwick Castle." *Zeitschrift für historische Waffen- und Kostümkunde* 14, n.s. 5 (1935-36):157-60, 2 b&w pls., 3 b&w figs. "Die Waffensammlung auf Warwick Castle." *Zeitschrift für historische Waffen- und Kostümkunde* 15, n.s. 6 (1937-39):49-54, 10 b&w figs. Translated by D. Michelly.
        Brief presentation of important collection of Greenwich, Milanese, and German arms and armor.

Worcester, Mass.

HIGGINS ARMORY MUSEUM

1532   *Catalogue of Armor,* by Stephen V. Grancsay, with forward by J.W. Higgins. Worcester, Mass.: John Woodman Higgins Armory, 1961. 128 pp., 120 b&w figs.
        Six-page introduction; seventy-three entries chronologically arranged of most important holdings of German and Italian plate armor, the majority dating from 1400-1600. Includes several finely etched suits and an important French embossed example.

7. EXHIBITION CATALOGS

Allentown, Pa.

ALLENTOWN ART MUSEUM

1533   *Arms and Armor.* Exhibition catalog introduction by Stephen V. Grancsay. Allentown, Pa.: Allentown Art Museum, 1964. 93 pp., 79 b&w figs.
        Choice holdings from the Grancsay Collection, the Metropolitan Museum, and the Higgins Armory, Worcester, Mass. 168 entries include 15th- and 16th-century European suits of armor, individual pieces, shields, spurs, stirrups, daggers, mail, swords, etc.

Flint, Mich.

FLINT INSTITUTE OF ARTS

1534   *The Art of the Armorer.* Exhibition catalog by G. Stuart Hodge. Introduction by Stephen V. Grancsay. Flint, Mich.: Flint Institute of Arts, 1967. 62 pp., 75 b&w figs.
        Summary catalog of 151 items including suits and components, swords and pommels, pole arms, crossbows, firearms, gunlocks, maces, horse armor, buckles, also brass rubbings and armorial tapestries of the 15th-17th century from the Metropolitan Museum, Higgins Armory, Detroit Institute of Arts, Walters Art Gallery, and two private collections.

Geneva

MUSÉE RATH

1535   *Armes anciennes des collections suisses.* Exhibiton catalog by Clément Bosson, René Géroudet, and Eugène Heer. Geneva: Musée Rath; Lausanne: Edita, 1972. 191 pp., 233 b&w figs.

Selection of 551 European arms and armor from the 11th to the 18th century in Swiss collections. Concisely written, well illustrated, and very useful as a reference to separate the various types of edged weapons, firearms, and basic elements of armor.

8. PRIVATE COLLECTION, AUCTION, AND DEALER CATALOGS

BREADALBANE COLLECTION

1536 FFOULKES, CHARLES. "Armour from the Breadalbane Collection." *Burlington Magazine* 31 (1917):70-76, 8 b&w figs.

Briefly describes major pieces (suits, components, a sword) from this collection auctioned 5 July 1917 at Christie's, London, including Maximilian suits, a Nuremberg half-suit by Konrad Lochner, a backplate in the style of Lucio Piccinino, etc.

CARL OF PRUSSIA COLLECTION

1537 HILTL, GEORG. *Waffen-Sammlung Sr. Königlichen Hoheit des Prinzen Carl von Preussen — Mittelalterliche Abtheilung.* Berlin: W. Moeser Hofbuchhandlung; Nuremberg: S. Soldan, 1876. 213 pp., 100 b&w pls. Reprint. Fridingen: Graf Klenau Verlags, 1981.

Catalog of 1,129 detailed entries for arms and armor in the collection of Prince Carl of Prussia. Arranged by type and then chronologically. Pieces range in date from the 15th to the 18th century with the majority being of the 16th.

ESTRUCH Y CUMELLA COLLECTION

1538 LLANSO, A. GARCIA. *Museo-Armeria de D. José Estruch y Cumella.* Barcelona: n.p., 1896. 4 pp., 166 b&w pls., 233 makers' marks.

Illustration of major examples of arms and armor from this collection in Barcelona, each plate accompanied by a brief description of its figures. Pieces date from antiquity to the 19th century, but most are productions from main armorer centers of the 16th century.

HEARST COLLECTION

1539 *European Arms and Armor of the XV-XIX Century from the William Randolph Hearst Collection.* Sale No. 1387 held in New York at Parke-Bernet Galleries 4 December 1952. 40 pp., 21 b&w illus.

166 lots comprised of firearms (including some 16th-century wheel-lock pistols, petronels, and arquebuses); edged weapons (swords, daggers); three complete suits (lots 118, 121, 140); a Milanese half suit of etched and gilt armor by Pompeo della Chiesa with designs representing mythological subjects (lot 120); a three-quarter suit (lot 124); helmets and component parts; crossbows, horse trappings, etc.

HEVER COLLECTION

See entry 114.

KUPPELMAYR COLLECTION

1540 KUPPELMAYR, RUDOLPH. *Waffen-Sammlung Kuppelmayr.* Munich: Privately Printed, 1895. 47 pp., 30 b&w pls.

643 entries of mostly 15th-16th-century European arms and armor in this Viennese collection, repertoried on forty-six pages. Useful illustrations.

LAKING COLLECTION

See entry 115.

STUYVESANT COLLECTION

1541   DEAN, BASHFORD. *The Collection of Arms and Armor of Rutherford Stuyvesant, 1843-1909.* Privately Printed, 1914. 174 pp., 51 b&w pls.
Ancient, Eastern, and European (15th-18th-century) arms and armor. Six-page introduction deals with Stuyvesant and his collection in Allamuchy, N.J.; catalog of 218 entries typologically arranged; includes 15th- and 16th-century suits of armor, individual pieces, head gear, shields, equestrian trappings, and a variety of weaponry. Pieces are of German, French, Italian, English, Spanish, Austrian, and Scottish origin.

WHAWELL COLLECTION

See entry 119.

Arms

1. DICTIONARIES AND ENCYCLOPEDIAS

1542   BOCCIA, LIONELLO G. *Armi difensive dal Medioevo all'età moderna.* Florence: Centro Di, [1982]. 191 pp., 74 b&w pls.
Technical lexicon (in Italian only) of proper terminology for the various types and components of armor (pp. 18-46); line drawings with detailed labeling (47-122); sample inventory cards (123-66); bibliography (167-82).

1543   GAMBER, ORTWIN, ed. *Glossarium armorum: Arma defensiva.* Vol. 1 in 7 parts (part 1, line drawings by Margarethe Schulz; parts 2-7, terminology in German, English, French, Italian, Danish, Czech, respectively; part in English by C. Blair, V. Norman, H.R. Robinson). Graz: Akademische Druck-u. Verlagsanstalt, 1972. Part I: 100 pp. of 4 line drawings per page; part 3: 35 pp.
Polyglot glossary of main types of defensive arms from ancient times to the 17th century, arranged chronologically as well as typologically. Indispensable for specialized terminology.

3. SURVEYS AND HISTORIES

Books

1544   BLAIR, CLAUDE. *Pistols of the World.* London: Batsford, [1968]. 216 pp., 851 line drawings.
Major survey on the subject, which describes and carefully illustrates practically every type of pistol produced from 1534 to 1900.

1545   BOCCIA, LIONELLO GIORGIO. *Nove secoli di armi da caccia.* Florence: Editrice Edam, 1967. 16 color figs., 174 b&w figs.

Hunting spears, ivory horn, daggers, crossbows, hunting-poles, firearms, powder horns—many chiseled or inlaid—used in hunting from the 8th through the 18th century are illustrated with captions of variable length. Twenty-eight-page introduction and two pages of makers' marks.

1546   HAYWARD, J.F. *The Art of the Gunmaker.* Vol. 1, *1500-1660.* London: Barrie & Rockliff, 1962. 303 pp., 5 color pls., 160 b&w figs.

Development, construction, decoration, and distinctive features of firearms in Italy, Germany, France, England, Spain, the Low Countries, and Scandinavia. For the 16th century, see chap. 1-7, 13. Appendix with description of main locks.

1547   OAKESHOTT, R. EWART. *The Sword in the Age of Chivalry.* London: Lutterworth, 1964. 152 pp., 1 color pl., 48 b&w pls., 134 line drawings.

European knightly swords of 1100-1500; classification of swords by type and period (those dating from 1400-1500 on pp. 56-79); forms of pommels, cross-guards, grips, scabbards; appendix of blade inscriptions.

1548   PAYNE-GALLWEY, RALPH. *The Crossbow, Mediaeval and Modern, Military and Sporting: Its Construction, History, and Management with a Treatise on the Balista and Catapult of the Ancients.* London, New York and Bombay: Longmans, Green & Co., 1903. 397 pp., 245 b&w line drawings.

Early study of European crossbows tracing their history with emphasis on types, sizes, range, and construction techniques. Particularly relevant to 15th-16th century are chaps. 18-33, 36 (pp. 90-160, 169-73). Also deals with projectile engines (balista, catapults, and trebuchets). Useful illustrations showing construction.

Articles

1549   BUTTIN, FRANÇOIS. "La Lance et l'arrêt de cuirasse." *Archaeologia* 99 (1965):77-178, 12 b&w pls.

The lance from the 13th to the 18th century; its form, purpose, manner of holding and using in jousts and battles; the adoption of the lance-rest to facilitate aiming the lance and couching it with one quick movement; extensive use of extracts from contemporary literature and documents.

1550   KALMAR, JOHANN VON. "Pfeilspitzen als Würdezeichen." *Zeitschrift für historische Waffen- und Kostümkunde* n.s. 6 (1937-39):218-21, 8 b&w figs.

Metal arrowheads with intricate etching: their ceremonial use during the 15th-16th century.

1551   THOMAS, BRUNO. "Die Artillerie im Triumphzug Kaiser Maximilians I." *Zeitschrift für historische Waffen- und Kostümkunde* n.s. 6 (1937-39):229-35, 6 b&w figs.

Cannons and other elements of Maximilian's artillery as represented in the Triumph of the Emperor of 1507-12 by Jörg Kölderer (Vienna, Albertina 25230).

1552   WETTENDORFER, EDUARD. "Zur Technologie der Steinbüchsen." *Zeitschrift für historische Waffen- und Kostümkunde* n.s. 6 (1937-39):147-54, 10 b&w figs.

Bombards composed of stone elements held by metal rings produced in the 14th-15th century.

6. PERMANENT COLLECTIONS

Florence

MUSEO NAZIONALE DEL BARGELLO

1553   GERSPACH. "La Collection Ressman." *Les Arts* 9 (1902):9-16, 13 b&w figs.
Highlights of this Paris collection of mostly Renaissance arms bequeathed to the Bargello.

New York

METROPOLITAN MUSEUM OF ART

1554   *Catalog of European Daggers Including the Ellis, De Dino, Riggs, and Reubell Collections.*
Catalog by Bashford Dean. New York: Metropolitan Museum, 1929. 196 pp. with 61
b&w text figs., 85 b&w pls.
Chronological range from the 6th through the 19th century with emphasis on Renaissance weaponry. Includes many daggers from the years 1400-1600 including basilards, roundels, kidney, dirks, eared, cinquedeas, sword hilted, landsknecht, poignards, and stiletto. Includes brief introduction dealing with development of daggers.

Vienna

KUNSTHISTORISCHES MUSEUM – WAFFENSAMMLUNG

1555   GAMBER, ORTWIN. "Die mittelalterlichen Blankwaffen der Wiener Waffensammlung." *Jahrbuch der kunsthistorischen Sammlungen in Wien* 57 (1961):7-38, 40 b&w figs.
Examines a group of bladed implements and weapons (various sword types, table knives, as well as scabbards and sheaths) from the collection mostly dating of the late 14th through early 16th century. Nearly all examples were made for royal or ducal patrons including Philip the Good of Burgundy, Maximilian I, Philip I of Spain, Frederick III, etc.

Zurich

SCHWEIZERISCHES LANDESMUSEUM

1556   *Waffen im schweizerischen Landesmuseum.* Vol. 1, *Griffwaffen.* Catalog by Hugo
Schneider. Zurich: Orell Füssli, 1980.
Swords, daggers, and other private arms in the museum dating from the 10th to the 16th century; many are of the period 1400-1600. (Initial volume of a projected three-volume catalog of the arms in the collection.)

8. PRIVATE COLLECTION, AUCTION, AND DEALER CATALOGS

SCHWERZENBACH COLLECTION

1557   FORRER, R. *Die Schwerter und Schwertknäufe der Sammlung Carl von Schwerzenbach-Bregenz.* Leipzig: Karl W. Hiersemann, 1905. 63 pp., 360 b&w text figs., 60 b&w pls.

Five hundred swords and pommels owned by this collector of Bregenz, Austria, with examples from the 13th through the 18th century. Those of the period 1400-1600 are on pls. II-XXVI, XXIX-LVIII—for catalog entries see pp. 51-60. Includes fifty-page introduction and two pages of marks.

SPITZER COLLECTION

1558   BEAUMONT, W. DE. "Collections de M. Spitzer: Les Armes." *Gazette des beaux-arts* 25 (1882):461-74, 12 b&w figs.
Collection of 16th-century arms and armor owned by the famed Parisian dealer-collector (see entry 138a).

Armor

3. SURVEYS AND HISTORIES

Books

1559   KLAPSIA, HEINRICH; THOMAS, BRUNO; and GAMBER, ORTWIN. "Harnischstudien." *Jahrbuch der kunsthisorischen Sammlungen in Wien.* Part 1, "Stilgeschichte des deutschen Harnisches von 1500 bis 1530," by Thomas, n.s. 11 (1937):139-58, 22 b&w figs.; part 2, "Der Prunkharnisch des Manierismus (geschichtliche Sinndeutung und geistige Grundlagen," by Klapsia, n.s. 11 (1937):159-64, 9 b&w figs.; part 3, "Stilgeschichte des deutschen Harnisches von 1530 bis 1560," by Thomas, n.s. 12 (1938):175-202, 36 b&w figs.; part 4, "Stilgeschichte des deutschen Harnisches von 1560 bis 1590," by Thomas, n.s. 13 (1944):255-300, 47 b&w figs.; part 5, "Stilgeschichte des Plattenharnisches von den Anfängen bis um 1440," by Gamber, n.s. 14 (1953):53-92, 71 b&w figs.; part 6, "Stilgeschichte des Plattenharnisches von 1440-1510," by Gamber, n.s. 15 (1955):31-102, 79 b&w figs.
Part 1: German armors of Nuremberg, Innsbruck. etc. made for the court of Maximilian I between 1500 and 1530; their style and construction as exemplified in the Waffensammlung, Vienna. Part 2: embossed parade armors of the second half of the 16th century produced in Germany, Milan, etc. as seen by examples made for Archduke Ferdinand of Tyrol, Emperor Rudolf II, Carlo Gonzaga, etc., now in Vienna. Part 3: the making of German parade armors from 1530 until 1560 in Augsburg, Innsbruck, Landshut, Nuremberg, by various masters including Koloman and Desiderius Colman, Master of the W Mark, Jörg Seusenhofer, Jörg Song, Wilhelm von Worms the Younger, Konrad Lochner, Hand Perkhamer, as primarily exemplified in the Vienna collection. Part 4: parade armor for rider and horse with niello decoration produced in Augsburg, Innsbruck, etc. for the imperial court of Ferdinand I and Maximilian II. Part 5: history of plate armor from the beginning to 1440 with examples drawn from many sources including sculptures, panel paintings, frescoes, miniatures, etc., pp. 66-84 deal specifically with the 15th century. Part 6: history of plate armor from 1440 to 1510 ending with an appendix of drawings of datable component parts.

1560   ZSCHILLE, R., and FORRER, R. *Der Sporn in seiner Formen-Entwicklung.* Berlin: Paul Bette, 1891. 25 pp., 20 pls. comprising 188 line drawings.
The development of the stirrup in all countries from the 3d century B.C. until the 18th century dealt with in short chapters in four pages of tables, and plates of line drawings; pp. 13-18, 23-25, and pls. VIII-XV deal with 15th-16th-century examples and are useful for dates provided.

Articles

1561   BURGESS, MARTIN. "Further Research into the Construction of Mail Garments." *Antiquaries Journal* 33 (1953):193-202, 3 b&w pls., 6 diagrams.
Explanation of the manner of giving mail armor shape and examination of individual rings (wire, diameter, joints) and of method of construction to help identify pieces originating from same shop.

1561a   BURGESS, MARTIN. "The Mail-Maker's Technique." *Antiquaries Journal* 33 (1953):48-55, 2 b&w pls., 4 line drawings.
Of interest for information on materials, tools, methods, the division of labor, the role of the master craftsman, that can help in identifying origin and relationship of individual pieces.

1562   CRIPPS-DAY, F.H. "'The Greatest Armour Collector of All Time' – Ferdinand Archduke of Austria 1529-1595." *Connoisseur*. Part 1, 115 (1945):86-93, 14 b&w figs.; part 2, 116 (1945):22-29, 18 b&w figs.
History and content of this once vast collection, which included armor of illustrious Austrian, German, Italian, and French sovereigns, nobles, and captains, assembled by the archduke in the castle of Ambras, near Innsbruck (now mostly in Vienna) and inventoried during his lifetime. Comparative material includes portraits, engravings, and a funeral effigy of the duke wearing, in some cases, extant armor.

1563   KLAPSIA, HEINRICH. "Deutsche und italienisch Plattnerkunst am Ende des Mittelalters." *Zeitschrift für historische Waffen- und Kostümkunde* n.s. 6 (1937-39):65-78, 12 b&w figs.
Relationship and stylistic differentiations between German and Italian armor of the 15th and 16th century.

1564   MANN, JAMES. "Gauntlets and the Meyrick Society." *Connoisseur* 146 (1960):97-102, 15 b&w figs.
German, Italian, English, and Flemish mostly 16th-century gauntlets representative of various styles and techniques and types (e.g., bell-cuffed, fluted, embossed, locking) from private collections and comprised in a small private exhibition in London.

1565   MANN, J.G. "Notes on the Armour of the Maximilian Period and the Italian Wars." *Archaeologia* 79 (1929):217-44, 55 b&w figs. on 17 pls.
Characteristics of Italian and of German armor, and the meshing of the two traditions, during the period of the Italian Wars (ca. 1494-1524), to form the Maximilian fashion of armor distinguished by rounded contours and channeled surfaces. Examples from European and U.S. public and private collections, as well as from sculpture and paintings.

1566   MANN, JAMES G. "Recollections of the Wilton Armoury." *Connoisseur* 104 (1939):10-16, 12 b&w figs.
Content of personal armory of the Earl of Pembroke dating of the 16th century auctioned at Sotheby's in three sales in 1921-23; includes important suits now at the Tower of London, Metropolitan Museum, Higgins Armory Museum, etc.

1567   THOMAS, BRUNO. "Die Münchner Waffenvorzeichnungen des Étienne Delaune und die Prunkschilde Heinrichs II. von Frankreich." *Jahrbuch der kunsthistorischen Sammlungen in Wien* n.s. 22 (1962):101-68, 61 b&w figs.

Embossed suit of armor and shields produced by Étienne Delaune for Henri II of France; adaptations of his designs by German and Netherlandish silversmiths.

6. PERMANENT COLLECTIONS

Innsbruck

KUNSTHISTORISCHES MUSEUM – SCHLOSS AMBRAS

1568   *Die Rüstkammern.* Catalog by Elisabeth Scheicher, Ortwin Gamber, and Alfred Auer. Vienna: Kunsthistorisches Museum, 1981. 106 pp., 12 color figs., 24 b&w figs.
Guide to this famous collection of mostly 16th-century parade armors with German, Italian, Hungarian examples briefly described.

London

TOWER OF LONDON

1569   *European Armour in the Tower of London.* Catalog by Arthur Richard Dufty, with introduction by William Reid. London: Her Majesty's Stationery Office, 1968. 75 pp., 1 color pl., 163 b&w pls.
Photographic corpus of selected armor in the Tower. Eleven-page introduction deals with history of the armory, inventories, formation, and scope of the collection. The majority of the pieces illustrated are from England, France, Germany, Italy, and Austria and date from the 15th and 16th century; includes full suits, harnesses, saddles, etc.

1570   BLAIR, CLAUDE. "King Henry VIII's Tonlet Armour." *Burlington Magazine* 125 (1983):16-20, 1 b&w fig.
Suit of armor probably worn at the "Field of Cloth and Gold" in 1520 and characterized by a "tonlet" (steel skirt) here suggested to have originated at the Burgundian-Hapsburg Court of Brussels.

New York

METROPOLITAN MUSEUM OF ART

1571   GRANCSAY, STEPHEN V. "The Mutual Influence of Costume and Armor: A Study of Specimens in the Metropolitan Museum of Art." *Metropolitan Museum Studies* 3 (1930-31):144-208, 28 b&w figs.
Influence of costume, mostly in the 15th and 16th century, on the contour of armor; laces on costume for attaching the latter to the armor; brigantines (armor plate) in turn covered with material; some armor in Germany worn with skirts.

1572   *A Loan Exhibition of Equestrian Equipment from the Metropolitan Museum of Art.* Exhibition held in Louisville at the J.B. Speed Art Museum. Catalog by Stephen V. Grancsay. Louisville: J.B. Speed Art Museum. 1955, 45 pp. (unpaginated), 19 b&w pls. often with many illustrations each.
158 brief entries describing spurs, saddles, stirrups, bits, and other equestrian trappings of the Middle Ages and Renaissance fashioned from iron, copper, brass, bronze, etc.

Paris

MUSÉE DE L'ARMÉE

1573   REVERSEAU, JEAN-PIERRE. *Les Armures des rois de France au Musée de l'Armée.*
Saint-Julien-du-Sault: Éditions F.P. Lobies, 1982. 142 pp., 9 color pls., 65 b&w figs.

Armor made for the French monarchs and their court (mostly parade armor) in the
collection. Of the 16th century are complete suits, components, helmets and shields, some
elaborately decorated with blued, gilded, or etched steel, or with richly embossed historiated
scenes made by Italian (among which the Negroli), German (Jörg Seusenhofer of Innsbruck),
and French armorers for Francis I, Henri II, Henri IV, and their retainers. Detailed descriptions placing objects in historic and artistic perspective and with examples from other collections.

Vienna

KUNSTHISTORISCHES MUSEUM – WAFFENSAMMLUNGEN

1574   BORN, WOLFGANG. "Armours of Kings and Captains. Examples in the Neue Hofburg, Vienna." *Connoisseur.* Part 1, 98 (1936):307-13, 1 color pl., 12 b&w figs.; part 2, 99
(1937):4-7, 7 b&w figs.

Relation among various styles and types of 15th-16th-century armor and their original
owners, famous princes and generals, as seen from examples from the collection of Archduke
Ferdinand of Tyrol (1529-95), nucleus of the armor collection in the Neue Hofburg, and contemporary portraits.

B. SINGLE COUNTRY OF ORIGIN

AUSTRIAN

Armor

3. SURVEYS AND HISTORIES

1575   BOEHEIM, WENDELIN. "Die Waffenschmiede Seusenhofer, ihre Werke und ihre
Beziehungen zu Habsburgischen und Anderen." *Jahrbuch der kunsthistorischen Sammlung des allerhöchsten Kaiserhauses* 20 (1899):283-320, 5 b&w pls., 14 b&w figs.

Armor produced by the metalsmith Konrad Seusenhofer of Innsbruck at the service
of the Hapsburgs in the first half of the 16th centrury. Parade armor for Charles V, Maximilian I, Henry VIII of England (gift of Maximilian), Ludwig II of Hungary, King Ferdinand,
etc.

6. PERMANENT COLLECTIONS

Baltimore

WALTERS ART GALLERY

1576 GRANCSAY, STEPHEN V. "A Late Medieval Helmet (Sallet)." *Journal of the Walters Art Gallery* 13 (1950):20-29, 3 b&w figs., 24 line drawings.
    History and technical development of the sallet in 15th- 16th-century Europe focusing on a particular Innsbruck example of 1490.

BRITISH
(ENGLISH AND SCOTTISH)

Arms and Armor

3. SURVEYS AND HISTORIES

1577 CALDWELL, DAVID H. "Royal Patronage of Arms and Armour Making in Fifteenth and Sixteenth-Century Scotland." In *Scottish Weapons and Fortifications, 1100-1800.* Edited by David H. Caldwell. Edinburgh: J. Donald; Atlantic Highlands: Humanities Press, 1981. Pp. 73-93, 8 illus.
    Royal encouragement to improve standards of workmanship and to increase Scottish production of arms and armor.

Arms

3. SURVEYS AND HISTORIES

1578 BLAIR, CLAUDE. "The Early Basket-Hilt in Britain." In *Scottish Weapons and Fortifications, 1100-1800.* Edited by David H. Caldwell. Edinburgh: J. Donald; Atlantic Highlands: Humanities Press, 1981. Pp. 153-252, 71 illus.
    Documentary and pictorial evidence leads author to conclude that these swords were in use in England as early as about 1540, that the Scottish form had developed by the 1560s, and that the basket guard was in use in Scotland by around 1570.

1579 SMITH, OTTO. "Herleitung des Claymore vom Wikingerschwert." *Zeitschrift für historische Waffen- und Kostümkunde* n.s. 6 (1937-39):25-31, 6 b&w figs.
    Adaptation of a Viking sword model in Western Scotland for hilts produced locally mostly during the 15th century.

6. PERMANENT COLLECTIONS

Glasgow

GLASGOW ART MUSEUMS AND ART GALLERIES – KELVINGROVE MUSEUM

1580   SCOTT, JACK G. "Three Medieval Swords from Scotland." In *Scottish Weapons and Fortifications, 1100-1800*. Edited by David H. Caldwell. Edinburgh: J. Donald; Atlantic Highlands: Humanities Press, 1981. Pp. 10-20, 4 illus.
    The evolution of swords with spatulate-terminal crosses as seen from three 15th-century swords in this collection and those depicted on tomb slabs.

London

WESTMINSTER ABBEY

1581   OAKESHOTT, R. EWART. "A Fifteenth-Century 'Royal' Sword Preserved in Westminster Abbey Library." *Connoisseur* 129 (1952):104-8, 128, 14 b&w illus.
    Dated by the author to the early 15th century on the basis of the style of its pommel, quillions, and blade in comparison with extant pieces and reproductions of swords in contemporary paintings and sculpture, and proposed to have been part of the offering made at the funeral of King Henry V.

Armor

3. SURVEYS AND HISTORIES

Book

1582   DILLON, HAROLD ARTHUR LEE. Introduction and notes to *An Almain Armourer's Album: Selections from an Original Manuscript in Victoria and Albert Museum, South Kensington*. London: W. Griggs, 1905. 33 hand-tipped color pls., 8 b&w figs.
    Partial reproduction with three-page introduction of an album of watercolor drawings of ca. 1562-75 recording the armors produced by German craftsmen at Greenwich for English noblemen; each is accompanied by a brief descriptive caption and biographical information.

Articles

1583   BLAIR, CLAUDE. "The Emperor Maximilian's Gift of Armour to King Henry VIII and the Silvered and Engraved Armour at the Tower of London." *Archaeologia* 99 (1965):1-52, 25 b&w pls., 10 line drawings.
    Documents and a related extant armor suggest that this suit of Henry VIII was probably made at Greenwich by the king's Milanese armorers between 1514 and 1516 (and therefore was not the one presented by Maximilian to Henry in 1514 as was long held), and was decorated by the English workshop of Paul van Vrelant of Brussels.

1584   GAMBER, ORTWIN. "Armour Made in the Royal Workshops at Greenwich: Style and Construction." *Scottish Art Review* 12 (1969):1-13, 30-32, 32 b&w figs.

Activity of the Royal Armoury established by Henry VIII from ca. 1511 and in Greenwich starting about 1525 attracting Milanese, German, Netherlandish, and French masters.

1585　HAYWARD, J.F. "The Armoury of the First Earl of Pembroke." *Connoisseur* 155 (1964):225-30, 9 b&w figs.

Discusses and transcribes (in part) an inventory dating of 1558 of the first earl of Pembroke from which it has been possible to identify eight extant Greenwich armors now dispersed between London, Glasgow, New York, and Toronto.

1586　HOLMES, MARTIN. "Genouilhac Reconsidered: A New Theory about a Famous Armour," *Connoisseur* 180 (1972):177-81, 6 b&w figs.

Holmes suggests that the helmet of this Greenwich armor has an old-fashioned visor and must therefore have been produced at an earlier date than the rest of the suit.

1587　NICKEL, HELMUT. "'A harnes all gilte' — A Study of the Armor of Galiot de Genouilhac and the Iconography of Its Decoration." *Metropolitan Museum Journal* 5 (1972):75-124, 69 b&w figs.

Examination of a rich garniture for rider and horse dated 1527, gilded and etched with late Gothic as well as Renaissance decorative motives. Stylistic evidence points that it is the work of a German armorer who had traveled to the Netherlands and who worked in England, while iconographic interpretations reveal the original owner to have been François II de la Tour d'Auvergne, Vicomte de Turenne, who was at the court of Henry VIII of England to negotiate a marriage between Princess ("Bloody") Mary and the duke of Orléans, later Henri II of France. The original owner may subsequently have given the armor to Galiot de Genouilhac, "écuyer du roi" and "grand maître de l'artillerie."

1588　WILLIAMS, A.R. "A Technical Note on Some of the Armour of King Henry VIII and His Contemporaries." *Archaeologia* 106 (1979):157-65, 67 b&w figs.

Detailed technical study of various armor components produced for Henry VIII in the workshop he established in Greenwich reveals that neither the Milanese of this workshop nor the subsequently imported German armorers ever mastered the very specialized techniques of Maximilian's South German craftsmen to produce armor of very great strength from very effectively hardened steel.

6. PERMANENT COLLECTIONS

New York

METROPOLITAN MUSEUM OF ART

1589　GRANCSAY, STEPHEN V. "Notes on Armor of the Greenwich School." *Metropolitan Museum Studies* 2 (1930):85-101, 23 b&w figs.

Various etched armor components identified as a product of a shop established by Henry VIII. Some pieces are recognized to have come from specific suits on the basis of the Greenwich Album and other pictorial sources.

8. PRIVATE COLLECTION, AUCTION, AND DEALER CATALOGS

CRIPPS-DAY COLLECTION

1590   CRIPPS-DAY, FRANCIS HENRY. "Der Helm König Heinrichs VI. von England."
Zeitschrift für historisches Waffen- und Kostümkunde n.s. 6 (1937-39):2-6, 3 b&w figs.
Helmet of King Henry VI of England (died 1471) in the collection of the author;
until the early 17th century it had been in Windsor over the funerary monument of the
sovereign.

CZECHOSLOVAKIA (BOHEMIAN)

Arms and Armor

6. PERMANENT COLLECTIONS

New York

METROPOLITAN MUSEUM OF ART

1591   NICKEL, HELMUT. "Ceremonial Arrowheads from Bohemia." *Metropolitan Museum
Journal* 1 (1968):61-90, 59 b&w figs.
The ceremonial use of the arrow is traced through a 15th-century arrowhead with
brass inlay at the Metropolitan Museum and compared with similar objects and their representation in paintings and prints. A more detailed rendition of the subject in German entitled
"Bohemische Prunkfeilspitzen" appeared in *Sborník Národního Muzea v Praze* 23 (1969):101-
63, 75 b&w figs.

Prague

NÁRODNI GALERI V PRAZE

1591a   DENKSTEIN, VLADIMÍR. "Böhmische Prunksporen aus dem 15. Jahrhundert."
Sborník Národního Muzea v Praze 23 (1969):166-93, 20 b&w figs.
Large and often fancifully worked spurs and stirrups in fashion during the 15th cen-
tury in the kingdom of Bohemia.

1591b   DENKSTEIN, VLADIMÍR. "Pavézy ceského typu, studie k dejinám husitské vojenské
tradice, jejího rozsírení a vlivu v 15. století." [Pavises of the Bohemian Type, Contribution
to the History of the Hussite Military Tradition, Its Dissemination and Influence in the
15th Century.] *Sborník Národního Muzea v Praze*. Part 1, 16 (1962):185-228, 2 color figs.,
53 b&w figs.; part 2, 18 (1964):107-94, 34 b&w figs.; part 3, 19 (1965):117-203, 12-page ad-
dendum, 64 b&w figs. Czech/English text.
Characteristics of 15th-century large infantry shields of Bohemian origin preserved in
Prague as well as in museums of other cities. Their important painted decoration and wide influence on similar shields of a later date produced elsewhere in Europe.

FRENCH

Arms and Armor

3. SURVEYS AND HISTORIES

1592   GRANCSAY, STEPHEN V. "Knights in Armor." *Metropolitan Museum of Art Bulletin* 6 (1948):178-88, 11 b&w figs.

Valuable information on French arms and armor—such as depiction of now rare or extant types and method of holding—can be drawn from contemporary tapestries.

8. PRIVATE COLLECTION, AUCTION, AND DEALER CATALOGS

TALLEYRAND-PÉRIGORD COLLECTION

1593   COSSON, BARON [C.A.] DE. *Le Cabinet d'armes de Maurice de Talleyrand—Périgord, duc de Dino: Étude descriptive*. Paris: Édouard Rouveyre, 1901. 119 pp., 23 b&w pls.

Important collection of over three hundred items of arms and armor owned by this family and formed primarily in the 16th century. Includes full and partial suits (helmets of Henri II and IV of France), swords, daggers, rondaches, halberds, etc., as well as ivory saddles and some 17th-century firearms (arquebus of Louis XIII) and shield of Louis XIV.

Arms

6. PERMANENT COLLECTIONS

Écouen

MUSÉE NATIONAL DE LA RENAISSANCE

1594   DEMANGE, FRANÇOISE and ERLANDE-BRANDENBURG, ALAIN. "Une Réduction de canon à l'emblématique de Catherine de Médicis." *Revue du Louvre* 30 (1980):109-14. 10 b&w figs.

Small-scale (55 cm. long) canon cast between 1559-89, one of four in the inventory of Catherine de' Medici.

Zurich

SCHWEIZERISCHES LANDESMUSEUM

1595   STÜBER, KARL. "Das Wappen Strassburgs auf dem Zwingli-Schwert." *Zeitschrift für schweizerische Archäologie und Kunstgeschichte* 38 (1981):290-2, 4 b&w figs.

Sword of the Zurich reformer Huldrych Zwingli produced ca. 1519 in Strasbourg and now in the museum of his native city.

Armor

3. SURVEYS AND HISTORIES

1596   FFOULKES, CHARLES. "The Armour of Jeanne d'Arc" *Burlington Magazine* 16 (1909-10):141-46, 2 b&w figs., 7 line drawings.
Author evaluates the reliability of representations of the maid's armor. Among anachronistic renderings is the incised slab in the crypt of St.-Denis.

1597   NORMAN, A.V.B. "A Pauldron in the Scott Collection of Arms and Armour." *Scottish Art Review* 7 (1960):8-11, 30; 5 b&w figs.
A left pauldron of the late fifteenth century in the German style bearing an unidentified armorer's mark, which appears on at least five other pieces in various collections, including a right pauldron in the Metropolitan Museum of Art. Perhaps the work of Romain des Ursins, a Milanese armorer working for the French court at Tours.

1598   THOMAS, BRUNO. "Die münchner Harnischvorzeichnungen des Étienne Delaune für die Emblem- und die Schlangen-Garnitur Heinrichs II. von Frankreich." *Jahrbuch der kunsthistorischen Sammlungen in Wien* n.s. 20 (1960):7-62, 61 b&w figs.
Drawings of Étienne Delaune, often with scroll patterns, preserved in the Staatlichen Graphischen Sammlung, Munich, which the artist made in relation to the decoration of armors produced for King Henri II of France.

1599   THOMAS, BRUNO. "Die münchner Harnischvorzeichnungen im Stil François Ier." *Jahrbuch der kunsthistorischen Sammlungen in Wien* n.s. 19 (1959):31-74, 50 b&w figs.
Series of 16th-century drawings relating to parade armor with mannerist forms and designs that can be associated with the School of Fontainebleau and the works of the Negroli family of armorers in Milan.

6. PERMANENT COLLECTIONS

New York

METROPOLITAN MUSEUM OF ART

1600   GRANCSAY, STEPHEN V. "The Armor of Henry II of France from the Louvre Museum." *Metropolitan Museum of Art Bulletin* 11 (1952):68-80, 28 b&w pls.
The "Medici" helmet in the collection compared to Henri II's armor in Paris; both of the "Louvre School" and dating of ca. 1560; their stylistic connection with the Fontainebleau School through designs by followers of Giulio Romano.

GERMAN

Arms and Armor

3. SURVEYS AND HISTORIES

1601   WILLERS, JOHANNES. "Nuremberg Weapons and Armour." *Connoisseur* 199 (1978):172-79, 4 color figs., 7 b&w figs.

Art of the armorer in Nuremberg from the 10th to the 18th century. Particularly relevant to the 15th and 16th century are swords, spears, halberds, and defensive armor. Also deals with guild divisions and statistics, foreign influences, and production.

6. PERMANENT COLLECTIONS

Moscow

GOSSUDARTSTVENNYJ ISTORITSCHESKIJ MUSEJ

1602   "Spoils of War in the State Historical Museum, Moscow." *Connoisseur* 165 (1967):1-3, 10 b&w figs.
Identification of nineteen 16th-century German suits (among them armor of Herzog Friedrich von Liegnitz by Konrad Seusenhofer), component parts, and arms formerly in the Zeughaus, Berlin, and the Musée de l'Armée, Paris, that were finally removed from East Germany by the Soviets in the aftermath of World War II.

Arms

3. SURVEYS AND HISTORIES

1603   ASH, DOUGLAS. "The Fighting Halberd." *Connoisseur* 125 (1950):101-5, 22 b&w figs.
Evolution of this pole weapon in Germany from ca. 800 to the 15th-16th century with examples drawn mostly from the author's collection and the holdings of the Bern Museum.

1604   BOHLMANN, ROBERT. "Über Jagd-, Schwein- und Landsknechtsschwerter." *Zeitschrift für historische Waffen- und Kostümkunde* n.s. 5 (1935-36):117-21, 11 b&w figs.
German hunting and fighting swords of the 16th century; variations in pommels and guards.

1605   THOMAS, BRUNO. "The Hunting Knives of Emperor Maximilian I." *Metropolitan Museum of Art Bulletin* 13 (1955):201-8, 14 b&w figs.
Attribution of a series of knives of the "Burgundian type" in Kremsmünster, the Wallace Collection, and the Metropolitan Museum, to Hans Sumersperger.

6. PERMANENT COLLECTIONS

Dresden

HISTORISCHES MUSEUM

1606   STARKE, HEIDRUN. "Ein Prunkschwert der deutschen Frührenaissance." *Dredener Kunstblätter* 15 (1971):144-48, 3 illus.
A ceremonial sword embossed on the front and etched on the back with leaf ornaments and two scenes of combat in the style of H. Aldegrever, made in Augsburg or Nuremberg after 1530.

New York

METROPOLITAN MUSEUM OF ART

1607   GRANCSAY, STEPHEN V. "A Wheellock Pistol Made for the Emperor Charles V."
Metropolitan Museum of Art Bulletin 6 (1947):116-22, 8 b&w figs.
Technical and historical examination of a double-barreled pistol with inlaid staghorn
and gilt and etched metal of ca. 1540—considered to be the most valuable firearm in the
museum's collection on account of its historic association, technical features and the workmanship of Peter Pech of Munich (bears his mark P).

Nuremberg

GERMANISCHES NATIONALMUSEUM

1608   WEGNER, WOLFGANG. "Eine Schwert von Daniel Hopfer im Germanischen Nationalmuseum in Nürnberg," *Münchner Jahrbuch der bildenden Kunst,* 3d ser., 5 (1954):124-30, 5
b&w figs.
A ceremonial sword dating of ca. 1536 wth intricate damascene decoration signed by
the engraver Daniel Hopfer.

1609   WILLERS, JOHANNES. "Firearms and Military Models from Nuremberg." *Connoisseur*
199 (1978):188-91, 3 color figs., 6 b&w figs.
Manufacture of firearms in Nuremberg in the 14th-16th- century; traces the development of types, technical progress, ornamentation, and makers' marks; illustrates 16th-century
guns, pistols, and canons from the Germanisches Nationalmuseum.

Weimar

STAATLICHE KUNSTSAMMLUNGEN – SCHLOSSMUSEUM

1610   SCHENK ZU SCHWEINSBERG, E. FRHR. "Ein Schwertriss Wenzel Jamnitzers von
1544." *Jahrbuch der preuszischen Kunstsammlungen* 47 (1926):38-47, 5 b&w figs.
Highly ornamented ceremonial sword of 1544 held to be the work of Wenzel Jamnitzer.

Armor

3. SURVEYS AND HISTORIES

1611   BUTTIN, CHARLES. "L'Armure et le chanfrein de Phillippe II." *Revue de l'art ancien
et moderne* 35 (1914):183-98, 3 b&w pls, 9 b&w figs.
Chamfron, roundels, and cubitieres from an armor produced by Desiderius Colman
and engraved by Jörg Sigman of Augsburg in 1549/50 for Phillip II of Spain.

1612   CRIPPS-DAY, F.H. "Some Armours of the Electors of Saxony and Portraits Depicting
Them." *Connoisseur* 112 (1943):71- 78, 17 b&w figs.
Armor and armored portraits of the 16th-early 17th-century electors housed in the
Historisches Museum at Dresden, and engravings of Shrenck's *Armamentarium heroicum*
published in 1601.

1613   GAMBER, ORTWIN. "Kolman Helmschmid, Ferdinand I. und das Thun'sche Skizzenbuch." *Jahrbuch der kunsthistorischen Sammlungen in Wien* n.s. 35 (1975):9-38, 56 b&w
figs.
Series of detailed drawings in the Thun-Hohenstein Library at Tetschen (Czechoslovakia) recording major armors made for Ferdinand I, Maximilian II, Charles V, etc., many
of which were produced during the first half of the 16th century by the master armorer Kolman Helmschmied.

1614   HAYWARD, J.F. "Some Augsburg Armours Etched by Jörg Sorg." *Burlington Magazine*
90 (1948):253-57, 6 b&w figs.
Author traces design of overlapping trilobed scales on chanfron (Victoria and Albert
Museum) made for Enriquez de Ribera, a Spanish nobleman, that he dates of 1550, to various
drawings in Jörg Sorg's pattern album, and matches armor elements with similar ornaments in
Turin, Metropolitan Museum of Art, and Victoria and Albert Museum, to Sorg's drawings of
armor made by Anton Pfeffenhausen for another Spanish patron, Don Alba de Bomont Dassa.

1615   MANN, JAMES G. "The Etched Decoration of Armour: A Study in Classification."
Proceedings of the British Academy 27 (1940):1-31, 21 b&w figs.
Regional styles of etched and engraved decoration in five centers of Germany:
Augsburg, Nuremberg, Landshut, Dresden, and Innsbruck; reproduction of complete suits
and single elements primarily of the 16th century.

1616   POST, PAUL. "Zum 'Silbernen Harnisch' Kaiser Maximilians I von Coloman Kolman
mit Ätzentwürfen Albrecht Dürers." *Zeitschrift für historische Waffen- und Kostümkunde*
n.s. 6 (1937-39):253-58, 8 b&w figs.
Drawings by Dürer at the Albertina for designs to be etched on a silver armor for
Emperor Maximilian I.

1617   REITZENSTEIN, ALEXANDER VON. "Der Landshuter Plattner Sigismund Wolf."
Münchner Jahrbuch der bildenden Kunst, 13 (1938):103-6, 2 b&w figs.
Visors produced by the mid-16th-century armorer Sigismund Wolf of Landshut.

1618   REITZENSTEIN, ALEXANDER VON. "Der Landshuter Plattner Wolfgang und Franz
Grosschedel," *Münchner Jahrbuch der bildenden Kunst,* 3d ser., 5 (1954):142-53, 10 b&w
figs.
Armors made by the German metalsmiths Wolfgang and Franz Grosschedel of
Landshut in the 16th century for the Hapsburgs and their courtiers.

1619   THOMAS, BRUNO. "Jörg Helmschmied d.j.—Plattner Maximilians I. in Augsburg und
Wien." *Jahrbuch des Kunsthistorischen Sammlungen in Wien* n.s. 16 (1956):33-50, 19 b&w
figs.
Breastplates and visors produced by the armorer Jörg Helmschmied the Younger
and Lorenz Helmschmied of Augsburg in the second half of the 15th century for the court of
Maximilian I.

1620   THOMAS, BRUNO. "Nürnberger Plattnerkunst in Wien." *Anzeiger des Germanischen
Nationalmuseums* (1963):89-99, 7 b&w figs.
Armor by the 15th-17th-century metalsmiths of Nuremberg Hans Grünewalt, Wohl
Konrad Poler, Valentin Siebenbürger, Kunz Lochner, Master HB, and Jörg Hardtmann.

1621   THOMAS, BRUNO. "Portions of the Rogendorf Armour in the Wallace Collection." *Burlington Magazine* 92 (1950):173-74, 3 b&w figs.

Description of an early 16th-century suit (Waffensammlung, Vienna) made by Koloman Colman of Augsburg for Wilhelm von Rogendorf, distinctive for its large "puffed" sleeves in imitation of contemporary costume and its unique etched decoration, and for its alternative (conventional) arm defense in the Wallace Collection and Vienna.

6. PERMANENT COLLECTIONS

Moscow

GOSSUDARTSVENNYJ ISTORITSCHESKIJ MUSEJ

1622   ARENDT, W. "Ein Werk des Kunz Lochner in der Moskauer Rüstkammer." *Zeitschrift für historische Waffen- und Kostümkunde* n.s. 5 (1935-36):69-72, 6 b&w figs.

Brief description of a matching armor for rider and horse with embossed and etched decoration, produced in 1550 by Kunz Lochner for the Margrave of Brandenburg.

Paris

MUSÉE DE L'ARMÉE

1623   REITZENSTEIN, ALEXANDER VON. "Der Ringlersche Harnische des Pfalzgrafen Ottheinrich." *Anzeiger des Germanischen Nationalmuseums* (1964):44-56, 15 b&w figs.

Set of armor for rider and horse by the Nuremberg metalsmith Hans Ringler made in 1532 for Count Palatine Otto Heinrich.

Stendal

ALTMÄRKISCHES MUSEUM

1624   BOHLMANN, ROBERT. "Ein gesteppter Waffenrock des 15. Jahrhunderts in Stendal." *Zeitschrift für historische Waffen- und Kostümkunde* n.s. 6 (1937-39):259-61, 5 b&w figs.

Quilted garment to be worn under wide shirtlike armor, both dating of ca. 1430-40.

Vienna

KUNSTHISTORISCHES MUSEUM – WAFFENSAMMLUNG

1625   THOMAS, BRUNO. "Der Wiener Ottheinrich-Harnisch von Koloman Colman: Stilkritik und Waffenkunde." *Zeitschrift für historische Waffen- und Kostümkunde* n.s. 6 (1937-39):116-23, 6 b&w figs.

The armor made by the Augsburg silversmith Koloman Colman (1470/71-1532) for Count Palatine Otto Heinrich.

1626   WENZEL, ERNST. "Die harnische Landgraf Philipps des Grossmütigen von Hessen." *Zeitschrift für historische Waffen- und Kostümkunde* n.s. 6 (1937-39):181-87, 9 b&w figs.

Etched armor of Philip, Count of Hessen, produced in 1534.

1627   THOMAS, BRUNO. "Kaiser Ferdinands I. Harnisch von Kunz Lochner." *Jahrbuch des kunsthistorischen Sammlungen in Wien* n.s. 14 (1953):131-36, 9 b&w figs.

Parade armor with niello decoration (elements in Waffensammlung) produced ca. 1545 in Nuremberg by Kunz Lochner for Emperor Ferdinand I who was portrayed wearing it by Titian.

1628   GAMBER, ORTWIN. "Der Turnierharnisch zur Zeit König Maximilians I. und das Thunsche Skizzenbuch." *Jahrbuch des Kunsthistorischen Sammlungen in Wien* n.s. 17 (1957):33-70, 89 b&w figs.
    Jousting armors of the time of Maximilian I studied through the examples made by Lorenz Helmschmied now in the Waffensammlung, and the drawings in a 15th-century codex now in Tetchen (Czechoslovakia).

ITALIAN

Arms and Armor

3. SURVEYS AND HISTORIES

1629   BOCCIA, LIONELLO G.; ROSSI, FRANCESCO; and MORIN, MARCO. *Armi e armature lombarde.* Milan: Electa, 1980. 279 pp., 67 color figs., 295 b&w figs.
    Pictorial survey of Lombard arms and armor of the 12th to the 19th century with three essays describing production, evolution of elements and styles, and characteristics of Lombard armor centers. Particularly useful large plates.

6. PERMANENT COLLECTIONS

Detroit

DETROIT INSTITUTE OF ARTS

1630   BOCCIA, LIONELLO G. "Arms and Armour from the Medici Court." *Bulletin of The Detroit Institute of Arts* 61, no. 1/2 (1983):58-64, 8 b&w figs.
    Of approximately a thousand pieces surviving from the Medici armories, two corslets of the late 16th century and a German wheellock gun of ca. 1610 formerly in the Hearst Collection, are now in Detroit.

Arms

3. SURVEYS AND HISTORIES

Books

1631   BOCCIA, LIONELLO G. and COELHO, EDUARDO T. *Armi bianche italiane.* Milan: Bramante, 1975. 462 pp., 43 color figs., 757 b&w figs., numerous line drawings and fac-simile armorers' marks.
    Comprehesive study of ornamentation of swords, daggers, lances, produced in all regions of Italy from the 13th to the 19th century through eight hundred examples with useful illustration and short catalog entries and preceded by a twenty- nine-page essay.

1632   GAIBI, AGOSTINO. *Le armi da fuoco portatili italiane dalle origini al Risorgimento.* Milan: Bramante, 1962. 527 pp., 71 color pls., 239 b&w pls. Italian/French/English captions.

    Authoritative study on Italian firearms from the first years of the 14th through the 19th century. Some 15th- and many 16th-century examples of hand guns, wall guns, barrels of portable firearms, muskets, arquebuses, crossbows, petronels, powder flasks, wheel-lock pistols, etc., most decorated with chiseling. Includes catalog with brief entries and an eighty-nine-page introduction.

Articles

1633   LAUTS, JAN. "Eine Gruppe ferraresischer Cinquedeen aus dem Ende des 15. Jahrhunderts." *Zeitschrift für historische Waffen- und Kostümkunde* n.s. 5 (1935-36):122-26, 6 b&w figs.

    Series of eight daggers produced in Ferrara at the end of the 15th century with niello decoration related to the frescoes of the Palazzo Schifanoia.

1634   NORTH, A.R.E. "A Late Fifteenth Century Italian Sword." *Connoisseur* 190 (1975):238-41, 6 b&w illus.

    A late 15th-century sword in a private collection is reassigned to North Italy or specifically Venice from a Moroccan attribution on the basis of hilts (grips and pommels), guards, and blades.

6. PERMANENT COLLECTIONS

London

VICTORIA AND ALBERT MUSEUM

1635   BLAIR, CLAUDE. "Cesare Borgia's Sword-Scabbard." *Victoria and Albert Museum Bulletin* 2 (1966):125-36, 14 b&w figs.

    Description and technique used in decoration of a scabbard with high relief and detailed modeling. Author proposes it was made in 1498 by "Herculis," a Milanese or Brescian metalsmith who signed a similar scabbard at the Musée de l'Armée, Paris, and a sword in a private collection, Rome.

Armor

3. SURVEYS AND HISTORIES

Book

1636   GELLI, J. and MORETTI, G. *Gli armaroli milanesi: I Missaglia e la loro casa.* Milan: Ulrico Hoepli, 1903. 117 pp., 56 b&w pls., many line drawings in text.

    Dated but still useful reference on one of the major Milanese armorer families. Also includes biographical information and mention of the activity of other workshops (Negroli, etc.) of the late 15th and especially the 16th century.

Articles

1637   BEARD, CHARLES R. "A New-Found Casque by the Negroli." *Connoisseur* 101 (1938):293-99, 399; 12 b&w figs.
Examines a previously unpublished helmet (London, unspecified location) bearing richly embossed classical and grotesque decoration and attributed here to the workshop of the Negroli brothers of Milan, 1545-50, on the basis of comparison of construction and style with other helmets in the Kunsthistorisches Museum, Vienna, and The Metropolitan Museum of Art.

1638   GAMBER, ORTWIN. "Der italienische Harnische im 16. Jahrhundert." *Jahrbuch der kunsthistorischen Sammlungen in Wien* n.s. 18 (1958):73-120, 79 b&w figs.
Italian suits of armor of the 16th century from extant examples and those depicted in sculpture and painting: particularities, components, major patrons, and master silversmiths are studied.

1639   KURZ, OTTO. "A Gold Helmet Made in Venice for Sultan Sulayman the Magnificent." *Gazette des beaux-arts* 74 (1969):249-58, 4 b&w figs. Reprinted in *The Decorative Arts of Europe and the Islamic East: Selected Studies.* London: Dorian Press, 1977.
Bejeweled helmet consisting of four crowns made in 1532 by the Venetian goldsmiths Luigi Caorlini and Vincenzo Lavriero for the purpose of selling it to the sultan and as recorded in an engraving of Agostino Musi Veneziano.

1640   PYHRR, STUART W. "Some Elements of Armor Attributed to Niccolò Silva." *Metropolitan Museum Journal* 18 (1983):111-21, 16 b&w figs.
Attribution, on the basis of ornaments and precision of draftsmanship, with reappraisal of attributions, of several unmarked pieces in the Metropolitan Museum and the Museo Stibbert, Florence, to this 16th-century documented armorer.

6. PERMANENT COLLECTIONS

Florence

MUSEO NAZIONALE DEL BARGELLO

1641   COSSON, C.A. DE. "Notizie su diversi pezzi d'armatura provenienti dall'antica armeria medicea esistenti nel Museo Nazionale di Firenze." *L'arte* 17 (1914):387-92, 7 b&w figs.
Breastplate and pauldrons from the Medici collection attributed to the armorer Bartolomeo Campi of Pesaro (active before 1456, died 1473), who worked at the court of Urbino.

MUSEO STIBBERT

1642   KÖNIGER, ERNST. "Ein Harnisch des Pompeo della Chiesa auf dem Bildnis eines jungen Mannes 'von Salomon Adler.'" *Anzeiger des Germanischen Nationalmuseums* (1964):104-5, 2 b&w figs.
Armor of the 1580s signed by the Milanese Pompeo della Chiesa is reproduced in the Portrait of a Young Man of 1679-91 by the painter Salomon Adler acquired by the Germanisches Nationalmuseum in 1963.

Madrid

REALE ARMERIA

1643 CORTÉS, JAVIER. "Armature italiane nella Reale Armeria di Madrid." *Antichità viva* 2, no. 6 (1963):33- 42, 1 color fig., 15 b&w figs.

Prestigious suits of armor for the Hapsburgs fashioned and often signed by Milanese armorers (Missagli, Negroli, Campi, etc.).

Mantua

S. MARIA DELLE GRAZIE

1644 MANN, J.G. "The Sanctuary of the Madonna delle Grazie, with Notes on the Evolution of Italian Armour during the Fifteenth Century." *Archaeologia* 80 (1930):117-42, 46 b&w figs., 16 line drawings.

The discovery of several complete suits and of component parts—probably from Gonzaga armories—displayed on early 17th-century life-size papier maché figures in the Franciscan monastery west of Mantua, provides important examples in the evolution of Italian armor.

1644a MANN, J.G. "A Further Account of the Armour Preserved in the Sanctuary of the Madonna delle Grazie near Mantua." *Archaeologia* 87 (1938):311-52, 126 b&w figs., facsimiles of armorers' marks.

Sequel to the author's previous article (see above). Detailed description and classification of six reassembled complete suits of the 15th century and many component parts of the 15th century and 16th century, all restored and revealing thirty-nine different Milanese armorers' marks.

1645 BOCCIA, LIONELLO GIORGIO. *Le armature de S. Maria delle Grazie de Curtatone de Mantova e l'armatura lombarda del'400.* [Milan]: Bramante, 1982. 303 pp., 20 color pls., 536 b&w figs.

This large collection of armor gives rise to a study of 15th-century Lombard and particularly Milanese suits and components. Includes catalog and sixteen-page appendix.

New York

METROPOLITAN MUSEUM OF ART

1646 GRANCSAY, STEPHEN V. "A Parade Shield of Charles V." *Metropolitan Museum of Art Bulletin* 8 (1949):122-32, 13 b&w figs.

Description of an embossed, gilded, silvered, and partially damascened shield depicting a scene from the Battle of Mühlberg (1547) based on a drawing by Maerten van Heemskerck and produced for Emperor Charles V in Milan ca. 1555 to commemorate his victory.

1647 GRANCSAY, STEPHEN V. "Museum Armor and a Van Dyck Portrait from Vienna." *Metropolitan Museum of Art Bulletin* 8 (1950):270-73, 4 b&w figs.

An Italian helmet and breastplate of ca. 1560 similar in decoration to the cuirass worn by a young knight in a Van Dyck portrait, corroboate the identification of the sitter as Ferdinando Gonzaga, duke of Mantua.

1648   GRANCSAY, STEPHEN V.   "Sculpture in Steel: A Milanese Renaissance Barbute."
Metropolitan Museum of Art Bulletin n.s. 21 (1963):182-91, 9 b&w figs.
Helmet of ca. 1470 bearing the mark of the armorer Jacobo de Canobbio detto
Bichignola, formerly in the Douglas and Cosson collections.

1649   GRANCSAY, STEPHEN V.   "Lucio Piccinino, Master Armorer of the Renaissance."
Metropolitan Museum of Art Bulletin n.s. 22 (1964):257-71, 20 b&w figs.
Half body armor with involved embossed decoration commissioned by the Duke of
Alba ca. 1470 is held to have been produced by the Milanese Lucio Piccinino on the basis of
Alessandro Farnese's full suit now in the Waffensammlung, Vienna.

Oxford

ASHMOLEAN MUSEUM

1650   LAKING, GUY.   "An Early Work of Lucio Piccinino." *Burlington Magazine* 31 (1917):26-
30, 2 b&w figs.
Attribution of an embossed pageant shield of the mid-16th century bearing a Medusa
mask in high relief to the Milanese armorer Piccinino producing designs similar in conception
to those of the Negroli but with his own distinctive method of applying gold decoration.

Vienna

KUNSTHISTORISCHES MUSEUM – WAFFENSAMMLUNG

1651   LAUTS, JAN.   "Eine neue Vorzeichnung zum Farnese-Harnisch der Wiener Waffensammlung." *Jahrbuch der kunsthistorischen Sammlungen in Wien* 10 (1936):207-9, 4 b&w figs.
Armor produced in 1565 by Lucio Piccinino of Milan for Alessandro Farnese.

SPANISH

Arms

3. SURVEYS AND HISTORIES

1652   BLAIR, CLAUDE.   "A Royal Swordsmith and Damascener: Diego de Çajas."
Metropolitan Museum Journal 3 (1970):149-98, 76 figs.
Inclusive study on this 16th-century Spanish artist and workshop whose damascened
arms were in great demand and of which thirty-seven pieces are now scattered among major
collections.

Armor

6. PERMANENT COLLECTIONS

Baltimore

WALTERS ART GALLERY

1653   GRANCSAY, STEPHEN V.   "An Historical Spanish Suit of Armor." *Apollo* 100 (1974):410-14, 5 b&w figs.
Suit of armor made for Alonso Pérez de Guzmán, 7th duke of Medina Sidonia (1542-1615) is attributed to the Spanish armor-making center of Eugui near Pamplona, which produced a hybrid style comprising Milanese, Augsburg, and Spanish characteristics.

SWISS

Armor

3. SURVEYS AND HISTORIES

1654   SCHNEIDER, HUGO.   "Harnischproduktion in der Schweiz am Beispiel von Zürich." *Zeitschrift für schweizerische Archäologie und Kunstgeschichte* 28 (1971):175-84, 7 b&w figs.
Breastplates produced in Switzerland in the late 16th to early 17th century, especially in Zurich; makers' marks and control stamps.

6. PERMANENT COLLECTIONS

Sion

MUSÉE DE VALÈRE

1655   SCHNEIDER, HUGO.   "Ein Kampfschild aus dem 14. Jahrhundert." *Waffen- und Kostümkunde* 23 (1981):77- 86, 13 b&w figs.
Five large oblong shields (pavises) of the 14th-15th century on which figure a painted image of the church.

XXIX. Textiles — Introduction

A. MULTI COUNTRY OF ORIGIN

1. DICTIONARIES AND ENCYCLOPEDIAS

1656   *Encyclopedia of Textiles,* by the editors of American Fabrics and Fashion Magazine. 3d ed. Englewood Cliffs, N.J.: Prentice-Hall, 1980. 702 pp., numerous b&w figs. (1st ed. 1960.)

      Source volume on textiles: history, types, design, manufacture, etc. Although dealing primarily with later works, pertinent to 1400-1600 are: the chronological history (pp. 161- 63); various chapters on specific textiles and manufacturing processes; dictionary of textile terms (515-601).

3. SURVEYS AND HISTORIES

Books

1657   *Aspetti e problemi degli studi sui tessili antichi. Il Convegno C.I.S.S.T. Firenze 1981.* Edited by Giuliana Chesne Dauphine Griffo. Florence: Edizioni C.I.S.S.T. Sezione Toscana, 1983. 159 pp., 10 color illus., 106 b&w figs.

      Series of twelve essays dealing with the conservation of major textiles dating mostly of the 14th-16th century in Italian museums produced not only in Italy but also in adjacent countries.

1658   BRANTING, AGNES, and LINDBLOM, ANDREAS. *Medieval Embroideries and Textiles in Sweden.* Translated by J.S. Herrström. 2 vols. Uppsala and Stockholm: Almqvist & Wiksells Boktryckeri-A.-B., 1932. 1:155 pp., 4 color figs., 119 b&w figs.; 2:40 color pls., 180 b&w figs.

      Wall hangings, ophreys, copes, chasubles, mitres, altar frontals in Swedish museums and churches. Characteristics and techniques of Swedish embroideries in silk, wool, gold and silver threads (pp. 19-78); Netherlandish (103-18), German (119-34), English (135-37) embroideries of the 15th century; Florentine Renaissance textiles (141-43).

1659   EMERY, IRENE. *The Primary Structures of Fabrics: An Illustrated Classification.* Washington: Textile Museum, 1966. 365 pp., 378 b&w figs.

Useful explanation of fabric types and manufacturing techniques (e.g., for lace, brocade, damask, embroidery, tapestry weave); basic terminology.

1660   GEIJER, AGNES. *A History of Textile Art.* Translated by Roger Tanner. London: Pasold Research Foundation in association with Sotheby Parke Bernet Publications and Philip Wilson Publishers, 1979. 378 pp., 113 b&w text figs., 4 color pls., 95 b&w pls.

Surveys world history of textiles from antiquity to the 20th century with much detailed technical information and discussion of specific topics: silk manufacturing, pile fabrics, dyeing and textile printing, and the textile trade. Includes useful information pertinent to the years 1400-1600.

1661   HUNTER, GEORGE LELAND. *Decorative Textiles.* Philadelphia and London: J.B. Lippincott Co.; Grand Rapids, Mich.: Dean Hicks Co., 1918. 480 pp., 27 color pls., 553 b&w figs.

Comprehensive work on coverings of all periods for furniture (chairs, screens, etc.), wall hangings, and floor rugs, including damasks, brocades, velvets, tapestries, laces, embroideries, tooled and embossed leather.

1662   SCHMEDDING, BRIGITTA. *Mittelalterliche Textilien in Kirchen und Klöstern der Schweiz.* Bern: Abegg-Stiftung, 1978. 325 pp., 29 color pls., 343 b&w figs.

Catalog of 296 medieval textiles in churches and abbeys of Switzerland arranged alphabetically by location. Emphasis is on technical description and conditions. Includes several liturgical textiles of the 15th century.

Article

1663   WESCHER, H. "Embroiderers and Painters of Flags." *Ciba Review* 77 (1949):2825-30, 5 b&w figs.

Silks, embroideries, painted linen—elements to produce banners in the 15th century and earlier periods.

4. BIBLIOGRAPHICAL GUIDES

1664   MARQUET DE VASSELOT, J.J., and WEIGERT, ROGER-ARMAND. *Bibliographie de la tapisserie, des tapis et de la broderie en France.* Paris: Librairie Armand Colin, 1935. 369 pp.

Bibliography (by and large without annotations) of twenty-seven hundred articles, books, or catalogs published from the 18th century until 1934 and dealing with French tapestries, carpets, embroidery, and lace produced from the 14th through the early 20th century. Presented under the following headings: references, techniques and marks, specific periods (Middle Ages and Renaissance, pp. 23-26), proper names, iconographic subjects, manufacturing centers, locations (of textile), model books; concludes with a forty-five-page index.

1665   WASHINGTON, THE TEXTILE MUSEUM, ARTHUR D. JENKINS LIBRARY. *Rug and Textile Arts: A Periodical Index, 1890-1982.* Edited by Katherine T. Freshley. Boston: G.K. Hall & Co., 1983. 485 pp.

Catalog reproducing library cards of selected articles from over three hundred international periodicals, most dating from 1920 to the present. Comprises two sections: Author and Subject/Title, the latter subdivided by geographical location and then by time period. A very useful tool.

6. PERMANENT COLLECTIONS

Cleveland

CLEVELAND MUSEUM OF ART

1666   *Textiles in Daily Life in the Middle Ages.*   Exhibition catalog by Rebecca Martin. Cleveland: Cleveland Museum of Art; Bloomington: Indiana University Press, 1985. 68 pp., 4 color pls., 41 b&w figs.
        Essays on ecclesiastical and secular textiles illustrated with seventeen representative examples, three oil panels, two miniatures, one engraving, ivory, furniture, all drawn, but for one (Philadelphia), from Cleveland's permanent collection, half dating of the 15th century.

Indianapolis

INDIANAPOLIS MUSEUM OF ART

1667   *Fabrics in Celebration from the Collection.*   Exhibition catalog by Peggy Stoltz Gilfay, with technical analysis by Katherine Dolk-Ellis, Indianapolis: Indianapolis Museum of Art, 1983. 391 pp., 33 color illus., 222 b&w figs.
        Catalog of 168 representative entries highlighting the museum's important textile collection (over seven thousand items). Catalog is geographically arranged, each section accompanied by a brief introduction. Comprehensive entries provide complete physical, including technical, descriptions and pertinent overview of those aspects of the art of weaving as they relate to the pieces. For 15th-16th-century European textiles, see cat. nos. 94-102, which include velvets, damasks, and embroideries from Italy, Spain, Switzerland, and England. Glossary, appended with structural analysis and condition report.

London

VICTORIA AND ALBERT MUSEUM

1668   *Textile Fabrics; a Descriptive Catalogue of the Collection of Church-Vestments, Dresses, Silk Stuffs, Needlework and Tapestries, Forming That Section of the [South Kensington] Museum,* by Daniel Rock. London: Chapman & Hall, 1870. 524 pp., 20 b&w figs.
        A 152-page introduction examines, in a rambling and dated style, the nature of different textiles, types of embroidery, tapestries. Entries, mostly descriptive, for the museum's extensive holdings of ecclesiastical vestments, altar frontals, textile fragments, and embroideries, many of the period 1400-1600, as well as some Flemish and German 15th-16th-century tapestries. Useful to gain an overview of the collection.

Lyon

MUSÉE HISTORIQUE DES TISSUS

1669   COX, RAYMOND. *L'Art de décorer les tissus d'après les collections du Musée Historique de la Chambre de Commerce de Lyon.* Paris: P. Mouillot; Lyon: A. Rey et Cie, 1900. 39 pp., 39 chromolithographs, 88 b&w pls.
Even though dated, this is still the most complete survey of this world famous textile collection, which includes many examples of European 15th-16th-century secular and ecclesiastical silks and embroideries, as well as tapestries.

Milan

MUSEO POLDI PEZZOLI

1670   *Arazzi, tappeti, tessuti copti, pizzi, ricami, ventagli.* Vol. 4 of museum catalogs, edited by Carlo Pirovano, with entries by Peggy Eskenazi, Mercedes Viale Ferrero, Alessandra Mottola Molfino, and Annapaola Zaccaria Ruggiu. Milan: Electa, 1984. 452 pp., 37 color figs. 666 b&w figs.
For the period 1400-1600 are Flemish and Italian tapestries (cat. nos. 1-3, pp. 17-19; figs. 1-17, pp. 21-32), Italian and Flemish lace (pp. 131-43, nos. 1-6, 8-40, 42-49, 51- 54, 74-78, 82; figs. 1-6, 8-33, 36-43, 45-48, 67-69, 73, pp. 181-91, 194-97, 204-5), and Italian and German embroideries (pp. 323-28, nos. 1-12, 18, 20-22, 25-27; figs. 1-12, 18, 20-22, 25-27, pp. 345-54). Three-page glossary.

Oxford

BODLEIAN LIBRARY

1671   *Textile and Embroidered Bindings.* Introduction by Giles Barber. Oxford: Oxford University Press, 1971. 11 pp., 30 b&w pls.
Handbook of choice velvet, silk, satin, and embroidered European bindings of the 15th-19th century; includes eleven plates of specimens dating 1400-1600. Seven-page introduction traces the history of such bindings and highlights the holdings at Oxford.

Zurich

SCHWEIZERISCHES LANDESMUSEUM

1672   *Textilien.* Catalog by Jenny Schneider. Zurich: Berichthaus, 1975. 251 pp., 28 color figs., 137 b&w figs.
Catalog of 165 textiles including some well-known tapestries, brocades, and embroideries of the 15th-16th century.

7. EXHIBITION CATALOGS

London

VICTORIA AND ALBERT MUSEUM

1673   *The Franco-British Exhibition of Textiles.* London: His Majesty's Stationery Office, 1922. 26 pp., 50 b&w pls.

259 examples of the 15th-18th century from French (mostly) and English public and private collections. Many Flemish and English and some Spanish, German, French, and Italian 15th-16th-century tapestries, ecclesiastical vestments, and embroideries (nos. 29-38, 58-59, 61-64, 85, 96-97, 101-10, 116, 119-21, 137-41, 143, 145-49, 160-70, 173-87, 203-9, 217-19); brief entries.

B. SINGLE COUNTRY OF ORIGIN

BELGIUM

3. SURVEYS AND HISTORIES

1674   VERSYP, J. "Enkele nieuwe gegevens betreffende gehistorieerd damastlinnen uit de late middeleeuwen." *Artes textiles* 1 (1953):25-30. French summary
Damascened and historiated tablecloths produced in Bruges, Brussels, Tournai, Ghent, and Malines from the mid-15th to the mid-16th century.

BRITISH (ENGLISH)

3. SURVEYS AND HISTORIES

1675   HUNTON, W. GORDON. *English Decorative Textiles: Tapestry and Chintz, Their Design and Development from the Earliest Times to the Nineteenth Century.* London: John Tiranti & Co., 1930. 9 pp., 181 b&w pls.
Pictorial survey preceded by a seven-page introduction. Twenty figures illustrates 16th-century tapestries.

FRENCH

3. SURVEYS AND HISTORIES

1676   WESCHER, H. "Fabrics and Colours in the Ceremonial of the Court of Burgundy." *Ciba Review* 51 (1946):1850-56, 6 b&w figs.
Specific circumstances and etiquette directing the fabric fittings of interiors as well as of clothing, both often lavish.

GERMAN

3. SURVEYS AND HISTORIES

Book

1677   JAQUES, RENATE. *Deutsche Textilkunst in ihrer Entwicklung bis zur Gegenwart.* Berlin: Rembrandt-Verlag, 1942. 320 pp., 6 color pls., 225 b&w figs.

Comprehensive, well-illustrated survey of German woven textiles (mostly tapestries) especially those of the Gothic and Renaissance period, even if some of the points made by the author have been criticized.

Articles

1678 WESCHER, H. "Fustian Weaving in South Germany from the Fourteenth to the Sixteenth Century." *Ciba Review* 64 (1948):2339-49, 15 b&w figs.
Cotton weft and linen warp weaving produced in Constance, Ulm, and elsewhere in Germany, a sizeable industry.

1679 WILCKENS, LEONIE VON. "Die Teppiche der Sebalduskirche." In *600 Jahre Ostchor St. Sebald, Nürnberg, 1379-1979.* Edited by Helmut Baier. Neustadt a.d. Aisch: Schmidt, 1979. Pp. 133-42, 12 figs.
Altar cloths, bench cloths, and other textiles in the church of St. Sebald recorded to have been in Nuremberg before 1525 and now dispersed among institutions in Munich, Cologne, Hamburg, Glasgow, and Nuremberg, or else lost.

6. PERMANENT COLLECTIONS

Nuremberg

GERMANISCHES NATIONALMUSEUM

1680 *Katalog der Gewerbesammlung des Germanischen Nationalmuseums.* 2 vols. Vol. 1, *Gewerbe und Wirkereien, Zeugdrucke,* by Theodor Hampe, Nuremberg: Verlag des Germanischen Museums, 1896, 182 pp., 14 b&w pls. Vol. 2, *Stickereien, Spitzen und Posamentierarbeiten,* by Hans Stegmann, Nuremberg: Verlag des Germanischen Museums, 1901, 80 pp., 17 b&w figs.
Catalog comprising brief entries for 3,653 textiles forming the museum's holdings from all countries and periods. Vol. 1: weavings, knittings, stamped textiles; vol. 2: embroideries and lace. The collection's emphasis is on Germany, many examples dating (and illustrated) to the period 1400-1600.

ITALIAN

3. SURVEYS AND HISTORIES

1681 ERRERA, ISABELLA. "Les Tissus reproduits sur les tableaux italiens." *Gazette des beaux-arts* 4 (1921):143-58, 21 b&w figs.
Fabrics represented in Italian paintings of the early 14th to the end of the 15th century compared to extant fragments in the Brussels Musée du Cinquantenaire and in the author's collection.

6. PERMANENT COLLECTIONS

Florence

MUSEO NAZIONALE DEL BARGELLO

1682   *Tessuti italiani del Rinascimento: Collezioni Fanchetti Carrand, Museo Nazionale del Bargello.* Exhibition held in Prato at the Palazzo Pretorio. Catalog by Rosalia Borito Fanelli and Paolo Peri. Prato: Palazzo Pretorio, 1981. 167 pp., 13 color pls., 59 b&w pls.

Fifty-nine representative examples of Renaissance fabrics — some full ecclesiastical vestments and many fragments — from the museum's extensive collection. Detailed entries, including precise technical data, state of conservation, iconographic and stylistic considerations. Four-page glossary.

8. PRIVATE COLLECTION, AUCTION, AND DEALER CATALOGS

KELEKIAN COLLECTION

1683   GUIFFREY, JULES M., and MIGEON, GASTON. *La Collection Kelekian: Étoffes et tapis d'Orient et de Venise.* Paris: Librairie Centrale des Beaux-Arts, n.d. 4 pp., 44 color pls., 56 b&w pls.

Textiles and carpets including a few 15th-16th-century Italian (mostly Venetian) examples, illustrated on pls. 78-84, 86-87.

PORTUGUESE

3. SURVEYS AND HISTORIES

See entry 1684.

SPANISH

3. SURVEYS AND HISTORIES

1684   RÉAL, DANIEL. *Spanische und portugiesische Gewerbe.* Berlin: Ernst Wasmuth A.G., n.d. 10 pp., 48 unbound pls. of which 6 are hand colored.

Spanish and Portuguese textiles from the 11th to the 20th century mostly from the Victoria and Albert Museum, the Musée du Cinquantenaire, Brussels, and the Musée des Arts Décoratifs, Paris. Five-page introduction, two pages of captions. Nos. 7-26 pertain to the 15th-16th century.

6. PERMANENT COLLECTIONS

Detroit

DETROIT INSTITUTE OF ARTS

1685   WEIBEL, ADELE COULIN. "Textiles from Old Spain." *Bulletin of The Detroit Institute of Arts* 13 (1932):73-76, 6 b&w figs.

XXIX. Textiles—Introduction

Author briefly surveys the recent gift to the museum of 187 specimens of Spanish textiles, including several 16th-century examples.

XXX. Secular Garments and Ecclesiastical Vestments

A. MULTI COUNTRY OF ORIGIN

1. DICTIONARIES AND ENCYCLOPEDIAS

1686   LELOIR, MAURICE. *Dictionnaire du costume et de ses accessoires, des armes et des étoffes, des origines à nos jours.* 2d ed. rev. and enl. by André Dupuis. Paris: Librarie Gründ, 1951. 390 pp., numerous line drawings. (1st ed. 1940?)

    Dictionary of costumes and accessories, fabrics, arms and armor from all periods and all countries. Alphabetically arranged descriptive (and mostly short) entries. No bibliography. Useful but limited in scope.

1687   WILCOX, R. TURNER. *The Dictionary of Costume.* 2d ed. London: B.T. Batsford, 1970. 406 pp., numerous b&w line drawings. (1st ed. New York: Charles Scribner's Sons, 1969.)

    Concise entries for clothing items and fabrics of all periods and countries; also bibliographical entries. No bibliography. Useful but cursory.

1688   YARWOOD, DOREEN. *The Encyclopedia of World Costume.* New York: Charles Scribner's Sons, 1978. 471 pp., 8 color pls., over 2,000 line drawings.

    Over 650 entries covering all aspects of costume through the ages to the present day and from all parts of the world. Entries include descriptions of specific items of clothing, etymology, influence of social, economic, and political change on the development of costume, interchange of influences. Also covers hairstyles, headdress, jewelry, and spectacles. Includes bibliography and a comprehensive index.

See also entry 6.

3. SURVEYS AND HISTORIES

Books

1689   BRAUN, JOSEPH. *Die liturgische Gewandung im Occident und Orient nach Urpsprun und Entwicklung, Verwandung und Symbolik.* Frieburg im Breisgau: Herdersche Verlagshandlung, 1907. Reprint. Darmstadt: Wissenschaftliche Buchgesellschaft, 1964. 821 pp., 316 b&w figs.
The standard survey dealing with the use of each ecclesiastical vestment.

1690   DAVENPORT, MILLIA. *The Book of Costume.* 2 vols. New York: Crown Publishers, 1948. 970 pp. (continuous pagination), 2,778 b&w figs.
A survey of dress through the ages. Chronologically arranged, each period introduced by an historical summary and outline of changes followed by a comprehensive pictorial documentation (subdivided by country) of costume as seen in manuscripts, drawings, paintings, and actual examples, with a detailed entry for each illustration. Also includes jewelry, clocks, and watches. Vol. 1 includes the 15th and part of the 16th century (pp. 242-468); discussion of the latter is continued in vol. 2 (469-503).

1691   DEMAY, G. *Le Costume au Moyen Âge d'après les sceaux.* Paris: D. Dumoulin, 1880. 510 pp., 13 pls., illus. Reprint, with intro. by J.-B. de Vaivre. Paris: Berger-Lavrault, 1978.
Medieval costume as shown on seals. The fact that most seals are precisely datable makes them important in dating works of art by costume style. Index.

1692   HOUSTON, MARY G. *Medieval Costume in England & France: The 13th, 14th and 15th Centuries.* London: Adams & Charles Black, 1939. 228 pp., 8 color pls., 350 line drawings.
Survey of ecclesiastical, courtly, military, and middle-class clothing. Author discusses various brocade patterns and concludes by providing a useful glossary of terms.

1693   LAVER, JAMES. *Costume and Fashion: A Concise History.* Rev. ed. New York and Toronto: Oxford University Press, 1983. 288 pp., 58 color figs., 264 b&w figs. (1st ed., *A Concise History of Costume,* 1909.)
Includes (pp. 64-102) garments worn by men and women of the 15th-16th century in France, Italy, England, Germany, and the Netherlands.

1694   PAYNES, BLANCHE. *History of Costume from the Ancient Egyptians to the Twentieth Century.* New York: Harper & Row, 1965. 620 pp., 585 b&w figs., 43 pattern drafts.
Chaps. 10-13 (pp. 199-324) deal with 15th-16th-century costumes (excluded are military uniforms and ecclesiastical vestments) with emphasis on national characteristics of fashion mostly in Italy, France, Germany, and England and illustrated by actual extant garments as well as paintings, prints, miniatures, and sculpture.

1695   RUBENS, ALFRED. *A History of Jewish Costume.* Rev. and enl. ed. London: Owen, 1981. 240 pp., 1 color pl., many b&w figs. (1st ed. 1967.)
Sartorial development and particularities in the West: secular and rabbinical dress. Islamic influences and restrictive laws.

Articles

1696   ARNOLD, JANET. "Three Examples of Late Sixteenth and Early Seventeenth Century Neckwear." *Waffen- und Kostümkunde* 15 (1973):109-24, 19 figs. and diagrams.
    This distinctive part of late Renaissance costume is discussed in relation to specific examples from the Victoria and Albert Museum, Rijksmuseum, Germanisches National-museum, and Bayerisches Nationalmuseum.

1697   BRAUN-RONSDORF, M. "The History of the Modern Handkerchief." *Ciba Review* 89 (1951):3203-10, 11 b&w figs.
    Evolved in mid-15th-century Italy as recorded in accounts and in paintings.

1698   HAYWARD, JANE. "Sacred Vestments as They Developed in the Middle Ages." *Metropolitan Museum of Art Bulletin* 29 (1970- 71):299-309, 18 b&w figs.
    Outlines the significant changes in liturgical vestments, especially chasubles, dalmatics, and miters, from the Early Church to the 16th century.

1699   TATTERSALL, C.E. CECIL. "A Set of 16th-Century Vestments." *Burlington Magazine* 29 (1916):49-56, 7 b&w figs., 3 line drawings.
    A cope, chasuble, and two dalmatics, dispersed among the Victoria and Albert, the Fitzwilliam, the Metropolitan Museum of Art, and a private English collection, are described, dated (1500-20), and proposed to be either made in Spain, under strong Flemish influences, or by Flemish hands, for use there, or possibly made in Flanders.

4. BIBLIOGRAPHICAL GUIDES

1700   COLAS, RENÉ. *Bibliographie générale du costume et de la mode: Description des suites, recueils, séries, revues et livres français et étrangers relatifs au costume civil, militaire et religieux, aux modes, aux coiffures et aux divers accessoires de l'habillement, avec une table méthodique et un index alphabétique.* 2 vols. Paris: Librairie René Colas, 1933. 1483 pp. (continuous pagination).
    Serious annotated bibliography of 3,121 works dealing with military and ecclesiastical dress and furnishings in all countries until 1933. Vol. 1, A-M; vol. 2, N-Z, indexes.

1701   HILER, HILLAIRE, and HILER, MEYER. *Bibliography of Costume.* Edited by Helen Grant Cushing, assisted by Adah V. Morris. New York: H.W. Wilson Co., 1939. 911 pp. Reprint. New York: Blom, 1967.
    Bibliography of international scope of approximately eighty-four hundred works on costume and adornment listed in a dictionary catalog with author, subject, and title entries covering every period and country from prehistoric times to the present. Useful introduction to pre-1939 literature and for tracking down references, but lacks critical apparatus.

1702   LIPPERHEIDE, FRANZ JOSEPH VON. *Katalog der freiherrlich lipperheideschen Kostümbibliothek.* 2 vols. Berlin: Lipperheide, 1896-1905. 1:645 pp., 310 b&w figs.; 2:840 pp., 293 b&w figs. Reprint. New York: Hacker Art Books, 1963.
    Expanded edition of the catalog of the Lipperheide collection comprising about twelve thousand books and thirty thousand prints relating to the history of costume. The catalog is arranged in twenty-five sections. Entries give complete, detailed bibliographical information including number and type of plates and frequently annotations. Vol. 1, nos. 403-75 (pp. 170- 234), deals with the 15th century; nos. 476-509 (pp. 235-52), with the Renaissance period. Vol. 2 includes a comprehensive index.

6. PERMANENT COLLECTIONS

Berlin

STAATLICHE MUSEEN PREUSSISCHER KULTURBESITZ, KUNSTGEWERBEMUSEUM

1703   SIMON, HERTHA. "Ein Jaghut des 16. Jahrhunderts." *Zeitschrift für historische Waffen-und Kostümkunde* n.s. 6 (1937-39):39-40, 1 b&w fig.
        Hunting cap of woven textile acquired by the Schlossmuseum in 1933, is said to date of ca. 1450-75 and to be either German or Spanish.

New York

METROPOLITAN MUSEUM OF ART

1704   GRANSCAY, STEPHEN V.   "The Interrelationships of Costume and Armor." *Metropolitan Museum of Art Bulletin* 8 (1950): 176-88, 14 b&w figs.
        Description of costumes worn with armor and the mutual influence of costume and armor in terms of line, form, and ornamentation. Mostly 15th-16th-century examples from the Metropolitan Museum and representations in early paintings.

1705   HUSBAND, TIMOTHY B. "Ecclesiastical Vestments of the Middle Ages: An Exhibition." *Metropolitan Museum of Art Bulletin* 29 (1970-71):285-90, 12 b&w figs.
        Overview of several rarely seen pieces, mostly 15th-century chasubles, from the collection.

B. SINGLE COUNTRY OF ORIGIN

BELGIUM
(BRABANTINE, FLEMISH, AND HAINUYER)

3. SURVEYS AND HISTORIES

1706   CALBERG, MARGUERITE. "Les Brodeies historiées de l'abbaye d'Averbode," *Revue belge d'archéologie et d'histoire de l'art* 23 (1954):133-96, 28 b&w figs.
        Embroidered liturgical vestments produced in Brabant mostly around 1546-65 for the Abbey of Averbode. Details on specific commisions.

1707   VERSYP, J. "Het parement van Maria van Boergondie in de O.L. Vrouwkerk te Brugge." *Artes textiles* 5 (1959-60):134- 48, 9 b&w figs. French summary.
        Embroidered altar cloth, cope, and shield of 1497-1551 produced by Jehan Marchant and Jehan Ghisbrecht, gift of Maximilian I to the church of Our Lady in Bruges, in memory of Mary of Burgundy.

6. PERMANENT COLLECTIONS

Genoa

DUOMO

1708 PODREIDER, F. "I parati della Cattedrale di Genova." *Bollettino d'arte* 26 (1933):515-24, 8 b&w figs.
Description of several copes in the rich collection of 15th-18th-century textiles in the treasury of the cathedral.

Glasgow

GLASGOW MUSEUMS AND ART GALLERIES – BURRELL COLLECTION

1709 NORMAN, A.V.B. "An Unknown Hercules Tapestry in the Burrell Collection." *Scottish Art Review* 8, no. 3 (1962):17-20, 5 b&w figs.
Examination of saddles, armor, and clothing as depicted in a ca. 1451 Tournai tapestry held to have been woven for the Burgundian court. Reality of details and interpretative conceptualization of weavers made apparent when compared with actual objects.

BRITISH

3. SURVEYS AND HISTORIES

Books

1710 ASHELFORD, JANE. *A Visual History of Costume: The Sixteenth Century.* London: B.T. Batsford; New York: Drama Book Publishers, 1983. 144 pp., 8 color illus., 148 b&w illus.
Survey of mostly English 16th-century costume and accessories through 157 annotated reproductions of period paintings, drawings, sculpture, brasses, woodblocks, embroideries, etc.

1711 CUNNINGTON, CECIL WILLET. *Handbook of English Costume in the Sixteenth Century.* 2d rev. ed. London: Faber & Faber, 1970. 244 pp., 1 color pl. (1st ed. 1954.)
Practical and historical information on men's, women's, and children's costume and furnishings such as aiglets, lace, panes, etc. Illustrated with line drawings after original sources. Glossary of materials, pp.212-27.

1712 CUNNINGTON, CECIL WILLET. *Handbook of English Mediaeval Costume.* 2d ed. London: Faber & Faber; Boston: Plays, 1969. 210 pp., illus., some in color. (1st ed. 1952.)
A basic handbook of historical and practical information on all types of costume from the 9th through the 15th century.

1713 MAYO, JANET. *A History of Ecclesiastical Dress.* London: B.T. Batsford, 1984. 192 pp., 6 color illus., 102 b&w figs.

Historical survey of evolution, style, and function of liturgical vestments (cope, maniple, chasuble, stole, cassock, surplice, mitre, etc.) in the British Isles from the 6th to the 20th century. Clearly organized with succinct descriptions of specific clothes considered in the context of contemporary society and as observed through illuminated manuscripts, paintings, prints, drawings, and sculpture. For the 15th-16th century see especially chap. 4 (Opus Anglicanum), 5 (Reformation), and 6 (Birth of Protestantism). Fifty-page illustrated glossary.

Articles

1714   NEVINSON, J.L. "The Earliest Dress and Insignia of the Knights of the Garter." *Apollo* 47 (1948):80-83, 8 b&w figs.
Description of the garter—a strap, probably blue with gold letters, and a buckle—the mantle, robes, and hood as recorded on brass monuments and in manuscripts.

1715   PERRY, MARY PHILLIPS. "A Medieval Chasuble at Barnstaple." *Burlington Magazine* 18 (1910-11):51-52, 2 b&w figs.
An early 16th-century damask vestment with embroidered Virgin and Child within gold rays, with angels and floral motifs.

1716   RIBEIRO, AILEEN. "'A Paradice of Flowers': Flowers in English Dress in the Late Sixteenth and Early Seventeenth Centuries." *Connoisseur* 201 (1979):110-17, 3 color illus., 8 b&w illus.
Widespread fashion of brocades of often delicate floral motifs in costumes of the Elizabethan and Jacobean periods. Illustration of actual fabrics and depictions in paintings of the period.

1717   WESCHER, H. "Dress and Fashion at the Court of Queen Elizabeth." *Ciba Review* 78 (1950):2843-49, 8 b&w figs.
The queen as setter of fashion, her courtiers emulating her, as exemplified in paintings, etc.

CZECHSLOVAKIA (BOHEMIAN)

3. SURVEYS AND HISTORIES

1718   DROBNÁ, ZOROSLAVA, and DURDÍK, JAN. *Medieval Costume, Armour and Weapons (1350-1450)*. Translated by Jean Layton. [London]: Andrew Dakers, n.d. 72 pp., 383 pls. of line drawings (some watercolored) by Eduard Wagner.
Overview of Czech military and civilian costume, the latter both feminine and masculine worn by various professions and levels of society. Generously illustrated with drawings after Bohemain manuscripts and paintings, photographs, and earlier publications.

FRENCH

3. SURVEYS AND HISTORIES

Book

1719   BEAULIEU, MICHÈLE, and BAYLÉ, JEANNE. *Le Costume en Bourgogne de Phil-lippe le Hardi à la mort de Charles le Téméraire (1364-1477).* Paris: Presses Universitaires de France, 1956. 220 pp., 24 b&w pls., 89 line figs.
Style and function of secular Burgundian dress through the reigns of the four dukes of Burgundy; plebeian as well as courtly dress for men and women, costume worn by officials and on special events, costume accessories, armor styles, fabrics, merchants. Study sources are sculpture, illuminated manuscripts, panel painting, stained glass, tapestries, seals, and a few rare extant examples of actual costumes.

Articles

1720   WESCHER, H. "Fashion and Elegance at the Court of Burgundy." *Ciba Review* 51 (1946):1841-48, 9 b&w figs.
Costumes worn by the dukes, their consorts, and courtiers from 1400 to 1500 as a reflection of changing styles and ceremonies.

1721   WESCHER, H. "French Fashions in the Sixteenth Century." *Ciba Review* 69 (1948):2522-30, 14 b&w figs.
Elements of masculine and feminine costume at the courts of Henri II and his sons.

GERMAN

3. SURVEYS AND HISTORIES

1722   POST, PAUL. "Des Kostüm der deutschen Renaissance 1480-1550." *Anzeiger des Germanischen Nationalmuseums* (1954-59):21-42, 30 b&w figs.
Study of the fashions and accoutrements of the German nobility and burghers—both men and women—in the period 1480-1550, based on contemporary paintings and prints.

1723   WILCKENS, LEONIE VON. "Kleiderverzeichnisse aus zwei Jahrhunderten in den Nachlassinventaren wohlhabender Nurnbergerinnen." *Waffen- und Kostümkunde* 21 (1979):25-41, 11 illus.
Presents lists of clothing from inventories and from a trousseau of seven wealthy women of Nuremberg between the years 1537 and 1701. Description of outer garments, underwear, fashionable accessories with headgear, gloves, stockings, handerkerchiefs, bags, fans, etc., and jewelry; monetary value presented for each article of clothing. Changes of fashion in Nuremberg discussed. Glossary.

ITALIAN

3. SURVEYS AND HISTORIES

1724 CAPPI BENTIVEGNA, FERRUCCIA. *Abbigliamento e costume nella pittura italiana.* 2 vols. Vol. 1, *Rinascimento.* Rome: Carlo Bestetti, 1962. 13 color pls., 553 b&w figs.
Pictorial survey of 15th-16th-century costume as seen through Italian paintings (and a few drawings). Brief introduction, short essays, quotations drawn from Renaissance writings.

1725 HERALD, JACQUELINE. *Renaissance Dress in Italy 1400-1500.* London: Bell & Hyman, 1981. 256 pp., 16 color pls., 160 b&w figs.
Sociocultural significance of fashions in Quattrocento Italy as revealed by chronicles and as exemplified in painting of the period. Discusses also manufacture and functions of costumes. Useful glossary of Italian terms for Renaissance dress and textiles.

1726 LEVI PISETZKY, ROSITA. *Storia del costume in Italia.* 5 vols. Vol. 2 (1964), 516 pp., 251 illus., many in color; vol. 3 (1964), 499 pp., 219 illus., many in color. Milan: Istituto Editoriale Italiano (Fondazione Giovanni Treccani degli Alfieri), [1964-69].
Fairly exhaustive history of Italian costume from the early Middle Ages to the early 19th century lavishly illustrated through reproduction of paintings, frescoes, miniature paintings, drawings, medals, and armor. Vol. 2 (pp. 211-500) deals with the Quattrocento, discussing taste, foreign influences, social conditions, and then specific items of feminine apparel from petticoats to shoes, the various elements of masculine clothing, also those of children, types of clothes, importance of various colors, etc. Vol. 3 (7-300) deals with the Cinquecento emphasizing the wide diffusion of Italian fashions throughout Europe and then discussing feminine and masculine (civil and military) costume as well as the dress of children. Concludes with descriptions of fabrics, theatrical costumes, and sumptuary laws.

1727 OZZOLA, LEANDRO. *Il vestiario italiano dal 1500 al 1550, saggio di cronologia documentata.* Rome: Fratelli Palombi, 1940. 223 pp., 205 b&w figs.
Survey of various forms of clothing in Italy in the first half of the Cinquecento.

1728 POLIDORI CALAMANDREI, E. *Le vesti delle donne fiorentine nel Quattrocento.* Rome: Multigrafica, 1973. 162 pp., 4 color pls., 76 b&w pls., line drawings. (1st ed. Florence. 1924.)
Feminine fashions in 15th-century Florence as exemplified in contemporary paintings, miniatures, prints, textiles, and medals. Author studies the sumptuary laws and the evolution of specific elements, and concludes with an eight-page glossary of Italian terms.

6. PERMANENT COLLECTIONS

Florence

MUSEO NAZIONALE DEL BARGELLO

1729 *Velluti operati del XV secolo col motivo delle "gricce. 1."* Catalog by Rosanna De Gennaro. Florence: Museo Nazionale del Bargello, 1985. 31 pp., 5 color figs., 17 b&w figs.
Catalog of fifteen Italian silk velvets of the Quattrocento with leaf patterns highlighting the important textile collection (985 items) bequeathed by Louis Carrand and Giulio Franchetti to the Bargello.

Venice

PALAZZO MOCENIGO

1730   *Tessuti, costumi e moda: Le raccolte storiche di Palazzo Mocenigo.* Exhibition catalog by Irene Ariano, Doretta Davanzo Poli, and Stefania Moronato. Venice: Centro Studi di Storia del Tessuto e del Costume, 1985. 81 pp., 58 b&w figs.
    Exhibition dealing with mostly Italian fabrics used in making fashionable secular and ecclesiastical attires from the Middle Ages through the 19th century. Includes forty items (mostly silks) dating of the 15th-16th century in the permanent collection.

NETHERLANDISH

3. SURVEYS AND HISTORIES

1731   BAART, J.M., et al. "Knopen aan het Hollandse kostuum uit de zestiende en zeventiende eeuw." *Antiek* 9 (1974):17-49, 4 color illus. 133 b&w illus.
    Buttons on 16th- and 17th-century Dutch costume with emphasis on decoration, material (bone, wood, thread, glass, pewter, nickel, brass, gold and silver — sometimes set with stones), and history of button-making in Holland.

SCANDINAVIA (SWEDISH)

3. SURVEYS AND HISTORIES

1732   FALKE, OTTO VON. "Kirchliche Textilien in Schweden." *Pantheon* 3 (1929):172-75, 5 b&w figs.
    Notes on the exhibition of ecclesiastical textiles (mostly silk weavings and embroideries) held at the Historical Museum of Stockholm. Included are works of the 15th century representative of major Swedish embroidery schools such as a bishop's mitre of 1460 made in the embroidery school of the Vadstena nunnery and incorporating Italian gold enamels of the 11th century.

SPANISH

3. SURVEYS AND HISTORIES

Books

1733   ANDERSON, RUTH MATILDA. *Hispanic Costume 1480-1530.* New York: Hispanic Society of America, 1979. 293 pp., 8 color figs., 569 b&w figs.
    Survey of mostly aristocratic fashions based on historical accounts and pictorial records; also hairstyles, headgear, body and outer garments, leg coverings, footwear and accessories, for men and women. Essay deals with customs and ceremonies.

1734   BERNIS, CARMEN. *Trajes y modas en España de los reyes católicos.* 2 vols. Vol. 1,
       Las mujeres (1978), 102 pp., 4 color pls., 44 b&w pls.; vol. 2, *Los hombres* (1979), 175 pp.,
       4 color pls., 128 b&w pls. Madrid: Instituto Diego Velázquez del Consejo Superior de
       Investigaciones Científicas.
            Spanish costume, feminine (vol. 1) and masculine (vol. 2), at the end of the 15th and
       the early 16th century; styles and social distinction in dress; relies on pictorial representations
       and cited documents.

   Article

1735   ANDERSON, RUTH MATILDA. "Spanish Dress Worn by a Queen of France."
       Gazette des beaux-arts 98 (1981):215-22, 14 b&w figs.
            Detailed analysis of each item of Spanish costume worn by Eleanor of Austria,
       spouse of Francis I, on the basis of six types of pictorial sources.

XXXI. Embroidery

A. MULTI COUNTRY OF ORIGIN

3. SURVEYS AND HISTORIES

1736   LEFÉBURE, ERNEST. *Embroidery and Lace: Their Manufacture and History.* Translated, enlarged, and with notes by Alan S. Cole. New York: G.P. Putnam's Sons; London: H. Grevel & Co., 1899. 326 pp., 156 b&w figs.
   Early but still useful overview of development and technique from antiquity to the present. Pertinent to 1400-1600 are pp. 80-134 for embroidery and 171-97 for lace.

1737   SYMONDS, MARY, and PREECE, LOUISA. *Needlework through the Ages: A Short Survey of Its Development in Decorative Art with Particular Regard to Its Inspirational Relationship with Other Methods of Craftsmanship.* London: Hodder & Stoughton, 1928. 446 pp., 8 color pls., 96 b&w pls.
   Chronologically and geographically arranged. Pertinent to 1400-1600 are pp. 217-33: 15th-century embroidery on Italian silks and velvets and on Flemish weavings, distribution through Hanseatic League, Golden Fleece vestments; 234-71: 16th-century ceremonial dress of London's Livery Companies, linen embroidery, embroidery on bookbinding and furnishings. Illustrations of ecclesiastical vestments and altar frontals, secular clothing, carpets, orphreys, curtains, bed valances, chair seats and backs, embroideries represented in paintings, etc.

B. SINGLE COUNTRY OF ORIGIN

BELGIUM

3. SURVEYS AND HISTORIES

1738　DUVERGER, J.; VERSYP, J.; HAUWERMEIREN-GROSSE, J. VAN; CASTEELS, M.; and DOUILLEZ, J. "'Engels' borduurwerk in de Nederlanden." *Artes textiles* 2 (1955):18-44, 6 b&w figs.; 3 (1956):3-13, 5 b&w figs.; 5 (1959-60):124-33. French summary.
　　　　Flemish embroideries inspired by English models in the South Netherlands illustrated by the late 15th- early 16th- century copes from Nonnen-Mielen (near St.-Trond) in the Vleeshuis of Antwerp, others in Notre-Dame in Liseuwege, St.-Sauveur in Bruges, the Musées Royaux d'Art d'Histoire in Brussels, the church of St. Roch in Blankenberghe, the Mayer van den Bergh Museum and the Elisabeth Gasthuis in Antwerp.

6. PERMANENT COLLECTIONS

New York

METROPOLITAN MUSEUM OF ART – CLOISTERS

1739　FREEMAN, MARGARET B. "The Legend of Saint Catherine Told in Embroidery." *Metropolitan Museum of Art Bulletin* 14 (1955):281-93, 16 b&w figs.
　　　　Iconography of two small 15th-century roundel embroideries in the Cloisters (part of a series of eight in other collections). In the style of Jacques Daret and Roger van der Weyden, they were probably made in Tournai or Arras, and possibly belonged to Duke Philip the Good of Burgundy.

BRITISH (ENGLISH)

3. SURVEYS AND HISTORIES

1740　LAWRENCE, WILLIAM. "Elizabethan Embroidery." *Old Furniture* 2 (1927):51-57, 1 color pl., 6 b&w figs.
　　　　Briefly describes the material, stitching, and decorative motives of embroidered caps and of a handkerchief in private collections.

1741　MADOU, MIREILLE. "Engels bourduurwerk in de Nederlanden: Bijdrage tot de oplossing van een omstreden probleem." *Nederlands kunsthistorisch jaarboek* 31 (1980):16-23, 2 b&w figs. English summary.
　　　　Large 16th-century copes embroidered in England and then　imported into the Netherlands and now in the Rijksmuseum and Catharijneconvent, Utrecht.

1742　WACE, A.J.B. "An Exhibition of Old English Needlework." *Old Furniture* 2 (1927):112-22, 12 b&w figs.
　　　　Brief description of several English 16th-century petit-point panels (as well as later pieces) from private British collections.

1743   WALLIS, W. CYRIL. "Petit Point Embroidery of the Sixteenth Century (with Special Reference to Mary Queen of Scots)." *Embroidery* 1 (1933):7-11, 3 b&w figs
  Two embroidery panels of the second half of the 16th century in Edinburgh worked in colored wool and silks representing Queen Elizabeth receiving an embassy and King Solomon and the Queen of Sheba.

6. PERMANENT COLLECTION

Glasgow

GLASGOW MUSEUMS AND ART GALLERIES – BURRELL COLLECTION

1744   WELLS, WILLIAM. "Heraldic Relics from Kimberley." *Scottish Art Review* 8, no. 4 (1962): 17-21, 1 color fig., 8 b&w figs.
  Throne with elaborate canopy produced in 1578 for the visit of Elizabeth I at Kimberley bearing the arms of Roger Wodehouse in the Burrell Collection.

London

VICTORIA AND ALBERT MUSEUM

1745   VAN DE PUT, A. "The Calthorpe Purse." *Old Furniture* 3 (1928):62-67, 1 color pl., 3 b&w figs.
  Describes an English embroidered purse of the 16th century with forty-three armorial quarterings of the Calthorpes of Norfolk, Suffolk, and adjacent counties.

1746   *Catalogue of English Ecclesiastical Embroideries of the XIII. to XVI. Centuries.* 4th ed. London: Board of Education, 1930. 84 pp., 41 b&w pls. (1st ed. 1907.)
  Eight-page introduction traces evolution of style and quality, describes specific vestments. Catalog of sixty-eight chasubles, copes, orphreys, dalmatics, altar frontals, chronologically arranged from the 13th to the early 17th century (nos. 20-48, 65-68, are of the 15th-16th century).

1746a   *Catalogue of English Domestic Embroidery of the Sixteenth and Seventeenth Centuries.* Catalog by John L. Nevinson. London: Board of Education, 1938. 136 pp., 1 color pl., 72 b&w pls.
  Fourteen-page introduction examines patterns and their sources, techniques, and colors. Catalog entries arranged by types and introduced by brief essays: embroidery for furnishings (table and floor carpets, cushion covers, hangings, bed valances, bookbinding), and for fashion (jackets, caps, gloves, purses, etc.).

1747   BRETT, GERARD. "Some Elizabethan Embroideries." *Burlington Magazine* 89 (1947):190-91, 2 b&w figs.
  Two cushion covers with equestrian figures and foliage sprays.

1748   LEVEY, SANTINA M. " An Elizabethen Embroidered Cover." *Victoria and Albert Museum Yearbook* 3 (1972):76-86, 1 color pl. (frontispiece), 13 b&w figs.
  A late 16th-century linen cover embroidered with silk and metal thread and bearing the arms of Grenville-Bevill is discussed for its unusual inclusion of twenty-two paired inscriptions in English and a mixture of French and Latin derived from copybooks of writing masters such as Thomas Trevelyon, also responsible for design patterns.

7. EXHIBITION CATALOGS

London

BURLINGTON HOUSE

1749 *Exhibition of English Embroidery Executed Prior to the Middle of the XVI Century.* Exhibition catalog introduction by A.F. Kendrick. London: Burlington Fine Arts Club, 1905. 87 pp., 10 color pls., 20 b&w pls.

Thirty-one-page historical introduction; catalog of 112 ecclesiastical vestments and altar cloths and frontals, over half dating of the 15th-16th century, mostly from British religious foundations and private collections.

VICTORIA AND ALBERT MUSEUM

1750 *Opus Anglicanum: English Medieval Embroidery.* Exhibition catalog by Donald King. London: Arts Council, 1963. 64 pp., 2 color pls., 24 b&w pls.

180 entries dating from the 11th to the 16th century: chasubles, maniples, albs, orphreys, copes, stoles, palls, altar frontal, banner, etc.: includes a few examples of furniture (cat. no. 167), ivories (168-69), metalwork (170-73) for comparison. For embroideries of 1400-1600 see 100-66.

8. PRIVATE COLLECTION, AUCTION, AND DEALER CATALOGS

RICHMOND COLLECTION

1751 KENDRICK, A.F. "Tudor Embroideries in the Collection of Sir Frederick Richmond, Bart." *Connoisseur* 99 (1937):145- 52, 2 color figs., 10 b&w figs.

Description of iconography (drawn from the Bible and classical mythology) of several Elizabethan embroideries, mostly petit-point panels.

WARD COLLECTION

1752 WACE, A.J.B. "Antique Needlework in the Collection of Frank Ward, Esq." *Old Furniture* 4 (1928):62-67, 1 color fig., 7 b&w figs.

Of the eight embroideries described, six are of Elizabethan style: women's caps, cap pieces, and cushion covers.

CZECHOSLOVAKIA (BOHEMIAN)

6. PERMANENT COLLECTIONS

Detroit

DETROIT INSTITUTE OF ART

1753 WEIBEL, ADELE COULIN. "A Late Medieaval Chasuble Cross." *Art Quarterly* 9 (1946):144-52, 6 b&w figs.

Author ascribes the orphrey with an embroidered Crucifixion on an early 15th century chasuble to Bohemian craftsmen working on a design in the style of the Master of Wittingau.

FRENCH

3. SURVEYS AND HISTORIES

Book

1754   FREEMAN, MARGARET B. *The St. Martin Embroideries: A Fifteenth-Century Series Illustrating the Life and Legend of St. Martin of Tours.* New York: Metropolitan Museum of Art, 1968. 132 pp., 2 color pls., 35 b&w pls., 81 b&w figs.
Two series forming forty embroidered roundels and panels for a chasuble and orphrey of ca. 1420, dispersed among U.S. and European collections, are studied for their iconography, style, and technique, and are attributed to Franco-Flemish workshops of ca. 1425 and ca. 1445.

Article

1755   EISLER, COLIN. "Two Franco-Flemish Embroideries—Suggestions for Their Settings." *Burlington Magazine* 109 (1967):571-80, 13 b&w figs.
Design of Franco-Flemish embroideries (see preceding entry) attributed to a miniature painter who produced the illustration of a *Roman de la rose* manuscript (Vienna, Nat. Bibl., Cod. 2583) and suggested to have been the gift of Duke Philip the Good to Pope Martin V.

6. PERMANENT COLLECTIONS

Geneva

MUSÉE D'ART ET D'HISTOIRE

1756   LAPAIRE, CLAUDE. "Trois broderies allégoriques de la fin du XVIe siècle." Genava 23 (1975):147.
Three French panels of ca. 1580 with embroidered moralizing subjects.

GERMAN

3. SURVEYS AND HISTORIES

1757   SCHEYER, ERNST. *Die kölner Bortenweberei des Mittelalters.* Augsburg: Dr. Benno Filser, 1932. 110 pp., 53 b&w figs.
Woven ornamental borders on Colognese vestments of the Middle Ages in various public collections in Germany. Most examples discussed are dated to the 15th century.

6. PERMANENT COLLECTIONS

Gdansk (Danzig), Poland

MARIENKIRCHE

1758   BURKE, J.T.A. "Some Embroidered Vestments at Danzig." *Burlington Magazine* 70 (1937):122-29, 9 b&w figs.
    15th-century cope and two chasubles said to be probably North German produced under English influence.

ITALIAN

6. PERMANENT COLLECTIONS

Boston

MUSEUM OF FINE ARTS

1759   TOWNSEND, GERTURDE. "A Fifteenth Century Italian Velvet." *Bulletin of the Museum of Fine Arts* 29 (1931):63-65, 1 b&w fig.
    A velvet panel with looped gold patterns dating of the second half of the fifteenth century seen in relation to a Florentine workshop associated with Maso Finiguerra and Antonio Pollaiuolo, on the basis of its modification of a traditional pattern and on its technical handling.

Cleveland

CLEVELAND MUSEUM OF ART

1760   SHEPHERD, DOROTHY G. "A Fifteenth-Century Florentine Embroidery." *Bulletin of The Cleveland Museum of Art* 41 (1954):211-13, 1 b&w pl. on p. 209.
    Roundel, probably from an antependium, representing the Coronation of the Virgin after paintings of Lorenzo Monaco.

Florence

MUSEO DELL'OPERA DEL DUOMO

1761   SCHWABACHER, SASCHA. *Die Stickerein nach Entwürfen des Antonio Pollaiolo in der Opera di S. Maria del Fiore zu Florenz.* Strasbourg: J.H. Heitz Ed., 1911. 121 pp., 37 b&w pls.
    Earliest full-scale study devoted to the series of embroideries of 1466-87 designed by Antonio Pollaiuolo.

1762   SABATINI, ATTILLIO. "Apunti sul Pollaiolo (a proposito dei ricami per i paramenti del S. Giovanni). *Rivista d'arte* 13 (1941):72-98, 16 b&w figs.
    Discussion of Antonio Polaiuolo's models for the embroidery series now in this museum amplifying Schwabacher, *Die Stickerein* (see preceding entry). Suggests relationship of compositional details to the work of other contemporary artists.

1763 JOHNSTONE, PAULINE. "Antonio Pollaiuolo and the Art of Embroidery." *Apollo* 81 (1965):306-9, 1 color pl., 4 b&w figs.

Embroidery panels with colored shading over gold thread (or nué) depicting scenes from John the Baptist's life were designed by Antonio Pollaiuolo ca. 1466-87.

Whalley, Lancashire

STONYHURST COLLEGE

1764 KENDRICK, A.F. "The Italian Exhibition. II—Textiles." *Burlington Magazine* 56 (1930):15-16, 2 b&w figs.

Chiefly discusses a cope of velvet and gold embroidered in Florence (ca. 1509) for the opening of Henry VII's chapel at Westminster Abbey, suggesting that it was designed by Pietro Torrigiani.

NETHERLANDISH

3. SURVEYS AND HISTORIES

1765 STECHOW, WOLFGANG. "Four Netherlandish Embroidered Panels." *Jahrbuch der Hamburger Kunstsammlungen* 28 (1973):43-54, 15 b&w figs.

Four embroidered panels, proably hangings of a canopy carried over the host in Corpus Christi processions; their style suggests a date ca. 1515-25 and a North Netherlandish provenance. Now dispersed among Oberlin, Denver, Baltimore, and Bloomfield Hills, Michigan.

6. PERMANENT COLLECTIONS

New York

METROPOLITAN MUSEUM OF ART

1766 STANDEN, EDITH APPLETON. "The Bulrushes in The Waves." *Metropolitan Museum of Art Bulletin* 14 (1956):181-85, 6 b&w figs.

Analysis of the iconography—with its political implications—of a dalmatic dated 1570 and probably made in Gouda, Holland.

POLISH (SILESIAN)

8. PRIVATE COLLECTION, AUCTION, AND DEALER CATALOGS

ILKÉ COLLECTION

1767 KURTH, BETTY. "A Silesian Gold Embroidery of the Fifteenth Century." *Connoisseur* 121 (1948):38-40, 3 b&w figs.

Attribution of a linen altar cloth of the Nativity in this Swiss collection, to Silesia, on stylistic and technical grounds.

SPANISH

3. SURVEYS AND HISTORIES

1768   F. L. "El arte del bordado y de los tapices en Valencia." *Archivo de arte valenciano* 18 (1932):45-58, 6 b&w figs.

Embroidered vestments and tapestries with devotional scenes produced in 14th-15th-century Valencia and now in local religious institutions.

6. PERMANENT COLLECTIONS

London

VICTORIA AND ALBERT MUSEUM

1769   KING, DONALD. "Medieval and Renaissance Embroidery from Spain." *Victoria and Albert Museum Yearbook* 2 (1970):55- 64, 13 b&w figs.

An altar frontal of ca. 1530 here attributed to a Toledo workshop, gives rise to an outline history of Spanish church embroideries from the 12th to the late 16th century as illustrated by examples in the museum's collection.

Seville

EGLESIA DE SANTIAGO

1770   TURMO, ISABEL. "La capa del Emperador Carlos V, de Santiago de Sevilla." *Archivo español de arte* 25 (1952):257-65, 3 b&w figs.

Embroidered copelike mantle with religious and secular motifs was worn by Emperor Charles V at his coronation in 1520.

SWISS

3. SURVEYS AND HISTORIES

1771   TRUDEL, VERENA. *Schweizerische Leinenstickereien des Mittelalters und der Renaissance.* Bern: Paul Haupt, 1954. 64 pp., 32 b&w pls., 16 b&w text figs.

Swiss embroidered linen of the 13th-17th century: material, technique (with twenty-five different stitches listed and illustrated), purpose (secular and ecclesiastical), dating, and decoration (motifs and iconography).

6. PERMANENT COLLECTIONS

Cleveland

CLEVELAND MUSEUM OF ART

1772   WARDWELL, ANNE E.   "The Holy Kinship: A Sixteenth-Century Immaculist Embroidery." *Bulletin of The Cleveland Museum of Art* 67 (1980):285-95, 12 b&w figs.

Large linen embroidery of Swiss or South German origin: iconography and design sources.

XXXII. Lace

A. MULTI COUNTRY OF ORIGIN

3. SURVEYS AND HISTORIES

Book

1773   LEVEY, SANTINA M. *Lace: A History.* London: Victoria and Albert Museum/W.S. Maney & Son, 1983. 140 pp., 24 b&w figs., 360 b&w pls.
Chronologically and typologically arranged; pertinent to the 15th-16th century are chaps. 1-2 (pp. 4-20): origins, technique and fashion for lace; examines bobbin lace, needle lace, pattern books, and the various styles and uses of lace in Flanders, England, and Italy. Illustrations include portraits that demonstrate the role of lace in contemporary costume. Glossary.

Article

1774   SCHUETTE, MARIE. "History of Lace." *Ciba Review* 73 (1949):2685-98, 14 b&w figs.
Deals mostly with the development of lace-making in Italy, France, and the Netherlands during the Renaissance and Baroque periods.

See also entry 1736.

7. EXHIBITION CATALOGS

Burano

MUSEO SCUOLA DI MERLETTI

1775   *Cinque secoli di merletti europei: I capolavori.* Exhibition catalog essays by Doretta Davanzo Poli, Rosalia Di Campo, Santina M. Levey, et al. Burano: Museo Scuola di Merletti, 1984. 384 pp., 257 figs. Summaries in English/French/German.

Masterpieces of 16th-19th-century lace from Italy, Great Britain, France, Belgium, Holland, Austria, Spain, Portugal, Greece, and the U.S.S.R.: handkerchiefs, altarcloths, tablecloths, decorative hangings, clothing. Catalog is arranged by country, each section preceded by an essay outlining the history of the specific lace-making region. Entries for exhibited pieces provide stylistic and often detailed technical analyses.

B. SINGLE COUNTRY OF ORIGIN

ITALIAN

3. SURVEYS AND HISTORIES

1776 RICCI, ELISA. *Old Italian Lace.* 2 vols. Vol. 1 (1913), 426 pp., 417 b&w figs.; vol. 2 (1912), 277 pp., 343 b&w figs. London: William Heinemann; Philadelphia: J.B.Lippincott Co.
Covers the 15th-18th century with emphasis on the Renaissance. Vol. 1 discusses techniques (lacis, drawn thread, buratto, punto a reticello, punto in aria) of needle-made lace; vol. 2, main production centers (Venice, Genoa, Milan, Abruzzi) of bobbin-made lace; contains references to inventories, and discusses lace production outside Italy, including Spain, France, and Flanders, Well illustrated, many examples as represented in paintings of the period.

6. PERMANENT COLLECTIONS

London

VICTORIA AND ALBERT MUSEUM

1777 POLLEN, MRS. JOHN HUNGERFORD. "Early Design in Lace." *Burlington Magazine* 19 (1911):73-79, 2 b&w pls.
Drawing from examples in the collection, the author proposes that the design of the famed punto in aria, for which Venice was preeminent in the 16th century, can be traced to Persia.

XXXIII. Silks

A. MULTI COUNTRY OF ORIGIN

3. SURVEYS AND HISTORIES

Book

1778   FALKE, OTTO VON. *Kunstgeschichte der Seidenweberei.* Tübingen: Ernst Wasmuth, [1950]. 55 pp., 10 color pls., 541 b&w figs., 53 text figs.
      History of silkweaving including Venetian, Florentine, and other Italian examples of the 15th century and also German and Spanish 15th-16th-century silks. Most textiles illustrated are in public German collections.

Article

1779   FALKENBERG, T. "A Collection of Old Textile Fabrics." *Old Furniture* 3 (1928):112-18, 10 b&w figs.
      Early textiles formerly in the Hugo Benario collection, Berlin (sold 1927); included some 15th-century Florentine, Venetian, and Spanish brocades.

7. EXHIBITION CATALOGS

Los Angeles

LOS ANGELES COUNTY MUSEUM OF ART

1780   *2,000 Years of Silk Weaving.* Exhibition catalog introduction by Adèle C. Weibel. New York: E. Weyhe, 1944. 63 pp., 1 color pl., 88 b&w pls. Exhibition also held at The Cleveland Museum of Art and The Detroit Institute of Arts.

484 short entries including 15th-century Italian (pp. 14-16) and Hispano-Moresque (18-21) silk and satin brocades and damasks; 15th-century European damasks (21-22), 15th-century Italian and Spanish velvets (22-28), 16th-century Italian, Spanish, Portuguese, French, German velvets and brocades (28-32). Examples on loan from dealers, from the Cleveland and Metropolitan museums, the Detroit Institute of Arts, and the Art Institute of Chicago, etc.

B. SINGLE COUNTRY OF ORIGIN

ITALIAN

3. SURVEYS AND HISTORIES

Book

1781   BUSSAGLI, MARIO. *La seta in Italia.* Rome: Editalia, 1986. 303 pp., 32 color pls., many b&w figs.
Well-illustrated overview of silkmaking in Italy from its inception in early medieval times until the present. Pp. 83-176 deal with medieval and Renaissance creations (mostly Florentine and Venetian) illustrated by extant examples and panel paintings in Italian collections. The appendix includes a reprint of the *Trattato dell'arte della seta* in the Laurenziana Library written in the mid-15th century by an anonymous Florentine.

Article

1782   FANELLI, ROSALIA BONITO. "I drappi d'oro: Economia e moda a Firenze nel Cinquecento." In *Le arti del principato mediceo,* Florence: Studio per Edizioni Scelte, 1980. Pp. 407-26, 5 b&w figs.
Activity of the Arte della Lana and Arte della Seta in 16th-century Florence; silk industries (velvets being most costly), fashions, and sumptuary laws.

6. PERMANENT COLLECTIONS

Florence

MUSEO BARDINI

1783   *Un parato della Badia fiorentino.* Exhibition catalog by Dora Liscia Bemporad and Alessandro Guidotti. Florence: Nardini Editore; Centro Internazionale del Libro, 1981. 63 pp., 3 color figs., 10 b&w figs.
A rare, complete set of Florentine-produced gold brocaded red velvet wall hangings with the repeated pomegranate design, here dated to ca. 1470, intended to entirely cover the walls of the Badia of Florence.

Los Angeles

LOS ANGELES COUNTY MUSEUM OF ART

1784   *Velvets East and West from the 14th to the 20th Century.* Exhibition held in Los Angeles at the Lytton Gallery. Catalog by Stefania and Eugene Holt. Los Angeles: Los Angeles County Museum of Art, 1966. 63 pp., 55 b&w figs.

Fifty-five short entries of velvets from the 14th to the 20th century in the permanent collection. Cat. nos. 1-17, 23 are Italian examples of the 15th-16th century including copes, banners, and hangings.

7. EXHIBITION CATALOGS

Milan

CASTELLO SFORZESCO

1785   *Tessuti serici italiani, 1450-1530.* Exhibition catalog by Chiara Buss, Marina Molinelli, Grazietta Butazzi, et al. Milan: Electa, 1983. 158 pp., 24 color figs., 82 b&w figs.

Fifty-one major examples of silk, mostly brocaded velvet and damasks, produced in Venice, Florence, Milan, Genoa, and elsewhere in Italy from 1450 to 1530 (over half from the Civiche Raccolte d'Arte Applicate in the Castello Sforzesco and never exhibited or studied before): fragments, ecclesiastical vestments, antependia, secular garments, even slippers. Detailed entries including technical analysis of threads and dyes. Pp. 17-68 comprise six essays dealing with dating, technique, dyes, restoration, Italian fashion, and inventories.

SPANISH

3. SURVEYS AND HISTORIES

Books

1786   BUNT, CYRIL G.E. *Hispano-Moresque Fabrics.* Leigh-on-Sea, England: F. Lewis, 1966. 9 pp., 52 b&w figs.

Useful for illustration of examples dating of the 10th-16th century in various U.S. and European museums.

1786a   BUNT, CYRIL G.E. *Spanish Silks.* Leigh-on-Sea, England: F. Lewis, 1965. 10 pp., 56 b&w figs.

Picture book of the sumptuous damasks and brocades produced from the 12th to the 18th century, the majority dating of the period 1400-1600 (figs. 24-53) and in the Victoria and Albert Museum. The black and white plates do not do justice to these rich textiles.

1787   MAY, FLORENCE LEWIS. *Silk Textiles of Spain: Eighth to Fifteenth Century.* New York: Hispanic Society of America, 1957. 286 pp., 6 color figs., 161 b&w figs.

Chap. 4 (pp. 171-248) discusses 15th-century pieces with Mudejar and late Gothic patterns; mentions various inventories and documents, Chinese and Italian influences; examples of copes, altar cloths, wall hangings, curtains, vestments, funeral palls, secular clothing, and bed coverings from Toledo, Seville, Valencia, Cordoba, etc.

Articles

1788   MARTÍN GONZÁLEZ, J.J. "Una cama rica de Felipe II." *Boletin del Seminario de Estudios de Arte y Arqueologia Valladolid* 19 (1952-53):133-35

Velvet and satin bedspread and canopy enlivened with gold, silver, and precious stones produced in 1574-75 in Augsburg for Philip II of Spain.

1789   WITTLIN, A. "The Development of Silk Weaving in Spain." *Ciba Review* 20 (1939):707-21, 19 b&w figs.
Organization of the Spanish silk industry from the 12th through the 17th century with emphasis on its heyday in the 16th century.

6. PERMANENT COLLECTIONS

Cleveland

CLEVELAND MUSEUM OF ART

1790   WARDWELL, ANNE E. "A Fifteenth-Century Silk from Muslim Spain." *Bulletin of The Cleveland Museum of Art* 70 (1983):58-72, 19 b&w figs.
Moorish curtain consisting of two large panels of silk, lampas weave with areas of compound tabby weave and Arabic inscriptions, likely to have been produced in Grenada for the Naspid dynasty.

London

VICTORIA AND ALBERT MUSEUM

1791   DIGBY, G.F. WINGFIELD. "Sixteenth-Century Silk Damasks: A Spanish Group." *Burlington Magazine* 74 (1939):222-28, 12 b&w figs. on 2 pls.
The author distinguishes silk weavings of Spain from those of Italy and ascribes a group of damasks in the museum to Spain on the basis of their particular technical characteristics and on their adaptation of Italian prototypes.

SWISS

6. PERMANENT COLLECTIONS

Beromünster

STIFTSKIRCHE ST. MICHAEL

1792   SUTER, ROBERT LUDWIG. "Die Altarornate des Stiftes Beromünster." *Zeitschrift für schweizerische Archäologie und Kunstgeschichte* 30 (1973):5-25, 25 b&w illus.
Unique series of fifteen altar hangings of silk dating of the 15th century.

XXXIV. Tapestries

A. MULTI COUNTRY OF ORIGIN

3. SURVEYS AND HISTORIES

Books

1793 COFFINET, JULIEN. *Métamorphoses de la tapisserie.* Paris: Bibliothèque des Arts, 1977. 225 pp., 76 color pls., 216 b&w figs.

The evolution of tapestry designs (style, iconography, and technique) chiefly in France and Flanders from the 14th to the 20th century with detailed consideration of major manufacturing centers (Paris, Arras, Tournai, Brussels) and their products; chaps. 3-12 (pp. 39-165) deal with 15th-16th-century French and Flemish tapestries. Two-page technical glossary.

1794 DEMOTTE, G.-J. *La Tapisserie gothique.* Parts 1-4. Preface by Salomon Reinach. Paris: Demotte, 1921-24. 14 pp., 100 b&w pls.

Major 15th- early 16th-century French and Flemish tapestries: the Apocalypse in Angers, the Bourbon series in the Cathedral of Sens, all the main tapestries of the Musée de Cluny and the Musée des Arts Décoratifs in Paris, and other examples in various private collections.

1795   GÖBEL, HEINRICH. *Wandteppiche.* 3 vols. in 6 parts. Vol. 1, *Die Niederlande,* Leipzig: Klinkhardt & Biermann, 1923, part 1, 680 pp., 1 color pl., 52 b&w figs., 24 pls. of town marks and weavers' monograms; part 2, 3 color pls., 452 b&w figs. Vol. 2, *Die romanischen Länder,* Leipzig: Klinkhardt & Biermann, 1928, part 1, 647 pp., 1 color pl., 20 pls. of town marks and weavers' monograms; part 2, 6 color pls., 552 b&w figs. Vol. 3, *Die germanischen und slawischen Länder,* part 1, *Deutschland einschliesslich Schweiz und Elsass (Mittelalter), Süddeutschland (16. bis 18. Jahrhundert),* Berlin: Klinkhardt & Biermann, 1933, 316 pp., 2 color pls., 241 b&w pls.; part 2, *West-, Mittel-, Ost-, und Norddeutschland, England, Irland, Schweden, Norwegen, Dänemark, Russland, Polen, Litauen,* Berlin: Brandussche Verlags-Buchhandlung, 1934, 334 pp., 3 color pls., 209 b&w pls. (with many figs.), 6 pp. weavers' marks. (A shortened version of vol. 1 was translated into English by Robert West, *Tapestries of the Lowlands,* New York: Brentano's 1924, 106 pp., 3 color pls., 510 b&w figs., 24 pls. of town marks and weavers' monograms.)

    Comprehensive survey of European tapestries and their manufacture, technique, dating, iconography, weavers, weaving centers, patronage, commissions, inventories, etc. from the 12th through 20th century; includes abundant illustration and facsimiles of town marks and weavers' monograms and signatures. Some peripheral items such as cushion covers and ecclesiastical vestments. Vol. 1: the Netherlands; vol. 2: France, Italy, Spain, Portugal; vol. 3, part 1: South Germany, Switzerland, Alsace; part 2: North, West, East, Middle Germany, England, Ireland, Norway, Denmark, Sweden, Russia, Poland, and Lithuania.

1796   GUIFFREY, JULES. *Les Tapisseries du XIIe à la fin du XVIe siècle.* Paris: Librairie Central des Beaux-Arts, n.d. 228 pp., 98 b&w text figs., 15 b&w pls.

    Historical survey of European tapestries, mainly 15th- and 16th-century French, German, Italian, Spanish, English, and Flemish works (pp. 23-210). Individual chapters deal with major manufacturing centers, weavers, and designers.

1797   GUIFFREY, JULES; PINCHART, ALEXANDRE; and MÜNTZ, M. EUGÈNE, *Histoire générale de la tapisserie.* Vol. 1, *Histoire de la tapisserie en France,* by Guiffrey, 159 pp. with 22 text figs., 50 pls.; vol. 2, *Histoire de la tapisserie dans les Flandres,* by Pinchart, 131 pp., 26 pls.; vol. 3, *Histoire de la tapisserie en Italie, en Allemagne, en Angleterre, en Espagne, au Danemark, en Hongrie, en Pologne, en Russie et en Turquie,* by Müntz, 130 pp. with 31 text figs., 26 pls. Paris: Société Anonyme de Publications Périodiques, 1878-85.

    Early, monumental study of European tapestries. Vol. 1: French tapestries of the 15th century (pp. 5-72) and Renaissance (73-116); covers all major and minor manufacturing centers and weavers with valuable references to inventories. Vol. 2: Flemish tapestries mostly of the 15th and 16th century; arranged by weaving center. Vol. 3: 15th- and 16th-century hangings from Italy (2-98; geographically arranged, with documents), Germany (for earlier period see 100-113), England (119-21), Spain (125-26), Denmark (128), Hungary, and Poland (129-30).

1798   HEINZ, DORA. *Europäische Wandteppiche.* Vol. 1, *Von den Anfängen der Bildwirkerei bis zum Ende des 16. Jahrhunderts.* Brunswick: Klinkhardt & Biermann, 1963. 366 pp., 15 color pls., 216 b&w figs., 16 pp. of town and makers' marks.

    Concise history of tapestry-making in Europe during the 15th-16th century. Particularities of each center briefly discussed and well illustrated.

1799   JARRY, MADELEINE. *La Tapisserie des origines à nos jours.* Paris, Hachette, 1968. 358 pp., 31 color pls., 185 b&w figs.

The making of tapestries from Coptic to modern times. Chap. 3 (pp. 51-93) deals with the workshops of Arras and Tournai in the 15th century; chap. 4 (95-136), with the rise of the Brussels workshops and the "millefleurs" around 1500; chap. 5 (137-83), Renaissance tapestries from Brussels, the cartoons of Raphael and Giulio Romano, Bernard van Orley and his successors, Italian and French mannerist productions, Swedish, Danish, and Norwegian tapestries.

1800   JOBÉ, JOSEPH, ed. *The Art of Tapestry.* Essays by Pierre Verlet, Michel Florisoone, Adolf Hoffmeisler, and François Tabard. Translated by Peggy Rowell Oberson. London: Thames & Hudson, 1965. 278 pp., 75 color pls., 54 b&w figs.
   Broad survey of the art of tapestry weaving from the Middle Ages to the present arranged in four parts: Gothic Tapestry (pp. 10-76); Classical Tapestry (79-88); Contemporary Tapestry; Weaver's Art (226-64), each by a different contributor and each of first three followed by a catalog of tapestries from various museums. Discusses usage, technique, and patronage in addition to style and iconography. Large plates with details, several appendixes.

1801   LESTOCQUOY, J. *Deux siècles de l'histoire de la tapisserie (1300-1500): Paris, Arras, Lille, Tournai, Bruxelles.* Arras: Mémoires de la Commission Départementale des Monuments Historiques du Pas-de-Calais, vol. 19, 1978. 140 pp., 13 color pls., 21 b&w pls.
   Reappraisal of archival documents and of historical writings dealing with tapestries woven in Paris, Arras, Lille, Tournai, and Brussels in the period 1300-1500 as well as those of Italian centers (mainly Milan, Ferrara, Florence, and Siena) that, according to Lestocquoy, are offshoots of Franco-Flemish ones.

1802   SARTOR, M. *Les Tapisseries, toiles peintes et broderies de Reims.* Preface by Jules Guiffrey. Reims: L. Michaud, 1912. 191 pp., 83 b&w figs.
   Monograph on tapestries in the cathedral and the Church of St.-Remi, Reims, including the 15th-century History of King Clovis (only two large panels remaining), a 16th-century Brussels tapestry series (seventeen panels) of the life of the Virgin, and ten others depicting events from the life of St. Remi.

1803   THOMSON, W.G. *A History of Tapestry from the Earliest Times until the Present Day.* London: Hodder & Stoughton, 1906. 506 pp., 4 color pls., 48 b&w pls., 23 b&w figs.
   Broad survey dealing with history and development of tapestry weaving as well as artists, workshops, designs, patronage, styles, technique, major centers of production, etc. For 15th-16th-century European productions, see chaps. 6-12. Includes extracts from early inventories, facsimile tapestry marks, list of artists and merchants, and a subject index.

Articles

1804   KURTH, BETTY. "Medieval Romances in Renaissance Tapestries." *Journal of the Warburg and Courtauld Institutes* 5 (1942):237-45, 8 b&w figs.
   Author traces the rare subject of three tapestries, in her opinion woven in Paris, to the Spanish poem "Carcel de Amor," and suggests that they were very possibly given by Francis I to Renée de France in 1528 on the occasion of her marriage to Ercole II d'Este of Ferrara. Author also examines the subject of two other tapestries perhaps woven in Tournai ca. 1500 depicting the death of Hercules, which was most probably taken from the *Recueil des histoires de Troie* ordered in 1464 by Philip the Good from Raoul Lefèvre.

1805   ROBERT, C.L. "The Wittelsbach Tapestries." *Connoisseur* 100 (1937):175-81, 8 b&w figs.

Author highlights some 16th-18th-century tapestries from the collection of 414 (as inventoried in 1896) amassed by Bavarian princes (60 are in the national museum and the Residenz in Munich; the remainder are in other Bavarian museums): 3 of a set of genealogical tapestries woven at Lauingen in 1540, many Brussels tapestries (by Maerten van Heemskerck, Franz Geubels, Theodor De Bry, Jan van Tiegen, etc.).

1806 STEPPE, JAN-KAREL, and DELMARCEL, GUY. "Les Tapisseries du Cardinal Érard de la Marck prince-évêque de Liège." *Revue de l'art* 25 (1974):35-54, 14 b&w figs.
Study of the tapestry collection of this prince-bishop of Liège (1505-38): iconographic subjects (allegories and religious); place of manufacture; formation of the collection based on political relationships and as known from recently discovered inventories dating of 1522-23 of his household effects (here published), and from later documents. Of the twenty-one series of hangings (232 pieces) in his possession between 1522 and 1533, six can be traced today.

1807 THOMSON, W.G. "German, Italian, and Other European Tapestries." *Apollo* 1 (1925):324-29, 9 b&w figs.
Useful, though somewhat dated account, that provides an introduction to tapestry-making in Germany, Scandinavia, Italy, and Spain.

1808 THURMAN, CHRISTA C.M. "Tapestry: The Purposes, Form, and Function of the Medium from Its Inception until Today." In *Acts of the Tapestry Symposium, November 1976.* San Francisco: Fine Arts Museums, 1979. Pp. 3-19, 17 b&w figs.
Concise yet comprehensive introduction to the subject: techniques, materials, sources, patronage, major centers of production, and methods and tools for studying and dating.

6. PERMANENT COLLECTIONS

Bern

BERNISCHES HISTORISCHES MUSEUM

1809 *Bildteppiche und Antependien in Historischen Museum Bern.* Catalog edited by Michael Stettler and Paul Nizon. Bern: Stämpfli & Cie., 1959. 53 pp. (unpaginated), 7 color pls., 21 b&w figs.
The important collection of Upper Rhenish, Brussels, and Tournai 15th-century tapestry series including those from the Burgundian booty at Grandson in 1476. Particularly important among the latter are the four hangings depicting the history of Julius Caesar of ca. 1465-70.

Boston

MUSEUM OF FINE ARTS

1810 TOWNSEND, GERTRUDE. "Eight Fragments of Fifteenth Century Tapestry." *Bulletin of the Museum of Fine Arts* 27 (1929):2-10, 8 b&w figs.
Description and historical background of Franco-Flemish fragments with the story of Penelope and self-destruction of the Cimbri Woman, which once formed part of two tapestries in a series of eight woven ca. 1480-83 for the Burgundian patron, Ferry de Clugny.

1811   *Tapestries of Europe and of Colonial Peru in the Museum of Fine Arts, Boston.* Catalog by
        Adolph S. Cavallo. 2 vols. Boston: Museum of Fine Arts, [1967]. 1: 249 pp., 26 b&w
        figs.; 2: 15 color pls., 87 b&w pls.
            Includes fifty-five European tapestries of which over thirty-five (German, Flemish
        [mostly], French) are of the period 1400-1600. Vol. 1: thirty-page introduction with history of
        the collection, weaving technique, followed by entries including origin, provenance, descrip-
        tion, condition, and some technical data. Vol. 2 consists of plates usually of particularly good
        legibility.

Glasgow

GLASGOW MUSEUMS AND ART GALLERIES – BURRELL COLLECTION

1812   TATTERSALL, C.E.C. "Sir William Burrell's Gothic Tapestries." *Old Furniture* 1
        (1927):111-22, 10 b&w figs.
            Cursory presentation of some items of this famous collection of Gothic tapestries:
        series of Labors of the Month, Charity Overcoming Envy, courtly scenes. Useful for illustra-
        tion.

1813   KURTH, BETTY. "Masterpieces of Gothic Tapestry in the Burrell Collection." *Connois-
        seur* 117 (1946):3-12, 15 b&w figs.
            Iconography, technique, localization of examples from Arras, Paris, Tournai,
        Touraine, and Brussels, including heraldic, millefleurs, and hunting tapestries, as well as
        several representing historical, mythological, and religious scenes.

1814   WELLS, WILLIAM. "Two Burrell Hunting Tapestries." *Scottish Art Review* 14, no. 1
        (1973):10-15, 2 color figs., 7 b&w figs.
            Late 15th-century Flemish tapestries of the Seven Sacraments and with ferreters by
        Pasquin Grenier, and a French tapestry of the early 1500s said to represent Francis I hunting.

1815   *Treasures from the Burrell Collection.* Exhibition held in London at Hayward Gallery.
        Catalog by William Wells. London: Arts Council of Great Britain, 1975. 51 pp., 64 b&w
        pls.
            Selection of 382 objects including (nos. 64-100) well-known German, Swiss, "Franco-
        Flemish," "Franco-Burgundian," and "Anglo-Netherlandish" tapestries of the 15th-16th century.

Leningrad

HERMITAGE

1816   BIRYUKOVA, N.Y. *The Hermitage, Leningrad: Gothic and Renaissance Tapestries.* Lon-
        don: Paul Hamlyn, 1965. 199 pp., 128 color figs.
            Highlights of Soviet Union's main holdings (introduction, pp. 9-30) with twenty-two
        examples of German, French, and Flemish hangings dating from the second half of the 15th to
        the early 16th century. Illustrations useful for details.

Lisbon

CALOUSTE GULBENKIAN COLLECTION

1817   NUNES RISO GUERREIRO, GLORIA. "Some European Tapestries in the Calouste
Gulbenkian Collection in Lisbon." *Connoisseur* 173 (1970):229-37, 1 color pl., 8 b&w figs.
        16th-18th-century Flemish, Italian, and French examples. Of the 16th century are
two Ferrarese hangings of ca. 1540 with Gonzaga arms after Giulio Romano designs probably
made in the workshop of Hans or Nicolas Karcher working as master weaver in Ferrara and
Mantua, and a tapestry of Vertumnus and Pomona made for Charles V bearing Brussels
marks and those of a weaver, perhaps Georges Wezeler.

London

VICTORIA AND ALBERT MUSEUM

1818   *Catalogue of Tapestries.* 2d ed. Catalog by A.F. Kendrick. London: Board of Education,
1924. 110 pp., 37 b&w pls. (1st ed. 1914).
        Catalog of 103 hangings, many of the 15th-16th century from England, the Nether-
lands, France, Germany, and Italy. Appendix with supplementary notes on heraldry.

New York

METROPOLITAN MUSEUM OF ART

1819   PHILLIPS, JOHN GOLDSMITH.   "The Museum's Collection of Renaissance
Tapestries," *Metropolitan Museum of Art Bulletin* 6 (1947): 123-29, 5 b&w figs.
        Brief synopsis of the change of function of tapestries from medieval times, and cur-
sory mention of some notable pieces in the museum, including a Brussels tapestry of the
Crucifixion and two with the Months of the Year woven after designs by Bernard van Orley,
two hangings produced by van Pannemaker, and a 16th-century tapestry of the Story of Diana
made in Paris after designs by Jean Cousin.

7. EXHIBITION CATALOGS

New York

METROPOLITAN MUSEUM OF ART

1820   *Masterpieces of Tapestry from the Fourteenth to the Sixteenth Century.* Exhibition catalog
by Geneviève Souchal. Introduction by Francis Salet. Translated by Richard A.H. Oxby.
New York: Metropolitan Museum of Art, 1973. 222 pp., 20 color figs., 126 b&w figs.
        Thirteen-page essay dealing with style, attribution, production, technique, and dating
of 14th-16th-century northern European (France and Burgundian Netherlands) tapestries.
Ninety-seven catalog entries of hangings from European and American collections; includes
major 15th-century works (nos. 6-17), the Hunt of the Unicorn (18-24), millefleurs tapestries
(25-36), Lady with a Unicorn (37-42), choir and heraldic tapestries (43-52), scenes from daily
life and allegories (53-73), and Brussels tapestries (74-97). Exhibition originated in Paris and
was shown there at the Galeries du Grand Palais in 1972.

Strasbourg

ANCIENNE DOUANE

1821   *Tapisseries du Moyen-Age à nos jours.* Exhibition catalog by Victor Beyer and Jean-Louis Faure. Strasbourg: Musées de la Ville de Strasbourg, 1966. 38 pp., 20 b&w pls.

Fifty-eight entries dealing with hangings in French collections (many in Strasbourg, most importantly that of Simon Mikaeloff) ranging from the 15th-20th century; pertinent to 1400-1600 are nos. 1-26 featuring primarily Flemish tapestries with hunting, allegorical, classical, or devotional scenes, millefleurs, and wild men.

8. PRIVATE COLLECTION, AUCTION, AND DEALER CATALOGS

FFOULKE COLLECTION

1822   FFOULKE, CHARLES MATHER, *The Ffoulke Collection of Tapestries.* Essay by Glenn Brown. Introduction by Ernest Verlant. New York: Privately Printed, 1913. 346 pp., 4 color pls., 71 b&w pls.

Collection of over 135 Brussels, Flemish, French, and Italian hangings of the 16th through the 19th century with biblical, mythological, and historical subjects, acquired for the most part from the Barberini family in 1889. By the time of the catalog's publication, several had in turn been sold to other collectors (Gardner, Hearst, Harriman, etc.). Entries with iconographic description, reproduction of marks, and dimensions.

GOULDEN COLLECTION

1823   *Catalogue des objets d'ameublement des XVIIe & XVIIIe siècles . . . tapisseries Renaissance, Régence et Louis XV, ancien tapis d'Orient, le tout provenant de la succession de M. le Pasteur Goulden de Sedan.* Sale held in Paris at Galerie Georges Petit 8-9 December 1919. Paris: F. Lair-Dubreuil, 1919. 31 pp., 16 b&w pls.

Among the 192 lots of this sale are 19 (nos. 156-74) French and Brussels tapestries of the late 15th to the late 16th century notable for their depiction of romances, biblical scenes, and Renaissance motifs.

MACKEY COLLECTION

1824   HUNTER, GEORGE LELAND. *Tapestries of Clarence H. Mackey.* New York: Privately Printed, 1925. 101 pp., 10 color pls., 49 b&w pls.

Catalog of New York private collection. Brief entries describe tapestries among which are two famous 15th-16th century Flemish (pp. 28-59) examples and four French (60-67) weavings now at the Metropolitan and Cleveland museums. Also included are Flemish furniture coverings (98-99).

MACOMBER COLLECTION

1825   ACKERMAN, PHYLLIS. *A Catalog of the Tapestries in the Collection of Frank Gair Macomber.* New York: Privately Printed, n.d. 107 pp., 38 b&w pls.

Collection of fifty-three woven panels of mostly secular iconography dating from the 15th through the 18th century. All 15th-16th-century tapestries cataloged as Flemish or German. Provides description and provenance for many whose whereabouts are now unknown.

PIERPONT MORGAN COLLECTION

1826   DE RICCI, SEYMOUR. *Catalogue of Twenty Renaissance Tapestries from the J. Pierpont Morgan Collection.* Paris: Typographie Philippe Renouard, 1913. 51 pp., 20 b&w pls.
     Selected Gothic, Renaissance, and later tapestries including important French and mostly Flemish examples.

London

V. AND C. STERNBERG

1827   *Four Centuries of Tapestry.* Catalog of private collection exhibited and offered for sale 2-23 November 1966. 101 pp. (unpaginated), 67 b&w figs.
     Eighty tapestries of unstated provenance, spanning the 16th through the 19th century and including twenty-two of the 16th century (nos. 1-16, 21-25, 30). Examples include a millefleurs (Loire region), and tapestries representing landscapes and depicting hunting, mythological, and biblical scenes, assigned to France or mostly Flemish centers (Brussels, Tournai, and Oudenaarde).

B. SINGLE COUNTRY OF ORIGIN

BELGIUM
(BRABANTINE, FLEMISH, AND HAINUYER)

3. SURVEYS AND HISTORIES

Books

1828   ASSELBERGHS, J-P. *Les Tapisseries flamandes aux États-Unis d'Amérique.* Brussels: Musées Royaux d'Art et d'Histoire, 1974. 62 pp. 36 b&w figs.
     Annotated checklist of Flemish tapestries in many U.S. museums (grouped by regions); particularly useful for collections that have been little published. Indexes of subject, weavers, centers of production.

1829   HULLEBROEK, ADOLPHE. *Histoire de la tapisserie à Audenarde du XVe au XVIIIe* siècle. Renaix: J. Leherte-Delcour, 1938. 255 pp., 142 b&w pls.
     Extensive if somewhat dated account of tapestry-making in the city of Oudenaarde and immediate surroundings from 1468 through the 18th century. Author discusses workshops, manufacturing, and cartoons. Concludes with a catalog of 188 hangings.

1830   HULST, ROGER-A.D'. *Tapisseries flamandes du XIVe au XVIIIe siècle.* Preface by H. Liebaers, with introduction by J. Duverger, 2d ed. Brussels: Éditions Arcade, 1966. 315 pp., 52 color pls., 76 b&w figs. (1st ed. 1960.)
     Twenty-five-page introduction surveys history and uses of Flemish tapestries between the 14th and the 18th century (for 15th- and 16th-century works consult particularly pp. XIV-XXVII). Detailed catalog (thirty-four entries) includes 15th- and 16th-century masterpieces (pp. 7-262) from Arras, Tournai(?), Brussels, and Grammont, some published for the first time. Large plates with many details.

Articles

1831 ASSELBERGHS, JEAN-PAUL. "Les Tapisseries tournaisiennes de la Guerre de Troie." *Revue belge d'archéologie et d'histoire de l'art* 39 (1970):93-183, 32 b&w figs.
Reconstruction of eleven large pieces of a tapestry depicting the Trojan War, woven in Tournai ca. 1465-90, the iconographic sources being the *Roman de Troie* of Benoît de Sainte-Maure and a French translation of Guido da Colonna. Duke Charles the Bold of Burgundy owned the original version.

1832 BACRI, JACQUES. "A New Fragment of the Guillaume de Hellande Tapestries." *Burlington Magazine* 101 (1959):402- 4, 3 b&w figs.
Partially preserved series of eleven tapestries depicting the Life of St. Peter commissioned in 1460 and now in the Beauvais Cathedral, Boston Fine Arts Museum, and French and U.S. private collections. It is held to have most probably been woven in Tournai.

1833 CRICK-KUNTZIGER, M. "Un Fragment de tapisserie de l'histoire de Thèbes." *Revue belge d'archéologie et d'histoire de l'art* 2 (1932):231-37, 1 b&w fig.
A 15th-century tapestry fragment (private collection) depicting an episode from the *Histoire de Thèbes* is connected to the workshop of Willaume Desreumaux of Tournai.

1834 CRICK-KUNTZIGER, M. "Tapisseries inédites à la vue de Bruxelles." *Revue belge d'archéologie et d'histoire de l'art* 22 (1953):105-8, 1 b&w fig.
Some 16th-century Brussels tapestries in public and private European collections with identifiable buildings and broad depictions of that city.

1835 CRICK-KUNTZIGER, MARTHE. "Les Tapisseries de la légende de Notre-Dame du Sablon." *Bulletin des Musées Royaux d'Art et d'Histoire,* 3d ser. 2 (January 1930):2-14, 5 b&w figs.
Attempt to reconstitute a famous Brussels 16th-century tapestry set of four panels depicting the Miracles of Our Lady of the Sablon from fragments that are in public and private collections.

1836 DUVERGER, ERIK. "Lucas van Leyden en de tapijtkunst." *Artes textiles* 4 (1957-58):26-38, 7 b&w figs. French summary.
Early 16th-century tapestries for which cartoons were made not by Lucas van Leyden himself but after his engravings, proposes the author.

1837 DUVERGER, J. "Giels van de Putte, tapijtwever en tapijthandelaar te Brussel (ca. 1420-na 1503)." *Artes textiles* 7 (1971):5-22, 3 b&w figs. French summary.
Tapestries in the Vatican, Brussels (Musée d'Art et d'Histoire), and a Madrid private collection attributed to the workshop of the Brussels weaver Gielis van de Putte (1420-1503) who may well have also produced an antependium for Cardinal Ferry de Clugny (fragment in the Museum of Fine Arts, Boston).

1838 DUVERGER, J. "Jan de Haze en de bourgondische wapentapijten te Bern." *Artes textiles* 6 (1965):10-25, 2 b&w figs. French summary.
Activity of the Flemish weavers Jan de Haze, perhaps from Brussels, and Perceval van Helsele of Bruges, both at the service of dukes Philip the Good and Charles the Bold, who produced floral tapestries with arms, now in Bern and Thun, as well as seat cushions.

1839   ERKELENS, LOUISE. "Drie fragmenten van een Hercules tapijt uit de laatste vijftien jaren van de XVe eeuw." *Bulletin van het Rijksmuseum* 2 (1954):9-14, 4 b&w figs. English summary.
Two panels of a late-15th-century Brussels tapestry depicting the Youth and Prowess of Hercules, in the Rijksmuseum and the Musée d'Art et d'Histoire, Brussels.

1840   GÖBEL, HEINRICH. "Die Hamburger Wandteppich-Manufaktur des Joos van Herseele." *Pantheon* 8 (1931):420-25, 3 b&w figs.
Brief history of the Hamburg tapestry workshop maintained by the Flemish weaver Joost II van Herseele from ca. 1589-1621; cursory descriptions of three hangings made for Bückeburg Castle depicting scenes from Roman history.

1841   HUNTER, GEORGE LELAND. "Scipio Tapestries Now in America." *Burlington Magazine* 29 (1916):59-66, 1 color pl., 2 b&w pls.
Description of four Brussels tapestries of ca. 1520-60 brought to New York (unspecified collection) from Madrid. Signed H.M., these hangings were made from designs after Giulio Romano.

1842   KENDRICK, A.F. "A Brussels Tapestry." *Apollo* 22 (1935):280-81, 1 color pl., 1 b&w fig.
Flemish tapestry depicting St. Veronica holding the veil with Christ's features. This weave is associated with the style of Quentin Metsys and is assigned to a Brussels workshop active ca. 1500-10.

1843   KURTH, BETTY. "Some Hitherto Unknown Tapestries with the Story of Jonathan Maccabeus." *Connoisseur* 120 (1947):22-25, 4 b&w figs.
Three tapestries (one from the Burrell Collection, Glasgow, and two of unknown whereabouts) are related on the basis of style and attributed to a Brussels workshop of the late 15th- early 16th century.

1844   SALMON, LARRY. "The Passion of Christ in Medieval Tapestries." In *Acts of the Tapestry Symposium, November 1976.* San Francisco: Fine Arts Museums, 1979. Pp. 79-101, 17 b&w figs.
Eight Flemish hangings dispersed in American and European collections and a set of nine monumental embroideries preserved in the collegiate church of Romans (France), all depicting scenes from Christ's Passion and drawn from the same design. Author reassesses past attributions.

1845   SOUCHAL, GENEVIÈVE. "The Triumph of the Seven Virtues: Reconstruction of a Brussels Series (ca. 1520-1535)." In *Acts of the Tapestry Symposium, November 1976.* San Francisco: Fine Arts Museums, 1979. Pp. 103-33, 24 b&w figs., 2 tables.
Analysis of the iconographic program of seventeen surviving tapestries of an important early Renaissance series, now dispersed in Europe and the U.S. Investigation into sources, differentiation and possible number of identical compositions, identity of owners of original weavings, and workshops.

1846   STANDEN, EDITH A. "Romans and Sabines: A Sixteenth-Century Set of Flemish Tapestries." *Metropolitan Museum Journal* 9 (1974):211-28, 24 b&w figs.
Tapestries at the Metropolitan and the Cleveland museums of art of the Rape of the Sabines designed by Nicolas von Orley and executed by Flemish weavers (perhaps in Italy) ca. 1570.

1847   UYTVEN, R. VAN. "De Leuvense legwerkers van het begin der XIVe tot het einde der XVIe eeuw." *Artes textiles* 5 (1959-60):5-30. French summary.
Activity of tapestry weavers in the town of Louvain from the early 14th century until the end of the 16th century as recorded by documents as well as by tapestry fragments in city offices of Louvain and the Musée d'Art et d'Histoire in Brussels.

1848   VERDIER, PHILIPPE. "The Tapestry of the Prodigal Son." *Journal of Walters Art Gallery* 18 (1955):9-58, 26 b&w figs.
Iconographic study of an allegorical tapestry in the Walters Art Gallery woven in Brussels ca. 1485 and of the first panel of the series to which it belongs in the J.B. Speed Museum, Louisville.

1849   VERSYP, JACQUELINE. "De Alexander en Aeneastapijten te Fabriano." *Artes textiles* 8 (1974):71-86, 10 b&w figs. French summary.
Tapestry set of the history of Aeneas and of Alexander—partly in Fabriano, Italy—probably bearing the monogram of Jan Stomman of Brussels and dating of ca. 1570.

1850   VERSYP, JACQUELINE. "Zestiende-eeuwse jachttapijten met het wapen van de Vidoni en aanverwante stukken." *Artes textiles* 7 (1971):23-46, 15 b&w figs. French summary.
Tapestries of the 16th century with hunting scenes and bearing the arms of the Vidoni family in the Palazzo di Venezia, Rome, and Castle of Laarne near Ghent, woven in Brussels by a still unidentified workshop.

1851   WELLS, WILLIAM. "The Marshal Remembers . . . an Allegorical View of French History." *Scottish Art Review* 14, no. 2 (1973):14-21, 1 color fig., 15 b&w figs.
Set of tapestries of ca. 1510 divided between Glasgow, the Corcoran Gallery, Washington, and the Musée de Cluny, Paris, proposed to have been designed by Jean Perréal and woven in Flanders, and to represent an allegory of Louis XII's marriage to Anne of Brittany.

1852   WOOD, D.T.B. "'Credo' Tapestries." *Burlington Magazine* 24 (1913-14):247-54, 309-16, 5 b&w pls.
Iconography of 15th-century Flemish tapestries in the Vatican and Museum of Fine Arts, Boston, panels of a 16th-century Flemish tapestry in a private Parisian collection and others whose whereabouts are unknown belonging to J. Pierpont Morgan, and three 16th-century French painted textiles in the Hôtel Dieu of Reims, described as illustrating the Credo, a recurring iconographic program in tapestries, according to 14th-16th-century inventories.

1853   WOOD, D.T.B. "Tapestries of the Seven Deadly Sins." *Burlington Magazine* 20 (1912). Part 1, 210-22, 9 b&w figs. [on 3 pls.]; part 2, 277-89, 16 b&w figs. [on 3 pls.].
Iconographic study of these eight Brussels hangings produced ca. 1500, and dispersed among the Louvre, Burgos Cathedral, Hampton Court Palace, and private collections. Author relates the panels to each other historically, stylistically, and iconographically, classifying them according to themes (1) the History of the Redemption, (2) the Allegory of Mankind, and (3) the Allegory of Virtues and Vices.

6. PERMANENT COLLECTIONS

Aix-en-Provence

MUSÉE DES TAPISSERIES

1854   *Les Tapisseries de la vie du Christ et de la Vierge d'Aix-en-Provence.* Exhibition catalog essays by Donald King, M.H. Krotoff, Jacques Paul, François Garnier, Yvonne Deslandres, Jean Jenkins, Michel Pastoureau, Madeleine Jarry, and Guy Delmarcel. Aix-en-Provence: Musée des Tapisseries, 1977. 111 pp., 26 color pls., several b&w figs.

Two tapestries woven in Brussels during the first quarter of the 16th century, one of the Life of Christ and one of the Life of the Virgin, remaining from the collection belonging to Saint-Sauveur Cathedral in Aix-en-Provence. Now in eight segments, these are composed of twenty-six scenes. Essays on their history, literary sources, iconographic program, costumes, musical instruments, and arms depicted, as well as on other series woven from the same cartoons.

Bakewell, Derbyshire

HARDWICK HALL

1855   ROETHLISBERGER, MARCEL. "The Ulysses Tapestries at Hardwick Hall." *Gazette des beaux-arts* 79 (1972):111-25, 12 b&w figs.

Eight previously unpublished tapestries with scenes from *The Odyssey,* dating of ca. 1560 and produced in the circle of Michiel Coxie. One bears the mark of the weaver Nicolas Hellinck.

Barcelona

MUSEU D'ART DE CATALUNYA

1856   DURAN I CANYAMERAS, F. "Els tapissos de l'audiència al nostre museu." *Butlletí dels Museus d'Art de Barcelona* 7 (1937):367-84, 22 b&w figs.

Outstanding cycle of Brussels tapestries illustrating Petrarch's Triumphs and biblical scenes produced (by F. Gembel? and others) in the late 16th century.

Bern

BERNISCHES HISTORISCHES MUSEUM

1857   SCHNEEBALG-PERELMAN, S. "La Tenture armoriée de Philippe le Bon à Berne." *Jahrbuch des bernischen historischen Museums* 39 (1959):136-63, 9 b&w figs.

Author refutes the theory of Crick-Kuntziger that this millefleurs tapestry bearing the arms of Philip the Good, duke of Burgundy, was made in Lille. She proposes instead that it was produced in Brussels by Jean de Haze in 1466 and heralds the series of the Dame à la Licorne in the Musée de Cluny, Paris.

Boston

MUSEUM OF FINE ARTS

1858   FLINT, SARAH GORE. "A Flemish Tapestry of the Sixteenth Century." *Bulletin of the Museum of Fine Arts* 7 (1909):5-7, 1 b&w fig.
Dated by the author 1450-1500, it is divided into four scenes: the Creation of Eve, the Baptism, Nativity, and Crucifixion, which are suggested to depend on paintings by Hans Memling.

1859   TOWNSEND, GERTRUDE. "Prophets and Apostles in the Creed Tapestry." *Bulletin of the Museum of Fine Arts* 26 (1928):64-70, 6 b&w figs.
Examining the iconography of this late 15th-century Flemish tapestry the author relates the order of appearance of the prophets and apostles to that in early 14th-century manuscripts.

1860   TOWNSEND, GERTRUDE. "The Passion Tapestry from Knole." *Bulletin of the Museum of Fine Arts* 29 (1931):98-104, 3 b&w figs.
Six hangings with scenes from the Passion suggested to have been woven in Brussels or Tournai after the same cartoons or designs as the Angers Passion tapestries.

1861   CRICK-KUNTZIGER, MARTHE. "Un Chef-d'oeuvre inconnu du Maître de la 'Dame à la Licorne.'" *Revue belge* 23 (1954):3-20, 7 b&w figs.
Tapestry series representing illustrious women destroyed in 1791 except for a fragment with Penelope in this collection attributed to the weaver who produced the Dame à la Licorne series in the Musée de Cluny, Paris. The master is held to have worked in Bruges for Mary of Burgundy or Ferry de Clugny, her counselor.

1862   CAVALLO, ADOLPH S. "The Redemption of Man: A Christian Allegory in Tapestry." *Bulletin of the Museum of Fine Arts* 56 (1958):147-68, 10 b&w figs.
The iconography of this large, early 16th-century Brussels tapestry, formerly in the Duke of Alba and Hearst collections, is based on the writings of Hughes de St.-Victor and St. Bernard.

Brussels

HÔTEL DE VILLE

1863   CRICK-KUNTZIGER, MARTHE. *Les Tapisseries de l'Hôtel de Ville de Bruxelles.* Antwerp: De Sikkel, 1944. 46 pp., 29 b&w pls.
Tapestries in Brussels's city hall dating from the 16th to the 18th century, all held to have been made in that city. Of the 16th century are those depicting David and Bathsheba, the Legend of the Virgin of the Sablon, the Credo, the Life of St. Paul, and a hunting scene.

MUSÉES ROYAUX D'ART ET D'HISTOIRE

1864   *Catalogue des tapisseries (XIVe au XVIIIe siècle),* by Marthe Crick-Kuntziger. [Brussels: Musées Royaux d'Art et d'Histoire, n.d.] 94 pp., 120 b&w figs.

Useful entries from this major collection of 115 tapestries including forty-three examples dating of the 15th-16th century (biblical scenes, Life of Christ, Triumphs after Petrarch, Hercules, verdures, etc.). The most renowned among these were woven in Brussels, Tournai, and in Flanders.

1865   *Tapeçarias antigas da Bélgica.* Exhibition held in Lisbon at the Museu Nacional de Arte Antiga. Catalog by Guy Delmarcel, with one-page survey of Brussels-made tapestries in Portugal by Maria José Mendonça. Lisbon: Ministério Belga da Cultura Neerlandesa; Brussels: Musée Royal d'Art et d'Histoire, 1978. 14 pp. (unpaginated). 12 b&w pls.
    Twelve 16th-18th-century mostly Brussels-made tapestries from the collections of the Musées Royaux d'Art et d'Histoire. Of the 16th century are cat. nos. 1-4: a Triumph of Love, two panels from a series of a History of Jacob after cartoons by Bernard van Orley, and one of a set of the Rape of the Sabine Women.

La Chaise-Dieu

ABBAYE ST. ROBERT

1866   POMMARAT, MICHEL, and BURGER, PIERRE. *Les Tapisseries de l'abbatiale Saint-Robert de la Chaise-Dieu.* Brioude: Watel, 1975. 147 pp., numerous color and b&w illus.
    Set of fourteen (Flemish?) tapestries commissioned between 1501-18 by Abbot Jacques de Saint-Nicaise.

Cleveland

CLEVELAND MUSEUM OF ART

1867   WARDWELL, ANNE E. "The Mystical Grapes, A Devotional Tapestry." *Bulletin of The Cleveland Museum of Art* 62 (1975):17-23, 10 b&w figs.
    Small Flemish tapestry of wool, silk, and metallic threads of ca. 1500 in the style of Joos van Cleve; relationship to similar woven panels.

Florence

GALLERIA DEGLI UFFIZZI

1868   YATES, FRANCES A. *The Valois Tapestries.* London: Warburg Institute, 1959. 170 pp., 48 b&w pls.
    Through detailed examination of the iconography of the eight hangings of this famous series representing the family of Catherine de' Medici—the festivals depicted, the portraits, many after drawings of the French court artist Antoine Caron—the author identifies a second artist, the Fleming Lucas de Heerg at the service of the House of Orange, as being responsible for the deliberate alteration of Caron's designs to gain Catherine de' Medici and Henri IV's support for the French venture in the Netherlands.

1869   GATTI GAZZINI, GIULIA. "Le feste dei Valois." *Antichità viva* 3. Part 1, no. 1 (1964):32-41, 1 color fig., 7 b&w figs.; part 2, no. 4 (1964):33-44, 10 b&w figs.; 55-63, 6 b&w figs.
    Series of Brussels-made tapestries glorifying the reign of Henri III of France are held to have been designed by Antoine Caron.

Ghent

OUDHEIDKUNDIG MUSEUM VAN DE BIJLOKE

1870   DELMARCEL, GUY. "Peter de Kempeneer (Campaña) as a Designer of Tapestry Cartoons." *Artes textiles* 10 (1981):155-62, 4 b&w figs. French summary.
De Kempeneer (1503-80) received official commission for cartoons in the town of Brussels in the 1560s. Tapestries in this collection are attributed to his design.

Glasgow

GLASGOW MUSEUMS AND ART GALLERIES – BURRELL COLLECTION

1871   WELLS, WILLIAM. "An Unknown Hercules Tapestry in the Burrell Collection: Iconography and Dating." *Scottish Art Review* 8, no. 3 (1962):13-16, 1 color fig., 3 b&w figs.
Important 15th-century tapestry suggested to have been woven in Tournai shortly after 1451 for the court of Burgundy.

Kansas City

NELSON-ATKINS MUSEUM OF ART

1872   ACKERMAN, PHYLLIS. "An Important Early XVIth Century Tapestry." *Apollo* 21 (1935):94-97, 1 color pl., 2 b&w figs.
An early 16th-century Brussels tapestry in the style of Jan II van Roome representing Christ Carrying the Cross is attributed to Jacob de Camp of Antwerp.

Kraków

PÁNSTWOWE ZBIORY SZTUKI NA WAWELU

1873   SZABLOWSKI, JERZY, ed. *The Flemish Tapestries at Wawel Castle in Cracow: Treasures of King Sigismund Augustus Jagiello.* Translated by Haakon Chevalier. Antwerp: Fends Marcator, 1972. 501 pp., 88 color pls., 43 b&w pls.
Series of outstanding 16th-century Brussels tapestries with biblical subjects influenced by Raphael's school; others of ca. 1560 with verdures and animals woven by Jan van Tiegham after Pieter Coecke van Aelst of Brussels; third set with mannerist grotesques bearing the arms of Poland and Lithuania.

London

VICTORIA AND ALBERT MUSEUM

1874   DIGBY, GEORGE WINGFIELD. "The Restoration of the Devonshire Hunting Tapestries." *Victoria and Albert Museum Bulletin* 2 (1966):80-92, 13 b&w figs.
Technical problems encountered in the 1958-66 restoration of three hangings from the famous 15th-century Flemish set.

1875   ASSELBERGHS, J.P. "Charles VIII's Trojan War Tapestry." *Victoria and Albert Museum Yearbook* 1 (1969):80-84, 5 b&w figs.

Famous Tournai tapestry of the late fifteenth century based on the poem of Benoît de Saint-Maure, bears the insignia of the French king.

1876 SOUCHAL, GENEVIÈVE. "Charles VIII et la tenture de la Guerre de Troie." *Revue belge d'archéologie et d'histoire de l'art* 39 (1970):185-89.

Tapestry of the Arrival of Penthesilea in Troy woven in late 15th-century Tournai as part of eleven sections dealing with the Trojan War. It bears the emblem of Charles VIII of France over an earlier shield as yet undeciphered.

1877 DIGBY, GEORGE WINGFIELD, assisted by HEFFORD, WENDY. *The Devonshire Hunting Tapestries.* London: Her Majesty's Stationery Office, 1971. 101 pp., 20 color pls., 31 b&w pls.

Thorough presentation of the four 15th-century hangings in this famous series seen in an historical perspective – hunting and hawking in medieval times and later, costumes and accoutrements of 15th-century lords and ladies – as well as from a stylistic standpoint. Five appendixes including a repertory of other hunting tapestry sets and notes on costume (by Madeleine Ginsburg).

1878 KING, DONALD. "The Devonshire *Hunts:* Art and Sport in the Fifteenth Century." *Connoisseur* 196 (1977):246-53, 2 color figs., 4 b&w figs.

Provenance, style, iconography, and costumes of these four well-known tapestries with hunting scenes, which are here dated ca. 1420-1440 and assigned to an anonymous group of four different designers, probably from Arras or Tournai.

Madrid

COLLECCIÓN REAL

1879 *Tapisseries des maisons royales en Espagne.* Exhibition held in Bordeaux at the Galerie des Beaux-Arts. Catalog by Paulina Junquera de Vega and Maria Teresa Ruiz Alcon, with the collaboration of Evelyne Baroux. Edited by Gilberte Martin-Mery. Bordeaux: Galerie des Beaux-Arts. 1968, 107 pp., 9 color pls., 26 b&w figs.

Selection of thirty tapestries from the Spanish royal collection. Includes twenty-one outstanding 16th-century Brussels examples. Well illustrated with scholarly entries and good bibliographical references.

1880 DELMARCEL, GUY. "The Triumph of the Seven Virtues and Related Brussels Tapestries of the Early Renaissance." In *Acts of the Tapestry Symposium, November 1976.* San Francisco: Fine Arts Museums. 1979. Pp. 155-169, 10 b&w figs.

Study of the diffusion of style and iconography in tapestries originally conceived for the Hapsburg Court and now in the Spanish royal collection.

PATRIMONIO NACIONAL

1881 KURZ, OTTO. "Four Tapestries After Hieronymus Bosch." *Journal of the Warburg and Courtauld Institutes* 30 (1967):150-62, 6 b&w figs. Reprinted in *The Decorative Arts of Europe and the Islamic East: Selected Studies.* London: Dorian Press, 1977.

Garden of Delights, Hay Wain, Feast of St. Martin, Temptation of St. Anthony probably made for the Duke of Alba ca. 1567 after a set borrowed from the Cardinal Nicolas de Granvelle.

Minneapolis

MINNEAPOLIS INSTITUTE OF ARTS

1882   "A Gothic Tapestry Based on the Moralities." *Bulletin of the Minneapolis Institute of Arts* 31 (1942):84-89, 4 b&w figs.
       Tournai tapestry of ca. 1515 depicting the Triumph of Virtue decribed in terms of its narrative and allegory.

New York

METROPOLITAN MUSEUM OF ART

1883   HUNTER, GEORGE LELAND.   "The Burgundian Tapestries in the Metropolitan Museum." *Burlington Magazine* 12 (1907-8):184-87, 2 b&w pls.
       Five fragments of the first half of the 15th century from a set with the seven sacraments.

1884   FORSYTH, WILLIAM H.   "A Tapestry from Burgos Cathedral." *Metropolitan Museum of Art Bulletin* 33 (1938):148-52, 3 b&w figs.
       Large tapestry of ca. 1500 depicting the Redemption of Man and formerly in Burgos Cathedral is attributed to the workshop of Pieter Coecke van Aelst of Brussels.

1885   STANDEN, EDITH A.   "The Twelve Ages of Man." *Metropolitan Museum of Art Bulletin* 12 (1954):241-48, 8 b&w figs.
       Four tapestries woven in Brussels around 1520 represent a subject dealt with in a series of early 16th-century Parisian books of hours.

1886   RORIMER, JAMES J.   "The Glorification of Charles VIII." *Metropolitan Museum of Art Bulletin* 12 (1954):281-99, 26 b&w figs.   (A summary version was published in *Connoisseur* 134 [1954]:112-13, 1 color pl.)
       Three long-separated panels reunited to form a hanging thirty feet long.   Made around 1490, the signed tapestry is associated with Jan van Roome of Brussels, and was most likely commissioned by Maximilian in honor of his son-in-law.

1887   FORSYTH, WILLIAM H.   "The Trojan War in Medieval Tapestries." *Metropolitan Museum of Art Bulletin* 14 (1955):76-84, 7 b&w figs.
       Iconography of tapestries produced in the workshop of Pasquier Grenier of Tournai, ca. 1470-90.

1888   STANDEN, EDITH A.   "Some Sixteenth-Century Flemish Tapestries Related to Raphael's Workshop." *Metropolitan Museum of Art Journal* 4 (1971):109-21, 11 b&w figs.
       Tapestries of the Adoration of the Kings (Brussels, ca. 1525), and the Story of Mercury and Herse (ca. 1550) are compared with paintings by Raphael's workshop and Bernard van Orley.

1889   FREEMAN, MARGARET B.   *The Unicorn Tapestries.*   New York: Metropolitan Museum of Art, 1976.   244 pp., 50 color figs., 255 b&w figs.

XXXIV. Tapestries

Examination of the set of seven late 15th-century tapestries in the collection; the unicorn in ancient and medieval literature; iconography and symbolism in medieval and Renaissance art (other tapestries, medals, miniatures, ivories, enamels, caskets, etc.); thematic study of various images of the tapestries including animals and birds, aspects of the hunt, landscape elements, their representation and significance in comtemporary art. Chapters on the monograms and original ownership, design and techniques, inventories and later history.

1890   STANDEN, EDITH A. "Ostentatio Christi and Ecce Homo: Two Sixteenth-Century Flemish Tapestries in the Metropolitan Museum of Art." *Artes textiles* 10 (1981):19-28, 8 b&w figs. French summary.
   After compositions of Quentin Metsys and Albrecht Dürer.

Paris

MUSÉE DE CLUNY

1891   VERLET, PIERRE, and SALET, FRANCIS. *The Lady and the Unicorn.* Contributions by Geneviève Souchal. Translated by R.D. Chancellor. London: Thames & Hudson, 1961. 47 pp., 18 color pls., 5 b&w pls.
   Famed set of six 15th-century tapestries: description and iconography (five perhaps represent the senses), artist and style, intended ownership.

1892   LANCKORONSKA, MARIA. *Wandteppiche für eine Fürstin: Die historische Persönlichkeit der "Dame mit dem Einhorn."* Frankfurt: Heinrich Scheffler, 1965. 80 pp., 6 color pls., 32 b&w figs.
   Author proposes that the lady in the Dame à la Licorne tapestry is meant to portray Margaret of York, wife of Charles the Bold, duke of Burgundy.

1893   SOUCHAL, GENEVIÈVE. "Le Tenture de David et la Bible." *Gazette des beaux-arts* 71 (1968):17-32, 10 b&w figs.
   Reinterpretation, in light of the *Second Book of Samuel,* of the narrative in the ten 16th-century Brussels-made tapestries of the life of David, and the proposed new sequence in which the hangings should be displayed.

1894   SOUCHAL, GENEVIÈVE. "La Tenture de David du Musée de Cluny." *Revue du Louvre et des Musées de France* 22 (1972):43-50, 1 color pl., 6 b&w figs.
   Series of ten monumental (75 x 4,55 meters) tapestries woven in Brussels ca. 1510-15, possibly after cartoons of Jan van Roome.

MUSÉE DU LOUVRE

1895   SCHNEEBALG-PERELMAN, SOPHIE. *Les Chasses de Maximilien: Les Énigmes d'un chef-d'oeuvre de la tapisserie.* Brussels: Éditions de Chabassol, 1982. 321 pp., 47 color figs., 133 b&w figs.
   Twelve so-called hunting tapestries of Emperor Maximilian each representing the hunt in a different month commissioned in 1540 by Charles V from François Borreman and Pieter Coecke van Aelst (cartoons) and Jean Ghieteels (weaving) in Brussels. Extensive comparative material.

Pittsburgh

CARNEGIE INSTITUTE

1896 STANDEN, EDITH A. "Tapestries in the Collection of the Museum of Art, Carnegie Institute." *Carnegie Magazine* 55 (1981):2-19, 3 color figs., 14 b&w figs.

Short catalog entries for a selection of the tapestries in the collection including two produced in 16th-century Brussels depicting the Holy Family Attended by Angels, and the Triumph of Hope.

Riggisberg

ABEGG-STIFTUNG BERN

1897 *Ein Brüsseler Bildteppich mit Taufe Christi,* by Robert L. Wyss. Riggisberg: Abegg-Stiftung Bern, 1977. 80 pp., 43 b&w illus.

Brussels tapestry of the first quarter of the 16th century with the Baptism of Christ; its iconographic precedents.

Saint-Quentin

MUSÉE ANTOINE LECUYER

1898 "Bijdragen tot de inventaris van vlaamse tapijten in Franse verzamelingen." *Artes textiles* 4 (1957-58):3-18, 4 b&w figs. French summary.

Three hangings depicting the early life of John the Baptist woven in early 16th-century Brussels and one tapestry made in the same town ca. 1520 representing the Return of Young Tobias to Ninive on commission of the English chancellor, Thomas Wolsey.

San Francisco

FINE ARTS MUSEUMS

1899 MASSCHELEIN-KLEINER, LILIANE. "Dyeing Techniques of Tapestries in the Southern Netherlands during the Fifteenth and Sixteenth Centuries." In *Acts of the Tapestry Symposium, November 1976.* San Francisco: Fine Arts Museums, 1979. Pp. 29-40, 11 b&w figs., 2 diagrams.

Identifies some medieval dyes and the organic materials from which they derive, examining particularly those in tapestries in the collection.

Sigmaringen, Germany

HOHENZOLLERNSCHES MUSEUM

1900 CRICK-KUNTZIGER, MARTHE. "Eine unveröffentlichte Wandteppich—Folge von Peter van Edinghen, Gennant van Aelst." *Pantheon* 17 (1936):193-98, 6 b&w figs.

Describes a set of six previously unpublished Flemish tapestry fragments of the Story of Bathsheba signed by Pieter Coecke van Aelst of Brussels and dating of ca. 1520.

Stuttgart

WÜRTTEMBERGISCHES LANDESMUSEUM

1901 GRÖNWOLDT, RUTH. "Two Hunting Tapestries of the Commander of the Teutonic Order, Hugo von Hohenlandenberg." *Connoisseur* 196 (1977):182-89, 6 color figs., 2 b&w figs.
Two 16th-century tapestries with hunting scenes were woven in Antwerp ca. 1578.

Tarragona

CATEDRAL

1902 BATTLE HUGUET, PEDRO. *Los tapices de la catedrale primada de Tarragona.* Tarragona: Sindicato de Iniciativa, 1946. 78 pp., 53 b&w pls.
Catalog of famed tapestry collection dating mainly of the 16th century. Includes Tournai and Brussels examples, "La Buena Vida" cycles with the Story of Joseph, of David, of Samson, allegories, verdure. Poor illustrations.

Vienna

KUNSTHISTORISCHES MUSEUM

1903 *Tapisserien der Renaissance nach Entwürfen von Pieter Coecke van Aelst.* Exhibition held in the Halbturn Schloss. Catalog by Rotraud Bauer. [Vienna]: Burgerlandischen Landesregierung, [1981]. 102 pp., 20 color pls., 21 b&w pls.
Exhibition of large Brussels tapestries from the holdings of the museum, woven in the 1530s after cartoons by Pieter Coecke van Aelst. Study of documents and iconographic sources. Very useful color plates.

Warsaw

ZAMKU KRÓLEWSKIM

1904 HENNEL-BERNASIKOWA, MARIA. "Une tapisserie inconnue de la collection de Sigismond-Auguste, roi de Pologne." *Artes textiles* 10 (1981):73-79, 2 b&w figs.
Tapestry depicting the Corruption of Humanity before the Flood from a series commissioned for Wawel Castle by King Sigismund-Auguste of Poland ca. 1550 from Brussels weavers and for which Michiel Coxie designed the cartoons.

Zamora

CATEDRAL

1905 GÓMEZ MARTINEZ, AMANDO, and CHILLON SAMPEDRO, BARTOLOMÉ. *Los tapices de la catedral de Zamora.* Zamora: Catedral, 1925. 121 pp., 22 b&w pls.
Discursive presentation dealing mainly with the iconography of the important sets of late 15th-16th-century Flemish tapestries in the cathedral: scenes of the Old Testament, Trojan War, Life of Hannibal, etc.

7. EXHIBITION CATALOGS

Brussels

MUSÉES ROYAUX D'ART ET D'HISTOIRE

1906   *Tapisseries bruxelloises de la pré-Renaissance.* Exhibition catalog by Anne van Ruymbeke, Anne van Ypersele de Strihou, Guy Delmarcel, Ghislaine Derveaux-Van Ussel, Van-Karel Steppe, and Sophie Schneebalg-Perelman. Brussels: Musées Royaux d'Art et d'Histoire, 1976. 256 pp., 3 color pls., 76 b&w figs.
      Thirty entries of hangings now in Belgium, France, Germany, and the U.S.S.R. produced in Brussels during the period 1510-25 and centering on the Cluny David and Bathsheba series, the Herkenbald tapestry of 1513, and the set made for the church of Notre-Dame du Sablon, Brussels. Twenty-five entries of drawings, sculpture, and paintings, reflecting the same style and iconography, followed by four essays on origins and development of the Brussels industry, inscriptions, and signatures, Jan van Roome, iconography.

8. PRIVATE COLLECTION, AUCTION, AND DEALER CATALOGS

HOLMES COLLECTION

1907   ACKERMAN, PHYLLIS. "Two 'Signed' Tapestries in the Collection of Mrs. Christian Holmes," *Apollo* 22 (1935):32-35, 2 b&w figs.
      Flemish tapestries in a U.S. collection attributed respectively to Jan 'II' van Roome and to a Jean 'I' de Camp on the basis of style and of cryptic signatures.

STEWART COLLECTION

1908   ADAMS-ACTON, MURRAY. "Gothic Tapestries in the Collection of Sir P. Malcolm Stewart, BT." *Connoisseur* 117 (1946):71- 72, 122, 2 color pls.
      Description of two hangings: a mounted knight bearing a pennon, Franco-Flemish of ca. 1480, and scenes from the Labors of Hercules woven ca. 1498 by the Fleming Joos of Oudenaarde after a cartoon of Pierre Peret of Tournai.

BRITISH (ENGLISH)

3. SURVEYS AND HISTORIES

Books

1909   HUMPHREYS, JOHN. *Elizabethan Sheldon Tapestries.* London: Oxford University Press, 1929. 27 pp., 13 b&w pls.
      History of the tapestry workshop founded by William Sheldon at Barcheston Manor, Warwickshire, in the mid-16th century, the earliest in England; its productions through records and extant examples such as the "map" series and others with biblical or armorial subjects ranging in date from 1564 to 1598.

1910   THOMSON, W.G. *Tapestry Weaving in England from the Earliest Times to the End of the XVIIIth Century.* London: B.T. Batsford; New York: Charles Scribners' Sons, [1914]. 172 pp., 3 color figs., 56 b&w figs.

Chaps. 3-9 (pp. 15-65) deal with the 15th-16th century: import of foreign tapestries into England; those commissioned for the royal household and those recorded in early inventories; the genesis of a native tapestry industry in England in the 15th century primarily due to emigrant weavers from Flanders and France; the Sheldon Workshops of the 16th century.

Articles

1911   CLARK, JANE. "A Set of Tapestries for Leicester House in The Strand: 1585." *Burlington Magazine* 125 (1983):283-84, 4 b&w figs.
Heraldic tapestry with arms of Robert Dudley, Earl of Leicester, in the Victoria and Albert Museum, and two smaller panels in the Burrell Collection, Glasgow, suggested to be by Richard Hicks, head weaver of the Sheldon tapestry manufactory at Barcheston in Warwickshire.

1912   THOMSON, W.G. "English Tapestries." *Apollo* 1 (1925):26-32, 6 b&w figs.
Synoptic and rambling presentation of tapestries produced in England from the late 14th century; several examples cited for the 15th and 16th century.

1913   WELLS-COLE, ANTHONY. "Some Design Sources for the Earl of Leicester Tapestries and Other Contemporary Pieces." *Burlington Magazine* 125 (1983):284-85, 8 b&w figs.
Prints of the Dutch artists Jan Vredeman de Vries (1527-1606), Cornelis Floris, and Jan van der Straet (ca. 1530-1605) here suggested to be the source of inspiration for several English tapestry weavers in the 1580s and 90s.

FRENCH

3. SURVEYS AND HISTORIES

Books

1914   LORIQUET, CH. *Tapisseries de la Cathédrale de Reims: Histoire du Roy Clovis (XVe siècle), Histoire de la Vierge (XVIe siècle).* Paris: A. Quantin; Reims: F. Michaud, 1882. 164 pp., 17 b&w pls.
Introduction deals with history and manufacture of tapestries in Reims highlighting specific shops and weavers; main scope of book is concerned with the style and iconography of the Legend of King Clovis (Franco-Flemish) and the Life of the Virgin (French) cycles in the cathedral.

1915   SALET, FRANCIS. *La Tapisserie française du Moyen-Age à nos jours.* Paris: Vincent, Fréal & Cie, 1946. 23 pp., 4 color pls., 100 b&w pls.
Pictorial presentation of French tapestries from medieval times to the present. Pls. 11-52, with very cursory captions, are of 15th-16th-century tapestries in public and private French collections.

1916   WEIGERT, ROGER-ARMAND. *French Tapestry.* Translation of 1956 French edition by Donald and Monique King, with addition of 4 color pls. London: Faber & Faber, 1962. 214 pp., 4 color pls., 64 b&w pls.

Survey from origins to the 20th century. The first chapter is a useful introduction to technique, material, training of weavers, designs and cartoons, borders, marks. Chaps. 3-6 (pp. 42-96) deal with 15th-century Franco-Flemish tapestries and French tapestries of the 16th century: workshops, guild regulations, subjects, and cycles.

Articles

1917   DIGBY, G.F. WINGFIELD. "French Tapestries at the Paris Exhibition." *Connoisseur* 119 (1947):3-13, 15 b&w figs.
        Major exhibit of 318 hangings is discussed with respect to changing function of tapestry in European history. Examples range from the 14th century to the Baroque period with many dating of 1400-1600: History of Clovis (Reims); Capture of Jerusalem (Saumur); Legend of St. Stephen (Paris, Musée de Cluny), etc.; mentions prominent owners of tapestries in history such as the dukes of Burgundy.

1918   GATTI GAZZINI, GIULIA. "Le arti decorative alla corte de Borgogna nel XV secolo." *Antichità viva* 2. Part 1, no. 2 (1963):36-44, 1 color pl., 6 b&w figs.; part 2, no. 4 (1963):47-56, color cover, 9 b&w figs.
        Author examines the Jourdain de Blaye tapestry, an Arras production, in the Museo Civico of Padua, in relation to tapestries owned by Philip the Good of Burgundy; discusses the two tapestries of the Epic of Alexander the Great in the Palazzo Doria, Rome, Tournai productions, in relation to the large Alexander series purchased from Pasquier Grenier of Tournai.

1919   KURTH, BETTY. "A 'Tree of Jesse' Tapestry Panel." *Connoisseur* 122 (1948):94-96, 3 b&w figs.
        Attribution to France and perhaps Reims of a tapestry (private collection), shown in Chicago in 1926 on the basis of iconographic relations with hangings in Reims and a woodcut of ca. 1515 in a book of hours for the use of Reims.

6. PERMANENT COLLECTIONS

Boston

MUSEUM OF FINE ARTS

1920   ERLANDE-BRANDENBURG, ALAIN. "Les Tapisseries de François d'Angoulême." *Bulletin de la Société de l'Histoire de l'Art Français* (1973):19-31, 9 b&w figs.
        A monogram and heraldic devices link a tapestry in this collection to the commission of this French patron of the early 16th century.

Cleveland

CLEVELAND MUSEUM OF ART

1921   SHEPHERD, DOROTHY G. "Three Tapestries from Chaumont." *Bulletin of The Cleveland Museum of Art* 48 (1961):158-77, front cover in color, 15 b&w figs.
        Depicting Triumph of Eternity, Youth, and Time, these weavings, related to contemporary productions, are attributed to a Loire Valley workshop and dated to 1500-1515.

7. EXHIBITION CATALOGS

Kyoto

KOKURITSU KINDAI BIJUTSUKAN

1922   *Merveilles de la tapisserie française.* Tokyo: Éditions d'Art Curieux-do, 1976. unpaginated, 46 pls., many with details and many in color. Preface, introduction and captions in French and Japanese.

    Pictorial presentation of forty-six masterpieces of French tapestries, mostly from the Musée des Arts Décoratifs, Paris, and also from the Musée des Tappisseries, Angers. Concise entries. Valuable for the excellent quality of the large, color details.

GERMAN

3. SURVEYS AND HISTORIES

Book

1923   KURTH, BETTY. *Die deutschen Bildteppiche des Mittelalters,* 3 vols. Vienna: Anton Schroll & Co., 1926. 1:320 pp., 91 b&w figs.; 2:168 b&w figs.; 3:176 b&w figs.

    Comprehensive in-depth study of German tapestries from the 11th to 16th century, organized chronologically and then geographically. Detailed entries for 344 panels and fragments in various public and private European collections.

Article

1924   WILCKENS, LEONIE VON. "Nuremberg Medieval Tapestries." *HALI* 29/8, no. 1 (1986):16-25, 94; 7 color figs., 3 b&w figs.

    Lively quality of dossals woven on narrow looms from the late 14th until the early 16th century in the city. Excellent illustrations.

6. PERMANENT COLLECTIONS

New York

METROPOLITAN MUSEUM OF ART

1925   FORSYTH, WILLIAM H. "A 'Credo' Tapestry: A Pictorial Interpretation of the Apostles' Creed." *Metropolitan Museum of Art Bulletin* n.s. 21 (1963):240-51, 22 b&w figs.

    Mid-16th-century German wool and silk tapestry with fifteen Old and New Testament scenes drawn from contemporary woodcuts.

Nuremberg

GERMANISCHES NATIONALMUSEUM

1926   FALKE, OTTO VON. "Ein Bombeckteppich im Germanischen Museum." *Pantheon* 2 (1928):392-94, 3 b&w figs.

A mid-16th-century tapestry by the German weaver Seger Bombeck with armorial bearings of the ducal House of Saxony, is evidence of Bombeck's training in the workshop of Willem van Pannemaker in Brussels.

ITALIAN

3. SURVEYS AND HISTORIES

Books

1927   FORTI GRAZZINI, NELLO. *L'arazzo ferrarese.* Milan: Electa,1982. 239 pp., 40 color pls., 124 b&w illus.

Comprehensive study of production, patronage, collecting, import and export of tapestries in Ferrara in the 15th-16th century; detailed analysis of themes, subjects, and their sources. Transcription of 1457-69 Este inventory; glossary; iconographic, and name and place indexes.

1928   VIALE FERRERO, M. *Arazzi italani.* Milan: Electa, 1961. 262 pp., 38 text figs., many in color, 82 color pls.

The most complete survey to date of Italian tapestry-making from the 15th through the 18th century. Concise introduction, followed by good color plates of details, touches on hangings made for the Sforzas in Milan, the Estes in Ferrara, and especially the Medicis in Florence.

1929   VIALE FERRERO, MERCEDES. *Arazzi italani del Cinquecento.* Milan: Antonio Vallardi, 1961. 95 pp., 7 color pls., many b&w figs.

Author focuses on mannerist Italy with special emphasis on the Medicean Workshop and the cartoons produced for the weavers by major court painters.

Articles

1930   ADELSON, CANDACE. "Cosimo I de' Medici and the Foundation of Tapestry Production in Florence." In *Firenze e la Toscana dei Medici nell' Europa del '500.* Vol. 3 *Relazioni artistiche, il linguaggio architettonico europeo.* Florence: Leo S. Olschki, 1983. Pp. 899-924, 18 b&w figs.

Commissions of the grand duke from 1545 until 1574 from Flemish weavers called to Florence and working after cartoons of local painters. Author critically reviews literature and announces her dissertation in progress for New York University, *The Tapestry Patronage of Cosimo I de' Medici 1545-1553,* of which this article is a synthesis.

1931   HEIKAMP, DETLEF. "Die Arazzeria medicea im 16. Jahrhundert; neue Studien." *Münchner Jahrbuch der bildenden Kunst* 20 (1969):33-74, 43 b&w figs.

Analysis of the activity of the 16th-century Florentine tapestry workshop in light of cartoons by Italian court artists, Netherlandish prints, and the publication of new documents from the Guardaroba Medicea.

1931a   HEIKAMP, DETLEF. "La Manufacture de tapisserie des Médicis. *L'Oeil* 164-65 (1968):22-31, 1 color pl., 19 b&w figs.

Activity of the tapestry workshop established in Florence in 1545 by Cosimo I who hired Netherlandish craftsmen working after cartoons by Bronzino, Pontormo, and Salviati.

1932   HEIKAMP, DETLEF. "Unbekannte Medici-Bildteppiche in Siena." *Pantheon* 37 (1979):376-82, 1 color fig., 18 b&w figs.

Eleven tapestry fragments from the Medici workshops discovered in the former Royal Palace in Siena intended for the Palazzo Vecchio or Poggio a Caiano and woven after designs by Jan van der Straet or Allesandro Allori. Includes a tapestry fragment depicting Cosimo il Vecchio with the model of the Abbey at Fiesole by Brunelleschi (1571-72); fragments showing Providentia (1597-1602), chase scenes (1567-68), Central and South American Indian hunting scenes (1578), and mythological representations (1579).

1933   VENTURI, ADOLFO. "Le arti minor a Ferrara nella fine del sec. XV: L'Arazzeria." *L'arte* 12 (1909):207-10.

A series of documents relating to the activity of Flemish and French tapestry weavers in Ferrara and outside acquisitions of the court during the last quarter of the 15th century.

6. PERMANENT COLLECTIONS

Ferrara

CATTEDRALE

1934   BARALDI, ANNA MARIA FIORAVANTI. "Gli arazzi della Cattedrale: Appunti per una storia della arazzeria estense." In *La Cattedrale de Ferrara (Atti del convegno nazionale di studi storici).* Ferrara: Belriguardo, 1979. Pp. 515-35.

Eight tapestries with hagiographic scenes executed in Ferrara in 1550 at the commission of Duke Ercole II by two Flemish weavers recorded as Giovanni and Nicolà (Jan and Nicholas) Karcher after cartoons by Camillo Filippi and Benvenuto Tisi da Garofalo.

Florence

PALAZZIO VECCHIO

1935   ADELSON, CANDACE. "Bachiacca, Salviati, and the Decoration of the Sala dell'Udienza in Palazzo Vecchio." In *Le arti del principato medioeco,* Florence: Studio per Edizioni Scelte, 1980. Pp. 141-200, 30 b&w figs.

Series of ten spalliere tapestries with decoration of grotesques woven in Florence in 1546 by Rost and Karcher on cartoons by Il Bachiacca for the lower parts of the walls of the Sala dell'Udienza in the Palazzo Vecchio. Author studies precendents, inventories, and the relationship with frecoes by Salviati for the same hall.

1936   *Gli arazzi della Sala dei Duecento.* Exhibition held in Florence at the Palazzo Vecchio. Catalog edited by Loretta Dolcini, with essays by eighteen contributors. Modena: Panini, 1985. 209 pp., over 222 figs., many in color.

Didactic exhibition on the restoration of the famous series of twenty large tapestries from the Sala dei Duecento in Palazzo Vecchio. These, on the life of Joseph, were woven by the Flemish Janni Rost and Nicholas Karcher between 1546-53 after cartoons by Pontormo, Bronzino, and Salviati in the Medicean workshop founded by Cosimo I. Essays on historical aspects and sources, and mostly on technical examination of threads, colors, technique, state of conservation, and methods of restoration.

Milan

CIVICHE RACCOLTE DE ARTE APPLICATA – CASTELLO SFORZESCO

1937   MARINELLI, GUIDO.   "Renaissance Tapestries from the Vigevano Workshop in the Castello Sforzesco, Milan: A New Attribution to Bramante of the Tapestries Depicting the Twelve 'Months' Made for Gian Giacomo Trivulzio at the Beginning of the Sixteenth Century." Translated by Minta Jones. *Connoisseur* 160 (1965):29-33, 7 b&w figs.
Reattribution of the cartoons for this tapestry series in Milan to Bramante rather than Bramantino.

1938   FORTI GRAZZINI, NELLO.   *Gli arazzi dei mesi Trivulzio: Il committente, l'iconografia.* Milan: Ripartizione Cultura e Spettacolo, 1982. 78 pp., 30 b&w figs.
The complex iconography of the series of twelve tapestries of the months woven by Benedetto da Milano after the cartoons of 1503-5 by Bramantino (or Bramante) for Gian Giacomo Trivulzio; sources, symbolism, and political significance.

NETHERLANDISH

3. SURVEYS AND HISTORIES

Book

1939   YSSELSTEYN, G.T. VAN.   *Geschiedenis der tapijtweverijen de noordelijke nederlanden: Bijdrage tot de geschiedenis der kunstnijverheid.* 2 vols. in 1. Leiden: N.V. Leidsche Uitgeversmaatschappij, 1936. 1:324 pp., 198 b&w figs. on 92 pls.; 2:653 pp., 4 b&w pls., 140 weavers' marks. Eighty-six-page summary in English.
Scholarly, well-documented history of tapestry in the northern Netherlands from the 15th through the 17th century. Includes transcription of archival documents and reproduction of marks in line drawings.

Article

1940   BANGS, JEREMY D.   "Tapestry Weaving before the Reformation: The Leiden Studios." *Nederlands kunsthistorisch jaarboek* 37 (1986):225-40, 21 b&w figs.
Activity in Leyden from 1540 to ca. 1570 of William Andriesz. de Raet of Brussels who supplied tapestries of biblical scenes and foliage compositions – after earlier Brussels weavings or models by local artists such as Pieter Cornelisz. Kunst, Dammas Claez. de Hoey, and Hans Liefrinck – not only to Leyden burghers and institutions but also to those of Gouda, Egmond, Haarlem,and Amsterdam.

SCANDINAVIA (SWEDISH)

3. SURVEYS AND HISTORIES

1941   CEDERLÖF, ULF.   "Paintings and Tapestries of the Hunt in Swedish Royal Collections." *Connoisseur* 196 (1977):254- 61, 11 b&w figs.
Deals primarily with later period but includes the tapestry of Meleager and Atalanta (ca. 1550) from the workshop of Paul de Bucher at Gripsholm Castle.

SWISS

3. SURVEYS AND HISTORIES

1942   FALKE, OTTO VON. "Gestickte Bildteppiche der Ostschweiz." *Pantheon* 9 (1932):20-25, 6 b&w figs.
Examines examples in Swiss and German museums of embroidered tapestries dating of the early 16th century made in eastern Switzerland and principally in Zurich.

1943   KURTH, BETTY. "Ein unbekannter Bildteppich aus der Klosterwerkstatt Gnadental in Basel." *Pantheon* 13 (1934):172-74, 1 b&w fig.
An early 15th-century tapestry in a private Viennese collection depicting the Presentation in the Temple is ascribed to the workshop of the Swiss monastery of Gnadental.

1944   KURZ, OTTO. "Metz Unmuss." *Zeitschrift für schweizerische Archäologie und Kunstgeschichte* 14 (1953):86-88, 3 b&w figs. Reprinted in *The Decorative Arts of Europe and the Islamic East: Selected Studies*. London: Dorian Press, 1977, 2d article (unpaginated).
Iconography of two Swiss allegorical tapestries of ca. 1430 in the Stadtmuseum, Cologne, and in Glasgow.

1945   WYSS, ROBERT L. "Medieval & Renaissance Tapestries & Wall Hangings in Switzerland." *Connoisseur* 152 (1963):22-30, 2 color figs., 10 b&w figs.
Selection of tapestries with busy compositions and embroidered hangings in museums of Basel, Zurich, and Bern, produced in the Upper Rhine, and mostly in Basel, in the 15th and 16th century.

6. PERMANENT COLLECTIONS

Glasgow

GLASGOW MUSEUMS AND ART GALLERIES – BURRELL COLLECTION

1946   WELLS, WILLIAM. "Swiss Altar Frontal." *Scottish Art Review* 7 (1959):18-19, 27; 3 color figs., 2 b&w figs.
Frontal of the Nativity, Adoration of the Magi, and Presentation in the Temple perhaps woven in the Dominican convent of Basel in the second half of the fifteenth century.

1947   WELLS, WILLIAM. "Vice and Folly in Three Swiss Tapestries." *Scottish Art Review* 8 (1961):13-16, 1 color fig., 4 b&w figs.
Hangings of secular iconography produced in Basel ca. 1450-80.

New York

METROPOLITAN MUSEUM OF ART

1948   OSTOIA, VERA K. "A Tapestry Altar Frontal with Scenes from the Life of the Virgin." *Metropolitan Museum of Art Bulletin* 24 (1966):286-303, 19 b&w figs.
Differences between German tapestries and those woven in France and the Lowlands as seen in Swiss Upper Rhine altar frontal of 1450-75; its iconography, style, and technique.

XXXV. Carpets

B. SINGLE COUNTRY OF ORIGIN

BRITISH

3. SURVEYS AND HISTORIES

1949   TATTERSALL, C.E.C. *A History of British Carpets from the Introduction of the Craft until the Present Day.* 2d ed., rev. and enl. by Stanley Reed. Leigh-on-Sea, England: F. Lewis, 1966. 139 pp., 176 pls., some in color. (1st ed. 1934.)

       Mostly carpets of later periods, but chap. 2 (pp. 20-36) deals with historical accounts of the introduction of imported carpets into English interiors in the 15th century, their increased use in the 16th century, and the beginnings of English manufactures at this time. Chap. 3 (37-40) is on "Turkey work," small pieces of hand-knotting used for upholstering chairs and benches, with references to 16th-century records. Limited scholarly apparatus.

SPANISH

3. SURVEYS AND HISTORIES

1950   THOMSON, W.G. "Hispano-Moresque Carpets." *Burlington Magazine* 18 (1910-11):100-111, 1 color pl, 6 b&w figs., 12 line drawings.

       Composition, styles, and varied influences (Saracenic, Coptic, Moorish) of 15th-16th-century examples in the Victoria and Albert Museum, Harris Collection, London, and the Kaiser Friedrich Museum (now Bode Museum in East Berlin).

1951   VAN DE PUT, A. "Some Fifteenth-Century Spanish Carpets." *Burlington Magazine* 19 (1911):344-50, 1 color pl., , 7 b&w figs.

XXXV. Carpets

Author reassigns a carpet with the Enriquez arms (Harris Collection, London) to the 15th century on the basis of style and similar carpets depicted in manuscripts and listed in the 1410 inventory of Martin the Elder of Aragon; describes the coat-of-arms on a carpet in the Spanish Art Gallery belonging to the Enriquez family and to Marina de Ayala; identifies the arms on a carpet formerly belonging to the convent of Santa Isabel la Real, Toledo, as those of Mary of Castille, Queen of Alfonso V of Aragon.

6. PERMANENT COLLECTIONS

Cleveland

CLEVELAND MUSEUM OF ART

1952   SHEPHERD, DOROTHY G. "A Fifteenth-Century Spanish Carpet." *Bulletin of The Cleveland Museum of Art* 41 (1954):188-90, b&w cover illus.
Mudejar carpet with large octagonal patterns woven in the Province of Murcia and probably in the town of Alcarez.

Washington

TEXTILE MUSEUM

1953   *Catalog of Spanish Rugs— 12th Century to 19th Century,* by Ernst Kühnel, with technical notes by Louisa Bellinger. 2 vols. Washington DC: National Publishing Co., 1953. 1:63 pp., 2:11 color pls., 33 b&w pls.
Includes eleven 15th-16th-century Mudejar carpets, one late Gothic, and five 16th-century Renaissance examples, all with single knot pile, briefly described from a technical and stylistic viewpoint.

7. EXHIBITION CATALOGS

Madrid

SOCIEDAD ESPAÑOLA DE AMIGOS DEL ARTE

1954   *Exposición de alfombras antiguas españolas.* Exhibition catalog by José Ferrandis Torres. Madrid: Sociedad Española de Amigos del Arte, 1933. 122 pp., 11 b&w text figs., 4 color pls., 48 b&w pls.
Useful catalog dealing with the making of rugs in Spain from the 15th through the 19th century. Exhibition of ninety-four examples drawn primarily from private collections: nos. 1-16 date of the 15th century, 17-44 of the 16th. Important ninety-six-page essay dealing with technique, style, and inventories.

XXXVI. Leather

A. MULTI COUNTRY OF ORIGIN

1. DICTIONARIES AND ENCYCLOPEDIAS

1955   ROBERTS, MATT T., and ETHERINGTON, DON. *Bookbinding and the Conservation of Books: A Dictionary of Descriptive Terminology.* Washington: Library of Congress, 1982. 296 pp., 13 color pls., diagrams, text figs.
    Comprehensive work, alphabetically arranged with succinct entries pertaining to history of the craft, materials, technical terms, notable binders, and publishers. Many entries deal with the period 1400-1600; cross-referenced.

3. SURVEYS AND HISTORIES

Books

1956   BRASSINGTON, W. SALT. *A History of the Art of Bookbinding, with Some Account of the Books of the Ancients.* London: Elliot Stock, 1894. 293 pp., 10 color pls., 270 b&w figs. and line drawings.
    Early but valuable general work useful as an introduction to the subject.

1957   DIEHL, EDITH. *Bookbinding, its Background and Technique.* 2 vols. New York: Reinhart & Co., 1946. 1:272 pp., 92 b&w pls., 2:412 pp. 190 b&w figs. (all but 2 are line drawings).
    Fundamental study of ancient to modern bindings with much relevant information for period 1400-1600. Vol. 1 deals with history, design, production, distribution, national styles, etc.; vol 2, with techniques. Useful glossaries.

1958   GALL, GÜNTER. *Leder im europäischen Kunsthanderk.* Brunswick: Klinkhardt & Biermann, 1965. 406 pp., 16 color pls., 305 b&w figs.

Thorough study of painted, tooled, and mostly embossed European leatherwork from Coptic times to the 19th century in all its varied forms: caskets, cases (e.g., for books, monstrances, pokals, knives), reliquaries, triptychs, parade shields, flasks, cabinets, Madonna reliefs, and even large-scale sculptural Pietà groups. Numerous 16th-century examples and some of the 15th.

1959 HOBSON, G.D. *Bindings in Cambridge Libraries.* Based on research by N.F. Barwell, H.M. Davies, and C.E. Sayle. Cambridge: University Press, 1929. 179 pp., 27 color pls., 45 b&w pls.

Catalog organized in seventy-two entries, which often include several types of bindings and binding stamps dating from the 12th through the 18th century. For 15th-16th-century examples for London, Cambridge, Bruges, Louvain, Paris, Milan, and Venice, see pls. III (an embroidered specimen) through XXXVII.

1960 HORNE, HERBERT P. *The Binding of Books: An Essay in the History of Gold-Tooled Bindings.* London: Kegan Paul, Trench, Trübner & Co., 1915. 248 pp., 9 b&w figs.

Early study with much pertinent information for the period 1400-1600. Includes chapters dealing with techniques and materials (pp. 1-54); early Italian bindings with emphasis on origin and development of gold tooling and collectors (55-98); French bindings with history of the guild, binders, and collectors (99-163); English bindings with emphasis on foreign influences and collectors (164-215).

1961 WATERER, JOHN W. *Leather in Life, Art and Industry.* London: Faber & Faber, n.d. 320 pp., 109 b&w pls.

Exposition on all aspects of the subject: historical overview, particularly concerning England, technical explanations for the layman, varied uses of leather. Provides useful general background and many sections relevant to the decorative arts.

Articles

1962 KUP, KARL. "Notes on a Fifteenth-Century Coffret." *Connoisseur* 140 (1957):62-66, 10 b&w figs.

Description of various types of caskets—cuir bouilli, wrought iron, leather-covered wood—made to store books, with focus on a leather-covered wood casket, with a pasted-in incunabula, in the New York Public Library.

1963 WATERER, JOHN W. "An Historical Forcer." *Connoisseur* 134 (1954):189-91, 3 b&w figs.

Examines a 16th-century forcer (jewelry casket) dated 1532, covered with incised parchment formerly decorated with tempera and gilding including representations of Charles V of Spain and Isabel of Portugal.

6. PERMANENT COLLECTIONS

London

BRITISH LIBRARY

1964 *The Henry Davis Gift: A Collection of Bookbindings.* Vol. 1, *Studies in the History of Bookbinding.* London: British Library Board, 1978. 352 pp., 36 b&w pls.

XXXVI. Leather

Selections of the 16th (many), 17th, and 18th century from this large collection. Twenty-five comprehensive essays provide detailed biographical data on the binders and bibliophiles and discuss the bindings in relation to others by the same bindery; each often accompanied by one or more appendixes. (Vol. 2 deals with North American bindings.)

VICTORIA AND ALBERT MUSEUM

1965 BUNT, CYRIL G.E. "Bookbindings at the Victoria and Albert Museum. I.—Some Italian Bindings of the Sixteenth Century. II.—English Bindings." *Apollo* 16 (1932). Part 1, pp. 21-25, 6 b&w figs.; part 2, pp. 98-105, 10 b&w pls.

Part 1: outstanding examples of Florentine and Venetian morocco bindings of the 16th century; part 2: select 16th-18th- century English examples with stamped and tooled designs; the source of some of their motifs.

1966 *Bookbindings.* Catalog by John P. Harthan. 3d rev. and enl. ed. London: Her Majesty's Stationery Office, 1985. 50 pp., 8 color pls., 91 b&w pls.

Thirty-page introduction traces the development of bookbinding design. Ninety-nine brief entries for selections from the museum's collection (all illustrated); entries for figs. 10-37 and color pls. 1-2 present German, French, Spanish, Netherlandish, English, and Italian bindings of the 15th-16th century. Illustrated six-page appendix describes bookbinding technique. One-page glossary.

Milan

BIBLIOTECA TRIVULZIANA

1967 SANTORO, CATERINA. *I tesori della Trivulziana: La storia del libro dal secolo VIII al secolo XVIII.* Milan: Biblioteca Trivulziana, 1962. 257 pp., 16 color pls., 144 b&w pls.

Illuminated manuscripts and early printed books dating from the 8th to the 18th century. Pp. 55-64 deal with 15th-16th-century Italian and French bindings: Milanese (including those for Jean Grolier with casts from plaquettes), Venetian, Neapolitan, Roman (with impressions from medals), Parisian, and one German example.

Munich

BAYERISCHE STAATSBIBLIOTHEK

1968 *Bucheinbände aus elf Jahrhunderten* by Ferdinand Geldner. Munich: S. Bruckmann, 1958. 46 pp., 108 b&w pls.

108 precious bindings dating of the 9th to the 19th century in the Bavarian State Library's collection. Figs. 31-46, 49-51, 53-79, 84-96, 99-107, 109, 113-14, all accompanied by descriptive entries, are of 15th-16th-century bindings, many from Germany (Regensberg, Bamberg, Augsburg, Munich, etc.), and also from Paris, Lyon, and Venice, made for all the great bibliophiles of the period (Francis I, J. Grolier, Thomas Mahieu, Kilian Berchtold, Georg Enhard, J.J. Fugger, Albrecht V, etc.).

New York

PIERPONT MORGAN LIBRARY

1969   *A Guide to an Exhibition of Armorial and Related Bookbindings 1500-1800.* Catalog by Betty Carson Tyson. New York: Pierpont Morgan Library, 1935. 71 pp.
English, French, and Italian bindings with armorial devices and personal book-stamps; 149 brief, unillustrated entries include many 16th-century examples.

1970   *Sixteenth-Century Gold-Tooled Bookbindings in the Pierpont Morgan Library.* Catalog by Howard M. Nixon. New York: Pierpont Morgan Library, 1971. 278 pp., 66 b&w figs.
Exemplary catalog for sixty-six important bindings produced in France, Italy, Germany, the British Isles, Netherlands, Spain, and Mexico for various rulers, ecclesiastics, and other well-known bibiliophiles such as Grolier, Thomas Mahieu, and Marx Fugger. Provides concise but informative study for each example as well as bibliographical references.

1970a   *Twelve Centuries of Bookbindings 400-1600.* Catalog by Paul Needham. New York: Pierpont Morgan Library, 1979. 338 pp., 7 color pls., 118 b&w figs.
One hundred exhaustive entries of holdings in the library. Includes some medieval bindings (silver-gilt, gold, ivory, jeweled — pp. 46-48, 52-54), and early examples of leather (74-307) dating before 1600. All entries illustrated.

Oxford

BODLEIAN LIBRARY

1971   BRASSINGTON, W. SALT. *Historic Bindings in the Bodleian Library, Oxford.* London: Sampson Low, Marston & Co., 1891. 108 pp., 24 color pls., 5 b&w figs.
Highlights of the collection with twenty-four examples. Thirty-six-page introduction traces the history of the library, bookbinding at Oxford, and the development of leather book-binding in Europe. Informative catalog entries (pp. 10-41) include mostly 15th-16th-century embroidered and leather bindings from Germany, France, and England.

1972   *Gold-Tooled Bookbindings.* Introduction by I.G. Philip. Oxford: Oxford University Press, 1951. 7 pp., 24 b&w pls.
Selection of bindings illustrating some of the styles of gold-tooling produced in Europe up to the 18th century. Includes fifteen plates of bindings dating from the 15th and 16th century and originating from Hungary, Italy, England, and France. Four-page introduction sketches history of such bindings.

Philadelphia

PHILADELPHIA MUSEUM OF ART

1973   GALL, GÜNTER. "Leather Objects in the Philadelphia Museum of Art." Translated by Susan G. Detweiler. *Bulletin. The Philadelphia Museum of Art* 62 (1967):260-75, 15 b&w figs.
Survey of the development of European leather decoration from the 14th century as seen through the examination of a casket (14th century), a Milanese parade shield of ca. 1560-70, and a Parisian jewelry casket of ca. 1585.

XXXVI. Leather

7. EXHIBITION CATALOGS

Baltimore

BALTIMORE MUSEUM OF ART

1974   *The History of Bookbinding 525-1950 A.D.* Exhibition catalog by Dorothy Miner. Baltimore: Walters Art Gallery, 1957. 275 pp., 106 b&w pls.

718 bookbindings from various public and private U.S. collections including examples of the 15th and 16th century, some from treasuries, (cat. nos. 17-18), 15th-century textile-covered books, some with goldsmiths' fittings (113-20, 122-23, 126-27), utilitarian bindings (128-31), Hispano-Moresque bindings (133- 40), blind-tooled bindings (141-66, 172-78), cuir ciselé bindings (167-71), and panel stamped bindings (127, 179-92); 16th-century examples include paper covers (193 A-D) and a wide assortment of European bindings in various materials and techniques (194-373).

Genoa

PALAZZO DELL'ACCADEMIA

1975   *Mostra di legature dei secoli XV-XIX.* Exhibition catalog by Luigi Marchini et al. [Genoa; 1976]. 143 pp., 60 b&w pls.

Twenty-page synthesis on the evolution of style in bookbindings in Europe from the 15th to the 19th century followed by entries for 440 examples belonging to various public institutions of Genoa.

New York

GROLIER CLUB

1976   *A Catalog of an Exhibition of Renaissance Bookbindings.* Exhibition catalog introduction by Lucius Wilmerding. New York: Grolier Club, 1937. 68 pp., 16 b&w pls.

Twenty-one-page essay traces the development of bookbinding and techniques; 107 short entries include representative examples of tooled leather from England, France, Germany, Austria, Italy, and Spain.

8. PRIVATE COLLECTION, AUCTION, AND DEALER CATALOGS

GOLDSCHMIDT COLLECTION

1977   GOLDSCHMIDT, E. PH. *Gothic and Renaissance Bookbindings—Exemplified and Illustrated from the Author's Collection.* 2 vols. London: Ernest Benn, 1928. 1:369 pp., 1 color pl., 2 b&w pls.; 2:110 b&w pls.

While describing, localizing, and dating specimens within his own collection, the author presents a history of 15th-16th-century bookbinding in Europe. Lengthy introduction deals with such topics as the earliest bindings, monastic bindings, regional types, distinguishing marks and names on bindings, the book trade, binding centers, types, tooling. Catalog of 268 entries follows; all examples date ca. 1400-1600 and originate from various European centers.

New York

CHARLES SCRIBNER'S SONS

1978   *Partial List of an Unique Exhibition of Historical and Famous Bindings Principally of the XVth and XVIth Centuries from the Libraries of Royal and Notable Personages.* New York: Charles Scribner's Sons, 1903. 53 pp., 30 b&w pls.

      Sales catalog of mostly French leather, metal, and embroidered bindings; ninety-nine brief entries.

B. SINGLE COUNTRY OF ORIGIN

AUSTRIAN

6. PERMANENT COLLECTIONS

Michelstadt

PFARRKIRCHE

1979   KEIL, C.A., and STAUB, K.H. "Ein zweibändige Bibel mit Einbänder des Wiener Buchbinders Mathias in der Kirchenbibliothek zu Michelstadt." *Gutenberg-Jahrbuch* 59 (1984):328-31.

      Leather bindings produced in 1463-69 by the Viennese binder Mathias for a two-volume Bible recorded to have originally been in the libarary of N. Matz of the same town.

BELGIUM (FLEMISH)

3. SURVEYS AND HISTORIES

1980   INDESTEGE, LUC. "Das Bild Karls V auf flämischen Einbänden des XVI Jahrhunderts." *Gutenberg-Jahrbuch* (1961):309-18, 6 b&w figs.

      Study of Flemish 16th-century bindings on which appears the portrait of Emperor Charles V. Nearly all are held to have been made in Antwerp.

1981   INDESTEGE, LUC. "Opschriften in afzonderlijke letterstempels op vlaamse boekbanden uit de vijftiende eeuw." *Gulden passer* 39 (1961):211-22, 2 b&w pls. English summary.

      Inscriptions (prayers, proverbs, and rebuses) found on Flemish leather bindings of the 15th century.

BRITISH (ENGLISH)

3. SURVEYS AND HISTORIES

1982   HOBSON, G.D. *English Binding before 1500. The Sandars Lectures (1927).* Cambridge: University Press, 1929. 58 pp., 55 b&w pls., 14 b&w figs.

The development of stamped and tooled bookbinding in England: designs, types of stamps, models, foreign influences, and binding centers. 15th-century Gothic bindings are discussed in chap. 1 and appendixes G, H, and J. Numerous full-page illustrations including a few leather boxes (pls. 41, 41a).

6. PERMANENT COLLECTIONS

London

BRITISH LIBRARY

1983   DAVENPORT, CYRIL. *Royal English Bookbindings.* London: Seeley & Co.; New York: Macmillan Co., 1896. 96 pp., 8 color pls., 27 b&w text figs.
General description of bindings in the library made for royalty including some made for Henry VIII, Edward VI and Queen Mary, Elizabeth I, and James I.

VICTORIA AND ALBERT MUSEUM

1984   BUNT, CYRIL G.E. "British Armorial Book Stamps." *Connoisseur* 107 (1941):233-39, 272; 17 b&w figs.
A selection of gold-tooled bookbindings dating of the 16th through 18th century from the collection of J.B.Clements, since bequeathed to the museum, of eleven hundred volumes each bearing a coat of arms, crest, or device of royal or other notable personages.

FRENCH

3. SURVEYS AND HISTORIES

1985   GUIGNARD, JACQUES. "Jean Grolier et la reliure en France au XVIe siècle." *Art de France* 1 (1961):306-10, 1 color pl., 2 b&w pls.
Library of three thousand volumes of the famed collector Jean Grolier (1479-1565) with outstanding French and Italian bindings, now dispersed or destroyed.

1986   MICHON, LOUIS-MARIE. "Les Reliures exécutées pour François Ier." *Gazette des beaux-arts* 7 (1932):309-22, 12 b&w pls.
Stages in the development of French bookbinding from the 15th century and through the 16th—the Italian influence and the subsequent new French style. Three different workshops producing bindings for King Francis I.

6. PERMANENT COLLECTIONS

Besançon

BIBLIOTHÈQUE MUNICIPALE

1987   PIQUARD, MAURICE. "Les Livres du Cardinal de Granvelle à la Bibliothèque de Besançon." *Les Trésors des bibliothèques de France* 7 (1942):16-29, 7 b&w pls.
Bookbindings made by six different French workshops for the enlightened 16th-century collector and statesman Antoine Perrenot de Granvelle.

Paris

BIBLIOTHÈQUE MAZARINE

1988   GID, D. *Catalogue des reliures françaises estampées à froid (15ᵉ-16ᵉ siècles) de la Bibliothèque Mazarine.* Paris: Éditions du CNRS, 1984. 741 pp., illus.
Major holdings of outstanding 15th-16th-century French bindings.

GERMAN

3. SURVEYS AND HISTORIES

1989   KYRISS, ERNST. *Verzierte gotische Einbände im alten deutschen Sprachgebiet.* 4 vols. Stuttgart: Max Hettler, 1951-58. Text vol.:166 pp.; 3 vols. of illus. comprising 364 pls.
Important repertory of 15th-16th-century German leather bindings including catalog entries and plates reproducing rubbings made from specific stamped decorative elements, inscriptions, etc., as well as illustrations of full flaps. Excellent for helping to localize Gothic bindings of German-speaking countries.

HUNGARIAN

7. EXHIBITION CATALOGS

Budapest

IPARMÜVÉSZETI MÚZEUM

1990   *Ateliers de reliure de la Renaissance en Hongrie: Exposition de reliures hongroises 1470-1520.* Exhibition catalog by Eva Sz. Koroknay. Translated (into French) by Margit Németh. Budapest: Iparmüvészeti Museum, 1967. 62 pp., 24 b&w pls., some b&w text figs.
Thirteen-page essay follows the evolution of Hungarian bookbinding in the 15th-16th century: the royal bindery at Buda; the different types of bindings particularly those of Mathias Corvinus; comparison with contemporary Italian bindings. Entries for eighty-three examples from various collections in Hungary.

ITALIAN

3. SURVEYS AND HISTORIES

Books

1991   DE MARINIS, TAMMARO. *La legatura artistica in Italia nei secoli XV e XVI.* 3 vols. Florence: Alinari, 1960. Illus., some color.
The major study produced on Italian bindings of the 15th-16th century. Vol. 1: Naples, Rome, Urbino, Florence; vol. 2: Bologna, Cesena, Ferrara, Venice; vol. 3: Verona, Milan, Bergamo, Perugia. Invaluable also for illustration.

1992   FUMAGALLI, G[IUSEPPE]. *L'arte della legatura alla corte degli Estensi a Ferrara e a Modena, dal secolo XV al XIX, col cataloga delle legature pregevoli della biblioteca estense di Modena.* Florence: 1913. 176 pp., 37 b&w pls.

        Still useful, if somewhat dated, survey of bindings produced for the Este court at Ferrara.

1993   HOBSON, G.D. *Maioli, Canevari and Others.* London: Ernest Benn, 1926. 178 pp., 6 color pls., 64 b&w pls.

        Renaissance bindings: those of the library of Jean Grolier, treasurer of France (1547-65), including Italian plaquettes by Moderno, IO.F.F., Antonio da Brescia; those with tooled architectural motifs; bindings made ca. 1550-60 for Thomas Mahieu, secretary of Catherine de' Medici; and others said to have belonged to the Genoese physician Canavari (1559-1625) that actually were the property of Pier Luigi Farnese, son of Pope Paul III.

Article

1994   ROSSI, FILIPPO. "De legature italiane del '500." *Dedalo* 3 (1922):373-95, 1 color pl., 16 b&w figs.

        Highlights of 16th-century Florentine, Venetian, and Roman bookbindings from the exhibition at the Pitti Palace, Florence, which spanned the 11th to the 19th century. Discussed are those with Oriental influence, the Venetian bindings of Aldo Manuzio's workshop, those with mosaiclike motifs, and those influenced by coins and medals. Reattribution of bindings made for bibliophile Tommaso Maioli to Italian, probably Venetian, workmanship, and not French, as hitherto held.

6. PERMANENT COLLECTIONS

Florence

BIBLIOTECA MEDICEA LAURENZIANA

1995   *Mostra di legature (secoli XV-XX).* Essay by Annarosa Garzelli. Florence: Biblioteca Medicea Laurenziana, 1978. 51 pp., 2 color pls.

        Exhibition of 165 bindings from the library's permanent holdings. Entry nos. 1-72 are of 15th-16th-century Roman, Venetian, Florentine, and two French bindings. Essay at end on the gilt-silver and enamel box made in Florence for Cardinal Cesarini to store the documents of the Council of 1439.

Padua

BIBLIOTECA CAPITOLARE

1996   BARZON, ANTONIO. "Saggi di rilegature." In *Libri stampatori Padova* (Misc. G. Bellini), Padua, 1959. Pp. 297-318, 7 b&w figs.

        Leather bindings of the 15th-16th century, others of the early 16th century with flaps encased in silver by Master Alvise.

7. EXHIBITION CATALOGS

Venice

FONDAZIONE GIORGIO CINI

1997   *Rilegature veneziane del XV e XVI secolo.* Exhibition catalog by Tammaro De Marinis. Venice: Neri Pozza Editore, 1955. 45 pp., 38 b&w pls.

   104 brief catalog entries of 15th-16th-century Venetian tooled leather bindings from Italian, French, English, and Austrian collections.

SPANISH

3. SURVEYS AND HISTORIES

1998   CLOUZOT, HENRI. *Cuirs décorés.* Vol. 2, *"Cuirs de Cordoue."* Paris: A. Calavas, [1928]. 12 pp., 48 b&w pls.

   Twelve-page introduction to the development of gilded and often embossed leather, of Lybian inspiration, worked in Spain as early as the 11th century and still in vogue throughout Europe—mostly in Spain, France, and Italy, through the 17th century: caskets, sheaths, and mostly wall panels. Of the 15th-16th century are pls. 1-3, 6, 8-10, 36.

1999   WATERER, JOHN W. *Spanish Leather: A History of Its Use from 800 to 1500 for Mural Hangings, Screens, Upholstery, Altar Frontals, Ecclesiastical Vestments, Footwear, Gloves, Pouches, and Caskets.* London: Faber & Faber, 1971. 130 pp., 16 color figs., 71 b&w figs.

   Survey covering the period 800-1800. Discusses origins in Moorish Spain, development and dissemination, gilding and techniques, utilitarian and ornamental uses, and production centers (geographically arranged, pp. 51-69). Seven appendixes including significant dates, manufacturing centers, technical terms, ordinances, geographical listing of extant leather hangings, etc.

7. EXHIBITION CATALOGS

Madrid

SOCIEDAD ESPAÑOLA DE AMIGOS DEL ARTE

2000   *Exposición de encuadernaciones españolas siglos XII al XIX.* Exhibition catalog by Francisco Huesco Rolland. Madrid: Sociedad Española de Amigos del Arte, 1934. 249 pp., 8 color pls., 53 b&w pls., 35 b&w text figs. and diagrams.

   Spanish bookbindings 12th-19th century. Brief essays on Gothic monastic examples (pp. 39-42), treasury bindings (43-45), important libraries and bibliophiles (46-56), the Renaissance (61-65), bookbindings at the Escorial (68-70), with heraldic decoration (71-78), from Valencia (89-90), library inventories (103-60). 534 catalog entries follow, many pertinent to years 1400-1600, of bindings from Spanish, mostly private, collections.

XXXVII. Musical Instruments

A. MULTI COUNTRY OF ORIGIN

1. DICTIONARIES AND ENCYCLOPEDIAS

2001   *The New Grove Dictionary of Musical Instruments.* Edited by Sadie Stanley, with many
contributors. 3 vols. Vol. 1 (A to F), 805 pp.; vol. 2 (G to O), 982 pp.; vol. 3 (P to Z),
921 pp. Numerous b&w figs. and line drawings throughout all vols. London: Macmillan
& Co.; New York: Grove's Dictionaries of Music, 1984.
   The most up-to-date and comprehensive dictionary of its type with numerous entries
by authoritative musicologists. Useful to grasp the history and evolution of specific instruments, also good descriptions and illustrations. Covers all countries and times. Many entries
apply to 15th-16th-century Europe.

3. SURVEYS AND HISTORIES

2002   GEIRINGER, KARL. *Musical Instruments: Their History in Western Culture from the
Stone Age to the Present.* Translated by Bernard Miall. 2d ed., with some changes in illus.
New York: Oxford University Press, 1945. 278 pp., 26 b&w pls. (1st ed. 1943.)
   Sparsely illustrated popular survey, with no art-historical information. Chaps. 3 and
4 (pp. 66-113) deal with the period 1300-1600. Useful as easy reference.

2003   SACHS, CURT. *The History of Musical Instruments.* New York: W.W. Norton & Co.,
1940. 505 pp., 24 b&w pls., 167 text figs.
   Scholarly, classic, study, but without art-historical information, from early times to
the 20th century. Chap. 15 (pp. 297-350) deals with "The Renaissance (1400-1600)."

2004   WILSON, MICHAEL I. *Organ Cases of Western Europe.* Montclair, N.J.: Abner
Schram, 1979. 91 pp., 264 b&w figs.
   Ten-page introduction deals with types of organs, principles of design, development,
styles, and settings. 264 short catalog entries inluding 15th- and 16th-century examples from
the Netherlands (nos. 1-11, 19, 43-46), Austria, Germany, Switzerland (65-71), Denmark (111-
12), France (119-27), Spain, Portugal (162-71, 173-74, 177), Italy (205-19, 221-25), and British
Isles (249-50). Particularly useful for plates.

2005 WINTERNITZ, EMANUEL. *Musical Instruments of the Western World*. London: Thames & Hudson, 1966. 259 pp., 56 color figs., 75 b&w figs., numerous engravings.

Appealing presentation with excellent color reproduction of one hundred instruments described as art objects rather than musical tools. Examples from all countries are drawn from major collections. Nos. 5-29 are of the 15th-16th century; examples include crecelle, lutes, chitarrone, lyres, harps, pochette, viola, spinets, organs, harpsichords, virginal, trumpets, and an organ, with fanciful reliefs, three-dimensional carvings, enamelings, intarsia work, or paintings.

6. PERMANENT COLLECTIONS

London

VICTORIA AND ALBERT MUSEUM

2006 *Catalogue of Musical Instruments*. Vol. 1, *Keyboard Instruments*. Catalog by Howard Schott. 2d ed. London: Her Majesty's Stationery Office, 1985. 148 pp., 119 b&w figs. (1st ed. 1968.)

Important collection of fifty-nine keyboard instruments, the first twelve (harpsicords, spinets, and a virginal with inlay and/or painted decoration) dating of the 16th century and originating from Italy, Flanders, England, and Germany.

B. SINGLE COUNTRY OF ORIGIN

BELGIUM (FLEMISH)

6. PERMANENT COLLECTIONS

New York

METROPOLITAN MUSEUM OF ART

2007 RORIMER, JAMES J. "A Double Virginal, Dated 1581 by Hans Ruckers." *Metropolitan Museum Studies* 2 (1930):176-86, 14 b&w figs.

One of the twenty-three extant spinets by this Antwerp master. It is decorated with colorful geometric ornaments, painted scenes of garden feasts, and gesso medallions representing Anne of Austria and Philip II of Spain.

BRITISH (ENGLISH)

3. SURVEYS AND HISTORIES

2008 PALMER, FRANCES. "Musical Instruments from the *Mary Rose*: A Report on Work in Progress." *Early Music* 11 (1983):53-59, 3 b&w figs., line drawings; MYERS, HERBERT W. "The *Mary Rose* 'Shawm'" *Early Music* 11 (1983):358- 60, 2 b&w figs.

Shawm, three-hole pipes, fiddles and bosun's pipe recovered from the wreckage of the *Mary Rose*, which sank off Portsmouth in 1545.

ITALIAN

3. SURVEYS AND HISTORIES

2009   HADAWAY, ROBERT. "The Cittern." *Early Music* 1 (1973):77-81, 5 b&w figs.
A popular string instrument of Renaissance Italy—often with fine carvings—of which there are extant examples in the Victoria and Albert and Kunsthistorisches museums.

2010   HEADLAM WELLS, ROBIN. "The Orpharion: Symbol of a Humanist Ideal." *Early Music* 10 (1982):427-40, 28 b&w figs.
Surviving examples of the "Lira da herraccio"—product of the humanist attempt to revive the musical practice of classical antiquity—including carved decorations of the scallop shell and rose, held to have amorous connotations.

NETHERLANDISH

3. SURVEYS AND HISTORIES

2011   BANGS, J.D. "The Sixteenth-Century Organ of the Pieterskerk Leiden." *Oud holland* 88 (1974):220-31, 12 b&w figs.
Built and carved by Jan Kerstantsz between 1540 and 1553; woodcarving related to contemporary prints and compared to other examples in Dutch churches.

XXXVIII. Furniture

A. MULTI COUNTRY OF ORIGIN

Works Dealing with Both Secular and Church Furniture

1. DICTIONARIES AND ENCYCLOPEDIAS

2012   ARONSON, JOSEPH. *The New Encyclopedia of Furniture.* New York: Crown Publishers,[1967]. 493 pp., 16 color pls., numerous b&w figs. and line drawings. (First published as *The Encyclopedia of Furniture,* 1938, 1941, 1965.)
    Handy reference book covering all aspects of subject: main characteristics and evolution of style according to country and period; definition of terms; explanation of techniques, material, etc., supplemented by a large illustration. Bibliography, pp. 467-79; glossary of designers and craftsmen, 480-84.

3. SURVEYS AND HISTORIES

Books

2013   BISHOP, ROBERT, AND COBLENTZ, PATRICIA. *Furniture I: Prehistoric through Roccoco.* Washington: Smithsonian Institution, 1979. 127 pp., 26 color pls., 99 b&w figs.
    General survey: chaps. 3 (pp. 26-33) and 4 (34-47) touch on late medieval and Renaissance furniture.

2014   BOGER, LOUISE ADE. *The Complete Guide to Furniture Styles.* Enl. ed. New York: Charles Scribner's Sons, [1969]. 512 pp., over 500 b&w figs. (1st ed. 1959.)
    Practical guide to the development of furniture styles from ancient to modern times; includes brief essays on 15th- and 16th-century English, French, Italian, Spanish, and Netherlandish furniture; subdivided by article of furniture. Bibliography.

2015   CHAMPEAUX, ALFRED DE. *Le Meuble.* Vol. 1, *Antiquité, Moyen Age et Renaissance.* 2d ed. Paris: Ernest Gründ, 1926. 330 pp., 75 line drawings. (1st ed. 1885.)

Furniture in antiquity, the Middle Ages, and the Renaissance with emphasis on the two latter periods in France (see pp. 92-256, subdivided into regional schools—Normandy, Brittany, Touraine, etc.), but also including chapters on Italy and Spain (257-86), and on Germany, Netherlands, England, and Scandinavia (287-317). Mentions of extant pieces but mostly seen from a historical perspective (accounts, inventories, and other contemporary writings).

2016   GRIMM, CLAUS. *The Book of Picture Frames,* with a supplement, "Frames in America," by George Szabo. Translated by Nancy M. Gordon and Walter L. Strauss. New York: Abaris Books, 1981. 343 pp., 489 b&w figs. (German edition, Munich: George D.W. Callwey, 1978.)
        Most inclusive compendium dealing with the history of picture frames. Series of 489 large (but often lacking in definition) illustrations with captions preceded by a thirty-five-page essay, a useful glossary, and bibliography. Nos. 24-138 are 15th-16th-century examples. Addendum by Szabo pp. 311-43 (nos. 434-89) includes six 15th-16th-century fames in U.S. institutions.

2017   JACKSON, F. HAMILTON. *Intarsia and Marquetry.* London: Sands & Co., 1903. 171 pp., 55 b&w pls.
        Still useful, if dated, survey of wood inlaying from antiquity to the 18th century. Much of the book deals with Italian and French Renaissance examples from the standpoint of technique and styles.

2018   JARMUTH, KURT. *Lichter Leuchten im Abendland: Zweitausend Jahre Beleuchtungskörper.* Brunswick: Klinkhardt & Biermann, 1967. 416 pp., 404 b&w figs.
        Valuable study dealing with the development of the chandelier and candlestick and their use in the Western world. Pp. 75-222 deal with the Gothic and Renaissance periods with emphasis on Germany, France, and Italy. Very useful illustration.

2019   RAVA, CARLO ENRICO. *La sedia.* Milan: Görlich, 1964. 222 pp., 8 color pls., 609 b&w figs.
        History of chairs in Europe. Thirty-page introduction and series of plates with descriptive captions. Figs. 41-54 deal with late Gothic examples; 55-116, with others of the Renaissance period.

2019a   SCHMITZ, HERMANN. *Das Möbelwerk: Die Möbelformen vom Altertum bis zur Mitte des neunzehnten Jahrhunderts.* Tübingen: Ernst Wasmuth, 1951. 80 pp., 683 b&w figs.
        Furniture through the ages. Pls. 31-135 illustrate mostly 15th-16th-century chests, stalls, paneling, cassoni, chairs, credenze from Germany, France, Italy, England, and Scandanavia.

2020   WINDISCH-GRAETZ, FRANZ. *Möbel Europas: Von der Romanik bis zur Spätgotik; mit einem Rückblick auf Antike und Spätanike.* Munich: Klinkhardt & Biermann, 1982. 333 pp., 8 color figs., 319 b&w figs.
        Survey of medieval furniture produced in Europe with emphasis on stools, choir stalls, chairs, thrones, tables, beds, cabinets, chests, and the differing manufacturing techniques used.

Article

2021   ADAMS-ACTON, MURRAY. "The Genesis and Development of Linenfold Panelling." *Connoisseur* 117 (1946): Part 1, 25- 31, 13 b&w figs.; part 2, 80-86, 10 b&w figs.

In situ English and French examples of the 15th and 16th century discussed in terms of origins (15th-century France), evolution, technique, and in conjunction with carved friezes and furniture decoration.

6. PERMANENT COLLECTIONS

Barcelona

MUSEU D'ART DE CATALUNYA

2022 MASERES, ALFONS. "La Col·lecció d'arquetes de Martí Estany." *Butlletí dels museus d'art de Barcelona* 7 (1937):357-67, 18 b&w figs.
Bequest of a series of 14th-16th-century boxes made of ivory, iron, or wood.

Chicago

ART INSTITUTE OF CHICAGO

2023 *The Art of the Edge: European Frames 1300-1900.* Exhibition catalog by Richard R. Brettell and Steven Starling, with an essay by José Ortega y Gasset. Chicago: Art Institute of Chicago, 1986. 124 pp., 15 color figs., 113 b&w figs.
Annotated catalog of seventy-three frames in the permanent collection including Italian, Austrian, Flemish, and French examples of the 15th-16th century. Useful introduction to the field with glossary and bibliography.

8. PRIVATE COLLECTION, AUCTION, AND DEALER CATALOGS

FIGDOR COLLECTION

2024 ECKHARDT, FERDINAND. "Furniture in the Figdor collection." *Collector* 9 (1930). Part 1, 21-28, 11 b&w figs.; part 2, 82-89, 12 b&w figs.; part 3, 122-28, 14 b&w figs.; part 4, 170-75, 11 b&w figs.
Largest private collection at the time of choice furniture amassed by Albert Figdor of Vienna auctioned in 1930 (see entry 102). Brief presentation with good photographs of major holdings: Tyrolian and Italian chests, door from the residence of Federigo da Montefeltro at Gubbio, cabinets from Auvergne, Tuscany, and Lyon, lecterns, desks, and ecclesiastical chairs, Italian folding chairs, Bavarian, Franconian, Lyonese tables of the Renaissance, secular chairs of the same period from Italy and France.

Secular Furniture

3. SURVEYS AND HISTORIES

2025 DIETRICH, GERHARD. *Schreibmöbel vom Mittelalter zur Moderne.* Munich: Keyserche Verlagsbuchhandlung, 1986. 231 pp., 7 color figs., 161 b&w figs.
This study surveys the development of desks and writing tables from the 10th through the 20th century. Pp. 9-39 provide a brief overview of the medieval and Renaissance periods in Germany, Italy, Spain, and France. Includes glossary.

2026   EAMES, PENELOPE. *Medieval Furniture.* London: Furniture Society, 1977. 317 pp., 132 b&w figs. Also published as "Furniture in England, France, and the Netherlands from the Twelfth to the Fifteenth Century," *Furniture History* 13 (1977), entire issue.

Thorough study based on documentary evidence (e.g., inventories, wills, household account books), extensively transcribed, and detailed examination including technical analysis of fifty-one extant examples of fixed and movable furniture of all materials and types (but excluding church stalls, altars, and pulpits, whose provenance and/or authenticity are unquestioned). Study is organized in sections by furniture type: armoires, buffets, dressoirs, beds and cradles, chests, seating, tables.

2027   EBERLEIN, HAROLD DONALDSON, and RAMSDELL, ROGER WEARNE. *The Practical Book of Italian, Spanish, and Portuguese Furniture.* Philadelphia and London: J.B. Lippincott Co., 1927. 254 pp., 144 b&w pls., 26 line drawings.

General overview, arranged by country and then chronologically. Pertinent to the period 1400-1600 are pp. 19-105 (Italy), 175-213 (Spain), and 243-46 (Portugal).

2028   FEDUCHI, LUIS. *A History of World Furniture.* Barcelona: Blume, 1977. 656 pp., 26 color pls., 1,213 b&w figs.

Chronologically and geographically subdivided survey of ancient and European furniture until the 20th century. General essay on each period includes many illustrations: French, Spanish, English, German, and Italian Gothic furniture (chairs, tables, cupboards, beds, cassoni, pp. 31-39, figs. 138-276); Italian, Spanish, French, English, German, and Netherlandish furniture of the Renaissance (pp. 41-68, figs. 277-595). Concludes with appendixes of characteristics of styles and of legs, and a glossary. Plate captions in English/Spanish; text in English.

2029   FEULNER, ADOLF. *Propyläen Kunstgeschichte.* Vol. 2, *Kunstgeschichte des Möbels.* Berlin: Propyläen Verlag, 1980. 396 pp., 28 b&w text figs., 42 color pls., 398 b&w pls.

History of furniture from Egyptian times to the 20th century. Pertaining to the Late Gothic and Renaissance periods are pp. 40-127 as well as many illustrations of primary examples, with useful caption entries printed in the form of a catalog.

2030   GLOAG, JOHN. *Guide to Furniture Styles: English and French 1450-1850.* London: Adam & Charles Black, 1972. 232 pp., 357 b&w figs.

Evolution of furniture styles in England and France: chairs, tables, beds, chests, paneling, cupboards, chimneypieces, etc. Relevant to the 15th-16th century are the introduction (pp. 7-12) and chaps. 1-3 (13-66) illustrated with numerous line drawings after examples mostly in the Victoria and Albert Museum and the Wallace Collection.

2031   *The History of Furniture.* Edited by Anne Charlish. London: Orbis, 1976. 344 pp., numerous color and b&w figs.

Overview of Western furniture styles. Two-page introduction by Francis Watson; essays pertinent to 1400-1600 by James Wheeler (pp. 11-23) and Geoffrey Beard (24-55) with cursory treatment of medieval and Renaissance chairs, beds, cassoni, chests, and cabinets with some reference to contemporary paintings; mainly useful for illustrated glossary (313-28).

2032   HUNTER, GEORGE LELAND. *Decorative Furniture.* Philadelphia and London: J.B. Lippincott Co.; Grand Rapids, Mich.: Good Furniture Magazine, Dean Hicks Co., 1923. 480 pp., 23 color pls. 397 b&w pls.

Broad and dated survey of furniture from Egyptian times through the early 20th century. Chaps. 3, 5-8 deal with French, Flemish, English, Spanish, and Italian Gothic and Renaissance furniture. Of some use for its many illustrations, most pieces being in public and private American collections.

2033   JERVIS, SIMON. *Printed Furniture Designs before 1650.* [London]: Furniture History Society, 1974. 63 pp., 449 b&w illus.

Good introduction to theoretical aspects of designs, the volume organizing, discussing, and illustrating the whole range of widely scattered printed European ornamental designs of the Renaissance and mannerist periods.

2034   KOHLHAUSSEN, HEINRICH. *Minnekästchen im Mittelalter.* Berlin: Verlag für Kunstwissenschaft, 1928. 114 pp., 66 b&w pls.

Extensive study of "engagement" boxes with carved wood or leather-tooled panels produced in Germany, northern France, Switzerland, Italy, Spain, England, from the 13th to the 16th century. Catalog includes 162 items, most of which date of the 15th century.

2035   ROCHE, SERGE; COURAGE, GERMAIN; and DEVINOY, PIERRE. *Mirrors.* Translated by Colin Duckworth and Angus Munro. New York: Rizzoli, 1985. 63 pp., 16 color pls., 224 b&w pls. Enl. ed. of Serge Roche's *Miroirs, galeries et cabinets de glaces,* Paris: Paul Hartmann, 1956.

Most complete work dealing with mirror frames. Pp. 13- 18, figs 40-51, 204-12 deal with portable (ivory, boxwood) and large carved examples of the 15th-16th century.

2036   ROEPER, ADALBERT. *Moebel aller Stilarten von Ausgange des Mittelalters bis zum Ende des 18 Jahrhunderts.* Introduction by Hans Bösch. Munich: Jos. Albert, n.d. 4 pp., 50 b&w pls.

Furniture from public and private German collections; includes 15th- and 16th-century German (mostly), French, and Italian cupboards, tables, beds, stalls, chests (pls. 1-18).

2037   SCHMIDT, ROBERT. *Möbel.* Berlin: Richard Carl Schmidt & Co., 1917. 256 pp., 196 b&w figs.

Early general handbook of furniture subtitled "for collectors and connoisseurs" published for a German public. Pp. 46-128 deal with late Gothic and Renaissance examples from Italy, Germany, and France typical of those represented in German collections of around 1900.

Articles

2038   ADAMS-ACTON, MURRAY. "Domestic Architecture and Decoration: The Decoration and General Aspect of the Interior of the House at Various Periods in the Past." *Apollo* 1 (1925). Part 1, 12-22, 4 b&w figs.; part 2, 69-79, 9 b&w figs.; part 3, 132-40, 7 b&w figs.; part 4, 211-18, 8 b&w figs.; part 5, 273-79, 4 b&w figs.; part 6, 338-44, 8 b&w figs.

The decor and furnishing of Gothic manors in England and France (parts 1-4) and in Italian Renaissance palazzi (part 5). Chatty presentation with good photographs of examples in various collections.

2039   ADAMS-ACTON, MURRAY. "Early Oak: Recent Additions to Notable Collections." *Connoisseur* 115 (1945):79-85, 10 b&w figs.

Early 16th century English cupboards, chests, chairs, and a table with linenfold panels, and a French cupboard with rich carving in private collections (Burrell, Hearst, etc.).

2040   RYDER, RICHARD D. "Three-Legged Turned Chairs." *Connoisseur* 190 (1975):242-47. 6 color illus., 11 b&w figs.
Brief survey of tripod chairs dating mostly of the 15th and 16th century. The technique of "turning," its origins, the evolution of style (comparative illustrations from illuminated manuscripts) are discussed.

2041   SYMONDS, R.W. "The Evolution of the Cupboard." *Connoisseur* 112 (1943):91-99, 1 color pl., 13 b&w figs.
The cupboard from a surface on which to lay food to a closed cupboard; its antecedents the ambry and the press; descriptions and definitions from inventories, accounts, contemporary literature, miniatures, and extant examples.

6. PERMANENT COLLECTIONS

Amsterdam

RIJKSMUSEUM

2042   *Catalogus van meubelen en betimmeringen.* Catalog by Th. H. Lunsingh Scheurleer. Amsterdam: Rijksmuseum, 1952. 374 pp., 89 b&w figs.
Seventy-page introduction (followed by a fifteen-page summary in English) presents a chronological overview of 15th- to 19th-century European furniture—description of types, evolution of styles—as exemplified by the museum's holdings. Catalog of 552 mostly Dutch and Flemish but also Italian, French, Spanish, English, and German pieces arranged first by place of origin and then by type; many of the 15th-16th century. Full descriptive entries with bibliographical references.

Frankfurt

MUSEUM FÜR KUNSTHANDWERK

2043   *Europäische Möbel von der Gotik bis zum Jugendstil.* Catalog by Margrit Bauer, Peter Märker, and Annaliese Ohm. Frankfurt: Museum für Kunstandwerk, 1976. 195 pp., 23 color pls., 253 b&w figs.
Major public collection of often outstanding examples of European furniture from the Gothic to Art Nouveau. Pp. 7-17 include ten 15th-century pieces (mostly chests), and five 16th-century Gothic examples; pp. 18-52 include fifty-one 16th-century Renaissance chairs, chests, etc., some with involved intarsia. All items are illustrated. Includes a four-page German glossary.

London

WALLACE COLLECTION

2044   *Wallace Collection Catalogues. Furniture.* Catalog by F.J.B. Watson. London: William Clowes & Sons, 1956. 360 pp., 121 b&w pls.
Entries for fourteen French and fifteen Italian 15th- 16th-century caskets, cupboards, dressers, cabinets, chairs, mirrors, and tables (pp. 1-7, 246-53).

New York

FRICK COLLECTION

2045 *The Frick Collection.* Vol.11, *Furniture, Oriental Carpets, English Silver.* Section on French and Italian Renaissance furniture by Pierre Verlet. New York: Frick Art Reference Library, 1956. 45 pp., 26 b&w pls.

Nine-page introduction on Renaissance furniture followed by detailed catalog entries for thirteen Italian and French cassoni, tables, a cabinet, and chairs (caquetoire, etc.).

Vienna

ÖSTERREICHISCHES MUSEUM FÜR ANGEWANDTE KUNST [formerly K.K. Österreichisches Museum für Kunst und Industrie]

2046 *Mittelalterliches Holzmobiliar.* 2d ed. Catalog by Jacob von Falke. Vienna: Anton Schroll & Co., 1897. 4 pp., 40 b&w pls. (1st ed. 1894.)

European furniture of the 14th-16th century: tables, chairs, chests, doors, cabinets, beds, cassoni and caskets, architectural details, etc. Useful for plates; includes checklist.

Church Furniture

1. DICTIONARIES AND ENCYCLOPEDIAS

See entry 6.

3. SURVEYS AND HISTORIES

2047 COURTENS, ANDRÉ. "Les Stalles sculptées du XIVe au XVIe siècle." *Gazette des beaux-arts* 60 (1962):317-26, 14 b&w figs.

Misericords and carved bench-ends in Flemish, French, and some English churches: their style and iconography.

2048 VERSPAANDONK, J.A.J.M. "Het vreemde houten gezelschap." *Antiek* 9 (1974-75):121-40, 2 color figs., 39 b&w figs.

General discussion of the rich iconography of late medieval choir stalls, its various sources: scriptures, proverbs, etc., as illustrated in churches of Holland, Germany, and Belgium.

B. SINGLE COUNTRY OF ORIGIN

BELGIUM
(FLEMISH AND LIÉGEOIS)

Secular and Church Furniture

3. SURVEYS AND HISTORIES

2049   PHILIPPE, JOSEPH. *Meubles, styles et décors entre Meuse et Rhin.* Liège: Wahle et Cie, 1977. 373 pp., 120 color figs., 439 b&w figs.
Furniture and furnishings in the region between the Meuse and the Rhine. Pp. 58-92 deal with 15th-16th-century chests, credenze, doors, a pulpit, choir stalls, a prie-dieu, etc.

2050   PHILIPPE, JOSEPH. *Le Mobilier liégeois (Moyen- Age- XIXe siècle).* Liège: Éditions Bénard et Centrale Réunies, 1962. 243 pp., 6 color pls., 123 b&w pls.
Sketchy outline of furniture produced in Liège. For a brief account of the 15th-16th century, see pp. 27-32, 91, pls. XXV-XXVIII.

Secular Furniture

3. SURVEYS AND HISTORIES

2051   DEFOUR, FRANS. *Zeven eeuwen meubelkunst in België: XIIIe tot XXe eeuw in Vlaanderen en Wallonië.* Lannoo: Mercatorfonds, 1977. 221 pp., 20 color figs., 117 b&w figs. English summary and captions.
Seven centuries of furniture-making in Belgium (Flanders and Wallonie). Of some use on account of paucity of works dealing with the subject. Pp. 22-57 illustrate carved chests and cabinets with tracery of linenfold decoration in public Belgian collections.

BRITISH
(ENGLISH, SCOTTISH, AND WELSH)

Secular And Church Furniture

1. DICTIONARIES AND ENCYCLOPEDIAS

2052   MACQUOID, PERCY, and EDWARDS, RALPH. *The Dictionary of English Furniture from the Middle Ages to the Late Georgian Period.* 3 vols. Introduction by H. Avray Tipping. London: Country Life; New York: Charles Scribner's Sons, 1924. 1: 302 pp., 19 color pls.; 2: 360 pp., 14 color pls.; 3: 340 pp., 16 color pls; numerous b&w figs. in all 3 vols.
Comprehensive and well-illustrated reference work. Forty-page introduction; entries (types of furniture, terms, styles, artists and craftsmen) arranged alphabetically. Vol. 1: A-Ch.; vol. 2: Ch.-M; vol. 3: Mo-Z. Numerous references to the period 1400-1600.

3. SURVEYS AND HISTORIES

Books

2053   CESCINSKY, HERBERT. *English Furniture from Gothic to Sheraton.* Garden City, N.Y.: Garden City Publishing Co., 1937. 406 pp., over 900 b&w figs.

English furniture of the 15th-19th century including interior woodworking and timber houses; brief chapters discuss Gothic pulpits, choir stalls, window tracery, 15th- and 16th- century paneling and oak furniture (chairs, chests, tables, buffets); valuable mainly for illustrations.

2054   MACQUOID, PERCY. *A History of English Furniture: The Age of Oak.* London: Lawrence & Bullen, 1904. 243 pp., 15 color pls., 215 b&w figs.

History, development, and evolution of English furniture of the period 1500-1600 subdivided as: Gothic, Elizabethan, and Jacobean. Deals with cupboards, chests, hutches, coffers, linenfold panels, stalls, chairs, English caquetoires, cabinets, stools, beds, with large and clear illustrations of pieces that are mostly in private collections.

Articles

2055   ADAMS-ACTON, MURRAY. "Wall Seats and Settles of the Sixteenth Century." *Connoisseur* 121 (1948):16-21, 10 b&w figs.

Benches with carved wooden backs (often linenfold panels), armrests, and sometimes a chest beneath the seat, found in churches, guildhalls, colleges, taverns, and secular dwellings in England.

2056   SYMONDS, R.W. "The Craft of the Joiner in Medieval England." *Connoisseur* 118 (1946). Part 1, 17-23, 10 b&w figs.; part 2, 98-104, 16 b&w figs.

The emergence of the craft, its historical context and various tasks performed on chairs, tables, paneling, chests, etc.

6. PERMANENT COLLECTIONS

London

VICTORIA AND ALBERT MUSEUM

2057   *Catalogue of English Furniture and Woodwork.* Vol.1, *Gothic and Early Tudor* by H. Clifford Smith, 2d ed., London: Board of Education, 1929, 100 pp., 61 b&w pls. (1st ed. 1923.) Vol. 2, *Late Tudor and Early Stuart,* London: Board of Education, 1930, 68 pp., 52 b&w pls.

Vol. 1: descriptive entries for 349 ecclesiastical and secular examples dating from the mid-14th to the mid-16th century. Arranged by types (e.g., misericords, lecterns, screens, bench-ends, doors, panels, chests, cupboards, tables, chairs, stools, beds) and then chronologically. Vol. 2: 193 examples dating fom 1558-1660: furniture arranged by types (beds, chairs, chests, cabinets, cupboards, tables), and panels, paneling, and chimneys.

Secular Furniture

3. SURVEYS AND HISTORIES

Books

2058   ROBINSON, FREDERICK S. *English Furniture.* London: Methuen & Co., 1905. 364
pp., 161 b&w pls.
        Standard if rather dated history from medieval times through the 19th century. Pp. 1-
65 deal mostly with the period 1400-1600: Gothic chairs, armoires, oak chests, the Renaissance house, paneled rooms, and bedsteads.

2059   ROE, FRED. *Ancient Coffers and Cupboards, Their History and Description from the Earliest Times to the Middle of the Sixteenth Century.* London: Methuen & Co.; New York:
E.P. Dutton & Co., 1902. 140 pp., 2 hand-colored pls., 98 b&w line drawings.
        The evolution of the two basic furnishings in England discussed in the perspective of
contemporaneous examples on the Continent. For the period 1400-1600, see chap. 6 (15th
century), 7 (16th century), 8 (linen panels), 9 (plain coffers).

2060   SMALL, JOHN WILLIAM. *Scottish Woodwork of the Sixteenth & Seventeenth Centuries.*
Edinburgh: David Douglas, [1878]. 100 pls. of line drawings.
        The first analytic presentation of Scottish furniture (chairs, tables, cabinets,
wardrobes, shutter boards, etc.), through selected examples from public and private collections. Each piece is briefly described, illustrated in full and then by several details of its ornamentation. Almost half of the cited examples are said to date of the 16th century.

2061   WILLS, GEOFFREY. *English Furniture 1550-1760.* London: Guinness Superlatives,
1971. 260 pp., 32 color pls., 195 b&w figs.
        Examples of tables, chairs, chests, cupboards, and beds from Elizabeth I's reign
(1558-1603) and broad history of furniture during the period (pp. 1-32).

Articles

2062   ADAMS-ACTON, MURRAY. "Benches and Wall-Seats. A Few Early Examples." *Collector* 9 (1930):139-47, 7 b&w figs.
        Discusses 15th-16th-century examples from Somerset and the West of England in
relation to French ones.

2063   CESCINSKY, HERBERT. "Two English Oak Cabinets of the Early Sixteenth Century."
Burlington Magazine 74 (1939):187-193, 2 b&w figs.
        Construction and decoration of two standing cupboards of ca. 1510 in the Acton
Surgly and Malcome Stewart collections, one being in the Gothic style and the other in the
new Renaissance mode.

2064   EAMES, PENELOPE. "Inventories as Sources of Evidence for Domestic Furnishings in
the Fourteenth and Fifteenth Centuries." *Furniture History* 9 (1973):33-40
        Availability, use, appreciation, and value of furniture such as chairs, stools, tables,
barrels, and cupboards in craftsmen's living quarters.

2065 FORMAN, BENNO M. "Continental Furniture Craftsmen in London: 1511-1625." *Furniture History* 7 (1971):94-120, 5 illus.

The migration to London of 477 furniture craftsmen from the Netherlands and Lower Rhine because of religious wars, and their influence on English furniture.

2066 STRANGE, E.F. "The Henry VIII Room at Bretton Park," *Old Furniture* 2 (1927):96-100, 3 b&w figs.

Linenfold paneling, a Tudor Gothic bed with ornate bedstead of carved figural representations, etc. in a Yorkshire house.

2067 SYMONDS, R.W. "The Bed through the Centuries." *Connoisseur* 111 (1943):34-43, 11 b&w figs.

Description of English beds and their vital position in the house from the 14th to 19th century as seen through inventories, wills, 15th-century miniatures, and actual examples; evolution of types and styles; terminology.

2067a SYMONDS, R.W. "The Chest and the Coffer: Their Difference in Function and Design." *Connoisseur* 107 (1941):15-21, 9 b&w figs.

Purpose, construction, and design of the English chest—furniture for the storage of household articles and often used as a seat—and the coffer—essentially a trunk designed for travel. Includes several illustrated examples of the 16th century.

2067b SYMONDS, R.W. "The Counter-Board and Its Use." *Connoisseur* 128 (1951):169-75, 16 b&w figs.

Examines the medieval counter—a board, either in table or chest form, or a separate table, marked with lines and used for calculation—and its accompanying cloth or carpet, also marked with lines. Illustrates some 16th-century chests with carved panels, proposed to have originally been counter- boards.

2067c SYMONDS, R.W. "The Craft of the Coffer-Maker." *Connoisseur* 107 (1941):100-105, 133, 9 b&w figs.

Evolution of the English coffer—designed for transport and travel—which by the 16th century had expanded into the production of elaborately upholstered (leather, velvet, cloth, lace, etc.) and embellished chairs, footstools, close tools.

2067d SYMONDS, R.W. "English Trestle Tables: 'The Festive Borde.'" *Connoisseur* 104 (1939):275-80, 301-2, 9 b&w figs.

Oak and chestnut table-boards of the 16th-17th century; their use.

2068 WENHAM, EDWARD. "Oak Motifs in English Furniture: The Elizabethan and Early Stuart Periods." *Connoisseur* 97 (1936):134-39, 10 b&w figs.

Cursory discussion of English adaptations of Italian Renaissance forms in elaborately decorated tables, chests, chairs, and buffets of the 16th-17th century.

6. PERMANENT COLLECTIONS

London

VICTORIA AND ALBERT MUSEUM

2069   *The Panelled Rooms.* Vol. 6, *The Waltham Abbey Room,* by H. Clifford Smith. London: Board of Education, 1924. 24 pp., 16 b&w pls.
    Early 16th-century room composed of 110 panels with carved medallion heads, perhaps portraits of the Denny family.

2070   *A Short History of English Furniture,* [by Ralph Edwards]. London: Her Majesty's Stationery Office, 1966. 32 pp., 100 b&w pls.
    Pictorial survey of furniture styles based on examples in the museum. Eighteen-page essay outlines the evolution of style. Illustrations of one hundred pieces with captions. For chests, cupboards, armchair, spinet, paneling, bedstead, and draw-table dating of the 15th-16th century, see nos. 2-13.

2071   *English Desks and Bureaux.* Catalog by J.F. Hayward. London: Her Majesty's Stationery Office, 1968. 22 pp., 40 b&w pls.
    Permanent collection includes one reading desk of the 15th century and two table desks of the 16th.

2072   *English Chairs.* Catalog by Ralph Edwards, revised by Desmond Fitz-Gerald. 3d ed. London: Her Majesty's Stationery Office, 1970. 28 pp., 1 color pl., 129 b&w pls. (1st ed. 1951.)
    Brief history with emphasis on form; five examples of box-chairs and caquetoires (nos. 5-7, 8), dating from 1525-1600.

8. PRIVATE COLLECTION, AUCTION, AND DEALER CATALOGS

HART COLLECTION

2073   SYMONDS, R.W. "The Craft of Furniture Making in the XVIth and XVIIth Centuries with Examples from the Collection of Mr. Geoffrey Hart." *Connoisseur* 99 (1937):130-37. 1 color pl., 10 b&w figs.
    The historical background of the craft in England: the woodworking companies and their regulations and apprenticeships, division of labor; includes some 16th-century examples.

Church Furniture

3. SURVEYS AND HISTORIES

2074   ANDERSON, M.D. *Animal Carvings in British Churches.* Cambridge: University Press, 1938. 99 pp., 43 b&w figs.
    Deals mostly with the lively bestiary, often imaginary, found on misericords.

2075   BOND, FRANCIS. *Screens and Galleries in English Churches.* London, New York, and Toronto: Henry Frowde, Oxford University Press, 1908. 204 pp., 152 b&w figs.

Study of all types of screens from all periods. Includes 15th-16th-century oak screens—their construction, cost, design, influences from other countries.

2076 BOND, FRANCIS. *Wood Carvings in English Churches.* Vol. 1, *Misericords.* London, New York, Toronto, and Melbourne: Henry Frowde, Oxford University Press, 1910. 256 pp., 241 b&w figs.

  Comprehensive study, organized by iconographic source (Eastern mythology, classical mythology, the *Physiologus*, medieval romances, Old and New Testament scenes, etc.) and with concise explanation of narrative and symbolism.

2076a BOND, FRANCIS. *Wood Carvings in English Churches.* Vol. 2, *Stalls and Tabernacle Work.* London, New York, Toronto, and Melbourne: Henry Frowde, Oxford University Press, 1910. 154 pp., 124 b&w figs.

  First publication solely devoted to stalls—their design, construction, cost, arrangement, types. Also bishops' thrones and chancel chairs.

2077 COX, J. CHARLES. *English Church Fittings, Furniture and Accessories.* New York: G.P. Putnam's Son; London: B.T. Batsford, [1923]. 329 pp., 274 b&w figs.

  Useful introduction to various types of church seating—misericords, bench-ends, manor pews—pulpits, lecterns, screens, ironwork, armor, coat of arms, hatchments, clocks, candelabra (see particularly chaps. 5-10, 14).

2078 COX, J. CHARLES. *Pulpits, Lecterns, & Organs in English Churches.* London, New York, Toronto, Melbourne, and Bombay: Humphrey Milford, Oxford University Press, 1915. 239 pp., 155 b&w pls.

  Church furnishings described within the context of religious practices. Includes many 15th-16th-century carved wood pulpits, 16th-century hourglass stands, mostly of wrought iron, brass, and wood lecterns, many eagle-shaped, and reading desks.

2079 GARDNER, ARTHUR. *Minor English Wood Sculpture 1400- 1550: An Essay on Carved Figures and Animals on Bench-Ends in English Parish Churches.* London: Alec Tiranti, 1958. 42 pp., 170 b&w figs.

  Carvings in East Anglia, the Midlands and the West Country; their iconography, mostly drawn form bestiaries.

2080 HOWARD, F.E., and F.H. CROSSLEY. *English Church Woodwork: A Study in Craftsmanship during the Mediaeval Period A.D. 1250-1550.* London: B.T. Batsford, 1917. 403 pp., 386 b&w illus., 66 line drawings.

  Comprehensive study of doors, reredos, canopies, sedilia, stalls, thrones, lecterns, pulpits, font covers, bench-ends, misericords, chests, cupboards, tombs, and reliquaries. Numerous illustrations for the many 15th-16th-century examples.

2081 LAIRD, MARSCHALL. *English Misericords.* London: John Murray, 1986. 128 pp., 160 b&w figs.

  Useful, concise introduction also meant to serve as a general guidebook. Deals primarily with iconography, chapter headings being the following: Humans, Animals, Monsters, Plants and Heraldry, the Bible and the Saints.

2082 RANDALL, GERALD. *Church Furnishing and Decoration in England and Wales.* London: B.T. Batsford, 1980. 240 pp., 262 b&w figs.

Study of English and Welsh church furniture of the 11th to the 20th century; eight-page historical survey. Includes 15th- and 16th-century porches, fonts, congregational and chancel pews, nave furniture, screens, eucharist furniture, stained glass, tomb monuments, and a wide range of miscellaneous objects such as altar frontals.

2083   REMNANT, G.L. *A Catalogue of Misericords in Great Britain,* with an essay on iconography by M.D. Anderson. Oxford: Clarendon Press, 1969. 263 pp., 48 b&w pls.

Six-page introduction deals with history and method of dating; eighteen-page essay on iconography. Following is a two-hundred-page catalog of misericords from the 13th to the 20th century in England, Scotland, and Wales, with a single entry for Ireland (Limerick Cathedral); many date of the 15th-16th century. Entries are arranged geographically according to county and city. The majority of works are in parish churches. Includes appendix and iconographic and proper names and indexes.

2084   WRIGHT, PETER POYNTZ. *The Rural Benchends of Somerset: A Study in Medieval Woodcarving.* Amersham: Avebury Publishing Co., 1983. 176 pp., 220 b&w figs. [on 55 pls.].

Comprehensive study of all-important rural carvings of West Somerset abounding in the 15th-16th century as a result of the new requirements for seating coupled with increased prosperity. Seven recurring iconographic subjects, their symbolism and style, are dealt with in some detail.

FRENCH

Secular and Church Furniture

6. PERMANENT COLLECTIONS

Paris

MUSÉE DES ARTS DÉCORATIFS

2085   *Le Bois.* Vol. 1, *Moyen Age—Renaissance,* by Louis Metman and Gaston Brière. Paris: D.-A. Languet, 1911. 15 pp., 60 b&w pls. comprising 800 figs.

Valuable pictorial corpus of 15th-16th-century French secular and ecclesiastical furniture and carved woodwork (beds, desks, doors, panels, chairs, caskets, choir stalls, lecterns, etc.) in the decorative arts museum.

Secular Furniture

3. SURVEYS AND HISTORIES

Books

2086   AGNEL, G. ARNAUD D'. *Le Meuble: Ameublement provençal et comtadin du Moyen-Age à la fin du XVIIIe siècle.* 2 vols. Paris: Lucien Laveur; Marseille: Alex Jouvène, 1913. 1:319 pp., 70 b&w pls.

Major study on furniture-making in Provence and the Comtat Venaissin (Avignon) from the 15th to 18th century; includes some Gothic chests and chairs, and many Henri II chests and cabinets. The emphasis is on descriptive and historical relationships with the work of craftsmen from other regions.

2087   BOUSSEL, PATRICE. *Les Styles du Moyen Age à Louis XIV.* Paris: Baschet et Cie, 1979. 190 pp., 32 color figs., 337 b&w figs.
French furniture, furnishings, and buildings from the 15th to 18th century. Chap. 1 (pp. 5-28) deals with Gothic period; chap. 2 (29-66) with Renaissance and Henri II examples. Of interest for illustrations especially of pieces in private collections.

2088   FÉLICE, ROGER DE. *French Furniture in the Middle Ages and under Louis XIII.* Translated by F.M. Atkinson. New York: Frederick A. Stokes Co., [1923]. 175 pp., 78 b&w figs.
Early work revealing history and styles with cursory exposition on particular types of furniture (e.g., tables, beds, cupboards, etc.). For the 15th-16th century see pp. 1-85.

2089   JANNEAU, GUILLAUME, and JARRY, MADELEINE. *Le Siège en France du Moyen Age à nos jours.* Paris: Paul Hartmann, 1948. 390 pp., 343 b&w pls. M. Jarry published an edition entitled *Le Siège français* in 1973 [Fribourg: Office du Livre.]
Brief history of chairs in France from the Middle Ages to the 20th century and types in existence during the Middle Ages and the Renaissance. Pls. 1-31 are of 15th-16th-century examples in public and private French collections, each with a brief entry.

2090   VIAUX, JACQUELINE. *Le Meuble en France.* Paris: Presses Universitaires de France, 1962. 192 pp., 8 color pls., 31 b&w figs.
Introduction to the history of French furniture from the Middle Ages to the Fourth Republic; specific types, development of style, technique, influence of ornamental designers. On the period 1400-1600 are pp. 37-58.

Articles

2091   ADAMS-ACTON, MURRAY. "French Chests." *Connoisseur* 101 (1938):309-14, 9 b&w figs.
Salient points of style and construction of 15th-16th- century coffers with richly carved panels.

2092   THIRION, JACQUES. "Gravures et panneaux sculptés de la Renaissance: Figures de vertus d'après Goltzius." *Pantheon* 33 (1975):207-15, 15 b&w figs.
Prints of Jacob Matham after compostitions of Hendrick Goltzius and other prints as source for the carving of decorative panels in 16th-17th-century French furniture.

2093   THIRION, JACQUES. "Panneaux sculptés d'après Philippe Galle aux Musées de Cluny et des Arts Décoratifs." *Revue du Louvre et des musées de France* 15 (1965):103-10, 10 b&w figs.
Author traces the source of design on six furniture panels in two Paris museums and two private collections to an album of classical deities by Philippe Galle (1537-1612), one of Antwerp's principal engraver-editors, and proposes that other Italianate influences in French Renaissance furniture also be traced to Dutch mannerists of the last third of the 16th century rather than to the School of Fontainebleau.

2094   VIAUX, J. HENRI. "French Domestic Furniture of the Middle Ages." *Connoisseur* 133 (1954):252-55, 13 b&w figs.
Brief description of design and construction of the coffer, chest, chair, credenza, and bed, with several 15th-century examples.

4. BIBLIOGRAPHICAL GUIDES

2095   VIAUX, JACQUELINE. *Bibliographie du meuble (mobilier civil français).* Paris: Société des Amis de la Bibliothèque Forney, 1966. 589 pp.
Bibliography of periodical articles dealing with domestic French furniture from the medieval period to the 20th century. Divided into ten chapters: furniture of each period, regional furniture, craftsmen, exhibitions, institutional and private collections, inventories, techniques, corporations. Entries within each are arranged chronologically.

6. PERMANENT COLLECTIONS

Budapest

IPARMŰVÉSZETI MÚZEUM

2096   VADÁSZI, ERZSÉBET. "Deux caquetoires." *Ars decorativa* 2 (1974):45-60, 12 b&w figs.
Two French Renaissance oak chairs in the collection with carved festoons and initials on their high backs, which are related to those of a series of panels at the Musée des Arts Décoratifs in Paris.

2096a   VADÁSZI, ERZSÉBET. "Buffet ou dressoir? L'Influence de Ducerceau sur un dressoir de Budapest." *Ars Decorativa* 5 (1977):17-41, 20 b&w figs.
The decorative motifs of a French Renaissance credenza in the museum as well as related pieces in the former Spitzer Collection, the Musée de Cluny, etc. are held to be based on Du Cerceau's *Recueil des meubles* published in 1550.

Paris

MUSÉE DE CLUNY

2097   *Le Mobilier de la Renaissance française: Collections du Musée de Cluny.* 3d ed. Catalog by Egon Hessling. Leipzig: A. Schumann, n.d. 16 pp., 2 b&w figs., 72 b&w pls.
Presentation of the major 16th-century French furniture in the permanent collection. Useful for its good illustrations, many of carved details.

8. PRIVATE COLLECTION, AUCTION, AND DEALER CATALOGS

GOUPIL COLLECTION

2098   *Catalogue des objets d'art de l'Orient et de l'Occident, tableaux, dessins composant la Collection de feu M. Albert Goupil.* Sale held in Paris at Hôtel Drouot 23-28 April 1888. Paris: Escribe; Paul Chevallier, 1888. 101 pp., 14 b&w pls., some text figs.
Dispersal of the collection (617 lots) of the late Albert Goupil of Paris. Though most is Near Eastern art or Western paintings and sculptures, lots 438-81 comprise a very fine collection of furniture including excellent examples of French Renaissance "Henri II" style.

Church Furniture

3. SURVEYS AND HISTORIES

2099   KRAUS, DOROTHY and HENRY. *The Hidden World of Misericords.* New York: George Brazillier, 1975. 206 pp., 169 b&w figs.
Photographic anthology of carved figures or groupings of symbols, sacred events, or scenes of daily life on 16th-century choir stalls mostly in French churches, with short introductions and some iconographic notes.

6. PERMANENT COLLECTIONS

Le Mans

CATHÉDRALE ST.-JULIEN

2100   BLIN, E. *Cathédrale du Mans: Dossiers des stalles du 16ᵉ siècle.* Sainte-Jamme: E. Blin, 1984. 55 pp., illus.
Exceptionally fine choir stalls and screens of 1560-75 with scenes from the life of Christ.

New York

METROPOLITAN MUSEUM OF ART

2101   FREEMAN, MARGARET B.   "Late Gothic Woodcarvings from Normandy." *Metropolitan Museum of Art Bulletin* 9 (1951):260-69, 26 b&w figs.
Thrity-seven oak panels with tracery work and scenes from the life of Christ and of the Virgin, said to have been commisioned for the Abbey of Jumièges in 1501.

GERMAN

Secular Furniture

3. SURVEYS AND HISTORIES

2102   FALKE, OTTO VON. *Deutsche Möbel des Mittelalters und der Renaissance.* Vol. 1 of *Deutsche Möbel vom Mittelalter bis zum Anfang des 19. Jahrhunderts,* edited by Otto von Falke and Herman Schmitz. Stuttgart: Julius Hoffman, 1924. 279 pp., 600 b&w figs.
Indispensable early classic on medieval and Renaissance German furniture. A fifty-eight-page essay discussing the development of types and styles is amply illustrated by examples in public European collections supplemented by representations of furniture in contemporary paintings, miniatures, and sculptures.

2103   KREISEL, HEINRICH. *Die Kunst des deutschen Möbels.* Vol. 1, *Von den Anfängen bis zum Hochbarok.* Munich: C.H. Beck, 1968. 390 pp., 10 color pls.,729 b&w figs.
German furniture from the 6th to the 17th century chronologically and geographically arranged: beds, tables, cupboards, chairs, caskets, etc.   The Gothic and Renaissance periods are discussed pp. 23-152.

2104   MÖLLER, LIESELOTTE. *Der Wrangelschrank und die verwandten süddeutschen Intarsienmöbel des 16. Jahrhunderts.* Berlin: Deutscher Verein für Kunstwissenschaft, 1956. 194 pp., 1 color pl., 240 b&w figs.

Most complete study of intarsia cabinets and table tops as well as paneling produced, respectively, in South Germany (mostly Augsburg) and Tyrol, during the second half of the 16th century. Includes a catalog of eighty-two typical examples. Valuable illustration.

6. PERMANENT COLLECTIONS

Berlin

STAATLICHE MUSEEN, KUNSTGEWERBEMUSEUM

2105   SCHMIDT, ROBERT. "Mittelalterliche Truhen aus Niedersachsen." *Pantheon* 13 (1934):184-88, 3 b&w figs.

A group of carved oak chests in the Schlossmuseum produced in Lower Saxony in the 15th and early 16th century, are discussed in terms of differences of style and construction as well as chronology.

Munich

BAYERISCHES NATIONALMUSEUM

2106   HEFNER-ULTENECK, J.H. VON. *Ornamente der Holzsculptur von 1450 bis 1820 aus dem Bayerischen National-Museum.* Frankfurt: Heinrich Keller, 1895. 6 pp. (unpaginated), 40 b&w pls.

Album illustrating carved ornamental panels, frames, etc. in the museum produced in Germany from the period 1450-1820, preceded by a two-page introduction and four pages of captions. Pls. 1-17 include numerous examples of the period 1450-1600.

Vienna

KUNSTHISTORISCHES MUSEUM

2107   RUPP, FRIEDERICH. "Ein deutsches Minnekästchen der Spätgotik," *Jahrbuch der kunsthistorischen Sammlungen in Wien* 50 (1953):107-20, 21 b&w figs.

The relationship between the carved decoration of a 15th- century German "engagement" casket in the collection and contemporary engravings.

8. PRIVATE COLLECTION, AUCTION, AND DEALER CATALOGS

FAIRHAVEN COLLECTION

2108   BEARD, CHARLES R. "The 'Tree of Jesse' Cupboard in the Collection of Lord Fairhaven." *Connoisseur* 97 (1936):202-5, 3 b&w figs.

Description and early provenance of an elaborately carved Rhenish cupboard bearing a date of 1509 at Anglesey Abbey.

HUNGARIAN

Secular and Church Furniture

6. PERMANENT COLLECTIONS

Budapest

MAGYAR NEMZETI MÚZEUM

2109   KOVALOVSZKI, JÚLIA. *The Treasures of the Hungarian National Museum. Gothic and Renaissance Furniture.* Translated by Lili Halápy. Budapest: Magyar Helikon-Corvina Kiadó, 1981. 35 pp., 7 color figs., 75 b&w figs.

Introduction (19 pp.) on formation of the collection followed by an illustrated catalog of a selection of seventy-five pieces dating from the 14th-18th century, most of which are of the period 1400-1600 and include painted chests, cupboard, candlesticks, lectern, bindings, elaborately carved stalls, intarsia work, etc.

Secular Furniture

3. SURVEYS AND HISTORIES

2110   BÁRÁNY-OBERSCHALL, MAGDA. *Hungarian Furniture.* Budapest: Officina Press, 1939. 30 pp., 32 b&w pls.

General twenty-nine-page introduction.   Small illustration of major examples of Gothic and Renaissance bookcase, chests, doors, chairs, etc. in public Hungarian collections.

6. PERMANENT COLLECTIONS

Budapest

IPARMÜVÉSZETI MÚZEUM

2111   VADÁSZI, ERZSÉBET. "Ungarische Kastentische." *Ars decorativa* 4 (1976):7-31, 28 b&w figs.

A Hungarian chest table of ca. 1500 with stylized decoration motifs in the collection.

Church Furniture

6. PERMANENT COLLECTIONS

Budapest

IPARMÜVÉSZETI MÚZEUM

2112   VADÁSZI, ERZSÉBET. "La Stalle de Gölnicbánya." *Ars decorativa* 6 (1979):47-70, 21 b&w figs.

Late 15th-century choir stalls from the parish church of Gölnicbánya now in the museum.

ITALIAN

Secular and Church Furniture

3. SURVEYS AND HISTORIES

Books

2113   ALBERICI, CLELIA. *Il mobile lombardo.* Mobili regionali italiani. Milan: Görlich, 1969. 264 pp., 28 color figs., 340 b&w figs.
Furniture in Lombardy. Pertinent to the 15th-16th century are chests (with painted, carved, or intarsia decoration), wardrobe, cabinets, tables, beds, a crib frame with gesso decoration, many in private and public Milan collections.

2114   ALBERICI, CLELIA. *Il mobile veneto.* Milan: Electa, 1980. 341 pp., 50 color pls., 441 b&w illus.
Survey of Venetian furniture of the 14th-19th century with emphasis on historical context. Includes (pp. 10-93) 15th- and 16th-century choir stalls, storage cabinets, altar frontals, cassoni, credenze, tables, chairs, beds, boxes, bookcases, architectural decoration, musical intruments, and assorted objects.

2115   BACCHESCHI, EDI. *Mobili italiani del Rinascimento.* Milan: Görlich, 1964. 131 pp. of 6 color figs., 165 b&w figs.
Pictorial survey of Italian Renaissance furniture, arranged according to types (cassoni and cassapanche, choir stalls, chairs, credenze, wardrobes and cupboards, beds, doors, miscellaneous) with short captions.

2116   BANDERA, LUISA. *Il mobile emiliano.* Mobili regionali italiani. Milan: Görlich, 1972. 202 pp., 7 color figs., 284 b&w figs.
Furniture of Emilia. Pertinent to the 15th-16th century are chests, doors, cabinets, bed, and wardrobes, as well as choir stalls and intarsia paneling in Modena, Parma, and Bologna.

2117   BOCK, ELFRIED. *Florentinische und venezianische Bilderrahmen aus der Zeit der Gotik und Renaissance.* Munich: F. Bruckmann, 1902. 144 pp., 103 b&w figs.
Classic study devoted to frames of Florentine and Venetian devotional panels and reliefs of the 14th-16th century.

2118   CERA, MAURIZIO. *Il mobile italiano dal XVI al XIX secolo: Gli stili, le forme, il mercato.* Milan: Longanesi & C., 1983. 293 pp., 550 b&w figs.
Pictorial presentation with brief captions of Italian cassoni, credenze, prie-dieu, tables, chairs, cabinet, frame, including a number of the 16th century, recently sold at auction. Hammer price provided for each piece.

2119   COLOMBO, SILVANO. *L'arte del legno e del mobile in Italia: Mobili, rivestimenti, decorazioni, tarsie dal medievo al XIX secolo.* Milan: Bramante, 1981. 335 pp., 609 color and b&w figs.

Survey, through generally excellent photographs, of Italian choir stalls and room paneling (Part 1) and furniture (Part 2) from medieval times through the 19th century. The essay of Part 2 is a reprint of the author's *L'arte del mobile in Italia* (see entry 2130), while the body of illustration of part 2 is larger and very often different. Figs. 23-98, 155-298, reproducing examples in public and private Italian collections, deal with the period 1450-1600. Six-page glossary.

2120   DEL PUGLIA, RAFFAELLA, and STEINER, CARLO. *Mobili e ambienti italiani dal Gotico al Floreale.* Vol. 1. Milan: Bramante, 1963. 98 pp., 65 color figs., 251 b&w figs.
        Italian furniture from the Gothic to the 17th century. Chapters on Gothic (pp. 13-23) and Renaissance (23-40) periods are well illustrated with cassoni, chairs, tables, cupboards, stalls, beds, and period rooms in public and private Italian collections. Includes lengthy descriptions underlining stylistic characteristics, types, origin, intended placement, and purpose.

2121   EBERLEIN, HAROLD DONALDSON. *Interiors, Fireplaces and Furniture of the Italian Renaissance.* New York: Architectural Book Publishing Co., 1916. 12 pp., 82 b&w pls.
        Twelve-page text with general overview of the Renaissance interior. Useful for illustrations of doorways, fountains, period rooms (secular and ecclesiastical), fireplaces, chairs, lecterns, stools, tables, desks, wardrobes, choir stalls, frames, door-knockers, candelabra, pulpits, etc., with very brief captions, however.

2122   MIOTTI, TITO. *Il mobile friulano.* Mobili regionali italiani. Milan: Görlich, 1970. 168 pp., 18 color figs., 150 b&w figs.
        Furniture of Friuli. Pertinent to the 15th-16th century are Alpine-style examples of chests, tables, chairs, squarish tables, cabinets from Udine, Tolmezzo, Gorzia, etc.; also church chests and stalls (Montalbano, Venzone, etc.)

2123   PIGNATTI, TERISIO. *Mobili italiani del Rinascimento.* Milan: Vallardi, 1961. 111 pp., 6 color pls., 177 b&w figs.
        Well-illustrated, general survey of Italian furniture of the 15th and 16th century.

2124   QUAGLINO, ELIO. *Il Piemonte: Mobili e ambienti dal XV all'inizio del XIX secolo.* Mobili regionali italiani. Milan: Görlich, 1966. 184 pp., 15 color pls., numerous b&w figs.
        Furniture of Piedmont. Pertinent to the 15th-16th century are credenze, chairs, tables, sacristy chest of Aosta's cathedral, carved chests, doors, room paneling, many of the best examples being in the Museo Civico, Turin.

2125   TERNI DE GREGORY, W. *Vecchi mobili italiani: Tipi in uso dal secolo XV al secolo XX.* Milan: Antonio Vallardi, 1960. 213 pp., 6 color pls., 12 b&w pls., 158 b&w figs., 32 pls. of line drawings.
        Various furniture types in use in Italy from the 15th to the 20th century. Particularly useful for the plates of line drawings and diagrams classifying methods of assembling furniture elements, types of ironwork used for assemblage, forms of each furniture type, decorative motifs, border types, leg types, drawers, handles, etc.

2126   TINTI, MARIO. *Il mobilio fiorentino.* Milan-Rome: Casa Editrice d'Arte Bestetti e Tumminelli, n.d. 78 pp., 320 b&w pls.

Florentine furniture mainly of the 15th-16th century. Text (pp. 7-70) deals with stylistic evolution, technique (carving and intarsia), principal makers of the 15th-19th century and their known works, types of furniture, followed by eight pages of entries for the plates, which include lecterns, ecclesiastical and library stalls, wardrobes, cassoni, cupboards, doors, architectural decoration, candelabra, beds, chairs, tables, and desks.

2127   TRIONFI HONORATI, MADDALENA. *Il mobile marchigiano.* Mobili regionali italiani. Milan: Görlich, 1971. 148 pp., 13 color figs., 207 b&w figs.
        Furniture of the Marches. Pertinent to the 15th-16th century are choir stalls and sacristy chests in various cathedrals, benches, tables, intarsia panels in the Palace of Urbino, a carved ceiling in Ascoli.

Article

2128   VENTURI, ADOLFO. "L'arte dell'intaglio e della tarsia a Ferrara nella fine del Quattrocento." *L'arte* 19 (1916):55- 57.
        The activity of the cabinetmakers Belfiore, Bartolomeo Spadari, Pietro de Rechardo, Cristoforo and Lorenzo da Lendinara, Iacomo di Dona Bona, and others creating intarsia works in late 15th-century Ferrara.

Secular Furniture

3. SURVEYS AND HISTORIES

Books

2129   BODE, WILHELM VON. *Italian Renaissance Furniture.* Translated by Mary E. Herrick. New York: William Helburn, 1921. 48 pp., 130 b&w figs. on 71 pls.
        Cassoni, caskets, benches, chairs, stools, tables, cabinets, pedestals, mirror frames with emphasis on regional characteristics, forms, and craftsmanship: Florence and Tuscany (pp. 7-26), Venice (27-40), Northwest Italy (41-43), Rome and Naples (44-47).

2130   COLOMBO, SILVANO. *L'arte del mobile in Italia.* Milan: Bramante, 1975. 246 pp., 81 color figs., 263 b&w figs.
        Pictorial survey, through generally excellent photographs, of Italian furniture from medieval times through the 19th century. Twenty-five-page essay composed of reflections on the subjects, followed by illustrations of 344 furniture pieces, each accompanied by a short entry: nos. 1-107, 109-13 date of the 15th-16th century.

2131   FAENSON, LIUBOV, ed. *Italian Cassoni from the Art Collections of Soviet Museums,* with entries by Faenson and five other contributors. Translated by Arthur Shkarovsky-Raffé. Leningrad: Aurora Art Publishers, 1983. 243 pp., 81 color pls., 177 b&w illus.
        Catalog of forty-nine examples — representative of all types of decorative carving, painting, gilding, and gesso work — mostly from the large collection of cassoni from the Hermitage but also from museums in Moscow, Kiev, Lvov, Sarotov, and Yaroslavl, all abundantly illustrated. Arranged by region (Florence/Siena, Venice and northern Italy, and Rome), and preceded by a seventeen-page introduction dealing with history, usage, decoration, and evolution.

2132 FERRARI, GIULIO. *Il legno e la mobilia nell'arte italiana: La grande scultura e la mobilia della casa.* 2d enl. ed. Milan: Ulrico Hoepli, n.d. 38 pp., 6 color pls., 344 b&w pls.

Pictorial compendium on Italian woodwork and furniture from the 11th to the 18th century, many examples dating of the period 1400-1600, including choir stalls, benches, doors, bookrests, ceilings, crucifixes, candelabra, organs, cassoni, tables, cassapanche, chairs, and frames. Cursory captions. Superior illustrations in the first (1909?) edition.

2133 GHELARDINI, ARMANDO. *Il mobile italiano dal Medioevo all'Ottocento.* Milan: Bramante, 1970. Unpaginated, 126 color figs., 437 b&w figs.

Useful photographic survey of Italian furniture organized by types. Relevant to the period 1400-1600 are: cassoni, money and bread chests (painted, carved, intarsiated), credenze, chests (cassettoni), tables, desks, wardrobes, doors, cabinets, beds, chairs, most of which are in private Italian collections.

2134 LIZZANI, GOFFREDO. *Il mobile romano. Mobili regionali italiani.* Introduction by Alvar Gonzalez Palacios. Milan: Görlich, 1970. 210 pp., 8 color figs., 359 b&w figs.

Furniture of Rome. Pertinent to the 16th century are mannerist tables, the Farnese marble table by Guglielmo della Porta, and carved chests.

2135 MARIACHER, GIOVANNI. *Specchiere italiane e cornici da specchio, dal XV al XIX secolo.* Milan: Görlich, 1963. 30 pp., 8 color pls., 150 b&w figs.

Italian mirrors from the 15th to the 19th century, mostly 18th-century examples but some dating of the 15th and 16th century (see pp. 10-13 and pls. 2-7) from public and private collections. Brief but informative introduction on woods, styles, and the particular place of mirrors in relation to other furnishings.

2136 MORAZZONI, GIUSEPPE. *Il mobile genovese.* Milan: Edizioni Luigi Alfieri, 1949. 117 pp., 124 b&w pls.

Genoese furniture from the 15th to the 19th century. Pp. 1-29 deal with the Quattro- and Cinquecento: historical circumstances, development of styles, influences, major Genoese families, artists, appurtenances of Genoese interiors (fabrics and tapestries, gilded leather, etc.). Pls. I-XIX (figs. 3-50), each accompanied by a descriptive notice, are of 15th-16th- century chairs, cassetoni, chests, tables, and cupboards, from private (mostly) and public Italian collections.

2137 ODOM, WILLIAM M. *A History of Italian Furniture from the Fourteenth to the Early Nineteenth Centuries.* Vol. 1. Garden City, N.Y.: Doubleday Page & Co., 1918. 354 pp., 352 b&w figs.

Vol. 1 deals with the period 1400-1600. Comprehensive, if somewhat outdated, most-ly useful for illustration of generally major pieces, many from the Bardini Collection in Florence.

2138 PEDRINI, AUGUSTO. *Italian Furniture: Interiors and Decorations of the Fifteenth and Sixteenth Centuries.* 2d rev. ed. London: A. Tiranti, 1949. Forward by Mario Ceradini. 30 pp., 256 b&w pls. (English ed. of *L'ambiente, il mobilio e le decorazioni del Rinascimento in Italia,* Turin: Casa Editrice Itala Ars, 1925.)

Pictorial corpus of Italian furnishings and interiors including fresco and ceiling decoration, doorways, mirrors, andirons, small bronzes, etc. in addition to actual furniture. Brief caption for each illustration, with measurements, former collections for some in a four-page index.

2139   SCHOTTMÜLLER, FRIDA. *Furniture and Interior Design of the Italian Renaissance.*
        2d rev. ed. New York: B. Westerman, 1928. 286 pp., among which 238 pls. (588 b&w
        figs.) (1st English ed. New York: Brentano's, 1921, of *Wohnungskulptur und Möbel der
        italienischen Renaissance,* Stuttgart: Julius Hoffman, 1921, 246 pp., 590 b&w figs.)
            Text (28 pp.) deals with furniture of the Italian home and touches on church and
        shop furnishings; examines construction methods and materials and woodwork decoration;
        surveys Renaissance coffers, cassapanche, cupboards, bedsteads, tables, chairs, benches, stall
        library desks, stands, wall brackets, fireplaces, frames, etc. Brief catalog entries for each of
        the illustrations. Still a very useful source survey.

2140   SCHUBRING, PAUL. *Cassoni: Truhen und Truhenbilder der italienischen Frührenais-
        sance.* 2 vols. and a supplement. Vol. 1 (1915), 479 pp., 46 b&w figs.; vol. 2 (1915), 10
        pp., 889 b&w figs.; supplement (1923), 6 pp., 4 color figs., 55 b&w figs. Leipzig: Karl W.
        Heirsemann.
            Still standard if somewhat dated study of Renaissance marriage chests. Vol. 1: text
        deals with their origins, interior placement, types and uses, decoration, literary references,
        masters and scenes; catalog (chronologically and geographically arranged) of 893 examples;
        vol. 2: plates. Supplemental volume includes catalog and illustration of fifty-one additional
        cassoni.

Articles

2141   BELLOSI, LUCIANO. "Ipotesi sull'origine delle terracotte quattrocentesche," In *Jacopo
        della Quercia fra Gotico e Rinascimento—Krautheimer Festschrift* (Atti del convegno di
        studi, Siena, 1975), edited by Giulietta Chelazzi Dini. Florence: Centro Di, 1977. Pp. 163-
        68, 27 b&w figs.
            On the basis of style, compares the panels of a cassone and a terra cotta relief of the
        Virgin and Child in the Victoria and Albert Museum and another Virgin and Child relief
        formerly in a private Berlin collection to the early works of Donatello, ca. 1410.

2142   CECCHI, ALESSANDRO. "Les Cadres ronds de la Renaissance florentine." Translated
        by Nadine Blamoutier. *Revue de l'art* 76 (1987):21-24, color cover, 9 b&w figs.
            Note on the stylistic evolution of frames made for circular pictures in Florence
        during the second half of the 15th century: activity of the workshops of Giuliano da Maiano,
        Del Tasso and Lorenzo Donati.

2143   CHELES, LUCIANO. "The Inlaid Decorations of Federico da Montefeltro's Urbino
        Studiolo: An Iconographic Study," *Mitteilungen des kunsthistorischen Institutes in Florenz*
        26 (1982):1-46, 35 b&w figs.
            Major example of late 15th-century inlay marquetry representing figures, animals,
        and objects with illusionistic effects, attributed to Baccio Pontelli. Primarily discussed are the
        symbolic meaning and iconography of the program and how these relate to the patron.

2144   GONZÁLEZ-PALACIOS, ALVAR. "Giovanni Battista de Curtis, Iacobo Fiamengo e lo
        stipo manierista napoletano." *Antologia di belle arti* 6 (1978):136-48, 24 b&w figs.
            Production in Naples during the late 16th and early 17th century of large ebony
        cabinets profusely decorated with engraved ivory plaques by a group of highly specialized
        craftsmen headed by the local Giovanni Battista de Curtis.

2145   HILDBURGH, W.L. "Some Italian Renaissance Caskets with Pastiglia Decoration." *An-
        tiquaries Journal* 26 (1946):123- 37, 14 b&w figs.

Description of Renaissance boxes in London with a "gesso" applied decoration suggested to have been produced in Perugia by makers of wafering-irons.

2146 MATHER, FRANK JEWETT. "Some Carved Chests of the High Renaissance." *Burlington Magazine* 24 (1913-14):69-74, 1 b&w pl.

Three richly carved chests in private New York collections, one, with the story of the slaughter of Niobe's children, said to be signed by Baccio Bandinelli and dated 1536; examination of iconographic sources.

2147 NICKEL, HELMUT. "Two Falcon Devices of the Strozzi: An Attempt at Interpretation." *Metropolitan Museum Journal* 9 (1974):229-32, 5 b&w figs.

Florentine furniture of the second half of the 15th century bearing the badge of Filippo Strozzi.

2148 WINTER, PATRICK M. DE. "A Little-Known Creation of Renaissance Decorative Arts: The White Lead Pastiglia Box." *Saggi e memorie di storia dell'arte* 14 (1984):9-42, 103-31, 72 b&w figs.

Study of the material, methods of production, and relationship with prints, small bronzes, etc. of these examples typical of Cinquecento culture and its craving for objects "all'antica." Catalog of 115 caskets in European and U.S. collections, with attributions to seven Venetian workshops. (See also entry 213 with addenda.)

6. PERMANENT COLLECTIONS

Florence

MUSEO DEGLI ARGENTI

2149 PIACENTI, KIRSTEN ASCHENGREEN. "Un tavolo granducale del Cinquecento." In *Le arti del principato mediceo,* Florence: Studio per Edizioni Scelte, 1980. Pp. 365-69, 6 b&w figs.

Table with base shaped as sphinxes recorded in 1574 to have been in the bedroom of Cosimo I at the Pitti, was executed ca. 1574 by the master carpenter Dionigi Nigetti.

PALAZZO DAVANZATI

2150 REDDIE, ARTHUR. "Italian Furniture from the Palazzo Davanzati." *Old Furniture* 3 (1928): part 1, "Tables", 92-100, 9 b&w figs.; part 2, "Chairs", 153-60, 10 b&w figs. *Old Furniture* 5 (1928): part 3, "Chairs", 54-60, 12 b&w figs.; part 4, "Chests", 217-25, 9 b&w figs. *Old Furniture* 6 (1929): part 5, "Chests" (cont.), 28-32, 9 b&w figs.; part 6, "Beds", 214-18, 5 b&w figs. *Old Furniture* 7 (1929): part 7, "Ironwork", 112- 17, 7 b&w figs.; part 8, "Ironwork" (cont.), 215-21, 13 b&w figs.

Somewhat general but useful essays on Italian furniture as exemplified in the famed Davanzati palace: (1) table construction of the Cinquecento from several regions of Italy; (2) types of 16th-century chairs; (3) mostly 16th-century armchairs from Tuscany and Lombardy with leather, embroidery, or tapestry upholstery; (4) and (5) function and style of 15th-16th-century chests; (6) bedsteads evolved from the cassapanca, canopied beds, and beds with footboards; (7) and (8) wrought iron andirons, candelabra, grilles, stands.

London

VICTORIA AND ALBERT MUSEUM

2151   JERVIS, SIMON, and BAARSEN, REINIER. "An Ebony and Ivory Cabinet." *V&A Album* 4 (1985):49-56, 8 color figs., 1 b&w fig.
   Fanciful ebony and ivory furniture fashionable at the courts of Henri III of France and those of Florence and Mantua of the 16th century, exemplified by a cabinet made in Naples ca. 1600 and now in the museum. To this piece can be related a group of ten others commissioned by Spanish courtiers and high-ranking Italian nobility.

Milan

CIVICHE RACCOLTE DI ARTE APPLICATA – CASTELLO SFORZESCO

2152   VICENZI, CARLO. "Mobili lombardi del Quattrocento nei Musei del Castello Sforzesco di Milano." *Dedalo* 3 (1922):482-501, 21 b&w figs.
   General characteristics of Lombard furniture of the 15th-16th century as represented by primary examples in the collection. Includes cassoni, caskets, sideboards, and chairs decorated in various techniques such as intarsia, painting, leather covering, and wrought iron.

Munich

ALTE PINAKOTHEK

2153   *Italienische Bilderrahmen des 14.-18. Jahrhunderts.* Exhibition catalog by Leo Cramer and Peter Eikemeier. Munich: Alte Pinakothek, 1976. 68 pp., 79 b&w figs.
   Unusual catalog devoted to sixty-nine Italian picture frames produced from ca. 1400 until the 19th century. Describes wood construction elements, carvings. Some details are reproduced.

Urbino

PALAZZO DUCALE

2154   VENTURI, LIONELLO. "Studi sul Palazzo Ducale di Urbino." *L'arte* 17 (1914):415-73, 47 b&w figs.
   Sculptural decoration of the Palace of Urbino by Francesco Laurana, Francesco di Simone, and Gian Cristoforo Romano; intarsia panels of the Cardinal Virtues, etc. executed by Baccio Pontelli on the designs of Francesco di Giorgio for the studiolo of Federico da Montefeltro.

7. EXHIBITION CATALOGS

Genoa

PALAZZO BIANCO

2155 *Civiltà del legno: Mobili dalle collezioni di Palazzo Bianco e del Museo degli Ospedali di S. Martino.* Exhibition catalog edited by Clelia Alberici, with essays and entries by six contributors. Genoa: Sagep, 1985. 113 pp., 12 color pls., 107 b&w figs.

Essays on the collections of Palazzo Bianco, Genoa, and of the city's hospitals, from which the furniture of this exhibition were borrowed; on the art and craft guilds from the 11th to the 18th century; and on furniture restoration. Detailed entries for twenty objects dating from the 15th to the 19th century, each accompanied by notes on its restoration and an essay on the development of that particular type of furniture. For the 15th-16th century, see pp. 28-45, cat. nos. 1-5: cassoni and cupboards.

Milan

NOVA TRIENNALE D'ARTE DECORATIVA

2156 RAGGHIANTI, LICIA COLLOBI. *La sedia italiana nei secoli.* Catalog of exhibition organized by Milan's Triennial of Decorative Arts. Milan: Centro Studi della Triennale, 1951. 223 pp., 160 b&w figs.

Useful anthology of the Italian chair from ancient times through the 18th century. Each example illustrated (from public/private Italian collections) is discussed in a short paragraph with bibliography; pp. 32-89 deal with 15th-16th-century types.

8. PRIVATE COLLECTION, AUCTION, AND DEALER CATALOGS

ACTON COLLECTION

2157 TRIONFI HONORATI, MADDALENA. "Mobili del Rinascimento toscano nella raccolta Acton a 'La Pietra.'" *Antichità viva* 8, no. 1 (1969):40-53, 2 color figs., 15 b&w figs.

Excellent examples of Tuscan furniture of the Quattro- and Cinquecento in the villa "La Pietra" outside Florence.

Church Furniture

3. SURVEYS AND HISTORIES

Book

2158 PERRICCIOLI, ALESSANDRA. *L'arte del legno in Irpinia dal XVI al XVIII secolo.* Naples: Società Editrice Napoletana, 1975. 196 pp., 11 color pls., 38 b&w pls.

Woodcarvings from the 16th through 18th century in churches and convents of the region outlying Avellino and Benevento. Includes 16th-century stalls, doors, paneling, sacristy furniture. Useful catalog of this little-known material.

XXXVIII. Furniture

Articles

2159   GRASSI, MARIA GIUSTINA. "Gli arredi lignei e l'intaglio negli edifici religiosi di Mantova e del Mantovano." *Arte lombarda* 42/43 (1975):97-112, 31 b&w figs.
        Church furniture and woodcarvings, mostly of the 16th century, in the churches of Mantua and its immediate surroundings: sacristy cabinets, chests, etc. with woodcarvings and intarsia; also wood sculpture, particularly that of Clemente Zamara.

2160   TRIONFI HONORATI, MADDALENA. "Note sui maestri legnaioli." In *Le arti del principato mediceo*. Florence: Studio per Edizioni Scelte, 1980. Pp. 371-82, 6 b&w figs.
        Activity of the cabinet makers in Florence (mostly) of the second half of the 16th century, Battista Botticelli and Dionigi Nigetti (ciborium in Santa Croce, cabinet in the sacristy of S. Maria Novella); Il Crocino who produced the benches for the Laurenziana, etc., based on the documentation published by M.B. Hall in *Renovation and Counter-Reformation; Vasari and Duke Cosimo in Sta Maria Novella and Sta Croce* (Oxford, 1979).

6. PERMANENT COLLECTIONS

Bologna

SAN DOMENICO

2161   ALCE, P. VENTURINO. *Il coro di San Domenico in Bologna*. Edited and with introduction by Renzo Renzi. Bologna: Edizioni L. Parma, 1969. 338 pp., 31 color pls., numerous b&w pls.
        Large series of intarsia panels of the choir stalls executed by Fra Damiano da Bergamo between 1542-1548. Also touches on other art works in this church.

Ferrara

CATTEDRALE

2162   FRISONI, FIORELLA. "Il coro ligneo della Cattedrale di Ferrara." In *La Cattedrale di Ferrara (Atti del convegno nazionale di studi storici)*. Ferrara: Belriguardo, 1979. Pp. 537-58, 11 b&w figs.
        The intarsia panels in the choir, the major production of Bernardino da Lendinara and collaborators, were executed between 1501 and 1546, much of the iconography being related to local monuments.

Florence

S. MARIA DEL FIORE

2163   GILLI, ROSSELLA. "Proposte per Maso Finiguerra: Le tarsie della Sacrestia delle Messe in Santa Maria del Fiore a Firenze." *Antichità viva* 19, no. 6 (1980):32-40, 18 b&w figs. English summary.
        Reinterpretation of the documents and literature dealing with Maso Finiguerra as draftsman and engraver as well as designer of the intarsia panels executed by Giuliano da Maiano and his workshop, and placed on the rear wall of the Sacrestia delle Messe in Florence's cathedral.

2164 HAINES, MARGARET. *The "Sacrestia delle Messe" of the Florentine Cathedral.* Florence: Cassa di Risparmio di Firenze, 1983. 336 pp., 48 color pls., 134 b&w figs.

In-depth study of the series of intarsia panels lining the north sacristy that were restored in the 1970s. These outstanding works were produced (from about 1436 to about 1475) by various Florentine workshops. They are examined and compared in terms of technique, condition, commissions, authorship, style, and iconography. Concludes with transcription of pertinent archival documents.

Modena

DUOMO

2165 MEZZETTI, AMALIA, and CAPRARA, OTELLO. *Il coro del duomo di Modena restaurato.* Modena: Soprintendenza alle Gallerie per le Province di Modena e Reggio Emilia, 1972. 62 pp., 42 b&w figs.

Restoration of the intarsia panels with representations of saints and trompe l'oeil forms of the choir stalls of Modena's cathedral. These are signed by the brothers Lorenzo and Cristoforo Canozi da Lendinara and dated 1466.

Spilimbergo

DUOMO

2166 FERRETTI, MASSIMO. "Il coro di Marco Cozzi." In *Il Duomo di Spilimbergo 1284-1984.* Edited by Caterina Furlan and Italo Zannier. Spilimbergo: Commune, [1985]. Pp. 254-74, 2 color pls., 32 b&w figs.

Carved and intarsiated choir stalls, lecterns of 1475-77 by Marco di Giampietro Cozzi in this edifice and also elsewhere in North Italy in the Friuli and Veneto.

Swaffham Bulbeck, Cambridgeshire

ST. MARY'S CHURCH

2167 WALSTON, FLORENCE. "The Swaffham Bulbeck Chest." *Collector* 10 (1930):152-57, 6 b&w figs.

15th-century North Italian wooden chest in a church near Cambridge is decorated with religious scenes in stippling technique.

Todi

DUOMO

2168 RIGHETTI, MARINA. *Le tarsie di Todi.* Milan: Franco Maria Ricci, 1978. 13 pp., 22 color pls.

Brief presentation of the choir stalls with intarsia work of 1530.

Venice

S. STEFANO

2169   STEFANI, F. "Il vero autore del coro di Santo Stefano a Venezia." *Archivio veneto* 29 (1885):193-96.
Carved choir stalls, late work of Marco di Giampietro Cozzi of Vicenza (died 1485), completed by his nephew(?) Marco da Vicenza.

Verona

S. MARIA IN ORGANO

2170   ROGNINI, LUCIANO. *Tarsie e intaglie di Fra Giovanni a Santa Maria in Organo di Verona.* Verona: Centro per la Formazione Professionale Grafica, 1985. 130 pp., 45 color pls., numerous b&w illus.
Complete pictorial presentation of the intarsia work and reliefs of the choir stalls produced between 1491 and 1499 by Fra Giovanni da Verona, including landscapes, still lifes, and religious subjects.

NETHERLANDISH

Secular Furniture

3. SURVEYS AND HISTORIES

2171   SLUYTERMAN, K. *Huisraad en binnenhuis in Nederland in vroegere eeuwen.* The Hague: Martinus Nijhoff, 1947. 355 pp., 470 b&w figs.
Concise history of the development of household furniture in Holland from the late Gothic to the early 20th century. Pp. 1-67 (with 74 illustrations) outline the characteristics of the Dutch interior during the period 1400-1600.

6. PERMANENT COLLECTIONS

Amsterdam

RIJKSMUSEUM

2172   *Hollaendische moebel im Niederlaendischen museum zu Amsterdam,* by Willem Vogelsang. Amsterdam: Scheltema & Holkema, 1909. 56 pp., 64 b&w pls. comprising 212 figs.
Dutch furniture in the permanent collection. A photographic survey preceded by a forty-six-page introduction and eight pages of captions (giving point of origin and cabinet-maker when known). Includes major examples of late Gothic and Renaissance doors, chimneys, cabinets, chests, beds, credenze, panelings, etc.

Glasgow

GLASGOW MUSEUMS AND ART GALLERIES – BURRELL COLLECTION

2173 WENTZEL, HANS. "Ein Christkindbettchen in Glasgow: Addenda aus der Burrell Collection." *Pantheon* 20 (1962):1- 7, 4 b&w figs. English summary.
Study of 15th-century Christ Child cradles: a highly ornamented 15th-century oak bed representing the Pietà and St. Martin, probably of Dutch origin.

Church Furniture

6. PERMANENT COLLECTIONS

Amsterdam

OUDE KERK

2174 VERSPAANDONK, J.A.J.M. *Misericorde-reeks: Amsterdam de koorbanken van de Oude Kerk.* Amsterdam: Buitjen & Schipperheijn; Alphen aan den Rijn: Repro Holland, 1984. 103 pp., 35 b&w figs. Dutch/French/German/English text.
Choir stalls with misericords, several with satirical subjects, partially dating of the 15th-16th century.

Bolsward

MARTINKERK

2175 VERSPAANDONK, J.A.J.M. *Misericorde-reeks: Bolsward de Martinkerk.* Amsterdam: Buitjen & Schipperheijn; Alphen aan den Rijn: Repro Holland, 1974. 159 pp., 54 b&w figs. Dutch/French/German/English text.
Choir stalls with misericords depicting subjects from the New Testament, lives of the saints, and grotesques, partially dating of the 15th-16th century.

Breda

VROUWEKERK

2176 VERSPAANDONK, J.A.J.M. *Misericorde-reeks: Breda de koorbanken van de grote of lieve Vrouwekerk.* Amsterdam: Buitjen & Schipperheijn; Alphen aan den Rijn: Repro Holland, 1983. 176 pp., 94 b&w figs. Dutch/French/German/English text.
Choir stalls with misericords, often with lively subjects and some illustrating proverbs, partially dating of the 15th-16th century.

Haarlem

SINT BAVOKERK

2177 VERSPAANDONK, J.A.J.M. *Misericorde-reeks: Haarlem, de grote of Sint Bavokerk.* Amsterdam: Buitjen & Schipperheijn; [Alphen aan den Rijn]: Repro Holland, 1972. 159 pp., 98 b&w figs. Dutch/English text.

Twenty-seven carved choir stalls produced in 1512 and shortly thereafter by Jaspar Piertersz. Some later additions.

London

VICTORIA AND ALBERT MUSEUM

2178   VERSPAANDONK, J.A.J.M. "Laatgotische Zuidnederlandse misericorden in het Victoria & Albert Museum te Londen." *Antiek* 21 (1986):12-21, 38 b&w figs.
Choir stalls of ca. 1435-50 from the South Netherlands in the museum, compared with examples in Louvain, Diest, and Breda.

PORTUGUESE

Secular Furniture

3. SURVEYS AND HISTORIES

2179   GUIMARÃES, ALFREDO, and SARDOEIRA, ALBANO. *Mobiliário artistico português (elementos para a sua história).* 2 vols. Porto: M. Abreu, 1924-25. 227 b&w pls., 112 b&w figs.
Scholarly history of Portuguese furniture from the Middle Ages to the end of the 19th century.

2180   PINTO, AUGUSTO CARDOSO. *Cadeiras portuguesas.* Lisbon: A.C. Pinto & J.F. Da Silva Nascimento, 1952. 119 pp., 4 color pls., 128 b&w pls.
Portuguese chairs from medieval times through the 19th century. General characteristics of those dating to the period 1400-1600 are discussed within pp. 35-50 and illustrated figs. 1-3 and in reproductions of five paintings and a sculpture.

6. PERMANENT COLLECTIONS

Lisbon

MUSEU NACIONAL DE ARTE ANTIGA

2181   *Artes decorativas portuguesas no Museo Nacional de Arté Antiga, séculos XV-XVIII.* Catalog contributions by Maria Helena Mendes Pinto, Marià Fernanda Passos Leite, and Carlos V. da Silva Barros. Lisbon: Museu Nacional, 1979. 236 pp., 6 color pls., 175 b&w figs.
175 examples of Portuguese furniture, iron work, textiles, silver, and glass. Deals predominantly with later period, but includes some examples of 15th- and 16th-century furniture (chairs, cabinets, credenze, caskets), all from the permanent collection.

SCANDINAVIA
(DANISH, SWEDISH, AND NORWEGIAN)

Secular and Church Furniture

7. EXHIBITION CATALOGS

Bergen

VESTLANDSKE KUNSTINDUSTRIMUSEUM

2182   *Norske møbler i fortid og nåtid: Middelalder 1100-1600, nåtid 1940-1967.* Exhibition catalog by Peter Anker, Alf Boe, and Inger Kjaer. Translated by Toni Ramholt. [Bergen: Vestlandske Kunstindustrimuseum, 1986.] 63 pp., 105 b&w pls. English summary and captions.

Sixty-three pieces of Norwegian furniture from ca. 1100- 1600 and forty-four modern examples of the period 1940-67. For the early period, deals with domestic and church examples: chairs and benches, chests and cupboards, tables. Cat. nos. 5, 13, 18, 23, 26-29, 31, 34, 39-41, 48-56, 58-60, 63 are bracketed in the years 1400-1600.

Secular Furniture

3. SURVEYS AND HISTORIES

2183   CLEMMENSEN, TOVE. *Danske møbler. Stiludviklingen fra Renaessance til klunketid.* Copenhagen: Thaning & Appels, 1945. 95 pp., 44 b&w figs.

Cursory survey of Danish furniture. Pp. 5-15, which include six illustrations, deal with the Renaissance period.

2184   WAAGEPETERSEN, CHRISTIAN. *Danske møbler for 1848: Typerne i billeder.* Copenhagen: Forum, 1980. 484 pp., 658 figs.

Comprehensive study of Danish furniture from the Middle Ages to 1848.

6. PERMANENT COLLECTIONS

Stockholm

NORDISKA MUSEETS

2185   *Nordiska Museets möbler från Svenska herremanshem.* 3 vols. Vol. 1, *1500- och 1600-talen, vasatiden och den karolinska tiden Renässans och Barock,* by Sigurd Wallin. Stockholm: Nordiska Museets Förlag, 1931. 229 pp., 6 color pls., 342 b&w figs.

Swedish furniture in the collection of the museum. Volume comprehensively examines examples of the period 1500 to somewhat beyond 1600. Twenty-six-page introduction followed by reproduction of cabinets, often with inlay, chest, beds, chairs.

SPANISH

Secular Furniture

3. SURVEYS AND HISTORIES

Books

2186 BACCHESCHI, EDI. *Mobili spagnoli.* Milan: Görlich, 1965. 131 pp., 6 color pls., 165 b&w figs.
Introduction to Spanish furniture of the 14th-19th century. One-page introduction followed by plates with captions arranged chronologically reproducing 15th-16th-century chests, cassoni, storage cupboards, chairs, desks, tables, and period rooms (pp. 10-32).

2187 BURR, GRACE HARDENDORFF. *Hispanic Furniture from the Fifteenth through the Eighteenth Century.* New York: Archive Press, 1964. 231 pp., 203 b&w figs. (1st ed. 1941.)
This very useful survey, one of the few in English, includes 15th-century Gothic (pp. 1-18) and 16th-century Renaissance (19-40) pieces presented for their design, construction, decoration, and within economic factors of their period. Illustrated are beds, benches, cabinets, chairs, chests, coffrets, desks, interiors, tables, wardrobes, and miscellaneous pieces from Spanish, English, and U.S. collections.

2188 DOMENÉCH (GALISSÁ), RAFAEL, and BUENO, LUIS PÉREZ. *Antique Spanish Furniture. Muebles antiguos españoles.* Translated by Grace Hardendorff Burr. New York: Archive Press, 1965. 142 pp., 60 b&w pls. English/Spanish text.
Six-page general introduction on techniques of Spanish furniture-making and its main characteristics followed by somewhat murky plates, accompanied by captions: several 16th-century chairs, chests (some with ivory inlays), elaborate vargueños, desks, in Spanish museums and private collections.

Articles

2189 AGUILÓ, MARÍA PAZ. "Muebles catalanes del primer tercio del siglo XVI." *Archivo español de arte* 47 (1974):249-71. 35 b&w illus.
Catalan chests and wardrobes of the early 16th century and their carved and painted decoration. Includes a catalog of thirty-one pieces, each illustrated.

2190 TRAMOYERES BLASCO, LUIS. "Los artesonados de la antigua casa municipal de Valencia: Notas para la historia de la escultura decorativa en España." *Archivo de arte valenciano* 3 (1917):31-71, 48 b&w figs.
Carved wood paneling dating of the 14th-16th century in secular buildings of Valencia. Relationship of designs with those on azuelos, change from Gothic grotesques and geometrical designs to classical elements in Renaissance times.

2191 WILLIAMSON, G.C. "An Old Carved Spanish Chest." *Burlington Magazine* 9 (1906):412-16, 1 b&w pl.
Large walnut chest in a private collection, London, with carved scenes dealing with the surrender of the Alhambra to Ferdinand and Isabel paralleling, in iconography and style, those on the reredos in the Capilla Real of Grenada, are by extension attributed to the sculptor Felipe Vigerni while the chest is suggested to be of royal commission.

6. PERMANENT COLLECTIONS

Budapest

IPARMÜVÉSZETI MÚZEUM

2192   BATÁRI, FERENC. "Meubles espagnols du XVIe au XVIIe siècle." *Ars decorativa* 4 (1976):51-67, 11 b&w figs.
      Important Spanish Renaissance furniture in the collection including a bone encrusted arquilla from Granada, an escritorio, and a vargueño of the 16th century.

New York

HISPANIC SOCIETY OF AMERICA

2193   BURR, GRACE HARDENDORFF. *Hispanic Furniture with Examples in the Collection of the Hispanic Society of America.* New York: Hispanic Society of America, 1941. 240 pp., 175 b&w figs.
      Survey of Spanish furniture of the 15th-18th century. Chap. 1 (pp. 1-18) deals with late Gothic furniture and chap. 2 (21-39) with Renaissance furniture: chests, beds, chairs, desks, sideboards, benches, vargueños, and wood panels. Chap. 6 (117-221) is a catalog of pieces in the collection of the Hispanic Society including some 15th- and 16th-century examples (117-33).

8. PRIVATE COLLECTION, AUCTION, AND DEALER CATALOGS

BLUMENTHAL COLLECTION

2194   FALKE, OTTO VON. "Ein gotisches Lesepult." *Pantheon* 3 (1929):49, 2 b&w figs.
      A Spanish walnut reading-desk of ca. 1425 with low relief Gothic carving in the George Blumenthal Collection (New York).

Church Furniture

3. SURVEYS AND HISTORIES

Books

2195   KRAUS, DOROTHY and HENRY. *The Gothic Choirstalls of Spain.* London and New York: Routledge & Kegan Paul, 1986. 218 pp., 104 b&w figs.
      Chatty overview of 15th-16th century choirstalls in Spanish cathedrals: notes include some useful references. Illustrations are small and often murky.

2196   MATEO GOMEZ, ISABEL. *Temas profanos en la escultura gótica española: Las sillerías de coro.* Madrid: Consejo Superior de Investigaciones Científicas. Instituto Diego Velázquez, 1979. 478 pp., 397 b&w figs.
      Iconographic study of subjects found on choir stalls and most particularly misericords in Spanish churches.

Articles

2197   LAFOND, PAUL. "Andrés de Nájera." *Burlington Magazine* 20 (1911):133-39, 5 b&w figs. [on 2 pls.].
    Examines the richly carved choir stalls of the cathedral of Santo Domingo de la Calzada in Rioja and those of the monastic church of San Benito el Real in Valladolid, both produced in a mixture of Gothic and Renaissance forms by the Spanish woodcarver Andrés de Nájera (active 1517-26).

2197a   LAFOND, PAUL. "Philippe de Bourgogne (Felipe Vigarny)." *Burlington Magazine* 15 (1909):285-97, 3 b&w pls.
    Burgundian woodcarver from Langres, active in Spain ca. 1495-1543 who made choir stalls, screens, etc. for the cathedrals of Burgos, Palencia, and Toledo.

6. PERMANENT COLLECTIONS

Sarria

MONESTIR DE SANTA MARIA DE PEDRALBES

2198   *El moble Català al Monestir de Pedralbes.* Catalog by Assumpta Escudero-Josep Mainar. Barcelona: Ajuntament de Barcelona, Museu d'Art de Catalunya, 1976. 129 pp., numerous b&w figs. and line drawings.
    Catalan furniture of the 15th-17th century in the monastery: cabinets, chests, boxes, credenze, chairs, tables, etc. Introductory text describing characteristics is followed by a catalog of over 225 entries. Also includes a series of line drawings that illustrate the construction of many of the pieces.

SWISS

Secular Furniture

6. PERMANENT COLLECTIONS

Zurich

SCHWEIZERISCHES LANDESMUSEUM

2199   *Renaissance-Möbel der deutschsprachigen Schweiz um 1520 bis 1570,* by Walter Trachsler. Bern: Paul Haupt, 1959. 16 pp., 23 b&w figs.
    Twenty-three pieces of furniture (wardrobes, chests, buffets, and chairs) produced in various areas of Switzerland between 1520 and 1570.

2200   TRACHSLER, WALTER. "Eine walliser Truhe von 1449 im schweizerischen Landesmuseum." *Zeitschrift für schweizerische Archäologie und Kunstgeschichte* 28 (1971):156-74, 13 b&w illus.
    Earliest dated Swiss chest (1449) with three secret interior drawers made by a Valaisian craftsman.

Author Index

1019-20, 1115, 1185, 1199, 1238, 1258-58a, 1284, 1290, 1294, 1329-30, 1348
Middione, Roberto, 548
Migeon, Gaston, 53, 55-55a, 130, 134-34a, 534, 1683
Mihalik, Sándor, 1141
Mikhailova, O.E., 410 (ed.)
Miles, Elizabeth B., 862
Milovanović, Duśan, 1111
Milward, Clement, 1508, 1516
Miner, Dorothy E., 180, 1974
Miodońska, Barbara, 253
Miotti, Tito, 2122
Mirabella Roberti, Mario, 70
Mitchell, H.P., 865, 1021, 1127-28, 1130, 1135, 1139
Moerman, W.L., 1400
Moitinho de Almeida, Fernando, 1066
Molen, J.R. ter, 1059
Molen-den Outer, B. ter, 1059
Molinelli, Marina, 1785
Molinier, Émile, 28, 52, 138a, 138c, 167, 273, 284, 772, 1120, 1273
Molle, F. van, 1357, 1417
Möller, Lieselotte, 2104
Mondfeld, Wolfram zu, 1391
Morales, Alfredo J., 541
Morales San Martin, B., 1096
Morant, Henry de, 29
Morassi, Antonio, 230
Morazzoni, Giuseppe, 2136
Moretti, G., 1636
Morey, C.R., 293a
Morgan, Nigel J., 188
Morigi, Giovanni, 1032, 1186
Morin, Marco, 1629
Morisson, Henry, 361-62
Morley, Henry, 371
Morley-Fletcher, Hugo, 326
Moronato, Stefania, 1730
Morpurgo, Enrico, 1489
Morris, Adah V., 1701 (ed.)
Morrison, Katharyn, 184
Mory, Ludwig, 1375
Mosca, Luigi, 492
Moschetti, Andrea, 246-47
Mosel, Christel, 568 (ed.)
Mottola Molfino, Alessandra, 71, 215, 1670
Müller, Hannelore, 797, 989
Muller, Priscilla E., 755, 1100
Müller, Theodor, 1129
Munari, L., 441 (ed.)
Munoa, Rafael, 1083

Muñoz, Antonio, 161
Munthe, Gustaf, 1077
Müntz, Eugène, 138a, 210, 240-40a, 1797
Murray, Maria D., 560
Myers, Bernard S. and Shirley D., 10 (eds.)
Myers, Herbert W., 2008
Mylius, Georg, 1225

Nannelli, Paolo, 211
Narozhnaya, V., 87
Natale, Mauro, 215
Needham, Paul, 98, 1970
Neeve, B.R.M. de, 1399
Neils, Jenifer, 332 (ed.)
Németh, Annamaria T., 991, 993
Nesbitt, Alexander, 571
Neumann, Erwin, 1485
Neurdenburg, Elizabeth, 526
Neverov, Oleg, 620
Nevinson, John L., 1714, 1746a
Newman, Harold, 318, 553, 697
Nicaise, Henri, 346
Nickel, Helmut, 220, 1521, 1587, 1591, 2147
Nicodemi, Giorgio, 1322
Nicola, Giacomo de, 158
Ninane, Lucie, 180
Niox, Général, 1522 (ed.)
Nixon, Howard M., 1970
Nizon, Paul, 1809 (ed.)
Nobles, J.H.B., 789
Nocq, Henri, 902
Norman, A.V.B./Vesey, 338, 517, 1499, 1514, 1543, 1597, 1709
Norman-Wilcox, Gregor, 870
Norris, Andrea S., 1197
Norris, Malcolm, 1353-53a
North, A.R.E., 1634
Nowé, H., 90
Nunes Riso Guerreiro, Gloria, 1817

Oakeshotte, R. Ewart, 1547, 1581
Oates, F.A. Harman, 725
Odom, William M., 2137
Ohm, Annaliese, 567, 2043
Ojetti, Ugo, 234
Olaguer-Feliu Alonso, Fernando de, 1430
Olds, Clifton C., 95
Oliver, Pierre, 376
Olrik, Jørgen, 1078
Oman, Charles C., 77, 714, 729, 773, 785, 832-34, 853-56, 868-69, 872, 881a, 1033, 1043, 1061, 1098
Ortega y Gassett, José, 2023

Subject Index

Includes media, object types, artists, sitters, patrons, and 15th-16th-century owners specifically mentioned in titles and/or annotations. For 19th-20th-century collections, see the Location Index. Specific objects (e.g., combs, luminaries [candlesticks, chandeliers, etc.]) have been included selectively and only when they have been produced from more than one medium. Objects that are associated with only one material – for example, forks, which are nearly always made of silver – have not been indexed.

Abaquesne, Masséot, 376
Abondio, Antonio, 306, 312, 656, 1188, 1203,
 1231, 1243, 1259, 1264c, 1292
Adelmann, Augustin, 1154
Adler, Salomon, 1642
Adriano de' Maestri, 1253
Aelst, Pieter Cocke van, 165, 345, 1873, 1884,
 1895, 1900, 1903
Aeneid Master, 49a, 138a, 1116, 1123, 1140
Agata, Francesco di S., 1184, 1305
Agrippa, Giovanni Guido, 1247
Alari-Bonacolsi, Pier Jacopo. See Antico
Alba, Fernando Alvarez de Toledo, duke of,
 1649, 1862
Alberti, Leon Battista, 216, 1235, 1237
Albrecht V, duke of Bavaria, 740, 1968
Albrecht of Prussia, duke, 1216
Albuzzi, Giovanni, 1264d
Aldegrever, Heinrich, 1058, 1156, 1606
Aldobrandini, Ippolito, cardinal, 79b, 793, 943,
 1011, 1037
Alexander VI, pope, 240a, 1272
Alfonso I d'Este, duke of Ferrarra, 1235
Alfonso V, king of Aragon, 493, 548, 1252b, 1257,
 1272
Allori, Alessandro, 749, 1923
Altdorfer, Albrecht, 1217
Altenstetter, David, 945
Alvise (goldsmith), 246, 1996
Amadeo da Ferrara, 1247
Amadio da Milano, 1235, 1238, 1259, 1265

Amber. See Chap. XIII and entries 62, 154, 796
Amerigo (Amerighi) di Giovanni, 1017
Amethyst. See Chap. XIII and entry 58
Amman, Jost, 741
Amulets, Spanish, 79, 756
Anastasio da Vitale, 1023
Andrea da Volterra, Fra, 515
Andrea di Leonardo di Paolo, 1017
Andrea di Nicolò da Viterbo, 1250
Andreoli, Giorgio, 50, 79, 145, 165, 332, 403,
 430a, 480, 482
Andrés de Nájera, 2197
Angoulême, François d', 1920
Anne, duchess of Saxony, 742
Anne of Austria, duchess of Bavaria, 740, 743
Anne of Austria, queen of Spain, 2007
Anne of Brittany, queen of France, 876, 1235,
 1851
Antico (Pier Jacopo Alari-Bonacolsi), 83, 1169,
 1188, 1190, 1197, 1202, 1240, 1265, 1269,
 1302, 1305, 1323, 1345-46, 1350
Anton Francesco della Seta, 246
Antoni van der Borch, 1367
Antonio da Brescia, Fra, 138a, 237, 1186, 1258,
 1269, 1292, 1993
Archimanno Battista da Viterbo, 1023
Ardenti, Alessandro, 1259
Arentsz van Griecken, Gysbrecht, 1058
Aretino, Caterina and Adria, 1245
Aretino, Pietro, 1230
Argenterio, Bartolomeo, 306

258, 260- 62

Gaffurri, Giorgio, 617a
Galateo, Antonio, 1268
Galeotti, Pietro Paolo, 660, 1264b
Galeotto dal Ferro, 1259
Galle, Philippe, 2093
Gambello, Antonio, 1247
Gasparo (founder), 1331
Gastaldo, Rolando, 1244
Gauvain, Jacques, 1209- 10
Gebel, Matthias, 60, 203, 1217
Gempel, Frans, 1856
Gems. *See* Semiprecious Stones and Chap. XIII
Genouilhac, Galiot, 1586-87
Gentile, Antonio, 74, 661-62, 769, 1013, 1022, 1027, 1038, 1042, 1333
Gerhard, Hubert, 83, 1203
Gessner, Abraham, 1103
Gesso, 65. *See also* Pastiglia
Geubals, Franz, 1805
Geverts, Willem, 1063
Ghiberti, Lorenzo, 1020, 1322
Ghiberti, Vittorio, 1024
Ghieteels, Jean, 1895
Ghisbrecht, Jehan, 1707
Ghisi, Giorgio, 49
Giambologna, 34, 54, 60, 82-83, 106, 118, 125, 132, 147-48, 154, 165, 175, 306, 1166, 1169, 1172, 1175, 1302, 1305, 1307, 1322-23, 1343-46, 1349-50
Giancristoforo Romano, 1260, 1269, 2154
Gielis van de Putte, 1837
Giolito de' Ferrari, Gabriele, 403
Giovanni Battista de Curtis, 2144
Giovanni da Verona, Fra, 2170
Giovanni delle Corniole, 1235
Giovanni Maria (of Castel Durante), 417, 449-50
Giuliano da Firenze, 1040
Giuliano da Maiano, 1242, 2163-64
Giulio della Torre, 1247, 1252a, 1252f, 1252n, 1258
Giulio Romano, 807c, 1012, 1600, 1799, 1817, 1841
Glass. *See* Chap. XII and entries 76a, 84, 98-99, 107, 123, 135, 734
  Belgium (Flemish), 107, 180
  British (English), 182
  Czechoslovakia (Bohemian), 61, 156
  German, 46, 60, 91, 103, 106-7, 109, 117, 125, 130, 137, 150, 156, 165, 176, 199, 204- 5
  Italian, 48-49a, 50, 58-59, 61, 71, 73, 76a, 83, 91, 103, 107, 109-10, 113, 116-17, 127, 130, 135, 137, 139, 150, 156, 165, 172, 176, 211-16, 217, 219-22, 227, 229, 238

  Netherlandish, 251-52
  Spanish, 172, 222, 257-58
Gnoss, Elias, 945b
Gold- and Silversmith Works. *See* Chaps. XVI, XIV-XV and entries 47-48, 52-53, 59-60, 63-64, 68-69, 71, 75, 79, 84, 88, 91-93, 98- 99, 102, 106-7, 109, 113, 115, 117-19, 127, 129a, 130, 132, 134a, 135-38a, 138c, 139, 142, 148, 152, 156, 158, 160, 163, 166, 173a-74, 670-71, 681-82, 1465
  Belgium (Flemish), 64a, 79, 140, 167, 175, 180, 673
  British (English and Scottish), 46, 81, 85, 125, 182, 184, 186-88, 673
  Czechoslovakia (Bohemian), 163
  French, 49a, 56, 64a, 67, 79b, 82, 124, 140, 145, 175, 193-94, 672-73
  German, 34, 49-49a, 58, 61-62, 64a, 65-67, 78, 86-87, 100-102, 105-6, 110, 116, 121, 124-5, 137, 140, 144, 151, 153, 156, 165-66, 168, 170, 175-76, 198-207, 237, 672
  Hungarian, 67, 79b, 153
  Italian, 49a, 58, 64a, 69-70a, 74, 77-78, 79b, 82, 100-101, 110, 114, 121, 124, 129a, 134a, 136, 140, 154, 162, 167, 170, 175, 178, 202, 209, 214, 219, 221, 227, 230-37, 237b, 239-40a, 241-45, 247-49
  Netherlandish, 673
  Polish, 253-54
  Portuguese, 78, 167, 255
  Spanish, 78-79, 100, 114, 119, 121, 140, 167, 258, 261, 673
  Swiss, 263
  U.S.S.R. (Russian), 100
Goltzius, Hendrick, 2092
Gonzaga, 248-49
  Carlo, 1559
  Francesco, 212
  Gianfrancesco, 1240
Gonzaga-Colonna, Giulia, 1240
Grand Dauphin (Delfin), 625
Grandi, Vincenzo, Gian Gerolamo and Workshop, 83, 1167, 1319
Grandio, Muzio, 662
Granvelle, Antoine Perrenot de, cardinal, 1195, 1881, 1987
Grasseck, Paulus, 908
Gratt, Gianfrancesco and Franceschina, 1252o
Grenier, Pasquin, 1814, 1887, 1918
Gretzinger, Christoph, 957
Grimani, Domenico, cardinal, 1230
Groet, Adriaan de, 1063

Location Index

Lists locations of permanent and private collections, and multi- owner exhibition catalogs included under the subheadings 6, 7, and 8. The reader will find many other topographical mentions in the literature within subheadings 1-5, as well as 6, 7, and 8.

Location Index